Microscope #3

BIOLOGICAL SCIENCE

An Ecological Approach

BSCS GREEN VERSION

Fifth Edition

PR#7

Q Mount 15/UNSOI)
name:
Password

OK

BIOLOGICAL SCIENCE

An Ecological Approach

BSCS Green Version
Fifth Edition

BSCS

833 W. South Boulder Road
Louisville, CO 80027

Revision Team

Richard R. Tolman, Supervisor, BSCS
Dorothy S. Curtis, United States Geological Survey,
  Denver, Colorado
Don E. Meyer, BSCS
Gordon E. Uno, University of Oklahoma,
  Norman, Oklahoma

Editor

Nancy Lehmann Haynes

Houghton Mifflin Company   **Boston**

Atlanta Dallas Geneva, Illinois Hopewell, New Jersey Palo Alto Toronto

Writers of Previous Editions and their addresses at the time of their participation

Norris Anderson, Burlingame High School, Burlingame, California — 1968

Richard G. Beidleman, Colorado College, Colorado Springs, Colorado — 1968

Harold Durst, Southeast High School, Wichita, Kansas — 1963

Donald S. Farner, University of Washington, Seattle, Washington — 1968

Robert DeWitt Ivey, Sandia High School, Albuquerque, New Mexico — 1973

Garland E. Johnson, Hoover High School, Fresno, California — 1978

Haven Kolb, Hereford High School, Parkton, Maryland — 1978 (supervisor of writing team, 1963, 1968, 1973)

Edward J. Kormondy, Evergreen State College, Olympia, Washington — 1973

Victor Larsen, Adelphi College, Garden City, New York — 1963, 1968, 1973

William V. Mayer, BSCS, Boulder, Colorado — 1968

William B. Miller, Rand McNally & Company, Chicago, Illinois — 1963

Elra M. Palmer, Baltimore City Public Schools, Baltimore, Maryland — 1963, 1968, 1973

Paul G. Pearson, Rutgers, The State University, New Brunswick, New Jersey — 1968

Elizabeth Perrott, University of Stirling, Stirling, Scotland — 1968

Karin Rhines, Science Writer, New York — 1978

Gordon E. Uno, University of Oklahoma, Norman, Oklahoma — 1978, 1982 (supervisor of writing team, 1978)

Bruce Wallace, Cornell University, Ithaca, New York — 1973, 1978

Jonathan Westfall, University of Georgia, Athens, Georgia — 1963

The members of the revision team for this edition are listed on the title page.

Printed in the United States of America

Student's Edition ISBN: 0-395-31249-3
Teacher's Edition ISBN: 0-395-31250-7

Cover and title page photograph by Byron Crader/TOM STACK & ASSOCIATES

Sections One, Two, and Six opening photographs by C. Allan Morgan
Section Three opening photograph Copyright © 1980, Photo Works
Section Four opening photograph by Neil G. McDaniel
Section Five opening photograph © Charles G. Summers, Jr.

The following teachers contributed suggestions and comments for this edition:

Vern W. Adams, Clearfield, Utah; Michael W. Antrim, Omaha, Nebraska; Ruth L. Barrett, Omaha, Nebraska; Obert Barstad, Bismarck, North Dakota; William P. Batycky, Calgary, Alberta, Canada; John C. Bennethum, Milwaukee, Wisconsin; Richard Beran, Omaha, Nebraska; Marilyn K. Bunnell, Albany, Oregon; Ron Cisar, Omaha, Nebraska; William G. Coleman, Lakewood, Ohio; Ray A. Cook, Brookfield, Wisconsin; L. L. Darrow, Omaha, Nebraska; David Delaine, Omaha, Nebraska; R. F. Derrah, Lewiston, Maine; Carol Donovan, Omaha, Nebraska; George Drinnin, Omaha, Nebraska; Marshall Floyd, Albuquerque, New Mexico; Helen M. Foster, Santa Fe, New Mexico; Gary Gonzales, South Omaha, Nebraska; Herbert D. Granbard, Albuquerque, New Mexico; Matt Green, San Jose, California; D. Jay Hess, Madison, Connecticut; O. R. Humphreys, Newport, Vermont; Fred Hunt, Calgary, Alberta, Canada; John E. Hutchins, Hanover, New Hampshire; Dave James, Omaha, Nebraska; John H. Jameson, Princeton, New Jersey; Lamont Jensen, Clearfield, Utah; John Johnette, Omaha, Nebraska; Richard E. Kangas, Selma, California; Mike Kennedy, Omaha, Nebraska; Jim Kinsey, Omaha, Nebraska; William Klang, Reedsburg, Wisconsin; Vern Krenzer, Omaha, Nebraska; Jim Kros, Omaha, Nebraska; Forrest Lambeth, Springfield, Missouri; Ronald A. Leeseberg, Lakewood, Ohio; Mike Lestina, Fargo, North Dakota; David E. Lewis, Omaha, Nebraska; David Lines, Omaha, Nebraska; Bill Lipp, Fargo, North Dakota; Lewis Lopez, Los Angeles, California; Horace M. Lucich, San Jose, California; Thomas McCawley, Omaha, Nebraska; Joline McFadden, Lewiston, Maine; Warren Marquiss, Omaha, Nebraska; Mrs. Blanca Martin, Las Vegas, Nevada; D. S. Martin, Calgary, Alberta, Canada; Arthur D. Meyer, Lakewood, Ohio; Mrs. Rusty Miller, Albuquerque, New Mexico; Nick Modrein, Omaha, Nebraska; Darlene F. Montgomery, Omaha, Nebraska; Victor Neuwirth, Sanford, Maine; Mike T. O'Connor, Omaha, Nebraska; Raylene Owen, Englewood, Colorado; Joe Perina, Omaha, Nebraska; Alma Phifer, Plymouth, Nebraska; D. Rankin, Omaha, Nebraska; Cheryl Reade, Casper, Wyoming; Bob Reeder, Lincoln, Nebraska; Paul W. Richard, Greeley, Colorado; Ray Roberts, Milwaukee, Wisconsin; George Royce, Omaha, Nebraska; D. L. Severson, Calgary, Alberta, Canada; Jim Shank, Omaha, Nebraska; Terry H. Shelsta, Omaha, Nebraska; Gerald Smith, Strattanville, Pennsylvania; Fred Sorensen, Omaha, Nebraska; Creighton Steiner, Omaha, Nebraska; Sally Swartz, Englewood, Colorado; Richard L. Taylor, Clearfield, Utah; Florence Turek, Ketchikan, Alaska; Pat Wallington, Omaha, Nebraska; Charles Watt, Omaha, Nebraska; Larry V. Weatherwax, Anchorage, Alaska; Steven Weinberg, Windsor, Connecticut.

114133

Contents

Preface to the Student

There are two major aims in studying biology. One aim is to become acquainted with scientific facts and with the ideas that are built on them. These ideas have shown us that we have a place in nature; we are not apart from it. They have made our lives today very different from those of our ancestors.

The second aim in studying biology is even more important. It is to understand what science is—to feel its spirit, to appreciate its methods, and to recognize its limitations. We need this understanding to make intelligent decisions in our science-oriented world.

Science is not magic. Science is a process by which we can arrive at reliable knowledge of our surroundings. It involves curiosity, creativity, observation, and thought. It is a progressive activity, each generation building on the accumulated knowledge of the past.

Science, then, is a human activity. If our lives are to flourish, every person must understand to some degree the aims, methods, and consequences of science. Thus all of us—not just scientists—must understand what science is.

Understanding can best be gained by doing the kinds of things scientists do in their laboratories. A laboratory is a place where the work of a scientist is carried on. It may be either outdoors or indoors, but it is always a place where scientists are asking questions of nature. No scientists, however, lock themselves alone in a laboratory. They need libraries, conversation with fellow scientists, and skill in reading and writing. Most importantly, they need an inquisitive mind that questions the information that is given to them.

This book contains part of what you will need. In addition, you will need materials and equipment. And you will need living things. But most important, your biology course requires *you*. It needs your eyes, your ears, your hands, your brain—all of your senses. And it needs your curiosity and your questions.

Study the career essays carefully. They show the variety of opportunities that exist in the exciting field of biology. Perhaps, someday, you will pursue a career in biology.

Richard R. Tolman
Supervisor, Green Version 5th Edition

Gordon E. Uno
Supervisor, Green Version 4th Edition

Haven Kolb
Supervisor, Green Version 1st, 2nd, and 3rd Editions

June 1, 1981

SECTION ONE

The World of Life: the Biosphere

THE WORLD OF LIFE: THE BIOSPHERE

How shall we start to study biology — the science of life?

We might begin grandly with the universe, work down to the solar system, to the planet Earth, to a pond somewhere, and then look at the abundance of life that finds a home there. We might look into some living thing to look at the smallest parts under our microscopes. We could study the ways in which these parts are put together in an individual and discuss the many relationships among different individuals. Or we might start with chemistry — with electrons, atoms, and molecules — because all living things are composed of atoms, and we find chemical processes wherever we find living things. We might even take a historical approach. We could search for clues to the beginning of life and examine the fossil record to trace the development of living things.

There are many ways to start a biology course. Let us begin with things that are familiar — with students, and with other living things that are not household pets but are easy to picture, like rabbits and raspberry bushes.

Chapter 1

The Web of Life

YOUR GUIDEPOSTS

In this chapter you will have an opportunity to explore these questions in biology:

- How do scientists work to improve investigative and problem-solving methods?
- Why is it difficult to investigate a living thing in isolation from its environment?
- What is biology? Ecology?
- Where do living things obtain the energy they require?
- How does living matter differ from other matter?
- What are some problems humans face in biology?

At the beginning of each chapter you will find several questions such as these. They are intended to guide your study of the chapter by showing you some of the broad problems that have directed discovery and understanding in biology. Refer to these frequently as you study the chapter.

A LEASE ON WILDLIFE

A high school biology class took up a new challenge. They set out to show citizens of their community that a small piece of land near their school should not be changed.

Students used the land for quiet walks, and for nature studies. Some people wanted to build homes and businesses there. One person even suggested the land be used for growing grapes for the wine industry.

Would the results of an investigation really support development? Would they support the use of the land as a vineyard? What were the facts?

Partly lowland, the land lay along a small river. As the students began to catalog the plants and animals that lived there, they discovered something else of importance to the land's use. During each rainy season, part of the land was flooded. This would mean the vineyard would be destroyed. For homes and businesses it would mean costly flood-control devices.

In a separate investigation students learned that the land

had historical value. Descendants of both the Indians and later Spanish settlers supplied historical accounts.

As the evidence accumulated, students began interviewing citizens of the community. They interviewed the people who wanted to buy and develop the land. They interviewed many others to sample community opinion. During all this time they continued to visit the land. They cataloged and accounted for more and more kinds of plants and animals that would be destroyed or displaced if the land were developed.

To the students the most important reason for leaving the land in its natural state was these plants and animals. A distinct and unusual collection of **organisms** was living along the river. Among them were three pairs of an endangered species of birds. Seventy-two other kinds of birds also gathered food or raised their young in the area. Other small animals were numerous, and grasses and shrubs supplied food and shelter under towering oaks.

organisms [OR guh niz umz; Greek: *organon*, tool or instrument, from *ergon*, at work]: a working thing, or, in modern use, a living thing

At length, the students concluded their investigations. Their teacher contacted their state senator. The senator, who was given all the records of the students, requested a hearing before the state wildlife conservation board. The board studied the evidence carefully, then recommended that the state purchase the land as an ecological preserve.

Facts and careful records won the case. No land is unused, and this particular piece of land was not even ideally suited to human use. It was already supporting the life for which it was ideal. And so the students entered the decision-making process.

Today the streamside site has been modified only by a planned trail system. No "inhabitants" were asked to leave. Humans are requested to stay on the trails.

Photos by Mandy Schuer

1–1 Studies of the riverside land go on today. Two students (*left*) collect a water sample. Plant growth along the stream (*right*) is very dense in summer.

1—2 Describe all the relationships you see here among the plants and animals and their environment.

SHARED ENVIRONMENTS

What are the relationships between organisms and their surroundings? To start a study, you can select any kind of organism. Rabbits will do very well. They have a way of turning up in almost every land environment. Though not mentioned, they were in the records of animals living on the streamside site the biology class investigated. Rabbits turn up even in the suburbs of our largest cities, living under door stoops.

A rabbit needs a place to hide. This is important. In nature an ideal place is under a wild raspberry bush. Everyone knows about raspberry bushes, or about the jam or the thorns that tear clothes and discourage animals that are chasing rabbits.

A rabbit under a raspberry bush, and something else important—the rabbit will need something to eat. The raspberries, or some of them, may be out of the rabbit's reach. Or, birds and insects may have eaten the fruit. The raspberry leaves are not very tasty to a rabbit. And so the rabbit ventures out of its hiding place, looking for grass and other leafy green food.

The nearest patch of native grasses is not far away. But neither is the nearest animal that eats rabbits. The rabbit begins to munch the grass blades. A fox, which has spied the rabbit's movement, is bearing down silently on the rabbit. And suddenly the rabbit looks up. *Alarm* — off the rabbit goes, with the fox almost upon it. The chase leads across a field toward a nearby farm. Was this quick thinking by the rabbit? (No, probably not, and in science it could be offered only as a *hypothesis* to be investigated — not as a conclusion.) At any rate, the rabbit is saved. The farmer's dog bays and charges the fox. The dog will get the fox if it can. If not, the dog will come back and look for the rabbit.

hypothesis [hy POTH uh sis; Greek: *hypo*, under, + *tithenai*, to place]: a suggestion placed under consideration; plural, hypotheses [hy POTH uh seez]

Meanwhile, the bird that was eating raspberries has flown a short distance and is in a tree. What does this have to do with our story?

It all started where a raspberry bush grows. The bush is a plant, rooted in one spot. The rabbit that was hiding under it, and the bird and insects that were feeding on raspberries, are all animals, able to move about. Grass, fox, and dog entered the scene. The picture began to get complex — a *web* of relationships.

The idea of a web comes from thinking of spiders. A spider's web could be in the raspberry bush. If not, there is sure to be one in the taller grass. If you find and watch one, a breeze may tug at it, pulling strands that tug back. The web holds, because everything is connected.

Everything also seems connected in the story of a raspberry bush, rabbit, grass, fox, and dog. The bird? It is a part of the web, too. Remember that it was eating raspberries. A few hours later, without warning, it will leave droppings somewhere. The droppings contain raspberry seeds that can start another raspberry bush growing. Here is one little circle in the middle of our web of relationships — the bird and the raspberry bush.

1 – 3 A spider's web.

Rue/Annan Photo Features

Over there, partly hidden in a hole, are little scraps of fur and flesh we have not mentioned to this point. They are last week's rabbit. The fox carried this rabbit back to its den. Now little wormlike creatures are crawling on the remaining scraps. Other organisms, too small to be seen without a microscope, are also feeding on the scraps. The remaining rabbit materials are being broken down to a very simple form. Mixed with soil, these materials will fertilize new plants. Other rabbits will feed on the plants. Another little circle in our web of relationships is being completed.

As changes go on, the web of life seems the same. But at later times the same kinds of plants and animals are really different individuals living in this one environment. They are connected by a web as real as the spider's web. They contribute to one another. They depend on one another.

Only natural disasters—fires, floods, and so on—upset such an environment suddenly. Or human beings may do it—this was what the biology class was concerned with in investigating the streamside environment near the school.

What role have people played in the environment? Many human beings are still unaware that they, too, are a part of the web of life.

Study of the unseen web of life—relationships among organisms and between all of them and their physical environment—is called *ecology.* Ecology is only one of the many areas of *biology,* the science of life. The scientists are called biologists, ecologists, and by other names depending on their specialties.

ecology [ih KOL uh jee; Greek: *oik,* house or vicinity, + *logos,* word, story, or study]

biology [by OL uh jee; Greek: *bios,* life, + *logos*]

Investigation 1.1   LOOKING AT LIFE   wrong

INTRODUCTION

To be alive is to face problems of living. Like the rabbit and the raspberry bush, we humans face biological problems. But we can recognize the problems and use our minds to cope with them.

On this and following pages are some pictures that present biological problems. Some of the scenes may be familiar to you, some unfamiliar. Some may be scenes you have read about but have not seen. Whether familiar or strange, the pictures should help you to begin thinking biologically.

PROCEDURE

1. There is a set of questions with each of the pictures in this investigation. Some of

these questions can help you think about how human activities affect other living things, as well as other humans.

2. After the members of your class have had an opportunity to exchange ideas about the pictures, summarize the discussion by considering the following: (1) On what questions was there greatest agreement? (2) On what questions was there least agreement? (3) What kinds of information would be needed to increase agreement? (4) On which questions would there be no agreement, even if more information were provided?

3. Scenes that raise biological questions occur around each of us every day. Look for some on your way home from school

Parks Canada

1–4 What is the biological problem here? An observation: Plants are growing successfully everywhere except in and near the barren strip. Why are plants stunted or absent in this strip? Why have the three clusters of woody plants died? Suggest a way to begin an investigation.

and while you are at home tonight. In your data book, record at least 3 scenes, as follows:

a. Describe the scene in a sentence or two. (For example, "While my dog was sleeping, its legs twitched," or "Our neighbors have the same kind of trees growing in their yard as we have, but theirs are larger.")

b. List biological questions that the scene brings to your mind. (For example, "Is my dog dreaming?" or "Are their trees older than ours?")

4. List the scenes reported by students in your class. (5) Are there any that you do not consider to be biological? If so, why not?

5. Keep in mind the available time. Select questions that your class thinks most interesting. For each such question, consider: (6) Can a satisfactory answer be obtained with the information you already have? If not, what additional information is needed? (7) Do you think biologists already have the additional information? If not, how might a biologist get such information? (8) If all the imaginable biological information were obtained, would the question be answered? If not, what else might affect answers to the question?

1–6 Compare this city with the one photographed in figure 1–7. Are they the same city? What do you think will happen to the city you see here? What advantages and disadvantages do you see in large cities and industries?

1–5 Is the view below of rubbish cluttering a stream or pond? Before you reach a conclusion, look for clues. Notice the cut tree stumps in the foreground. What made these chiseled cuts? Why are all the cut trees and branches piled together and heaped with mud? How would you ask the right biological question?

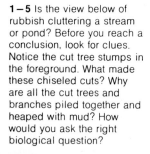

BSCS photo by Faith Hickman

Copyright Herb Ferguson

1–7 Was this a lucky day? Or was something done about the air pollution? Two rivers come together to form one, the Ohio River, in this photograph. Do you find two rivers that are coming together in figure 1–6? What city is this?

Copyright Herb Ferguson

James L. Lee/EARTH IMAGES

1–8 Mt. Saint Helens began erupting anew in 1980. Many miles away, people in Washington and Oregon lived under a severe but natural form of air pollution from volcanic ash (figure 1–9). Have you ever thought about natural causes of pollution, as opposed to human causes? Can you name examples of each? What biological problems do they cause?

© Terry Domico/EARTH IMAGES

1–9 "On a clear day you can see forever . . . ," but clear days may not occur within a hundred miles of an active volcano. Why is the man wearing a mask over his nose and mouth? How many different biological problems can you name that are caused by volcanic eruptions?

NASA

1–10 Do you see any biological problems? In what ways? This astronaut is on the moon. Why do people explore outer space? How do you feel about this? Do you think we should try to find life elsewhere in space? Can you think of any place we might find undiscovered life forms on Earth?

BSCS photo by John B. Thornton

1–11 The structure illuminated by its own destruction is a grain elevator. What biological problems are caused by fires like this one? By fires in nature? How do fires of both types affect food problems? Living space? Can you suggest how world food problems for humans could be solved?

A BIOLOGIST'S VIEWPOINT

Biologists are not the only people who observe and study living things. An artist might look at living things for their beauty of color and form. An engineer or a farmer might look for ways to manage them. A philosopher might try to find a meaning to life in the universe. You have been looking at living things scientifically, as a biologist does.

As a science, biology does not deal with value judgments such as what is beautiful, or even what you would be happiest studying in your biology class. Beliefs and value judgments differ from person to person. Biology is concerned mainly with *facts*—topics of information that do not differ from one person to another. Biologists collect and organize facts about organisms, and then use them in systematic ways to learn more facts. Some interesting ideas have to be excluded from biology because there is no way known to investigate them factually.

How does a dictionary define *fact*?

Can you name examples?

Like other people, a biologist studies a problem through use of the senses. Gaining information about your surroundings through the use of your senses is called *observation.* In Investigation 1.1 you made many observations. After you made them, you saw problems. Your problems were stated in the form of good questions. Learning how to ask good questions is an important part of the work of the biologist.

Any good question such as "What attracts bees to one kind of flower?" may state a problem for investigation. The first

1–12 (continued on opposite page) What activities of scientists do you think are illustrated in these photographs? The caribou is tranquilized and is not harmed by the tagging. It is being radiotagged for a year-round study of caribou migratory habits.

National Center for Toxicological Research, Jefferson, Arkansas

Courtesy Miami Seaquarium®

step is to find out whether it has already been investigated successfully. Thus, a biologist does <u>library research</u>. If the answer is not known, at least some facts related to investigating the answer may be found. Reading and thinking about the problem may produce a thought such as "Bees may be attracted to one kind of flower by its scent." Like the thought of whether or not the rabbit was clever to head for the farm when pursued by the fox, this thought about bees is a <u>hypothesis</u>. A good hypothesis is simple and clear. It often suggests how to collect evidence that would either support or disprove the hypothesis. A hypothesis *must* be stated to make an investigation possible, using the methods of science. Otherwise it may become another one of the interesting ideas with which science cannot deal. Sometimes hypotheses are retained for later investigation. New techniques or equipment that will make their investigation possible may be in development.

The ideal situation if for a hypothesis to be directly testable by **experiment.** The statement about the bees makes possible a **prediction:** if bees are attracted to a particular kind of flower by its scent, then putting that scent on another kind of flower to which they are not normally attracted should attract them there, too. Now you can see that an experiment is possible because of the prediction. Of course the flowers differ in many ways that are called **variables.** The variables are size,

Marg and Bill Staley

1—13 A bee in a flower.

experiment [ik SPER uh munt; Latin: *ex*, out, + *periri*, to try]: a test that provides evidence for or against a hypothesis

prediction [prih DIK shun; Latin: *prae*, before, + *dicere*, to say]

variables [VAIR ee uh bulz; Latin: *variabilis*, from *variare*, to vary]

1—12 (continued)

C. Allan Morgan

David Fritts

See Investigation 1.2. What do all the controls have to do with your findings?

data [DAY tuh; Latin: *datum*, thing that is given]; singular, datum

microscope [Greek: *mikros*, small, + *skopein*, to look]

shape, color, scent, and so on. To _control_ as many of them as possible, you will try to select a second kind of flower of the same size and color and general shape as the first. The major difference should be their scent, so far as you can determine. Scent is the **experimental variable** that you will change for the second kind of flower, to make the scent like that of the first.

In the actual experiment your control of the variables cannot be perfect. If you can tell the flowers apart, you know this. Many experiments may prove necessary before all the facts are in. But your experiment will provide certain facts, or **data.** The data are whatever the bees do, and also whatever they do not do, under the conditions of the experiment.

The bee/flower scent hypothesis is limited to bees of one kind. It does not apply to all bees or to other animals attracted to flowers by scent. Are moths and butterflies attracted to flowers by scent? Are rabbits? (Rabbits will eat flowers; does this imply they can smell the flowers?) Are humans attracted to flowers by the scent? Most hypotheses in biology, like this one about bees, are stated for a particular kind of organism and experiments with it. Only a relatively few hypotheses are stated to include many or most organisms. However, a major example is the hypothesis that when you look through the **microscope** at the structure of any organism, you will find little boxlike or saclike units. Organisms are composed of these units of structure, called **cells.** This hypothesis has received so much support for more than 150 years that it is generally accepted for all or most organisms. It would be stated simply as fact except for two things:

1. Not every part of every organism will ever be examined under the microscope. The task is impossible.

2. Rare exceptions have been found. Certain organisms, such as slime molds, do not show cells. If they originally had cells, the evidence has been lost as they grew and developed.

Clearly the hypothesis of cell structure may never be proved. Yet it appears generally true. The evidence supporting it is almost overwhelming, with only a few known exceptions. Biologists accept it as a **theory** — the cell theory. It may be modified, but it will not be proved entirely false when so many hundreds of thousands of kinds of organisms have already been shown to have cell structure.

Theories in biology are great organizers of knowledge. They are much more than just hypotheses. They are supported by the best available evidence and even predict future events. Yet they contain allowances for modification, if necessary, with new discoveries. No reputable biologist would ever present the world with a theory that could not be modified.

CHECK YOURSELF

A. Why is it difficult to describe one organism's way of life without describing the ways of life of other organisms in the same environment?
B. What is the relation between observations and facts? Between hypotheses and facts?
C. Why is it important for biologists to record and report their work accurately? How does this affect the library research another biologist might do before working on a related problem?
D. Describe briefly the essential features of a scientific investigation.
E. How does identification and control of variables help set problem-solving in science apart from problem-solving in everyday life?

Investigation 1.2   BEE ATTRACTION TO FLOWERS

INTRODUCTION

In this investigation you will consider how to control variables while testing a hypothesis.

PROCEDURE

1. Study the observation and hypothesis about what attracts bees to flowers. (See diagram at right.)
2. Examine Experiment 1: the scent of a flower that attracts bees is added to a flower that does not attract bees. (See also at right.)
3. Is scent the only variable? Identify as many other variables as you can think of between these two types of flowers.
4. Study the redesigned experiment (Experiment 2) on the following page. Be prepared to defend or criticize it. A, B, and C show three different possible outcomes for Experiment 2.

1—14

OBSERVATION:
Bees are attracted to Flower 1.

FLOWER 1   **FLOWER 2**

HYPOTHESIS:
Bees are attracted to Flower 1 by scent.

EXPERIMENT 1:
Add scent of Flower 1 to Flower 2.

FLOWER 1   **FLOWER 2**
                      scent added

What does the experiment lack?

EXPERIMENT 2: Experiment 1 is redesigned after consideration of the variables. The new experiment with three different possible outcomes appears below.

A

FLOWER 1 **FLOWER 2**
(control)

FLOWER 2
scented spray added

FLOWER 2
unscented spray added
(control)

B

FLOWER 1 **FLOWER 2**
(control)

FLOWER 2
scented spray added

FLOWER 2
unscented spray added
(control)

C

FLOWER 1 **FLOWER 2**
(control)

FLOWER 2
scented spray added

FLOWER 2
unscented spray added

DISCUSSION

Compare Flower 2 in Experiment 1 with Flower 2 in Experiment 2. (1) What variables are being controlled by the choice made for Flower 2 in Experiment 2?

In Experiment 2, the scent-producing substance from Flower 1 is dissolved in a liquid (water or another solvent harmless to flowers) to produce a spray. (2) What is the purpose of the control flowers with nothing sprayed on them? (3) Of the control flowers sprayed with unscented spray?

(4) What hypotheses would account for Outcome A in Experiment 2? (5) Outcome B? (6) Outcome C?

(7) How does Outcome B illustrate the difference between the two sets of control plants? (8) What further controls, if any, can you think of that might be helpful?

(9) Why would you want to try the experiment with more than one group of the kind of bees you are studying? (10) How would you interpret the results if the *numbers* of bees visiting each kind of flower differed noticeably?

INTERRELATIONSHIPS

How do biologists study the web of life when there are more variables than they can control? In many nonexperimental investigations control of variables is not necessary. Each condition or variation in organisms and in their environment is a part of how the organisms live. You would be changing that if you identified and controlled every variable—even if you could. Instead you try to make accurate observations of organisms in their environment while *accepting* the natural variables.

In a sense you *ignore* the variables, but you really are

aware that they exist and are at work. Thus, in winter it can become too cold for foxes to be out chasing rabbits. On the coldest days foxes may not come out of their dens at all. This doesn't mean that foxes do not hunt rabbits. You only need to come around again on a warmer day. Then the **interrelationships** among the foxes, rabbits, and other organisms can become very complex, provided that *you* remain undiscovered.

interrelationships [IN tur rih-LAY shun ships; Latin: *inter*, among, + *relatus*, carried back]; the ways in which different organisms affect each other

Does this interrelated web of life hold true of other environments? Let us begin again. This time we will be looking at the organisms in a special way. In another field of grass far away from the first field with the raspberry bush, we see—it appears to be another rabbit. Rabbits are everywhere. We also see two other kinds of animals that eat grass—a horse and two sheep. The sheep are a ewe and her lamb.

Why is it important not to be detected as an observer in an environment?

1—15

What does the arrow from the grass to the rabbit mean? From the grass to the horse? To the ewe? Why doesn't an arrow go from the grass to the lamb? Instead you see an arrow from the ewe to the lamb. What does this arrow mean?

There are no foxes here, but there are coyotes. Let us add a coyote. Along with it you see two more arrows. Now let us add the human being to whom the pasture, horse, and sheep belong —and another arrow:

1—16

The pathway from the grass to the horse is a *food chain.* The longer pathway from the grass to the rabbit to the coyote is another food chain. The still longer pathways from the grass to the ewe to the lamb—and branching there, in one direction to the coyote and in the other direction to the human being— are two more food chains. The last two differ only in their last link.

If the coyote eats the rabbit and the human eats the lamb, all will be fed. But suppose this is another lucky rabbit. Then, in the dead of night, the coyote may get the baby lamb, which unlike the rabbit cannot run away.

The next day, the carcass of the dead lamb, following the coyote's meal, has flies buzzing about it. The flies lay eggs on the dead flesh. The eggs hatch into maggots that feed on the flesh. In the next figure you see the dead lamb, with an arrow leading from it to the hovering flies. There is also another arrow, from the lamb to the soil. This arrow represents tiny organisms that invade the lamb flesh and feed on it. (You probably would say that the carcass "rots" or "decays," but this process is really brought about by the feeding of the tiny organisms.) The little organisms break down the lamb's flesh to simple materials that are returned to the soil. In the soil these materials fertilize more grass growth.

The arrow from the lamb to the human being still appears. This particular lamb is no longer in the human's food chain. However, other lambs still are.

1—17

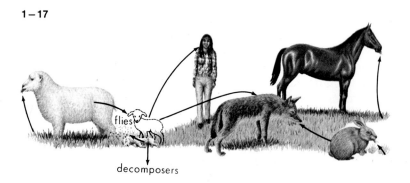

flies

decomposers

You can see from the figure that a web of life is taking shape, just as it did around the rabbit and the raspberry bush. This time all the food chains have been diagramed. Together all the food chains make up a *food web.*

The food web is not complete. It does not show other animals that feed on the grass or its seed. It does not show other animals that the coyote eats. It also does not show the other animals—and the fruits and vegetables—that the human being eats.

The food web represents the web of life. However, it is not the whole web of life. It does not show the relationship between the human being and the horse. The human being owns, feeds, and rides the horse. The food web also does not show the relationship between the human being and the coyote. The human being considers the coyote a competitor and may try to kill or live-trap the coyote to prevent it from slaughtering more lambs. In this case the coyote will not be taken for food. However, it is likely to be removed from the environment as effectively as if it had been killed and eaten.

In one more way this food web does not show a full relationship. The arrow from the lamb to the human being represents food. However, the sheep may be raised primarily for their wool or for sale as breeding stock. Only an occasional lamb may become food.

A food web diagram, therefore, is not as complete as the web of life. Biologists let it stand for the web of life because it is the most obvious and important part.

ENERGY IN A FOOD WEB

The data that an observer of a food web collects are **qualitative.** They tell *what* but not *how much.* They describe an environment, the plants and animals in it, and the interrelationships among them. Instruments that extend the senses are helpful— a binocular, a microscope, a camera.

qualitative [KWAL uh tay tiv; Latin: *qualitas,* kind or quality]

Qualitative data are obtained without direct measurement. This does not mean they are guesses or opinions. In fact, **verification** by other biologists is necessary before the data are accepted. Qualitative data are very important in biology.

verification [ver uh fuh KAY-shun]; Latin: *verus,* true, + *facere,* to make]: repetition and confirmation of the observations and experiments of others

Another kind of data is always obtained with **measurement.** **Quantitative** data help eliminate differences of interpretation when questions like how many, how big, how hot or how cold, and so on, can be investigated and answered as part of solving a biological problem. Metersticks, thermometers, balances, stopwatches, and other **instruments of measure** are nearly always associated with quantitative data. An exception is in counting. (To say "There were 43 sheep in the flock" is quantitative but does not require a measuring instrument.)

quantitative [KWAN tuh tay tiv; Latin: *quantitas,* amount]

Quantitative data must be verified, too. This is not because of opinion or guesswork but because of errors that are sometimes made even in measurement.

Which kind of data do biologists prefer when there is a

choice? Probably every biologist you might meet would say, "Quantitative." But the key words are, ". . . when there is a choice." To help make this choice possible when studying food webs, biologists reduce events to common terms. They describe the movement of *matter* and *energy* through food webs—rather than the movement of so many different kinds of organisms individually.

All activity requires energy; it *uses* energy. No activity would ever occur without energy to activate it. And so whenever you see biological activity, you can ask, "Where does the energy come from?"

Ask the question when you have lunch. It may require some imagination to look at a hamburger and a pile of french fries and see energy. Do most people even see the food chains? One food chain is from potato plant to you. Another is from grasses and corn to cow to you. Still another is from wheat (and other sources) to baked hamburger bun to you. The energy used in this example is *chemical energy*. Such energy is found in bonds that hold together the molecules of a substance. There are many forms of energy—electrical, mechanical, heat, light, and so on. But the only forms in which energy is stored for long periods of time are nuclear energy and chemical energy.

A battery provides electricity. But the energy stored in it is chemical. An automobile provides mechanical energy. But the energy stored in the gasoline is chemical. A nuclear power plant provides electricity for homes and industries. But the energy stored in the power plant's fuel is nuclear energy.

The energy in food chains and food webs is chemical energy. But where does it come from? The only things the cow eats are grasses and grain. The same is true for rabbits and

1–18 For a hamburger with french fries, these are your main sources of energy. But where did they get *their* energy?

sheep, which eat mostly grasses rather than grain. Chickens eat grain, not grasses. Whatever their dietary differences, all these animals are plant-eaters.

A grass plant does not eat any other organism. Neither does a corn (or other grain) plant, or a potato plant. Where does their energy come from? In Chapter 12 you will perform some experiments in answer to this question, and one experiment to get some quantitative data on how much energy is stored in different foods.

But basically you already have an idea of where the food energy comes from. Plants grow in light, absorbing some of the *light energy* of the sun. Most plants are green. The green color is caused by **chlorophyll.** Chlorophyll is a plant pigment that absorbs light energy and changes it to chemical energy. This process is called **photosynthesis.** Photosynthesis supplies almost all the food energy in the world. Only a few bacteria are able to make their own food in other ways. No animal can make

chlorophyll [KLOR uh fil; Greek: *chloros*, green, + *phyllon*, leaf]

photosynthesis [FOH tuh SIN-thuh sis; Greek: *photos*, light, + *syn*, together, + *thesis*, putting in order, arranging]

1—19 Radiations from the sun form a continuous series, from those of very short wavelengths to those of very long wavelengths. Different parts of the series have been given names. The range of radiations that organisms can detect with their eyes—visible light—is roughly the same range used by producers.

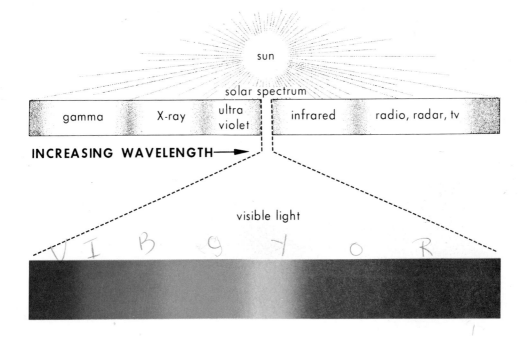

its own food. For you, the only two chemical processes light activates are in your eyes, leading to vision, and in your skin, leading to the conversion of one substance into vitamin D. But, interestingly, one kind of bacteria uses a pigment like your eye pigment to make food.

Plants and other organisms that capture light energy or use another energy source to make food are called ***producers.*** Falling sunlight can be measured, and the amount used by plants in photosynthesis calculated. This is the beginning of gathering quantitative data about energy in food chains.

Animals are all ***consumers.*** They cannot make their own food by photosynthesis. The animals that eat producers directly are called ***herbivores.*** (They are also called first-order consumers.) The cow, the sheep, the horse, and the rabbit in our examples are all herbivores. So are the bird and the insects that were eating raspberries.

herbivores [HUR buh vorz; Latin: *herba,* grass, green crops, + *vorare,* to eat]

Animals that eat other animals are called ***carnivores.*** (They are second- and higher-level consumers.) The fox, the dog, and the coyote in our examples are all carnivores.

carnivores [KAR nuh vorz; Latin: *carnis,* flesh, + *vorare*]

You are both a herbivore and a carnivore, or an ***omnivore.*** Bears and pigs are other examples of omnivores.

omnivore [OM nuh vor; Latin: *omnis,* all, + *vorare*]

A plant uses much of the energy it captures. Each kind of organism uses some of its food energy for its own life activities. That is one reason why figure 1−21, a food energy pyramid, gets smaller from the base up. Even if you could eat a whole cow's worth of hamburgers, you would not get most of the energy the cow obtained from the grass and grain it ate. The cow used most of its energy in its own growth, movement, and body heat, and in other ways. The energy that was stored in its muscles (meat) is what you get.

In careful experiments, the energy passed along in a food chain can be measured. It averages about 1/10 of what each food organism originally obtained for its own use. The 9/10 of the energy that is used does not disappear. It goes back into the environment in forms other than chemical energy. The chief form of energy return is heat. No organism can convert the heat back into chemical energy. The result is that energy flows in a one-way path through the web of life.

decomposers [dee kum PO zurz; Latin: *dis,* apart, + *compositus,* put together]

1−20 What kind of consumer is this mushroom?

GAF Corporation

Not all consumers "eat." At least they do not feed like you do. The tiny organisms that feed on the decaying lamb flesh are an example. Mushrooms are another. Mushroomlike organisms that grow on dead trees are still another. All these organisms break down, or decompose, animal and plant remains into simpler substances that are returned to the soil. These organisms are a special kind of consumer, ***decomposers.*** Decomposers are neither herbivores nor carnivores.

1—21 A food energy pyramid. Each level is one-tenth the equivalent of the level below it. Every organism carries on activities that use or release most of the energy it obtains. Only a fraction of the energy is passed along in a food chain.

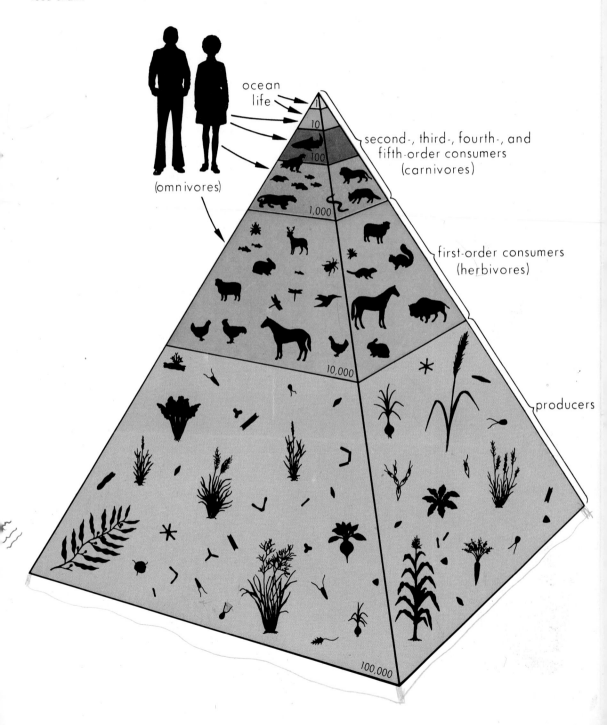

CHECK YOURSELF

F. How does a food web represent a web of life?
G. What is the source of energy for the living world?
H. Why is photosynthesis important to life on Earth?
I. How do consumers differ from producers?
J. What happens to the amount of energy available to organisms as it passes from one organism to another in a food chain?
K. Why are decomposers a special kind of consumer?

MATTER IN A FOOD WEB

The energy in a food web comes from the sun, but the food substance—or matter—comes from the earth. You probably already know something about matter. An *element* is matter that is made of a single kind of atom. A *mixture* and a *compound* are matter containing more than one kind of atom. In a mixture, you can sort the elements out individually if you know an efficient sorting method. In a compound, new **chemical bonds** have formed; that is, *atoms of the different elements share or exchange some of the particles of which they are made.* The different elements are locked into their new chemical structure until a chemical change occurs that may free them as elements again.

Organisms contain matter in all three forms: elements, mixtures, and compounds. There are also three *states* of matter: solid, liquid, and gas. Organisms contain matter in all three states. For almost all organisms, the matter is organized into

What is an example of a solid substance in organisms? A liquid? A gas?

ELEMENT	SYMBOL	APPROXIMATE % (BY WEIGHT) OF A HUMAN	APPROXIMATE % (BY WEIGHT) OF EARTH'S CRUST
Oxygen	O	65.	49.
Carbon	C	18.	0.09
Hydrogen	H	10.	0.88
Nitrogen	N	3.3	0.03
Calcium	Ca	1.5	3.4
Phosphorus	P	1.0	0.12
Potassium	K	0.35	2.4
Sulfur	S	0.25	0.05
Sodium	Na	0.24	2.6
Chlorine	Cl	0.19	0.19
Magnesium	Mg	0.05	1.9
Iron	Fe	0.005	4.7
Manganese	Mn	0.0003	0.08
Silicon	Si	trace	25.

1–22 Some of the elements that occur in organisms, mostly in compounds formed from the elements. Compare the percentages in humans with those in the earth's crust.

PRODUCERS   FIRST CONSUMERS   SECOND CONSUMERS   THIRD CONSUMERS

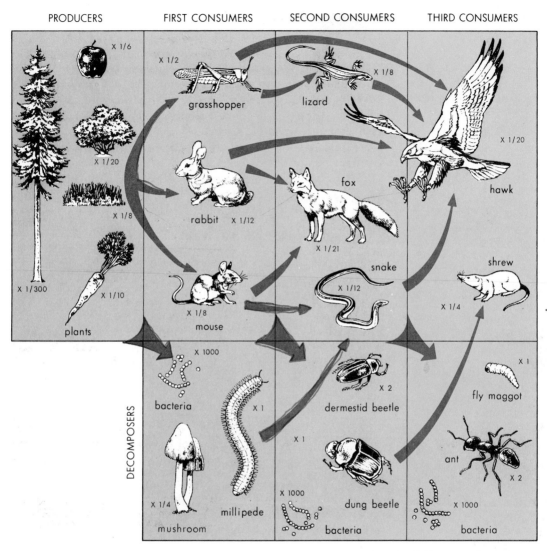

1—23 How many food chains can you trace?

cells (page 12). The cells are organized into the larger parts of the organisms' bodies.

Living things are so different from nonliving objects that for a long time scientists believed that special elements in organisms were not found in nonliving matter. However, this turned out not to be true. Biologists know today that organisms are made of a number of the same elements found elsewhere on the earth.

Of 100 or more elements, only about 30 are used in the makeup of organisms. Some of these are among the most abundant elements. Others are rare. Together they account for all living matter.

Photosynthetic organisms take from the environment relatively simple compounds that are called *inorganic.* Carbon dioxide and water are the chief examples. Inorganic compounds contain either no carbon at all or single carbon atoms per molecule. They never have carbon atoms linked to other carbon atoms. Inorganic molecules are all small. They contain chemical energy, but not in amounts useful to, or obtainable by, organisms.

Photosynthetic organisms take up inorganic compounds from the earth and air. These organisms use the energy of sunlight to build larger, *organic* compounds containing stored chemical energy. Typically the molecules of organic compounds are built with long carbon-to-carbon chains. Atoms of other elements are bonded to the carbon atoms in the chain. The usable food energy is stored mainly in the chemical bonds that link hydrogen atoms to the carbon atoms. When these carbon-to-hydrogen bonds are broken, the usable energy is released along with the hydrogen.

We can define both *foods* and *fuels* (like coal and oil) as organic substances containing carbon-hydrogen bonds. Indeed, a fuel to human beings — oil or wood — may be a food to some kinds of bacteria (which feed on oil) or to mushroomlike organisms (which feed on wood). Both foods and fuels, except for nuclear fuels, contain energy once trapped from sunlight by photosynthetic organisms.

A food is distinguished from a fuel by the biological differences among organisms. That is, an organism itself figures in the definition of a food. A *food* is an organic substance that an organism can break down and draw energy from for its body maintenance and repair — along with matter that can either be changed and used, or eliminated.

Unlike the flow of energy in a food web, the flow of matter is not one-way. Plants take up carbon dioxide, water, and other substances to begin photosynthesis. These are the same compounds that animals and decomposers give off again after using foods. Producers build up big molecules and store energy in them. Consumers change the molecules and tear many down. Consumers take usable energy and return carbon dioxide, water, and a few other substances to the environment again. Plants take up these materials and start over, with more photosynthesis. The only thing left out is that producers consume some of their own foods.

What we see is that the same matter is used over and over again. Matter travels in *cycles* from the nonliving environment to organisms, through their food webs, and back to the non-living environment. It then enters the food webs again in photosynthesis.

The carbon cycle. Like the rim of a wheel, a cycle has no beginning and no end. You break in somewhere to study the flow. The inorganic compound carbon dioxide (CO_2), mentioned earlier, is a good starting point. Carbon dioxide occurs in air and dissolved in water (figure 1–24). Certain other compounds on land and in water also release carbon dioxide readily (they are not shown in the figure). The organisms in the figure are familiar examples.

Follow the carbon dioxide around to the right. Plants take up carbon dioxide in photosynthesis. They return some of it to the atmosphere (see arrow) as they use their own foods. The rest of their foods, labeled "organic carbon," go mainly to animals and decomposers. The animals become food for other animals. All animals, and the decomposers, break down the organic compounds in foods and return carbon dioxide to the atmosphere. Notice that the decomposers get parts of both the plant and the animal organic carbon (see the short arrow from the rabbit and sheep to the decomposers).

Two other arrows in the figure indicate that carbon dioxide

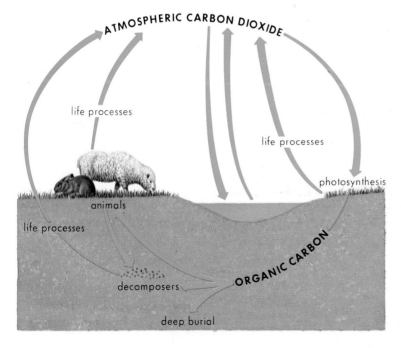

1–24 The carbon cycle. Use the text to explain the diagram. Where would you place humans in this cycle?

passes back and forth between the air and water. Also shown is that some organic compounds "get away" from the carbon cycle after photosynthesis. On land they are buried where decomposers cannot get at them. In the ocean they are buried in the sediments at the bottom. These energy-rich compounds slowly change in form and become sources of fuels—coal, oil, and natural gas. When the fuels are burned, the carbon is returned to the carbon cycle.

The water cycle. Organisms have more water (H_2O) in their bodies than any other compound. Water is necessary to life in many ways. It is one of the compounds plants use in photosynthesis. And in all organisms water combines chemically with certain other substances. It is released only when these substances are decomposed. Land plants absorb water from the soil. Land animals drink water or get it in their foods. Water constantly bathes organisms that live in ponds, lakes, rivers, and the oceans.

Water also evaporates from the surface of all bodies of water and from land. Plants and animals lose water, too, but by different processes.

The water cycle is probably the most familiar cycle to you. All the water comes from the nonliving environment (figure

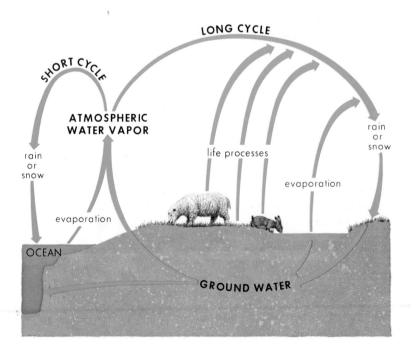

1−25 The water cycle. Explain the difference between the long and short cycles in terms of living things.

1–25). It all returns from the organisms to the nonliving environment.

The calcium cycle. The calcium cycle (figure 1–26) is different from the previous cycles. Calcium does not pass through the atmosphere. It cycles between organisms and soil, rock, and water. The calcium compounds are often buried and

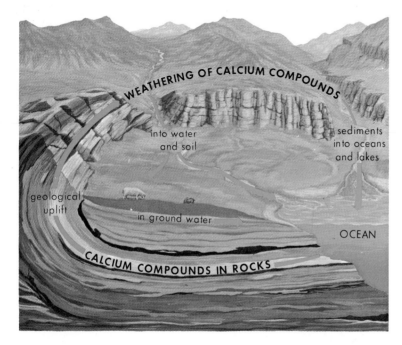

1–26 The calcium cycle. Unlike the preceding two cycles it occurs only on and below the ground's surface. It does not extend into the atmosphere. Many other elements follow identical cycles in earth, water, and rock.

"stored" for millions of years before they surface again. The same characteristics are true of the phosphorus cycle and of certain other cycles.

Organisms usually take in calcium compounds dissolved in water. Land plants obtain calcium compounds from soil water. Animals obtain calcium from plant foods and from water they drink. In the oceans, clams and oysters take calcium from the water and use it in building their shells. In other organisms, including humans, calcium is used in forming bones. These hard parts of organisms' bodies are often buried when the organisms die. The calcium compounds eventually become part of rock. Later, when the rock is exposed to rain or to circulation of underground water, calcium compounds are dissolved out of the rock again. Many of these calcium compounds are again taken from the water by organisms.

The calcium, water, and carbon cycles suggest that matter can be traced through food webs. This is the advantage of identifying the matter of which the food organisms in the food web are composed. Many thousands of quantitative experiments have been carried out. They provide data that let biologists know when an environment is gaining, losing, or remaining balanced in some of its materials.

CHECK YOURSELF

L. What is the source of all the matter that makes up the bodies of organisms?
M. How does the flow of matter differ from the flow of energy in a food web?
N. What do consumers do with organic compounds that return carbon dioxide to the environment and keep the carbon cycle going?
O. How do land organisms get water?
P. How do organisms get calcium and similar matter that is in the rocks of the earth?
Q. How are the cycles of matter useful to biologists in making quantitative studies of food chains in food webs?

Investigation 1.3   RELATIONSHIPS BETWEEN A PLANT AND AN ANIMAL

INTRODUCTION

In this investigation you will study a segment of the carbon cycle by setting up closed systems with plants and animals. (A closed system does not let materials in or out.) You will test for the presence of carbon dioxide using a dye. The dye is an indicator that changes color when a chemical reaction you ordinarily cannot see has taken place. Bromthymol blue is the indicator dye; it becomes green or yellow in the presence of an acid. Carbon dioxide (CO_2) forms a weak acid when dissolved in water. Therefore, in this investigation bromthymol blue is used to indicate, indirectly, the presence of CO_2.

MATERIALS
(per team)

8 screw-cap culture tubes, 20 × 150 mm
glass-marking crayon
2 test-tube racks
4 small water snails
4 pieces of elodea
bromthymol blue solution
container of melted paraffin
about 150 ml dechlorinated tap water
light source
box, large enough to cover 4 test tubes
small brush
white paper or white card

PROCEDURE

1. Read through the whole procedure. Then state the hypothesis that you think the procedure seems designed to test.
2. Prepare 2 sets of 4 culture tubes each, and label them *A1, A2, A3, A4,* and *B1, B2, B3, B4.*
3. Pour dechlorinated water into each tube to approximately 20 mm from the top. (Tap water becomes dechlorinated on standing for 24 hours. The chlorine in the water escapes into the air.)
4. Add 3 to 5 drops of bromthymol blue solution to each tube. Add nothing more to Tubes A1 and B1.
5. To Tubes A2 and B2 add a snail; to Tubes A3 and B3 add a leafy stem of elodea; and to Tubes A4 and B4 add both a snail and a leafy stem of elodea (figure 1−27).
6. Place a cap on each tube and tighten it. Brush melted paraffin onto the capped end of each tube to seal it. After the paraffin cools, test the seal by turning the tubes upside down for about 5 minutes.

1−27 Experimental setup.

liquid only   snail   elodea   snail and elodea

7. When all tubes are watertight, place one set (A1 to A4) in strong artificial light. Place the second set (B1 to B4) in a box, where it can be kept in the dark.
8. After 24 hours, observe both sets of tubes. Place a white card or sheet of white paper behind the tubes, so that it will be easier to determine color. In your data book, record changes in the color of the indicator and in the condition of the organisms. Record the letter and number of each tube you have observed.
9. Place the *A* series in the dark and the *B* series in the light.
10. After another 24 hours have passed, repeat your observations.
11. Switch the *A* series back to light and *B* back to dark. After several days observe the tubes again.

DISCUSSION

(*1*) In which tube did organisms die first? Snails and elodea usually live well in an aquarium or a pond. We might, therefore, hypothesize that being cut off from air had something to do with their deaths. (*2*) What substance in air may have been needed? Another possibility is that death may have resulted from the accumulation of a poisonous material in the water.

(*3*) What does the indicator show? Recall what you have read about photosynthesis and the carbon cycle. (4) Use this information and your answers to the previous questions to explain your data. (5) Why do you think Tubes A1 and B1 were used in this investigation even though no organisms were placed in them? (*6*) Did the indicator change color in Tubes A1 and B1? If so, how might you explain this? (7) What results might you expect if all the tubes were kept in total darkness?

(*8*) Do the data support your hypothesis? Explain (9) If not, try to devise a hypothesis that is consistent with (agrees with) all your observations.

HUMANS IN THE BIOSPHERE

After studying many food webs, biologists have concluded that all organisms are part of one worldwide web of life. Everywhere in this web, the organisms are tied to the matter and energy of the nonliving world. The living world forms only a thin layer around the nonliving world. This layer, including organisms, air, rock, soil, and water, is called the *biosphere.* It is deepest where oceans occur. Life exists all the way to the ocean bottom, as well as up from the ocean surface into the air. On land, the maximum depth life extends into the soil varies from a few meters to the depth of life-supporting underground caves. In studying small parts of this worldwide web of life, we can concentrate on any area that is convenient, such as the land along a river near a school, as in the high school biology class's study.

biosphere [Greek: *bios*, life, + *sphaira*, sphere].

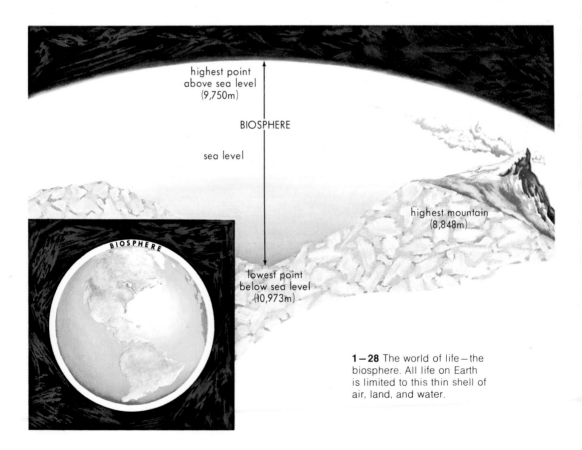

highest point
above sea level
(9,750m)

BIOSPHERE

sea level

highest mountain
(8,848m)

BIOSPHERE

lowest point
below sea level
(10,973m)

1—28 The world of life—the biosphere. All life on Earth is limited to this thin shell of air, land, and water.

Being a living thing, you too are a part of the biosphere. Your way of life keeps you occupied with your interrelationships with your family, friends, and other human beings. But according to the biosphere concept, you also have relationships with all other organisms. Your relationships to the plants and animals you eat are very direct. However, you can often miss seeing these relationships because you buy the edible parts of these plants and animals at a grocery store. The relationship between you and a grasshopper, which eats and damages some of your plant food, is less direct. But any damage to your food plants can affect your food supply.

What people have been longest in discovering is that the damage they do in changing the environment for their own uses has far-reaching effects all over the biosphere. Data being studied today show that many of our human activities worldwide are straining and destroying the balance in the biosphere. Fortunately, most other organisms that have been affected have established different food webs and balances where this has been possible. But humans keep pushing and making changes as though really independent of the rest of the living world. This has become a problem that not even biologists can solve without cooperation from leaders, industries, and people everywhere. Cooperation is not easy to get—people resist changes in their life-style. They want to see proof now that the ways they are using the biosphere will cause increasing problems better dealt with today than later.

What this means is that as a student you will enter a study of biology but as a citizen never leave it. Every public issue will have a biological meaning. You will use over and over the knowledge you acquire about ecology—about the relationships among organisms and between them and their nonliving environment.

CHECK YOURSELF

R. How do biologists define the biosphere?
S. Why is it useful to think of humans as a special kind of organism in the biosphere? How does this lead so many people to feel they are independent of the rest of the organisms in the biosphere?
T. How many ways can you name in which humans continue changing the biosphere?
U. What is the problem in getting people to anticipate the effects of human changes piling up in the biosphere?

Careers in Biology: Ecologist

Bill Knauer is an ecologist for the U.S. Fish and Wildlife Service. This federal agency has primary responsibility for managing the nation's birds, mammals, and fish for the enjoyment of all people. Part of Bill's past experience has been evaluating the effects of flooding stream valleys behind proposed dams. How will the wildlife respond to people's disruptions?

In a day Bill may be called upon to assess the effects of a deer-hunting season on nearby roosting bald eagles, to answer a letter from a congressperson asking why livestock grazing is restricted on a National Wildlife Refuge, and to speak to a high school biology class. He has caused a major U.S. highway to be moved a few feet, to preserve a trout and smallmouth bass stream. He then consulted with the highway engineers about planting trees and shrubs along the new route.

Although ecologists generally start out doing field research, many of them eventually move into offices. The most important part of Bill's job is telling other people what he has learned. Much of his time is spent consulting with biologists, engineers (**A**), and administrators from other agencies and organizations. As a result, communication skills are every bit

A. Bill consults with engineer John Kendal in the field.

U.S. Fish and Wildlife Service by Kent Olson

Photos by William W. Knauer II

B and C. Damming of a stream changes the streamside habitat from what you see on the left to the lake on the right. Instead of raccoons and deer, crappies and bass abound.

as important as biological knowledge.

All across our country, dams are being built (**B and C**), coal and other minerals strip-mined (**D and E**), and fields and farms converted to suburban development. All of this destroys habitats (homes) for fish and wildlife. The impact of development must be assessed for each group of animals, and ways must be found to reduce this impact. After some types of development the areas may be reworked and planted to again provide a place for wildlife.

D and E. Energy development by strip-mining depletes the habitat for animals such as antelope.

Betty R. Seacrest

All organisms need a place to live. For people, not only living space and food, but the energy to produce our necessities must be extracted from the natural environment. The interrelationships of fish and wildlife with water, land, people, and industry are very complex. Ecologists attempt to ensure that the development of our nation's resources is in the best interests of all our people and takes into account all the many kinds of wildlife (**F**).

The U.S. Fish and Wildlife Service is only one of the places where ecologists like Bill Knauer may be found. State fish and game departments, conservation organizations, private consulting firms, and other industries hire ecologists to assist in their operations. There are many pressures on ecologists, especially when a developer wants to destroy the habitat of an endangered species. The ecologist must be a true diplomat and negotiator in order to achieve the best solutions for all concerned.

F. Bill and an Administrative Officer of the Fish and Wildlife Service, Ann Miller, bring together field experience and administrative planning. They are reviewing plans for a proposed visitor contact station at the Sand Lake National Wildlife Refuge in South Dakota.

U.S. Fish and Wildlife Service by Kent Olson

Investigation 1.4   STUDYING A PIECE OF THE BIOSPHERE

INTRODUCTION

In Investigation 1.1 you studied small pieces of the biosphere in pictures. Then you studied living organisms, and, finally, a small piece of the biosphere in your laboratory. Now you should study a piece of the biosphere out of doors. It need not be a very large piece — just large enough to contain several kinds of organisms that show interrelationships with each other. Different schools have different opportunities for outdoor studies. Therefore, procedures will have to be worked out by your class and your teacher to fit the piece of biosphere that is most convenient to your school. Read the following sections carefully to get an overview of what you might do.

Selecting a study area. You may not have much choice, but let us examine some alternatives. A forest is complex and provides opportunities to collect abundant data, but it is most difficult to picture as a whole. A prairie is almost as complex and is somewhat easier to study. Cultivated areas, such as cornfields, and pastures are relatively simple to study. They are as important as forests and prairies because they now cover a large part of the land area of our country.

Pieces of the biosphere suitable for study can also be found in cities. Many schools have lawns with trees and shrubs. Here there may be fewer kinds of organisms than in the country, but you can be more thorough in your study. You also can study vacant lots and spaces between buildings. Even cracks in paving, gutters, and the area around trees often contain a surprising number of organisms.

Organizing the work. After deciding where to make the study, your class must next decide what kinds of data to collect. The questions in the discussion for this investigation should give you some ideas. Different teams should gather different kinds of data.

Each team must decide what materials it needs and arrange to obtain them. A team may draw up a form on which data can be recorded quickly. Each team should select a leader to see that all parts of the work are completed as planned by the team. Each individual has special abilities. Use these when deciding on tasks within the team.

All of the procedures in Investigation 1.4 can be expanded, depending on the wishes of your class. In many cases, further procedures can be found in E. A. Phillips, 1964, *Field Ecology,* a BSCS Laboratory Block, D. C. Heath & Co., Lexington, Mass., and in A. H. Benton and W. E. Werner, 1972, *Manual of Field Biology and Ecology,* 5th ed., Burgess Publ. Co., Minneapolis. Your teacher can suggest additional references or procedures.

Collecting the data. It may be easier to handle sheets of paper on a clipboard than to take data books into the field. Paste the sheets into data books when you return to the laboratory.

No biologist can identify every organism she or he sees. There are two ways to deal with this problem. One is to identify kinds only by general group names — for example, "trees," "spiders," "grass," "beetles," "turtles." These may be sufficient for developing many ideas about interrelationships. Another method is to collect a **specimen** — a sample individual or, in the case of large plants, a characteristic part (a leaf, for example). Assign the specimen a letter (*A, B,*

C, etc.) and whenever you need to refer to that kind of organism, refer to its letter. You may be able to identify your specimen, after you return to the laboratory, by looking it up or showing it to an expert.

Some descriptions of plants you may find in your study area may be useful to you. A **tree** is a tall woody plant with a single stem (trunk). A **shrub** is a woody plant that branches at or near the ground and lacks a trunk. A **sapling** is a young tree with a trunk 1 to 5 cm in diameter. An **herb** (urb) is a nonwoody plant that dies back at least to ground level in winter. A tree **seedling** is a very young tree with a trunk less than 1 cm in diameter.

Searching for animal data. This activity should be carried out after the studies of plants have been completed. Do this on a later day, if possible. Work in pairs, with one person searching, the other recording. Turn over stones, dead logs, and other cover to find animals. (All sheltering stones, logs, and so on, should be returned to their original position.) Look on plants, too, especially in flowers. And look for animal droppings.

Make notes of the kinds, numbers, and activities of animals you find. If it is permitted in the area where you are working, collect specimens of unknown kinds for identification.

Netting insects. In thick forests it may be difficult to catch flying insects, but you can beat the shrubs and saplings with a stout net, holding the open end up. In open fields sweep your net through the plants. When you have a number of insects in the net, place the net in a large plastic bag with several drops of chloroform. (Do not inhale the fumes.) Close the bag tightly around the net and wait a few minutes. Pick out the organisms and place them in jars of alcohol or formalin. Label the jars with your team number and the date.

Studying larger animals. Your searching

procedure may uncover toads or snakes. (*Caution: Do not pick up any animals or touch any plants unless you can identify them as harmless.*) To study reptiles, birds, and other large animals, you will need to cover larger areas than the ones we have been considering and observe the areas over longer periods of time. Unless there is some good reason to keep the animals, do not collect them.

Birds may not be present or active when your class is collecting data. A few students may want to look for them at different times over a period of several days. Around daybreak and dusk are usually the best times.

The most convenient way to begin studying larger animals, other than birds, is to trap them alive and unharmed. One of the easiest traps to make uses a 0.91 kg (2-lb) coffee can or a 1.5 kg (48-oz) juice can. Remove the top and bury the can so that the top rim is level with the soil surface. For bait, mix peanut butter and oatmeal and roll this into balls.

Even if you decide not to trap the animals, be sure to look for animal tracks and animal droppings. In cities you are likely to see birds, rats, mice, dogs, and cats. And don't forget to look for signs of humans.

PART A: A FIELD STUDY

MATERIALS
(per team)

hammer or mallet
8 stakes, 18 to 25 cm long
rope, heavy string, or plastic
　clothesline, 12 m, marked at
　0.5 m intervals
about 60 m twine
right triangles
glass-marking crayon

PROCEDURE

1. In a forest, study areas for different organisms should be of different sizes. These can be set up as shown in figure 1−29. Square or rectangular study areas are called **quadrats**.

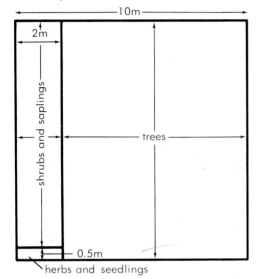

1−29 Plan of quadrats for use in the study of a forested area.

2. In unforested areas, quadrats should be 2 to 4 m on a side without internal divisions.
3. In vacant city lots, cultivated fields, and pastures, use smaller teams (of 2 to 3) and more of them. Each team should work on a quadrat 1 meter square (figure 1−30).
4. Drive a stake into the ground. Measure off 10 m in any direction from it, using the marked rope or clothesline. Drive another stake at this point.
5. Stretch twine from the 1st to the 2nd stake, tying it to each. You will need to make a right angle at the stake for the 2nd side of your quadrat. Use a right triangle or a carpenter's framing square to get your right angle, or apply your knowledge of geometry and use a meterstick to get the angle.
6. At 10 m from the 2nd stake, drive a 3rd stake and connect it with twine to the 2nd.

Continue around the square. You may want to divide the large study quadrat into smaller quadrats to make your counting easier. If the forest is thick, the quadrat may not be precisely square, because trees and bushes stand in the way. Be as accurate as possible.

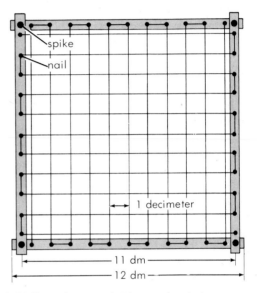

1−30 Frame for a quadrat in an unforested area.

7. If there are not many plants, an area may be set off by a stiff wire circle with a circumference of 345 cm. Laid on the ground, this circle encloses an area equal to 1 square meter (1 m² or 10,000 cm²).
8. In a forest it is convenient to divide plants into 5 groups: trees, shrubs, saplings, herbs, and seedlings. Trees over 5 cm in diameter (about 16 cm in circumference) should be studied in the main quadrat (figure 1−29). Observe trees that form the **canopy** (the forest top, which receives direct sunlight) separately from those that do not reach the canopy. Make a count of the trees, either by kinds or just as "trees." Count shrubs and saplings in an area smaller than that used for the trees. Also

count herbs and seedlings in small quadrats. In each small quadrat estimate the proportion that is covered by very small plants forming a mat over the ground.

9. Special problems may arise. In a lawn, for example, there is no need to count blades of grass. However, a count of the "weeds" might be worthwhile, especially if comparisons are made between well-trodden areas and protected ones. A frame (figure 1–30) may be useful for this work.

PART B: ORGANISMS IN LITTER AND SOIL

Many small organisms live just beneath and just above the soil surface. Collect them in samples of the upper part of the soil and in samples of *litter*—loose organic matter on the surface of the soil.

MATERIALS
(per team in the field)

plastic bags (1 per sample)
rubber bands
glass-marking crayon
wire circle, 35.4 cm in
  circumference (enclosing
  0.1 m²)
centimeter ruler
trowel with a 10-cm mark
  on the blade

(per team in the laboratory)

ether or chloroform
medicine dropper
white enameled pan or
  large sheet of white paper
light source
forceps
bottles or jars, with caps
alcohol or formalin, 50 ml
  per bottle
microscope
Berlese apparatus (figure
  1–31)
glass-marking crayon

PROCEDURE

1. Before going into the field, label the plastic bags with your team number and date of collection. Use the wire circle to mark out an area. Scrape loose litter from inside the circle. Place the litter in a plastic bag. Tightly fasten the bag with a rubber band.

2. In the same 0.1-m² circle from which the litter was taken, insert the trowel to a depth of 10 cm. Remove a sample of soil. Place the sample in a separate plastic bag and fasten with a rubber band.

3. At least 2 such pairs of samples (litter and soil) should be taken from different places in the large forest quadrats. On smaller quadrats in other kinds of areas, 1 soil sample per quadrat may be enough. If you are working in cracks in a paved area, a measured soil sample may not be possible.

4. In the laboratory, place a few drops of ether or chloroform in the bags containing the litter. Do not breathe the fumes. Close the bags tightly and wait 5 minutes. (*Caution: Do not use ether or chloroform near an open flame.*)

5. Empty the contents into a white enameled pan or onto a table covered with white paper. Shine a strong light on the litter.

6. Pick through the litter carefully with forceps. Put all the organisms you find into a small jar of alcohol or formalin.

7. Loosen each soil sample and, if very dry, moisten it slightly. Then place the samples in the Berlese apparatus (figure 1–31).

8. The heat and light from the bulb cause small organisms to crawl downward and fall into the preservative. Label the vials with your team number and the date of collection.

9. Leave the Berlese funnel in operation about 2 days. If the funnel becomes misshapen, you can reinforce it by adding pipe-cleaner "ribs."

1–31 Berlese funnel.

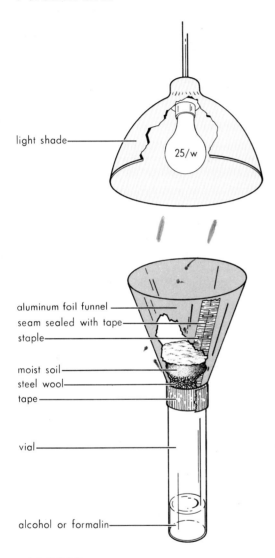

light shade

25/w

aluminum foil funnel
seam sealed with tape
staple

moist soil
steel wool
tape

vial

alcohol or formalin

DISCUSSION

When your field and laboratory work have been completed, place your team data on stencils from which copies can be made for the class. Using all the data from the study areas, carefully consider as many of the following questions as your information allows.

If different kinds of areas were included, make comparisons wherever possible.

(*1*) What producers are in the area? Answer in general terms—trees, shrubs, and so on—or by naming the organisms you were able to identify. (*2*) Are producers abundant or rare? (*3*) Do you have any evidence that there are seasonal changes in the kinds and numbers of producers? (*4*) Are there different groups of producers? If so, which one contributes the most toward producing the food that is present in the area? (*5*) Are there layers of producers? If so, what relationships can you find among the producers in the different layers? (*6*) Does the area produce all its own food, or is food carried in from beyond its boundaries? What evidence do you have for your answer?

(*7*) What consumers are in the community? Answer in general terms, such as insects, spiders, birds, and so on, or with names of those you identified. (*8*) Which consumers are herbivores and which are carnivores? What evidence supports your answer? (*9*) What relationships can you find between the numbers of a particular herbivore and the numbers of a carnivore that eats it?

(*10*) Using the information you have, construct an energy-flow diagram for the area. (*11*) Do you have any evidence that one kind of organism affects another in ways other than those involving food relationships? If so, what is the evidence and what is the relationship it shows?

An investigation such as you have made should raise more questions than it answers. In studying the data, part of your job is to look for questions that need answering. (*12*) List as many questions about the organisms in your area as you can.

Although your data from these investigations are incomplete, you have taken a biologist's first step in describing a study area.

PROBLEMS

The following problems require thinking or research. Some involve applications of your understanding of the text and the laboratory. Others require further study.

1. Draw a food web including at least four plants and four animals that you use for food. Show as many interrelationships as possible, including yourself. Be sure that the food chain for each animal is traced back to a producer.

2. How can the energy in coal and oil be related to the activities of producer organisms?

3. What might happen to the balance in the food web of life in a pond if the number of one kind of organism suddenly increased greatly? How long do you think such an increase would last? Is your prediction affected by the kind of organism involved? For example: first, think about a producer; then, a consumer.

4. What pathways do the calcium cycle and the water cycle share? What does this mean in terms of matter cycling through living organisms?

5. In making a journey into outer space, astronauts must take along a part of our biosphere. Try to design an efficient "package" of the biosphere for such a journey.

6. The President of the United States has a science advisor. Should he appoint a physicist, a chemist, or a biologist to the position? Explain your reasoning.

7. Many people have careers related to biology. How does the career of your school cafeteria's nutritionist relate to energy flow and materials cycles in a food web?

8. Read about the careers of a veterinarian, a botanist, and a wildlife conservation officer. Explain how each might affect a food web. Use the food web with grass, a rabbit, a ewe and her lamb, a horse, a coyote, and a person as the example.

SUGGESTED READINGS

British Museum of Natural History. 1978. *Nature at Work: Introducing Ecology.* Cambridge University Press, New York. Well-illustrated look at life in an oak woodland and on a rocky seashore. Traces food chains.

Dorfman, L. 1975. *The Student Biologist Explores Ecology.* Richards Rosen Press, New York. Discussion of the principles of ecology.

Gosz, J. R., R. T. Holmes, G. E. Likens, and F. H. Bormann. 1978. The Flow of Energy in a Forest Ecosystem. *Scientific American,* March. Describes how a forest partitions solar energy.

Janick, J., C. H. Noller, and C. L. Rhykerd. 1976. The Cycles of Plant and Animal Nutrition. *Scientific American,* September. Deals with how energy and nutrients are processed by organisms in food chains.

Kormondy, E. J. 1976. *Concepts of Ecology.* Prentice-Hall, Englewood Cliffs, N. J. Fairly advanced reading.

Likens, G. E., R. F. Wright, J. N. Galloway, and T. J. Butler. 1979. Acid Rain. *Scientific American,* October. Describes how mass burning of fuels increases the acidity of rain.

Mariner, J. L. 1975. *Understanding Ecology.* Independent School Press, Wellesley Hills, Mass. Readable introduction to the principles of ecology.

Reid, K., J. A. Lauwerys, J. Joffe, and A. Tucker. 1974. *Man, Nature and Ecology.* Doubleday, Garden City, N. Y. Refreshing look at human impact on the world ecosystem.

Chapter 2

Individuals and Populations

YOUR GUIDEPOSTS

In this chapter you will have an opportunity to explore these questions in biology:

- How are individual organisms grouped into populations?
- How do populations change?
- How is the density of populations calculated?
- How do environmental factors affect population size?
- What principles of biological investigation does the study of populations illustrate?

INDIVIDUALS

In general, life processes occur in separate "packages." You are such a package. You carry on the processes of life within your own body, separate and distinct from the life processes in the bodies of your parents or brothers or sisters. Each person is an *individual*. So, too, is each cow in a herd, each bee in a hive, each tree in a forest.

individual [Latin: *individuus*, indivisible]

Sometimes individuals are so close together that several seem to be one. From a distance, a flock of ducks in a pond may look like a single living mass. Of course, you have only to startle the flock into flight to see that it is made up of individuals. It is more difficult to untangle the individual grass plants in a lawn.

Look at figure 2–1. You see many small organisms with waving tentacles. Each organism seems to be separate from the others—an individual. But if you examine the coral more closely, you find that all the tentacle-waving organisms are connected. Is each an individual, or is the whole mass an individual?

tentacles [TENT ih kulz; Latin: *tentare*, to touch, feel]. See page 129.

41

S. A. Reed

2 – 1 Coral. Is this one individual or many?

geranium [juh RAY nee um]. See figure 8–5.

originate [uh RIJ uh nayt; Latin: *origo*, beginning, source]

X 1/10

2 – 2 From above ground how many iris plants do there seem to be? How many when the soil is removed?

There is still another difficulty. You can break off a piece of geranium, put it in soil, and see the piece grow and become a new individual. Or you can watch a chick hatch from an egg that was laid by a hen. In each case the new individual is clearly a piece of the old. The chick is more than that, with pieces of not only the hen but also the rooster. Apparently, new individuals always originate from existing individuals. Life is continuous in this way, yet it is divided into separate individuals.

We may have difficulty deciding just what we mean by "individuals" in corals and irises, or just when an egg becomes an individual separate from the hen. But, in most cases, it is easy to distinguish individuals. When we are studying a species in which individuals are difficult to identify, we investigate all possible characteristics, then define what the term "individual" applies to in this species.

POPULATIONS

Rarely in nature is a single individual totally isolated from all others of its kind. This is as true for mountain lions as it is for maple trees, even though we may have to look a little farther and harder to find more than one mountain lion. Groups of such similar individuals are called ***populations.*** Populations are an important factor in research, because biologists are interested in verifiable observations. Seldom do biologists rely on their observation of a single individual to test a hypothesis. Instead, they observe many individuals from a population.

Investigation 2.1   STUDY OF A YEAST POPULATION

INTRODUCTION

Yeast organisms are useful for studying populations. They reproduce rather rapidly and are conveniently small. You will observe a *culture* (population) of yeast cells growing on a broth *medium* (plural, media). To prevent other organisms from growing in your cultures, the medium has been sterilized. That is, all the living things that may have been in it have been killed.

You have already worked with variables. In Investigation 1.3 all the test tubes that were kept in the light were alike except in one way. That is, all variables except one were controlled. The experimental variable was the different organisms (elodea or snail) placed in the test tubes. You were testing what effect the organisms would have on the solution in the test tubes.

MATERIALS
(per team of 10 students)

glass-marking crayon
10 test tubes, each containing
   10 ml of sterile medium
2 test-tube racks
yeast culture
medicine dropper or 1-ml pipette
formalin
30 to 40 cover-slip fragments
10 microscope slides
10 medicine droppers
10 cover slips
5 microscopes
15 test tubes containing 9 ml of water

Read through the procedure for this investigation. (*1*) What is the experimental variable? (*2*) State a hypothesis that is appropriate for the procedure.

PROCEDURE

1. Using a glass-marking crayon, mark each tube of sterile medium with your team symbol. Number the tubes from *0* to *9*. Assign one numbered tube to each team member.
2. Stir the yeast culture thoroughly with a medicine dropper. Immediately transfer 10 drops of the culture to each tube. Uncap and recap each tube quickly and carefully.
3. Add 20 drops of formalin to Tube 0. (Formalin kills the yeast organisms and preserves them until you can count them.)
4. Place all the tubes except Tube 0 in a warm, dark place (*incubate* them). On each succeeding day, add 20 drops of formalin to the tube with the next higher number (Tubes 1, 2, 3, etc.).
5. After the last culture in the series (Tube 9) has been treated with preservative, count the yeast organisms in all 10 tubes. To do

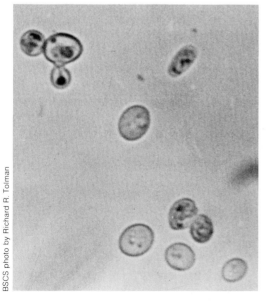

BSCS photo by Richard R. Tolman

2–3 Yeast. Note the small buds still attached to two yeast cells. These buds will separate from the parent cell and become new individuals. × 600

Team _____   Culture No. _____   Dilution Factor_____

MEMBER OF PAIR	FIELDS					TOTAL	AVERAGE	AVERAGE X DILUTION FACTOR
	1	2	3	4	5			
A. Your name								
B. Partner								

2−4 Chart for population counts.   Pair   Average _____

this, team members should work in pairs. Each student should count the yeast in his or her own tube and in his or her partner's tube.

6. Before you begin counting, prepare a chart like figure 2−4 in your data book. Carefully place 3 to 5 fragments of broken cover slip in the center of a microscope slide; position them to support an unbroken cover slip. Shake your test tube thoroughly to distribute the yeast organisms evenly. Immediately place 2 drops of the culture on the slide between the cover-slip fragments. Place a clean cover slip on the fragments without putting any pressure on it. Position the slide on your microscope stage. (Be careful not to tilt the stage.) Focus with low power; then switch to high power.

7. Count the number of individual organisms in 5 different high-power fields, as shown in figure 2−5. (Note: Yeast organisms are difficult to see if the light is too bright.) Refer to figure 2−3 for the appearance of yeast organisms. The cells often stick together, but count each cell in any clump separately. Buds also count as individuals. Record your 5 counts on the chart in your data book on line A.

2−5 Approximate positions of fields for counts.

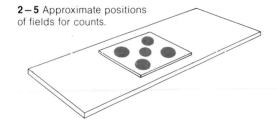

8. If the fields are too crowded for each counting, dilute the culture. Obtain a test tube containing 9 ml of water; label this tube with your culture number and *D1* (for "dilution one"). Shake the yeast culture until the organisms are evenly distributed. Immediately transfer 20 drops (1 ml) of the culture into the dilution tube. Rinse the medicine dropper several times with clean water. Mix the contents of the dilution tube thoroughly. Immediately transfer 2 drops from the dilution tube to a slide as directed above and count the yeast organisms.

9. If the field is still too crowded for easy counting, transfer 20 drops of the contents of Tube D1 to another test tube containing 9 ml of water. Mark this dilution *D2*. It may even be necessary to use a 3rd dilution (see figure 2−6).

10. In Tube D1, the culture is diluted 10 times; in Tube D2, 100 times; in Tube D3, 1,000 times. If you make dilutions during counting, record the proper number (10, 100, or 1,000) after "Dilution Factor" on the data chart. If you make no dilutions, the dilution factor is 1.

11. Now have your partner make 5 counts of a new sample taken from your culture, using the same procedure. If dilutions are necessary, use a new set of tubes and label them properly. Record these counts on the chart in your data book on line B.

12. After recording all the data, compute the total of the 5 counts across each line, and divide by 5 to get the average for the line. If your average (line A) and your partner's

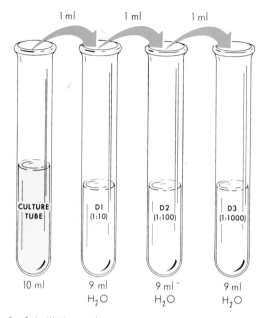

1 ml   1 ml   1 ml

| CULTURE | D1 | D2 | D3 |
| TUBE | (1:10) | (1:100) | (1:1000) |

10 ml   9 ml   9 ml   9 ml
             H_2O H_2O H_2O

2-6 A dilution series.

average (line B) differ by more than 10 organisms, check your calculations. If no mathematical error is detected, prepare new slides and repeat the counts.

13. Repeat the entire procedure using samples from your partner's tube. Enter your counts of your partner's culture on line B of his or her chart.

14. You have already filled the "Total" and "Average" columns in your data chart. Now multiply the average number on each line by the dilution factor. For example, if you made a count from Tube D2, the dilution factor is 100. If your average count was 15, the number in the last column should be 1,500. To find the "Pair Average," average the 2 numbers in the last column. Record the "Pair Average" on the master chart on the board.

DISCUSSION

In this investigation, you obtained an *estimate* of the populations in the tubes by a method called *sampling.* To increase the accuracy of your estimate, you took certain

precautions. You shook each tube to distribute the organisms evenly. By using the coverslip fragments of the same thickness, you made each count in the same volume of culture. You counted the organisms in 5 different fields of view. Averaging these 5 fields smoothed out chance differences. After 2 people made counts from the same tube, you averaged their counts. On the master chart, you averaged the figures obtained by all teams. These steps further smoothed out chance differences between the tubes. The final count for the population, at each period of incubation, is the average number of organisms per high-power field of view.

On a sheet of graph paper, list the ages of the cultures (in days) on the horizontal axis. Then, list the numbers of organisms on the vertical axis. Plot the data from each team separately, using a different color for each team. Then use black to plot the average data of all teams.

(3) On the basis of your discussion of this investigation, explain similarities and differences among the graph lines representing data from different teams. (4) Is there any general trend in the graph line representing the average data of all teams? If so, describe it. (5) Do the average data support your hypothesis? Explain.

FOR FURTHER INVESTIGATION

1. Does temperature affect the growth of a yeast population? Repeat the procedures, but incubate the cultures at a constant temperature 15°C above or below the average temperature at which the tubes were incubated before.

2. Does the amount of food energy available affect the growth of a yeast population? The medium you used in this investigation contained 4% glucose, a sugar that is used as food by yeast. Your teacher has directions for making a 1%- and a 2%-glucose medium. Repeat the procedures using one of these media.

CHARACTERISTICS OF POPULATIONS

censuses [SEN sus suz; Latin: *censere*, to enroll, tax]

The study of human population size has been going on for a long time. Ancient Romans and Chinese took censuses regularly, primarily for tax purposes. The study of population in modern science began in 1798, when Thomas Malthus published *An Essay on the Principle of Population as It Affects the Future Improvement of Mankind.* Malthus was interested primarily in social problems. He presented evidence to show that all kinds of organisms tend to multiply up to the limit of their food supply. When this happens, the results are misery, sickness, and starvation for many individuals. Malthus' conclusion started arguments and investigations that are continuing today.

imply [im PLY]: not directly stated but suggested by accompanying statements

In defining population, you need to identify the kind of individuals you are talking about and their limits in *time* and *space*. Thus, you can refer to the population of pigeons during August, 1978, in Chicago, or the population of catfish during a given year in a particular lake. The kind of individuals, the time, and the place are always involved, though sometimes we may imply one or more of these.

POPULATION CHANGES

rate [Latin: *ratus*, fixed by calculation]

reforestation: process of planting new trees on land once forested

The size of any population continually changes. Whenever the amount of one thing varies with respect to the amount of another thing, we can express the change as a ***rate***. How can we calculate the rate at which the size of a population varies during some period of time?

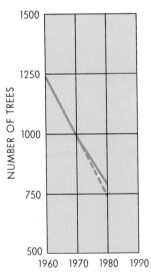

Suppose a biologist counted 1,225 living white pines in a reforestation area in 1960 and 950 pines in 1970. The difference in time, ΔT (delta T), is $1970 - 1960 = 10$ years. The difference in population size (number of trees), ΔN (delta N), is $950 - 1,225 = -275$. (The population sizes must be written in the same order as the dates.) Divide the difference in population size by the difference in time: $\dfrac{-275 \text{ trees}}{10 \text{ years}} = -27.5$ trees per year. The negative number indicates a decrease in population size. A positive number would indicate an increase.

This arithmetic can be summarized in the formula $R = \dfrac{\Delta N}{\Delta T}$.

That is, the rate at which the population size changes is equal to the change in number of individuals divided by the change in time. Suppose there are 770 living trees in the reforestation area in 1980. Using the formula, we have:

2—7 Changes in a white-pine population. The dotted line continues the 1960–1970 rate.

$$R = \frac{770 - 950}{1980 - 1970} = \frac{-180}{10} = -18 \text{ trees per year from 1970 to 1980.}$$

Figure 2–7 shows the data for this white-pine forest in graph form. The population decrease was slower in the decade 1970–1980 than in the decade 1960–1970. The reduced slope of the second part of the line on the graph shows the decrease.

Such a slope as that in the pine graph may become horizontal, but it can never become vertical. Why not?

INCREASES AND DECREASES

What accounts for the decrease of 455 pines during the 20-year period? Since pines do not wander away, they must have died. The decrease in the pine population per unit of time is called the death rate, or **mortality.** Death rate can be a characteristic only of a population. Since each individual dies only once, an individual cannot have a death rate.

mortality [Latin: *mortis,* of death]

Figure 2–8 shows that different kinds of organisms have different patterns of mortality. Some, like human populations in Western nations, have very low mortality rates among the young, but mortality rates increase rapidly among people who are 60 to 65 years old. Other organisms, like some fish and birds, have constant death rates. A chickadee, for example, is just as likely to die between the ages of five and six years as it was at the age of one or two years. Still others, like oysters and redwood trees, have very high mortality rates among young individuals. Those that survive this period, however, are likely to live a full life. For redwoods, a full life may mean 2,500 years!

2–8 Mortality graphs for three kinds of organisms.

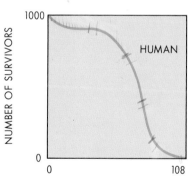
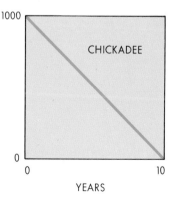
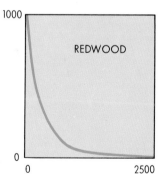

Mortality can change over periods of time. The death rate of the human population of the United States has declined steadily during the 20th century. In 1900 the death rate per 1,000 was 17.2. This means that, out of every 1,000 living persons of all ages, 17.2 died that year. In 1925 the rate was down to 11.7. Since 1948 it has varied between 9.0 and 9.9.

Our white-pine example may be too simple. While some individuals were being removed from the population, others might have been added. Perhaps no new trees were planted,

What do you think might be responsible for this drop in death rate?

but the trees already there could have produced seeds that added to the population. As death decreases a population size, reproduction increases it. Mammals are born, birds are hatched, seeds of plants germinate—we have a number of terms for the reproductive process. But the term customarily used for reproductive rate is **birth.** The rate at which reproduction increases the population is the birthrate, or **natality.** Again, note that this is a characteristic of a population, not of an individual.

natality [Latin: *natus,* born]

As was the case for mortality, different kinds of organisms have different natalities. Even different populations of the same kind of organism may have different natalities. For example, among humans, the birthrate in 1980 was 6 times higher in certain African nations than in West Germany. And natality also changes with time. In the United States, the birthrate in 1910 per 1,000 was 30.1. That is, there were 30.1 live births for every 1,000 living persons of all ages. In 1930 the rate had dropped to 20.2; in 1976 the rate was 15.0; in 1980 the rate was 16.0.

What do you think might be responsible for this change in birthrate?

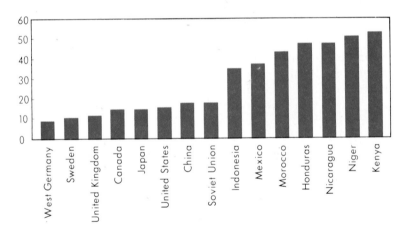

2—9 Natality (number of births per 1,000 persons) in various countries in 1980.

motile [MOH tul]

Pine trees do not move about. However, for **motile** organisms, those that can move about, we must take into account two other causes of change in population size. A population of rats, for example, may be increased by individuals coming from other places—**immigration.** Or the population may be decreased by individuals going to other places—**emigration.**

immigration [Latin: *in,* in, + *migrare,* to move from one place to another]

emigration [Latin: *e,* out, + *migrare*]

As mortality and natality change with time, so do movements into or out of a population. Human immigration to the United States, for example, was over 5.5 million in the period 1911 to 1920, but just over 500,000 between 1931 and 1940. By contrast, human emigration from the United States was 2 million in the period 1911 to 1920 and just under 500,000 between 1931 and 1940.

Since 1965 a limit has been placed on the number of immigrants into the U.S. each year. Check a recent almanac for information.

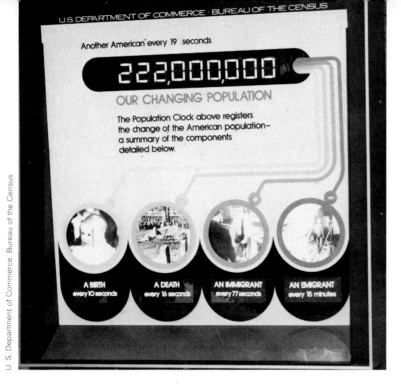

2–10 The population meter of the U.S. Bureau of the Census. Each of the pictures shows one of the four population determiners. The sum of these four rates sets the speed at which the numerals turn in the population estimate. The estimate shown is for April 1, 1980.

INTERACTION OF RATES

Suppose you are studying the pigeon population in a certain city. During some period of time, say, a year, some pigeons are hatched and some die. Some pigeons also wander into the city, and some wander out. All four causes of change in the size of the pigeon population can be calculated as rates. Natality and immigration *increase* the population; mortality and emigration *decrease* the population. Will the pigeon population in the city be greater or less at the end of a year? The answer depends on the relative sizes of the two sets of opposing rates.

Suppose the student population of your classroom is 35. You can assume that there is neither mortality nor natality. If students immigrate at the rate of 5 every minute and emigrate at the rate of 5 every minute, what is the population size at the end of any 1-minute period? Mathematically, we can express this as $35 + 5 - 5 = 35$. Thus, the population is the same at the end of a minute as it was at the beginning. The individuals in the room may not be the same individuals that were there before, but no change in population size has occurred. Now suppose that 5 enter and 10 leave every minute. What is the population size at the end of the first minute? We have $35 + 5 - 10 = 30$. The population size has decreased.

What would be the size at the end of *three* minutes?

This mathematical method can also be applied to natality and mortality. Like immigration and emigration, these factors work in opposite directions. The size of any population at any given time is the result of the numerical relationships among natality, mortality, immigration, and emigration. We may call these four rates the *determiners* of population size. In any experimental study of populations, these determiners must be considered as possible variables.

Investigation 2.2   POPULATION CHANGES: A MODEL

INTRODUCTION

Just as we need physical tools such as microscopes to extend our powers of observation, we also need mental tools to extend our thinking. One such mental tool is called a *model.* Here the word does not mean an object. Instead, it means something we construct in our minds. A mental model simplifies a complex real situation, so that we can understand it more easily. Because a model is a simplification, it differs in some respects from the real situation. To simplify a situation, we make *assumptions.* That is, we assume certain things that may be only approximately true. We must keep these assumptions in mind whenever we use a model to look at a real situation.

If a specific model gives results similar to the observations we make in some real situation, we conclude that the real situation works in the same way the model does. Of course, this conclusion *may* be wrong; a different model also might give results that fit the real situation.

PROCEDURE

1. Let us begin with real organisms — house sparrows. Imagine an island. For our model we will start with a hypothetical (imaginary) population of house sparrows. In the spring of 1981, there were 10 sparrows: 5 male-female pairs. Our assumptions are:
Assumption 1: Every breeding season (spring), each pair of sparrows produces 10 offspring, always 5 males and 5 females.

MATERIALS
(per student)

4 sheets graph paper (arithmetic)
1 sheet semilogarithmic graph paper

2–11 House sparrow.

X 1/2

Assumption 2: Each year, before the next spring, all the breeding (parent) birds die.
Assumption 3: Each year all offspring live through the next breeding season. (In most real situations some parents would live and some offspring would die. But taken together, Assumptions 2 and 3 balance each other to reduce the difference between the model and a real situation.)
Assumption 4: During the study, no other sparrows arrive on the island, and none leave.

2. Now let us use this model. Calculate the size of the hypothetical population at the beginning of each breeding season. Ac-

cording to Assumption 1, in the spring of 1981 there are 5 pairs of birds. Each of the 5 pairs produces 10 offspring, a total of 50. According to Assumption 1, there are 25 males and 25 females: 25 pairs. According to Assumption 2, the 10 breeding birds of 1981 die before the next spring. According to Assumption 3, all of the 50 offspring live to the spring of 1982. Thus, at the start of the 1982 breeding season, there are 25 pairs of house sparrows on the island. Using these assumptions, calculate the island's sparrow population at the *beginning* of the breeding season in 1983, 1984, 1985, and 1986.

3. You now have a series of numbers. To get a clearer idea of the population change, plot the numbers on a line graph. Show the years along the horizontal axis and the number of birds along the vertical axis. Be sure to make the vertical scale large enough to show the 1986 population. Plot the 6 generations.

4. Now plot your data using another tool — semilogarithmic (usually called semilog) graph paper. You do not need to understand fully the mathematics of logarithms to use this tool. Your teacher will explain what you need to know to plot the data. Construct your semilog graph with the same data you used before. (*1*) What advantage(s) does the semilog graph have over the arithmetic graph for plotting data on population growth?

DISCUSSION

Look first at the arithmetic graph. (*2*) How does the slope of the line connecting the plotted points change as you read from left to right (from year to year)? (*3*) What does this mean in terms of rate of population change? (*4*) Now compare the graphs. What kind of line shows the same thing on the semilog graph? (*5*) If you continued using the same assumptions to calculate populations for an indefinite number of years and plotted them on a graph, what would happen to the slope

of the line of the arithmetic graph? (*6*) What would happen to the slope on the semilog graph?

(*7*) In one or two sentences, summarize the change in a population that is supported by the assumptions stated in the model. (*8*) Do you think any real population might change in this way? Why or why not?

EXTRA credit

FOR FURTHER INVESTIGATION

Sometimes a model gives results that are very different from any observed situation. To make the model more useful, you can change one or two of the assumptions and compare the new results with reality. The closer the results of a model are to the observed situation, the more useful the model is. Some suggestions for changing assumptions follow. In each case calculate the populations, plot the data on arithmetic and semilog graph paper, and compare these results with your original graphs. Describe how the change of assumption has affected the hypothetical population.

1. Change Assumption 2 as follows: Each year 2/5 of the breeding birds (equally males and females) live to breed again a second year and then die. All other assumptions remain unchanged.

2. Change Assumption 3 as follows: Each year 2/5 of the offspring (equally males and females) die before the beginning of the next breeding season. All other assumptions remain unchanged.

3. Change Assumption 4 as follows: Each year 20 new house sparrows (equally males and females) immigrate to the island. None leave. All other assumptions remain unchanged.

4. Change Assumption 4 as follows: Each year 40 house sparrows (equally males and females) emigrate from the island. None arrive. All of our other assumptions remain unchanged.

5. You can devise more complex problems by changing two or more assumptions simultaneously.

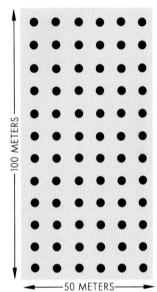

2–12 Plan of an orchard. Each dot represents one tree. What is the density of trees in the orchard?

DENSITY

Consider again the student population of your classroom. You might say there are 35 students per 150 square meters (150 m²). This depends, of course, on the area of your room. You also might say 35 per 450 cubic meters (450 m³), depending on the volume of the room. In each case you are talking about population *density* — the number of individuals in a population in relation to the amount of space they occupy at a given time.

Which space unit to choose depends on your purpose. Biology teachers interested in setting up a laboratory activity may want to know the number of students per square meter. But architects who designed the building had to allow for sufficient air, and needed to know the number of students per cubic meter.

In working with land organisms, biologists usually use two-dimensional units of space, such as square meters. But if they are considering the fish population in a pond, they may use three-dimensional units of space, such as cubic meters. To find the density (D) of a particular population, measure the space involved, count the number (N) of individuals in the population, and divide the number of individuals by the num-

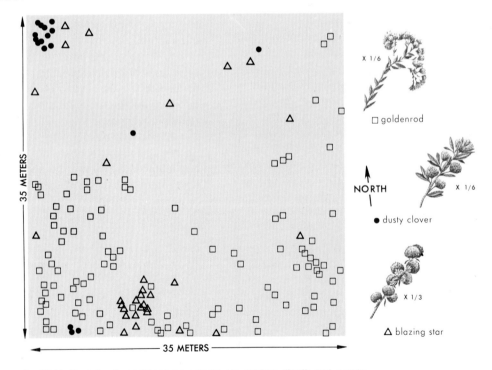

2–13 Under natural conditions organisms are seldom distributed evenly. Calculate the density of dusty clover in the field as a whole and then only in the northwest quarter. Compare.

ber of units of space (S), or $D = \dfrac{N}{S}$. The teacher would calculate

$D = \dfrac{35 \text{ students}}{150 \text{ m}^2} = 0.23$ student per m². For the architect:

$D = \dfrac{35 \text{ students}}{450 \text{ m}^3} = 0.08$ student per m³.

Biologists are often more interested in population density than in total population size. In 1970 the human population of Rhode Island was 949,723 and the population of Maine was 993,723. You might think that the human populations in Rhode Island and Maine were rather similar—until you learn that Rhode Island occupies 3,145 km² and Maine 86,049 km².

The determiners of population size are also determiners of population density. A formula similar to the one you used to calculate the rate of change in population size can be used to calculate the rate of change in population density: $R = \dfrac{\Delta D}{\Delta T}$.

Calculate the densities of the human populations in the two states.

Obtain the population figures of your state for the last two censuses. Also obtain your state's area. Calculate the rate of change per year in density of human population.

CHECK YOURSELF

A. Why is it difficult to say exactly what is meant by the term "individual"?
B. Why do biologists study populations?
C. What idea about human populations did Thomas Malthus suggest?
D. What three things define a population?
E. How can you calculate the rate at which a given population is increasing or decreasing?
F. Why are the terms "mortality" and "natality"—as defined in this text—not applicable to individuals?
G. Distinguish between immigration and emigration.
H. Which rates tend to increase population size? Which tend to decrease it?
I. What is the purpose of a mental model?
J. Describe in words what this formula states in symbols:
$D = \dfrac{N}{S}$.

KINDS OF POPULATION CHANGES

If you measure the density of a population at intervals over a period of time, you seldom find that any two consecutive measurements are the same. Density increases or decreases continually. Biologists have made many such studies of population densities, and they have been able to make some *generalizations* about how populations change. That is, they have summarized many specific observations in a few general statements that hold true for most of the data.

CLOSED AND OPEN POPULATIONS

The yeasts in the tubes of Investigation 2.1 are *closed populations.* They cannot emigrate, nor can others immigrate. Many closed populations of small organisms actually have been set up in laboratories to test hypotheses about population changes.

Figure 2–14 is based on data from an experiment involving diatoms (small photosynthetic organisms). As in the case of your yeasts, a few diatoms were placed in a favorable medium and samples from the population were counted on succeeding days. Compare your yeast data with the diatom data. Experiments with closed populations of other small organisms have produced similar data. Notice that the growth of the diatom population during the first eight days was similar to the growth of the hypothetical house-sparrow population (Investigation 2.2). The model used in your investigation agrees, then, with a real situation—up to a point. Unlike the model, a real population does not continue to grow indefinitely.

diatoms [DY uh tomz]. See page 168.

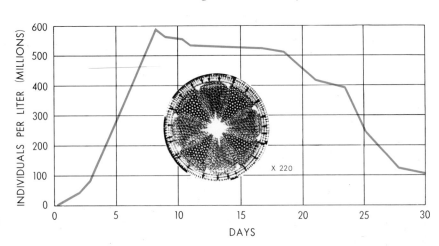

2–14 Changes in a laboratory population of a kind of diatom.

Is the human population of Earth open or closed?

Closed populations are found chiefly in laboratories. Most natural populations, on the other hand, are *open populations.* Individuals are free to enter or leave. Therefore, patterns represented by the diatom graph and by your yeast experiment cannot be assumed to apply to natural populations.

POPULATION FLUCTUATIONS

fluctuations [fluk chew AY-shunz]

The graph in figure 2–15 is based on data collected during population studies of Norway rats in Baltimore, Maryland. In 1942 the city health department conducted a poisoning campaign that apparently wiped out the rat population in the city block from which the data were collected. Since it is difficult to count individuals in natural populations, there may have been one or two rats remaining or a few rats may have immigrated. In either case, a "new" rat population started early in 1945, much as you started "new" yeast populations in Investigation 2.1. Compare the graph of figure 2–15 from early 1945 to late 1946 with your graphs from Investigations 2.1 and 2.2 and with figure 2–14.

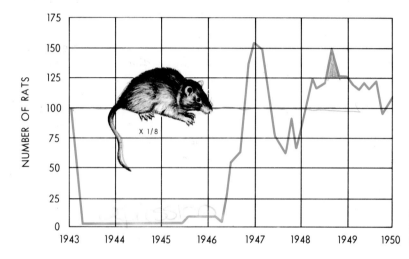

2–15 Changes in the Norway-rat population of a city block.

In the rat-population graph the line from mid-1945 to the end of 1946 is somewhat similar to the first part of the graph line of the diatom population. But look at the line for the later years of the rat study. As in the closed laboratory population of diatoms, the population decreased after a peak density was reached. The decrease in the rat population, however, did not continue. Open populations usually increase again — as the rat population did. After such a population peaks, it again decreases. Natural populations show such *fluctuations* — ups and downs — on graphs of population counts. These fluctuations are caused by variables in the environment — often in climate, available food, or the activities of natural enemies.

In the past, human populations undoubtedly have fluctuated like open populations of other organisms. During the Middle Ages the population of western Europe decreased sharply several times as a result of such plagues as the Black Death and then rose again. Within the last few centuries, however, such fluctuations have disappeared in many countries. For the world as a whole, we have a human population situation that looks rather like your graph of a hypothetical population in Investigation 2.2.

See figure 2–32.

POPULATION CYCLES

Sometimes population fluctuations are very regular, and the peaks on a graph are at approximately equal distances. Data gathered in Canada show that populations of snowshoe hares

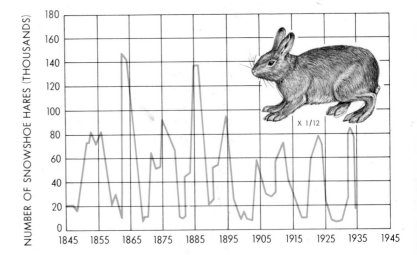

2–16 Changes in the snowshoe-hare population (Canada) based on skins traded at Hudson's Bay Company posts.

X 1/3

2–17 Lemming. These mouselike animals live in the northern parts of North America and Eurasia.

peak about every ten years. Similarly, populations of lemmings reach peaks every three or four years. A number of other organisms have such *population cycles.* Most of them are animals that live in the northern parts of Europe, Asia, and North America. But these observations do not explain why such cycles occur. Although the data show very regular cycles when plotted on a graph, some biologists think that this regularity is misleading. They point out that a combination of purely chance events can produce apparently regular cycles.

CHECK YOURSELF

K. Describe the usual form of a line graph that represents the growth of a closed population in a favorable environment.

L. How do most natural populations differ from most laboratory populations?

M. Describe the usual form of a line graph that represents changes in a well-established population under natural conditions.

N. How has human population size changed in recent centuries compared to earlier in history?

O. A cycling population is a special case of a fluctuating population. Explain.

Investigation 2.3   POPULATION CHANGES: FIELD DATA

INTRODUCTION

Gathering data on natural populations requires a lot of time and patience. You can observe some of the characteristics of population changes by using data that have already been obtained by biologists. Then you can compare these population data with the data from your hypothetical sparrow populations and from the laboratory yeast population that you investigated.

PROCEDURE

Cotton mouse. The data in figure 2–19 came from a study of cotton mice. The density is given as the number of mice caught per

2–18 Cotton mouse.

DATE	NUMBER PER 100 TRAPS PER NIGHT
September 24, 1949	25
October 9	45
October 30	38
December 4	30
January 7, 1950	20
February 26	14
March 12	13
April 16	8
May 8	7
June 16	11
July 16	4
August 16	13

2–19 Data on density of cotton mice (Florida).

MATERIALS
(per student)

2 sheets graph paper (arithmetic)
red pencil

100 traps per night. As is often the case in studying natural populations, the actual number of animals present in the area is not known. Thus, even in this real situation, we have to make an assumption. We assume that the number of mice caught was always in proportion to the actual density of the population.

1. Plot the data on a sheet of graph paper, using a vertical scale that will place the highest point for the population near the top.
2. Compare the graph of the cotton-mouse population with the arithmetic graphs you made in Investigations 2.1 and 2.2. (1) What part of this mouse graph is similar to the other graphs? (2) How does the mouse graph differ from your graph in Investigation 2.2? (3) How do you explain the differences? (4) How does the mouse graph differ from your graph of the yeast population? (5) How do you explain the difference? (6) Which (if any) of the 3 populations was an open population? (7) In which season of the year do you think natality was highest? (8) When do you think mortality and emigration were greatest?

Ring-necked pheasant. A few ring-necked pheasants (native to Eurasia) were introduced on Protection Island, off the coast of Washington, in 1937. They were brought in as game birds for hunters. Counts of the population each spring and fall for the next 5 years are presented in figure 2–21.

1. Plot the data on a sheet of graph paper and connect the points with a lead pencil. (9) How do you explain the regular fluctuations shown on your graph?

2–20 Heath hen (*left*) and ring-necked pheasant (*right*).

x 1/11

YEAR	SEASON	POPULATION SIZE
1937	Spring	8
	Fall	40
1938	Spring	30
	Fall	100
1939	Spring	90
	Fall	425
1940	Spring	300
	Fall	825
1941	Spring	600
	Fall	1520
1942	Spring	1325
	Fall	1900

2–21 Numbers of ring-necked pheasants (Washington).

2. Using a red pencil, connect all the points representing spring counts, skipping the fall counts. (*10*) What does this line tell you about the population? (*11*) If spring counts had been made after 1942, what do you think they might have shown? Remember that this is a natural population.

Heath hen. Heath hens were once com- mon birds along the Atlantic coast from New England to Virginia. By 1880 they had dis- appeared from all locations except Martha's Vineyard, an island off Cape Cod. Figure 2– 22 shows the result of a careful study of this population. Biologists believe several factors account for changes in the heath-hen popu- lation: pressure of hunting by humans, then extreme efforts at preservation, disease, ef- fects of forest fires, and an excessive number of males.

(*12*) What do you think happened about 1907? (*13*) How does the heath-hen graph between 1907 and 1916 compare with your graph of the pheasant data? (*14*) How might an excess of males affect the determiners of density? (*15*) What do you think would have happened to this population if there had been an excess of females? (*16*) What term is ap- plied to a population that reaches the point attained by the heath hens in 1932?

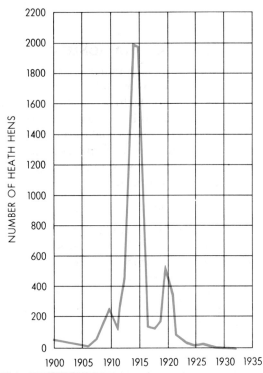

2–22 Numbers of heath hens (Martha's Vineyard, Massachusetts).

DISCUSSION

You should now be able to draw some general conclusions from your investigations of population change. (17) Does the growth of a population tend to follow a basic pattern? If so, what are the characteristics of this pattern? (18) What is the chief difference between the graph for the hypothetical population (Investigation 2.2) and the graphs for the real populations (Investigations 2.1 and 2.3)? (19) How do you account for the difference? (20) How does the web of life (Chapter 1) affect populations?

FOR FURTHER INVESTIGATION

Figure 2–23 presents data on a population of Italian bees. Plot the data on arithmetic graph paper. Does this graph most closely resemble the graph for the house-sparrow, the yeast, or the cotton-mouse population? On the bee graph, what is beginning to happen toward the end of the graph line? Can you predict what probably happened soon after the collection of data was discontinued? Which of the population determiners mentioned in the text is involved in your prediction?

2–23 Numbers of Italian bees in an experimental colony.

DAYS

0	7	14	21	28	35	42	49	56	63	70	77	84	91	98	105	112	119
1	1.5	2.5	4	8	16	22	32	40.5	50.3	55	62.5	72	72.5	71	82	78	81

POPULATION OF COLONY
(IN THOUSANDS)

POPULATIONS AND ENVIRONMENT

Population sizes and densities change. These changes result from interactions of mortality, natality, emigration, and immigration. But what factors cause the numerical values of these four determiners to increase or decrease?

If we can discover what these factors are, we may be able to make some predictions about population growth and decline. Making predictions is an important part of scientific work. Predictions can result in hypotheses that lead to further discovery.

SOME EXPERIMENTS

Let us first look at some experimental studies. Several biologists at the University of Wisconsin studied populations of house mice. In one experiment, they established a small population of mice in the basement of an old building. They provided the mice with 250 g of food each day. At first, this amount of food was not completely consumed in one day. But the population grew, and eventually the mice were eating all the daily food supply. Soon the biologists began to capture mice on the upper floors of the building, where they had not previously been found. Evidently the population had increased until there was a shortage of food within the experimental space. Emigration

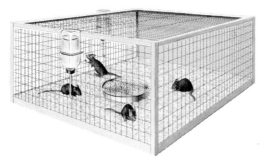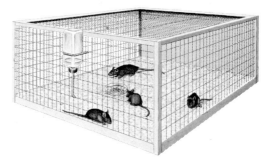

2-24 A population experiment. In the pen on the left, more than enough food is always provided for the mice. In the pen on the right, a food shortage may develop as the population grows. Emigration is impossible in both pens.
What do you predict will happen to the populations of the mice in both pens?

Was this an open or a closed population?

famine [FAM un; Latin: *fames*, hunger]: an extreme scarcity of food

maintained the population density in the basement at a level the food supply could support. There was no evidence that either mortality or natality had *changed*.

Earlier, the same investigators had performed a similar experiment. This experiment had one important difference: the mice were confined in pens. In this case, when the population grew to the point where a food shortage developed, emigration was impossible. Remembering Malthus (page 46), we might expect that there should have been famine and starvation—an increased mortality. Instead, when the daily food supply became insufficient to support the increased population, fewer young were born—a decreased natality. Thus a single factor (food shortage) may operate through different determiners (emigration or natality) to limit population growth.

In a third experiment, mice were confined in pens, but *more than enough* food was always provided. As the population size increased, there was a decline in space per mouse. The density of the population increased; the pen became crowded. This experiment was performed in different places, with different results.

At the University of Wisconsin, when the population became crowded, chasing and fighting increased greatly. Females stopped taking care of their nests and young. Mice continued to be born, but many newborn mice died from neglect. Eventually, mortality of young mice approached 100 percent. Thus further increase in population size was prevented by increased mortality in the young.

Another experiment designed to test the effect of space shortage when food is abundant was conducted in England. There, the investigators found little of the chasing, fighting, and neglect of nests that had been observed at Wisconsin. And there was no mortality among the young. Instead, after the population had increased to the crowded point, natality declined almost to zero.

In both experiments, the population growth rate leveled off. But at Wisconsin this came about through high mortality; in England it came about through low natality.

Seemingly similar experiments produced different results. Could one or both groups of biologists be mistaken about their results? Here we see the self-corrective nature of science, which comes from the fact that scientists deal with verifiable observation. Close examination of the published descriptions of these experiments showed that the experiments were not really the same. There were differences in the construction of the pens and nesting boxes. Still other tests have shown that the strain of mice used in the experiment influences the determiner that controls final population size.

EFFECTS OF ENVIRONMENT ON POPULATIONS

Most of the factors influencing the determiners of population density in the experiments just described came from outside the animals. Everything surrounding and affecting an organism is its *environment.* Earlier uses of the word "environment" sometimes did not refer to both living and nonliving things. But both are included. How is environment related to population density? To find out, we must get into ecology.

environment [en VY run munt]

2 – 25 Plants growing through a crack in a rock. What biotic and abiotic factors affect these plants?

Gordon E. Uno

biotic [by OT ik; Greek: *bios*, life]

Ecologists find it convenient to divide environment into two parts. The ***biotic*** environment is everything in an organism's surroundings that is alive or was recently alive. Thus all other organisms are a part of *your* biotic environment. Your classmates, your dog, the fleas on your dog, the yeasts in your test tubes, the trees along the street, even the people in another country are all included in your biotic environment. Obviously, some of these are closely connected to you in the web of life. For others this connection is very distant. The ***abiotic*** environment is everything in an organism's surroundings that is not alive. This includes such things as soil, solar radiation, rain, and waves on the seashore. Close to you, as a human being, are a wide variety of manufactured things—automobiles, houses, and electric lights, for example.

abiotic [AY by OT ik; Greek: *a*, without, + *bios*]

solar [SOH lur; Latin: *sol*, sun]

NUTRIENTS

In the mouse experiments food was one of the important variables. All consumers must have a source of food. Producers make their own food using solar energy and various kinds of matter. But organisms need more than food energy. (Review how the term "food" was used in Chapter 1.) All needed substances that an organism obtains from its environment—except oxygen, carbon dioxide, and water—are nutrients.

Many nutrients contain no food energy. How, then, are the terms "food" and "nutrient" related?

What makes a nutrient important as a factor affecting population determiners is not its quantity, but its availability. When the amount of food remained constant in the mouse experiments, its availability also remained constant as long as mice were free to emigrate. But when the mice were confined and the amount of food remained constant, the amount of food per mouse decreased as the population density increased. The availability of food decreased. When any nutrient is abundant in relation to the number of individuals, it is not a factor in limiting population density. When the nutrient becomes scarce, its importance increases.

availability: the extent to which a thing can be obtained

abundant [Latin: *ab*, from, + *undare*, to flow]: overflowing, more than enough

For producers the availability of nutrients depends on the chemical nature of the soil or water in which they grow. For example, even when magnesium and calcium are abundant in a soil, a plant may not be able to take in sufficient calcium. This happens because of chemical interference between these two elements.

SPACE

Every individual requires living space. Some organisms require less space than others. For example, individual corn plants often touch each other. Pumas (mountain lions), on the other hand, usually stay several kilometers away from each other. Motile organisms usually require more space than nonmotile ones.

X 1/26

2 – 26 Puma (also called cougar and mountain lion).

You might predict that the amount of space an organism requires is related to the availability of nutrients. This certainly is true to some extent. Consider the mouse experiments. Even when food was provided in abundance, a time came when the *space per mouse* became too small for normal activities to continue. Energy was used in fighting, chasing, and hiding, which maintained space between mice. Under lower population densities, this energy could have gone into producing and caring for young. Some organisms, raccoons, for example, need a particular kind of space. Two woodlands may be the same size and have equally good food supplies, but have very different-sized raccoon populations. The difference in raccoon density may be due to a difference in the number of hollow trees, which are homes for raccoons.

How much space does a human being need?

raccoons. See figure 15–31.

WEATHER

The mouse experiments do not show the effects on organisms of the abiotic environmental factors that we call weather. These factors include **precipitation** (rainfall, snowfall, and the like); temperature; **humidity** (amount of water vapor in the air); evaporation; and wind. Each may be measured separately, but they all affect each other.

In the northern part of the United States, almost all the adult mosquitoes are killed by the first heavy frost. In the autumn swallows fly south, so their population in the north drops also, though not as suddenly. Both these population changes are decreases, and both can be related to one weather factor — temperature. This factor changes the mosquito population through mortality, but it changes the swallow population through emigration.

It rarely rains in the deserts of southern Arizona. But after it does, blankets of small, bright flowering plants quickly appear

precipitation [prih sip uh TAY-shun; Latin: *praeceps*, falling headlong]

humidity [hew MID uh tee; Latin: *umere*, to be moist]

mosquito. See figure 7–8.

X 1/5

2–27 Barn swallow.

Josef Muench

2–28 Desert plants (*in the foreground*) that quickly germinate, flower, and wither after a rain.

on the formerly bare and baked desert soil. In a few days the density of visible flowering plants per km² springs from zero to thousands. Again the population change is clearly related to a single weather factor, in this case, rainfall. Rain provides the moisture needed for seeds to sprout, thus increasing natality.

OTHER ORGANISMS

The mouse experiments also fail to show the effects of other kinds of organisms, an important biotic factor. Under natural conditions consumers such as snakes, foxes, and hawks catch and eat mice. And microscopic organisms that live inside the mice may weaken them so much that they die. Populations of producers, as well as those of consumers, are influenced by other kinds of organisms. We will consider this topic more thoroughly in Chapter 3.

INTERACTION OF FACTORS

When changes in the density of a population are thoroughly investigated, we usually find that they involve the interaction of many factors. Consider tomato plants in a southern New Jersey field. In some years the density of living plants may be nearly as high in July as when the plants were set out in April. In other years it may be much lower, almost zero. Four weather factors are involved: temperature, rainfall, wind, and humidity. (The last is a consequence of the other three.) If temperature, rainfall, and humidity are high and wind is light, tomato plants usually grow very well. But there is a biotic factor in the toma-toes' environmental situation, too. A certain fungus also thrives in such weather. It may vigorously attack the tomato plants and greatly reduce their populations. This is, of course, a disaster for the tomato-grower.

fungus [FUNG gus]; plural, fungi [FUN jy]. A similar fungus is shown in figure 7–4.

How does this disaster affect a city dweller?

Some environmental factors are difficult to place in any of the groups we have been discussing. For example, radiation from the sun is the driving force behind all weather factors. For producers solar radiation is an environmental factor that controls the food supply, because it supplies the energy for photosynthesis. The amount of solar energy a producer receives depends on still other factors. A raspberry plant in the United States receives more solar radiation at noon than at eight o'clock in the morning. It receives more in June than in December, and more if it grows among grass plants than if it grows in a forest. Because of daily and seasonal variations in solar radiation, a plant in northern Minnesota receives less total annual energy than a plant in Tennessee. Time of day, season, shade, and *latitude* all influence the amount of solar radiation a plant receives.

Can you show that the amount of solar radiation received on any cm² of surface depends on the angle of the sun's rays?

latitude: angular distance, measured in degrees, north or south from the equator

terrestrial [tuh RES tree ul; Latin: *terra*, earth, land]

So far we have been discussing *terrestrial* organisms—

Richard G. Beidleman

2–29 The scene is in Colorado, as we look toward the east. Try to explain the striking patterns of plant distribution. North is to the left; south to the right.

those that live on land. *Aquatic* organisms are those that live in water. Aquatic organisms are affected by water conditions that correspond to the atmospheric conditions we call weather, but they do not vary as much. These water conditions include temperature, currents, salt concentration, and light. Aquatic producers get their nutrients from the water. For them, water corresponds not only to atmosphere but also to soil. The factors that influence aquatic populations are somewhat different from those on land. Nonetheless, the general principle—that environmental factors influence the four determiners of population density—applies to both land and water environments.

aquatic [uh KWAT ik; Latin: *aqua*, water]

DENSITY ITSELF A FACTOR

If lightning strikes a pine tree in the woodlands of northern Arizona, the tree may be set afire and killed. But its neighbors are not likely to be damaged, because the trees are far apart (the population density is low). If, however, lightning strikes a pine tree in northern Idaho, a whole forest may be destroyed. This may happen because the trees grow very close together (the population density is high).

A single freeze in Vermont may not kill all adult mosquitoes. Mortality depends on how many find shelter. If the density of mosquitoes is low, then most may find shelter from the freeze. In this case, mortality will be low. If the density of mosquitoes is high, then many will not be able to find shelter. The mortality will then be high. Thus the effect of a single factor on population density may itself be influenced by the density of that population.

2–30 Two ponderosa-pine forests. What environmental factors might influence the difference in population density?

U. S. Forest Service

U. S. Forest Service

CHECK YOURSELF

P. What was the experimental variable in each of the mouse experiments?

Q. How do the mouse experiments show the characteristics of scientific investigation?

R. What is meant by the environment of an organism?

S. Under what conditions does a nutrient affect the size of a population?

T. How does the amount of space per individual affect population density?

U. Give two examples of ways that weather influences the density of a population.

V. How might major environmental factors interact to determine population size?

W. How can the original density of a population affect the way an environmental factor may change that density?

Investigation 2.4 ENVIRONMENT AND NATALITY

INTRODUCTION

Brine shrimp are small aquatic animals that live in such places as Great Salt Lake, Utah. Unlike the eggs of most other aquatic animals, those of brine shrimp can survive drying. Indeed, the dried eggs may still hatch after a year or more. This fact has made the eggs useful to tropical-fish fans, for the eggs can be kept easily until needed, then hatched and used as food.

A number of environmental factors influence the hatching rate (natality) of brine-shrimp eggs. Read the following procedure. (1) Then state one or more hypotheses concerning the relation of environmental factors to brine-shrimp natality.

MATERIALS (per team)

glass-marking crayon
6 petri dishes
graduated cylinder
10 ml distilled (or deionized) water
sodium chloride solutions (1%, 2%, 4%, 8%, 16%), 10 ml of each
volume measure (medicine dropper with mark 3 mm from tip)
brine-shrimp eggs
refrigerator
incubator
stereomicroscope
medicine dropper

PROCEDURE

1. Using a glass-marking crayon, number 6 petri dishes on the rims of the bottom halves. Place your team symbol on each dish. Mark a large + on the bottom of each dish to divide it into 4 quadrats. Number the quadrats from 1 through 4.

2. Pour 10 ml of distilled (or deionized) water into Dish 1.

3. Into Dish 2, pour 10 ml of 1% sodium chloride (salt) solution.

4. Into Dishes 3 through 6, pour 10 ml of 2%, 4%, 8%, and 16% sodium chloride solutions, respectively.

5. Using the volume measure, measure dry brine-shrimp eggs as directed by your teacher. Scatter them on the surface of the water in Dish 1. Scatter the same volume in each of the other dishes.

6. Cover the dishes and stack them in the place designated by your teacher. Some teams' dishes will be left at room temperature. Some will be placed in a refrigerator and some in an incubator at a temperature 10° to 15°C above room temperature.

7. Check the temperature at the place where your dishes are to be kept and record it in your data book.

8. Recheck and record the temperatures on each of the following 2 days.

9. Two days after setting up the cultures, use a stereomicroscope to count the hatchlings in each dish. You may find that a rough count will be satisfactory. Or you may use a medicine dropper to remove each young brine shrimp as it is counted. The + on the bottom of the dish will help you to be sure you check the entire dish. Record each number (indicating whether an estimate or a count) in your data book.

DISCUSSION

Assemble data from all teams on the chalkboard. For each of the 3 temperature conditions, total the data for each of the 6 dishes. Then calculate an average for each dish. Set up your graph with the number of individuals on the vertical axis and salt concentrations on the horizontal axis. Use O's to plot the points for the low-temperature dishes. Use X's for the room-temperature dishes and +'s for the high-temperature dishes. Connect the O's with 1 line, the X's with a 2nd line, and the +'s with a 3rd line.

(2) What conclusion can you make about the effect of temperature on brine-shrimp natality? (3) About the effect of salt percentage on brine-shrimp natality? (4) Do your data indicate any interaction of temperature and salt percentages?

POPULATION CHANGES

From your study of populations and of the interactions between populations and environment come three major generalizations. First, when a few organisms are introduced into a favorable environment, a characteristic pattern of growth follows. Second, after the initial growth period, a population in a closed system develops differently from a population in an open system. Third, populations in open systems fluctuate between some upper and lower limits. Each is like a swing, back and forth between greater and lesser numbers. We need to explore the third generalization somewhat further.

initial [in ISH ul; Latin: *in,* in, + *ire,* to go]: indicating or occurring at the beginning

CARRYING CAPACITY

What limits the fluctuations of a population on the lower side? There is little information that helps us answer this question. But we do know that the size of a population may reach zero. This is the same as saying that the population has become extinct. Your study of heath hens in Investigation 2.3 suggested factors that can result in this.

What limits the population on the upper side? Any of the factors we have been discussing may cause a population to stop growing. In the long run, however, the size of a population is limited by the amount of matter or energy, the **resources,** available to it. If a population is so large that it uses all the available water or food, it can grow no larger. The number of individuals that any space can support with its available resources is called its *carrying capacity.*

The carrying capacity of a space is not constant. It too fluctuates. More solar energy is available to producers in summer than in winter. Little water is available to desert plants and animals except during rare but heavy rainfalls. So, in any given space, there is some limit to energy and matter. In other words, resources are *finite.*

See figure 2–28.

finite: [FY nyt; Latin: *finis,* end]

An example. Suppose that a deer population in a certain area is increasing. Gradually the kinds of plants that deer eat become scarce. A few deer may emigrate and look elsewhere for food. Those that remain will not be as well nourished as they were before. They will be caught more easily by carnivores, such as pumas, that eat deer. Or they may be more affected by disease than they were before. As the population continues to increase, more deer emigrate and more deer are killed. But, since emigration and mortality tend to reduce populations, the deer population begins to decrease. So fewer plants are eaten. As the plants continue to grow, more food becomes available for the remaining deer. Deer may stop emigrating. In fact, attracted by food within the area, deer may immigrate from elsewhere. With more food the deer are better fed and are not killed so easily. Some carnivores may even stop trying to catch deer and look for other sources of food. Thus immigration and a reduction in

2–31 A pair of mule deer.

National Center for Atmospheric Research

mortality tend to start the deer population increasing again. And this is where we started.

homeostasis [hoh mee oh STAY-sis; Greek: *homoios,* like, same, + *stasis,* condition]

This example illustrates the process called *homeostasis.* By means of this process, populations are maintained within limits. In homeostasis, an increase of something causes an environmental change. This change eventually stops the increase and starts a decrease. A decrease of something also can cause an environmental change. In this case, the change eventually stops the decrease and starts an increase.

A theory. Homeostasis is known to act in many kinds of situations both in living and nonliving systems. Ecologists have observed many cases that are similar to the example of the deer population. They have stated their observations in a general form: environmental changes tend to prevent populations either from becoming very large or from disappearing. This is a theory. It explains a recurring pattern of observations of different organisms. It is useful to scientists as a guide for developing hypotheses that lead to further observations. Using the theory, ecologists can predict what will happen to a given population in a given environment. At present, our theory of population change is supported by many observations, but at any time new observations might modify it.

Compare this theory with the cell theory introduced on page 12. What features do both theories share?

HUMAN POPULATION

When considering carrying capacity, why must we think of the earth as a whole for human beings but not for house sparrows or pine trees?

The human population of the 20th century depends on the entire earth for its resources. Wheat is transported from the United States and Canada to all other countries. The factories of Europe and America depend on raw materials from all over the world. The Middle East is the major supplier of oil, our prime energy resource. Given this interdependence, let us think about the carrying capacity of Earth for the human population.

Fluctuations in numbers of people once characterized isolated human populations. This has disappeared temporarily. In much of the world, mortality has decreased because of improvements in the medical treatment of children. Natality, however, has not decreased or has decreased only slightly. Because there is no immigration or emigration from Earth as a whole, you can calculate that the human population must be increasing. And, indeed, it is—rapidly.

Scientists disagree about the carrying capacity of Earth. If food were the only limiting factor, some claim that 30 billion persons might be fed. Others believe 7 to 10 billion is a more reasonable estimate. Still others consider the high standard of living of Western countries cannot continue. And they believe that the current population of more than 4 billion cannot be maintained indefinitely.

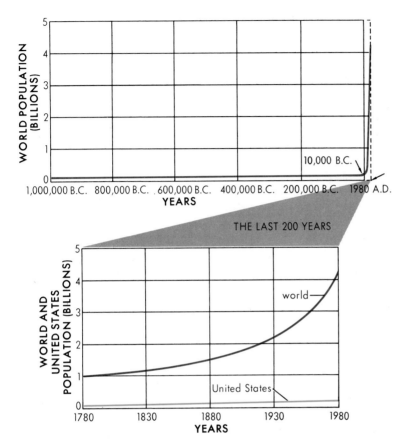

2-32 World and U.S. population growth.

Large amounts of energy are required to produce food by modern agricultural techniques. Energy is used to manufacture and operate farm machinery, to produce fertilizers and other farm chemicals, and to transport materials to and from farms. But our usual energy resources — coal, oil, and natural gas — are *finite*. Many scientists think that using up these resources will place a limit on the amount of food that can be raised in the future. Finally, severe overcrowding is seen by others as the limiting factor for human populations. Under crowded conditions the behavior of mice changed, sometimes dramatically and violently. But people are not mice. Scientists are unsure of the effects of crowding on humans.

Biologists are uncertain about which factor — food, energy, or space — will ultimately limit the number of persons on Earth. However, everything that is known about populations indicates that the number of people will be limited. The earth is fi-

2—33 Earth as seen from space. What will limit the growth of the human population?

NASA

nite and its carrying capacity is finite. The only question that seems to face us is "How?" Will mortality, through starvation, disease, and war, rise to equal present-day natality? Or will present-day natality be lowered to match the low death rates of today?

CHECK YOURSELF

X. How do salt concentration and temperature interact to affect natality in brine shrimp?

Y. What is meant by the carrying capacity of any given space?

Z. Use the example of the deer to illustrate the meaning of homeostasis.

AA. Name some ways in which scientific theories are useful to scientists.

BB. Discuss the present relationship between the human population and Earth's carrying capacity.

PROBLEMS

1. In a certain city 1,056 human beings and an estimated population of 1,400 rats lived in an eight-block area. Then the old buildings in the area were torn down and replaced with modern apartments. The area was then occupied by 2,480 human beings and an estimated population of 160 rats. Calculate the change in population density per block of both organisms. What determiners probably were most important in effecting the changes in density?

2. A team of biologists studied a population of box turtles in an Ohio woodlot for a period of ten years. They determined that the natality averaged 40 per year, the mortality 30 per year, immigration 3 per year, and emigration 8 per year. Was the population increasing or decreasing? Was the area supplying box turtles to other places, or vice versa? What was the average annual change due to immigration and emigration? If the initial population was 15 turtles, what was the population at the end of ten years?

3. Obtain the census data for your state. Make a graph of these data, beginning with the first census after your state entered the Union. Why is it unnecessary (except in the case of Virginia) to refigure these data for density? How does the form of this graph compare with that for the population of the United States as a whole? Try to explain any differences.

4. It is seldom possible to count all the individuals in a natural population. How can a biologist study population densities without such data?

5. Do some library research to explain what people in the following careers can add to population studies of the kinds in this chapter: biogeographer; climatologist; wildlife migration analyst.

6. Obtain some duckweed, an aquatic plant that grows on the surface of ponds. Tap the mass of plants with your finger to separate a single individual. Place the single duckweed plant in pond or aquarium water in a petri dish. At intervals of 2 to 4 days make counts of the numbers of individuals. Keep a record of dates and numbers. Construct a graph to show the growth of the duckweed population.

7. Grains, such as wheat and rice, are a basic food throughout the world. The 1975 worldwide production of grains was approximately 1.1 billion tons. This was enough grain to provide 3 billion people with enough food energy for normal activity for a year. Still, hundreds of thousands of people in Asia, Africa, and South America were malnourished and thousands of others starved to death. How can you explain this? *The World Almanac* and books such as *Not By Bread Alone*, by Lester Brown, may give you some insights.

8. Today we are still discussing the ideas Thomas Malthus presented in *An Essay on the Principle of Population as It Affects the Future Improvement of Mankind.* Think about his central idea as described in this chapter. Use other ideas in this chapter and your own experience with human populations to write a statement that either supports or disagrees with Malthus' idea.

SUGGESTED READINGS

Benton, A. H. and W. E. Werner. 1974. *Field Biology and Ecology.* 3rd ed. McGraw-Hill, New York. Good descriptions of some methods of population study. Fairly easy.

Brewer, R. 1979. *Principles of Ecology.* W. B. Saunders, Philadelphia. A comprehensive introductory text requiring minimal background. Advanced.

Brown, L. R. 1976. *By Bread Alone.* Pergamon Press, New York. Readable discussion of the world food situation.

BSCS. 1975. *Human Population.* Book IV, Environmental Resource Papers. Addison-Wesley, Menlo Park, Calif.

Gray, E., D. Dodson, and W. F. Martin. 1975. *Growth and Its Implications for the Future.* Dinosaur Press, Branford, Conn.

Kormondy, E. J. 1976. *Concepts of Ecology.* Prentice-Hall, Englewood Cliffs, N.J. Excellent account of some modern principles of population. Advanced.

Moran, J. M., M. D. Morgan, and J. H. Wiersma. 1980. *Introduction to Environmental Science.* W. H. Freeman, San Francisco. Chapters on many animal populations and on human populations specifically.

Myers, J. H. and C. J. Krebs. 1974. Population Cycles in Rodents. *Scientific American,* June. This article suggests that some cycles result from changes in the genetic makeup of a population.

Odum, E. P. 1975. *Ecology.* Holt, Rinehart and Winston, New York. Includes an excellent treatment of growth and fluctuations of populations. Advanced.

Quick, H. F. 1974. *Population Ecology.* Bobbs-Merrill, Indianapolis. Population dynamics and their consequences.

Scientific American. 1974, September. Population Issue. Articles relating to some aspects of human and nonhuman population studies.

Chapter 3

Communities and Ecosystems

YOUR GUIDEPOSTS

In this chapter you will have an opportunity to explore these questions in biology:

- How can we make sense from the many ways in which we observe populations affecting each other?
- How are abiotic environmental factors related to biotic ones?
- How does the concept of ecosystems help us to understand the biosphere?
- How do the complex activities of human beings affect ecosystems?
- How can we measure the biotic and abiotic factors in ecosystems?

COMMUNITIES

No population lives alone. Every population interacts with other populations in a complex web of relationships. The set of interacting populations at a particular place in a particular time is called a *community.*

In Investigation 1.4 you studied a community. You found many kinds of organisms living together and affecting each other in various ways. However, classes in different schools study different communities, find different organisms, and discover different relationships. So, to provide a background to which all students can refer, a brief description of a particular community follows.

AN EXAMPLE

Our sample community is located in the short rivers along the west coast of Florida. Since a community is a web of interac-

3–1 A Florida river.

tions, it is convenient to begin a description with one kind of organism. Let's see how river turtles relate to other kinds of organisms in the community.

Adult river turtles are herbivores. They eat many of the kinds of plants that grow in the rivers, though they do not eat all kinds in equal amounts. Most often they select tape grass. Unlike the adults, young river turtles are not entirely herbivorous. They eat snails, which are themselves herbivorous. The young turtles eat aquatic insects, many of which are carnivorous. And they eat worms, some of which may be third consumers in a food chain.

Other organisms eat river turtles. The highest mortality probably occurs in the egg stage. Turtle eggs are laid on land, in holes dug by the females. The nests are frequently discovered by skunks, raccoons, or snakes, all of which eat turtle eggs. The unhatched turtles are also killed by molds that live in the soil and grow through the thin shells of the eggs. If the eggs survive, the hatchlings may be picked up on the riverbank by snakes or raccoons. Once in the water, they may be eaten by some kinds of fish, by herons, or by a kind of snapping turtle.

When river turtles become larger, few organisms can kill them directly. Adults could be attacked by alligators, but there is little evidence of this. Leeches attach themselves to turtles and suck their blood but do not kill them. However, turtles do die of disease, accidents, and old age. Then their bodies become food for decomposers that finally return all the substances in the turtle's body to the nonliving world.

tape grass. See figure 3–3.

raccoons. See figure 15–31.

survive [sur VYV; Latin: *super*, over, + *vivere*, to live]: to continue to live

alligators. See page 122.

leeches. See page 131.

Plants, besides serving as food, play another part in river-turtle life. The mats of floating vegetation, the tangled tree roots along the bank, the sunken logs all provide places for young turtles to hide from animals that would eat them.

Each of the community relationships we have described so far is a *direct* relationship between a river turtle and another kind of organism. River turtles also have *indirect* relationships with other organisms. Snails eat tape grass. The tape-grass population varies greatly; sometimes it is plentiful and sometimes scarce. When tape grass becomes scarce, both turtles and snails may continue to eat it for a while. But eventually the snails begin eating algae, which are tiny green plants that grow on the rocks. (See page 168.) They can scrape algae off the rocks while turtles cannot. The turtles, on the other hand, can grasp and eat mats of larger plants that have floated away from the land.

Humans trap skunks, kill snakes, and catch some of the fish that eat young river turtles. This indirectly reduces the mortality of river turtles. But humans also may dredge the rivers, destroying the tape grass, which would increase turtle mortality.

Another kind of turtle, the musk turtle, eats nothing but snails. By reducing the number of snails that eat tape grass, musk turtles have an indirect effect on the river turtles. The musk turtles never eat all the snails, however, because the snails are not easy to find among the beds of tape grass. Moreover, many animals that kill musk turtles also kill young river turtles. Thus the more musk turtles there are in the river, the less likely it is that young river turtles will be caught.

3–2 Three animals that eat young river turtles.

skunk   X 1/20

X 1/25

great blue heron

X 1/14

alligator snapping turtle

◄ **3–3** Tape grass, spiral-shelled snails, musk turtle (*left*), adult river turtle (*right*), and pond turtle (*below*).

Draw a diagram to summarize the interrelationships in the Florida river community.

When tape grass is abundant, pond turtles, which usually do not live in rivers, temporarily join the community. Since pond turtles leave as soon as the tape-grass supply begins to decline, they have very little effect on river turtles.

We have been looking at the community as if through the eyes of a river turtle. If we had started with some other organism, we might have developed a somewhat different picture. To understand the community completely, we would have to look at all the relationships among all the organisms. Clearly, the study of a community—even a small one such as this—is not easy.

Try to describe the community of organisms that you found during Investigation 1.4 in the way this river community has been described.

CHECK YOURSELF

A. What is a community?
B. Why must the relationships of adult and of young river turtles with other organisms be considered separately?
C. How do direct and indirect relationships differ?
D. Give an example from the Florida river community of a relationship that is *not* part of a food web.

X 1/10

3–4 Black vulture.

Would you call yourself a predator when you eat a hamburger?

parasitism [PAIR uh syt iz um]

KINDS OF COMMUNITY RELATIONSHIPS

In the Florida river community you easily recognize some kinds of relationships that were discussed in Chapter 1. For example, tape grass, algae, and other green plants are producers; river turtles and snails are herbivores. But many other kinds of relationships help to form the community web of life.

Predation. Snapping turtles eat young river turtles. Musk turtles eat snails. Snakes swallow turtle eggs. In other communities, robins catch and eat earthworms; house cats kill and eat mice; spiders catch flies and suck the juices from them. A consumer that kills another living organism and eats it, regardless of whether it kills it before or during the eating process, is a *predator.* The organism that is eaten is called the *prey.*

However, we will not use these terms for herbivores and the plants they eat. There are also other relationships in which it is difficult to decide whether an organism is a predator. Vultures usually eat animals that are already dead. If a vulture finds an animal injured by an automobile, however, it may not wait for the animal to die before beginning to eat. On the other hand, snapping turtles are predators most of the time. But if they find something that is already dead, they will eat it.

Parasitism. Leeches cling to a turtle's skin and suck blood. Microorganisms within the turtle absorb food directly from its blood. In other communities dogs have worms in their intestines, fish may be attacked by molds, and humans can be killed by tuberculosis microorganisms in their lungs. Plants may be inhabited by molds or microorganisms. Larger microorganisms may have smaller microorganisms within them. Organisms that live on or in other *living* organisms and obtain their food from them are called **parasites.** The organisms from which parasites obtain their food are called **hosts.**

Predators kill their prey; parasites *may* kill their hosts. But the death of its host is a disadvantage and often a disaster for a parasite. When parasites kill, they usually kill indirectly. They produce substances that are in some way poisonous to their hosts.

What happens to tuberculosis microorganisms when a tubercular person dies?

Difficulties. How long does an organism have to live on or

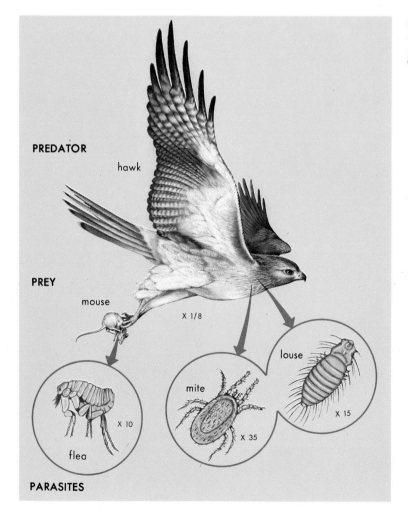

3–5 Some ecological relationships. Could the flea population have any effect on the hawk population?

PREDATOR

hawk

PREY

mouse

X 1/8

louse

X 15

mite

X 35

flea

X 10

PARASITES

in another before we can call it a parasite? Once tuberculosis microorganisms get into the body of a human host, they stay. And they may multiply there through many generations. A leech may stay attached to its turtle host for weeks, but it does not spend its entire life there. Most biologists would agree to call both of these parasites. But what about a mosquito? It consumes its victim's blood, just as the leech does. But it stays only long enough to obtain one meal—often a rather short one. Further, we have seen that some consumers sometimes eat organisms that are already dead and at other times act as predators.

precise [prih SYS]: sharply or exactly stated

Obviously, the terms we have been using are not precise. But this does not mean that they are not useful. It merely means that they are used in those cases where their lack of precision does not matter. For example, it is quite safe to say that snapping turtles are predators of young river turtles, even though they also eat dead flesh.

As ecologists gain more precise information about communities, they need more precise terms with which to discuss their findings. So they are developing some new approaches to the description of community relationships.

benefit [BEN uh fit; Latin: *bene,* well, + *facere,* to do]: to do good

One approach is to consider the benefit or harm that a relationship brings to the organisms. The relationship between an individual predator and its prey seems to be beneficial to the predator and harmful to its prey. The relationship between herbivore and producer is of the same kind as that between predator and prey or parasite and host. It is beneficial to one, harmful to the other. As yet, however, ecologists do not have any one term to apply to this kind of relationship.

remora [REM uh ruh]

Commensalism. A remora is a fish that has a kind of suction disk on the top of its head. By means of this disk, it attaches itself to some large sea animal, most often a shark. The effect on the shark is probably neutral, but the remora benefits. First, it uses very little energy in moving about, because it is carried by the shark. Second, it swallows pieces of the shark's prey that float by. This kind of relationship—in which one organism is benefited and the other is unaffected—is called *commensalism.*

neutral [NEW trul]: here, neither benefit nor harm

commensalism [kuh MEN suh-liz um; Latin: *cum,* with, together, + *mensa,* table]

Commensalism does not necessarily involve a food relationship. For example, most of the holes used by bluebirds for nesting are chiseled out by woodpeckers. Bluebirds use a woodpecker hole after it has been abandoned. Thus the presence of woodpeckers is beneficial to bluebirds. This is a commensal relationship like the one between a remora and a shark. It is neutral for one organism and beneficial for the other.

lichens [LY kunz]. See figures 3–7 and 5–34.

Mutualism. Growing on rocks or the bark of trees, you may find small plants that have no roots, stems, or leaves. These organisms are called *lichens.* Unlike mosses, which are often

3 — 6 Shark with remoras
attached underneath.

found in the same places, they are never bright green. Instead, lichens are a dull gray-green, yellow, or orange. Each lichen is composed of two different plants living in very close association. One is an alga, a producer that makes food by photosynthesis. The other is a fungus, a consumer that obtains food from the alga. The fungus protects the alga from drying out. Without the fungus the alga probably could not long survive in the places where lichens grow. Thus both organisms benefit. Such a relationship — one that is mutually helpful — is called *mutualism.*

    Competition. Both snails and river turtles eat tape grass. The tape grass that a turtle eats is clearly not available for a snail to eat, and vice versa. Thus the presence of the turtle can be harmful to the snail, and the presence of the snail can be harmful to the turtle. This relationship is an example of *competition.* Whether snail and turtle actually do compete depends on the amount of tape grass and other food plants available. If both tape grass and other plants are scarce, competition for tape

mutualism [MEW choo uh liz um; Latin: *mutuus,* exchange]

competition [kom puh TISH un; Latin: *cum,* with, together, + *petere,* to seek]

3 — 7 Lichens on a tree.

Do pond turtles compete with river turtles for tape grass?

starlings. See also figure 8–47.

How many examples of competition between humans and other organisms can you think of?

grass might be strong. Note that competition is always *for* something.

Competition does not always involve food. Both bluebirds and starlings nest in holes in trees, poles, and fence posts. Since neither is able to dig holes for itself, both are dependent on holes already available. Thus the presence of either of these birds may be harmful to the other.

3 – 8 Starling (*right*) and eastern bluebird. What is their relationship to each other and to woodpeckers?

EVALUATING RELATIONSHIPS

The terms we have been discussing are based on the idea that some ecological relationships are beneficial, some harmful, and some neutral. Now what do we mean by this? Clearly, when a musk turtle kills and eats a snail, that individual snail is harmed. But in the study of communities, ecologists are not concerned with individuals; they are concerned with populations. The question is, "Does the musk-turtle population harm the snail population?"

To investigate this problem, ecologists must define "harmful" in such a way that they can collect data to prove or disprove hypotheses. They might define "harmful" to mean that an increase in the musk-turtle population brings about a decrease in the snail population. "Beneficial" would then mean that an increase in one population brings about an increase in another population. "Neutral" would mean that a change in the size of one population has no effect on the size of another population. Often ecologists can obtain numerical data by measuring the sizes of the populations over a period of time. Because the preferred evidence in science is always quantitative (numerical data), these meanings of "harmful," "beneficial," and "neutral" are, in fact, the ones ecologists use.

From what you have learned about the nature of science, why do you think scientists prefer numerical data?

Definitions of this kind indicate the kind of data that must be collected. Here is an example: Lynxes undoubtedly eat snowshoe hares. But does the size of the hare population affect the size of the lynx population? You have already seen graphed data for the Canadian snowshoe-hare population (figure 2–16). Figure 3–9 adds data on the Canadian lynx population. Now we can think about the predator-prey relationship quantitatively. The graph shows that fluctuations in the lynx population closely follow fluctuations in the hare population. This evidence suggests that the abundance of hares is a factor in the abundance of lynxes. It is possible, however, that a third factor affects the sizes of both populations. Thus even good quantitative data do not necessarily lead to definite conclusions.

Measuring populations — particularly animal populations — is difficult. Because of this, knowledge of most community relationships is still very imperfect.

lynxes [LINGKS uz]. Also called bobcats.

Often when human populations become more dense, rat populations do also. Explain.

For some methods by which ecologists measure natural populations, see E. A. Phillips, 1963, *Field Ecology*, a BSCS Laboratory Block, D.C. Heath, Lexington, Mass., and R. L. Smith, 1974, *Ecology and Field Biology*, 2nd ed., Harper & Row, New York.

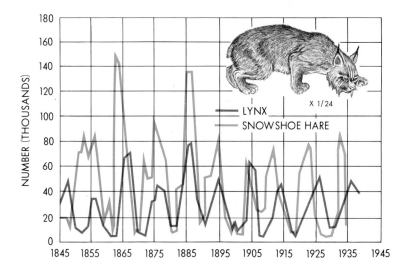

3–9 Population fluctuations of lynx and snowshoe hare in Canada, according to the records of the Hudson's Bay Company.

CHECK YOURSELF

E. How does a predator differ from a parasite?

F. A predator affects the population density of its prey, but a parasite may not always do so. Explain.

G. Distinguish between commensalism and mutualism.

H. Describe the relationship involved in lichens.

I. In ecological competition, what is the effect on both of the organisms?

J. How might an ecologist determine whether the effect of one kind of organism on another is beneficial, harmful, or neutral?

Investigation 3.1 RELATIONSHIPS BETWEEN TWO KINDS OF PLANTS

INTRODUCTION

Many unusual ecological relationships occur in communities that have been formed
by humans. Plants that would never occur
together naturally often are found together
in gardens and cultivated fields. To farm or
garden successfully, it is important to understand the relationships among such plants.

In this investigation you can examine
the relationships between two kinds of
plants during the early stages of growth.
(1) Read the procedure. Then form a hypothesis about the growth of radish and
tomato seedlings.

MATERIALS
(per team)

3 plastic or wooden boxes, at
  least 30 × 20 × 10 cm
sterile potting soil to fill 3 boxes
trowel
wood block, about 4 × 8 × 8 cm
sharp pointed stick (or pencil)
about 450 tomato seeds
about 450 radish seeds
3 pieces sheet glass or clear
  plastic wrap a little larger
  than the area of the boxes
beaker, 1,000-ml
paper towels
balance

PROCEDURE

1. Place the soil in the boxes and smooth to
   form a level surface. Use a block of wood
   to press the soil down firmly, but do not
   pack it tightly. If necessary, add soil to
   obtain a firmed depth of at least 7 cm.
2. Label the boxes A, B, and C. Sprinkle the
   soil with water and allow the water to soak
   in.
3. Using the pointed stick or pencil, draw fur-
   rows on the surface of the soil parallel to
   the long side of each box. Make them
   about 0.5 cm deep and 5 cm apart.
4. In Box A place tomato seeds 1 cm apart in
   each furrow. In Box B place radish seeds 1
   cm apart. In Box C place tomato and radish seeds alternately 1 cm apart. Each box
   should contain the same number of seeds.
   Record this number for each box. Use the
   wooden block to firm the soil along the
   lines of planting. By doing this, you will
   barely cover the seeds with soil.
5. To reduce evaporation, cover each box
   with a sheet of glass or clear plastic wrap.
   Put all the boxes where they will receive
   strong light but even temperature.
6. Remove the glass or plastic before the

seedlings press against it. By this time the
seedlings may be gently sprinkled with
water without being disturbed. Keep all
boxes equally moist. If they are kept on a
windowsill, turn them daily so that seedlings on each side will receive about the
same amount of light.

7. When the plants are 8 to 15 cm high, harvest them without mixing the plants from
   the 3 boxes. To do this, gently pull all the
   tomato plants in Box A. Rinse the soil from
   the roots and dry the plants on paper towels. Do the same with the radish plants
   from Box B. Remove, wash, and dry the
   tomato plants in Box C separately from the
   radish plants.
8. Count and determine the mass of all the
   plants together from Box A. Then repeat for
   all the plants from Box B. Do the same with
   all the tomato plants from Box C, and then
   with all the radish plants from Box C.
9. There were only half as many radish seeds
   and tomato seeds in Box C as in Boxes A
   and B. So before you compare masses of
   tomato plants and radish plants, divide
   the A and B masses by 2.

DISCUSSION

Organize your data in the form of a bar graph, with mass on the vertical axis. Arrange the 4 bars along the horizontal axis, left to right, in the order in which you obtained the masses. (2) Is there a difference between the total mass of the tomato plants grown in Box A (divided by 2) and the total mass of those grown in Box C? If so, how do you account for the difference? (3) Is there any difference between the total mass of the radish plants grown in Box B (divided by 2) and the total mass of those grown in Box C? If so, how do you account for the difference?

(4) If you found a difference in mass, do you think growing tomatoes and radishes together has more effect on the tomatoes or on the radishes? Or are the effects equal? (5) Try to explain how any effect you noted may have occurred. (6) What term would you apply to the relationship between tomatoes and radishes shown in this experiment? (7) Did every seed germinate? If they did not, how could you correct your data for differences in germination?

You examined this relationship in terms of masses of plants. This is different from the measurements of community relationships discussed on pages 82–83. (8) Why can the masses of the plants be considered indirect evidence of population relationships?

Each experiment must have a control. The **control** represents the normal situation and is used as a basis for comparison. When we test a hypothesis, we compare the results of the control to the results of the varied situation (the variable). (9) Which 2 of the 3 boxes of plants in this investigation were the controls? (10) Why are there 2 control boxes?

ECOSYSTEMS

A community cannot exist without an abiotic environment. This is true of small communities such as those in a Florida river. It is also true in the great world community of all living things. The world community, together with the world abiotic environment, is called the biosphere.

Refer to figure 1–28.

But the biosphere is too big to study as a whole. So ecologists study pieces of it—a forest, a farm, a pond, an aquarium, or even a vacant city lot. Even though each is only a part of the biosphere, each is a system in which organisms interact with one another and with their abiotic environment. Each is an *ecosystem.*

ecosystem [EE koh sis tum; Greek: *oikos*, house, + *syn*, together, + *histanai*, to place]

We have been studying the biotic part of ecosystems—that is, communities. Now we need to take a look at the abiotic part of ecosystems.

ABIOTIC ENVIRONMENT

It is certainly important for the Florida river community that the water does not freeze. If it did, many of the kinds of organisms we have described could not exist. Temperature, light (or darkness), and chemicals are among the abiotic factors that affect all ecosystems. Their effects differ, however, especially between aquatic and terrestrial ecosystems. Air temperature over a Flor-

Peter D. Behrendt

3–10 What abiotic environmental factors can you identify in this photo? What potential effects could these factors have on the human population?

What are the principal abiotic factors that are affecting you at this moment?

injurious [in JEUR ee us]: harmful

ida river may change 10°C in 12 hours. But a few centimeters below the water surface temperature may change less than 1°C. Bright sunlight on the surface of the water becomes dimmer with depth, because water absorbs and reflects light. Therefore, most photosynthesis occurs near the surface. If heavy rainfall washes mud into the river, the depth of light penetration decreases. If something should happen to cut off the flow of water, the Florida river community would disappear.

Water is a chemical substance—perhaps the most important chemical environmental factor. Oxygen and carbon dioxide occur in both aquatic and terrestrial ecosystems. But water holds less of each than air does. The inorganic nutrients that producers require are also chemical abiotic factors. They are not equally abundant in all ecosystems. And chemical substances that are injurious to organisms are found in some ecosystems. The kinds of substances present and their abundance determine whether a particular community can exist in any given place.

3–11 What abiotic environmental factor has produced the effect shown here?

EFFECTS OF ORGANISMS ON ABIOTIC ENVIRONMENTS

The current in Florida rivers—an abiotic factor—is not very strong. If it were, tape grass would not grow. But when tape grass is abundant, it clogs the rivers. This makes the current even slower. Thus the interaction between the abiotic environment and a community works in both directions.

Give some other examples of ways in which organisms affect abiotic environmental conditions.

Of all organisms, humans have the greatest ability to affect the abiotic environment. Very early in history, humans covered themselves with clothes. And they built houses that they warmed by fires. In this way they extended a bit of tropical climate into colder regions. With the invention of agriculture, they had much greater effects on the abiotic factors of ecosystems. Humans cleared and plowed the land. They spread the waters of rivers onto parched land. They added many chemical substances to ecosystems. Since the invention of power machinery, humans have become a force upon the landscape equal to earthquakes and hurricanes. And now, because of human ability to release vast amounts of chemical compounds and nuclear radiation, it is possible that we could destroy the entire biosphere.

What other organisms did they permit to spread poleward by these activities?

What chemical substances made by humans may be injurious to other organisms?

Investigation 3.2   **ABIOTIC ENVIRONMENT: A COMPARATIVE STUDY**

INTRODUCTION

The abiotic factors you will investigate are temperature and **relative humidity.** Relative humidity is a measure of the moistness of air. It is defined as the percentage of water vapor actually in the air at any given temperature, compared with the amount of water vapor that the air *could* hold at that temperature, In general, organisms lose water faster in an atmosphere with low relative humidity than in an atmosphere with high relative humidity. Therefore, this environmental factor is important to land organisms.

PROCEDURE

1. Team members should work in 3 groups. One member of each group will read the instruments. Another will fan the thermometer with stiff cardboard and record the data. Before starting, the 3 recorders should synchronize their watches and agree on the time at which each measurement is to be made.

2. Record your data on a form similar to this:

Location _____

	HEIGHT			
	0 cm	30 cm	90 cm	150 cm
TIME				
DRY-BULB TEMPERATURE				
WET-BULB TEMPERATURE				
RELATIVE HUMIDITY				

3. Each team will make measurements in 3 kinds of environment. One group of stu-

MATERIALS
(per team)

3 watches
3 metersticks
3 thermometers (−10° to +100°C)
3 thermometers (of same range, with cotton sleeves over the bulbs)
3 bottles (with screw tops) containing 30–50 ml distilled water
3 pieces stiff cardboard
3 umbrellas or other shade devices
table of relative humidities

dents will work in a dense cover of vegetation. Choose a woods, preferably, or a thicket, or a mass of shrubbery in a park. A 2nd group will work in a place that has a single layer of herbaceous vegetation. Select a meadow or a lawn (preferably not cut close to the ground). A 3rd group will work in a place that has no vegetation. Find some bare ground or a tennis court. The 3 environments should be as close together as possible.

4. Each group will make 4 sets of measurements: at ground level, at 30 cm above the ground, at 90 cm above, and at 150 cm above.

5. Take readings on both types of thermometers at the same time. Position the thermometers as described in steps 3 and 4 at least 5 minutes before readings are to be taken. (If the 1st reading is to be taken at 1:30 P.M., both thermometers should be in the 1st position at 1:25 P.M.) To make the wet-bulb reading, soak the sleeve of a thermometer in water and fan it vigorously for at least 2 minutes; then read the thermometer. Schedule at least 8 minutes between readings. You will need time to move both thermometers to the next posi-

tion and leave them there for 5 minutes. Use the umbrellas to shield the thermometers from the direct rays of the sun.

6. Your teacher will supply a relative-humidity table. To find the relative humidity on the table, you will need both your dry-bulb and wet-bulb thermometer readings. When you know these 2 temperatures, you can determine the amount of water vapor actually in the air compared with the amount that the air could hold at that temperature. The necessary calculations were made when the table was constructed.

DISCUSSION

(1) At ground level which environment is coolest and most humid? (2) At ground level which is warmest and least humid? (3) How do these 2 environments (Items 1 and 2) compare in temperature and humidity at higher levels above the ground? (4) At which level above the ground are all 3 environments most alike in temperature and humidity? (5) How does the greatest temperature difference *within* the same environment compare with the greatest temperature difference *among* the environments? (6) What differences among the 3 environments may account for differences in temperatures and relative humidities? (7) How does this show interaction of biotic and abiotic factors in an ecosystem?

You have been examining the differences among environments. Now turn to differences within an environment. (8) How does the temperature in each environment vary with respect to elevations? (9) Is the variation the same for each environment? If not, in which is the variation greatest? (10) How does the humidity in each environment vary with respect to elevation? (11) Is the variation the same for each environment?

In weather forecasts, temperatures predicted for the center of a city often differ from those predicted for the suburbs. (12) Relate this fact to the situations you have been observing. (13) What differences in temperature and humidity would be experienced by a beetle crawling on the ground in a meadow and a gnat hovering at 1.5 m above the meadow? In a general sense, we may say the beetle and the gnat are in the same environment, but small differences within an environment are often important to the existence of some organisms. We can therefore distinguish small environments within larger ones on the basis of measurements such as those you have made in this investigation. (14) Would it be useful to measure such differences if you were studying the ecological relationships among cows in a meadow? Explain.

CHECK YOURSELF

K. Distinguish between a community and an ecosystem.

L. In addition to factors that might be called "weather," what other abiotic factors can you name?

M. What kind of organism has the greatest effect upon abiotic factors of the environment? List three effects of this organism.

N. What is relative humidity?

ECOSYSTEM STRUCTURE

To study an ecosystem, it is important to collect data on populations of organisms as well as abiotic environmental factors. For this reason ecologists study physics and chemistry in addition to biology. From such broad studies they try to understand both the structure and the function of ecosystems.

CONTINUITY OF ECOSYSTEMS

What are the limits of an ecosystem? In our Florida example we would have clear boundaries for the ecosystem if it could be limited to the water. But turtles crawl onto the banks to lay their eggs, which then serve as food for land animals. Herons get almost all their food from the river but nest in tall trees. Frogs spend much time in the river. Here they are food for snapping turtles. But, while on the banks, frogs may also be caught and eaten by raccoons, which are land animals. Frogs eat insects, which they catch outside the river. Many insects spend their early lives in the river.

3–12 What is the boundary of this ecosystem?

George Silk, *Life* Magazine © Time, Inc.

This is not a special case. All ecosystems have relationships, both biotic and abiotic, with other ecosystems around them. Ecologists set boundaries primarily for convenience of study. Of course, some boundaries make more ecological sense than do others. Organisms that spend most of their time on land probably share more relationships with one another than they do with organisms that live in water. Water organisms probably share more relationships with each other than they do with land organisms. Therefore, the edge of the river makes a boundary that is both convenient for study and reasonable.

Nevertheless, all ecosystems are linked to other ecosystems around them. A forest ecosystem connects with a river ecosystem; a river ecosystem blends gradually into a saltwater ecosystem of the sea. All ecosystems on Earth are connected to one another, forming one great world system, the biosphere.

Ecosystems also have continuity in time. We can recognize producers preserved in ancient rocks. We can find evidence of extinct organisms that, from their structure, must have been herbivores. We can find others that were clearly predators on these herbivores. Ancient organisms undoubtedly received energy from the sun. They were affected by temperatures, winds, tides, and precipitation, and otherwise responded to factors in their abiotic environment.

Kinds of organisms have changed. Climates and landscapes have changed. But the system of interactions among organisms and environment seems to have remained much the same for millions of years.

STRUCTURE IN DEPTH

The Florida river ecosystem obviously has structure in three dimensions—length, breadth, and depth. Some of its organisms are usually found floating near the surface. Others swim deep in the water or crawl over the bottom. In water, it is easy to see that an ecosystem has volume.

On land, however, ecologists usually measure out study areas, as you probably did in Investigation 1.4. In some cases, it may be possible to overlook the third dimension—depth. But terrestrial ecosystems, like aquatic ecosystems, always have a volume. In forests an ecosystem may be many meters in depth, stretching from the canopy of the trees down through shrubs, herbs, moss, and into the soil. Other ecosystems—a pasture, for example—may seem much more shallow than a forest ecosystem. But the air above the plants is an important part of the ecosystem. Some substances that our technology puts into the atmosphere are harmful to human health. This makes us aware that every ecosystem exists in three dimensions.

Is the political boundary of a city a reasonable ecological boundary? Explain.

How did Investigation 3.2 show the effects of depths?

technology [tek NOL uh jee; Greek: technologia, systematic treatment]: application of science to provide objects for human life and comfort

ENERGY STRUCTURE

According to the principles discussed in Chapter 1, we would expect the following. First, every ecosystem must have a source of energy. Second, this energy must flow through the ecosystem. Third, the energy must eventually leave the ecosystem. Unlike the biosphere, the smaller ecosystems that ecologists actually study do not always receive their energy from the sun by way of photosynthesis. There are some ecosystems that receive no sunlight and therefore have no producers. An example is the ecosystem of a stream in a deep cave. All the energy for the organisms in such an ecosystem must come from elsewhere as food. Such an ecosystem has only consumers and decomposers.

The great majority of ecosystems, however, obtain all or most of their energy through the photosynthesis of their producers. Therefore, measuring the amount of energy that the producers get from the sun is a key to understanding an ecosystem. This measurement is the ***productivity*** of the ecosystem.

An important part of an ecosystem's total productivity is its ***net productivity.*** Net productivity is the energy that is available as food for the consumers. This can be measured in several ways. One is to find the mass of the producers (see Investigation 3.1). Much of the mass of living organisms is water. Water does not provide energy to consumers, and often varies in amount in the producers. So the producers are dried for truer comparisons by dry mass. Another measurement (heat during burning) then indicates the energy content of the producers.

Can you think of another example?

productivity [proh duk TIV uh tee]. See page 293.

3–13 A wheat field in Colorado. How would a farmer measure productivity?

BSCS by Bert Kempers

In many cases all the productivity of an ecosystem does not remain in that ecosystem. Coastal salt marshes, for example, have high productivity. Yet much of this is carried away by the tides and nourishes the consumers in the waters of bays or the nearby ocean.

Where does most of the productivity of a cornfield go?

ECOSYSTEM STABILITY

In describing the Florida river ecosystem, we named more than a dozen kinds of organisms and referred to many others in general terms. A careful biologist undoubtedly could find hundreds. The community that you studied in Investigation 1.4 surely had many more kinds than you were able to find.

No matter how many kinds of organisms there are within a given space, there are always more individuals of some kinds than of others. In any given volume of a Florida river, there are many tape-grass plants, fewer snails, still fewer river turtles, and *very* few alligators.

When we study the ***macroscopic*** organisms in most ecosystems of middle latitudes, we may find a large number of individuals. Many of these individuals, however, probably will be the same kind of organism. A careful inventory would show that only a few different kinds of organisms are present. As a result, most of the energy that passes through these ecosystems passes through a few kinds of organisms. On the other hand, there are usually many other *kinds*, but only a few of each. Only

macroscopic [mak ruh SKOP ik; Greek: *makros*, large, + *skopein*, to view]: large enough to be seen without a microscope

3–14 An ecosystem in a harsh environment, a desert in Utah. Would you say that this is a stable ecosystem?

Marg and Bill Staley

Into how many kinds of
producers does a wheat farmer try
to get solar energy to pass?

a small part of an ecosystem's energy passes through these organisms.

The biotic structure characteristic of most ecosystems in the middle latitudes usually is not found elsewhere. In a given space in most tropical ecosystems, there are only a few individuals of any one macroscopic kind, but there are a great many kinds. In high latitudes—ecosystems of Antarctica, for example—and in other severe environments, only a few kinds of organisms can exist. These have the energy supply to themselves, and the number of individuals of each kind is comparatively large.

Tropical ecosystems are rather stable and middle-latitude ones are somewhat less so. Those of severe environments, however, often experience wide fluctuations in population densities. It seems, then, that the greater the number of kinds of organisms—and the greater the number of links in food webs—the more effective is the homeostasis in an ecosystem.

ECOLOGICAL NICHES

analyze [AN uh lyz]: to think
about a thing in a way that
separates it into its parts

niche [NICH]

Some ecologists try to analyze the complexity of ecosystems by concentrating on the relationships of a single kind of organism. The sum of all relationships between any one kind of organism and its environment is called its ecological **niche.** Most dictionary definitions of "niche" stress location. The ecological definition concerns a *way of living.* Of course, any particular way of living occurs in a suitable place—a **habitat.** But, in describing the niche of an organism, ecologists do not tell where it lives; they tell *how* it lives.

habitat [HAB uh tat; Latin:
habitare, to live in a place]

The habitat of river turtles, for example, is a rather warm, slow-moving river. In describing the niche of a river turtle, however, ecologists must include all the relationships described on pages 75–78. They also must discover all the ways in which the abiotic environment affects river turtles. The temperature of the water, the flow of the current in the river, the clearness of the water, the nature of the soil where the turtles dig their nests must all be considered. Further, ecologists must include all the ways in which river turtles affect both their biotic and abiotic environments.

Seals and whales. See
Appendix 3 and page 120.

River turtles live in one habitat. Some other kinds of organisms live in several habitats and may have different niches in each. A human population that lives by hunting seals and whales has a different niche from that of a human population that lives by raising rice. Much of the study of human geography is the study of human ecological niches.

CHECK YOURSELF

O. Why is it impossible to draw sharp boundaries between ecosystems?

P. Why can we conclude that ecosystems have continuity through time?

Q. What is the productivity of an ecosystem?

R. What are some ways in which net productivity may be measured?

S. How does the number of kinds of organisms in an ecosystem seem to relate to the stability of that ecosystem?

T. How can organisms living in the same habitat be said to occupy different niches?

HUMANS IN ECOSYSTEMS

When humans lived in small groups and had few tools, they were clearly a part of a local ecosystem. They had a niche in their ecosystem. Their effects upon it were not much more noticeable than those of other organisms. Now such small, primitive human groups have almost disappeared.

Today, humans are numerous. The effects of our technology are great. Our activities greatly influence organisms and abiotic environments far away from where the activities occur. Corn plants growing in Kansas, tomatoes growing in New Jersey, sugarcane growing in Hawaii, and potatoes growing in Maine are all producer organisms for people living in all parts of the United States.

3–15 Human activity radically changes natural ecosystems. How has your ecosystem changed because of human activity?

X 1/8

3–16 A thistle.

pollution [puh LOO shun; Latin: *polluere*, to pour over]

The changes that we make in ecosystems usually reduce the number of kinds of organisms. For example, we have changed forests and prairies, which contained many kinds of plants, into cultivated fields with only one kind, such as corn. Of course, we cannot succeed in reducing the community to just corn. But by simplifying the community, we produce an ecosystem that can have wide fluctuations in population densities. The corn density may be great; then we have a good crop. But we must spend much time and energy to prevent other populations, such as smut or thistles, from overwhelming the corn. Thus an agricultural ecosystem is not much like natural ecosystems in any kind of environment—it is unstable.

To grow crops more effectively, we move things from all parts of the world into our fields. We bring in some chemical substances to increase plant growth and others to decrease populations of organisms that eat plants. Water and wind may carry these chemicals away from our fields. We bring in machines made of metals from many parts of the earth. Worn-out machines are placed together and their metal is left unused. We bring in gasoline and oil, and the wastes from their burning are carried into the air. Streams are used to carry away human and animal wastes. In short, human activities tend to result in the *pollution* of the environment—that is, to make it a more difficult environment in which to survive.

3–17 One of a city's many links to the world ecosystem. What are some others?

USDA

Clearly we can now understand ourselves ecologically only when we consider ourselves as being a part of the whole biosphere. In a city it is easy to forget our relationships to the world ecosystem. Here we have covered the land with streets and buildings. The producers are far away. Most of the decomposers are in a distant sewage system or garbage dump. Yet without them both—somewhere—a city ecosystem could not exist.

A city is mainly an aggregation of organisms of a single kind—humans. Yet we are not alone in a city. An urban community contains a number of organisms that, in one way or another, have adapted to urban conditions. The chief requirement is the ability to get along with people. Some organisms— dogs, cats, even pigeons—are deliberately cared for. Others— rats, mice, starlings, cockroaches—manage quite well without encouragement. Trees and shrubs that can live in the polluted urban atmosphere are planted along streets and in parks. Hardy herbs spring up, unwanted and untended, in vacant lots and even in the cracks of city sidewalks. And, of course, microorganisms are everywhere.

aggregation [ag rih GAY shun; Latin: *ad*, to, + *gregare*, to collect]: a group that has been brought together

urban [UR bun; Latin: *urbs*, city]

X 1/2

3 – 18 A cockroach.

M. Fredric Stein

3 – 19 Humans dominate ecosystems only through ceaseless effort. What is happening here?

Outward from the center of a city, we share space more generously with other organisms. There is more vegetation in the suburbs, though most of it is planted deliberately. Rabbits and squirrels manage to exist with humans' pets. Many kinds of birds survive, with or without the encouragement of feeding stations and birdhouses. In the South, various kinds of lizards get along nicely in gardens and even in houses.

There is a strange biological sameness in human-dominated communities. It is true that the palms of Los Angeles are missing from Boston, and crickets may not chirp everywhere between Miami and Seattle. But grass and a few trees, dogs, rats, pigeons, and houseflies are frequent companions of humans.

In recent years we have become more aware that we humans are part of the web of life. Regulations are being established to control pollution of air and water. Scientists are searching for better ways to protect crops from pests. More people are conscious of the need to conserve our limited resources. We humans are not yet living in harmony with nature. But we are beginning to understand past mistakes and are trying to prevent them in the future. Understanding and solving human ecological problems will be an important area of science for years to come.

CHECK YOURSELF

U. What two things have made human effects on ecosystems so great today?

V. Why does a farmer have difficulty in maintaining a single crop in a field?

Investigation 3.3   A LABORATORY ECOSYSTEM

INTRODUCTION

In this laboratory exercise you will investigate several variables at the same time. Such an investigation must provide separate setups for each variable. This makes it possible to distinguish results determined by any one variable from results determined by the others. (1) Read through Part A of the Procedure to find what variables are present. Then state a hypothesis for the effect of each variable.

PROCEDURE

A. Setting up the cultures

1. Using a glass-marking crayon, label the jars from A to E and mark your team symbol on each.

2. Pour 400 ml filtered pond water into each jar.

3. Stir the mixture of pond organisms. Then add 50 ml to each of the jars. Each jar now contains a culture of several kinds of producers and consumers in pond water.

4. To Cultures A and B add nothing more. To Culture C add 1 g fertilizer. To Culture D add 0.1 g pesticide. To Culture E add 0.3 g peptone and 0.5 g glucose.
5. Cover all cultures with plastic wrap.
6. Place Cultures A, C, D, and E where each will get the same amount of light. Cover Culture B with a box to keep it in darkness and place it with the other cultures.

B. Sampling the cultures

1. Choose a partner. Each pair should choose one of the team's 5 cultures. Your pair will be responsible for the sampling of this culture for the entire investigation. On the first day of the investigation remove a sample from your culture, as follows: Stir the culture. Then, using a pipette, transfer 5 ml of the culture to a vial.
2. Add to the vial about 20 drops of formalin and 20 drops of glycerin. Formalin kills the organisms, and glycerin preserves them after the water and formalin evaporate.
3. On the vial, mark your team symbol, letter of the culture, and date of sampling.
4. Cover the vial with a piece of lens paper held by a rubber band. Place it in a warm spot to allow the water to evaporate.
5. Finally, to maintain the volume in Culture A, add 5 ml filtered pond water to the culture jar.
6. Sample your culture in this way every 2 or 3 days for 2 weeks.

C. Counting the organisms

1. The counting procedure is that used in Investigation 2.1. In this investigation, however, more than one kind of organism is present. Your teacher will provide you with drawings to help you identify the different kinds. Count the organisms in each of 5 fields on a microscope slide, with 2 people making a count of each sample. Wash the medicine droppers thoroughly

MATERIALS

For Part A
(per team of 10 students)

glass-marking crayon
5 jars, about 1,000-ml
2,000 ml filtered pond water
300 ml mixed pond organisms
graduated cylinder, 100-ml
1 g balanced fertilizer
0.1 g pesticide
0.3 g peptone
0.5 g glucose
5 squares plastic wrap, about
    15 × 15 cm
box, large enough to cover jar

For Part B

5 cultures (from Procedure A)
5 pipettes, 5-ml
7 vials, 10-ml
2 medicine droppers
5 ml formalin
5 ml glycerin
glass-marking crayon
7 pieces lens paper, about 4 × 4 cm
7 rubber bands
filtered pond water

For Part C

2 medicine droppers
culture samples (from
    Procedure B)
4 microscope slides
broken cover slips
4 cover slips
microscope
10 sheets graph paper
colored pencils

before using them with each sample.
2. In your data book, prepare a chart like figure 3–20. In the chart, blocks have been divided into triangles. Record your data in the upper triangle and your partner's data in the lower one.
3. Obtain the average number of individuals from your counts. Then obtain the average combining yours and your partner's.

3 – 20 Chart for counting cultures.

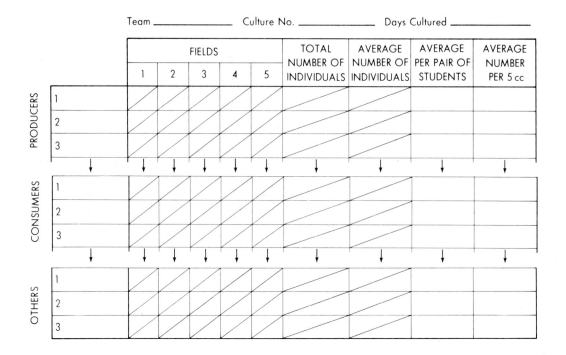

Team _____ Culture No. _____ Days Cultured _____

4. Finally, you must take into account the fact that you concentrated the sample by evaporating the water. To do this, multiply the average by 1/5.
5. Transfer the data from the last column of your chart to the class chart that your teacher has prepared.

DISCUSSION

Construct graphs of the class data. On the horizontal axis, place the ages of the cultures in days. On the vertical axis, list numbers to represent the population densities. Using a different-colored pencil for each kind of organism, plot the average data from Culture A. Make similar graphs for each of the other cultures. When you are finished, you should have 5 graphs, each with as many lines as you have organisms.

(2) What is the purpose of Culture A in the design of the experiment? (3) What changes, if any, occurred in the populations of the different organisms in Culture A during the 2-week period? (4) What changes, if any, occurred in each of the other cultures? (5) Compare the changes in each of the cultures with those in Culture A. (6) For each of your hypotheses, state a conclusion. (7) Make a general statement about the effects of abiotic variables on population changes in ecosystems that contain a mixture of aquatic producers and consumers.

PROBLEMS

1. Rivers that run underground through caves (as in Kentucky) are ecosystems that have few kinds of organisms. None of these are producers. Explain why producers are lacking. Explain how an ecosystem can exist without them.

2. Ecological relationships that increase a population are called "positive." Those that decrease a population are called "negative." How might a negative ("harmful") effect on a population actually benefit the population in the long run?

3. Here are two parasite-host relationships: (a) A fungus is the parasite; a chestnut tree is the host. The effect on the host is called "chestnut blight." (b) A bacterium is the parasite; a human is the host. The effect on the host is called "whooping cough." Investigate these two parasite-host relationships. Read about their history and the effects on the parasite and host populations. Find out how humans have tried to control these relationships. Then compare the relationships and attempt to explain any differences.

4. What terms do you think are most appropriate to describe the ecological relationships between (a) humans and rats, (b) humans and sheep, (c) humans and horses, (d) humans and dogs? Do you think any of these relationships have changed during history?

5. Investigate the community in a city. Gather evidence to support tentative answers to such questions as these: (a) To what extent does the biological energy in this community come directly from the photosynthetic activity of its producers? (b) How does the community get the rest of its biological energy? (c) Which organisms in the community get their energy through the first source? Which organisms get it through the second? (d) Which organisms are present because humans are members of the community? (e) Which organisms are encouraged by humans? Which organisms exist in spite of human activities? (f) Which organisms would be present whether humans were present or not?

6. Medical doctors, nurses, and veterinarians are three examples of people whose careers involve studying interactions between organisms in their environments. How many other careers can you identify that are involved with such interaction between living organisms?

7. Weather forecasters, farmers, toxicologists, and people in the artificial fertilizer industry provide examples of careers involving study of biotic and abiotic factors in interaction. How many other careers can you name that deal with interaction of biotic and abiotic factors?

SUGGESTED READINGS

Amos, W. H. 1977. Unseen Life of a Mountain Stream. *National Geographic*, April, pp. 562–580. Beautiful photos of smaller inhabitants of the mountain stream ecosystem.

Brewer, R. 1979. *Principles of Ecology*. W. B. Saunders, Philadelphia. Pages 120–246 deal with community and ecosystem ecology.

BSCS. 1976. *Environmental Biology*. W. B. Saunders, Philadelphia. An audio-tutorial program that deals with ecosystems.

Cheng, T. C. 1970. *Symbiosis: Organisms Living Together*. Bobbs-Merrill, Indianapolis. Devoted to various kinds of ecological relationships. Fairly easy.

Cody, M. L. and M. J. Diamond (eds.). 1975. *Ecology and Evolution of Communities*. Harvard University Press, Cambridge. An advanced treatment of biological communities.

Goreau, T. F., N. I. Goreau, and T. J. Goreau. 1979. Corals and Coral Reefs. *Scientific*

American, August. Describes one of the richest ecosystems on earth.

Kemp, W. B. 1971. The Flow of Energy in a Hunting Society. *Scientific American,* September. How energy is channeled in an Eskimo village. Advanced reading.

Kormondy, E. J. 1976. *Concepts of Ecology.* Prentice-Hall, Englewood Cliffs, N.J. Advanced reading.

Leshan, E. et al. 1965. Sabino Grove Ecology Study. *Natural History,* May. Study made by high school students in California.

Odum, E. P. 1975. *Ecology.* Holt, Rinehart and Winston, New York. Chapter 2. Fine description of the ecosystem concept by an ecologist who helped develop it. Advanced.

Rappaport, R. A. 1971. The Flow of Energy in an Agricultural Society. *Scientific American,* September. Study of energy routes in primitive farming in New Guinea.

SECTION TWO

Diversity
among Living Things

DIVERSITY AMONG LIVING THINGS

Every day crowds of curious people throng to zoos. They come to watch lions and elephants, owls and eagles, snakes and turtles. Just as popular are aquariums. Here hundreds of kinds of animals that live in water—sharks and whales, eels and starfish, crabs and clams—can be seen. Many people enjoy botanical gardens, where living plants from other parts of the world are grown—some in the open, others in greenhouses.

Of course, you don't have to live near a zoo, an aquarium, or a botanical garden to learn at firsthand about many different kinds of living things. You can visit a forest, a meadow, or a pond. In backyards of cities and suburbs, you will find many different kinds of organisms.

Wherever you observe living creatures, you will soon get an impression of overwhelming diversity. For the casual visitor to the zoo, this may be only an impression and nothing more. But if you have caught the spark of science, this impression of diversity arouses questions.

Biologists know of greater diversity than can be seen in any zoo or botanical garden. They know that almost 1½ million kinds of living organisms have been described and that more are discovered every year. How can we keep track of all of them? No language in the world has over a million words. How can we even find names for all the organisms? And why are there so many kinds of living things?

These questions provide the framework for Section Two. We are not going to describe every kind of organism. That would be impossible. But we can find out how biologists keep track of all life forms. We can discover ways to put some order into diversity. We can look into the way in which biologists name organisms. And we may even begin to find clues to the way in which so many different kinds of living things have appeared on the earth.

The grasshopper pictured on the reverse side of this page is a Lubber grasshopper from southeastern Arizona. These grasshoppers are common in the rocky and grassland areas from Montana, North Dakota, and Minnesota to Arizona, Texas, and Mexico. The wings are reduced. The numbers of these grasshoppers sometimes reach destructive levels.

4

Animals

YOUR GUIDEPOSTS

In this chapter you will have an opportunity to explore these questions in biology:

- What are the purposes of a biological classification system?
- How have biologists been able to keep track of the enormous number of different kinds of organisms?
- What does a biologist mean by a "kind" of organism?
- In what major ways do animals differ from each other?

PRINCIPLES OF CLASSIFICATION

Long before the beginning of agriculture, humans roamed far and wide searching for game and edible or medicinal plants. To survive, they had to distinguish useful organisms from those that were predatory, poisonous, or otherwise dangerous to them. Early humans probably grouped organisms as "good," or useful, and "bad," or harmful. By doing this, they took the first step toward classifying living things.

medicinal [muh DIS uh nul; Latin: *medicus*, physician]

Then people began to look beyond the groupings "useful" or "harmful." They became curious about more than just what organisms do to people or what people can do with them. This curiosity was the beginning of science. Because of this new way of looking at things, organisms had to be grouped in new ways. Perhaps these early observers began by recognizing the groups "animal" and "plant."

TWO METHODS OF CLASSIFICATION

The basic idea of classification is not difficult to understand. We all do some informal classifying. Almost anything may be classified—stamps, rocks, clouds, even the kinds of weather. The words in a dictionary are classified. They are classified according to their spelling—that is, alphabetically.

Suppose a supermarket manager arranged the merchandise alphabetically. Think of the different goods to be found under

What are the practical difficulties of this system?

4 – 1 How are these people classifying the living things around them?

the letter *A:* almonds, ammonia, apples, and many more. These would be followed by bacon, baking powder, and beans. Actually, in supermarkets we find the merchandise grouped according to the nature of the product. In one section we find canned goods; in another, fresh fruits and vegetables; in a third, meats. And each of these sections may be further divided. Familiarity with this system of classification enables shoppers to locate groceries easily and quickly.

Thus we can classify in either of two ways: according to likenesses in names or according to likenesses in the objects themselves. For biological classification names of organisms are of much less importance than characteristics. So the alphabetical method is not satisfactory.

A BASIS FOR BIOLOGICAL CLASSIFICATION

diversity [dih VUR suh tee; Latin: *dis*, away, + *vergere*, to bend]

As we look about us at the great number of organisms, we are first impressed by the differences between them — by their ***diversity.*** But when we look at them closely, we begin to see likenesses — many kinds of likenesses. What kind of similarities shall we choose as a basis for classifying organisms?

We might decide to look for likenesses in color. We could lump together organisms that are blue: bluebirds, bluegrass, bluefish, blue crabs, blue spruces. Or we might classify organisms according to where they live. If we lumped together those found in human households, then dogs, geraniums, canaries, rats, and fleas would belong to the same group. But most of the organisms in such groups share only one characteristic. Such broad groupings are not very useful to biologists. When we examine organisms carefully, however, we find that some are very similar in structure and others are less similar. For example, bluebirds and canaries are more similar than bluebirds and bluegrass. Therefore, we can group organisms according to similarities in structures we consider important. Structure provides a consistent and useful basis for classifying organisms.

structure [STRUK chur; Latin: *struere*, to heap together, arrange]

BIOLOGICAL CLASSIFICATION   Kind of organism (Guidepost)

How much structural similarity must a group of individuals have to be thought of as one kind of organism? First, we must decide what we mean by a "kind" of organism. Since science is concerned with verifiable knowledge, the organisms used in any biological investigation must be identified. If they are not, there is no way to ensure that the results of the investigation can be verified by other experimenters.

But classification is also important to nonbiologists. If an insect buzzed into your room, would you react in the same way if it were a fly as you would if it were a bee? Suppose you wanted to plant a shade tree. To order "a shade tree" would be as indefinite as to order "a meal" in a restaurant. The tree salesperson might ask whether you wanted a silver maple, a red oak, or a eucalyptus tree. Your choice could not be a matter of preference only. You also would need to consider which kind of tree would grow well and which would die in the environment outside your home. So the need to distinguish between kinds of organisms is not limited to **taxonomists,** the biologists who specialize in problems of classification.

A donkey differs from a horse. The donkey is smaller, has larger ears, a shorter mane and tail, and brays rather than neighs. You and a biologist agree that donkeys and horses are different kinds of animals—but a biologist would say different **species.**

horse

X 1/60

donkey

4–2 Two different species.

eucalyptus [yew kuh LIP tus]

taxonomists [tak SON uh musts; Greek: *tassein*, to arrange, + *nomos*, law]

species [SPEE sheez; Latin: *specere*, to look at]: hence, a shape or appearance

WHAT IS A SPECIES?

Organisms may look very different from each other and still be recognized by both you and a biologist as the same species. If we look at all dogs, we can easily see that there are many inter-

mongrels [MUNG grulz]: animals of mixed parentage

fertile [FUR tul; Latin: *ferre*, to bear, produce]

sterile [STER ul; Latin: *sterilis*, barren]

mediate mongrels between such different breeds as Great Danes and greyhounds. This is so because breeds of dogs can **interbreed.** This means they can mate with each other and produce offspring that differ in various ways from both parents. These offspring can also mate and produce offspring that may be even more different than their parents. Extremely different dogs, such as the Great Dane and Pekingese, do not interbreed because of physical differences. They nevertheless are part of one related series, because they can mate with intermediate breeds. All dogs, therefore, are grouped into a single species. On the other hand, two groups of individuals that may look alike are considered separate species if they do not interbreed and produce vigorous, **fertile** offspring. Fertile offspring are those that are capable of reproducing.

The distinctness of a species is maintained in several ways. In many cases, one species cannot physically mate with another. Clearly, an elephant and a crab cannot mate and produce offspring. In other cases, offspring are formed but die when young. If the eggs of a bullfrog are fertilized by a leopard frog, they develop for a short time, then die. In still other cases, mating occurs and vigorous offspring are produced. However, they are usually **sterile,** that is, unable to reproduce. Mules, which result when horses and donkeys are mated, are almost always sterile.

GREAT DANE

COLLIE

PEKINGESE

BEAGLE

TERRIER

4-3 Five breeds of dogs. Beginning with the Great Dane in the upper left, breeds are represented by every other dog. Mongrel offspring are intermediate between the breeds.

Sometimes individuals of two different species are able to form vigorous and fertile offspring in captivity but seldom do otherwise. In these cases, distinctness of the species is maintained not by lack of ability to interbreed but by other means. Alaska brown bears and polar bears in the Washington Zoo mated and produced vigorous, fertile offspring. In the wild no such cross has ever been discovered. Since brown bears live in forests and polar bears live on snowfields and ice floes, they rarely, if ever, see each other — except in zoos.

Generally, then, we can say that a species is a population of individuals that are more or less alike and that interbreed and produce fertile offspring under natural conditions. But this concept of species is far from perfect. For example, it cannot be used for the many very small organisms that reproduce by simply dividing into two parts. In such cases the word "interbreed" is meaningless. In addition the definition is dependent on the behavior of the organisms under *natural* conditions. That polar bears and brown bears may reproduce successfully in a zoo is not reliable evidence that they are of the same species.

These difficulties are not so important as to keep us from using the species definition. In many cases we must identify species without knowing all the facts about interbreeding. We often rely on the opinions of taxonomists who use structural and other characteristics to classify organisms.

X 1/75

4–4 Polar bear (*above*) and Alaska brown bear (*below*).

FURTHER GROUPINGS

Having grouped individuals into a species, taxonomists next look for similarities among different species. Dogs, coyotes, and wolves are separate species, but they are similar in many ways. Some breeds of dogs closely resemble wolves, and many people have mistaken a coyote for a dog. Species with many similar characteristics are grouped into the same **genus.** Some people may think that foxes are also very doglike, but not taxonomists. They have placed all the doglike animals in one genus, *Canis,* and foxes in a separate genus, *Vulpes.* Taxonomists have thus expressed their belief that more important structural similarities exist among dogs, wolves, and coyotes than between wolves and foxes. (Do not worry about the Latin names. You should understand methods of classification before you tackle the problem of naming.)

genus [JEE nus; Greek: *genos,* race]

Canis [KAY nus; Latin: dog]

Vulpes [VUL peez; Latin: fox]

Similar genera (plural of "genus") are grouped together in a ***family.*** All taxonomists agree in placing *Vulpes* with *Canis* in the family Canidae. In some ways weasels resemble dogs and wolves, but they are less like them than are foxes. Taxonomists express this difference by placing weasels in a separate family, Mustelidae. Bears, which also are furry predators, are structurally different from weasels or foxes in several ways. So, taxono-

Canidae [KAN uh dee]

Mustelidae [muh STEL uh dee; Latin: *mustela,* weasel]

Ursidae [UR suh dee; Latin: *ursa*, bear]

Carnivora [kar NIV uh ruh; Latin: *carnis*, flesh, + *vorare*, to devour, eat]

Mammalia [muh MAY lee uh; Latin: *mamma*, breast]

phylum [FY lum; Greek: *phylon*, tribe]

4–5 Some common animals in the order Carnivora. Which two look most alike?

mists place them in still another family, Ursidae. These three families (Canidae, Mustelidae, Ursidae) are grouped with other similar families into the **order** Carnivora.

Wolves, weasels, and bears have many differences, but they still share many likenesses. Certainly these animals have more likenesses among themselves than they have with monkeys. Monkeys, therefore, are placed in a different order, Primates. But monkeys—and rats, cows, horses, and many other organisms—do share some characteristics. These similarities are the basis for putting them all together in the next larger grouping—at the **class** level—Mammalia.

Continuing with this method of grouping, most taxonomists place the classes containing birds, frogs, fish, and snakes with the Mammalia into the **phylum** Chordata. And finally, chordates, snails, butterflies, and thousands of other organisms are grouped into the **kingdom** Animalia. This kingdom contains all the living things we think of as animals.

X 1/30

coyote

X 1/27

wolf

X 1/18

fox

X 1/10

weasel

X 1/36

bear

4–6 Examples of biological classification. In addition to the seven principal levels, intermediate levels are often used. For example, a *subphylum* level may be placed between phylum and class.

LEVEL	DOG	WOLF	HUMAN	BLACK WIDOW SPIDER	CORN	PARAMECIUM
Kingdom	Animalia	Animalia	Animalia	Animalia	Plantae	Protista
Phylum	Chordata	Chordata	Chordata	Arthropoda	Tracheophyta	Ciliophora
Class	Mammalia	Mammalia	Mammalia	Arachnida	Angiospermae	Ciliata
Order	Carnivora	Carnivora	Primates	Araneae	Poales	Holotricha
Family	Canidae	Canidae	Hominidae	Theridiidae	Poaceae	Parameciidae
Genus	Canis	Canis	Homo	Latrodectus	Zea	Paramecium
Species	familiaris	lupus	sapiens	mactans	mays	caudatum

As we go from species to kingdom, the organisms that are grouped together share fewer characteristics at each succeeding level. At the species level the individuals are so much alike they can interbreed. At the kingdom level very few characteristics are shared among all the individuals.

A taxonomic classification is not a fact. It results from the interpretation of facts. It shows what the facts mean to the classifier. That cats and eagles and alligators have claws is a verifiable fact. But whether these three kinds of organisms should be grouped together is a matter of opinion. There is no total agreement about the place at which organisms fit into the classification scheme. This is true even though all taxonomists base their classifications on a system of levels. The more taxonomists know about organisms and the methods of classification, the better their opinions will be. But, taxonomists of equal knowledge and experience sometimes differ greatly in their views.

Chordata [kor DAY tuh; Greek: *chorde*, string of musical instrument]

adult male

immature male

X 1/2

indigo buntings

Acadian flycatcher

X 1/2

least flycatcher

4 – 7 Appearance may be unreliable as a guide to grouping individuals in species. The two dissimilar birds are of the same species, while the two similar birds are from populations that do not interbreed.

CHECK YOURSELF

A. What is diversity?
B. What is the basis for biological classification? What advantages does it have over other possible bases?
C. Why should both biologists and nonbiologists be able to distinguish different kinds of organisms?
D. What are some of the means by which members of one species are kept from interbreeding with members of other species?
E. Why is the biological definition of the word "species" inadequate?
F. How does the number of characteristics shared by all members of a classification level change as you progress from species to kingdom?
G. Why is it possible for equally experienced taxonomists to differ from each other about the classification of a particular species?

Investigation 4.1   **LEVELS OF CLASSIFICATION**

INTRODUCTION

You will investigate some of the structural characteristics that taxonomists use in separating animal groups at different classification levels. Because you will be using the observations of other persons (recorded as drawings), your conclusions can be no more valid than those drawings.

PROCEDURE

1. Prepare 4 forms like the one in figure 4-8.
2. Label the first form "Chart 1." In the spaces under "Animals," list "human," "chimpanzee," and "gorilla." In the spaces under "Characteristics," copy the italicized key words in each of the following questions. These words should remind you of the full questions when you review the chart.

a. How does the *length of the arms* of the animal compare with the length of its legs?

Chart _____

CHARACTERISTICS	ANIMALS		
	1.	2.	3.
a.			
b.			
c.			
d.			
e.			
Classification level ___			

4-8 Classification chart.

b. Are the *canine teeth* [...] or are they *small* as compared with [...] teeth of the same organisms?
c. How many *incisor teeth* are present in the upper jaw?
d. Is the *brain case* of the skull *large* or is it

small as compared with the brain cases of the other organisms on the chart?

e. Is there an *opposable first toe on the foot?* (An opposable toe is one that can be pressed against all the others, just as your thumb can press against your other fingers.)

3. Study figure 4 – 9. For each of the animals, fill in all the spaces in Chart 1 with your answers. Then write "Family" in the space following "Classification level." Refer to Appendix 3 to find the family into which

each of these organisms has been placed. Write this information in the spaces at the bottom of the chart.

4. Label the second form "Chart 2." Under "Animals," list "human," "dog," and "cat." Under "Characteristics," copy the italicized words in each of these questions:

a. How many paired *appendages* (arms and legs) does the animal have?

b. Are *nails or claws* present on the toes of the foot?

c. How does the size of the *canine teeth*

4 – 9

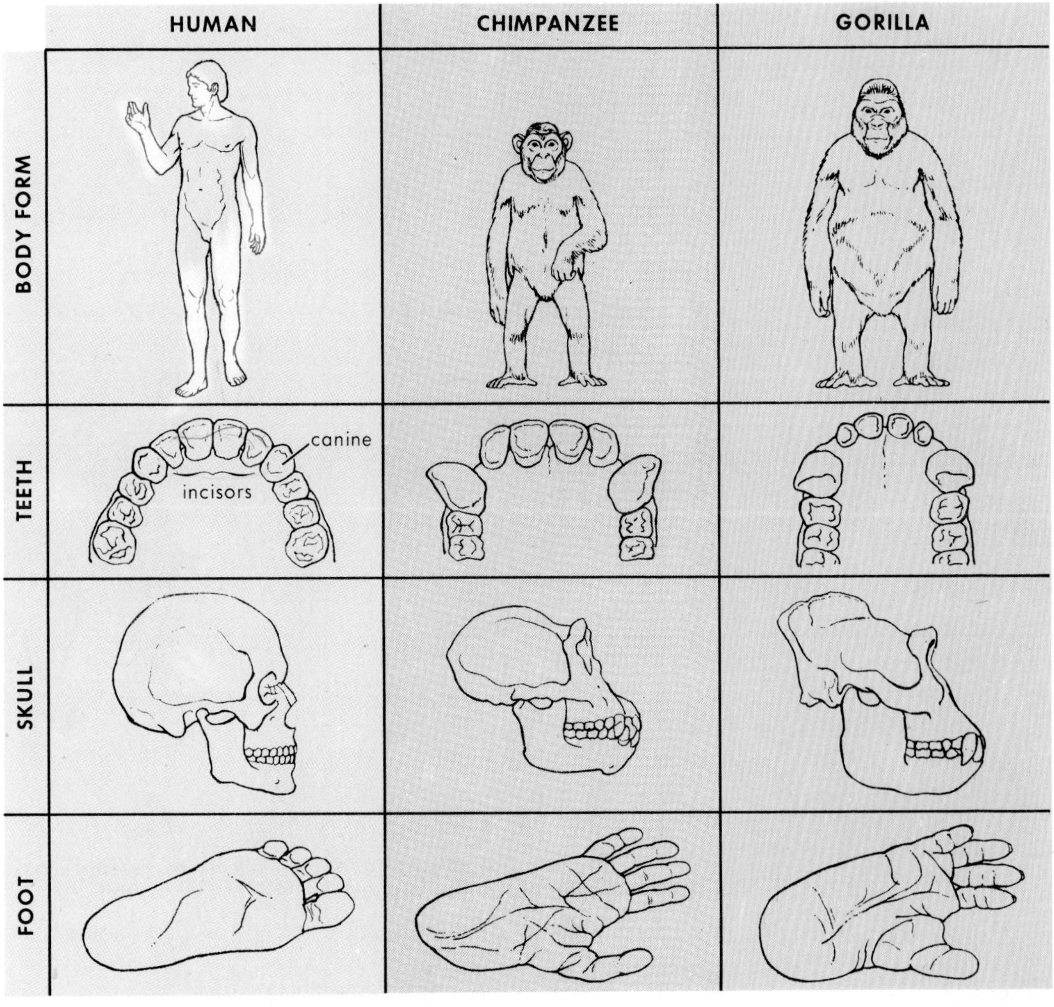

	HUMAN	CHIMPANZEE	GORILLA
BODY FORM			
TEETH	canine / incisors		
SKULL			
FOOT			

compare with that of other teeth in the lower jaw?

d. How many *incisor teeth* are present in the lower jaw?

e. How does the size of the *collarbone* compare with that of the other organisms?

5. Study figure 4–10. For each animal, fill in the spaces in Chart 2 with your answers to the questions. Write the word "Order" in the blank space following "Classification level." From pages 760–763 select the order into which each of these organisms

has been placed. Enter this information in the chart.

6. For Chart 3 use the information in figure 4–11 and the following questions:

a. What kind of *body covering* (hair, feathers, scales, none) does the animal have?

b. How many paired *appendages* (arms and legs) does the animal have?

c. Do the *ears project from* the surface of *the head?*

d. Is the *body temperature* similar to the temperature of the environment, or is it quite different?

4–10

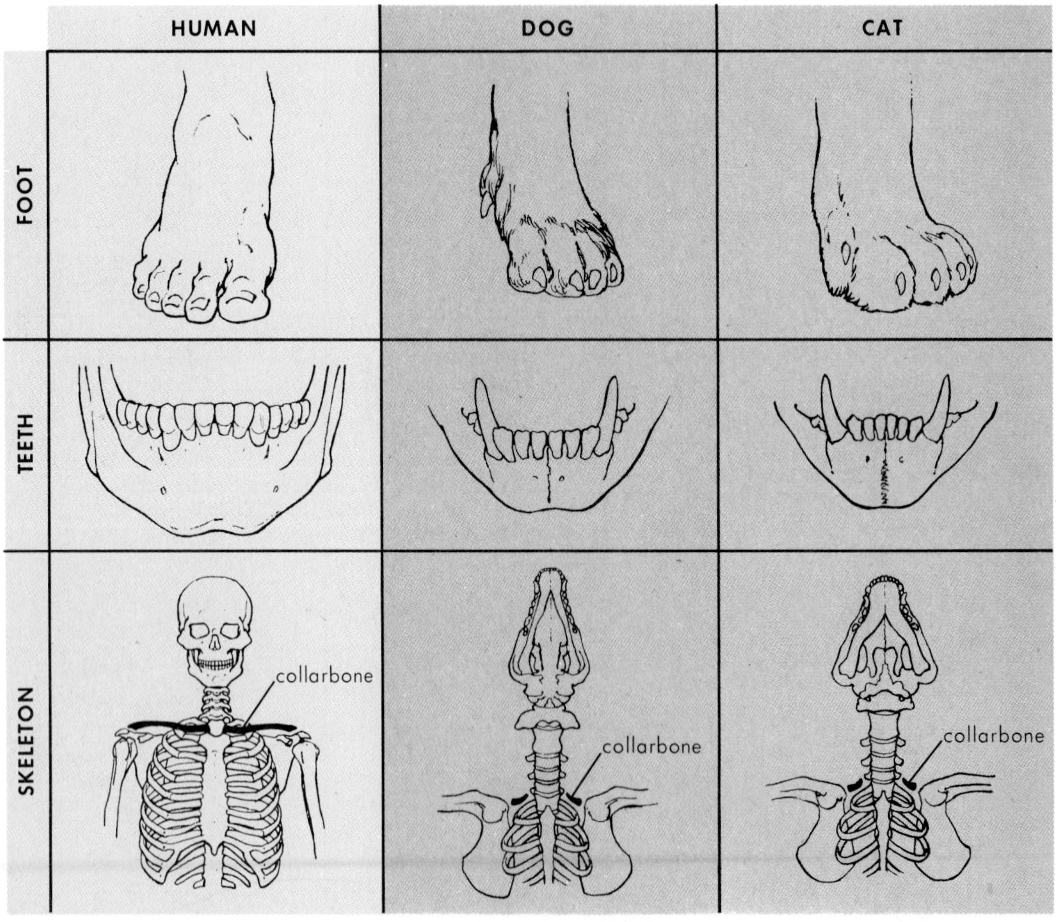

	HUMAN	DOG	CAT
FOOT			
TEETH			
SKELETON	collarbone	collarbone	collarbone

e. How many *ventricles* are *in the heart?*

7. The "Classification level" for this chart is "Class." Determine the class for each organism in figure 4 – 11 and write it in the chart.

8. For Chart 4 use the information in figure 4 – 12 and the following questions:

    a. What kind of *skeleton* (internal or external) does the animal have?
    b. Is the *position of* the *nerve cord* along the back or along the belly?
    c. Compared with the rest of the nervous system, is the *brain* large or small?
    d. Are paired *appendages* present or are they absent?
    e. Are there *grooves behind the head region* of the very young organism?

9. Write "Phylum" in the space following

"Classification level" and add the name of the phylum into which each animal in figure 4 – 12 is placed.

DISCUSSION

There are more structural similarities between chimpanzees and gorillas than between chimpanzees and humans. (*1*) How does the classification system you used express this fact? Focus on the levels in the classification system into which these organisms are placed together.

Apply this same question to the following: There are more structural similarities (*2*) between dogs and cats than between dogs and humans; (*3*) between humans and dogs than between humans and frogs; (*4*) between humans and birds than between humans and crayfish; (*5*) between humans and chimpan-

4 – 11

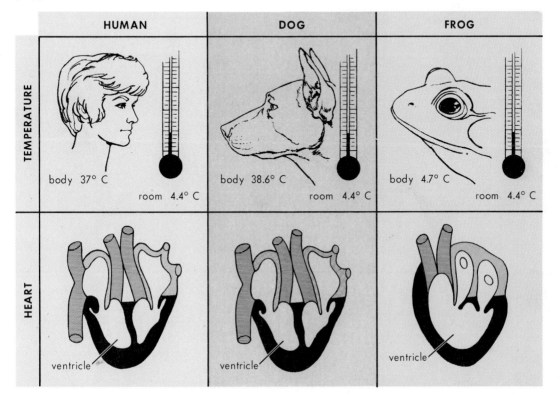

HUMAN	DOG	FROG
body 37° C	body 38.6° C	body 4.7° C
room 4.4° C	room 4.4° C	room 4.4° C
ventricle	ventricle	ventricle

zees than between humans and dogs.

(6) You are told that Species A and B are classified in the same kingdom but different phyla. You are also told that Species C and D are classified in the same phylum but different classes. What general statement can you make about similarities among Species A, B, C, and D?

4—12

	HUMAN	BIRD	CRAYFISH
SKELETON			
NERVOUS SYSTEM			
YOUNG ORGANISM			

THE ANIMAL KINGDOM

Let us see how classification can guide us through the diversity of organisms. In this chapter we shall consider only animals. All animals are motile for some part of their lives and are able to react to their environments rather quickly. They never carry on the process of photosynthesis. Not much more can be said, for organisms at the kingdom level share few characteristics.

CHORDATES

Look at the animals in figure 4–13: a sunfish, a frog, a bat, a robin, a rattlesnake, and a small shark. Can we unite these in one phylum? If so, we must find some structural likenesses among them. The bat and robin have paired wings; the shark and sunfish have paired fins; the frog has paired legs. We can group wings, fins, and legs as similar structures, calling them *appendages.* But on this structural basis, the snake would obviously not belong to the group.

appendages [uh PEN dih juz; Latin: *ad,* to, + *pendere,* to hang]

    A *zoologist* is a biologist specializing in the study of animals. If we sought help from one, we would learn that all these animals have similar internal skeletons. Each has a backbone made up of pieces called *vertebrae.* Some vertebrae are separate; others are fused in groups. The total backbone encloses a tubular nerve cord called the *spinal cord.*

zoologist [zoh OL uh just; Greek: *zoion,* animal, + *logos,* word, speech, reason]

vertebrae [VUR tuh bree; Latin: *vertere,* to turn]; singular, vertebra

4–13 What characteristics do all these animals share?

X 1/18

X 1/2

X 1/3

rattlesnake

bat

frog

X 1/4

X 1/24

shark

robin

X 1/4

sunfish

lancelet [LAN slut; Latin: *lancea,* spear]

notochord [NO tuh kord; Greek: *noton,* back, + *chorde*]

4 – 14 Lancelet. This animal lives partly buried in the sand of ocean shallows.

Suppose the zoologist now wants to add a small, fishlike animal called a lancelet to the group we already have. But close examination shows that the lancelet has no vertebrae. Instead, it has a kind of flexible rod, called a ***notochord,*** in nearly the same position as the backbone of the other animals. Just above this (closer to the back surface) is a nerve cord. It seems much like the spinal cord in the other animals we have examined.

Lorus and Margery Milne

embryos [EM bree oze; Greek: *en,* in, + *bryein,* to swell]

pharyngeal [far un JEE ul; Greek: *pharyngos,* of the throat]

dorsal [Latin: *dorsum,* back]

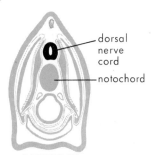

LANCELET

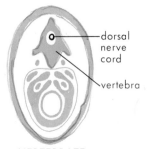

VERTEBRATE

4 – 15 Comparison of lancelet and vertebrate cross sections.

After a bit of dissection, the zoologist points out a pair of slits. One is on either side of the lancelet's body just behind its mouth. We might then look at some lancelet ***embryos.*** Embryos are organisms in the early growth stages, before birth or hatching. In the lancelet embryos we could see a series of paired pouches that grow outward in the throat region. We also would find corresponding series of paired grooves that push inward from the body surface. When these ***pharyngeal*** pouches and the grooves meet in the fully developed lancelet, paired pharyngeal slits are formed.

Both the shark and the sunfish have similar slits. But what about the frog, bat, robin, and snake? The zoologist tells us that such pharyngeal slits are present in frog tadpoles. The slits disappear before the frog becomes an adult. In the bat, robin, and snake, pharyngeal pouches and grooves are formed early in the developing embryo. These fail to meet, however and no openings are formed. In all of these animals a notochord like that of the lancelet also is present in the embryo. As development proceeds, it is replaced by the vertebrae of the backbone.

Here, then, is a new idea. To detect the basic structure of an organism, we may have to study its adult form *and* its embryonic stages. On the basis of such a study, zoologists group all the animals we have been studying into one phylum, the chordates. Although they differ greatly, all the animals in this phylum share *at some stage of their development* (1) a notochord, (2) pharyngeal pouches, and (3) a ***dorsal*** nerve cord – that is, one that is near the upper side of the body.

Turn now to Appendix 3, "A Catalog of Living Things" (pages 758–782), where other animal phyla are pictured. All the animals in each phylum have one basic pattern of structure in common, just as the chordates have a basic structural pattern. In the remainder of Chapter 4 we shall consider only a few of these phyla—those that include the kinds of animals many of us are likely to meet. Use "A Catalog of Living Things" to find pictures and information about other organisms as they are mentioned in later chapters of this book.

VERTEBRATES

All the animals in figure 4–13 are *vertebrates.* In these chordates the notochord is replaced during early development by a backbone of vertebrae. At the **anterior** end, the front end of a moving animal, the nerve cord is enlarged. This enlargement, the brain, is enclosed in a protective case—a skull. Most of the larger animals that you know fit this description of vertebrates.

anterior [an TIR ee ur; Latin: *ante,* in front of]

Mammals. All zoologists probably agree on which vertebrate animals should be called *mammals,* a class of vertebrates. From a tiny shrew to a giant blue whale 30 meters long (the largest animal that has ever lived), all mammals share two characteristics. First, all have hair. It is sometimes not very evident, and in some whales it is completely absent after birth. Second, all species of mammals feed their young with milk, a fluid secreted from mammary glands in the skin. These glands function only in females, but they are present in males as well. Further, mammals are usually *warm-blooded.* This means their bodies maintain constant temperature regardless of the environmental temperature. Mammals share this characteristic with birds.

Although they have many characteristics in common, mammals show great diversity in size, structure, and color. Much of this diversity comes from modifications that enable organisms to function in particular ecological niches. Such modifications are called structural *adaptations.* For example, mammalian hair may be greatly modified—it appears as quills in porcupines; as horns in rhinoceroses; as odd, flattened plates in pangolins; as wool in sheep. Zoologists know that these are modifications of hair from studies with developing embryos.

modifications [mod uh fuh KAY-shunz]: changes in a basic plan

adaptations [ad ap TAY shunz; Latin: *ad,* to, + *aptare,* to fit]

Birds. All birds have feathers, and all animals with feathers are birds. No other class of animals is so easy to characterize. All birds have wings, too, though not all can fly; and all birds hatch from eggs that have hard shells. Like mammals, birds are warm-blooded, but, unlike mammals, they have no mammary glands.

Many structural adaptations are found in both the feathers and the wings of birds. Feathers form the soft down of ducks, the long beautiful plumes of ostriches, and the waterproof coat

4 – 16 Diversity among mammals.

X 1/2

vampire bat

X 1/15

baboon

X 1/200

blue whale

X 1/30
porcupine

X 1/36
cheetah

X 1/36

impala

X 1/2

shrew

X 1/40

rhinoceros

X 1/10

pangolin

4–17 Diversity among birds.

albatross

X 1/20

X 1/2

X 1/10

hummingbird

flamingo

X 1/10

penguin

of penguins. Penguins never fly, but they use their short, broad wings for swimming. Albatrosses, which have long, slim wings, spend almost all their lives gliding on air currents. Yet diversity among birds is not so striking as it is among mammals. The difference between a hummingbird and a penguin is great. But the difference between a bat and a whale is startling. Modification of structures such as feet and beaks has been important in the adaptation of birds to many kinds of ecosystems.

    Reptiles. Turtles, snakes, lizards, and alligators are grouped in the **reptile** class. Reptiles may or may not have legs. One of their most studied characteristics is their jaws. Their eggs have leathery shells and are laid on land. Reptiles have skin outgrowths called **scales** (these are not like the scales of fish), but so do birds and some mammals. They breathe by means of lungs all their lives; so do birds and mammals. A

reptile [REP tul; Latin: *repere*, to creep]

4 – 18 Some reptiles.

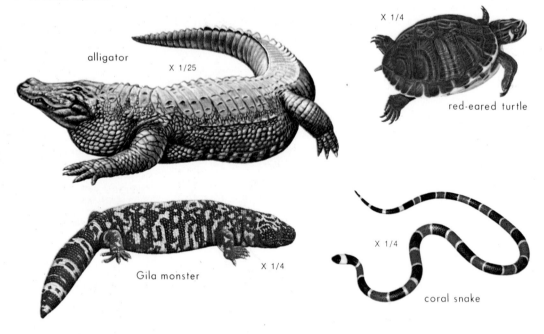

alligator

X 1/25

X 1/4

red-eared turtle

Gila monster

X 1/4

X 1/4

coral snake

ventricles [VEN trih kulz; Latin: *ventriculus*, little stomach]. See figure 4–11.

amphibians [am FIB ee unz; Greek: *amphis*, on both sides of, + *bios*, life]

X 1/2

tree frog

reptile's heart is like the heart of a mammal or bird because it has two **ventricles.** In most reptilian species, however, there is an opening in the wall between them. Body temperature in reptiles varies with the environmental temperature. That is, like amphibians and fish, they are *cold-blooded.*

Amphibians. Although some *amphibians* are shaped like lizards, there are many differences between the amphibians and the reptiles. Unlike most reptiles, very few amphibians have either claws or scales. The eggs of amphibians never have shells, so they must be laid in water or in places where humidity is high. Young amphibians, such as the tadpoles of most frogs and toads, may live in the water, but almost all adult amphibians breathe air.

4 – 19 Two amphibians.

X 1/2

tiger salamander

Bony fishes. Most people know more about catching or eating fish than about classifying them. You may be surprised to learn that living fishes are usually placed in three separate classes. However, almost all the fishes you are likely to know, especially if you do not live near the ocean, are "bony fishes." These fishes have skeletons made of the hard substance we call bone. Unlike animals in the other classes we have seen, almost all fishes, both young and adult, obtain their oxygen through gills. In bony fishes the gills are in the pharyngeal slits. They are covered by flaps and so are not visible from the outside.

Among bony fishes there is great diversity that involves structural adaptation to many aquatic ecosystems. In fact, of all the vertebrate classes, this one has the most species, and the bony fishes have invaded almost all the waters of the earth.

How does the shape of a fish relate to the manner in which it swims? What structural adaptations do bottom-living fish have? You may be able to answer these questions by carefully observing fish in an aquarium.

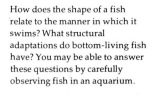

4–20 A few bony fishes.

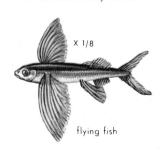

X 1/8

flying fish

X 1/5

American eel

X 1/10

tuna

Cartilaginous fishes. At first glance a shark seems to be as much a fish as a minnow is. Like other fishes — and also like amphibians — a shark is cold-blooded and has a heart with only one ventricle. However, some basic structural differences have led taxonomists to place sharks in a separate class. They think the differences between a minnow and a shark are as important as those between a snake (reptile) and a rabbit (mammal). The principal characteristic of this class is an internal skeleton made up entirely of *cartilage* rather than of bone. Cartilage is the substance that gives shape to your ears and nose. It is stiff enough to give support but is more flexible than bone. Also, nearly every cartilaginous fish has no flap over the pharyngeal slits. Besides sharks, the class contains rays, animals that have oddly flattened bodies. Perhaps this adapts them to feeding on the sea bottom.

cartilage [KART ul ij]

4—21 Two cartilaginous fishes.

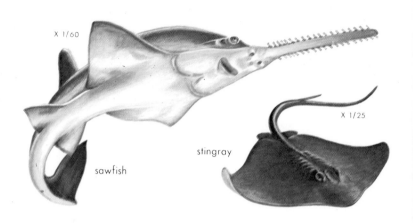

X 1/60

X 1/25

stingray

sawfish

CHECK YOURSELF

H. The vertebrates were once grouped as a phylum. Why are they now classified with such animals as lancelets?

I. At what level of classification have we placed human, dog, and cat together? What are some characteristics that they share at this level?

J. Give some examples of structural adaptations within the orders of mammals.

K. Which classes of vertebrates are cold-blooded? What does "cold-blooded" mean?

○ INSECT ARTHROPODS
  NONINSECT ARTHROPODS
○ NONARTHROPODS

4—22 Relative numbers of animal species.

arthropods [AR thruh podz; Greek: *arthron*, joint, + *pous*, foot]

ventral [Latin: *venter*, belly]

ARTHROPODS

Arthropods are as widespread in the world as chordates. More than three-quarters of all the species of living animals on Earth belong to the arthropod phylum. This means that arthropod structure has been adaptable to many kinds of environment.

The easiest way to understand basic arthropod structure is to compare it with basic chordate structure. An arthropod's main nerve cord is close to its *ventral* body surface. This is the lower body surface, which is usually toward the pull of gravity. In a chordate the main nerve is close to the dorsal surface. A chordate's nerve cord is a tube, but an arthropod's nerve cord is solid and often double. An arthropod's skeleton is outside the muscles and is called an *exoskeleton.* A chordate's skeleton is inside the muscles and is called an *endoskeleton.* The body of an arthropod is usually made up of a series of more or less similar *segments,* or sections, and their appendages are jointed.

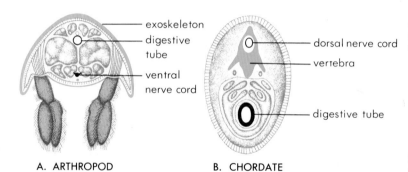

exoskeleton
digestive tube
ventral nerve cord

A. ARTHROPOD

dorsal nerve cord
vertebra
digestive tube

B. CHORDATE

4 – 23 Comparison of arthropod and chordate structures.

insects [IN sekts; Latin: *in*, into, + *secare*, to cut]

antennae [an TEN ee]; singular, antenna [an TEN uh]

thorax [THOR aks]

abdomen [AB duh mun]

Insects. All *insects* are arthropods. Besides having all the arthropod characteristics, insects have characteristics of their own. An insect's body is divided into three regions. It has a head, with a pair of *antennae*, or "feelers." Its middle part, a *thorax*, has three pairs of legs. The rear section, an *abdomen*,

4 – 24 Examples of insects.

X 1/2

butterfly

grasshopper X 1

housefly X 2

louse X 5

wasp X 2

dragonfly X 1/2

cucumber beetle X 2

mayfly X 1

silverfish X 5

moth X 1/2

usually is clearly segmented. In most adult insects one or two pairs of wings are attached to the thorax. All young insects lack wings, and many are quite wormlike. Some insects, such as lice, never develop wings.

You can easily find many species of insects. In a house you may find flies, ants, silverfish, and moths, not to mention the unpleasant possibility of fleas or lice. Many insects live close to humans — some very close indeed! On plants, in the soil, and flying in the air, you may find grasshoppers, aphids, beetles, butterflies, wasps, and many more insects. In fresh water (ponds, streams, or even a little water collected in a tin can), you may find many immature forms of dragonflies, mayflies, and mosquitoes. Insects walk, fly, burrow, and swim. Of all the major habitats on the earth, only the oceans, which support so much other life, lack insects.

arachnids [uh RAK nudz; Greek: *arachne,* spider]

Arachnids. Of all the arthropods, *arachnids* are most likely to be confused with insects. They differ from insects in having four pairs of legs, only two body regions, and no antennae.

Spiders are the most familiar arachnids. Most spiders make webs and all have poison glands, which they use in capturing and killing their prey. Only a few, however, are dangerous to humans. Scorpions, which are fairly common arachnids in the Southwest, are poisonous, but only a few are really dangerous.

Some less familiar arachnids such as mites are actually more dangerous than spiders or scorpions. In the United States mites merely cause irritating skin rashes. But in parts of the Far East and the South Pacific certain mite species carry the germs of scrub typhus, a serious disease. Ticks, better known than mites because they are larger, also carry disease germs.

What kinds of arachnids that are dangerous to humans live in the region of your home?

4 – 25 Several arachnids.

tick   X 3

X 1/2   scorpion

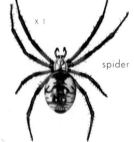

X 1   spider

crustaceans [kruh STAY shunz; Latin: *crusta,* rind]

Crustaceans. Most of the arthropods we have discussed so far are terrestrial animals, at least as adults. But one class of arthropods, the *crustaceans,* are primarily aquatic. All crustaceans have two pairs of antennae and breathe by means of gills. Most familiar are the large ones that are good to eat — lobsters, crabs, and shrimp. But most crustaceans are small, almost microscopic, animals that exist in huge numbers in bodies of water. In the ocean these crustaceans are the basic food supply for many animals—from tiny fishes to giant whales.

Although they are primarily an aquatic group, a number of crustaceans have adapted to a life on land. In the humid Pacific tropics some crabs spend most of their lives on land. They climb coconut palm trees and break open the coconuts with their stout claws. They do, however, return to the sea to lay their eggs. In the United States sow bugs are crustaceans that lead an entirely terrestrial existence. Although they may be found far from water, they do live in damp places.

These crabs breathe by gills. What adaptations might allow them to live on land?

4—26 Two crustaceans.

sow bug
X 1

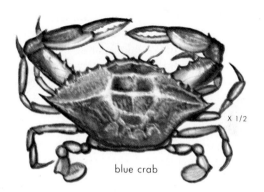
X 1/2
blue crab

4—27 Body symmetry.

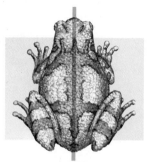

BILATERAL SYMMETRY

RADIAL SYMMETRY

ECHINODERMS

In the chordates and arthropods each animal has a "front end," that is, an anterior end. The opposite end—the end that usually trails along behind—is the *posterior* end. If you divide such an animal as shown in figure 4—27 (upper), you get right and left sides that are very much alike. This kind of body design is called *bilateral symmetry.*

In *echinoderms* the body has a different kind of symmetry. A starfish is a well-known member of this phylum. You immediately see that a starfish has no anterior and posterior ends and no definite left and right sides. There are many ways you could cut through the center of a starfish and get approximately equal halves. This kind of body design is termed *radial symmetry.* The body parts radiate from a center as spokes radiate from the hub of a wheel.

Just beneath its skin, an adult starfish has a hard skeleton with many little bumps and projections. In some echinoderms these projections are long spines. In sea cucumbers, however, the skeleton is reduced to a few small, hard particles in the leathery skin. No echinoderms are found on land or in fresh water. But they live in every part of the marine environment, from shallow shores to the greatest depths.

posterior [pos TIR ee ur; Latin: *post*, behind]

bilateral symmetry [by LAT uh rul SIM uh tree; Latin: *bis*, twice, + *latus*, side; Greek: *syn*, together, + *mentron*, measure]

echinoderms [ih KY nuh durmz; Greek: *echinos*, hedgehog, + *derma*, skin]

4 – 28 Some echinoderms. What examples of structural adaptation can you find here?

X 1/3

sea cucumber

X 1/2

sea urchin

X 1/3

sand dollar

mollusk [MOL usk; Latin: *mollis*, soft]

MOLLUSKS

Like members of the other phyla we have discussed, a **mollusk** has a nervous system, a heart that pumps blood, and a tubular digestive system—an ***alimentary canal.*** Unlike chordates and arthropods, mollusks are not segmented. Although some are bilaterally symmetrical, many show no symmetry at all. The most distinctive characteristic of a mollusk is an organ that, in most species, secretes a hard shell.

alimentary [al uh MENT uh ree; Latin: *alere*, to nourish]

Most mollusks are aquatic. They are abundant in the seas, but many species live in fresh water. And many snails live completely terrestrial lives. Mollusks are present in most ecosystems and show great structural diversity. Some are single-shelled, and some, such as clams and oysters, have shells in two parts. Some mollusks have jointed shells, and some, like the octopus, have very small shells buried inside their bodies.

4 – 29 Three mollusks.

X 1/10

octopus

X 1

garden snail

clam　　X 1/3

COELENTERATES

Around an island in the South Pacific is a habitat where the water is always clear and warm. Brightly colored fish swim through the waters. Snails, starfish, sea urchins, and crustaceans, in great variety of form and color, crawl or slither or creep about. But the reef itself is fashioned by still other organisms—for the most part, by **corals.** Taxonomists place these organisms in a phylum we have not yet examined, the ***coelenterates.***

corals. See figure 2–1.

coelenterates [sih LENT uh rayts; Greek: *koilos*, hollow, + *enteron*, intestine]

The body of a coelenterate is little more than a bag that

4 – 30 Some coelenterates.

X 4

Obelia

X 1/2

sea anemone

X 1/3

Aurelia

shows radial symmetry. Digestion occurs in the central cavity of the bag. Food is taken in and undigested particles are thrown out through the same opening. Around the opening to its digestive cavity, a coelenterate has **tentacles** that bear many small stingers. These can paralyze small organisms and, in some cases, large ones. Stinger-bearing tentacles are the most distinctive characteristic of the phylum.

tentacles: long protrusions around an animal's mouth or head

SPONGES

It is rather difficult to think of **sponges** as animals. This is not just because the adults stay in one place, attached to some solid support as do corals and oysters. Rather, it is because sponges lack the organs and systems normally associated with animals.

Basically, the body of a sponge is a bag pierced by many holes — **pores.** Water is pushed inward through these pores by the action of long, hairlike projections. This motion brings microscopic food particles into the sponge. The water flows back out of the body cavity through an opening called a "mouth." The body wall is supported by interlocking particles of hard or tough material — a kind of skeleton.

Sponges as a group show considerable diversity. Some have skeletons of hard materials that are chemically similar either to glass or to the shells of mollusks. Others have skeletons of a tough substance similar to that in a cow's horn. A few sponges have radially symmetrical shapes, but most are quite unsymmetrical.

4 – 31 Two sponges.

X 1/10

fringed basket

X 2

Scypha

FLATWORMS

In Old English "worm" meant any creeping or crawling animal. The hero, Beowulf, fought a "great worm." This doesn't sound too heroic until it is translated more accurately as "dragon." Today the word "worm" implies something small and lowly. In ordinary language it is applied quite carelessly to many different animals. In biology, also, "worm" has no clear-cut meaning, but, with various adjectives, it is used to refer to various groups of animals.

One of the main characteristics of the **flatworm** phylum is indicated by its name. A flatworm has no **circulatory system**, no system of tubes through which blood is circulated. Flatworms do not have a digestive tube. Instead they have a hollow sac with only one opening. Through this opening food enters and undigestible particles leave. This system is similar to that of the coelenterates.

There are free-living flatworms in fresh water and in the ocean. There are flatworms that have either commensal or mutualistic relationships with other organisms. But most flatworms are parasitic. Some — tapeworms, for example — have a striking adaptation to the parasitic life. Living inside the digestive systems of other animals, they completely lack digestive systems of their own. They simply absorb the digested food that surrounds them.

4 — 32 Flatworms.

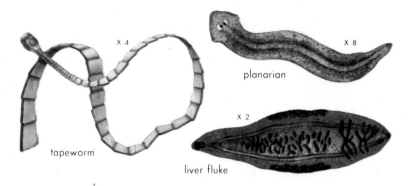

planarian

tapeworm

liver fluke

ANNELIDS

annelids [AN uh lidz; Latin: *anulus*, ring]

Annelids belong to another phylum of worms. As the name suggests, an annelid's body consists of a series of ringlike segments. We have seen segmentation in arthropods, but in annelids it is developed much further. Each segment of an annelid is a compartment that is more or less similar to the next compartment. Many internal body organs are repeated in one compartment after another. These worms are more complex than flatworms. Annelids have a complete digestive tube, not just a sac. They also have a circulatory system.

How might lack of appendages in earthworms favor burrowing?

Many annelids have appendages, but these are not jointed as in arthropods. They have solid nerve cords in a ventral position that are often paired — just as in arthropods.

The most familiar annelids are terrestrial, like earthworms, but the majority are aquatic. Some marine species reach a length of nearly a meter. Swimming around on the surface of the sea, annelids like this may have given rise to stories of sea serpents. But many marine annelids burrow in sand or mud. From hiding places they reach out with their sharp jaws and seize small passing animals. Leeches show another kind of annelid diversity. They are parasites that suck blood. A leech has a flat body without appendages, but it has one obvious structural adaptation. It possesses a pair of suction disks, one at each end of its body, with which it clings to its host.

4 – 33 Annelids.

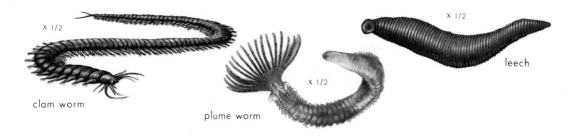

x 1/2

clam worm

plume worm

x 1/2

x 1/2

leech

CHECK YOURSELF

L.   Name three characteristics that all insects share.

M.   How do arachnids differ from insects?

N.   How does radial symmetry differ from bilateral symmetry?

O.   List some examples of diversity among mollusks.

P.   Why is it difficult to think of sponges as animals?

Q.   Compare and contrast flatworms with annelids.

Investigation 4.2   OBSERVING STRUCTURAL CHARACTERISTICS

PROCEDURE

A. Observing animal specimens

1. Draw 2 charts in your data book similar to the ones in figure 4–34. Your teacher will tell you how many columns you will need on the right side of each chart.

2. Some animal species are displayed at several numbered stations in your classroom. You may find both living and preserved specimens at some stations. The preserved specimens may be partially dissected so you can make further observations.

MATERIALS
(per class)

animal specimens
hand lenses or
  stereomicroscopes

3. Divide your class into as many groups as there are displays. Each group will begin making observations at a different display.

4. You will spend a definite amount of time at each station. At the end of each time period, move to the station with the next

4 — 34 Structural
characteristics charts.

Chart 1.

SKIN STRUCTURES / APPENDAGES / SKELETON / TEETH / JAWS	NAME OF ANIMAL		
	Class	Class	Class
SKIN STRUCTURES — Hair present			
Feathers present			
Scales present			
None of the above present			
APPENDAGES — Wings present			
Legs present			
Fins present			
None of the above present			
SKELETON — Bony			
Cartilaginous			
TEETH — Present			
Absent			
JAWS — Present			
Absent			

Chart 2.

	NAME OF ANIMAL		
	Phylum	Phylum	Phylum
EXOSKELETON — Present			
Absent			
BODY SYMMETRY — Radial			
Bilateral			
Part bilateral, part spiral			
JOINTED WALKING LEGS — 3 pairs present			
4 pairs present			
More than 4 pairs present			
Absent			
BODY SEGMENTATION — Present			
Absent			
TENTACLES — More than 4 present			
4 or fewer present			
Absent			
ANTENNAE — 2 or more pairs present			
1 pair present			
Absent			

higher number, until you reach your starting point.

5. Begin by deciding whether each animal you are studying is a vertebrate (has a backbone) or an *invertebrate* (has no backbone). If it is a vertebrate, record its common name on Chart 1 in one of the spaces under the heading "Name of Animal." If it is an invertebrate, follow the same procedure but use Chart 2.

6. At the left side of each chart is a list of characteristics to help you make observations. Each section includes two or more characteristics. After studying the speci-

mens, place a check after each characteristic you observe.

Suppose that the 1st specimen you study is a cat. A cat has a backbone. Write "Cat" in the space at the top of the 1st vertical column in Chart 1. Now look at the 4 choices indicated in the section "Skin Structures." Only 1 of the choices applies to the cat: "Hair present." Therefore, you put a check in the box that is under "Cat" and to the right of "Hair present." Next look at the choices in "Appendages." Again there is only 1 choice that applies to the cat, so you check the box under "Cat" and to the right of "Legs present." Proceed down the column in this manner. When you can't make a decision on any point, leave the space blank.

B. Using a key

Organisms are difficult to identify because there are so many of them. One tool biologists use is called a key. There are several different kinds; you will be using a **dichotomous key.** In this kind of key you must continue to choose between two characteristics until you reach the identity of the organism.

1. With the information you have recorded in Chart 1, use Key 1 (figure 4–35) to determine the class to which each of the animals belongs. Begin at the top of the key with Item 1, where you have choices 1a and 1b. If the animal you are considering has hair, your choice is 1a. Following the 1a line to the right side of the key, you find that it belongs to the class Mammalia. If the animal does not have hair, follow the 1b line to the right. Here you find that you are to go to Item 2 in the key, where two more contrasting characteristics are indicated, 2a and 2b. Again make a choice and, if necessary, continue down the key to the group with which the animal is classified. Write the name of the class in Chart 1. Repeat the process for each vertebrate animal.

4–35

KEY 1

Dichotomous Key to Classes of the Subphylum Vertebrata

1a. Hair present . . . . Class Mammalia
1b. Hair absent . . . . go to 2

2a. Feathers present . . . . Class Aves
2b. Feathers absent . . . . go to 3

3a. Jaws present . . . . go to 4
3b. Jaws absent . . . . Class Agnatha

4a. Paired fins present . . . . . . go to 5
4b. Paired fins absent . . . . go to 6

5a. Skeleton bony . . . . Class Osteichthyes
5b. Skeleton cartilaginous . . . Class Chondrichthyes

6a. Skin scales present . . . . . Class Reptilia
6b. Skin scales absent . . . . . . Class Amphibia

4–36

KEY 2

Dichotomous Key to Selected Invertebrate Phyla

1a. Body symmetry radial . . go to 2
1b. Body symmetry not
radial . . . . go to 3

2a. Tentacles present,
body soft . . . . Phylum Coelenterata
2b. Tentacles absent,
body hard and rough . . Phylum Echinodermata

3a. Exoskeleton present . . . go to 4
3b. Exoskeleton absent . . . . go to 5

4a. Jointed legs present . . . Phylum Arthropoda
4b. Jointed legs absent . . . . Phylum Mollusca

5a. Body segmented . . . . . . Phylum Annelida
5b. Body not segmented . . . Phylum Platyhelminthes

2. Use Key 2 (figure 4–36) to determine the phylum for each invertebrate in Chart 2. Record the phyla in the columns at the bottom of Chart 2.

3. Finally, use Key 3 to determine the class in which each of your arthropod animals has been placed. Record this information in your data book following Chart 2. (Keys can be made to carry identifications all the way down to the species level.)

4 – 37

KEY 3

Dichotomous Key to Selected Classes of the Phylum Arthropoda

1a. Walking legs,
      more than 5 pairs . . . . go to 2
1b. Walking legs,
      5 or fewer pairs . . . . go to 3

2a. Legs, 1 pair for each
      body segment . . . . Class Chilopoda
2b. Legs 2 pairs for each
      body segment . . . . Class Diplopoda

3a. Antennae present . . . . go to 4
3b. Antennae absent . . . . Class Arachnida

4a. Antennae, 1 pair . . . . Class Insecta
4b. Antennae, more than 1 pair . . . Class Crustacea

---

4. The simplified keys in this investigation will not always indicate a correct classification for every animal. A key gives you a correct identification *only* if it is used with the group of organisms for which it was constructed. If, for example, you attempt to classify a squid or a slug by using Key 2, the key will indicate the phylum Platyhelminthes; both are actually mollusks. Unless you use a key to unlock only the doors for which it was designed, you will end up in the wrong house! Check your identifications by using references such as those listed at the end of this chapter.

DISCUSSION

Having classified all the animals of your laboratory study, refer again to Charts 1 and 2. Once you know that an animal is a vertebrate, you need only determine a single characteristic—possession of hair—to place it in the class Mammalia. (*1*) Is there any other *single* characteristic that enables you to place a vertebrate in its class at once? If so, what characteristic is it, and in which class should the vertebrate be placed? (*2*) Does any single characteristic enable you to place an invertebrate you have studied in its phylum? If so, what is the characteristic and which phylum does it indicate? (*3*) Is there any single characteristic that enables you to place an arthropod in its class? If so, what is the characteristic and which class does it indicate?

FOR FURTHER INVESTIGATION

Select 10 students including yourself. Construct a dichotomous key using characteristics that will enable another person to identify each student in the group.

THE MEANING OF BIOLOGICAL CLASSIFICATION

In classifying organisms, we arrange them at different levels according to their structural characteristics. When we look over the results of this classification, some questions arise. Isn't it strange that *every* animal with an exoskeleton and jointed appendages also has a ventral nerve cord? Isn't it strange that *no* animal with a saclike digestive system has a circulatory system?

Why do animals with the annelid body plan *always* lack skeletons? Why do animals with the mollusk body plan *always* lack segmentation? All of these questions add up to one big question. By arranging organisms into groups according to their structural likenesses have we revealed some meaning?

Why do all the Wu children in Hong Kong have a fold in the upper eyelid and black hair? Why do all the Pedersen children in Copenhagen have blue eyes and wavy hair? Why do all the Perez children in Guatemala have dark eyes and straight, black hair? In all three cases, of course, the characteristics go together because they are family characteristics—they have "run in the family" for generations. They have been inherited together.

Perhaps it also is reasonable to assume that patterns of likeness are shared by organisms in a phylum or other taxonomic grouping because the organisms are related—in the kinship sense. On this assumption, we could say that all chordates have dorsal, tubular nerve cords, pharyngeal pouches, and notochords, because all are descended from ancestors that had the same characteristics. All insects have three pairs of legs and one pair of antennae, because all are descended from ancestors that had those characteristics.

This idea did not come directly from a study of classification, however. It arose as evidence accumulated from fossils and later from experimental studies of heredity. Early taxonomists had a hint of the idea, but, like many people, they were blinded to new thoughts by the ideas they had grown up with. Nevertheless, about a century ago, most biologists accepted the theory that species of organisms are related through their ancestry. Ever since then, taxonomists have tried to express the evidence of relationship in classification.

WORK OF MODERN TAXONOMISTS

A modern taxonomist does not look only at structural characteristics of organisms. *Any evidence of relationship* is used in the classification process. Such evidence may come from the way organisms develop during their early lives. Other important information may be obtained from the chemical materials in their bodies or even from their behavior.

Two factors, however, still make structural characteristics particularly important. The first is that a taxonomist can observe structural characteristics in preserved specimens, and these observations can easily be verified. In addition, structural evidence is all we are ever likely to have for organisms known to us only from fossils. We can make some good guesses about the activities of such organisms, but our guesses are based on

If all these families moved to, say, Chicago or Honolulu, the characteristics might get mixed up in a few generations.

4 – 38 A taxonomist at work.

structure. Knowledge of organisms of the past is important when we try to figure out the relationships of living ones because they may be the ancestors of the living ones.

EXPRESSING RELATIONSHIPS

Recall reading the following at the beginning of this chapter. "As we go from species to kingdom, the organisms that are grouped together share fewer characteristics at each succeeding level." Now we can say, "As we go from species to kingdom, the organisms are less closely related at each succeeding level." Thus we can say that all dogs are so closely related they form an interbreeding population, a species. Dogs and wolves do not ordinarily interbreed, but it is not impossible. Using structural and behavioral evidence, most zoologists believe that dogs and wolves had a common ancestry not so long ago. Taxonomists express this belief by putting them together in one genus (*Canis*), as figure 4 – 6 shows. By placing foxes in a separate genus (*Vulpes*), they show that they believe foxes are less closely related to dogs and wolves than these animals are to each other. By placing the genera *Canis* and *Vulpes* in the same family, taxonomists show that dogs are related to foxes — but less closely than to wolves.

common. Here, the word means "shared by two or more individuals or groups," as we speak in mathematics of a "common denominator."

This is somewhat similar to saying that you are closely related to your sister, but you are less closely related to your first cousin. You and your sister have the same mother and father but you and your first cousin have only one pair of grandparents in common. By placing the dog family (Canidae), the bear family (Ursidae), and the weasel family (Mustelidae) together in the order Carnivora, taxonomists imply that all of these animals descended from a common ancestral group—but probably long ago. As we continue up the list of levels, the relationships become more distant. Thus, when taxonomists place a dog and a goldfish in the same subphylum but in different classes, they imply a very distant relationship indeed.

CONFLICTING PURPOSES

Have we abandoned the original purpose of classification—to catalog organisms for convenient reference? Not at all. Modern taxonomists attempt to arrange organisms in a way that will both show relationships and allow convenient reference.

Of course, anyone who tries to do two things at once usually gets into trouble. The more evidence taxonomists obtain, the more complex the relationships of organisms appear to be. Taxonomists also differ in how they interpret the evidence. As a result, many schemes of classification exist, all designed within the same framework of levels. Classifications that are used to arrange museum specimens often lean toward convenience and neglect relationships. In contrast, classifications in advanced and specialized textbooks usually lean toward relationships and neglect convenience. Classifications for general use—as in this book—are often compromises between the two aims.

CHECK YOURSELF

R. What is a dichotomous key?

S. How does a classification reflect a taxonomist's ideas about kinship relationships among organisms?

T. What different kinds of information does a taxonomist use to determine relationships between two organisms?

U. Give two aims of a taxonomist.

Investigation 4.3   DIVERSITY IN ANIMALS: A COMPARATIVE STUDY

PROCEDURE

Make an enlarged copy of the chart shown in figure 4–39. It should extend across two facing pages in your data book. Each of the 13 spaces should allow for several lines of

MATERIALS
(per class)

pencils
paper
materials supplied by your teacher

4 – 39 Comparative chart.

CHARACTERISTICS	HYDRA	PLANARIA	EARTHWORM	CRAYFISH	FROG
1					
2					
3					
↕	↕	↕	↕	↕	↕
13					

writing. Copy the following questions, each in a separate space, in the column headed "Characteristics." (If more than one question follows a number, copy only the first.) The 13th space is for any additional observations you may make.

1. What do you think is the habitat of the animal? Does it live in water, on land, or in both places?
2. Is body symmetry radial or bilateral?
3. Does the animal have a skeleton? If it has, is it an endoskeleton or an exoskeleton?
4. Is the animal's body segmented or is it unsegmented?
5. Which does the animal have, an alimentary canal or a digestive sac?
6. Does it have paired appendages?
7. How does the animal obtain oxygen? (Through lungs, gills, skin, or a combination of these?)
8. Are there any sense organs visible? If so, what kinds are they, and where are they located?
9. How does the animal move from one place to another?
10. Does it make any kinds of movement while it remains more or less in one spot?
11. How does the animal capture and take in food?
12. How does it react when touched lightly with a dissecting needle or a small water-color-type brush?

All the specimens of one species of animal and the materials and equipment needed for observing them are arranged at one station. Each team will have a turn at each station.

Following are directions for observing each species. Some will help you make the observations needed to answer the questions. Some will direct your attention to additional observations that you should record in the 13th space of your chart. You may find some observations impossible to make. Therefore, you may have blank spaces on your chart. Do the best you can. Remember that you are recording *your observations,* not what you have read or heard about the organism.

Station 1. Observing hydras

a. Observe food capture and feeding in hydras under a stereomicroscope or hand lens. Place a single hydra in a small watch glass with some of the same water in which it has been living. Wait until the animal attaches itself to the dish and expands its tentacles. Then slowly add a few drops of a *Daphnia* culture.

b. Observe the hydra's reactions when it is gently touched with the water-color brush.

c. Examine a prepared slide of a longitudinal section of hydra under a monocular microscope. Try to determine the presence or absence of a skeleton and of an alimentary canal.

Station 2. Observing planarians

a. Use a stereomicroscope or hand lens. Place 1 or 2 planarians in a small watch glass that contains pond or aquarium water. Add a small piece of freshly cut raw liver. Record your observations.

b. Use a monocular microscope to examine cross sections of planarian. Examine whole mounts with a stereomicroscope. Determine the presence or absence of skeleton and alimentary canal.

Station 3. Observing earthworms

a. Pick up a live earthworm and hold it gently between your thumb and forefinger. Observe its movements. Are there any regions on the body surface that feel rough? If so, examine them with a hand lens and record your observations.

b. Watch a worm crawl about on the slightly moistened tabletop until you determine which is its anterior end. Use a hand lens to examine both ends of the animal. How do its anterior and posterior ends differ in structure?

c. Place an earthworm on some loose soil and observe its movements as it burrows.

d. Using a monocular microscope, examine cross sections of the body under low power and high power. Try to determine whether it has a skeleton.

Station 4. Observing crayfish

a. Observe the movements of the appendages and the pattern of locomotion of a live crayfish in an aquarium. Observe the antennae. Touch them gently with the water-color brush. Note the animal's reaction.

b. Put a small piece of liver in a dish with the crayfish. Observe how the crayfish eats.

Station 5. Observing frogs

a. Examine the prepared skeleton of a frog. Compare it with a dissected preserved specimen. Determine the position of muscles and other soft tissues in relation to the bones.

b. Study the breathing movements of a live frog that is not moving about. To do this, observe from the side, with your eyes at the level of the animal.

c. Observe the movements of a frog swimming in an aquarium. How do these movements compare with those of a frog hopping and moving about on a laboratory table? Your teacher will show you how to catch and hold a frog so as not to injure it.

d. If a hungry frog is available, your teacher may be able to show you how it captures food.

DISCUSSION

When you have completed your observations and recorded the data, review what you have learned about each of the items in the chart. By reading across the chart, you should be able to compare and contrast the characteristics of the 5 animals you have studied.

For each animal, select 5 functions that it performs as part of its way of life. Describe how, in each case, its structure enables it to perform these functions.

Careers in Biology: Plants and Animals

Do you have a Pekingese, a parakeet, or a prayer plant? Did you adopt this "pet" because you wanted to study its life cycle or its behavior? You probably would answer, "No, I just enjoy plants or animals." You may own a pet strictly for pleasure, not for scientific investigation. But, without special training, you must rely on other people with biological skills and knowledge to help raise your pet and keep it in good health.

Potted plants are raised in greenhouses — large sheds made mostly of glass. The glass lets in sunlight and keeps out cold. Some greenhouses are heated, so tropical plants can grow in them even in freezing weather.

Beth Thacker and Debbie Mangis (**A**) work at a greenhouse. They are horticulturists — they grow plants for sale and further research. Among other tasks, Beth and Debbie mate plants from closely related species or plants that are different varieties of the same species. This is done in an effort to produce new varieties with more beautiful and fragrant flowers. Many new kinds of roses are produced in this way.

Beth and Debbie also are involved in propagating plants by grafting. Grafting is simply the joining together of stems from two different plants. In one kind of graft, a shoot and adjoining stem of one plant are united with the stem and adjoining root of another plant. The two parts then grow together as one plant. For example, consider a tree that produces seedless oranges. It cannot reproduce by seeds. But its life can be extended by grafting. Individual branches of the seedless-orange tree can be grafted onto rootstocks of other orange trees. The result will be a large number of trees that produce seedless oranges.

Where can you find cacti from Arizona together with rhododendrons from China and lilies from Africa? You might see all of these and many more kinds of plants at a botanical garden. Here, many different species of plants are grown — often in garden plots that resemble their native habitats. Botanists, like Gary Hannan (**B**), are trained in the science of plants. They know how to care for plants, how to identify and classify them, and how to cure their diseases. At a botanical garden in California, Gary waters the orchids, vines, and palm trees in the tropical plant house and feeds flies to the insectivorous plants.

Zoological gardens, or "zoos" for short, house members of the animal

BSCS by Oliver Ask

A. Beth and Debbie often work on producing new varieties of plants. They are setting out one of their experimental groups and are hoping to get some encouraging results.

BSCS by Oliver Ask

B. In order to grow tropical plants in this greenhouse, Gary must maintain a very moist environment.

C. A young bobcat was not receiving proper care from its mother, so Cindy became its foster parent. The animal needs regular care and feeding several times a day.

kingdom. At most zoos you will find animals from all over the world. Zookeepers, who tend the animals, must have extensive biological training before they can begin work. Cindy Bickel (**C**) put her training to good practice when she cared for a young bobcat. The most difficult task was finding the right milk formula for the young cat.

What happens if one of the animals at a zoo becomes ill or is injured? A zookeeper may call a veterinarian, just as you would do if your pet became ill. Some veterinarians take care of house pets only (**D**). Doug James, a veterinarian in the city, often diagnoses and treats kittens with pneumonia or dogs with broken bones. Other veterinarians may work only with farm animals—horses, cattle, and pigs.

If you like plants and animals, you might consider a career that involves working with them.

American Veterinary Medical Association

BSCS by Oliver Ask

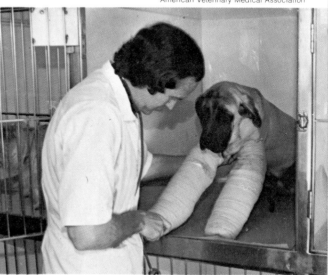

D. This family pet was hit by a car, and two of its legs were broken. A local veterinarian set the bones and is now examining them to make sure they are healing properly.

PROBLEMS

1. Suppose that by the year 2005 every kind of living organism on Earth will have been discovered, described, and classified. Do you think the development of taxonomy would then end? Explain.

2. How can you explain the fact that many attached or slow-moving animals are radially symmetrical, but many unattached, fast-moving animals are bilaterally symmetrical?

3. Disregard relationships and use structure as a basis to devise a new classification of all the vertebrates you know.

4. Some apparently similar vertebrates are placed in separate classes by taxonomists. What characteristics would enable you to distinguish between the following: (a) an eel and a lamprey? (b) an eel and a snake? (c) a lizard and a salamander? (d) a turtle and an armadillo? (e) a bat and a bird? (f) a shark and a whale?

5. Many years ago all living species of mollusks were placed in four classes. In 1957 a deep-sea dredge brought up some mollusks so different that taxonomists had to place them in a separate class. Look up the story of this discovery. During the last century what other major changes in classification have resulted from finding previously unknown organisms?

SUGGESTED READINGS

Emmel, T. C. 1975. Adaptation on the Wing. *Natural History*, October.

Goodall, J. 1979. Life and Death at Gombe. *National Geographic*, May, pp. 592–620. Recent studies of chimpanzees.

Hanson, E. D. 1972. *Animal Diversity*. 3rd ed. Prentice-Hall, Englewood Cliffs, N. J. Stresses aims of the modern taxonomist. Rather difficult.

Hutchins, R. E. 1975. *Insects and Their Young*. Dodd, Mead, New York. Excellent and useful entomology text.

Keast, A. 1974. Fish Are What They Eat. *Natural History*, January. A fish's mouth reveals a lot about the animal.

Kurten, B. 1974. *The Age of Mammals*. Columbia University Press, New York. Readable account of mammalian history.

McFarland, W. N., F. H. Pough, T. J. Cade, and J. B. Heiser. 1979. *Vertebrate Life*. Macmillan, New York. An advanced, but general, coverage of vertebrates.

Russell-Hunter, W. D. 1979. *A Life of Invertebrates*. Macmillan, New York. A broad view of the "lower" animals. College level.

Each of the following is a series of books that treat the classification and identification of certain parts of the animal kingdom.

Golden Nature Series. Edited by H. S. Zim. Western Publishing, New York. Includes volumes on reptiles and amphibians, fishes, mammals, birds, spiders, insects. Simple; many colored pictures.

Peterson Field Guide Series. Edited by R. T. Peterson. Houghton Mifflin, Boston. Volumes on birds, mollusks, butterflies, mammals, reptiles, amphibians, insects. These books do not use keys but are copiously illustrated. Most are quite complete for the area and taxonomic group covered.

Chapter 5

Plants

YOUR GUIDEPOSTS

In this chapter you will have an opportunity to explore these questions in biology:

- Why are scientific names important?
- What are the basic rules of the system for naming plants and animals?
- How is a key for the identification of plants made and used?
- What are the basic parts of a plant?
- How do groups of plants differ as to structure and habitat?

CLASSIFYING PLANTS

Plants, like animals, show much variation in size, shape, and color. However, many people do not observe plants carefully and tend to take them for granted. Most people recognize some large plants as trees, or take pride in the grass of their lawns, or, perhaps, know a rose when they see one. But being acquainted with trees, grass, and a few flowers is only the beginning, for there are nearly 350,000 known species of plants!

For many centuries plant classification was based on the groupings made by the early Greeks: tree, shrub, and herb. These Greeks were some of the first *botanists* — biologists who study plants. As botanists increased their knowledge, they found that the simple Greek system of classification was neither convenient nor a good indicator of relationships. It was not convenient because plants of the same kind might grow to be trees in one climate but shrubs in another. It was not a good expression of relationship between plants because some trees shared more characteristics with herbs than with other trees.

What structures in plants should be used as the basis for classification? Early in the 18th century, part of the answer to

G. R. Roberts

5–1 Do you recognize this plant?

botanists [Greek: *botane*, plant]

143

Carolus Linnaeus [KAR uh lus
luh NEE us]: 1707–1778

this question came from a young Swedish botanist named Carolus Linnaeus. His idea was to use the reproductive parts of
plants — flowers, in the more familiar plants — as a basis.

Today plant taxonomists still consider reproductive structures important for classification. Reproductive structures show
less variation within a species than do other plant characteristics. Therefore, they are reliable bases for classifying plant species. Like animal taxonomists, botanists take into consideration
characteristics other than structure. Types of cells in the plant,
development of the embryo, and chemicals in the plant may
also be important.

A TAXONOMIC PROBLEM

nomenclature [NOH mun klay-
chur; Latin: *nomen*, name, +
calare, to call]

We have discussed a number of problems that taxonomists face.
So far, however, we have ignored the problem of **nomenclature** — the problem of giving names to the kinds of organisms.

DEVELOPMENT OF NAMES

As long as there have been languages humans have had names
for the organisms that were important to them. Before the time
of written history the only plants named were those useful to
humans as spices, medicines, foods, and drugs or for religious
purposes. These so-called common names are still very useful. If

Sequoia sempervirens
[sih KWOI yuh sem pur VY runz]

you go into a lumberyard and ask for some *Sequoia sempervirens*
fence posts, you are not likely to get what you want. A request
for redwood posts works much better. Why, then, do biologists
need any other names than the ones in common use? Where do
these biological names come from?

The first attempts to give names to *all* known organisms,
and not just to those of special interest to farmers and hunters,
were probably made by the Greeks. At that time Latin was the
language used among most educated people — scholars, clergy,
and physicians. Since they were the only ones interested in all
organisms, they gave the plants and animals Latin names.

During the Middle Ages efforts were made to fit the names
used by the Greeks to the plants and animals of the rest of Europe. But this did not work. The plants and animals of England,
Germany, and other northern lands were often different from
those of Greece. The differences had to be recognized. This was
usually done by simply attaching a new adjective to the old
name of a similar plant or animal.

Then came the Age of Exploration. Year after year, explorers sent back to European scientists strange new organisms —
from Africa, South America, North America, the East Indies.
The scientists kept adding words to names to indicate differ-

ences between the newly discovered organisms and those already known. By the 18th century this practice made names very difficult to use. Here is the name that was used at that time for the carnation plant: *dianthus floribus solitariis, squamis calycinis subovatis brevissimis, corollis crenatis.* This means "the pink (a general name for the carnation) with solitary flowers, the scales of the calyx somewhat egg-shaped and very short, the petals scalloped."

For many years both botanists and zoologists fumbled for an easier system of nomenclature. The solution to the problem was developed by Linnaeus in 1753. His system was first designed as a shortcut in difficult cases. It later became the basis of modern biological nomenclature.

X 1/2

5–2 A carnation.

THE BINOMIAL SYSTEM

Linnaeus' **binomial system** is simple. He used only two words to name each species. The first word indicates a group of similar species. Linnaeus called this larger group a genus. This is described in the scheme of classification we discussed in Chapter 4. Thus all species of pinks are in a group named *Dianthus*. (The first letter of a genus is always capitalized.) The second word indicates a group of similar individuals. It is the species name, and is usually an adjective describing the genus. For the common carnation Linnaeus picked the word *caryophyllus.* Neither the word indicating the genus nor the word for the species is, by itself, the name. The name consists of both words.

binomial [by NOH mee ul; Latin: *bis,* twice, + *nomen,* name]

Dianthus [dy AN thus]

caryophyllus [kar ee oh FIL us]

The first rule of the system is that *Dianthus* can never be used for any other genus—only for pinks. The second rule is that *caryophyllus* can never be used for any other *Dianthus* species, but it might be used with some other genus. This does not create duplication, since the scientific name of a species always has *two* words. Thus the carnation plant is *Dianthus caryophyllus.* As long as Linnaeus' rules are followed, no other species can have this name.

With these rules a binomial (two-word) system of biological nomenclature began. It has been used for more than 200 years to name hundreds of thousands of organisms. Though there have been many refinements, the two basic rules remain unchanged.

A few misunderstandings about biological ("scientific") names need to be cleared up. First, the words used may seem strange, but they are not always long or difficult to pronounce (*Rosa,* roses; *Poa,* bluegrasses). Many words for genera have been absorbed into the English language. As common names they are properly spelled without a capital first letter—for example, iris, petunia, aster. The strangeness of words disappears as we use them.

How many other examples can you find?

Using biological names is necessary for scientific exactness. For one thing, there is no other single set of names available for all organisms. Further, different languages have different names for the same organisms—as "carrot" in English, "zanahoria" in Spanish, and "Mohrrübe" in German. Worse still, the *same* word may refer to different organisms: in Florida "gopher" refers to a turtle; in Kansas, to a rodent.

Tsuga [SOO guh]

Biological names are *not* a part of the Latin language. They are Latin simply because Linnaeus and other early scientists wrote in Latin. Although Latin and Greek word roots are frequently used, the words may be from any language or may be entirely manufactured. *Tsuga* (the hemlocks) comes from Japanese. *Washingtonia* (a genus of palms) is obviously not Latin. But all such names are given Latin endings. The names, however, always look the same. Thus, in a Russian or Chinese biology book, biological names are printed in the same form as they appear in this book, though the rest of the printing is different.

5–3 A short section on poisonous mushrooms from a Chinese BSCS biology book. Note the scientific name.

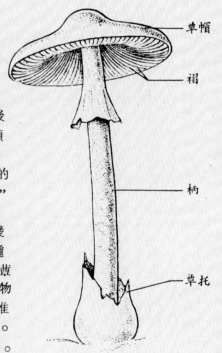

有些蕈菌含有毒性化合物，稱為瓢菌素，若誤食後會引起呼吸及循環的失常，對人類是有害的。蕈類約有70種，其中以瓢菌 Amanita verna 最毒（圖 12—6），它有潔白的子實體，雖僅食用少許的蕈帽，也必在一日之內致死，所以俗稱"死神蕈"，真是名符其實。通常這類毒蕈，柄的基部有一"杯狀物"（圖 12—6），這杯狀物常深藏土中不易發現，毒蕈與可食蕈的區別，普通傳述有如下的幾種謬見："銀匙與 毒蕈共煮則呈黑色"；"可食的蕈帽易於剝落，毒 蕈則不然"；"若昆蟲或其他動物吃過的蕈，人亦 可食之"等等，其實皆不可信。惟一可靠的選擇方 法是由市場購買人工栽培的食蕈。如從野外採來的 ，就應先經專家檢定後方可食用。

草帽

褶

柄

草托

圖 12—6 瓢菌 Amanita **verna** 圖示蕈托
杯狀物位在柄的基部（或藏地下）。這是許多頭毒蕈的特徵。蕈帽下放射狀蕈褶是蕈的特徵。

Adapted from Chinese BSCS Yellow Version, 1968, Science Education Center, Taiwan

There is nothing wrong with using common names when you do not need to be exact. Up to this point in our biology course, we have managed to get along without biological names. But sometimes it is better to say *"Pinus strobus"* instead of "white pine." There are several species of trees called white pines, and a biologist may need to state exactly *which* species is being studied.

Pinus strobus [PY nus STROH bus]

CHECK YOURSELF

A. Why is a classification system that is based on the differences between trees, shrubs, and herbs a poor one?

B. Why did it become necessary for biologists to have a system of nomenclature?

C. What are the basic rules of the binomial system of nomenclature?

D. Why is the use of biological names necessary for scientific exactness?

E. Why is it incorrect to think of modern biological names as Latin names?

Investigation 5.1   DIVERSITY AMONG PLANTS: LEAVES

INTRODUCTION

Suppose a visitor to Earth from another planet were to wander into a fruit market. Because the visitor does not yet know the names of the fruits and vegetables there, you might provide the identification chart shown in figure 5–4.

You probably will recognize that the chart is a kind of dichotomous key. When such a key is made, a group of objects is repeatedly divided into smaller groups. Each division is based on sharply contrasting characteristics. Wherever possible, the characteristics used at any point in the key lead to a division into 2 subgroups of about the same size. Eventually, the divisions result in each object being separated from all the others.

MATERIALS
(per team)

10 leaves (Set A): 1 each from 10 plant species, mounted on cards. The cards, numbered *1–10*, are labeled with the plant names.

10 leaves (Set B): 1 each from the same 10 species as Set A, mounted on cards. Each card has the same number as the card holding the corresponding leaf in Set A, but no name.

PROCEDURE

1. Construct a dichotomous identification chart for the leaves in Set A. Begin by spreading all the leaves on the table in front of you. Study each leaf. In what ways does it resemble the others in the set and in what ways does it differ?

2. What kinds of characteristics should you look for? A few suggestions follow:

Be all y B c
Can be!.

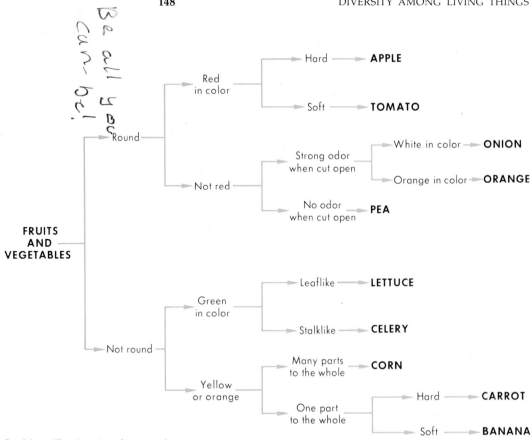

5—4 Identification chart for some fruits and vegetables.

Are there 2 distinct regions in the leaf —a stemlike portion (**petiole**) and a flattened part (**blade**)?

Is the blade all in one piece or is it divided into separate **leaflets?**

Is the edge of the blade smooth or is it notched?

Is the blade uniformly green or are other colors present?

Is the blade heart-shaped, oval, or spear-shaped?

3. Following the same arrangement as that used in the chart, draw a box at the left margin of a left page in your data book. Label it "All Leaves in Set." (You will probably need both the left and the right pages for the complete chart.) Now select a characteristic that gives you 2 choices and divides all the plants into 2 groups, such as

"shape—round or not round."

4. Draw 2 more boxes to the right of the 1st box. Label them with the characteristics you used to divide Set A into 2 groups. Draw lines that will show this division.

5. Study 1 of the 2 groups. Find a pair of contrasting characteristics that divides the group into 2 subgroups of approximately equal size. Using labeled boxes and lines, place these characteristics in the appropriate positions on your chart. Then do the same for the other group.

6. Continue this process until you have completed a key in which there is a single box or line for each of the 10 kinds of leaves. Label each of these boxes or lines with the name of the plant from which the leaf was obtained, but do *not* include the identifying number.

7. Use your chart to identify each of the leaves included in Set B. Since no two leaves are exactly alike, you may need to change some of the characteristics used in your chart, so that it will work with both sets of leaves.

8. Exchange with another team the chart and Set B (but *not* Set A). Using their chart, identify the leaves in their set. Write the number of each leaf next to the name of the species indicated. When you have finished, obtain their Set A (which includes both names and numbers) and check your identifications. If you have not achieved complete success, repeat the keying-out process. If differences still turn up, discuss them with the other team. (Two sources of error can occur — one is with the key itself, the other is in the use of the key.)

FOR FURTHER INVESTIGATION

Go back to the dichotomous keys in Investigation 4.2 (pages 133–134). In these keys each pair of contrasting characteristics is identified by a number-letter combination. Determine the principle used in this arrangement. Then convert your leaf key from chart form to the number-and-letter system.

UNDERSTANDING PLANT DIVERSITY

Even before reading Chapter 4, you probably would have had little difficulty in deciding that a mosquito and a mouse should be placed in different groups of animals. The contrast between insect and mammal is obvious. To most people, however, contrasts among plants are not so clear.

In walking through a forest, you might see a clump of green plants that cover a fallen tree (figure 5–5A). A botanist calls these "true mosses." A little later, you might pick up another mossy plant that is growing between fallen leaves on the forest floor (figure 5–5B) — a "club moss." Another small, greenish plant that grows in the Arctic (figure 5–5C) is called "reindeer moss." Finally, the picture of the mossy plant shown in figure 5–5D is a "moss campion." These four "mosses" are somewhat alike in both appearance and common name. Surely you would think they should be placed in the same family, if not in the same genus, of plants.

It turns out, however, that these four plants are usually classified in completely different groups. They all share certain obvious characteristics — they are mossy. But evidently botanists use characteristics that are not so obvious in working out taxonomic relationships among plants. Therefore, most people find an understanding of plant diversity more difficult than an understanding of animal diversity. Examples of this diversity can be found in "A Catalog of Living Plants" in Appendix 3. It will introduce you to a number of plant groups you are likely to encounter.

5-5 (A) True moss; (B) club moss;
(C) reindeer moss; (D) moss campion.

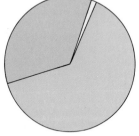

● FLOWERING TRACHEOPHYTES
NONFLOWERING TRACHEOPHYTES
● NONTRACHEOPHYTES

5-6 Proportion of plant species in various taxonomic groups. Compare this graph with figure 4-22.

tracheophytes [TRAY kee uh fyts; Greek: *tracheia*, windpipe, + *phyton*, plant]

vascular [VAS kyuh lur; Latin: *vasculum*, little container]

THE PLANT KINGDOM

Botanists usually group plants broadly in *divisions*. The word "phylum" is more often used with protists and animals. All other classification levels are the same for plants as for protists and animals—class, order, family, and so on.

Generally, plants do not move from one place to another. Chemically, most of them contain *cellulose*, not found in animals. The cellulose gives plant bodies firmness and support.

VASCULAR PLANTS

The chances are very good that almost all the plants you can name are *tracheophytes*. Every plant in this division has a continuous system of tubes (a *vascular system*) through its roots, stems, and leaves. By means of this system, water and substances dissolved in it move from one place in the plant to an-

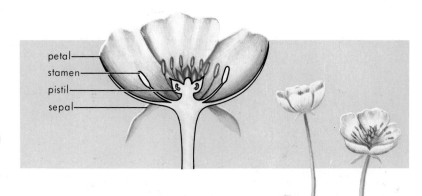

petal—
stamen—
pistil—
sepal—

5—7 Buttercup plant and
diagram of its flower
structure.

X 1

other. For land plants, movement of water upward from the soil
is very important. Any land plant that stands as much as a meter high is almost certainly a tracheophyte.

ANGIOSPERMS

Botanists place all the flowering plants in the **angiosperm** class.
They think of a flower as a short branch bearing groups of
leaves. Some of these may resemble ordinary leaves. Others are
so different in structure that it is hard to think of them as leaves
at all. If you examine the flower of a buttercup, for example, you
see on the underside a number of green, leaflike structures —
sepals. Before the bud opens, the sepals enclose and protect the
other parts of the flower. The most conspicuous flower parts in
a buttercup are the **petals.** They also are leaflike in shape but are
quite a different color. Just inside the petals are a number of
stamens, each having an enlarged tip. Grouped together in the
center of the flower are the small, rounded structures called **pistils,** each with pointed tip. Despite their shape, both stamens
and pistils are believed to be modified leaves.

A flower is a reproductive structure. Stamens produce **pollen** grains. When these grains are transferred to the tips of the
pistils, **seeds** may develop inside the pistils. Each seed contains
a tiny new plant, an embryo. The sepals and petals are not directly involved in seed formation, so a flower can function without them. In fact, in a few plants a flower may consist of only a
single stamen or a single pistil.

Much of the diversity among angiosperm species lies in
their flowers. There is no better way to appreciate this than to
examine different flowers you can find in a field, in a greenhouse, or in a vacant lot. This diversity is usually related to the
way the pollen is transferred from one flower to another. If pollen is transferred from stamen to pistil by insects, the petals of
the flower are often large and brightly colored. The petals, moreover, often have small glands that produce a sugar solution.
These adaptations attract pollinating insects. On the other

angiosperm [AN jee uh spurm;
Greek: *angeion,* container, +
sperma, seed]

sepals [SEEP ulz; Greek: *skepe,*
covering]

petals [PET ulz; Greek: *petalos,*
outspread]

stamens [STAY munz; Latin:
stare, to stand]

pistils [PIS tulz; Latin: *pistillus,*
pestle]

pollen [POL un; Latin: *pollen,* dust]

Gary Hannan

James R. Eckert

5—8 Comparison of wind-pollinated silk tassel flowers (*left*) with insect-pollinated thimbleberry. The many pollen-producing flowers of the silk tassel hang down in tassels. The pistil-bearing flowers are found in the axils of many branches.

hand, flowers in which pollen is transferred by wind usually have small sepals and petals or none at all. They are often located high up on the plant and produce an abundance of pollen. Their pistils commonly have large, long, or feathery structures at the tips, which are covered with a sticky fluid. These adaptations increase the likelihood of wind pollination.

After pollination, seeds begin to develop. As this happens, the pistils become *fruits,* which contain the seeds. Part of the embryo in the seed consists of one or two modified leaves, called **cotyledons.** Another part is a beginning of a root. Each seed also contains a supply of food that is used when the embryo starts to grow. The food may be stored in a special part of the seed called the **endosperm,** or it may be stored in the embryo itself, usually in the cotyledons.

cotyledons [kot uh LEE dunz; Greek: *kotyle,* anything hollow]

endosperm [EN duh spurm; Greek: *endon,* within, + *sperma*]

Seeds and fruits show as much diversity as flowers. In many cases, part of the pistil becomes thick and fleshy, as in the fruits of peach, plum, and tomato. Fleshy fruits are often eaten by animals. The seeds in many such fruits have thick coats that permit them to pass through an animal's digestive system unharmed. They are dropped later at some distance from the parent plant. Many fruits are not fleshy but have other adaptations that aid in scattering their seeds.

What kind of ecological relationship exists between plant and animal in this case?

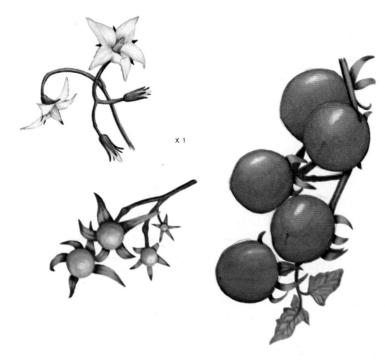

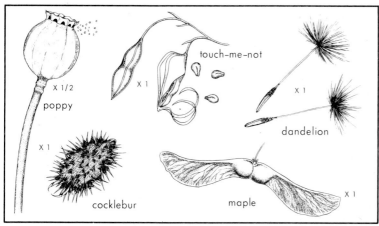

5–10 Diversity among fruits. How does each of the structural adaptations shown here provide for seed scattering?

In addition to the diversity in their flowers, there is great diversity in the size of angiosperms and in the life span of their *shoots*—the parts that appear above ground. Many angiosperms are trees. A tree bears its leaves well above the ground, where they are likely to receive more light than do those of shorter plants. Because of their size, trees can store large reserves of food in trunks and roots and can survive through bad years. Trees have relatively long life spans. A tree species prob-

What are the oldest known trees?

ably will survive even though the entire seed crop of any one year may be destroyed. But most species of angiosperms are not trees. Some, such as roses and raspberries, are woody shrubs. Others, such as ivy, grapes, and hundreds of tropical species, are woody vines, which grow on rocks, on walls, or on other plants. Most, however, are neither shrubs nor vines, but non-woody plants — herbs.

herbaceous [hur BAY shus]

Many of these herbaceous plants have roots that remain alive in the soil during winter while their shoots die. At the beginning of each growing season the root sends up new shoots. These are *perennial* herbs, such as goldenrod, iris, and asparagus. Others are *annuals.* These (for example, garden beans, sunflowers, and corn) produce seeds and die after growing for only one season.

perennial [puh REN ee ul; Latin: *per,* through, + *annus,* year]

Monocotyledons. Botanists divide angiosperms into two large subclasses. Figure 5–12 shows the characteristics on which these groups are based. Keep in mind that the figure is a summary and does not take all known angiosperms into consideration. The basic characteristic of the monocotyledons (*monocots*), as the name of the group indicates, is that the embryo contains a single cotyledon.

monocotyledons [mon uh kot uh-LEE dunz; Greek: *monos,* one, single, + *kotyle*]

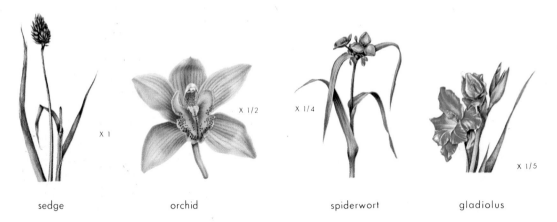

sedge   orchid   spiderwort   gladiolus

5–11 Some monocots.

In addition to grains, what other monocot plants are important for human food?

The monocots include grasses and grasslike plants. Many of the plants most economically important to humans are monocots. These include grain-producing plants, such as wheat, rice, and corn. Their fruits, the familiar grains, are a major source of biological energy for humans. The pasture grasses that feed cattle, another source of human food, are also monocots. It is safe to say that without the monocots the human population could never have reached its present size.

dicotyledons [dy kot uh LEE-dunz; Greek: *dis,* two, double, + *kotyle*]

Dicotyledons. This subclass is much larger than the monocot subclass. Most of the fruits and vegetables that are used as

MONOCOT   DICOT

FLOWER

petal

sepal

stamen

pistil

STEM

pith

conducting tissue

conducting tissue

pith

LEAF VENATION

netted

parallel

SEED

endosperm

embryonic shoot

cotyledon

embryonic root

5—12 Comparison of monocot and dicot characteristics.

5–13 Some dicot examples.

X 1/2

dandelion

wild rose

X 1/2

X 1/2

morning glory

X 1/2

columbine

human food come from dicotyledons (**dicots**). In addition, the so-called hardwoods used in furniture, flooring, hockey sticks, and baseball bats come from dicot trees. Almost all shade trees are dicots, also.

CHECK YOURSELF

F. Why is "moss" a rather indefinite term?
G. What is the principal structural characteristic of the tracheophytes?
H. What does a botanist mean by the word "flower"?
I. How is diversity among flowers related to ways in which pollination occurs?
J. What structural characteristics of fruits seem to be adaptations that are related to seed dispersal?
K. In what ways do dicots and monocots differ?

Investigation 5.2   "PRIMITIVE CHARACTERISTICS"

INTRODUCTION

Biologists sometimes use the terms "primitive" and "advanced" when discussing diversity among organisms. These terms are linked with the idea developed near the end of Chapter 4 — that species existing today are related to each other through their ancestors. From this comes the further idea that some of the species living today retain more of their ancestors' characteristics than do other species. A species that has

MATERIALS
(per class)

**10 labeled specimens of
  plants of various divisions
monocular microscopes
hand lenses
stereomicroscopes
microscope slides
cover slips**

changed little from its ancestors is said to be primitive. A species that has few of the characteristics of its ancestors is said to be advanced. Of course, there can be many degrees of advancement, so "primitive" and "advanced" are not absolute terms. They are useful only in making comparisons.

Botanists have studied many kinds of evidence, chiefly fossils. They have reached fairly general agreement about which plant characteristics are very ancient and which have appeared more recently. Figure 5–15 is based on such studies.

PROCEDURE

1. Determine the "Advancement Score" for each of the labeled specimens. Start at the left of figure 5–15. Arrows from the starting point lead to two descriptions. Choose the one that fits the plant you are scoring.
2. Proceed across the chart by following the arrows and choosing the descriptions that best fit the plant.
3. At each description there is a number. In your data book record these numbers in the 2nd column of a chart like figure 5–14. Continue as far as the arrows go. The "Advancement Score" for the plant is the sum of all the numbers appearing after the descriptions you used in working through the chart. The more alike two plants are, the more alike their scores will be. The greater the difference between two plants, the greater will be the difference in their scores. Advanced plants will have high scores (maximum 26), and primitive plants will have low scores (minimum 3).

4. When you have the "Advancement Score" for each of the plants, give the plant with the lowest score a rank of "1" and the plant with the highest score a rank of "10." Then rank all of the others according to their scores. Record the rankings in the column at the right side of your chart.

DISCUSSION

(1) Assuming that today's plants have developed from simpler, fewer, and older species, would you expect to find less diversity or greater diversity in the plant kingdom as time goes on? Explain.

(2) Basing your conclusions on the way the plant score chart was designed, list some of the most important differences among plants. (3) What are some of the less important differences? (4) On what basis do you distinguish between the important differences and those that are less important?

(5) Using the information included in the chart, list the characteristics you would expect to find in a primitive plant. (6) Do the same for a highly advanced plant. (7) In what ways does the plant score chart resemble the dichotomous key constructed in Investigation 5.1? (8) In what ways does it differ from the key?

5–14 Student data chart.

NAME OF PLANT	NUMERICAL VALUES OF CHOICES MADE	TOTAL "ADVANCEMENT SCORE"	RANK
1.			
2.			
3.			
10.			

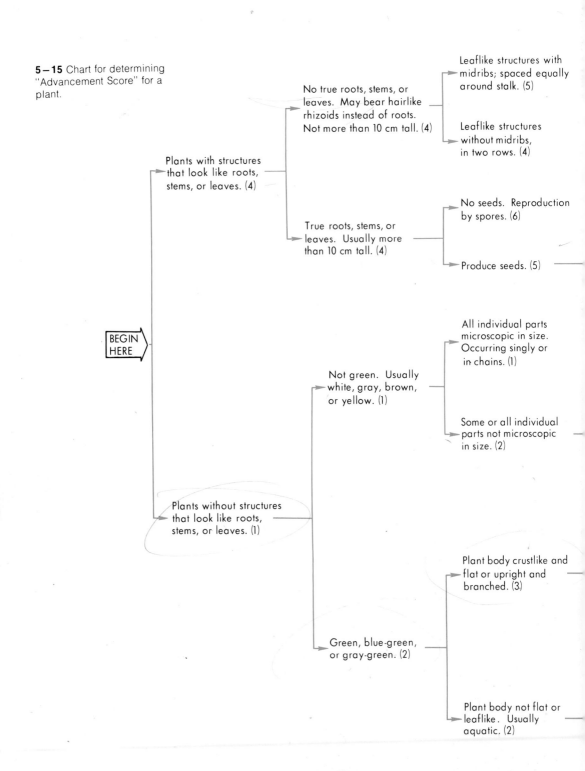

5 – 15 Chart for determining "Advancement Score" for a plant.

BEGIN HERE

Plants with structures that look like roots, stems, or leaves. (4)

No true roots, stems, or leaves. May bear hairlike rhizoids instead of roots. Not more than 10 cm tall. (4)

Leaflike structures with midribs; spaced equally around stalk. (5)

Leaflike structures without midribs, in two rows. (4)

True roots, stems, or leaves. Usually more than 10 cm tall. (4)

No seeds. Reproduction by spores. (6)

Produce seeds. (5)

Plants without structures that look like roots, stems, or leaves. (1)

Not green. Usually white, gray, brown, or yellow. (1)

All individual parts microscopic in size. Occurring singly or in chains. (1)

Some or all individual parts not microscopic in size. (2)

Green, blue-green, or gray-green. (2)

Plant body crustlike and flat or upright and branched. (3)

Plant body not flat or leaflike. Usually aquatic. (2)

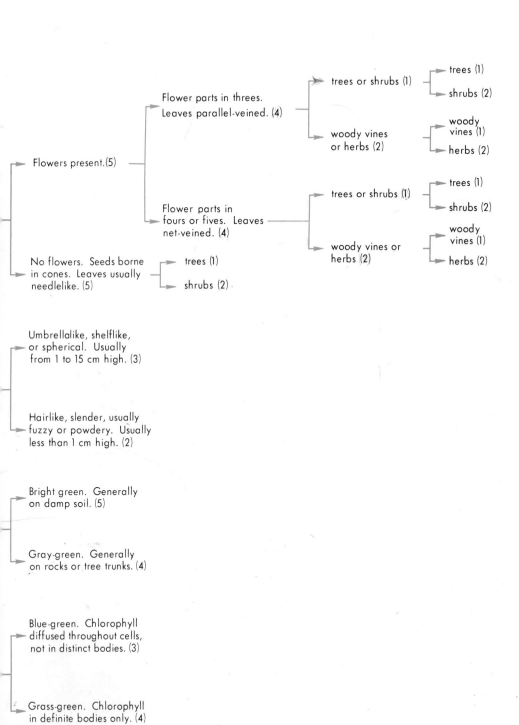

Flower parts in threes.
Leaves parallel-veined. (4)

trees or shrubs (1)

trees (1)

shrubs (2)

woody vines
or herbs (2)

woody
vines (1)

herbs (2)

Flowers present.(5)

Flower parts in
fours or fives. Leaves
net-veined. (4)

trees or shrubs (1)

trees (1)

shrubs (2)

woody vines or
herbs (2)

woody
vines (1)

herbs (2)

No flowers. Seeds borne
in cones. Leaves usually
needlelike. (5)

trees (1)

shrubs (2)

Umbrellalike, shelflike,
or spherical. Usually
from 1 to 15 cm high. (3)

Hairlike, slender, usually
fuzzy or powdery. Usually
less than 1 cm high. (2)

Bright green. Generally
on damp soil. (5)

Gray-green. Generally
on rocks or tree trunks. (4)

Blue-green. Chlorophyll
diffused throughout cells,
not in distinct bodies. (3)

Grass-green. Chlorophyll
in definite bodies only. (4)

GYMNOSPERMS

gymnosperm [JIM nuh spurm;
Greek: *gymnos*, naked, + *sperma*]

Like angiosperms, plants in the ***gymnosperm*** class produce seeds. But the seeds do not develop within pistils, and there are no fruits. Instead, the seeds are attached to the upper surfaces of

BSCS photo by Manert Kennedy

BSCS

5–16 Three contrasting gymnosperms – a South African cycad (*above left*), a Rocky Mountain juniper (*above right*), and an unusual low-growing form, *Welwitschia*, from Southwest Africa (*right*).

Edward S. Ross

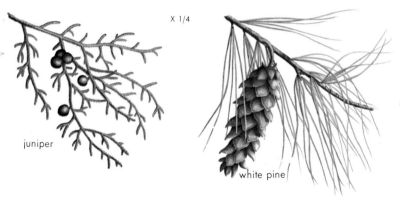

X 1/4

juniper

white pine

ginkgo

5—17 Diversity of gymnosperm leaves.

scales. In the most familiar gymnosperms, the **conifers,** these seed-bearing scales are grouped together in cones. A seed developing in a cone may be protected by the scales, somewhat as a small coin may be concealed between the pages of a book. The term "gymnosperm" may therefore seem misleading.

Almost all gymnosperms are trees or shrubs, and all are at least somewhat woody. Many have leaves that are like needles or scales, and most of these plants are evergreen. Though the number of species is small, the number of individual gymnosperms is enormous. In some parts of the world, most of the vegetation is forest made up of such conifers as pines and spruces. From these trees comes the greater part of the North American lumber supply—the so-called softwoods.

conifers [KON uh furz; Latin: *conus*, cone, + *ferre*, to bear]

Why is the term "gymnosperm" somewhat misleading?

To what extent are the lumberyard terms "hardwood" and "softwood" justified?

5—18

cone scale bearing seed on its upper surface

winged seed detached from scale

FERNS

The plants in this class, **ferns,** lack seeds, but they have other reproductive structures. At certain times of the year, small brown spots develop either on the undersides of fern leaflets or on special leaves. Each spot consists of a group of knob-shaped cases containing large numbers of **spores,** which are almost microscopic in size. Spores are far simpler than seeds. A spore contains no embryo and only a small amount of food.

When a spore case is ripe, it opens and throws the spores out into the air. Spores are very light and can be carried for incredible distances by the wind. If a spore falls in a suitably moist place, it germinates and develops rapidly into a thin, green, heart-shaped plant that is rarely over 1 cm in diameter. This small plant is seldom noticed in the woods, and it is different from the familiar fern with large leaves. From this small plant a conspicuous spore-bearing fern plant eventually grows. From the spore comes the small plant that produces the large plant that produces spores. This life cycle is the same for most of the ferns.

5 – 19 Fern examples.

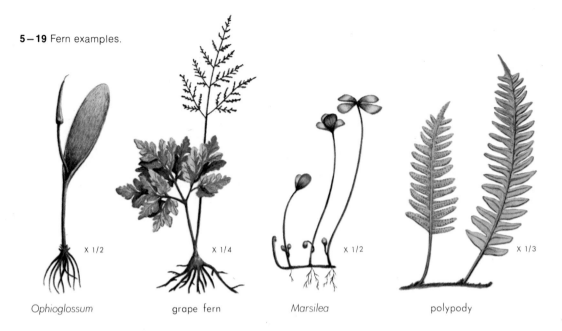

Ophioglossum   X 1/2   grape fern   X 1/4   Marsilea   X 1/2   polypody   X 1/3

The ferns native to most of the United States are shade-dwelling perennials with underground roots *and* stems. From these stems new sets of upright leaves appear above ground each spring. In the state of Hawaii and elsewhere in the tropics, however, many species of ferns have stems that grow upright. These tree ferns may reach a height of 20 m.

5 – 20 Tree fern on the island of Sumatra.

Edward S. Ross

CLUB MOSSES

The *club moss* subdivision includes low-growing evergreen plants that seldom become more than 40 cm tall. Their branching, horizontal stems grow on the surface of the soil or just below it. The most noticeable part of a club-moss plant is an upright branch growing from one of these stems. Club mosses reproduce by spores, which are produced on modified leaves. In many species these leaves form club-shaped cones at the tips of short, upright stems. From this feature, the name "club moss" is derived. Club mosses are rather common plants in much of the eastern and northwestern United States and are often used to make Christmas wreaths. They cannot grow in the dry states of the Southwest.

HORSETAILS

In this subdivision, *horsetails,* the plants have hollow, jointed, upright branches that grow from horizontal underground stems. Their small leaves are arranged in a circle around each stem joint. At the tips of some of the upright branches are conelike structures. In these the spores are produced. In middle latitudes horsetails rarely reach a height of 2 m, but in the American tropics one species may grow to 12 m.

Horsetails are harsh to the touch; their tissues contain silica, a compound present in sand. American pioneers scrubbed pots and pans with them, whence came their common name "scouring rushes."

BRYOPHYTES

All plants in the **bryophyte** division are less than 70 cm tall, and very few are taller than 20 cm. Most bear structures resembling stems and leaves, but they lack vascular (conducting) tissue. The largest class of bryophytes is the *true mosses.* They usually grow in clumps (figure 5–5A). An individual moss plant from such a clump is simply an upright stalk with threadlike structures called *rhizoids* growing out of its base. The rhizoids absorb water and help to hold the plant in place. A large number of flat, green, leaflike structures are attached spirally along the stalk. If you examine sections of a moss under a microscope, you find no vascular tissue. Since true roots, stems, and leaves have vascular tissue, these terms are not used in describing mosses.

True mosses reproduce by spores. A spore grows into a mass of green threads. From this mass the familiar moss plant arises. Most mosses grow in fairly damp places, and a few grow in water. Some, however, become dormant during droughts.

5–21 A club moss.

X 1/2

Lycopodium

5–22 Horsetails.

X 1/3

Equisetum

silica [SIL ih kuh; Latin: *silex*, any hard stone]. This same glasslike substance forms the skeletons of some sponges (page 129).

bryophyte [BRY uh fyt; Greek: *bryon*, moss, + *phyton*, plant]

rhizoids [RY zoidz; Greek: *rhiza*, root, + *eidos*, shape]

dormant: inactive

Many mosses photosynthesize in weak light, so they are often found on the ground in forest ecosystems.

5—23 Two moss species.

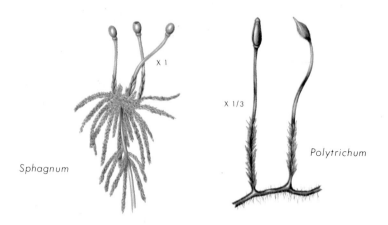

Sphagnum

X 1

X 1/3

Polytrichum

FUNGI

fungi [FUN jy]; singular, fungus [FUNG gus]

hyphae [HY fee; singular, hypha; Greek: *hyphe*, a web]

Mushrooms—and plants called by such names as mold, mildew, rust, and smut—are collectively known as *fungi.* All the organisms in this division have three characteristics. They have no vascular tissues; they reproduce, at least in part, by means of spores; they lack chlorophyll. Most of a fungus plant is a mass of slender white threads called **hyphae.** These grow in soil that contains large amounts of dead plant and animal matter—food for the fungus.

Most fungi are decomposers. You often can find white hyphae growing among decaying leaves or rotten wood in a forest. Some fungi are parasites on crops, and certain species are used for baking breads, making alcoholic beverages, and producing drugs. Because the hyphae of most fungi look very much alike, classification of fungi is based primarily on differences in reproductive structures. Since fungi have so many characteristics different from plants, some taxonomists believe they should be placed in a separate kingdom.

X 1/2

Coprinus

5—24 A club fungus species.

How can you tell an edible mushroom from a poisonous one?

How are commercial mushrooms grown?

CLUB FUNGI

The fungi in this class produce spores on the surfaces of club-like structures. Therefore, they are called *club fungi.* Many have rather large and conspicuous spore-bearing parts. Most species of mushrooms, both edible and poisonous, are club fungi. Many club fungi are parasites of plants that are important to humans, such as wheat and corn.

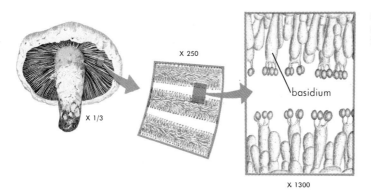

X 250

X 1/3

basidium

X 1300

SAC FUNGI

In this class of fungi, spores are produced in sacs. Some of the *sac fungi* are important in the manufacture of cheeses. The distinctive flavor and appearance of Roquefort cheese is, in part, the result of the growth of a sac fungus, *Penicillium roqueforti*. In Camembert cheese another fungus, *P. camemberti*, is involved. Still another species, *P. notatum*, produces the drug penicillin. Yeasts also are included among the sac fungi, since, under unfavorable environmental conditions, many of them produce spores enclosed in a sac. Among the many parasitic sac fungi is a species that causes Dutch elm disease. This has destroyed many of the elm trees in parks and along streets.

5-26 A sac fungus.

x 250

Neurospora

Penicillium roqueforti
[pen uh SIL ee um rok FOR tee]

camemberti [kam um BER tee]

notatum [noh TAH tum]

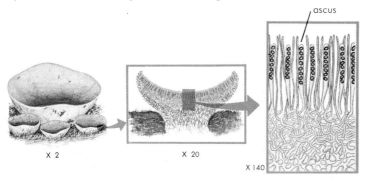

ascus

X 2

X 20

X 140

5-27 Reproductive structures of a sac fungus. Where are the spores?

ALGALIKE FUNGI

Algalike fungi lack chlorophyll, but otherwise resemble certain green algae. The fungi in this class are distinguished from other fungi by a lack of cross walls in the hyphae. Their spores are borne in various kinds of cases. Black bread mold (genus *Rhizopus*) is the most familiar member of this class. It is a decomposer that can be destructive to human foods—not only to bread but to fruits such as grapes, plums, and strawberries. Many of these fungus species are parasitic, and some attack crop plants. In 1845 and 1846 one species ruined the potato crop in Ireland, resulting in a disastrous famine there.

5−28 Comparison of an algalike fungus (*left*) with a sac fungus (*right*).

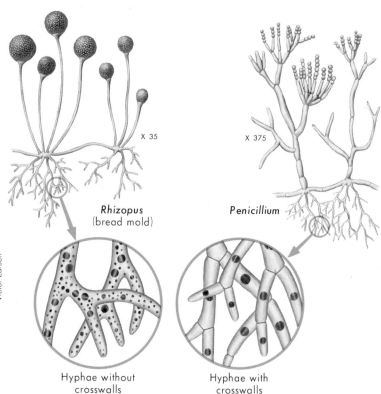

Rhizopus (bread mold)

X 35

Penicillium

X 375

Hyphae without crosswalls

Hyphae with crosswalls

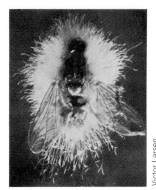

Victor Larsen

5−29 An algalike fungus (*Saprolegnia*) growing on a drowned fly in an aquarium. Only the hyphae, not the reproductive structures, appear here.   × 8

CHECK YOURSELF

L. If a taxonomist refers to an organism as "primitive," what idea is being expressed?

M. What are gymnosperms?

N. What is a spore?

O. Why is it improper to use the terms "root" and "leaf" when you are referring to bryophytes?

P. How do fungi differ from most other plants with respect to ecological relationships?

Q. What kinds of characteristics are used in classifying fungi?

RED ALGAE

Plants grouped in the **red algae** division are aquatic and almost all are marine. They occur mostly as feathery plants along the rocky coasts of warm oceans. The macroscopic kinds are among the plants commonly called seaweeds. All have chlorophyll, but it is usually masked by red pigments. Red algae have complex life histories by which botanists distinguish them from other plants. They also differ from most other plants in storing food not as starch but as a related chemical compound.

5–30 Some red algae.

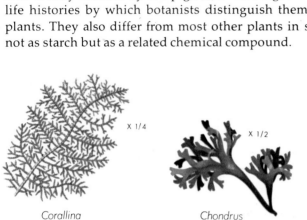

Corallina   *Chondrus*   *Polysiphonia*

BROWN ALGAE

Like the red algae, all **brown algae** are aquatic and most species live in the seas. Members of this division grow abundantly along rocky coasts in temperate regions. These algae range in size from small, almost microscopic, forms to very large seaweeds over 30 m long. Their chlorophyll is usually masked by brownish pigments. They store food as a carbohydrate related to starch. A compound of many brown algae may be used to provide a smooth texture in marshmallows, ice cream, certain

5–31 A few brown algae.

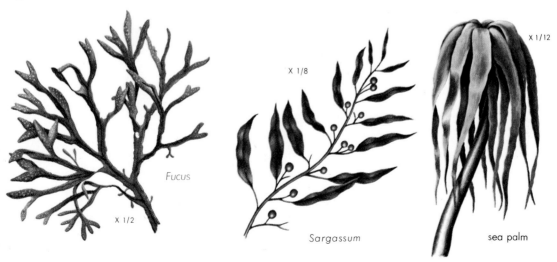

Fucus

Sargassum

sea palm

cheeses, and paint. Some species of brown algae are used for food by people of the islands and coasts of the eastern Pacific Ocean.

GOLDEN ALGAE

The **golden algae** are mostly microscopic aquatic plants, though some members of this division may grow in damp places on land. They have chlorophyll, but it is usually masked by yellow pigments. Some are threadlike in form. These often grow in masses at the edges of ponds or streams or on moist flowerpots in greenhouses. Within this division is a large group of plants commonly called diatoms. Diatoms have shells made of silica and store food in the form of oil. They are abundant in both fresh and marine waters, where they are the principal producer organisms in many food webs.

5–32 Several diatoms.

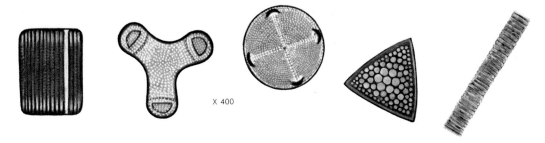

X 400

GREEN ALGAE

5–33 Green algae.

Green algae belong to a division of aquatic plants of both marine and fresh waters. Their chlorophyll is not usually masked

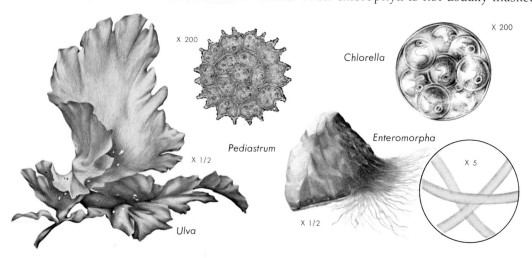

X 200

X 200

Chlorella

Pediastrum

X 1/2

Enteromorpha

X 5

Ulva

X 1/2

by other pigments. So they look bright green. They store food as starch, as do most plants. Some green algae are rather small seaweeds, and many are microscopic. The microscopic ones are sometimes so abundant that they color the water of ponds and lakes green.

SOME PROBLEMS OF PLANT CLASSIFICATION

Taxonomists find many difficulties in trying to make a classification system that is convenient to use and that also shows kinship relationships.

See page 137.

ALGAE

In some biology textbooks you may find a chapter entitled "The Algae." This implies that there is a group of plants similar in enough characteristics to be grouped under one name. In our text, however, there is no such group. But there are four divisions that have the word "algae" as part of their common names. The term is a convenient one and it is useful to many kinds of biologists, such as ecologists. But plant taxonomists have become convinced that the four algae divisions have little relationship to each other. For taxonomists to include all these organisms in a single group would, therefore, be misleading.

The common names that are used for the algal divisions are left over from a time when botanists did not know as much as they now do about plant relationships. A few plants that have all the other characteristics of "green algae" are actually reddish. Some "brown algae" are yellow-green, and at least one of the "red algae" is a beautiful violet-green. Again, you have an example of how an apparently convenient way to classify organisms can be misleading.

LICHENS

lichens. See pages 260–261.

On the bark of a tropical tree, on a tombstone in New Hampshire, buried under arctic snow, on a rock in Arizona—you can find lichens in all these places. In Chapter 3 we discussed the mutualistic relationship between an alga and a fungus that make up a lichen. Yet, so definite are the form, color, and other characteristics of each of these partnerships that for several hundred years biologists described lichens as if they were single organisms.

The body of a lichen has a framework of fungal hyphae. In its upper layers are many groups of small algae. These algae can grow independently, and many can be recognized as species that also are known to live alone. The lichen fungi, on the other hand, do not grow well when separated from their partners.

Carlye Calvin

5—34 Lichens.

If you were classifying lichens as a group in the plant kingdom, at which taxonomic level would you place them?

They can be placed in the known classes of fungi—mostly in the sac fungi—but they are unlike any of the species that live alone. None of this matters much when we view the world ecologically. But what can taxonomists do with lichens? They have described more than 15,000 "species" of them. And they have based the name of the lichen on the fungus partner.

"IMPERFECT" FUNGI

The classes of fungi are based on characteristics of their spore-bearing structures. But many fungi seldom produce such structures. Botanists have studied certain species for years without discovering spore-bearing structures. Some of these species resemble another species whose spore-bearing structures *are* known. It is a good assumption that the first should be placed in the same group with the second. For many species, however, there are no such resemblances. Some of these are species important to the interests of humans—parasites that grow on crop plants and even on our skin. Something must be done with such important organisms. So, for convenience only, taxonomists place these "imperfect" fungi together in a separate group. Whenever a botanist discovers spore-bearing structures in one of these plants, it can then be shifted to one of the fungal classes.

CHECK YOURSELF

R. How do humans use brown algae?

S. Why do many taxonomists put the plants commonly called algae into several different divisions?

T. How do the characteristics of lichens cause a taxonomic problem?

U. What do botanists mean by the term "imperfect" fungi?

A

B

E

5–35 Into which taxonomic group would you classify each of these plants?

C

D

PROBLEMS

1. How many of the taxonomic groups discussed in Chapter 5 are represented in your locality? Consider wild and cultivated plants, indoor and outdoor plants, aquatic and terrestrial plants.

2. Name some plant-related careers of people in and around your community. Include agronomist and plant geneticist. Do library research on these two careers.

3. Criticize the following statement: "All plants that are producers are green, because they contain the green pigment chlorophyll."

4. What advantages and disadvantages does a seed-producing plant have compared with one that produces only spores? How do you interpret the words "advantage" and "disadvantage" here?

5. The plant parts that furnish the greatest amount of human food are either seeds, roots, or underground stems. Explain this.

6. Observe the plants that grow without human help in a city. Try to discover the characteristics that enable them to live successfully in an urban environment.

7. Choose some cultivated plants. Investigate the history of their domestication. Examples: wheat, apple, potato, cotton, corn, cabbage, sugarcane.

SUGGESTED READINGS

Bold, H. C. and C. L. Hundell. 1977. *The Plant Kingdom*, 4th ed., Prentice-Hall, Englewood Cliffs, N. J. Introduction to plant diversity.

Kline, R. N. 1978. *The Green World*. Harper & Row, New York. Emphasizes the aspects of plant biology that affect humankind.

Litten, W. 1975. Most Poisonous Mushrooms. *Scientific American*, March.

Milne, L. J. and M. Milne. 1975. *Because of a Flower*. Atheneum, New York. Introduction to the nature of flowers, fruits, and seeds, and animal relationships to them.

Page, N. M. and R. E. Weaver, Jr. 1975. *Wild Plants in the City*. Quadrangle/New York Times, New York. Descriptive list of the common plants in many cities.

Ross, I. K. 1979. *Biology of the Fungi*. McGraw-Hill, New York. Comprehensive coverage of this important group.

Trainor, F. R. 1978. *Introductory Phycology*. John Wiley & Sons, New York. Introduction to freshwater and marine algae.

Each of the following is a series of books that treat the classification and identification of certain parts of the plant kingdom.

Golden Nature Series. Edited by H. S. Zim. Western Publishing, New York. Flowers, trees, orchids, nonflowering plants.

Peterson Field Guide Series. Edited by R. T. Peterson. Houghton Mifflin, Boston. Flowers, trees, shrubs, and ferns.

Chapter **6**

Protists

YOUR GUIDEPOSTS

In this chapter you will have an opportunity to explore these questions in biology:

- What are the arguments for and against using more than two kingdoms to classify organisms?
- Are viruses living or nonliving?
- Who were the early scientists that studied microorganisms?
- What role did the microscope play in the history of biology?
- What characteristics distinguish the phyla of micro-organisms from each other?

WHAT ARE PROTISTS?

The diversity of living things is like a color spectrum. But, instead of colors, we observe species as we move across the spectrum of living things. At one end of the diversity spectrum, organisms are unmistakably animals—such as monkeys and fishes. At the other end, they are obviously plants—such as pine trees and orchids. But what about the central zone? As we move from either end toward the center, we reach a place where the organisms—mostly microscopic—are neither clearly ani-

Figure 1–19 shows a section across a color spectrum.

6–1 A spectrum of living things. It is easier to classify organisms at either end of the spectrum than in the middle.

Ernst Haeckel [HEK ul]:
1834–1919. German biologist

Protista [proh TIS tuh; Greek:
protos, first (here, most
primitive)]

mals nor clearly plants. They possess some characteristics of both groups. Yet they are different from either group.

More than a century ago Ernst Haeckel proposed a third kingdom, **Protista.** It included all those organisms that could not definitely be classified as plants or animals. For a long time this proposal received little support. During the past few decades, however, taxonomists have adopted it. But they still do not agree on which organisms should be placed in a protist kingdom. Two more kingdoms have since been proposed— one to help resolve difficulties in classifying protists and one to remove mushrooms and their relatives from the plant kingdom. Meanwhile, protists—or most of them—are still called protists.

Most organisms considered protists are microscopic. Some are macroscopic. Some animals are microscopic. So size is not the only guide to classifying protists, as we shall see.

Investigation 6.1   A GARDEN OF MICROORGANISMS

PROCEDURE

1. Mark each finger bowl with your team symbol and number the bowls *1* through *8*.
2. Place materials in the bowls as follows:
   Bowl 1 — Fruit, cut to fit into the bowl.
   Bowl 2 — Water from a pond or river, containing bottom materials.
   Bowl 3 — Enough hay to cover the bottom of the bowl and 200 ml tap water.
   Bowl 4 — A few dried beans and 200 ml tap water.
   Bowl 5 — Cream cheese, spread over the bottom of the bowl about 1 cm deep.
   Bowl 6 — Two pieces of stale bread, moistened (not soaked) with tap water. Expose to air for 24 hours. Then cover.
   Bowl 7 — Place a piece of filter paper on the bottom of the bowl. Mix 5 g cornstarch with 95 g rich garden soil. While mixing soil and starch, add enough water to give the mixture a doughlike consistency. Spread the mixture smoothly on the filter paper, using a spatula. Keep the soil mixture moist throughout the investigation.

MATERIALS
(per team)

very ripe fruit
hay or dried grass
dried beans
cream cheese
stale bread
cornstarch
peppercorns
pond or river water with some
    bottom materials
rich garden soil
8 finger bowls
2 or 3 glass covers for finger bowls
glass-marking crayon
filter paper
spatula

(per pair of students)

hand lens or stereomicroscope
monocular microscope
forceps
2 dissecting needles
microscope slide
medicine dropper
cover slip

Bowl 8—1 g peppercorns and 200 ml tap water.

3. Place the bowls in stacks of 3 or 4 and cover each stack with a piece of glass or an empty bowl. Do not place in direct sunlight. If any of the bowls fit very tightly together, place the flat end of a toothpick between them.

4. Examine the bowls each day. In your data book, record the following: (A) Date of observation. (B) Number of bowl. (C) Macroscopic appearance of bowl's contents. (D) Appearance under a hand lens or stereomicroscope. (E) Anything else that you can notice with any of your senses.

In describing organisms, consider color first, then size. Some of the following descriptive terms may be useful: fuzzy, cottony, powdery, smooth, rough, shiny, glistening, dull, compact, spreading, irregular. You should not, of course, limit yourself to these terms.

5. After good growth has been obtained, make observations with a monocular microscope. From a solid medium, use forceps to transfer bits of the visible growth to a clean slide. From a liquid medium, draw up a drop or two with a medicine dropper and place on a slide. Then, for either kind of preparation, add a cover slip.

6. Record your observations by making sketches. Attempt to place organisms in taxonomic groups. Do this using references provided by your teacher and by referring to the protists illustrated in "A Catalog of Living Things" in Appendix 3.

DISCUSSION

(1) Did you find any evidence that different groups of organisms grow better on one or another kind of food? If so, what is it? (2) Which group of organisms did you find growing in the largest number of dishes? What reason can you suggest for this? (3) What happens to the food materials as the organisms grow? Explain.

FOR FURTHER INVESTIGATION

1. You have seen what microorganisms do to their food substances, some of which are also foods for humans. Clearly, it is desirable for us to try to prevent such effects. Chemicals are often added to human foods to discourage introduction and growth of microorganisms. Commercial bread and catsup usually contain such chemicals. These must be mentioned on the label of the product. By comparing the growth of microorganisms on homemade bread and catsup with growth on the commercial products, you can test the effectiveness of such chemicals.

2. Choose one food and investigate the growth of microorganisms on it at various temperatures.

DISCOVERY OF MICROORGANISMS

Behind words like "animal" and "plant" lies a long history. But when we turn from the familiar, visible world to the world revealed by the microscope, we encounter something comparatively new to human experience. It is so new that we can chart the history of its exploration.

LEEUWENHOEK AND THE "LITTLE ANIMALS"

This world was discovered in the 1670's by Anton van Leeuwenhoek. Leeuwenhoek was a cloth merchant of Delft, Holland. His hobby was grinding lenses for magnification. He also con-

Anton van Leeuwenhoek [LAY vun heuk]: 1632–1723. Dutch lens-maker and naturalist

6—2 Anton van Leeuwenhoek holding one of his microscopes.

6—3 A replica of a Leeuwenhoek microscope, about natural size. The specimen was placed on the metal point in front of the lens. The turnscrews adjusted the focus.

Leeuwenhoek's instruments were made with simple lenses, but so carefully were they ground that he could obtain clear magnifications of 200 ×.

natural philosophers: scientists. The latter term did not replace the former until the first half of the 19th century.

structed metal frames to hold the lenses. He became interested in things he could see with his instruments. Others were examining the fine structure of large plants and animals, but Leeuwenhoek alone had the idea of peering into drops of water from rain, wells, and other places. By 1675 Leeuwenhoek had observed in such water—apparently for the first time by anyone—some of the living things that we now call protists. He called them *tierken*, Dutch for "little animals."

Leeuwenhoek wrote about his observations to the Royal Society for the Improvement of Natural Knowledge, London. The Royal Society's *Philosophical Transactions* was the first scientific journal in the English language. In it, a paper appeared (vol. 11, 1677) with this title: "Observations communicated to the publisher by Mr. Anton van Leeuwenhoek in a Dutch Letter of the 9th of October, 1676, here English'd: Concerning little animals by him observed in Rain-Well-Sea-and Snow water; as also in water wherein Pepper had lain infused." In 1680 Leeuwenhoek also reported seeing the organisms we now call yeasts. In 1683 he reported seeing what we call bacteria. All these were "little animals" to him.

The fame of the Royal Society was great then and it is still flourishing today. The distribution of its *Transactions* was so wide that the news soon spread among natural philosophers.

But when we look back now, progress in exploring the world of microorganisms seems to have been remarkably slow. To scientists of the 18th century the study of microorganisms seemed unimportant. There were many beautiful and interesting plants and animals being discovered all over the world. So, scientists did not choose to spend time on things that were so hard to see. They were there and then gone so quickly. In his 18th-century classification of all organisms, Linnaeus took little notice of the microscopic world.

BEGINNINGS OF MICROBIOLOGY

After 1800, following the Industrial Revolution, the manufacture of microscopes improved rapidly. This led to an increased study of **microbes,** as microscopic organisms began to be called. But it was not until the middle of the 19th century that biologists focused their attention on microbes. At that time, a series of discoveries clearly showed the importance of microbes to humans.

microbes [MY krobz; Greek: *mikros*, small, + *bios*, life]

In this period the name of Louis Pasteur stands out. Pasteur showed the importance of microbes in the making of wine, beer, and cheeses. This linked the world of microscopic life to commercially important enterprises. Pasteur also furthered (though he did not originate) the idea that microbes are associated with diseases of larger organisms, including humans. Thus biologists came to see that, despite their small size, microbes are important organisms. Studying them soon became an important part of biology.

Robert Koch, a physician, concentrated on the relationship of microbes to disease. To study this relationship, Koch had to be able to grow and study the microbes. For nearly 40 years, he and his colleagues invented methods and instruments for culturing and examining microbes. One student invented the petri dish. Another suggested the use of agar, a substance derived from seaweed. These are still in use today. Koch set up the experimental procedure by which a particular microbe could be associated with a particular disease. He used the procedure to identify the microbe of tuberculosis. Building on the work of Pasteur, Koch founded the science of **microbiology** — the study of microscopic organisms.

colleagues [KOL eegz]: persons who work together

agar [AH gar]

tuberculosis [tew bur kyuh LOH-sis]: disease in which tissues of the host—most often in the lungs—are destroyed

Throughout the 18th century, scientists experimented and debated the hypothesis that living organisms could come into being by **spontaneous generation.** Spontaneous generation, or **abiogenesis,** was used to explain such observations as: Fish and frogs appeared from dry pond bottoms after a rain, and mice suddenly appeared in old clothing where no mice had been seen before.

spontaneous [spon TAY nee us; Latin: *sponte*, of one's own accord]

abiogenesis [ay by oh JEN uh sis; Greek: *a*, without, + *bios*, life, + *genesis*, birth]

6–4 Redi's experiment: (*A*) Maggots developed on meat left in an open dish.
(*B*) Another dish was covered with cloth, and no maggots developed on the meat. However, flies' eggs were found on the cloth. And maggots hatched from these eggs.

A 17th-century Italian physician, Francesco Redi, conducted an experiment to test the spontaneous generation of maggots in rotting meat. The result showed that the maggots did not just "appear." They hatched from eggs laid on the meat by living flies. The concept of living things coming only from other living things, *biogenesis,* was supported by his experiment.

A   B

Investigation 6.2   SPONTANEOUS GENERATION

INTRODUCTION

Do microbes arise without parents from the nonliving materials in meat broths— abiogenesis? Or do they come from living ancestors (biogenesis) that have somehow gotten into the broths? At the time of the American Revolution, an Italian, Lazzaro Spallanzani (lah TZAH roh spal lan TZAH-nee), conducted experiments in an attempt to answer the question. Later, in the middle of the 19th century, Pasteur carried out more carefully designed experiments.

In this investigation you will perform experiments similar to those of Spallanzani and Pasteur. You will use some techniques developed since their day, but the principles involved in your procedure will be the same.

MATERIALS
(per team or class)

bouillon cube or 8 g peptone
2 pieces glass tubing (30 cm long)
1 piece glass tubing (8 cm long)
7 erlenmeyer flasks, 250-ml
bunsen burner with wing tip
3 1-hole stoppers to fit flasks
2 solid stoppers to fit flasks
beaker, 1,000-ml
beaker (for melting paraffin)
stirring rod
funnel
ring stand to fit funnel
graduated cylinder
forceps and wad of cotton
paraffin
autoclave or pressure cooker
heat source
triangular file
filter paper

PROCEDURE

1. Using a wing-tip burner, bend one of the 30-cm lengths of glass tubing into a J

shape. Bend the other into an S shape (figure 6–5). Trim the tubes to look like those in the illustration. Insert them into 1-hole stoppers. Insert the straight piece of glass tubing into the 3rd 1-hole stopper. (Caution: While inserting the glass tubing through the rubber stoppers, wrap a piece of paper toweling around the glass tube to protect your hands.)

2. Dissolve 1 bouillon cube in 500 ml warm water. When cool, filter. The broth must be clear.

3. Pour 70 ml of the broth into each of 7 flasks.

4. Using a lead pencil, number each flask on the small white area on its side. Treat them as follows:

   Flask 1 — Plug with a solid stopper. Do not heat.

   Flask 2 — Add 10 ml water to the broth. Boil gently for 15 minutes. About 10 ml of water will boil off, making the level approximately the same as in the other flasks. Leave open.

   Flask 3 — Add 10 ml water to the broth. Boil gently for 15 minutes, with the solid stopper resting at an angle in the mouth of the flask. Plug immediately with the stopper. To seal, melt paraffin in a beaker; apply it with a wad of cotton held in forceps.

   Flask 4 — Heat in an autoclave or a pressure cooker for 15 minutes at 15-lb pressure. Leave open.

   Flask 5 — Plug with the stopper through which a straight glass tube was inserted. Heat as for Flask 4. Then seal with paraffin around the neck of the flask and around the tube where it comes through the stopper.

   Flask 6 — Plug with the stopper through which the J-shaped glass tube was inserted. Heat as for Flask 4. Seal as for Flask 5.

   Flask 7 — Plug with the stopper through which the S-shaped glass tube was inserted. Heat as for Flask 4. Seal as for Flask 5.

5. Record the date on which the experiment is set up. Place all flasks on a laboratory table but not in direct sunlight or over a radiator.

6. Look for changes in the flasks each day for 1 week, then each week for 5 weeks. Record any changes in the clearness of the broth, noting the number of the flask and the date. Record other observed changes in the broth such as appearance of scum, mold colonies, etc. At the end of the experiment, open the flasks and note the odor of the broth in each.

DISCUSSION

Flasks 2 and 3 represent Spallanzani's experiment. (1) What differences did you observe in these flasks during the 5 weeks? (2) How can you explain the differences? (3) In your experiment, Flask 3 may or may not have developed cloudiness. Spallanzani's sealed

6–5 Completed setup for Investigation 6.2.

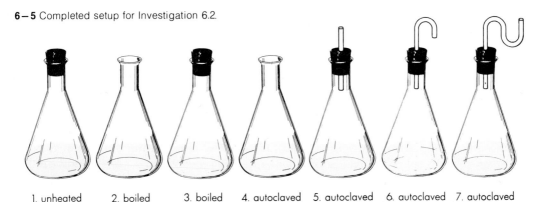

1. unheated   2. boiled   3. boiled   4. autoclaved   5. autoclaved   6. autoclaved   7. autoclaved

flask developed no cloudiness or putrid odor. But biologists of his day denied that this showed microbes had to get into the broth from outside. They clung to the theory of spontaneous generation. How do you think they defended their point of view against Spallanzani's evidence?

Flasks 4 to 7 represent some of Pasteur's work. (4) In the experimental setup, what is the function of Flask 4? (5) How do you explain the result obtained in Flask 7? (6) What is the function of Flask 1 in this investigation? (7) Compare your observations of Flask 1 with those of Flasks 2 and 4. Explain any likenesses and differences in these results.

(8) In the light of the results of these experiments, discuss the question raised in the introduction to this investigation: "Do microbes arise without parents from the nonliving materials in meat broths? Or, do they come from living ancestors that have somehow gotten into the broth?"

CHECK YOURSELF

A. What are some arguments for a more-than-two-kingdom classification system?
B. Why was progress in studying microorganisms very slow for a century and a half after Leeuwenhoek's discovery?
C. Why is the science of microbiology dated from Pasteur and Koch rather than from Leeuwenhoek?
D. What evidence led biologists to discard the theory of spontaneous generation?

THE PROTIST KINGDOM

The two aims in classification — convenience and the expression of relationships — often conflict. The protist kingdom is a grouping of convenience. There is little evidence of relationship among most of the protist phyla. But many organisms that have been placed in this kingdom have both animal and plant characteristics. If we do not place these puzzling organisms in a separate kingdom, we must place them in *both* animal and plant kingdoms. By assigning them to a third group, we can define the animal and plant kingdoms more clearly.

As you read this section, refer to the career essay on pages 194 and 195.

SLIME MOLDS

Members of the **slime mold** phylum usually grow among damp, decaying leaves and other dead plant material. If you search through such material soon after a heavy rain, you may find a slime-mold **plasmodium.** It is a glistening sheet that may be several centimeters, or even a meter, across. A plasmodium is a living mass that crawls slowly from one place to another. Its body has no definite shape.

plasmodium [plaz MOH dee um; Greek: *plassein*, to mold, + *eidos*, form]

6-6 Slime-mold plasmodia crawling over a woodpile.

As it crawls, it picks up small bits of dead organic matter for food. After feeding, a plasmodium moves to a drier location and slowly changes into a number of spore cases. These cases are on stalks and usually are not more than a few millimeters high. Many are brightly colored. Large numbers of spores are formed inside each case. When a case breaks, spores are released into the air and carried by the wind. If they land in a suitable spot where water is available, the spores give rise to tiny organisms with *flagella.* After swimming about for a short time, these organisms lose their flagella and fuse in pairs. By feeding and growing, each pair develops into a new plasmodium.

flagella [fluh JEL uh; singular, flagellum; Latin: *flagellum*, little whip]: long, hairlike projections that cause movement

6-7 Slime-mold spore cases.

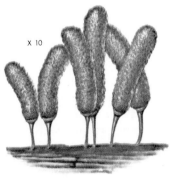

X 10

Arcyria

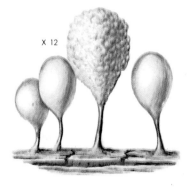

X 12

Hemitrichia

CILIATES

Some *ciliate* species are 0.25 mm long — visible to the unaided eye when seen in good light against a dark background. However, most species are microscopic. Some ciliates are commensal or parasitic, but the majority are free-living.

The name of the phylum indicates its principal characteristic. Ciliates have great numbers of *cilia* covering their bodies. The cilia beat in rhythm, driving the organisms through the

cilia [SIL ee uh; singular, cilium; Latin: *cilium*, eyelash]: short, hairlike projections on the surface of an organism. Many cilia are usually found together.

6 – 8 A few ciliates.

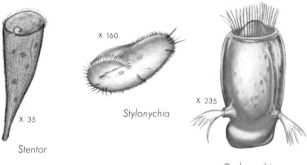

X 160

Stylonychia

X 235

X 35

Stentor

Cycloposthium

If a ciliate requires one second to swim across the low-power field of your microscope, what is its speed in meters per hour?

water. In some species the beating of the cilia causes a current that sweeps food particles toward the organism. A few species have poisonous tentacles that are used to capture prey or in defense against predators.

All ciliates have definite shapes. Some species that live attached to solid objects in water have radial symmetry. The many species that are active swimmers have definite anterior and posterior ends but are usually unsymmetrical.

6 – 9 A predator that is smaller than its prey. From the left, four stages are shown as one ciliate (*Didinium*) consumes another (*Paramecium*).

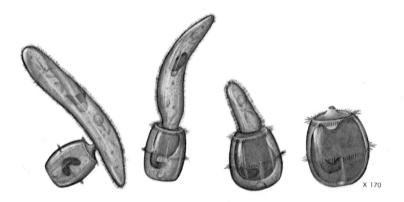

X 170

SPOROZOANS

sporozoans [spor uh ZOH unz; Greek: *spora*, seed, + *zoion*, animal]

All **sporozoans** are microscopic. Organisms in this phylum have three characteristics in common. First, all are parasites. Second, they have no means of locomotion (at least, not as adults). Third, a parent sporozoan reproduces by forming large numbers of tiny spores, which are released into the environment.

Some species of sporozoans affect their hosts only slightly, if at all. Others have such a weakening effect that the hosts become ill. Still others frequently cause the death of their hosts. Malaria is one of the human diseases caused by sporozoans.

X 100

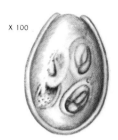

X 1000

Plasmodium vivax   Eimeria

6—10 Two sporozoan species.

SARCODINANS

The most famous microorganisms of pond water are amebas, which move around on the undersides of lily pads and across the pond bottom. Amebas are barely visible to the unaided eye, but under the low power of a microscope they look like granular, grayish masses.

An ameba has no definite shape. Its body substance is constantly flowing into *pseudopods* (fingerlike extensions), and often into more than one at a time. One pseudopod outgrows the others, and the organism flows in the direction of that pseudopod. Pseudopods also serve in obtaining food (figure 6–11). Pseudopods are the characteristic structures of the *sarcodinan* phylum. In some species, pseudopods are less numerous than in amebas. In others, they are more numerous and do not constantly change position.

One group of sarcodinans has shells of silica, a substance similar to sand. Many long, stiff pseudopods radiate from their

sarcodinans [sar kuh DY nunz; Greek: *sarx*, flesh, + *eidos*]

amebas [uh MEE buz; Greek: *ameibein*, to change]

pseudopods [SOO duh podz; Greek: *pseudes*, false, + *podion*, little foot]

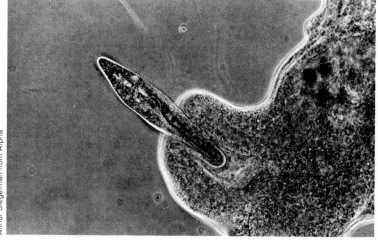

6—11 Pseudopods of an ameba taking in food—a paramecium.   × 160

shells. Another group build shells of calcium carbonate—chemically the same as clam shells. During past ages great numbers of such shells have accumulated at the bottom of seas and have solidified into rock.

Many amebalike sarcodinans live in ponds, puddles, and damp soil. Most of the shell-bearing kinds live in the seas. Other species live with larger organisms in various kinds of relationships—some as commensals, some as parasites.

6–12 Examples of sarcodinans.

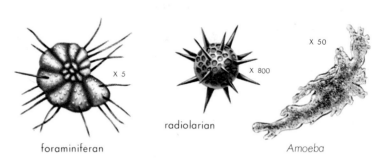

X 5

X 800

X 50

foraminiferan

radiolarian

Amoeba

Would you call the flagellate-termite relationship described below a mutualistic relationship? If so, what advantage do the flagellates gain?

FLAGELLATES

Flagellates are microscopic or very nearly so. Members of this phylum move by means of flagella. Some contain chlorophyll and synthesize their own food when light is present. When light is not present, they may digest food particles in the surrounding water and then absorb the products. Other species that lack chlorophyll capture smaller microorganisms and digest them internally. Such a mixture of plant and animal characteristics has made the classification of flagellates puzzling.

Flagellates are abundant in damp soil, in fresh water, and in the ocean. Many live in close relationships with other organisms. These relationships may be parasitic or mutualistic. For example, some live in the alimentary canals of termites. There they digest the wood eaten by the insects. Without the flagellates, the termites would starve to death, just as you would on a wood diet, for neither you nor the termites can digest this material.

6–13 Flagellate representatives.

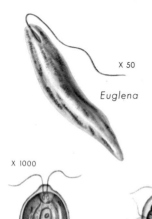

X 50

Euglena

X 1000

Chlamydomonas

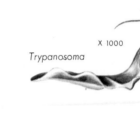

X 700

Pandorina

Trypanosoma

X 1000

X 300

dinoflagellate

BLUE-GREEN ALGAE

You may be surprised to find in the protist kingdom a phylum of organisms called "algae." The name goes back to a time when biologists did not know as much about these organisms as they do now. *Blue-green algae* contain chlorophyll, but it is not organized into distinct structures as it is in plants. Moreover, blue-green algae lack other plant characteristics and in some ways resemble bacteria. They are mostly microscopic organisms, but many grow in colonies that are easily visible and that have characteristic forms.

Blue-green algae are among the most hardy of organisms. They grow in almost any place that has a little liquid water: in ponds and streams, on moist soil and tree bark. They even grow on the surface of snowbanks and in hot springs where the temperature can reach 85° C.

6 – 14 Some blue-green algae.

X 600

Nostoc

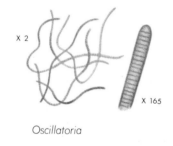

X 2

X 165

Oscillatoria

Gloeocapsa

X 375

All the individuals grouped in the *bacteria* phylum are invisible to the unaided eye. Some are among the smallest things that can, with certainty, be called living. Most bacteria range from 0.001 to 0.005 mm (1 to 5μm) in size.

Bacteria have few visible characteristics besides shape. Most individuals are shaped like a rod, a sphere, or a coil. Early

μm is the symbol for micrometer. One micrometer is equal to one millionth of a meter; 1,000 μm = 1 mm.

6 – 15 Different shapes of bacteria.

X 325

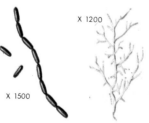

X 2200

X 1500

X 1200

spirilla (stained)   cocci (stained)   bacilli (stained)   actinomycete

in the history of microbiology, it became clear that there are many more species than shapes of bacteria. Therefore, bacterial taxonomists began to use characteristics other than structure for classification. The foods bacteria use, the waste materials they produce, their reactions to stains, and their colonies—all are used to identify species of bacteria.

Most bacteria are consumers. They obtain their energy from foods produced by other organisms. Some are parasites, but many are decomposers. A few have pigments that are chemically similar to chlorophylls in plants. These bacteria carry on a kind of photosynthesis that produces food but does not produce oxygen. A few other bacteria obtain their energy from inorganic substances that contain iron, sulfur, or nitrogen. They are the *only* known organisms that do not depend, directly or indirectly, on radiant solar energy.

6–16 Colonies of four kinds of bacteria growing in a laboratory culture.   × 2

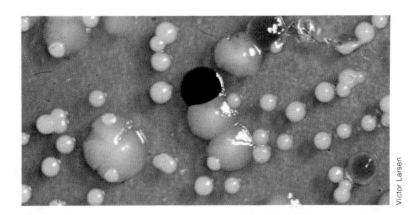

Victor Larsen

Many bacteria move by using a flagellum. Most reproduce simply by splitting into two bacteria that are exactly like the parent. Under favorable conditions, many species may divide every 20 minutes. This may explain why food sometimes spoils so rapidly.

The best-known bacteria are those that cause diseases. Tetanus, tuberculosis, and strep throat are caused by bacteria, as are many other diseases. Many bacteria, however, are bene-

George B. Chapman and Luis J. Archer

6–17 An electron micrograph of a dividing bacterium.   × 4,500

ficial. People use certain ones to produce vinegar, several vitamins, butter, various cheeses, and certain drugs and hormones.

There are organisms still smaller than most bacteria, which are classified in the same phylum. Rickettsias are an example. Rickettsias measure about 0.00035 by 0.00025 mm (0.35 by 0.25μm). They are, therefore, barely visible under a light microscope. However, they can be studied with an *electron microscope.* This is an instrument that uses beams of electrons rather than of light to produce an image on film or on a screen. Electron micrographs show that a rickettsia has an internal structure much like that of a bacterium. In fact, some microbiologists think rickettsias may be very small bacteria that became parasitic in the past and can now live in no other way. With the exception of one known species, they can be grown only in living cells of other organisms.

rickettsias [rik ET see uz]: named for Howard T. Ricketts, 1871–1910, American pathologist

electron micrographs: pictures taken by means of streams of electrons instead of by rays of light

National Center for Atmospheric Research

6–18 Compare this electron microscope with Leeuwenhoek's microscope and with the microscopes in your laboratory. Many interesting science careers involve the use of microscopes.

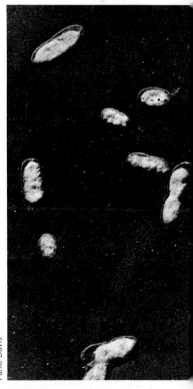

Parke Davis

6–19 Electron micrograph of rickettsias.   × 24,000

CHECK YOURSELF

E. Which characteristics of slime molds are animallike and which are plantlike?
F. What is a flagellum?
G. How do ciliates move?
H. In what ways does an ameba use its pseudopods?
I. Why are blue-green algae placed in the protist kingdom in our classification?
J. What are some characteristics used in distinguishing among the kinds of bacteria?
K. What are some differences between bacteria and rickettsias?
L. What kinds of ecological relationships are found among protists?

Investigation 6.3   **MICROBIAL TECHNIQUES: POPULATIONS**

If you have a mixed population of horses, cattle, and sheep in a pasture, it is easy to separate the 3 kinds of animals and determine the number of each. But if you have a mixed population of invisible microorganisms, how can you separate the kinds? How can you obtain a *pure culture* – a population of one species growing in a medium? And how can you count individuals?

There is a further difficulty. Occasionally horses and cattle may be dangerous, but at least you can see them coming. How can you protect yourself from dangerous kinds of microorganisms? You will follow sterile procedures that have been developed. During the work, keep your hands away from your eyes, ears, nose, and mouth. Wash and disinfect your hands afterward.

PROCEDURE

The following directions will be supplemented with demonstrations by your teacher.

A. Preparing the cultures

1. Stand 4 tubes of nutrient agar in a 1,000-

MATERIALS
(per team)

mixed culture of bacteria
4 culture tubes, containing 15 ml sterile nutrient agar
2 beakers, 1,000-ml
4 sterile petri dishes
inoculating loop or micropipette
test-tube rack
ring stand
bunsen burner or alcohol lamp
thermometer ($-10°$ to $+110°C$)
glass-marking crayon
paper towels
disinfectant soap or solution for hands

ml beaker. Add water to a level above that of the agar in the tubes.

2. Place the beaker on a ring stand and heat. (*Caution: Bunsen burners and alcohol lamps should never be used in the same classroom. Alcohol is highly flammable and should never be allowed to come in contact with an open flame. If safety goggles are available, use them when heating all substances.*) When the agar has melted, transfer the tubes to a 2nd 1,000-ml beaker containing water at

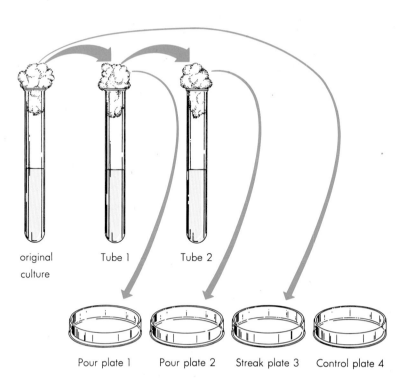

original culture

Tube 1

Tube 2

Pour plate 1   Pour plate 2   Streak plate 3   Control plate 4

44°C. Check the temperature of this water bath occasionally. When necessary, heat gently to maintain approximately 44°C.

3. Wash the top of the laboratory table with a soapy paper towel. Place 4 sterile petri dishes on the table. Number the dishes *1* through *4*, using a glass-marking crayon. Write on the bottom of each dish, near the edge. Include a symbol to designate your team.

4. Remove the plugs from one of your tubes of melted agar. Immediately pour it into Dish 3. Pour the agar from a 2nd tube into Dish 4. Do not allow the tube lip to touch

6–21 Pouring a culture plate.

the dish (figure 6–21). Allow the medium to solidify.

5. Sterilize an inoculating loop or micropipette in the flame of a bunsen burner or alcohol lamp. (*See caution in step 2.*)

6. Remove the plug from the mixed culture of bacteria and from one of your two remaining tubes of melted agar. With the sterilized loop, transfer a loopful of the culture to the tube of sterile medium.

7. Replug both tubes immediately and reflame the loop. Mix the bacteria and agar thoroughly by rolling the tube between your palms for about 15 seconds. Keep the plugged end up so that the cotton remains dry. Using the crayon, label this tube with a *1*.

8. Again, flame the loop. Transfer a loopful of the mixture in Tube 1 to a 2nd tube of melted medium. Replug the tubes and reflame the loop. Mix in the same way you mixed Tube 1. Label this 2nd tube with a *2*.

9. Return Tubes 1 and 2 to the 44°C water

bath for 1 minute to make sure all the agar is melted.

10. Remove Tube 1 from the water bath and dry it with a paper towel. Remove its plug and flame the mouth of the tube. (*Caution: Be sure to keep the cotton plug a safe distance away from the flame.*) Pour the contents of Tube 1 into Dish 1. Immediately, cover the dish. (The dish is called a "plate" once it is inoculated — has had the microorganisms added.) Swirl the plate very gently, keeping it on the tabletop. This should distribute the medium evenly over the bottom of the plate. Repeat for Plate (Dish) 2.

11. As soon as the agar is solid in Dish 3, flame the loop. Take a loopful of the original mixed culture and streak the surface of the agar, as shown in figure 6–22. Use one of the patterns shown in figure 6–23. Flame the loop. Record the pattern used.

12. Dish 4 receives no treatment.

13. As soon as the agar is solid, set all the plates upside down in a place designated by your teacher. Observe daily until many bacterial colonies are clearly visible in at least one of the plates.

6–22 Streaking a culture plate.

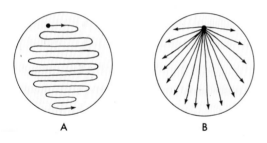

A   B

6–23 Two patterns for streaking culture plates.

B. Counting the colonies

1. Ignoring differences in appearance, count the separate colonies of bacteria that have developed in each of the poured plates (1 and 2) and record the counts.

2. In some cases the colonies may be very crowded. You can estimate the number by using the following sampling technique. First, using black ink, draw a square 1 cm on each side on a piece of white paper. Second, position Plate 1 on the paper so you can see the colonies of bacteria against the background of the square. Count the number of colonies in the square. Move the square to another position under the plate. Count the colonies again. Repeat until you have 5 counts from different parts of the plate. Third, add all the counts and divide the total by 5. This will give an average count per cm^2.

3. Estimate the number of colonies on the whole plate. To do this, multiply the number of colonies per cm^2 by the surface area of the entire plate. (This is 78.5 cm^2 for petri dishes with 100-mm diameter.) (*1*) How many colonies do you estimate Plate 1 contains?

4. Repeat calculations for Plate 2. (*2*) How many colonies do you estimate Plate 2 contains?

5. Examine Plate 4 (control). If there are colonies present in this plate, count them. (*3*) What correction in your original counts should be made if colonies are present in this control plate? Make such a correction, if necessary.

DISCUSSION

When you have completed counts of Plates 1 and 2, you are ready to estimate the population density of organisms (number per cm^3) in the *original* mixed culture of bacteria. You will need the following information:

    The volume of liquid held in your inoculating loop was about 1/200 cm^3. Therefore, the loopful of material introduced into Plate 1 contained about 1/200 of the number of bacteria in each cm³ of the original culture.

Let's assume that each organism in Plate 1 produced a visible colony. Then, the number of colonies in Plate 1 multiplied by 200 gives the number of bacteria per cm³ in the original culture. (4) What do you estimate was the density of bacteria in the *original* culture?

Now estimate the density of bacteria (per cm³) in the original culture *again*. This time use the data from Plate 2. To do this, multiply the estimated number of colonies in Plate 2 by 600,000. (5) What is the density (per cm³) of bacteria in the *original* culture based on these data?

You now have 2 separate estimates of the number of organisms present per cm³ (density) in the original culture. (6) How closely do these compare with each other? Also compare with other teams. (7) If there is any difference, how do you account for it? (8) Which calculation do you think is more accurate? Why?

Next examine Plate 3—the streak plate. Compare the pattern of colonies with the pattern of streaking that you recorded. (9) Are the patterns different or similar? (10) How many *kinds* of colonies have developed? In what ways do they differ? (11) How many kinds of bacteria were in the original culture? (12) What seems to be the principal way in which the colonies of these bacteria differ macroscopically? Suppose you were to lift a part of one colony with a sterile inoculating loop and streak it on a plate of sterile medium. (13) How many kinds of colonies would you expect to develop? (14) What would you call such a culture? (15) Which steps in the procedure are concerned only with determining the population density of microorganisms? (16) Which steps are concerned only with obtaining a pure culture? (17) Formulate a set of rules for working safely with microorganisms. (18) Suggest a method of disposing of the cultures after you have finished studying them.

FOR FURTHER INVESTIGATION

1. You did not actually complete the procedure for producing a pure culture. Carry out the last step. How can you determine that you have been successful?

2. Use the methods of this investigation to determine the population density of microorganisms in a sample of stream or pond water. How might differences in kinds of culture medium and in incubation temperature affect your results?

3. Observe the microorganisms in the mixed culture under a microscope. Use the staining techniques your teacher has in a teacher's edition of the textbook (page T763F).

VIRUSES

After Koch showed the relationship between a species of bacterium and the disease tuberculosis, many biologists began to look for microbes in diseased organisms. In 1892 Dimitri Iwanowski was studying the mosaic disease of tobacco plants. He forced the juice of diseased plants through porcelain filters. When this filtered juice was injected into healthy plants, they developed the mosaic disease. This was puzzling, because bacteria could not pass through such filters. Iwanowski concluded that some *toxin* (poisonous substance) produced by bacteria passed through and affected the healthy tobacco plants. But he could not find the bacteria themselves.

Dimitri Iwanowski [duh MEE tree ee vuh NOF skee]: 1864–1919. Russian microbiologist

Martinus W. Beijerinck
[BY uh ringk]: 1851–1931. Dutch
microbiologist

Six years later M. W. Beijerinck, who was studying the same disease, verified Iwanowski's observations. Beijerinck repeated the experiment many times—and always with the same result. In addition, whatever was affecting the plants seemed to be reproducing in them. Toxins do not do this. Therefore, Beijerinck concluded that the mosaic disease could not be bacterial. It must result from what he called a "living fluid"—something that was able to pass through porcelain filters *and* to reproduce. Today we know that such diseases are not caused by a fluid but by tiny particles called ***viruses.***

viruses [VY rus uz; Latin: *virus,*
slimy, poisonous liquid]

Scientists have learned much about viruses. Although they are too small to be seen with even the best light microscopes, we can obtain pictures of virus particles with an electron microscope. Viruses are of different sizes and shapes. They are found not only in plant diseases but also in those of animals and even of bacteria. They occur in many familiar human diseases—for example, measles, mumps, influenza, and colds.

6–24 Electron micrograph of three viruses. The two small spherical viruses cause a diseased condition in monkeys. Between them is the rodlike tail of a larger virus (*center and above*) that attacks bacteria. × 275,000

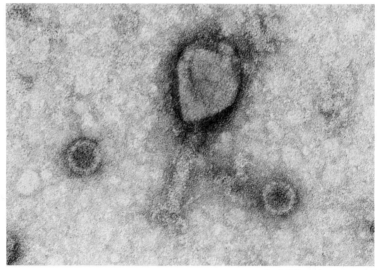

Scott M. Brown (work supported
by NIH Grant AI-14994)

Until recently, viruses could be grown only in living things. Some can now be grown in complex culture media containing substances obtained by finely grinding up parts of living things. Nevertheless, viruses are still most easily cultivated in other organisms. Some—such as those of influenza—are grown in developing chick embryos.

Are viruses alive? They have two characteristics we usually associate with living things: the ability to reproduce and the ability to undergo changes in hereditary characteristics. Yet, what we call viral reproduction differs from reproduction of bac-

hereditary [huh RED uh ter ee]:
carried from parent to offspring

teria or other microbes. A virus cannot produce copies of itself without another organism. It must rely on the life processes or parts of another species. When a bacteriophage attaches itself to a bacterium, only part of the virus moves inside. This part has the instructions for making duplicate viruses. In about 20 minutes the affected bacterium falls apart, releasing 200 or so new bacteriophages.

bacteriophage [bak TIR ee uh fayj]: Greek: *bakterion*, a little rod, + *phagein*, to eat]: a virus that attacks bacteria

In 1935 tobacco mosaic virus was crystallized in much the same way as salt or sugar can be crystallized from a solution. Crystallized virus can be stored for long periods of time on a laboratory shelf like a jar of salt. Once they are rubbed into a tobacco leaf, however, the virus particles multiply. So viruses seem to be a link between the living and nonliving worlds.

In classifying living things, we have seen organisms that do not fit neatly into our groupings. Viruses present a similar problem.

6—25 TYMV (turnip yellows mosaic virus) in cabbage.

BSCS photo by Richard R. Tolman

CHECK YOURSELF

M. What steps are necessary in preparing a pure culture of microorganisms?

N. How were viruses discovered?

O. What is a toxin?

P. Why might we consider viruses living things? Why might there be disagreement?

Q. What is a bacteriophage?

Careers in Biology:
Investigating Slime Molds

Photos by Gordon E. Uno

Ray Collins is a science professor at the University of California in Berkeley. He teaches biology and botany (**A**). Ray is a mycologist—a person who studies fungi. His special interest is the life cycle and mating habits of slime molds. He is a pioneer in this field of research.

Ray Collins was born and raised on a farm in Louisiana during the Depression. With his brothers, Ray worked in the fields of his father's farm. Later, when his father was busy with carpentry and working at a butcher shop, Ray took charge of the farm.

But he wasn't satisfied with his work there. So Ray jumped at a chance to work in a dog and cat hospital in a big city—Houston. There he became fascinated by the scientific names of the animal diseases. His work at the hospital was one reason Ray decided to go to college and study biology. This was a giant step for Ray, since no one else in his family had gone to a university.

Ray can remember distinctly his first scientific experiment. It was an experiment on diffusion. Instead of plastic tubing (such as you will use), Ray used a pig's bladder. To measure the results, he used a metric rule—for the first time. In his biology course, Collins found answers to the questions he had asked when he lived on the farm.

There was a reason why moss grew on the north side of the trees—it was moister there. And the decaying logs he had seen were not oozing liquid, as Ray had thought. Actually, the "liquid" consisted of slime molds that lived on the rotting wood. He became interested

A. Ray helps a graduate student plan a research project.

in slime molds and studied them in graduate school. He wanted to learn about their life cycles. At that time no one but Ray thought that slime molds could mate. He hoped to "set the record straight" about the reproductive activities of slime molds.

Ray's first attempts at research were frustrating. It was difficult to isolate the microscopic slime-mold spores from the spore cases. And he had to find out what conditions would cause spores to germinate. After hundreds of experiments, he finally succeeded. The germinated spores became tiny, one-celled organisms (**B**). He placed two of these microscopic organisms in a culture tube.

Later, he inspected the culture tube. Instead of two small cells, he found one large cell. This indicated to him that the slime-mold organisms had mated. Had he discovered something that no one else had seen? Indeed he had. But it took many more experiments before he convinced other mycologists that slime molds do mate.

As head of the Botany Department at Berkeley, Collins divides his time between administrative duties and the things he loves most. Besides his family, these include researching and teaching. He is pleased when he sees the look of understanding on the faces of his students (**C**). And his satisfaction is great when an experiment is successful.

Why did Ray turn to science? He explains that science is the way he hopes to find answers to his questions about the natural world.

B. Ray looks for the microscopic organisms that develop when the slime-mold spores germinate.

C. Ray discusses plant cell structure with his students.

D. When he made his discovery about mating in slime molds, Ray wrote a report describing the experiment. He read it carefully to make sure it was accurate before having it published.

195

PROBLEMS

1. Under favorable environmental conditions, an individual bacterium may divide once every 20 minutes. Suppose you begin with a single bacterium at noon on a certain day. Assume that no bacteria die and that each divides every 20 minutes. How many bacteria would there be at noon on the next day?

2. In addition to rickettsias, other organisms in the size range between bacteria and viruses are known. Investigate the characteristics of pleuropneumonia organisms (PPO) and of pleuropneumonia-like organisms (PPLO).

3. Pasteur, with the help of other early microbiologists, established the idea that microorganisms and other forms of life arise only from similar living things.

There is evidence, however, that at first the earth was without life. If life began once, why does it not begin again?

4. Explain what each of the following careers has to do with protists. Do some library research if necessary.

baby bottle sterilizer manufacturer	frozen-food packager leather tanner
baker	operating-room
cancer researcher	nurse
cheesemaker	pharmacist
dentist	freezer manufacturer
doctor	rust-resistant-
dried-food processor	wheat breeder
epidemiologist	school nurse
food canner	vaccine producer

5. Long before humankind knew that microbes exist, many people were making use of them. What are some of these uses? What industries depend on microbes?

SUGGESTED READINGS

Ashworth, J. M. and J. Dee. 1975. *The Biology of Slime Moulds.* Crane, Russek, New York. Introductory book following developmental stages of two species of slime molds.

Berg, H. C. 1975. How Bacteria Swim. *Scientific American*, August.

Campbell, A. M. 1976. How Viruses Insert their DNA into the DNA of the Host Cell. *Scientific American*, December. Discusses virus reproduction.

Frobisher, M. et al. 1974. *Fundamentals of Microbiology.* 9th ed. W. B. Saunders, Philadelphia. Useful for beginners or professionals. Covers many topics in microbiology.

Gasner, D. 1975. Natural History of Influenza. *Science Digest*, March.

Henle, W., G. Henle, and E. T. Lennette. 1979. The Epstein-Barr Virus. *Scientific American*, July. Shows a virus to be a cause of infectious mononucleosis and linked to human cancers.

Patent, D. 1974. *Microscopic Animals and Plants.* Holiday House, New York. Basic guide to microscopy with a survey of microscopic life.

Reid, R. 1975. *Microbes and Men.* Saturday Review Press, New York. Fascinating introduction to the history of microbiology.

Walsby, A. E. 1977. The Gas Vacuoles of Blue-Green Algae. *Scientific American*, August. Special vacuoles help these organisms float.

SECTION THREE

Patterns
in the Biosphere

PATTERNS IN THE BIOSPHERE

We have seen how individual organisms may be grouped as populations. From an ecological viewpoint, populations may be studied as parts of communities and ecosystems. From a taxonomic viewpoint, species populations may be grouped to form a classification. Now we turn to another aspect of biology—to the distribution of organisms in the biosphere.

No species lives everywhere. Some are widespread, and some are found only in a few places. Some are living on the earth today, and some have become extinct. Species are not scattered helter-skelter over the earth. Different species live in different places and at different times. That whales do not live in Nebraska today and that echinoderms live only in the seas and apparently never lived elsewhere are facts of distribution. So are the facts that palms once lived in Greenland and that the bacterium of tuberculosis lives in humans and cows but not in dogs. Some are obvious facts; some are facts that have been established only after much patient searching for evidence. But do these facts make any sense?

A British scientist once said, "Science is not the mere collection of facts, which are infinitely numerous and mostly uninteresting, but the attempt of the human mind to order these facts into satisfying patterns." In Section Three we shall attempt to find some satisfying and meaningful patterns within the multitude of facts about the distribution of organisms in the biosphere.

What patterns in the biosphere are represented in the photo on the preceding page?

Chapter 7

Life in the Microscopic World

YOUR GUIDEPOSTS

In this chapter you will have an opportunity to explore these questions in biology:

- Where in the biosphere are microorganisms found?
- How has interest in disease grown from a narrow treatment of human ills to a broad concern with biological principles?
- How can disease be studied as an ecological process?
- What role do microorganisms play in soil ecosystems?
- How does the nitrogen cycle illustrate the interdependence of organisms in the biosphere?

Investigation 7.1   **DISTRIBUTION OF MICROORGANISMS**

INTRODUCTION

In Chapters 5 and 6 you were introduced to a variety of microorganisms. Now let us see how these organisms fit into your ecosystem. A person working in a laboratory may need to know what kinds of microorganisms are present, how abundant they are, and how they move or are carried from one place to another. These also may be very important concerns to anyone who has ever had a cold.

MATERIALS
(per team)

7 sterile petri dishes with
    nutrient agar
sterile cotton swabs
glass-marking crayon
transparent tape
dissecting microscope

PROCEDURE

1. Do not yet open any of the petri dishes containing nutrient agar. On the bottom of all 7, write your team's name and the date. Give each dish a number from 1 through 7.
2. Do nothing to Dish 1.
3. Remove the cover from Dish 2. Expose the dish to the air in your laboratory for 10 minutes. Then cover the dish again.
4. Using a sterile cotton swab, rub the surface of some part of a team member's face, hair, or hands. Carefully lift one side of the cover of Dish 3 without completely removing it. Slip in the swab and rub it over part of the surface of the agar. Be sure the swab does not cut into the surface of the agar.
5. You may want to divide Dish 3 into several parts and test samples from different parts of your body. If you do this, be sure to use another sterile swab for each sample. Indicate each part of the body tested on the bottom of the dish.
6. Using another cotton swab, wipe an area in your laboratory that has not been cleaned. Lift the cover of Dish 4, and streak the entire surface of the agar.
7. Using another clean swab, wipe an area in your laboratory that has been cleaned with soap and water. Streak the agar surface of Dish 5 with this swab.
8. Your team must decide how to expose the remaining 2 dishes. Try to make a comparison between 2 different conditions or areas in your school. For example, you may want to place 1 open dish in the corridor of your school for 10 minutes and compare the results to a dish that is left open in a quiet broom closet for 10 minutes. You may wish to cough or sneeze directly onto the agar surface of either of these dishes.
9. Tape all petri dishes closed. Incubate all the plates at room temperature for 3 or 4 days. Keep all the plates upside down. This will prevent water droplets that may

condense inside the cover from dripping onto the agar.
10. Observe all plates daily, and record your observations. (*Caution: At no time should you remove the cover of any petri dish. This is because harmful microorganisms can be picked up and cultivated even on this simple nutrient agar.*) Observe all your colonies through the cover. You may want to use a dissecting microscope to help in your observations.
11. Make sketches of the different kinds of colonies and write a description of each. Mold colonies are fuzzy and they are larger than bacterial colonies. Count the number of each kind of colony per plate. On the 4th day, answer the following questions.

DISCUSSION

(1) What are the results in Plate 1? What was the purpose of Plate 1? (2) What are the results in Plates 2 through 7? (3) How do you account for the presence or absence of microorganisms on the examined surfaces?

(4) Coughing or sneezing may spread droplets from mouth and nose to a distance of 3 m or more. The water in these droplets evaporates rapidly, leaving microscopic bits of dry matter that contain bacteria. Microorganisms from many other sources also may be carried on dust particles. How can you use this information to help interpret the class data? (5) Are microorganisms transmitted by touch alone? (6) Are microorganisms present in equal abundance throughout your school? (7) In your daily living how can you protect yourself and others from contamination by microorganisms?

FOR FURTHER INVESTIGATION

Does the kind of medium used in the petri dishes affect the count obtained at any one location? Does the temperature at which the plates are incubated affect the count? Design and carry out experiments that test hypotheses based on these questions.

Brian G. Platte

7−1 Two extremes in natural ecosystems where microorganisms might be found. A hot springs in Yellowstone National Park during the winter.

ECOLOGY OF MICROORGANISMS

Microorganisms live in all natural ecosystems. They grow on snowbanks at the poles. They live in hot springs that would scald larger organisms. Microorganisms live without free oxygen in the dark depths of lakes and seas. They can survive when carried high into the cold, thin atmosphere many kilometers above the earth.

When you study a biotic community, macroscopic plants and animals attract your attention. But in this same community there may be millions of unseen microorganisms. From an ecosystem viewpoint microorganisms are closely related to macroorganisms. Their patterns of distribution, however, are not so closely related. The distribution of macroscopic organisms is linked to geography. The distribution of microorganisms is not. For example, pond fishes in one region of the world may be different from those in other regions. Pond microorganisms, on the other hand, are likely to be much the same in all ponds. Ecologists often study patterns of distribution among microorganisms separately from those among macroscopic organisms.

Can you suggest a reason for this difference in distribution?

In your school you have discovered some habitats where microorganisms are found. Now let's consider two ecological relationships in which microorganisms are especially important. These are relationships in disease and in soil.

Henry Caserotti

MICROORGANISMS AND DISEASE

Dictionaries often define *disease* as a departure from a healthy state. Health is defined as the absence of disease. These definitions make the words "health" and "disease" like "hot" and "cold." Neither word of a pair has meaning without the other.

Biologists picture health in terms of the total life of the individual, and of the condition of every part of the body. Anything that affects the individual's best functioning may contribute to disease. A "germ" may be only one step.

You are certainly acquainted with some human diseases. Anyone who has a pet dog or cat knows that other animals also get diseases. Every person who grows potted plants knows that they, too, can become diseased. Diseases even occur among protists. All diseases are of interest to biologists, and the principles of **pathology** (the science of disease) apply to all organisms.

Find in Chapter 6 a condition of bacteria that might be called a disease.

pathology [Greek: *pathein,* to suffer, + *logos,* speech, reason]

SOME HISTORY

An early and common idea was that human disease came from evil spirits that entered the body. Obviously, then, the cure for illness was to get the spirits out. They might be frightened out or coaxed out. This became the function of witch doctors, with their masks, rattles, and charms. Even ancient people, however, did not rely entirely on magic. It was all right for the witch doctor to chase a toothache demon away, but, in the meantime, an application of coca leaves eased the pain.

7–2 Plants used in both ancient and modern medicine. *Datura metel* of India (*right*) contains a drug used as a calming drug for asthma. *Erythrozylon coca* of South America (*below*) is used for relieving pain.

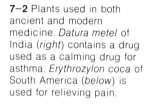

Field Museum of Natural History

John R. Clawson

Thus early people discovered practical remedies for certain illnesses. In fact, many of the drugs we use today have long histories — aspirin, for example. An extract of willow bark had long been used in folk medicine to relieve pain. The pain-relieving substance in the bark was synthesized by a German chemist in 1835. It was named salicylic acid. Later it was found that salicylic acid is more effective in combination with other chemicals. This compound was given the trade name Aspirin.

synthesized [SIN thuh syzd; Greek: *syn*, together, + *thesis*, an arranging]: here, meaning to form a more complex chemical substance from simpler substances

Physicians of ancient Greece developed some theories that led to better treatment for their patients. They developed the idea that health is related to the food we eat. And they began to investigate the effects of diet in illness. But there was little progress in the centuries that followed.

salicylic [sal uh SIL ik; Latin: *salix*, willow]

Do you remember what a theory is? See pages 12 and 70.

The first evidence that disease might be the result of the activities of microorganisms did not involve humans or any other animals. It came from the study of a plant disease. Late in the summer of 1845, potato plants throughout northern Europe were struck by a disease, a ***blight.*** Almost overnight whole fields of potatoes became black masses of rotting plants. In Ireland the consequences were disastrous, because most of the

blight [blyt]

7−3 Navajo healing ceremony. The medicine man (*right*) and a helper construct a design with colored powders. The young patient will sit in the middle of the design when it is finished.

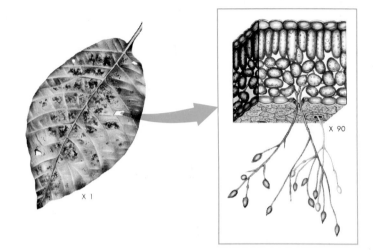

7–4 Late blight of potato. Infected leaflet (*left*). Section through the leaflet with hyphae of the fungus growing from it (*right*). The hyphae bear spore cases. (Note that the cube on the right is a very small piece lifted from the leaf on the left.)

people depended on potatoes as their main food. During the next two years nearly half a million Irish died in the *famine,* and two million emigrated to America.

Crop failures and famine had occurred many times in the past. The difference this time was that a scientific investigation could be made. It was soon found that the dead plants were full of fungal hyphae. But did the fungus appear because the plant was dead, or did it kill the plant?

Can you use terms from Chapter 3 to rephrase this question?

Early in the 19th century a French scientist formed a hypothesis that a certain fungus caused a disease of wheat. The evidence, however, did not strongly support the hypothesis. But the observations made on the potato blight could not be ignored. By 1861 another scientist had gathered convincing evidence that the blight was caused by the fungus in the potato plants.

By the end of the 19th century most scientists agreed that microorganisms caused disease. Just as all diseases were once blamed on evil spirits, it now seemed that all diseases might be caused by microorganisms. But diseases are not so simple. Today pathologists recognize many diseases in which microorganisms have little or no part.

CLASSIFYING DISEASES

Diseases may be classified in a few broad groups. First, we have diseases that are caused by microorganisms — *infectious diseases* ("germ diseases"). By "germ" we mean a microorganism that can reproduce. Viruses are certainly disease germs even though we may not call them living. Colds and influenza are infectious diseases.

infectious [in FEK shus; Latin: in, in, + facere, to make]

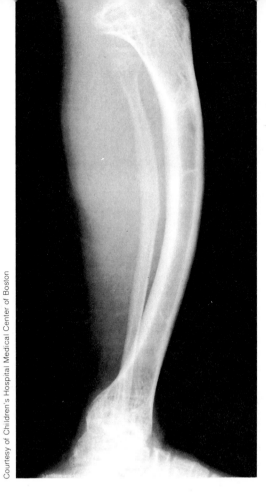

Courtesy of Children's Hospital Medical Center of Boston

USDA

7—6 A deficiency disease. Lack of iron affects the new leaves of a soybean plant.

7—5 Rickets, a disease resulting from lack of vitamin D.

There are many kinds of noninfectious diseases. **Deficiency diseases** develop when some necessary substance is lacking in an organism's diet. Scurvy, for example, is a human disease caused by the lack of vitamin C. **Vitamins** are organic substances that are essential in regulating or carrying on certain body activities. There are **environmental diseases**. These result from reaction to substances that invade the body of an organism but do not reproduce there. Asthma is such a disease. It often results when people inhale plant pollen. **Hereditary diseases** are disorders passed on by inheritance from one generation to the next. Sickle-cell anemia, a condition resulting in large-scale abnormality of red blood cells, is an example. There are also **degenerative diseases**, which are disorders in the functioning of an organism's body — usually as it becomes old. Arthritis and most heart diseases are examples.

Cancer is difficult to classify. Cancer is second only to heart diseases as a cause of death in the United States, but there is still much to be learned about it. A cancer is a rapidly spreading group of abnormal cells. The different types of cancers are

deficiency [dih FISH un see]

scurvy: characterized by weakness, spongy gums, and bleeding from mucous membranes

asthma [AZ muh; Greek: *azein*, to breathe hard]

degenerative [dih JEN uh rayt iv; Latin: *de*, away, + *genus*, race or kind]

arthritis [ar THRYT us; Greek: *arthron*, joint, + *itis*, (now) inflammation of]

named for the organ in which they are usually found. As a person grows older, the risk of some cancers seems to become greater. There are several hypotheses about how a cancer begins. At present, many medical scientists think most cancers are started by chemicals in the environment. These may be tars in tobacco smoke, chemicals used in manufacturing plastics, or nuclear wastes. On the other hand, many cancers have been found to contain viruses. And hereditary factors in an individual seem to be necessary for some cancers to start. Although this sounds complicated, scientists who study cancer see a pattern in these facts. Chemicals that cause cancer also cause hereditary changes. These changes in parents may cause cancer in their offspring. Also, viruses that may cause cancer could be passed from one generation to the next. Thus cancer, as a category of disease, may be environmental, infectious, *and* hereditary.

CHECK YOURSELF

A. How does study of ecological patterns of microorganisms differ from such study of macroorganisms?
B. With what is the study of pathology concerned?
C. What ideas of disease did early peoples and tribes accept?
D. What discoveries that are still useful did primitive people make in the treatment of disease?
E. How did biologists come to associate microorganisms with disease?
F. What are some of the major groups of diseases?
G. How does cancer fit into the classification of disease?

INFECTIOUS DISEASES

An infectious disease results from an interaction between two organisms. They are a *pathogen* — usually a microorganism — and a host. It is a kind of ecological relationship. Pathogen is not a synonym for parasite because not all parasites are pathogens. For instance, a parasite may live at the expense of another organism without producing *symptoms* (signs of illness). On the other hand, an organism that is not a parasite may still be involved in a disease. Examples are the fungi associated with athlete's foot and with ringworm. Neither is a parasite, but both are decomposers living on the dead layers of our skin. Yet the uncomfortable symptoms of athlete's foot certainly indicate a disease.

Transmission. An infectious disease is a *relationship* between pathogen and host. This means that the disease itself cannot be

pathogen [PATH uh jun; Greek: *pathein*, + *genes*, born]

symptoms [SIMP tumz; Greek: *syn*, together, + *piptein*, to fall]

transmission [trans MISH un; Latin: *trans*, across, + *mittere*, to send] *transmitted* (carried) from host to host. Rather, it is the pathogen that is transmitted. Scientists study the ways in which pathogens are transmitted to learn how to control infectious diseases.

Syphilis is a disease that results from infection of a human host by a protist called *Treponema pallidum*. This organism dies in seconds when exposed to light and air, but it survives inside the human body. There it multiplies and eventually may inhabit every part of the host. The first symptom of syphilis is a small open sore at the point of infection. The syphilis pathogens from this sore are easily transmitted when the sore touches any moist membrane of another person. This occurs most often during sexual intercourse. From two to six months after the appearance of the first sore, new symptoms appear—rashes, blotches, and more sores. By this time, the person with the disease no longer can transmit the organism. Symptoms may then disappear for a period of 10 to 20 years, while the protists attack internal body parts, especially nerves and the brain. Eventually this leads to blindness, deafness, or insanity. The human body cannot get rid of the organism that causes syphilis without some outside help, such as treatment with **antibiotics.** Antibiotics are chemicals that kill or slow the growth of microorganisms.

Malaria is a disease that results from infection of a host by protists of the genus *Plasmodium*. For infection to occur, the pathogenic organisms must first enter the host's bloodstream. They travel through the bloodstream to the liver, where they multiply. Their offspring move back into the blood, and enter red blood cells. As they continue to multiply, they destroy these cells. This destruction of blood cells takes place at definite intervals. At these times the host experiences alternating violent chills and high fever, the principal symptoms of the disease.

If an infected person happens to be bitten by a female mos-

syphilis [SIF uh lus]

Treponema pallidum
[trep uh NEE muh PAL uh dum]

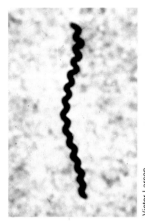

Victor Larsen

7−7 The pathogen of syphilis is a spirochete bacterium.   × 3,000

antibiotics [ant ih by OT iks; Greek: *anti*, against, + *bios*, life]

Why do you think only female mosquitoes bite and feed on the blood of animals?

7−8 Transmission of malaria. What would be the best way to stop the spread of this disease?

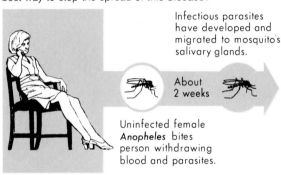

Infectious parasites have developed and migrated to mosquito's salivary glands.

About 2 weeks

Uninfected female **Anopheles** bites person withdrawing blood and parasites.

Human with forms of parasite in blood.

About 10 days

Infected mosquito bites healthy human.

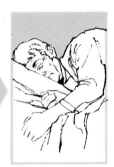

Parasites have developed and moved to person's blood.

Anopheles [uh NOF uh leez]

salivary glands [SAL uh ver ee glandz]. Saliva produced by these glands prevents the blood of a mosquito's victim from clotting.

contagious [kun TAY jus; Latin: *cum*, together, + *tangere*, to touch]

vector [Latin: carrier]

What other human diseases do you know that are considered contagious?

7—9 A housefly walked over the nutrient medium in this petri dish before incubation. How do you explain the results?

alternation [OL ter NAY shun; Latin: *alter*, other]

Rocky Mountain spotted fever is actually most common in the Atlantic coastal states. It has caused many deaths.

African sleeping sickness affects the nervous system of the mammalian host.

tsetse [TSET see]

How have populations of *Anopheles* mosquitoes been reduced?

What precautions should you take when a scratch or cut occurs in your skin?

virulence [VIR uh lunz; Latin: *virus*, poison]

quito of the genus *Anopheles*, the pathogens may be picked up by the insect. In the mosquito's body they undergo many changes. These microorganisms migrate through the mosquito's body to its salivary glands. When the mosquito bites another human, it injects saliva into the blood of its victim. If the mosquito has malarial parasites in its salivary glands, these are injected along with the saliva. In this way the disease is transmitted to a new host.

Syphilis is a **contagious** (or contact) **disease.** Because the syphilis protists do not survive drying, they must be transmitted directly from a moist surface of one person to a moist surface of another. Normally such contacts occur only in the regions of the mouth and the sexual organs. Malaria, on the other hand, is a **vector disease.** That is, the pathogen can get from one human host to another *only* when some other thing carries it. The vector of malaria is the mosquito.

The use of the word "vector" often implies a point of view. For humans, mosquitoes are vectors of malaria parasites. For mosquitoes, however, humans are the malarial vectors. From the biological point of view, we think of such relationships as involving an **alternation of hosts.**

Alternation of hosts is far from unusual. The hosts of Rocky Mountain spotted fever are ticks and humans (or rodents). African sleeping sickness involves tsetse flies and humans (or cattle). Human diseases with alternate-host transmission are not common in the United States today. We have been able to control most of the alternate hosts through sanitary measures. Malaria, for example, has almost disappeared wherever *Anopheles* mosquito populations have been destroyed.

Merely transmitting pathogens from one host to another does not necessarily result in disease. To be effective, a pathogen must enter the host. Many microorganisms exist at all times on human skin, but they are unable to get through the dead outer layers. However, any break in the skin may provide an entry. And certain microorganisms, such as those of syphilis, can get through moist inner membranes.

Virulence and resistance. How serious an infectious illness is depends on characteristics of both host and pathogen. The capability of a pathogen to affect its host is called its **virulence.** The ability of a host to cope with a pathogen is termed **resistance.** A pathogen with high virulence may cause death in a host with low resistance and severe illness in a host with medium resistance. Only mild symptoms may appear in a host with high resistance.

What determines the virulence of a pathogen? This is a complex problem, but consider some evidence. With diphtheria, damage to the host is the result of a poison produced by the pathogen *Corynebacterium diphtheriae*. Pure cultures of *C. diphtheriae* obtained from different sources produce different amounts of poison even though they are grown under identical conditions. In other words, different varieties of this bacterium have different virulences. Virulence (at least in *C. diphtheriae*) seems to be inherited. This, of course, is only a first step in investigating the problem of virulence.

Corynebacterium diphtheriae [kor uh nee bak TIR ee um dif-THIR ee ee]

Many microorganisms normally live on or in human bodies, especially on the skin or in the digestive system. One of the many that live in the intestines is the bacterium *Escherichia coli*. Usually it causes no harm there. It is usually a commensal. However, the distribution of microorganisms may change within the human body. *E. coli* has been found in human bladders, where it can cause disease. It also has infected the kidney and the heart. These changes in where we find *E. coli* are related to changes both in the human environment and in human behavior. The widespread use of antibiotics has affected other intestinal microorganisms. This may have allowed *E. coli* to move into organs where it is normally not found. The use of unsterilized needles by persons using drugs may have led to the presence of *E. coli* in heart infections. Thus *E. coli* has in some cases changed from a commensal to a pathogen.

Escherichia coli [esh uh RIK ee-uh KOH lye]

Why is *E. coli* referred to here as a commensal?

Immunity. Why do different individuals of the same host species have different degrees of resistance? This is another complex problem. We can develop varieties of domestic plants and animals that are more resistant to particular diseases than are other varieties. It seems, therefore, that some resistance involves inherited characteristics.

immunity [im YEW nut ee]

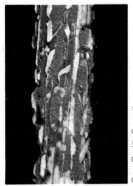

On the other hand, much resistance is not inherited. It may be acquired during the lifetime of an individual. When a human host is invaded by a pathogen, or any other foreign protein, the host produces ***antibodies.*** Antibodies combat the pathogen or the poisons produced by it. If the host survives the infection, its body may retain the ability to produce these antibodies. Then, if a new infection by the same kind of pathogen occurs, the host's body can act immediately against it. Such resistance is called ***immunity.***

Antibodies may be produced even though the virulence of a pathogen is too low to produce symptoms. Thus a person may become immune without knowing it. By the time they reach adulthood, many people have had some contact with the pathogens of poliomyelitis and tuberculosis and have acquired some immunity to these diseases.

Each kind of antibody is effective only against the particular pathogen that brought about its production or sometimes

Crop Quality Council

7–10 Stem rust of wheat. The pathogen, a fungus, has barberry as an alternate host. Some varieties of wheat have an inherited resistance to the disease.   × 1

poliomyelitis [poh lee oh my uh-LYT us]: a disease in which a virus attacks nerves of its host, frequently leaving the host crippled

typhoid fever: a disease centered in the digestive system of the host

against very similar pathogens. For example, an antibody produced as the result of an infection by typhoid bacteria has no effect on diphtheria bacteria.

Sometimes immunity does not last long, as with the common cold. Sometimes it is lifelong, as with mumps. The strength of immunity to a disease may vary too. An organism's immunity may be strong enough to ward off an attack by a weakly virulent variety of a pathogen, but it may not be effective against a strongly virulent variety.

The immunity discussed so far occurs as a result of chance infection. Fortunately, we do not have to depend entirely on inherited resistance or natural immunity. We can produce immunity in various artificial ways.

artificial [art uh FISH ul; Latin: *ars*, art, + *facere*, to make]

Edward Jenner: 1749–1823. English physician

In the late 18th century smallpox was a common and often fatal disease. Edward Jenner observed that people who worked with cows seldom had smallpox, although they usually had been infected by a mild disease of cattle called cowpox. Jenner concluded that a person might become immune to smallpox by being deliberately infected with cowpox. He developed this idea into a successful medical procedure — *vaccination.*

vaccination [vak suh NAY shun; Latin: *vacca*, cow]. Why is it improper to use this term as a synonym for "immunization"?

Today we have several ways of bringing about artificial immunity. The kind of antibody formed in a host depends on the kind of pathogen rather than on the kind of host. It is possible, then, to inject a pathogen into a nonhuman host, such as a horse, where antibodies are produced. These antibodies can be removed from the blood of the horse and then injected into a person. Sometimes the pathogens themselves, weakened or dead, can be injected into a human being to stimulate the production of antibodies without producing symptoms of disease. This method is used in immunizing against poliomyelitis.

Antibiotics. For some diseases, such as syphilis, no effective

7–11 A cartoonist of Jenner's day shows the fears that vaccination aroused.

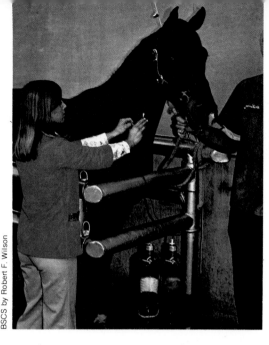

7–12 Drawing blood containing antibodies that will be used in treating a human disease. What advantage do horses have for this purpose?

BSCS by Robert F. Wilson

artificial immunity has been developed. Syphilis can often be controlled with penicillin, an antibiotic. Antibiotics are natural products of microorganisms, especially certain bacteria and fungi. Many can be developed in the laboratory. Such antibiotics are used to combat some infectious diseases. Antibiotics cannot be formed by the human body as antibodies are.

Antibiotics are selective. A particular antibiotic may kill or slow the growth of one kind of organism but not another. Those that act against disease-causing organisms without being toxic to humans are of most medical interest. Penicillin was discovered when an English scientist, Alexander Fleming, noticed that one of his culture plates was contaminated with a mold. The blue-green mold was a species of *Penicillium* similar to what you may find on a spoiled orange. Fleming observed that no bacteria were growing around the mold though they could be found in all other parts of the plate. He concluded that the growth of the bacteria had been inhibited by some substance produced by the mold. Fleming isolated the substance and named it penicillin. It is still commonly used today to control infections.

If antibiotics can control infectious diseases, why do we still suffer from many pathogen-caused illnesses? For one thing, there are many infectious diseases that no antibiotic can control. Virus-caused colds and other virus diseases are good examples. Sometimes, when antibiotics have been used to control a disease, disease organisms that are resistant to the treatment appear. In such cases larger doses of the antibiotic are used to combat the pathogen. But sometimes they are ineffective. Another major problem is that some patients are allergic to an antibiotic. The reaction to the antibiotic may be more violent than to the pathogen. In addition, some antibiotics may kill beneficial bacteria in the body.

CHECK YOURSELF

H. What is the difference between a pathogen and a parasite?
I. Contrast the ways in which the pathogens of syphilis and malaria are transmitted.
J. What is meant by an alternation of hosts?
K. Why do different host individuals react differently to infection by the same kind of pathogen?
L. In what ways may resistance to a specific infectious disease be acquired?
M. What is an antibiotic substance?
N. Why can't antibiotics control all infectious diseases?

Investigation 7.2   CONTROL OF BACTERIA

INTRODUCTION

In this investigation you will observe some relationships of bacteria and substances used to control them.

PROCEDURE

1. With a glass-marking crayon, mark the *bottoms* of the plates as follows: Label your 4 plates *A, B, C,* and *D*. Divide each plate into 4 sections. Number the sections *1, 2, 3,* and *4*. On Plates B and D print "control."

2. In this investigation you should follow the same *sterile procedures* and *cautions* as in Investigations 6.3 and 7.1.

   Sterilize an inoculating loop in the flame of a bunsen burner. Streak the entire surface of Plates A and B with *Sarcina lutea* as shown in figure 6–23.

3. Streak the entire surface of Plates C and D with *Escherichia coli*.

4. Use forceps to place 1 disk with no chemical in each section of Plates B and D.

5. Your teacher will have a variety of antiseptic, disinfectant, and antibiotic solutions. Choose any 4 of these. Make cer-

MATERIALS
(per team)

4 antiseptic disks
4 antibiotic disks
8 disks with no chemicals
broth cultures of *Sarcina lutea* and *Escherichia coli*
4 sterile nutrient agar plates
glass-marking crayon
forceps
inoculating loop
bunsen burner
transparent tape

tain, however, that at least 1 disk is dipped into an antibiotic.

6. Using forceps, pick up a clean disk. Dip it into one of the solutions you selected. Remove the disk. Gently shake off excess liquid. Quickly place it in section 1 of Plate A. Dip another disk into the same solution. Dry it, and place it in section 1 of Plate C. Be sure the disks are stuck to the agar surface, but do not break through it.

7. Repeat this procedure with 3 other solutions, placing them in sections 2, 3, and 4 of Plates A and C.

8. In your data book, record the section in which you place each disk. Also record the substance in which you dipped each disk.
9. Cover and tape all 4 plates. Invert them and incubate at 37°C.
10. Observe all plates after 1 or 2 days. Record your observations.

DISCUSSION

(1) What do the clear areas indicate? (2) What evidence do you have that the inhibition of microorganisms is due to the chemicals on the disks and not the disks themselves? (3) Which of the 2 species of bacteria is more sensitive to all the chemicals? (4) Which product would you use to control *Sarcina lutea*? To control *Escherichia coli*?

E. coli are normally harmless bacteria that live in the human intestines. (5) Does the reaction of *E. coli* to antibiotics suggest that antibiotics should be used only when necessary? Explain. (6) How does an antibiotic differ from a disinfectant?

FOR FURTHER INVESTIGATION

Test different concentrations of the same antibiotic. Be sure to have at least 1 antibiotic disk and 1 antiseptic disk in each plate to compare their effects.

ENVIRONMENT AND DISEASE

During famines more people die from disease than from starvation. At such times a moderately virulent pathogen may produce serious illness. Environmental factors, such as lack of food, may affect the host, the pathogen, or both. A host that is poorly nourished has much less resistance than it would have if well fed. The improved diet of the United States population in the past half century probably has been an important factor in reducing cases of tuberculosis and other diseases. Environmental factors also may affect the ability of a pathogen to infect its host. For example, fungi that attack human skin grow best in a warm, moist atmosphere. In some parts of the tropics these pathogens are very active. In much of the United States they usually find such favorable conditions only inside clothing. Athlete's foot fungi, for example, grow inside shoes and stockings.

Combating infectious disease involves much more than killing pathogens. It is a complex ecological problem involving the pathogen, the host, and the environment in which they interact.

Medical scientists have learned to control many infectious diseases and have begun to investigate environmental diseases. These diseases are caused by environmental substances other than "germs." Many such substances are produced by human activities. They are **pollutants.** In the United States heavily industralized regions show high percentages of persons with certain environmental diseases. But there are many sources of pollution. Coal miners may develop "black lung," an environ-

pollutants [puh LOOT unts]

mental disease caused by breathing coal dust. Asbestos workers develop lung and other diseases caused by intake of asbestos particles. Some disease-causing pollutants affect everyone in the community. The waste gases from automobiles have
become a general threat to human health. Among other poisonous substances in automobile waste gas is lead. In some cities
the amount of lead in smog has become large enough to affect
the activity of people who live there.

POPULATIONS AND DISEASE

Modern physicians recognize that disease is an ecological problem. Many devote much time and thought to disease in populations — what is often called "public health." Some physicians
today never see individual patients. Instead, they specialize in
controlling disease in whole populations. To do this, they study
changes in the frequency of diseases in populations. They also
study the geographical distribution of diseases and the ways in
which diseases spread.

Public health departments often have a large staff that operates behind the scenes to protect your health. In this country,
milk, meat, other foods, water, and air are tested regularly to
determine their effects on human health. For example, meat
must be checked by government inspectors before it can be sold
in public markets.

epidemic [ep uh DEM ik; Greek: *epi*, upon, + *demos*, the people]

Epidemics. An *epidemic* is a severe outbreak of a disease in
a host population that often causes alarm and panic. An epidemic can be understood best in relation to the usual, *endemic,*
situation. In the endemic situation a pathogenic species may
only occasionally successfully infect members of its host
species. Many infectious disease organisms exist in the endemic state and can cause epidemics given the right conditions.
These "right conditions" generally include increased chances
for transmitting the pathogen from one host to another. This
could happen when a sick person walks into a room crowded
with potential hosts. The right conditions may be lowered resistance in the host population or increased virulence in the
pathogen population.

endemic [en DEM ik; Greek: *en*, in, + *demos*]

An epidemic does not always affect the entire population of
a species. Most human adults have acquired immunity to measles and today most children are vaccinated against the disease.
Before the days of artificial immunization, however, measles
epidemics occurred among children. Syphilis, gonorrhea, and
other *venereal* diseases have long been endemic. Venereal diseases are those in which the pathogens are transmitted mainly
by sexual contact between host individuals. Within recent years
they have become epidemic in the 15- to 25-year age group of

Epidemics of noninfectious diseases can occur. Can you find any examples?

venereal [vuh NIR ee ul; Latin: *Venus*, goddess of love]

Why do you think this epidemic has occurred?

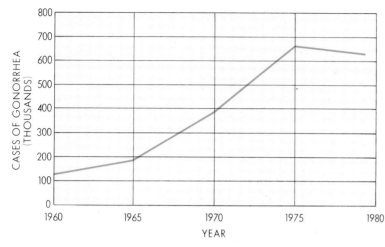

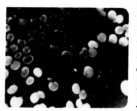

7–13 The bacterium of gonorrhea, *Neisseria gonorrhoeae.*   × 15,200

7–14 Number of cases of gonorrhea among people ages 15–24 in the United States.

urban and suburban populations. Immunity to these diseases either does not exist or is very short.

Epidemics sometimes occur when control methods break down. Typhoid fever is not common in the United States, but its pathogen, *Salmonella typhi*, is not an extinct organism. Any careless treatment or disposal of sewage could result in a typhoid epidemic in any city.

Perhaps the worst epidemics have occurred when diseases were introduced into populations that had no hereditary resistance. Measles seldom kills Europeans (except infants). However, it became a deadly disease when it was introduced among Pacific island people by European explorers and colonizers.

Geography of disease. Many human infectious diseases are now almost worldwide. Examples are colds and influenza. With modern transportation they have spread everywhere. They persist wherever the human population is dense enough to support them.

Through history the geographic patterns of human diseases have shifted greatly. We have just mentioned the introduction of measles into the Pacific islands. We know, too, that many infectious diseases of the Old World, such as smallpox, were absent from America until European explorers brought them here. It is also possible that the New World contributed diseases to the Old. Syphilis suddenly became prominent in Europe about 1500 A.D. Some medical historians have supposed that it was brought back by Columbus' sailors. This is by no means certain. Old descriptions of diseases and epidemics are usually incomplete and difficult to interpret.

Salmonella typhi [sal muh NEL uh TY fy]: the pathogen of typhoid fever; not related to typhus fever, in which the pathogen is a rickettsia

A pathogen that requires an alternation of hosts can occur only in places where both hosts live. African sleeping sickness, for instance, is transmitted by tsetse flies. This disease is found only where tsetse flies and humans are found together. It is thought that yellow fever also originated in Africa. The vector of this disease is a species of mosquito, *Aedes aegypti*. Breeding in the water kegs of ships, the mosquitoes were carried from Africa to the New World. Today constant checking by public health specialists prevents transportation of disease organisms around the world.

Aedes aegypti [ay EED eez ee JIP ty]

7-15 Yellow fever in the American tropics. Forest mosquitoes (*shown on white circle*) transmit the pathogen from one monkey to another. People in the forest may acquire the pathogen from these mosquitoes. Infected people, in turn, may be the source of infection for others if *Aedes* mosquitoes (*on orange circle*) are not controlled.

7-16 Distribution of tsetse flies in Africa. Into what parts of the world is African sleeping sickness most likely to spread?

Can you name some of these substances?

Changing patterns of human disease. Long ago, human populations were small and scattered. The most common diseases were probably those infectious ones people shared with wild animals. The infectious organisms were carried by vectors back and forth between human hosts and other animals. As human populations increased, the spread of infectious diseases increased. As late as 1920, they were the leading cause of death in the United States.

During the 20th century, deaths from infectious diseases have declined greatly all over the world. This is a result of increased knowledge of their causes and spread. Many ways have been developed to combat diseases. We use substances that kill the microorganisms or their vectors. In some countries, including the United States, the improvement of general health through abundant good food has helped also. Today, in the United States, degenerative diseases cause more deaths than any other. There are signs that environmental diseases, involving various pollutants, are becoming a leading cause of death.

CHECK YOURSELF

O. How may environmental factors affect an infectious disease?

P. Why must any infectious disease be considered an ecological problem?

Q. Why have environmental diseases become an increasing health problem?

R. What is the difference between endemic- and epidemic-disease situations?

S. How have the geographical patterns of infectious diseases changed?

T. Why are some human infectious diseases found only in certain geographic regions?

U. Why have the kinds of diseases that are the leading causes of human death changed through history?

SOIL ECOSYSTEMS

Farmers often pick up a handful of soil and let it trickle through their fingers. From its feel, odor, and appearance, they can tell a great deal about its condition and the kinds of crops that can be grown in it. They know that they hold in their hands the source of their livelihood. The rest of us — 95 percent of the United States population — often forget that we, too, depend on this soil. Our dependence, of course, is by way of the supermarket.

What source of human food does *not* depend on soil?

COMPONENTS OF SOIL

Soil is a complex mixture of substances derived from rocks, air, and remains of living things. It also contains living things themselves. Soil is an ecosystem.

components [kum POH nunts; Latin: *cum*, together, + *ponere*, to put, place]: substances that are part of a more complex substance

Inorganic components. Heating and cooling, freezing and thawing, wetting and drying weaken the structure of rocks. Minerals in rocks react chemically with water and air that enter through tiny cracks and crevices. Thus rocks break up, and the loose, weathered material becomes the basic ingredient of soil.

derived [dih RYVD]: obtained from a source

7–17 Boulder of granite weathering into mineral soil particles. Rock surface peels off like the layers of an onion.

J. R. Stacy/USGS

Each rock particle holds a thin layer of moisture. In the spaces between particles are tiny pockets of gases, mostly the gases of the atmosphere. If the soil is very wet, the spaces between particles may be filled with water and not much air. Many substances that soil organisms need are dissolved in soil water. Some of these are organic and some are inorganic. From rock particles come inorganic compounds containing sulfur, calcium, potassium, magnesium, and other elements mentioned in Chapter 1.

What are the principal gases of the atmosphere?

7−18 Inorganic substances in soil. Water clings to mineral particles. Usually, the larger the particles, the larger are the air spaces. Dissolved substances are not visible at this degree of magnification.

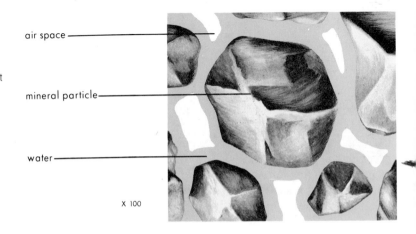

air space

mineral particle

water

X 100

humus [HEW mus; Latin: ground, soil]

decomposition [dee kom puh ZISH un]

Humus. Terrestrial organisms obtain the materials for their bodies directly or indirectly from soil. At death, their bodies return to the soil. Much energy and many nutrients are locked up in them. Soil organisms get the remaining energy out of these dead substances. Through this *decomposition* process the substances are eventually returned to such inorganic forms as minerals, gases, and water.

Much decomposition is accomplished by microorganisms. It occurs most rapidly under the warm, moist conditions that favor their growth. However, in all climates this activity takes time, so organic substances usually occur in soil in various stages of decomposition. When decomposition has reached a point where the original organisms can no longer be distinguished, the remaining organic substance is called *humus.*

Give some reasons why desert soils have low percentages of humus.

bog: wet, spongy ground in marshes and swamps

In general, the darker a soil is, the more humus it contains. Because humus is derived from dead matter that falls onto the surface, most of it occurs in the top layer of soil. The proportion of humus in the top layer varies from about 1 percent in desert soils to 70 percent in some bog soils.

USDA

USDA

7 – 19 Sections through soils. A forest soil in North Carolina (*left*).
A prairie soil in Nebraska (*right*). Which appears to have more humus?

Humus increases the water-holding ability of soil and the amount of air space. It also helps to control the soil temperature. These functions of humus tend to improve the soil as a habitat for living organisms. But there can be too much of a good thing. Humus also increases the acidity of soils. This makes bog soils unfavorable to most organisms — including many of the decomposers themselves.

How does this help to explain the high percentage of humus in bog soils?

Soil organisms. Ground squirrels and other rather large animals dig into soil. Though they have few direct relationships with soil communities, they affect soil environments and belong to soil ecosystems. Moles seldom go above ground, so they have more direct ties to soil communities. Earthworms are full-time members of soil ecosystems.

ground squirrels. See figure 8–1.

When have you seen earthworms come out of the soil ecosystem on their own?

The majority of soil organisms are small animals. Arthropods — centipedes, millipedes, mites, isopods, and insects — are abundant in soil. Microscopic animals live in soil water along with some protists.

isopods [EYE suh podz; Greek *isos*, equal, + *poda*, foot or feet]

Bacteria are more widely distributed in the biosphere than any other organism. The importance of bacteria in soils was

BSCS by Bert Kempers

7 – 20 Two members of a soil community, an isopod (sow bug) and an earthworm.

actinomycetes [ak tuh noh MY-seetz; Greek: *aktinos*, ray, + *myketes*, mushrooms]

cellulose [SEL yuh los]

Why would algae be unlikely to grow deep in soil?

first pointed out in 1900. It was not until the 1920's, however, that soil microbiologists began to take much interest in them. When they cultured soil samples, 30 to 40 percent of the colonies that appeared belonged to a group of bacteria called actinomycetes. Some of these decompose cellulose, one of the most abundant materials in plant remains. They also are responsible for the pleasant, earthy smell of freshly turned soil.

More than 60 different species of algae have been found in soil samples. Algae sometimes develop as green, slimy growths on wet soils. In rice paddies, algae contribute to the nitrogen and oxygen content of the soil and help to increase crop yields.

CHECK YOURSELF
   V. Why is soil called an ecosystem?
   W. What are the nonliving components of a soil?
   X. Why is decomposition an important process?
   Y. What is humus?
   Z. What are the principal groups of organisms in a soil ecosystem?

Investigation 7.3 MEASURING SOIL pH

INTRODUCTION

Several abiotic factors, such as the size of soil particles and soil temperature, affect soil macroorganisms and plants. Farmers and soil scientists are interested in the concentrations of nitrogen, phosphorus, and oxygen and in the acidity of the soil.

Whether a solution is acid or basic is indicated by a series of numbers from 0 to 14 called the *pH scale.* The pH numbers below 7 indicate *acid* solutions (the smaller the number, the greater the acidity). The pH numbers above 7 indicate *basic* solutions (the larger the number, the lower the acidity).

The pH scale is a tool that indicates the *concentration* (number) of hydrogen *ions* present in a solution. At each step on the pH scale, from 0 to 14, the concentration of hydrogen ions is 10 times greater than at the next step. Ions are electrically charged chemical particles. An uncharged particle is chemically very different from its ion.

Water molecules are made up of 2 particles of hydrogen to 1 particle of oxygen. In any water sample a few water molecules break up into their ions. Each of these water molecules then forms 1 hydrogen ion with a positive electrical charge (H^+) and 1 *hydroxide* ion with a negative charge (OH^-). In pure water there are equal numbers of hydrogen and hydroxide ions. Such water is *neutral* and has a pH of 7.

If the amount of liquid remains the same, but pH has changed from 7 to 6, the concentration of hydrogen ions is 10 times greater than it was at pH 7. When pH is 8, the concentration of hydrogen ions has been reduced to 1/10 of what it was at pH 7. A pH of 9 indicates that the number of hydrogen ions is now 1/10 that of pH 8 (or 1/100 that of pH 7).

The pH of a solution is measured most accurately by means of electrical instruments. It can also be measured with chemical indicators. Many soluble *pigments* (colored substances) change chemically when there is an increase or a decrease in the pH of the water in which they are dissolved. This chemical change in the pigment changes its color.

For many such pigments the pH at which the color change occurs is known. These pigments can be used as indicators to determine the pH of an unknown solution. Often it is more convenient to use indicator paper than a pigment solution. Indicator paper is prepared by soaking porous paper in a pigment solution and then allowing it to dry. A number of pigments may be combined in the same paper, so that different ones do not have to be tried separately.

PART A: ACTION OF INDICATORS
PROCEDURE

MATERIALS
(per team)

3 dropping bottles, 10-ml, 1 for
   each of the following:
   distilled water
   0.1N hydrochloric acid solution
   0.1N sodium hydroxide solution
pH test paper, wide-range
forceps
2 glass microscope slides
glass stirring rod

1. Place one drop of the hydrochloric acid solution on one end of a clean glass slide. *(Caution: Be careful not to touch the test solutions. If you do, wash your hands immediately and consult your teacher.)*
2. Using the forceps, touch a 1-cm piece of pH paper to the acid solution.
3. Record your observations. Measure the pH by comparing the color of the paper with

the color scale on the package.

4. On the other end of your slide, place one drop of sodium hydroxide solution.
5. Touch a 1-cm piece of pH paper to the solution and record your observations.
6. Place a drop of distilled water on the end of another slide and test it with the pH paper.
7. Place a drop of hydrochloric acid on the other end and add a drop of sodium hydroxide. Mix with the glass stirring rod. Test this mixture with the pH paper.

PART B: pH OF SOIL SAMPLES
PROCEDURE

MATERIALS
(per team)

3 or more soil samples
pH test paper, wide-range,
   1 cm per soil sample
distilled water
test tubes, 1 per soil sample
microscope slide, 1 per soil
   sample
glass stirring rod
graduated cylinder, 25-ml
mortar and pestle
test-tube rack
glass-marking crayon
plastic bags for soil samples

1. Collect soil samples from at least 3 different environments around your school or home. Give each sample a number. For each location record the following: kind of vegetation that grows in the soil (grass, shrubs, trees); kind and amount of dead plant material (litter) lying on the ground. Also record any soil organisms that you may find in your sample.
2. Place about 10 g soil from one sample in a mortar. Add 10 ml distilled water. Grind.
3. Pour the mixture into a test tube labeled with the number of the soil sample.
4. Wash the mortar and pestle and rinse with distilled water before preparing the next sample.
5. Repeat this procedure for each sample. Let the tubes stand 10 minutes.
6. Place one microscope slide in front of each test tube. Put a small piece of pH test paper on each slide.
7. Dip a glass stirring rod into the 1st sample and transfer a drop of the liquid to the test paper. Note the color of the test paper where the drop has been placed and compare it with the color scale that comes with the paper. Record the pH of the sample.
8. Repeat this procedure for each sample, washing and drying the stirring rod before each test.

7–21 A group of students study soil characteristics, including pH and soil organisms.

BSCS photo by Richard R. Tolman

DISCUSSION

(1) According to the introduction, what should the pH of distilled water be? How did your results compare with this? (2) What was the pH of the acid solution? Of the hydroxide solution? (3) What would be the pH of a solution made up of equal amounts of an acid (pH 5) and a base (pH 9)? (4) What was the pH of the acid-hydroxide mixture you made?

(5) What are the pH ranges of your soil samples? (6) From what kind of environment did your most acid soil come? (7) From what kind did your most basic soil come? (8) Suggest reasons for the differences in soil pH.

COMMUNITY RELATIONSHIPS IN SOIL

Most soil organisms are consumers. Algae, which are producers, can live only at the surface and are rare in many soils. A soil ecosystem, therefore, is like a city: its food supply comes from outside. In soil some food comes into the roots of plants from their green parts, which are in the sunlight. But most of the food supply comes from the remains of organisms. Therefore, decomposers are important organisms in soil communities.

Decomposer relationships. In a dead leaf or twig lying on the soil surface, there are large amounts of complex organic substances such as starch. Likewise, in a dead animal there are complex organic substances such as fats and proteins. These are used as food by beetles and other small animals living in the upper soil or on its surface. But other substances, such as cellulose in plant bodies and chitin in insect bodies, can be used only by microorganisms. Microorganisms that use cellulose and chitin leave simpler organic substances as waste products. These wastes still contain energy. Other microorganisms then use these waste products. Even these decomposers may not extract all the energy. They may leave very simple substances — such as sugars — that still other kinds of organisms may use. Thus, one decomposer organism depends on another for its food supply. Such a food chain is like an assembly line in reverse. Instead of building step by step from simpler to more complex things, the food chain breaks down complex organic substances. At the end of the chain, only inorganic substances, such as carbon dioxide, water, and mineral compounds, remain.

Some substances that soil organisms produce harm other organisms. Such an antibiotic substance accumulates in the soil around the organism that forms it. It then reduces growth of competing organisms. We have seen how some of these antibiotic substances are used for combating bacterial infections in humans. The drug Aureomycin, derived from an actinomycete, is an example.

On the other hand, a number of soil organisms produce

Haven Kolb

7–22 Fungi grow from humus of a forest soil.

chitin [KYT un]: a substance that forms part or most of the exoskeletons of arthropods

Aureomycin [or ee oh MYS un]. What other antibiotics that are used in medicine do you know?

7–23 (*A*) A shrub, *Salvia leucophylla*. (*B*) A bare area about 2 m wide bordered by small herbs. (*C*) Grassland. Try to explain this interrelationship of plants.

promote [pruh MOT; Latin: *pro*, forward, + *movere*, to move]: here, to further or to advance

What kind of ecological relationship would you call this?

mycorrhizae [my kuh RY zee; Greek: *mykes*, fungus, + *rhiza* root]

7–24 Pine roots without mycorrhizae (*left*). Pine roots with mycorrhizae (*right*). What differences do you see?

substances that promote the growth of other organisms. Some species of yeast increase the growth of certain neighboring bacteria. Some species of bacteria are more abundant around the roots of certain plants than elsewhere in the soil. This pattern of distribution seems to be caused by substances these roots give off.

If you trace fungal hyphae in loose soil, you often find that many lead to plant roots. There the fungi form feltlike covers around branches of the roots. Some of the fungal hyphae grow into the other parts of the roots and form masses of tissue there. These associations between fungi and roots are called *mycorrhizae.*

Mycorrhizal pine seedlings were compared with nonmycorrhizal seedlings of the same species, growing in the same kind of soil. The mycorrhizal seedlings took up almost twice as

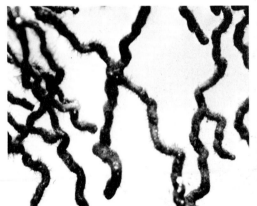

much nitrogen and potassium and more than three times as much phosphorus. All three of these substances are needed for the growth of the seedlings. In many such experiments plants definitely benefited from the mycorrhizal relationship. Some plants—orchids, for example—either do not grow or grow poorly if their mycorrhizal fungi are not present. The mycorrhizal fungi also benefit from the association. They absorb food from the roots of their plant partners.

What kind of ecological relationship occurs in mycorrhizae?

Parasites and predators. The parasite-host relationship is frequent in soil communities. In farm soils nematodes are important parasites. This is because many species attack the roots of crops and may damage or kill them. On the other hand, some species of nematodes parasitize insects that damage crops. In these two cases the parasite-host relationships are similar. But from the human viewpoint one is good and the other is bad.

Check "A Catalog of Living Things," Appendix 3.

Predator-prey relationships also occur among soil organisms. Centipedes and beetles prey on smaller animals. Slime molds, amebas, and ciliates feed on bacteria. Predatory protists act as one of the chief biotic factors influencing populations of soil bacteria.

How are the words "good" and "bad" being used here? Would this statement be true if the insects attacked by the nematodes were honeybees?

In soil ecosystems even plants act as predators. Several species of soil fungi form hyphae with tough branches that curl into loops. The tips of the loops from adjacent hyphae intermesh, forming a network that produces a sticky fluid. Nematodes are caught and held fast despite violent struggles. Other hyphae then grow into the bodies of the captive nematodes and consume them.

adjacent [Latin: *ad,* toward, near, + *jacere,* to lie]

Robert Bjork/USDA

7—25 Golden nematode infection of potato roots. Swollen females—the berrylike objects—bear eggs, which can live in soil from year to year.

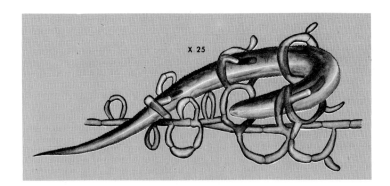

7–26 A nematode trapped in fungal hyphae.

CHECK YOURSELF

AA. What is the principal part played by microorganisms in a soil ecosystem?

BB. What kind of community relationship is represented by mycorrhizae?

CC. What evidence is there for this relationship?

DD. How can a single, ecological relationship be both "good" and "bad" from a human viewpoint?

EE. Give some examples of predation in a soil ecosystem.

Investigation 7.4   CELLULOSE DECOMPOSITION

INTRODUCTION

If all the water were removed from your body, your tissues would contain 15 to 20 percent carbon, on a dry-mass basis. The ultimate source of all this carbon is the atmospheric gas, carbon dioxide. As you read in Chapter 1, carbon dioxide is used by producers to build plant tissue. Consumers eat the producers, and the carbon is passed on to them. When producers and consumers die, their bodies are reservoirs of carbon compounds. After a long period of time, our source of carbon would be depleted if there was no way to release this

MATERIALS
(per team)

trowel (for collecting soil)
2 plastic bags (for soil samples)
500 ml sterile distilled water
5 sterile test tubes containing filter-paper strip and salt solution
4 empty test tubes
2 pipettes, 1-ml
test-tube rack
incubator
balance
glass-marking crayon
paper
pencil

trapped carbon.

We eat carbon-containing food. In our bodies, energy and nutrients are removed from the food, and carbon dioxide is released to the atmosphere when we exhale. But our bodies cannot break down all materials that contain carbon.

The most common carbon compound in plants and probably the most abundant compound in nature is cellulose. Most macroorganisms cannot break down cellulose. How, then, is the carbon in cellulose returned to the atmosphere?

In this activity you will investigate this question using soil samples. As a source of cellulose, you will use filter paper. (Most paper is made from wood products, and wood contains cellulose.)

PROCEDURE

1. Collect a soil sample from an area near your school or home. Note the vegetation at the location of the sample and the amount of litter.
2. Label 4 empty test tubes *1, 2, 3,* and *4.* Place 9 ml sterile distilled water in each tube.
3. Prepare soil dilutions of 1/10, 1/100, 1/1,000, and 1/10,000. To do this, carefully weigh and add 1 g soil to Tube 1. Place your thumb over the top of the tube and shake vigorously 50 times.
4. Using a sterile pipette, transfer 1 ml of the solution in Tube 1 to Tube 2. Shake.
5. Continue the dilution series. Between each dilution, rinse the pipette with distilled water.
6. Label 5 sterile test tubes (containing salt solution and the filter-paper strip) *A, B, C, D,* and *E.* Put your team symbol on each tube.
7. Using a clean pipette, transfer 1 ml of the 1/10 soil dilution from Tube 1 to Tube A.
8. Transfer 1 ml of the 1/100 solution from Tube 2 to Tube B.

9. Transfer 1 ml of the solution in Tube 3 to Tube C, and 1 ml from Tube 4 to Tube D. Do nothing to Tube E.
10. Place Tubes A – E in a test-tube rack and incubate at 28°C.
11. Examine these tubes periodically for evidence of decomposition in the strip of filter paper.
12. After 14 days, make your final observations. Describe the changes in each tube.
13. Shake Tube 1 vigorously. Note and record evidence of the amount of deterioration of the paper.

DISCUSSION

(*1*) What is the evidence that the paper has been decomposed? (*2*) What is the result in each tube? (*3*) Why was Tube E used? (*4*) Compare your results with other teams. In which type of soil was cellulose decomposition greatest?

(*5*) How does this relate to the vegetation and the amount of litter found at each sample site? (*6*) Young plants may be eaten by herbivores, but woody plants are difficult to eat. Both types of plants contain cellulose. Would it take longer for carbon to be returned to the atmosphere if the plants are eaten or if they are left to decompose? (*7*) What do you think caused the decomposition of the paper?

FOR FURTHER INVESTIGATION

To observe the possible cause of decomposition, remove a fragment of partially decomposed paper with forceps. Transfer the paper to a microscope slide. Tease the paper fibers apart. Fix by immersion in ethanol. Stain for 2 to 3 minutes with a solution of 1% erythrosin and 5% phenol in water. Wash in distilled water. Stain for 5 to 10 minutes with 0.1% aqueous solution of crystal violet. Observe under a microscope. Observe the microorganisms and their positions in regard to the cellulose fibers.

THE NITROGEN CYCLE

Refer to Chapter 1.

Soil microorganisms are essential in the chemical cycles of the biosphere, particularly in the nitrogen cycle.

Nitrogen gas makes up about 78 percent of the atmosphere. Yet the great majority of organisms cannot use it. We ourselves take it in at every breath and breathe it out unused. Likewise, elemental nitrogen, in air or dissolved in water, enters most plants and animals and leaves unused. Yet nitrogen compounds occur in the substance of all organisms. Therefore, a source of usable nitrogen is necessary for all organisms.

All consumers get nitrogen-bearing compounds in the things they eat. All food, of course, can be traced to producers. Producers get their nitrogen-bearing compounds from the soil (or the water) in which they grow. This brings us back to soil ecosystems.

Many soil organisms decompose the complex nitrogen compounds in dead bodies. They take most of the energy from

7–27 Diagram of the nitrogen cycle.

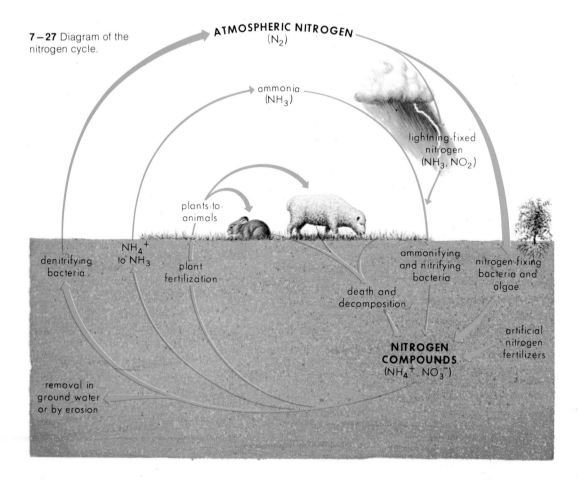

them and leave simpler substances. Among these simpler sub-stances, the chief one that contains nitrogen is ammonia (NH_3). Ammonia is a gas, but it dissolves readily in water. In soil water, ammonia reacts chemically with hydrogen ions to form ammonium ions (NH_4^+). In the form of ammonium ions, nitrogen may be absorbed by the roots of plants. It is then built into living material again by the plants.

However, other things may happen. Two groups of bacteria in soil are called *nitrifying* bacteria. One group changes ammonium ions (NH_4^+) to nitrite ions (NO_2^-). Then another group rapidly changes the nitrite ions to nitrate ions (NO_3^-). In general, plants cannot use nitrites, but they can use nitrates. In fact, nitrates are their main source of nitrogen. Thus there is another available form of nitrogen to plants, in the nitrogen cycle.

nitrifying [NY truh fy ing]

nitrite [NY tryt]

nitrate [NY trayt]. Note: Do not confuse these closely similar words.

Nitrifying bacteria operate only under *aerobic* environmental conditions. That is, they operate when oxygen is available in the soil water. Oxygen dissolves into soil water from the air spaces that normally occur in soil. Sometimes, all the spaces become filled with water, leaving no room for air. When this happens, the soil water has no source of oxygen and the soil environment becomes *anaerobic.*

aerobic [a ROH bik; Greek: *aer*, air, + *bios*]. In biology the term is applied specifically to oxygen, not to air in general.

Under anaerobic conditions, nitrifying bacteria cannot carry on their activities. *Denitrifying* bacteria, however, thrive in anaerobic environments. They change remaining nitrates to nitrogen gas. The gas gradually escapes into the atmosphere, where it is lost to most organisms. Some ammonia (NH_3) also escapes into the atmosphere.

anaerobic [Greek: *an*, without, + *aer* + *bios*]

denitrifying [dee NY truh fy ing]

Fortunately, the nitrogen gas and ammonia are not lost to all organisms. Lightning changes some atmospheric nitrogen back to nitrogen compounds. Much more important is the action of *nitrogen-fixing* organisms in soil and on the roots of certain plants. They change elemental nitrogen (N_2) to nitrogen compounds that can be used by other organisms.

Centuries ago, farmers discovered that soils in which clover has been grown produce better crops than do other soils. Early in the 19th century, a French chemist showed that this results from an increase in the nitrates in such soils. Clover and other plants of the legume family such as peas, beans, and alfalfa have this effect. Much later in the 19th century, the great Dutch microbiologist, Martinus Beijerinck, discovered that legumes themselves do not fix nitrogen. Rather, bacteria of the genus *Rhizobium* living on legume roots fix nitrogen. These bacteria form swellings called nodules on the roots. Under favorable conditions, root-nodule bacteria can fix as much as 225 kg of nitrogen per hectare per year.

Rhizobium [ry ZOH bee um]

nodules [NOJ oolz; Latin: *nodulus*, small knot]

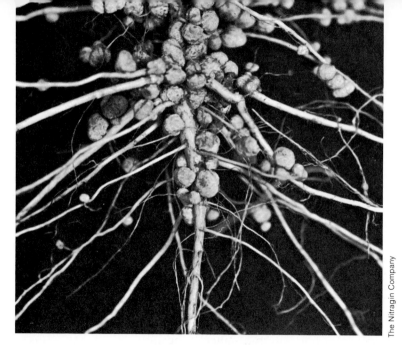

7–28 Soybean roots bearing abundant nodules formed with a species of *Rhizobium*. Why are these root outgrowths considered mutualistic, but those of figure 7–25 infectious?

The Nitragin Company

During the 20th century, much more has been learned about nitrogen fixation. Microbiologists now know that different species of *Rhizobium* live in different kinds of legumes. They have found that some actinomycetes have a similar relationship with roots of a few plants that are not legumes. Alder trees are an example.

A few free-living bacteria also are known to be nitrogen-fixers. Even some of the blue-green algae carry on nitrogen-fixing. In agriculture, however, most of the nitrogen fixed comes from *Rhizobium* bacteria. Artificial nitrogen fertilizers add to this source, as the diagram of the nitrogen cycle shows. Current experiments are under way to produce more crops that will support nitrogen-fixing bacteria on their roots.

CHECK YOURSELF

FF. Why don't most organisms get their required nitrogen from the air?

GG. Where do most consumers and producers obtain nitrogen?

HH. What are the principal nitrogen-bearing nutrients used by producers?

II. What is the difference between aerobic and anaerobic environments?

JJ. How is nitrogen returned from organisms to the atmosphere?

KK. What is nitrogen-fixing?

LL. Where do the principal nitrogen-fixers live?

PROBLEMS

1. Investigate an infectious disease, using the following outline of topics: history, symptoms, pathogen, vector (where appropriate), treatment, epidemiology. Investigate plant diseases as well as those of humans and other animals. Suggested diseases: anthrax, bacterial meningitis, Dutch elm disease, filariasis, tsutsugamushi fever, hoof-and-mouth disease, black stem rust of wheat, brucellosis, fire blight of pears, legionnaire's disease.

2. Malaria was the world's most widespread major disease until massive spraying of DDT and other insecticides reduced the vector population (*Anopheles* mosquitoes). The World Health Organization hoped to bring the disease under control, but recent epidemics have occurred again. Suggest some of the reasons why.

3. Scientists are aware that some infectious diseases have not been identified. First cases, or infrequent cases, may go unrecognized. The first epidemic draws attention to the disease. This was the case with the human disease now called legionnaire's disease. It is named after the American Legion convention at which an epidemic occurred. A number of people died. Consider such an epidemic, its victims, and their autopsies (studies of blood and other body parts after death). How would you employ people in each of the following careers in attempting to identify the cause of the disease? (Do library research on the careers.)

biochemists   microbiologists (virolo-
food inspectors   gists, bacteriologists)
medical doctors   pathologists
metallurgists   toxicologists

4. In recent years epidemics of virus-caused influenza have occurred and spread over many parts of the world. Yet vaccination against influenza viruses is common. Why are the vaccines ineffective against a new epidemic that is given a new name? (Examples: "Asian flu," "Hong Kong flu," and so on.) Use your understanding of pathogens, resistance on the part of both host and pathogen, and acquired immunity to answer the question.

5. How antibodies are made and produce immunity against a disease is very complicated. Consult L. E. Hood et al, *Immunology*, on the "Suggested Readings" list to find the answer.

6. Collect a sample of soil that supports good plant growth. Use sieves of different sizes to separate the soil particles into size groups. Study the groups and their proportions and identify all the soil components you can. Then begin on your own and manufacture a completely artificial soil. Select and use a rock and a hammer to crush it (wear safety goggles). Also use dried plant remains (peat moss is effective), a small amount of dried animal manure or artificial fertilizer, and water. Add any other needed soil components you have identified from your study. Try growing a plant in your soil.

7. A farmer divided a field into two halves, A and B. Rye was planted in Plot A. When the rye was almost full-grown, it was plowed under; then potatoes were planted in both plots. More potatoes were produced in Plot B than in Plot A. Without further treatment of the soil, potatoes were planted in both fields the following year. In the second year, more potatoes were harvested from Plot A than from Plot B. Explain the differences in potato production in the two years, using your understanding of soils and plant needs.

SUGGESTED READINGS

Ayres, J. C., J. O. Mundt, and W. E. Sandine. 1980. *Microbiology of Foods.* W. H. Freeman, San Francisco. Covers the beneficial and harmful relationships of microorganisms to foods.

Cooper, M. D. and A. R. Lawton. 1974. The Development of the Immune System. *Scientific American*, November.

Croce, C. M. and H. Koprowski. 1978. The Genetics of Human Cancer. *Scientific American*, February. A single human chromosome may contribute to the origin of cancerous cells.

Devoret, R. 1979. Bacterial Tests for Potential Carcinogens. *Scientific American*, August. Demonstrates how bacteria can be used in place of laboratory animals to identify cancer-causing chemicals.

Frobisher, M., R. D. Hinsdill, K. T. Crabtree, and C. R. Goodheart. 1974. *Fundamentals of Microbiology.* 9th ed. W. B. Saunders, Philadelphia. Contains materials on many aspects of infectious diseases and on soil microorganisms. Advanced.

Gasner, D. 1975. Natural History of Influenza. *Science Digest*, March.

Harley, J. L. 1971. *Mycorrhiza.* Oxford University Press, London. Well-illustrated pamphlet that describes experimental investigations of mycorrhizae.

Henderson, D. A. 1976. The Eradication of Smallpox. *Scientific American*, October. Discusses the disappearance of this once dread disease.

Hood, L. E., I. L. Weissman, and W. B. Wood. 1978. *Immunology.* Benjamin-Cummings, Menlo Park, Calif. Paperback. A basic text in immunology for the advanced student.

Kaplan, M. M. and H. Koprowski. 1980. Rabies. *Scientific American*, January. Traces the search for ways to control this deadly disease.

Nicolson, G. L. 1979. Cancer Metastasis. *Scientific American*, March. Describes the ability of certain cells to travel through the body and establish new tumors.

Pilgrim, I. 1974. *The Topic of Cancer.* Thomas Y. Crowell, New York. Discusses what cancer is and what we don't know about it. Also relates disease to humans.

Rubenstein, E. 1980. Diseases caused by Impaired Communication Among Cells. *Scientific American*, March. Introduces a new concept of a disease-causing mechanism.

Chapter 8

Life on Land

YOUR GUIDEPOSTS

In this chapter you will have an opportunity to explore these questions in biology:

- Why do different kinds of organisms live in different places on Earth?
- How do climates influence the kinds and activities of organisms?
- How can we explain the orderly changes that occur in ecosystems within a given climate?
- What factors hinder or help the spread of organisms from one place to another?
- How have human activities changed ecosystems?

MEETING THE ENVIRONMENT

Consider all the species of organisms found within 100 kilometers of your school. You probably know many by name. Others you may know in a general way but cannot name. And many exist quite unknown to you. Even if you are not well acquainted with the *biota* (all living things) of your region, you undoubtedly realize that some organisms do not "belong" there. In the hills of Kentucky, you expect oaks and ferns, gray squirrels and woodpeckers. On the plains of Wyoming, you find pronghorn, ground squirrels, and horned larks. But palm trees do not grow in Kentucky or Wyoming. They are not part of the biota of either area.

Gray squirrels are a part of the biota of Kentucky and Kansas. But the *geographic range* of this species does not include Wyoming. So gray squirrels are not a part of the biota of that state. On the other hand, the geographic range of *ground* squirrels includes both Wyoming and Kansas but not Kentucky. Thus, with respect to squirrels, the biota of Kansas resembles

biota [by OH tuh; Greek: *bios,* life]

pronghorn. See figure 8–26.

The geographic range of a species is its distribution over large areas of land.

233

X 1/3

X 1/4

8–1 Horned lark (*above*) and thirteen-lined ground squirrel (*right*).

Haven Kolb

8–2 Coconut palms (Florida).

Jim Annan

8–3 Gray squirrel burying a nut.

caimans [KAY manz]

8–4 Young caiman.

X 1/2

that of both Wyoming and Kentucky. With respect to many other organisms, however, the biota is completely different. As we will see, each region tends to have its own characteristic biota.

SURVIVAL

You may have dandelions in your lawn or rats in your neighborhood. These organisms are immigrants to this continent. Geographic ranges, then, are not permanent. Like everything else in the biosphere, they are constantly changing. That dandelions and rats exist here today is evidence that they are able to exist in the environmental conditions of this continent.

Every year visitors to Florida buy small caimans as souvenirs. They carry them northward to New England and the Middle West. As the pets grow larger and become bothersome, they are often dumped into the nearest river or pond. Although this has been going on for many years, the Ohio and Connecticut rivers still have no adult caimans living in them.

What determines the **survival** of a species in a particular ecosystem? Here, "survival" does not mean mere existence. It means active living—growing and reproducing. Many individuals may be able to exist in an environment, but this still does not make that species a part of the ecosystem. Only when a species continues to grow and reproduce does it become an ecosystem member. It is evident that caimans cannot survive in the northern United States.

TOLERANCE

If a household geranium is left outdoors during a Minnesota winter, it dies. If a blacksnake is exposed in a shadeless cage to the July sun of Georgia, it dies. Household geraniums do not tolerate long periods of freezing temperatures. Blacksnakes do not tolerate long periods of high temperatures. **Tolerance** is the ability of an individual or a species to withstand particular environmental conditions.

Working with any one measurable environmental factor, we can, by experiment, determine the tolerance limits of a species. To do this, we must find the upper limit (maximum) and the lower limit (minimum) of tolerance. Likewise, we can determine the range of conditions most favorable for growth and reproduction for that species. These are called the **optimum** conditions for the species. This seems clear-cut, but several complications arise.

The **duration** of the condition is important. Its duration is especially important in determining maximum and minimum limits. For instance, geraniums can withstand *short* periods of freezing temperature but not long ones. Another complication is **variation** (differences) within a species. Variation is found between populations that come from different parts of that species' geographic range. A jellyfish, *Aurelia aurita*, has an optimum temperature for swimming. This is between 5° and 18°C for the population that lives off the coast of Maine. But the optimum is between 28° and 30°C for the population in the waters off the southern Florida coast.

In addition, variation occurs among the individuals of a species. If many flies are sprayed with a pesticide, some may die and some may survive. Which individuals die is not a matter of chance. It is a matter of individual differences in their resistance to the pesticide. A test population of flies was sprayed with pesticide, and the survivors were allowed to reproduce. The offspring of these hardy survivors were sprayed with the pesticide. The proportion of survivors among the offspring was higher than that of the original population. It appears that some of the individual differences in the test flies may have been passed on to their offspring.

X 1/4

8—5 Household geranium.

blacksnake. See figure 18–21.

tolerance [TOL uh runs; Latin: *tolerare*, to endure]

optimum [OP tuh mum]

duration: here, length of time

Aurelia aurita [aw REEL yuh aw-RY tuh]. See page 749.

X 1/6

8—6 Kangaroo rat in its native, dry habitat.

relative humidity. See Investigation 3.2.

Spizella pusilla [spuh ZEL uh pew SIL uh]

X 1/3

8—7 Field sparrow.

Can you outline a plan for an experimental investigation of this hypothesis?

Further complications arise when different factors interact. When relative humidity is near zero, people can withstand very high temperatures. With increasing humidity, however, our tolerance for temperatures above 40°C is very low. As you discovered in Investigation 3.2, relative humidity can vary considerably among the microhabitats of an area. The relative humidity on a California desert may be quite low during the day. Yet within its burrow the relative humidity surrounding a kangaroo rat will be high. For land animals the effects of humidity and temperature are so closely related that there is little point in measuring one without the other.

THE ENVIRONMENT AS A WHOLE

Consider now the interrelationship of tolerances in determining geographic range. Field sparrows (*Spizella pusilla*) can survive northern winter temperatures in the United States if they have enough food. Sparrows need more food in the winter, because more heat is lost from their bodies than in summer. Sparrows can hunt food only during the day, and winter days are short. Which, then, is the tolerance factor that sets the northern winter boundaries of field sparrows? It could be any one, or any combination of, temperature, length of day, or food supply.

Abiotic conditions that are within a species' tolerance limits may allow it to survive in a particular ecosystem. But these conditions do not guarantee that the species will survive there. The species may fail because it has to compete with other organisms. For example, bald cypresses grow naturally in swampy areas. But if we plant and carefully tend them on a hilltop, they also grow well. It seems they can tolerate much less moisture than that found in swamps. Perhaps cypresses fail to grow naturally on hills because trees that are more tolerant of low moisture crowd them out. Or we may look at the matter from the opposite direction. Bald cypresses are tolerant of flooded ground, and few other tree species are. Perhaps, then, cypresses grow in swamps, not because they require a swamp environment, but because the competition there is less.

These examples remind us that the whole organism encounters the whole environment. Individuals respond in certain ways when a particular environmental factor is changed. Ecologists can partially understand the whole situation of an organism by studying these factors one at a time. One major aspect of ecology is the study of the tolerance limits of different species.

8–8 Bald cypress tree in a Georgia swamp. Other, younger cypress trees appear in figure 8–23.

CHECK YOURSELF

A. How are the ideas expressed by the ecological terms "biota" and "geographic range" related?
B. What must occur if a species is to survive as a part of a particular ecosystem?
C. What are three terms used to describe the tolerance of a species to any one environmental factor?
D. Give an example in which two environmental factors interact to determine the tolerance of a species.
E. Explain why species may be able to survive a given set of abiotic conditions in an ecosystem but still not become a part of the ecosystem.

Investigation 8.1   ENVIRONMENTAL TOLERANCE

INTRODUCTION

The seeds of some desert plants will not **germinate** (sprout) until sufficient rainfall washes out chemicals in the seeds that inhibit germination. Other seeds must pass through the digestive tracts of animals before they will germinate. Some wheat seeds will not germinate until they have been exposed to low temperatures for a certain period of time. In this investigation you will examine the tolerance that some seeds have to some environmental abiotic factors.

Before beginning work, read through the procedure. (1) Set up hypotheses on the basis of the experimental design.

PROCEDURE

1. Label the beakers *tomato, radish, vetch,* and *lettuce.* In each beaker, place 50 seeds of the species named. Add enough fungicide to cover the seeds. Allow them to soak for the period of time recommended by your teacher.

2. Place 4 disks of paper toweling in each petri dish. Moisten the paper thoroughly with distilled water. Divide each dish into 1/4 sections by inserting cardboard dividers, as shown in figure 8–9.

8–9 Experimental setup.

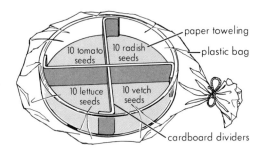

3. Pour the fungicide solution from the beakers, and rinse the seeds with water.

4. Using forceps, place 10 tomato seeds in 1 section of each dish. Repeat with the other 3 kinds of seeds in the remaining 3 sections of each dish.

5. Label the dishes with your team symbol and number them from *1* to *5.* Place each dish in a clear plastic bag. Tie the bag closed with a piece of string.

6. Place each dish in a different environment, as follows:
   Dish 1 – continuous light and cold – a refrigerator that has the light adjusted to remain on when the door is closed.
   Dish 2 – continuous dark and cold – a lighttight box in a refrigerator. (Try to maintain temperature at 10° to 12°C.)

MATERIALS
(per team)

4 beakers, 50-ml
50 seeds each of radish,
    vetch, tomato, and lettuce
150 ml fungicide
5 petri dishes
5 clear plastic bags
5 20-cm pieces of string
2 shallow cardboard boxes
    with covers
20 pieces of paper toweling,
    cut to fit petri dishes
20 cardboard strips, cut to fit
    diameter of petri dishes
forceps
glass-marking crayon
refrigerator
incubator
2 thermometers (−10° to +110°C)

Dish 3 – continuous light and warm – an incubator with a light.
Dish 4 – continuous dark and warm – a lighttight box in an incubator. (Try to maintain temperature at 30° to 32°C.)
Dish 5 – variable temperature and light – on a windowsill.

7. Each day, count the number of seeds that have germinated. Record the counts in your data book. A suggested form:

Dish No. _____   Environment _____

KIND OF SEED	NUMBER GERMINATED		
	Day 1	Day 2 ←———→	Day 10
tomato		←———→	
radish		←———→	
vetch		←———→	
lettuce		←———→	

8. Combine the data of all teams. (2) Why should this be done?

DISCUSSION

(3) In which environment did the greatest percentage of tomato seeds germinate? Of radish seeds? Of vetch seeds? Of lettuce seeds? (4) Did any seeds of one species germinate fastest in one environment, but have the greatest number of germinated seeds in another environment? If so, which species and environments are involved?

(5) Which kind of seed has the greatest tolerance for continuous light? (6) Which kind has the greatest tolerance for low temperature? (7) Does any kind germinate similarly in all the experimental environments? If so, which?

(8) Check your results with your hypotheses. Recall that the establishment of a species in an ecosystem depends on both its tolerances and its competition with other species. (9) Which do you think would give a species a greater advantage — rapid germination or germination of á large percentage of seeds? Why? (10) On the basis of your experimental results, describe an ecosystem in which each species you studied in this investigation might have an advantage.

FOR FURTHER INVESTIGATION

From a grocery store obtain seeds of plants that grow in a variety of climates, such as avocados, dates, grapefruits, oranges, pomegranates, lentils, and many kinds of beans. Test these for germination in experimental environments. In some cases you may have to lengthen the time allowed for germination.

ECOLOGICAL DISTRIBUTION OF LIFE ON LAND

Tolerance to environmental factors determines the kinds of organisms that can live in an ecosystem. There are many different ecosystems on Earth. Most have no sharp boundaries between them. But biologists can distinguish them, with or without exact boundaries, by differences including abiotic factors.

CLIMATE AND BIOMES

Large ecosystems can be described in terms of their *climate,* or long-term weather patterns. An ecosystem's climate results from the interaction of several abiotic factors. These include radiant (solar) energy, temperature, wind, precipitation, humidity, and evaporation rate.

climate [KLY mut]: originally, slope of Earth from the equator toward the poles

Radiant energy is important to an ecosystem for two reasons. First, it is the form of energy that producers trap and make into food. Almost all organisms in the ecosystem depend on this supply of food. Second, the temperature of the ecosystem is determined by the amount of radiant energy it receives. The energy is absorbed at the earth's surface and is returned to the air as heat.

The earth is an odd-shaped sphere, and is tilted with respect to its orbit around the sun. As a result, the earth receives unequal amounts of solar energy at different places on its surface. The circulation of the atmosphere is powered by solar energy. The movement of the atmosphere helps to distribute the

8–10 Summer shower in Arizona desert.

NOAA

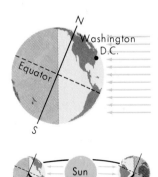

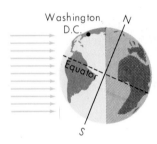

8–11 Distribution of solar energy on the earth's surface.

climatograms [kly MA tuh gramz; Greek: *klima*, latitude, + *gramma*, writing, record]

arid [AR ud]

biome [BY ome; Greek: *bios*, + *oma*, group, mass]

radiant energy that is converted to heat. At the same time, the circulating atmosphere carries water vapor from the oceans over land surfaces, where it falls as rain.

Climates occur in broad belts that encircle the earth. The boundaries of these belts are disrupted by lands and oceans. Climates are modified further by mountains and ocean currents. It is rather easy to map the distribution of a particular factor of climate. It is difficult, however, to map a climate as a whole. This is because climatic factors overlap and mix with one another in complex ways. This overlap also makes it difficult to measure climates. To simplify, ecologists frequently use *climatograms.* These summarize monthly measurements of temperature and precipitation.

In each major kind of climate, a characteristic kind of vegetation develops and maintains itself. Warm, arid (dry) climates, for example, are associated with desert vegetation. Semiarid climates usually are covered with grassland. Moist climates support forests. The vegetation and animals living in a particular climate are thought of together and are called a *biome.*

BIOMES AND RADIANT ENERGY

You need not study all biomes in detail to understand something about the distribution of terrestrial life. We will describe only some selected biomes. We begin with biomes near the North Pole and end near the equator. The annual amount of radiant energy received in these biomes increases as you move away from the pole.

8–12 (*opposite*) Climatograms. Average monthly temperatures in blue (degrees Celsius); average monthly precipitation in gray (centimeters).

TUNDRA

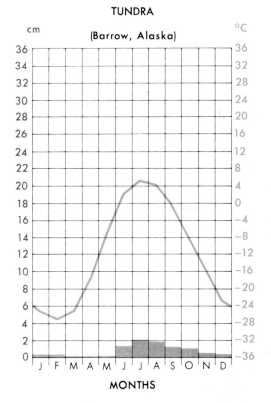

(Barrow, Alaska)

MONTHS

CONIFEROUS FOREST

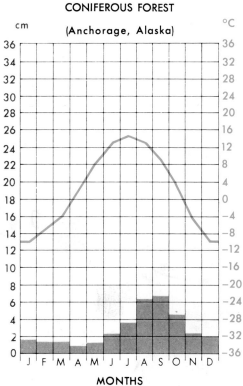

(Anchorage, Alaska)

MONTHS

MID-LATITUDE DECIDUOUS FOREST

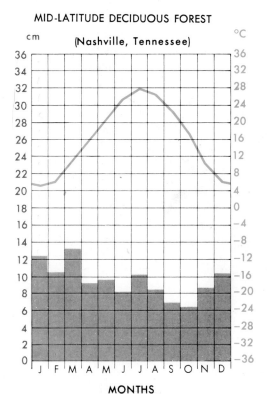

(Nashville, Tennessee)

MONTHS

TROPICAL RAIN FOREST

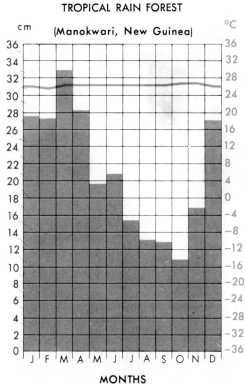

(Manokwari, New Guinea)

MONTHS

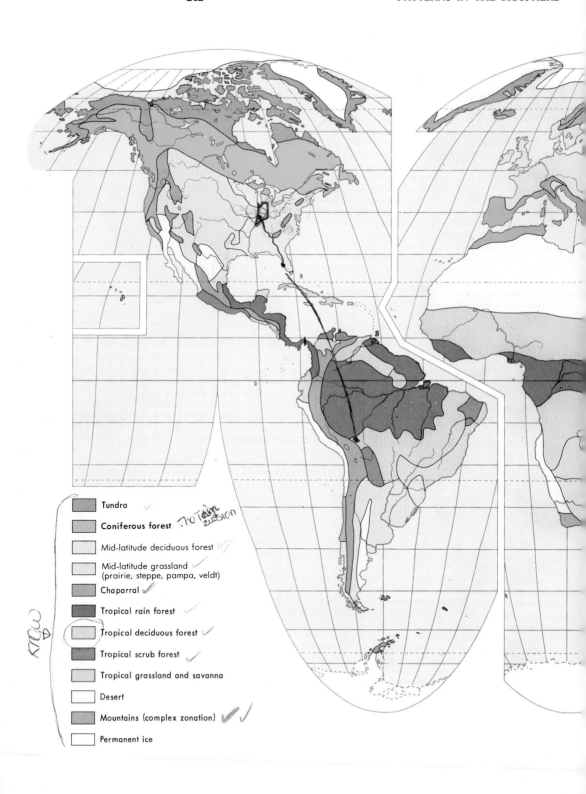

Tundra

Coniferous forest   The Taiga zussion

Mid-latitude deciduous forest

Mid-latitude grassland
(prairie, steppe, pampa, veldt)

Chaparral

Tropical rain forest

Tropical deciduous forest

Tropical scrub forest

Tropical grassland and savanna

Desert

Mountains (complex zonation)

Permanent ice

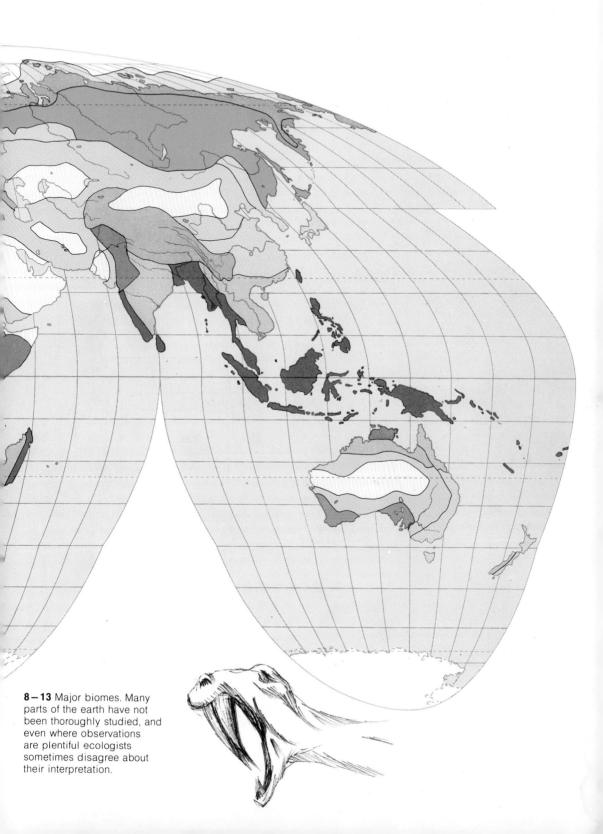

8—13 Major biomes. Many parts of the earth have not been thoroughly studied, and even where observations are plentiful ecologists sometimes disagree about their interpretation.

8-14 Tundra (Alaska). Note pond in the foreground.

tundra [TUN druh]

permafrost [PUR muh frost; Latin: *per*, through, + *manere*, to remain, + frost]

dominate [DOM uh nayt; Latin: *dominus*, master, lord]

Tundra. The *tundra* biome circles the earth in the Northern Hemisphere. It lies just south of the ice-covered polar seas where no vegetation is found. In the Southern Hemisphere there is no tundra. North of the ice-covered Antarctic continent, the climate would permit tundra but the earth is covered by ocean.

In the tundra the sun is always low in the sky. Little radiant energy is received at any time. In summer, however, the total radiant energy is greater since the days are very long. The top layer of soil thaws, but the ground beneath, the *permafrost*, always remains frozen. Melting snow cannot drain into permafrost, so water collects on the surface and in the top layers of soil. For six to eight weeks the tundra is a land of ponds and marshes. This is true even though the yearly precipitation is small. In this short growing season, plants must synthesize a whole year's food supply.

Grasses and sedges dominate tundra. Great areas also are covered by low mats of lichens and mosses. The few woody plants, such as willows and birches, grow close to the ground.

8-15 A tundra willow. What environmental conditions limit the growth of this woody plant?

They seldom become more than a few centimeters tall. Leaves of most plants are small. Many are hairy or have margins rolled inward, which reduces the evaporation of precious water from a leaf surface. Flowers appear rapidly and seeds develop quickly.

These are adaptations of structure and function to the abiotic environment. Try to explain them.

During summer, tundra teems with animal life. Large flocks of water birds raise their young in the long days that allow around-the-clock food gathering. Few species of insects live here, but the number of individuals is great. Caribou graze on grasses and lichens. Ptarmigan, arctic foxes, and snowshoe hares are present in their brown summer coats. Lemmings scurry along runways among the plants. When the lemming population is high, predators such as snowy owls and weasels are numerous.

Use the Index of this book and "A Catalog of Living Things" (Appendix 3) to help you locate illustrations of some unfamiliar animals.

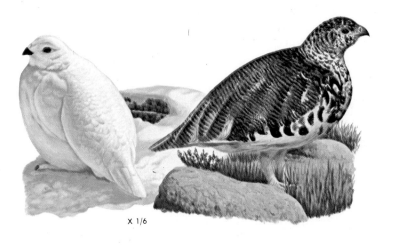

X 1/6

8−16 Ptarmigan in winter (*left*) and summer (*right*). How can you explain the difference in the coloration of the feathers?

Change from summer to winter is rapid. Lakes and ponds freeze—the shallower ponds freeze all the way to the bottom. Snowfall is light, and high winds sweep open areas free of snow. Daylight hours are few or lacking. During the winter much of the tundra receives *no* sunlight. Photosynthesis stops during these dark periods.

In the cold and darkness food is scarce. The water birds leave, flying far to the south. Among mammals the chief migrants are caribou, which move south to the forests. Some animals, such as gulls and foxes, migrate to the seashores. There they become commensal with seal-hunting polar bears. But some animals stay in the tundra all year. The invertebrate animals become dormant. Lemmings avoid the windswept bare ground and burrow under the snow in sheltered spots. There they eat plant roots or seeds that they stored during the summer. Ptarmigan burrow into the snow during storms. At other

How does a snow cover provide protection?

8—17 Tundra mammals: musk oxen (*left*) and caribou (*right*).

A bud is a small swelling on a plant that develops in late summer, from which a new leaf, flower, or shoot grows the following spring.

times they feed on buds of plants that stick out above the shallow snow. Only musk oxen face the tundra winter's full force. Living on lichens, they seek out uncovered plants or paw away the snow cover.

Coniferous forest. As you travel south in the tundra, you begin to find scattered clumps of dwarf trees in sheltered places. Eventually tundra gives way to the great *coniferous forest* biome. This forest extends in a broad zone across Europe, Asia, and North America. In the Southern Hemisphere there is no similar biome.

The coniferous forest receives more radiant energy, both daily and annually, than does tundra, because it lies closer to the equator. Summer days are not so long as those in the tundra. They are, however, warmer and the ground thaws completely. Winters are not so long, but a few places have days without sunlight. In winter, snow is deeper here than in the tundra. Under the cover of the trees, the snow is not easily blown away and is kept from melting by the dense shade.

Until 10 to 20 thousand years ago, most of this region was covered by a great sheet of ice. Grinding its way slowly across the continents, the ice dug out depressions. As the ice melted, it left piles of dirt and rocks that often formed dams across streams. Many ponds and lakes were created this way.

Can you think of a coniferous tree that is not evergreen?

Most coniferous trees are evergreen. Throughout the year they keep out sunlight, so there is little vegetation near the ground. Therefore, the production of food takes place mostly in the upper parts of the trees. Many insects attack the conifers, and a large number of small birds eat the insects. Porcupines nibble the tree bark, and deer munch the young leaves. Moose wade into the ponds and eat aquatic vegetation.

hibernate [HY bur nayt; Latin: *hibernus*, wintry]: to spend the winter in a dormant state

During the winter many animals *hibernate.* As winter approaches, they find shelter. Their body processes slow down and little energy is needed to keep them alive while they are hibernating. Many other animals migrate southward. The large

8–18 Coniferous forest in Canada.

feet of hares and lynxes serve as snowshoes. Deer, moose, and the caribou that arrived in autumn from the north wade through the snow on their long legs. They browse on buds and twigs of the trees.

Mid-latitude deciduous forest. As you go south in the coniferous forest, you find trees with broad leaves rather than needles. These trees usually shed their leaves each fall. They are *deciduous.* In eastern North America — Massachusetts, southern Michigan, or southern Wisconsin — such deciduous trees are most common. This is the *mid-latitude deciduous forest.*

deciduous [dih SIJ uh was; Latin *de,* from, + *cadere,* to cut]

This biome is not continuous. It is found in eastern North America, in western Europe, and in eastern Asia. In the Southern Hemisphere a small similar forest occurs in southern Chile. The following description applies in general to all of these areas, but the organisms mentioned are North American.

Because figure 8–13 is quite simplified, you will find this biome mapped at two other Southern Hemisphere areas, but they are rather different from the biome described here.

In summer the sun is high in the sky and days are long. As a result, much radiant energy is available. In June, at the latitude of Philadelphia, the daily supply of radiant energy is *greater* than it is in the tropics on all but a few days of the year. Of course, in December little radiant energy is received. So the *annual* supply of radiant energy is much less in Philadelphia than in the tropics. Precipitation in the deciduous forest is high and steady. Droughts are infrequent and not severe. In winter, snow may be heavy, but it usually melts rapidly and the ground is seldom snow-covered for long. In summer, heat and humidity may both be high. But at any time cool, dry masses of air may flow down from the north.

What effects might such conditions have on producers?

There are many species of deciduous trees. The tallest ones form a canopy, an upper layer of leaves that catch the full sunlight. Leaves of deciduous trees are rather thin, and much radiation filters through them. Thus there is enough light to provide energy for a lower layer of trees. But even these trees do not use all the energy. There is still enough to support a layer of shrubs beneath. And finally, close to the ground, mosses and ferns receive the remaining faint light.

canopy. See page 37.

8—19 Seasons in mid-latitude deciduous forest (New Jersey). All of these pictures show the same area. What effects do these changes have on herbivores such as deer?

Winter

Spring

Summer

Fall

Photos by Murray F. Buell

This large mass of producers supports a large number of consumers. Squirrels collect nuts and berries from trees. Deer mice climb in the shrubs and search on the ground for seeds. White-tailed deer browse on shrubs and the lower branches of trees. In summer, insects are abundant in the soil and all layers of the forest. ***Insectivorous*** birds prey upon them. Red-eyed vireos consume canopy insects. Acadian flycatchers catch insects flying below the canopy. Ovenbirds search out insects on the ground. Woodpeckers extract boring insects from the bark of trees. There are few large predators in most of this biome, except for human hunters.

deer mice. See figure 18-27.

insectivorous [in sek TIV uh rus]: feeding chiefly on insects; the "-vorous" ending means "feeding on"

How does this paragraph illustrate the concept of niches?

In autumn the leaves of the deciduous trees turn yellow, orange, red, or brown. Then they drift down, covering the ground with a thick mass of organic matter. Nuts and acorns fall, too. Berries cover the lower trees and shrubs. Many mammals fatten on the abundant food, and some store it. Woodchucks form thick layers of fat and then hibernate in burrows. Reptiles, much more abundant here than in the coniferous forest, also hibernate. Many insectivorous birds migrate to the tropics.

X 1/4

8–20 Red-eyed vireo.

In winter, the leafless trees use and lose little water. Many mammals rest during cold spells. They resume activity when warm masses of air move in from the south. Then small insects may fly in swarms above brooks. A few butterflies may appear in the weak midday sun. Winter birds are more abundant here than in the coniferous forest. They eat seeds and fruits, and search out dormant insects and insect eggs from cracks in tree bark.

In spring, solar radiation becomes strong before air temperatures are high enough to bring the trees into leaf. A great number of herbs spring up on the forest floor. Their leaves and flowers grow quickly. By the time the shade from the trees has closed over them, the herbs have finished photosynthesis for the year. Food is stored in roots or underground stems; seeds mature and then scatter. The herbs die back to the ground until the next spring.

Tropical rain forest. In three separate places along the equator there is a biome called ***tropical rain forest.*** The largest area is in the Amazon Basin of South America. The second in size is found in the East Indies, and the smallest is in the Congo Basin of Africa.

In tropical rain forest the noon sun is almost directly overhead throughout the year. Thus the energy supply is large and fairly constant. Rain falls almost every day, and the humidity is always high. Temperatures vary little throughout the year. Beneath the canopy, temperature remains about the same day and night. No other terrestrial biome has such a uniform climate.

How are such conditions favorable to living things?

8–21 Within tropical rain forest. How can you explain the predominant color of this scene? Note the buttresses supporting the tree.

Ralph Buchsbaum

8–22 Section through tropical rain forest.

epiphytes [EP uh fyts; Greek: *epi*, upon, + *phyton*, a plant]

buttresses [BUH truh suz]: the broadened base of a tree trunk

Why does a "wall of vegetation" occur in such places?

Vegetation deeply covers the land. The canopy reaches an average height of about 50 m. Some individual trees may even grow to 80 m or more. Thus the vegetation is much deeper than in mid-latitude deciduous forest (averaging 30 m), coniferous forest (15 m), or tundra (0.1 m at most). Beneath taller trees are shorter ones that are tolerant of shade. Beneath these are still others that are even more shade-tolerant. Weaving through the branches are many woody vines.

The trunks and branches of the trees and the twisting stems of the vines serve as perches for many kinds of *epiphytes.* These plants get no nourishment from the other plants; they simply use them for support. Since epiphytes have no contact with the ground, they must get water and minerals elsewhere. Some have roots that absorb moisture from the humid atmosphere in the same way that blotting paper soaks up water. Many catch the daily rain in special hollow leaves. Mosquitoes, water beetles, other aquatic insects, and even a species of frog may live in such treetop puddles.

The dense layers of trees absorb most of the light, so only shade-tolerant plants grow on the forest floor. The trees are supported in the damp soil by huge braces called *buttresses* (figure 8–21). Vines coil upward into the dim green of the canopy. Only along rivers or at the edges of clearings does a thick wall of vegetation extend down to the ground, blocking the traveler's way. The way through the forest — once you are in it — is clear.

Ripe fruits drop to the forest floor — a food supply for some ground dwellers. Although the trees are always green, leaves die and fall continuously for most of the year. In the warm,

8–23 Epiphytes on trunks of cypress trees in a Florida swamp.

moist environment huge numbers of insects, fungi, and bacteria attack this food supply rapidly. Therefore, organic remains do not build up on the ground. Large herbivores, such as hoofed mammals, are rare or live only near riverbanks. Predators and parasites are abundant at all levels of the forest.

What environmental factors are related to the rarity of large, hoofed herbivores?

All forests have some animals that live in the trees—*arboreal* animals. In tropical rain forest many animals live in the canopy. In one study of rain forests 90 percent of the birds were found to feed mostly in the canopy. For birds this may not be surprising. But in this biome a large number of mammals, over 50 percent of the species, also are arboreal. Moreover, there are many tree snakes, tree lizards, tree frogs, and an untold number of arboreal insects.

arboreal [ar BOR ee ul; Latin: *arbor*, tree]

CHECK YOURSELF

F. Why is radiant energy important to an ecosystem?

G. What are biomes?

H. What adaptations of structure and function are found among tundra organisms? Describe the adaptations for summer residents and for year-round residents.

I. What is the most noticeable difference between tundra and coniferous forest landscapes?

J. What is hibernation?

K. What are some of the noticeable differences between the landscapes of mid-latitude deciduous forest and coniferous forest?

L. Describe vegetation in mid-latitude deciduous forest and vegetation in tropical rain forest. Why are these different?

M. What happens in mid-latitude deciduous forest as the seasons change?

N. What are epiphytes?

O. Many arboreal animals live in tropical rain forest. Why is this true?

BIOMES AND PRECIPITATION

The principal variable in the biomes we have described was radiant energy. In each biome, precipitation during the growing season was sufficient for the plants that could tolerate the temperatures. In many biomes, however, lack of water is a factor that limits the biota.

Similar areas are found in other mid-latitude regions of the world. See figure 8–13.

Mid-latitude grassland. In mid-latitude deciduous forest, droughts occur but they seldom kill the trees. As you go west in the mid-latitudes of North America, however, you eventually leave the trees behind. Grasses become the dominant natural vegetation. The *mid-latitude grassland* extends from the Mississippi River to the Rocky Mountains and from central Canada

8–24 Mid-latitude grassland (Illinois).

Harold R. Hungerford

8–25 Mid-latitude grassland (eastern Nebraska). What other herbivores besides bison might you find here?

Grant Heilman

8−26 Mid-latitude grassland (South Dakota). How does this grassland differ from that shown in figures 8−24 and 8−25? What kind of animal is pictured?

to the Gulf of Mexico. The change from forest to grassland occurs gradually. In Illinois, for example, much grassland lies east of the Mississippi River. In Missouri and Arkansas, deciduous forest extends far west along the moist riverbanks.

The radiant energy supplies for deciduous forest and this grassland are similar, because both biomes stretch through the same latitudes. Along this line grassland is found in the west and deciduous forest in the east. Temperature differences, between day and night and between winter and summer, are

8−27 Compare these climatograms with those in figure 8−12.

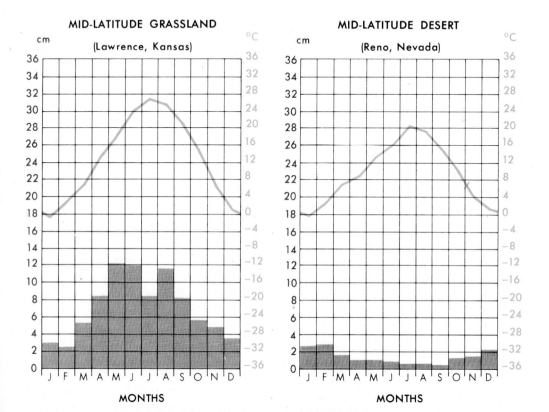

X 1/12

8 — 28 Black-tailed jackrabbit.

X 1/12

8 — 29 Badger.

X 1/6

8 — 30 Meadowlark.

You should now be able to make a generalization about the relationships between production of vegetation (in kg/hectare/year) and the abiotic environment.

What does this abiotic-environment factor (temperature) suggest about desert animals, especially cold-blooded ones?

greater in the grassland than in the forest. The principal difference between the two biomes, however, is in the precipitation. It is consistently less in the grassland than in the forest. Grasses can tolerate the frequent droughts that occur in central North America, but trees cannot.

The height of the grasses varies from more than 2 m near the Mississippi River to less than 0.5 m near the Rocky Mountains. Though the depth of vegetation is much less than in forests, in some wetter parts of the grassland vegetation is very dense. During summer the grass leaves grow continuously from their bases. Therefore, as herbivores eat the tops, the grass crop is renewed. Many other herbs grow among the grasses, but shrubs are rather rare, except along streams.

The most conspicuous first-order consumers are hoofed mammals. Once there were many bison and pronghorns in North American grasslands. Now most of them have been replaced by cattle and sheep. Less conspicuous herbivores are jackrabbits and ground squirrels. Many kinds of insects also feed on the vegetation. At times grasshopper populations reach huge sizes. Then swarms of them may devour the plants down to ground level.

Wolves and coyotes were once the chief large predators. Today, wolves have been nearly exterminated, but coyotes survive. Rattlesnakes and badgers are important predators on ground squirrels. There are many insectivorous birds, such as meadowlarks. Hawks and owls prey upon small rodents and birds.

Mid-latitude desert. In North America the western edge of the grassland is bordered by *desert.* The situation is complicated by mountains, but, between the western ranges, deserts occur from eastern Washington south into Mexico.

When we think of a desert, we think of an area with little precipitation. Just as important in defining a desert, however, is the rate of evaporation. In a desert evaporation rate is always high compared with the precipitation. This is partly a matter of latitude. The amount of precipitation that produces a desert at the equator can support a fine grassland at higher latitudes. When precipitation does occur in a desert, it is likely to be heavy but brief. Also, much of the water runs off instead of sinking into the soil.

Loss of heat from the earth's surface is greatly slowed down by water vapor in the air. Because desert air is very dry, heat that builds up in the soil during the day is quickly lost at night. Air and soil temperatures at the soil surface vary greatly between day and night. Temperatures underground, however, are much more stable.

8–31 "Hot" desert (Arizona). What characteristics do many of the plants have in common?

The roots of most desert plants spread far in all directions from the stems and are only a short distance below ground. When rains occur, these widespread, shallow roots soak up the moisture rapidly. The water is then stored in the tissues of the plants. For example, 100 or more liters of water may be stored in the thick stems of large cacti. Thorns and spines are numerous on desert plants. Most desert plants have small leaves or none at all. This feature reduces the amount of water lost from the plant into the air.

Here are more statements of fact that require ecological explanations.

Few hoofed herbivores live in **mid-latitude deserts,** but rodents are numerous. Most of these rodents are burrowers. They get water in their food or from early morning dew. Pocket mice, for example, survive without drinking much water. Instead, they use water that is produced from the chemical breakdown of foods in their bodies. As in all terrestrial biomes, there are many insect herbivores.

Many birds and some reptiles, especially lizards, are insectivorous. Scorpions also prey upon insects. Among larger predators are coyotes, hawks, and rattlesnakes. All of these depend primarily on rodents and rabbits as food.

X 1/2

8–32 Pocket mouse.

SOME OTHER BIOMES

Use figure 8–13 to locate regions of tropical deciduous forest.

Tropical deciduous forest. The seasonless rain forests with a uniform climate cover a rather small part of the tropics. Most tropical regions have seasons. Instead of being warm and cold seasons, however, they are wet and dry. In higher latitudes winter is the season when frozen soil limits available moisture. Snow and ice are frozen water that cannot be used by plants. Most of the broad-leaved trees and shrubs of high latitudes are deciduous in winter, a dry season. In the tropics many woody plants also lose their leaves during the dry season. These tropical regions with uniform temperatures but wet and dry seasons produce a *tropical deciduous forest* biome.

In this biome the canopy is not as dense as that in rain forest. Light filters all the way to the forest floor. A dense mass of undergrowth thrives during the rainy season. People can penetrate this mass only by cutting their way through with axes or large knives. It is this biome that best matches the common idea of a "jungle."

Many animals become dormant during the dry season. This response to unfavorable environmental conditions is somewhat

8–33 Tropical deciduous forest (Thailand). In what season do you think this picture was taken?

A. W. Kuchler

similar to hibernation. Because this is a response to heat and dryness rather than cold, it is called *aestivation.* Insects and reptiles, in particular, are likely to aestivate.

aestivation [es tuh VAY shun; Latin: *aestas*, summer]

Savanna. Where tropical dry seasons are long and severe, trees grow far apart. Between the trees the ground is covered with tall grasses. This is *savanna,* a biome that covers large areas in South America and Africa.

savanna [suh VAN uh; Spanish: *zabana*, treeless plain] Use figure 8–13 to locate regions of Savanna.

In Africa, savanna is the home of many large hoofed mammals that graze and browse. Zebras, gazelles, and antelopes are among the many herbivores. These first-order consumers are followed by predators such as lions, leopards, and cheetahs. The kills of these big cats are cleaned up by commensals such as hyenas and vultures.

If you traveled from savanna to still drier regions, what changes would you expect to find in the vegetation?

8–34 Tropical savanna in eastern Africa. Elephants, zebras, and giraffes (*background*); gnu and ostrich (*foreground*). What predators might you find here?

Mid-latitude rain forest. A narrow band along the coast from southern Alaska to northern California has cool summers and mild winters. In addition, there is abundant precipitation. These climatic conditions produce a *mid-latitude rain forest.*

The trees here are mostly conifers, but they are much larger than those of coniferous forest. Some even exceed the height of trees in tropical rain forests. The "coast" redwoods of California are located in the rain forest and may grow over 100 m tall. The

8—35 Within mid-latitude rain forest (Washington).

G. E. Johnson

canopy is much simpler than in the tropics, and there are relatively few species of trees. Moss, fern, and lichen epiphytes are
abundant. Shrubs are fairly numerous, but herbs and vines are
few. The ground is covered with deep cushions of moss.

Elk and deer browse on the shrubs. Many birds and rodents live largely on conifer seeds. Compared with the tropical
rain forest, this forest has few arboreal vertebrates, but it has
many insects. Small invertebrates live in the deep layers of
humus on the forest floor. These are food for populations of
ground birds, such as thrushes.

Chaparral. In California most of the precipitation comes in
winter. The summers are very dry. South Africa, western
Australia, central Chile, and the region around the Mediterranean Sea have similar climates. The biome characteristic
of this kind of climate has several names. In America the term
chaparral is used.

Chaparral is composed of large shrubs with small, evergreen leaves that are thick and often coated with waxy material.
The canopy is low and often dense. In some cases, no herbs
grow under the shrubs. The shrubs have thick underground
stems that survive the dry summers and the frequent fires that
burn through the chaparral. The fires burn off all the plant parts
above the ground. The thick stems of the shrubs near the
ground remain alive, however, and sprout new plants. Rodents
and reptiles are numerous here. As in tropical deciduous forest,
aestivation occurs in the dry season.

Dennis Brokaw

8–36 Chaparral (California). At what season do you think this picture was taken?

MOUNTAIN BIOMES

Because air is heated at the earth's surface, the air becomes cooler at higher altitudes. Temperature drops (on the average) about 2.7°C for each 500 m of elevation. By climbing only a few hundred meters up the side of a mountain, you get the effect of going many kilometers poleward. This means that at the base of a mountain you may find climate suitable for grassland. But near the top of the same mountain you may find a climate suitable for tundra plants. Ecosystems that resemble the biomes of higher latitudes develop as beltlike zones circling mountains.

We might attempt to relate these zones to the similar biomes we have read about. The similarities, however, are somewhat superficial. For example, in the upper mountain, or alpine, region of the Rocky Mountains, the landscape looks much like the tundra of the north. Many species of organisms are the same in both alpine and tundra. But in mountain biomes there is no permafrost and no long period of darkness in the winter. The amount of radiant energy received here in summer is much greater than that received at any time in the northern tundra. It seems best, therefore, to think of mountainous regions as often having familiar biomes with certain distinctive characteristics.

alpine: a mountain zone above the altitude at which trees grow

Even at the equator, mountains rise above the tree zone. Use geography books to find some such places.

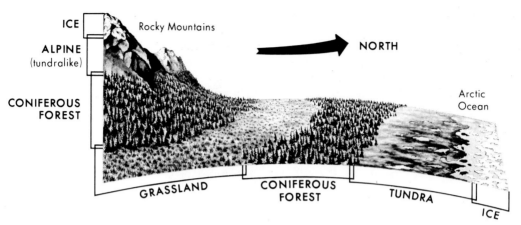

8–37 Comparison of effects of altitude and latitude in western North America.

erosion [ih ROH zhun; Latin: *e*, from, away, + *rodere*, to grow]

How might fires be started naturally?

Study figure 8–38 as you read the next paragraphs.

BIOMES AND SUCCESSION

In the coniferous forest region, the great sheets of ice that were once there have melted. They have left bare rock and soil in many places. In all regions of the world, erosion constantly exposes bare rock. In many biomes, fire is a natural factor. Floods, blowing sand, and volcanic eruptions also may destroy the vegetation of an area and leave bare ground.

If a fire burns a part of a spruce (coniferous) forest, most of the life is destroyed. Much of the organic matter on the soil may be burned also. Soon, however, seeds and spores are blown in from neighboring areas. At first, only lichens, mosses, and annual plants grow in the bare soil or in the cracks of rocks. This community of small plants begins to cover the area. As the plants die, their remains are added to the soil. The plants change other factors of the abiotic environment, too. Their roots hold more moisture in the soil. The temperature of the soil may become suitable for the germination of seeds of other plant species. Within a few years a community of perennials, including grasses and sedges, may crowd out the first plants. A meadow is formed. Again the environment is slightly changed.

Somewhat later an aspen may grow from a seed or an unburned root. An aspen forest replaces shorter plants that are unable to tolerate the shade. On the other hand, seedlings of spruce and fir *can* survive in the shade of the young aspens. After many years the conifers push up through the aspens. Since aspens cannot survive in the shade of the taller conifers, the aspen community is replaced by the coniferous forest community.

succession [suk SESH un; Latin: *sub*, under, after, + *cedere*, to go]

This series of different communities replacing each other is called **succession.** Succession begins with bare soil or rock and ends with a community that is determined by the climate. The community that ends a succession is called the **climax**

community. It differs from the other communities in the succession process because it is not replaced by any other community. If a single spruce dies of old age, the space that it occupied is too shaded by neighboring spruces for aspen to grow. A young spruce, tolerant of shade, will probably take its place. Thus, once established, the climax community is relatively permanent.

Although other factors such as soil may play an important role, the climax is determined mainly by the climate of the region. In some areas, for instance, the climate is unsuitable for trees and the climax community is dominated by grasses. These climax communities make up the biomes we have been studying.

Try to find successional
ecosystems in your biome.

8 – 38 Succession on rock. How might succession differ if it were to begin on a sandbar?

A

B

C

D

David S. Galusha

BSCS by Robert F. Wilson

David S. Galusha

BSCS by Robert F. Wilson

262

8—39 Successional stages and animals of coniferous forest.

porcupine X 1/25

whitetail deer X 1/60

crossbill X 1/5

red squirrel X 1/8

elk X 1/80

meadow vole X 1/6

bare rock ⟶ lichen ⟶ meadow ⟶ aspens ⟶ spruc

SUCCESSION FROM ROCK

CLIM

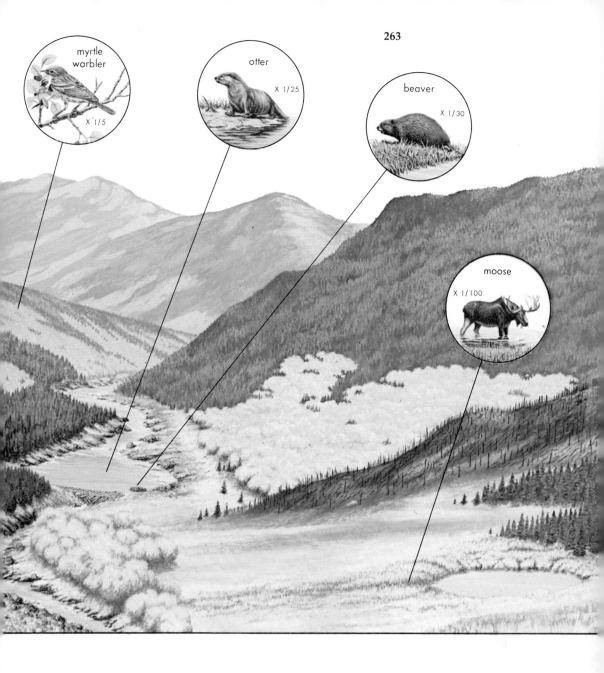

myrtle warbler X 1/5

otter X 1/25

beaver X 1/30

moose X 1/100

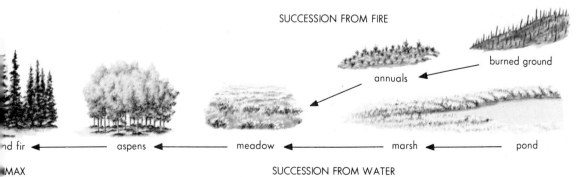

SUCCESSION FROM FIRE

burned ground

annuals

nd fir ← aspens ← meadow ← marsh ← pond

IMAX

SUCCESSION FROM WATER

CHECK YOURSELF

P. Why are there grasslands in the same latitudes as forests?

Q. What two abiotic environmental factors must be considered together in describing desert climate?

R. How are plants adapted to desert conditions?

S. What climatic factor explains the presence of deciduous trees in the tropics?

T. Compare and contrast hibernation and aestivation.

U. Describe the savanna biome and the abiotic factors that influence it.

V. What vegetation grows in mid-latitude rain forest?

W. What is chaparral?

X. How do conditions in an alpine ecosystem on mid-latitude mountains resemble conditions in the tundra? In what ways do the two sets of conditions differ?

Y. What kinds of conditions start natural ecological succession?

Z. What is meant by a climax community?

Investigation 8.2   TEMPERATURE, RAINFALL, AND BIOMES

INTRODUCTION

Climatograms show monthly variations in only two climatic factors, precipitation and temperature. Although other factors also affect climate, a climatogram *does* give a rough idea of the climate in a particular area.

By daily observation you can associate the climate of your own locality with the biome found there. Only by extensive travel, however, can the worldwide relationship of particular climates with particular biomes be learned. This investigation is a substitute for such travel. As you proceed through the investigation, refer frequently to pictures and descriptions of biomes. This will help you visualize relationships between the

MATERIALS
(per student)

3 to 17 sheets graph paper
pencil

abiotic and biotic features in some of the earth's major ecosystems.

PROCEDURE

1. Draw climatograms from the data in Group 1 (figure 8–40). When these are completed, you will have 10 climatograms (6 being on pages 241 and 253) that represent the major land biomes of the earth.

2. Obtain monthly averages of precipitation and temperature from the weather station closest to your school. These data may be

8–40 Group 1 data.

GROUP 1

T = temperature (in degrees Celsius)   P = precipitation (in centimeters)

a. Tropical Deciduous Forest: Cuiabá, Brazil

	J	F	M	A	M	J	J	A	S	O	N	D
T	27.2	27.2	27.2	26.7	25.6	23.9	24.4	25.6	27.8	27.8	27.8	27.2
P	24.9	21.1	21.1	10.2	5.3	0.8	0.5	2.8	5.1	11.4	15.0	20.6

b. Chaparral: Santa Monica, California

	J	F	M	A	M	J	J	A	S	O	N	D
T	11.7	11.7	12.8	14.4	15.6	17.2	18.9	18.3	18.3	16.7	14.4	12.8
P	8.9	7.6	7.4	1.3	1.3	0.0	0.0	0.0	0.3	1.5	3.6	5.8

c. Savanna: Moshi, Tanzania

	J	F	M	A	M	J	J	A	S	O	N	D
T	23.2	23.2	22.2	21.2	19.8	18.4	17.9	18.4	19.8	21.4	22.0	22.4
P	3.6	6.1	9.2	40.1	30.2	5.1	5.1	2.5	2.0	3.0	8.1	6.4

d. Tropical Desert: Aden, Aden

	J	F	M	A	M	J	J	A	S	O	N	D
T	24.6	25.1	26.4	28.5	30.6	31.9	31.1	30.3	31.1	28.8	26.5	25.1
P	0.8	0.5	1.3	0.5	0.3	0.3	0.0	0.3	0.3	0.3	0.3	0.3

expressed as inches of precipitation and degrees Fahrenheit. If so, convert the data to centimeters and degrees Celsius, using Appendix 1 (pages 731 and 732). From your local data, draw a climatogram.

3. From the data in Group 2 (figure 8–41), draw climatograms as they are assigned by your teacher.

DISCUSSION

Compare your climatogram based on local data with the 10 climatograms on pages 241 and 253 and in Group 1. (1) Which one of these does your local climatogram most nearly resemble? (2) In what ways are the two similar? Different? (3) Do they represent the same biome? If so, which is it? (4) If they do not, what climatic differences account for the biome differences? If they do, what charac-

teristics of climate seem to be related to characteristics of the biota in your biome?

Try to associate biomes with the climatograms drawn from data in Group 2. Use the generalizations you made from studying climatograms of known biomes. Of course, you are working with only two variables. You have no data on winds or cloud cover, and you can only judge humidity indirectly. Nevertheless, by careful thinking you can make fairly accurate deductions.

Write the name of your hypothesized biome at the top of each graph. (5) Relate the characteristics of the biota of each biome to the characteristics of its climate. Your teacher will give you the location of the places from which the data come. You can then check your reasoning.

8—41 Group 2 data.

GROUP 2

		J	F	M	A	M	J	J	A	S	O	N	D
a.	T	1.1	1.7	6.1	12.2	17.8	22.2	25.0	23.3	20.0	13.9	7.8	2.2
	P	8.1	7.6	8.9	8.4	9.2	9.9	11.2	10.2	7.9	7.9	6.4	7.9
b.	T	10.6	11.1	12.2	14.4	15.6	19.4	21.1	21.7	20.0	16.7	13.9	11.1
	P	9.1	8.9	8.6	6.6	5.1	2.0	0.5	0.5	3.6	8.4	10.9	10.4
c.	T	25.6	25.6	24.4	25.0	24.4	23.3	23.3	24.4	24.4	25.0	25.6	25.6
	P	25.8	24.9	31.0	16.5	25.4	18.8	16.8	11.7	22.1	18.3	21.3	29.2
d.	T·	12.8	15.0	18.3	21.1	25.0	29.4	32.8	32.2	28.9	22.2	16.1	13.3
	P	1.0	1.3	1.0	0.3	0.0	0.0	0.3	1.3	0.5	0.5	0.8	1.0
e.	T	−3.9	−2.2	1.7	8.9	15.0	20.0	22.8	21.7	16.7	11.1	5.0	−0.6
	P	2.3	1.8	2.8	2.8	3.2	5.8	5.3	3.0	3.6	2.8	4.1	3.3
f.	T	19.4	18.9	18.3	16.1	15.0	13.3	12.8	13.3	14.4	15.0	16.7	17.8
	P	0.0	0.0	1.5	0.5	8.9	14.7	12.2	8.1	2.0	1.0	0.3	0.8
g.	T	−22.2	−22.8	−21.1	−14.4	−3.9	1.7	5.0	5.0	1.1	−3.9	−10.0	−17.2
	P	1.0	1.3	1.8	1.5	1.5	1.3	2.3	2.8	2.8	2.8	2.8	1.3
h.	T	11.7	12.8	17.2	20.6	23.9	27.2	28.3	28.3	26.1	21.1	16.1	12.2
	P	3.6	4.1	4.6	6.9	8.1	6.9	6.4	6.6	8.9	5.1	5.6	4.6
i.	T	23.3	22.2	19.4	15.6	11.7	8.3	8.3	9.4	12.2	15.1	18.9	21.7
	P	5.1	5.6	6.6	5.6	2.8	0.9	2.5	4.1	5.8	5.8	5.1	5.3
j.	T	17.2	18.9	21.1	22.8	23.3	22.2	21.1	21.1	20.6	19.4	18.9	17.2
	P	0.3	0.5	1.5	3.6	·8.6	9.2	9.4	11.4	10.9	5.3	0.8	0.3
k.	T	−20.0	−18.9	−12.2	−2.2	5.6	12.2	16.1	15.0	10.6	3.9	−5.6	−15.0
	P	3.3	2.3	2.8	2.5	4.6	5.6	6.1	8.4	7.4	4.6	2.8	2.8
l.	T	−0.6	2.2	5.0	10.0	13.3	18.3	23.3	22.2	16.1	10.6	4.4	0.0
	P	1.5	1.3	1.3	1.0	1.5	0.8	0.3	0.5	0.8	1.0	0.8	1.5

GEOGRAPHIC RANGES

At the Arctic and Antarctic, climate and other abiotic factors are similar. Yet only in the Arctic do polar bears roam the ice floes. In the Antarctic they are absent. Only in the Antarctic do penguins waddle about. In the Arctic there are none. Why are there no polar bears near the South Pole and no penguins near the North Pole?

From observations such as these, we must conclude that tolerance to environmental factors does not entirely explain

8—42 Adelie penguins in Antarctica. How far north do penguins travel?

geographic ranges of organisms. Because an organism *can* live in a particular place does not necessarily mean that it *does* live there. To understand the geographic ranges of polar bears, penguins, and other organisms, we need additional facts.

We can start our search with two hypotheses. All species once occurred everywhere and later disappeared from some places. Or, each species originated in a particular place and then spread into other places. For the first of these hypotheses, biologists have little evidence. For the second, the evidence is strong. Scientists have studied fossils from all parts of the world. The evidence indicates that species populations originated in small areas and then spread.

DISPERSAL

Every farmer knows that if fences are not kept in good repair, the cattle will wander away. In all populations it is easy to observe this tendency of living things to spread from places where they are to places where they are not. This spreading of organisms is called **dispersal.**

In the case of motile organisms, dispersal may be accomplished by flying, swimming, walking, running, crawling, or burrowing. In the case of nonmotile organisms, dispersal is passive. Seeds, spores, and eggs can remain in a dormant state for long periods. During this time they may be carried great distances in currents of air or water or in mud on the foot of a bird. Even motile organisms may be carried much farther than they could travel themselves. A polar bear may be carried hundreds of kilometers on floating ice. A spider may be blown long distances by air currents.

Dispersal alone, of course, does not change a species' geographic range. Unless the organism can survive and reproduce in the new location, its range has not changed.

dispersal [dis PUR sul; Latin: *dispergere,* to scatter abroad]

passive: inactive but acted upon

How does this relate to the statement on page 201 about the geographical distribution of pond microorganisms?

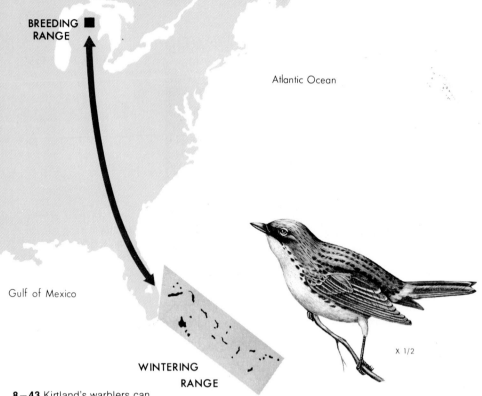

BREEDING RANGE ■

Atlantic Ocean

Gulf of Mexico

WINTERING RANGE

X 1/2

8–43 Kirtland's warblers can fly very well, yet they are found only in the small areas shown on the map. How might you explain this situation?

This is exactly what has happened in the case of at least one macroscopic species. Which?

What barrier has probably kept tsetse flies out of South America?

BARRIERS

Every kind of organism has some means of dispersal. It seems reasonable, therefore, to expect that eventually all species might be found wherever suitable environmental conditions are found. Actually, such a broad geographic range is the exception rather than the rule. What, then, limits the dispersal of organisms? In the case of pastured cattle, it is a fence — a **barrier.** In nature, too, barriers prevent dispersal.

For most terrestrial animals large areas of water are effective barriers. For aquatic animals the land may be a barrier. Mountains and rivers are barriers to many organisms. Besides such physical barriers there are ecological barriers. For organisms adapted to life in a forest, grassland or desert areas may be barriers. For grassland species, a forest region may limit dispersal.

Some barriers are behavioral. It seems reasonable to suppose, for instance, that flying birds would be found almost everywhere. But many birds that can fly great distances remain in very restricted regions. The Amazon River, in Brazil, serves as a boundary of the ranges of many forest birds. Most of these birds could fly across the river, but apparently they seldom try to do so.

268

NOAA

8—44 A tornado near Union City, Oklahoma.

An increase in the population of a motile species encourages emigration to less populated areas. Dispersal may take place rapidly as the population grows. But, when barriers are great, dispersal may be slow even though the population is increasing rapidly. In passive dispersal the means of transportation may be the most important factor in determining rate of spread. Species of trees whose seeds are carried away and buried by squirrels have been estimated to spread about 1.6 km every 1,000 years. By contrast, organisms swept up in a tornado may be carried 30 km in a few hours.

What tree species have seeds that are easily carried by wind?

RESULTS

If our reasoning is correct, we can now explain the absence of polar bears from the Antarctic. We first assume that polar bears originated in the Arctic. Their ecological requirements are such that the tropical environment is a barrier to their dispersal. This wide barrier has existed throughout the existence of the polar bear species. Thus far no part of the population has been able to move across the barrier. Therefore, no polar bears are found in the Antarctic. Similar reasoning can be applied to the dispersal of penguins.

X 1/13

8—45 Cattle egret. This native of Africa is now found in much of America. Try to find out how it got here.

HUMAN INFLUENCE ON TERRESTRIAL ECOSYSTEMS

Flying from Cleveland, Ohio, to Nashville, Tennessee, you cross the biome of mid-latitude deciduous forest. You see only a few traces of forest, however. Flying from Chicago, Illinois, to Lincoln, Nebraska, you cross the eastern part of the North American grassland. Here, too, you see only traces of the original climax ecosystem. In fact, in these two flights the landscapes below appear to be remarkably alike. Although in both cases climate remains an important factor, the present landscape has been shaped by people.

Photo by Frank Grant of G/W Photography Ltd.; courtesy of Rio Algom Limited

8–46 An aerial view of Elliot Lake, Ontario. How have humans influenced the ecosystem?

DISPERSAL

Our species has wandered more widely than any other. In our travels we have carried other organisms with us. At first, perhaps, this meant merely the dispersal of parasites such as lice. Later, mice and rats may have been transported accidentally. Today, dandelions and other weeds are carried along with crop plants. And airplane travel has made easy the rapid dispersal of insects and microorganisms.

intentional [in TEN chun ul; Latin: *in*, into, + *tendere*, to stretch]: done purposely

People began cultivating plants about 10,000 years ago. Since then we have become agents of intentional dispersal. Many organisms have been carried over barriers they might never have been able to cross themselves. Oranges and lemons were taken from southeastern Asia and were introduced to all warm regions of the earth. Wheat and barley were taken from southwestern Asia. They now replace huge areas once covered by forest and grassland. Cattle and horses from Asian grasslands now graze in almost every biome except tundra.

Choose several domesticated animals or plants. Find out where they originated and how they reached your region.

To bring banana plants to Pennsylvania in hopes of starting a plantation is ecologically absurd. But it is not always so easy to determine if an organism will thrive or fail in a new area. In some cases organisms have easily become part of the ecosystem in the new area, as have wheat and oranges. When humans brought a few European rabbits to Australia, the rabbits quickly spread over much of the continent without the help of humans. In other cases, however, organisms continue to exist only through constant human protection. Wheat has been grown in England for 2,000 years. But it probably would not be found there if it were not cultivated. Dozens of species of European birds have been transported to North America. But fewer than

What are they?

half a dozen of these species have become a real part of the North American biota.

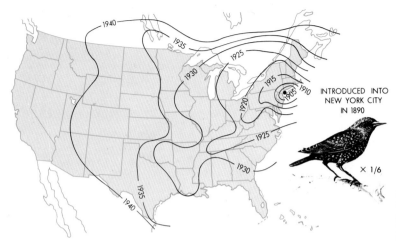

INTRODUCED INTO
NEW YORK CITY
IN 1890

× 1/6

8−47 Expansion of the range of the European starling in North America. It now extends to the Pacific. The first reported sighting near the west coast was at Lake Tahoe, California, on January 10, 1942.

Attempts to transplant species fail more often than they succeed. But there is always danger that in a new environment an organism may adapt *too* well to suit human interests. The Australian rabbits became disastrous pests in pastures. Governments now require careful studies of the ecological relationships of any organism proposed for introduction into a new area. And most governments have set up inspection services at their borders to examine incoming automobiles, ships, and planes. In this way they hope to prevent accidental introduction of undesirable organisms.

CULTIVATION

By transporting organisms and cultivating them in new regions, people have changed whole ecosystems. In some cases the change has been small. Wheat, a grass from Asia, adapts well to the former grassland of Kansas, because its tolerances are similar to those of the native grasses. A Kansas wheat field is a grassland similar to the native grassland it replaces. The wheat field, however, is composed of one species instead of a mixture. Wheat fields also do well in Virginia, but there humans had to remove deciduous forest to plant the wheat. To the organisms that were a part of the Virginia forest ecosystem, the wheat-field ecosystem is an intolerable place to live. Many organisms of the Kansas grassland, on the other hand, can adapt to the wheat-field ecosystem.

In many parts of the world, cultivation has changed ecosystems even more than in the Virginia example. In some places, agricultural land has actually been made. The Dutch have drained land once covered by the sea. The Filipinos have built terraces for rice on steep slopes in tropical forests. Many countries, such as Israel, have irrigated deserts to make productive

Many of the weeds of cultivated fields in eastern North America are immigrant species from Eurasia. Can you explain this?

8 – 48 Pattern formed in cornfields watered by center-pivot irrigation systems.

farmlands. And there are millions of hectares of irrigated land in the United States today.

We have had difficulty in trying to cultivate certain ecosystems. In the short-grass plains of the North American grassland, there are periodic droughts and strong winds. The native grasses can survive the droughts. Their matted roots protect the soil from wind erosion. In the early part of the 20th century, these native grasslands were plowed, and cultivated fields were established. In the 1930's and again in the 1950's, great droughts occurred that lasted several years. With the perennial native grasses gone and the cultivated crops destroyed by drought, winds swept up the dry, rich topsoil in great dust storms. Many areas were left barren. With the return of normal rains, neither the cultivated crops nor the native grasses could be reestablished easily on the poor soil that remained.

8 – 49 Dust-storm damage (Oklahoma), April, 1936.

SUCCESSION

What occurred in the short-grass plains was a case of setting a biome back to an early stage of succession. Many human activities do this. Plowing exposes bare earth. Dams and dikes cover land with water. Hundreds of hectares of concrete and asphalt roads and parking lots are built each year in the United States. These create a kind of bare-rock condition similar to the result of an earthquake or landslide. Lumbering sets back succession several stages, much as do fires.

We have said that a cultivated field is an artificial ecosystem. Perhaps it is equally reasonable to say that a wheat field in Virginia is an early stage in a succession toward deciduous forest. Either viewpoint might be supported. Suppose a Virginia wheat field is abandoned. In the first year we might observe that the field becomes covered with annual weeds, such as ragweed. In the second year perennial plants—goldenrods, asters, and grasses—become conspicuous. By the third or fourth year young woody plants are large enough to be seen among the herbs. Within a decade young trees shade out the earlier perennial herbs. As the trees grow larger, their fallen leaves begin to form a humus soil in which seeds of forest herbs and shrubs can germinate. After nearly two centuries some abandoned Virginia fields could develop an ecosystem almost identical to the original climax deciduous forest.

X 1/8

8–50 Ragweed.

8–51 A lodgepole-pine forest (Wyoming). What is happening here?

Haven Kolb

CHECK YOURSELF

AA. In what ways does dispersal of organisms occur?

BB. In addition to knowledge of biological tolerances, what information do you need to explain the geographic ranges of species?

CC. How can a barrier to the dispersal of one species be a pathway for dispersal of another?

DD. In what ways have humans been agents of dispersal for other organisms?

EE. How has human dispersal of other organisms affected the biota of North America?

FF. What human activities produced "grassland landscapes" in mid-latitude deciduous forests?

GG. What human activities produced, at least temporarily, a "desert" in a grassland biome?

HH. How is succession that has been modified by human activities related to the natural succession pattern of the biome?

Investigation 8.3   EFFECTS OF FIRE ON BIOMES

INTRODUCTION

Fire is an important ecological factor in terrestrial ecosystems. Some fires start from natural causes. But many are caused by people — deliberately or accidentally. No matter how they begin, fires have many effects on the organisms in their paths. The most easily observed effects are on vegetation.

PROCEDURE

As you read each of the following sections, base your answers to the questions on study of figures 8–52, 8–53, and 8–54.

1. Fire in mid-latitude grassland. Figures 8–52A to 8–52D picture a series of events that occur in the southern part of the North American grassland. Two kinds of populations are involved: grasses of various species and mesquite shrubs. Study figures 8–52A and 8–52B. *(1)* What is happening to the sizes of the populations?

Roots of mesquite have been found in mine shafts many meters below the surface of the soil. *(2)* What competitive advantage might this kind of root growth give mesquite over grasses? *(3)* If occasional droughts strike the area (as actually happens), what kind of community do you think might result?

Now refer to figures 8–52C and 8–52D. In these figures plant parts shown in light color at or below ground level represent unharmed tissue. *(4)* Do both kinds of plants survive fires? *(5)* In which kind has more growing tissue been killed? Grasses usually reach maturity and produce seeds in 1 or 2 years; mesquite usually requires 4 to 10 years. *(6)* Which kind of plant has lost more in terms of growing time? *(7)* In figure 8–52D which kind of plant occupies most of the land? *(8)* What might you expect this area to look like 4 or 5 years after a fire?

Now you can make a generalization on

8–52 Fire in mid-latitude grassland.

A

B

C

D

the effect of fire in this community. (9) Describe the probable landscape if fires did not occur at all. (10) What would be the appearance of the landscape if fires occurred every few years? (11) What environmental factor seems to be necessary for maintaining grassland in this region?

2. Fire in a forest of the Great Lakes region. Around the Great Lakes of North America is a region of transition between the coniferous and mid-latitude deciduous forests. In many places much of the forest consists of pines (figure 8–53A). But, early in the settlement of the region, Europeans brought about a great change in the landscape (figure 8–53B). (12) What was this change?

Fires apparently had been rare in this

8–53 Fire in a forest of the Great Lakes region.

A

B

C

D

region, but following the change they became more frequent. (*13*) What might have brought about the increase in the number of fires? (*14*) If fire does not occur, what might the area shown in figure 8–53B look like in later years?

Study figures 8–53B, 8–53C, and 8–53D, which picture jack pine. (*15*) What characteristic of jack pine gives that species a competitive advantage when there is a fire?

8–54 Fire in a forest of the southeastern United States.

A

B

C

D

(*16*) Describe the probable appearance of the area shown in figure 8–53D 5 or 6 years later. Jack pines produce cones in 8 to 10 years but do not live to a very great age. Their seedlings do not thrive in shade. Suppose no fires occur for 200 years. (*17*) What changes in appearance might take place in this area during that period? Suppose fires occur about once every 20 years. (*18*) What might the area look like at the end of 200 years?

3. Fire in a forest of the southeastern United States. In the southeastern United States are great forests in which longleaf pine is almost the only large tree. Occasionally there may be seedlings and saplings of deciduous trees. Between 3 and 7 years of age longleaf pines look somewhat like clumps of grass (figure 8–54A). While in this "grass stage," the young trees develop deep roots in which food is stored. (See cutaway, lower corner of figure 8–54A.)

Fires in these forests generally are confined to the ground, where they burn grasses and the sparse growth of deciduous shrubs and saplings (figure 8–54B). (*19*) What is the effect of fire on young longleaf pines? (*20*) What is the effect on the deciduous shrubs and saplings? (*21*) Which plants have a competitive advantage after a fire?

After the "grass stage," longleaf pines grow rapidly in height and develop a thick, fire-resistant bark. (*22*) What is the effect of ground fires at this stage in the development of the pines (figure 8–54C)? (*23*) Which plants have a competitive advantage when fires do not occur (figure 8–54D)? (*24*) What

factor seems to maintain a forest of longleaf pines within the deciduous-forest biome?

DISCUSSION

Knowledge of the ecological effects of fire on biomes can be useful to humans. (*25*) If you were interested in raising cattle in a mid-latitude grassland, would occasional fires be an advantage or a disadvantage? Why?

Jack pine is not as valuable a lumber tree as are other trees of the Great Lakes region. (*26*) If you were a landowner in that region, would fire be an advantage or a disadvantage? Why? (*27*) If you were interested in maintaining a longleaf-pine forest to obtain turpentine, would ground fires be an advantage or a disadvantage? Why?

Suppose you wanted bobwhites (game birds that nest on the ground) in your turpentine forest. (28) What effect might this have on your management of the forest? (29) What things must ecologists know before deciding whether to recommend fire as a method of management to a landowner?

FOR FURTHER INVESTIGATION

Investigation 8.3 is based on case studies of fires in forest and grassland management (originally published in *Scientific American*). Recent controversy over fire as a means of control of diseases of forest trees, and of replacement of older trees by younger ones, has been discussed in many newspaper articles. A useful and comprehensive reference is T. T. Kozlowski and C. E. Ahlgren (eds.), 1974, *Fire and Ecosystems,* Academic Press, New York.

PROBLEMS

1. Make a list of terrestrial organisms that human beings have brought into your locality. Divide the list into two parts: organisms that (in your opinion) survive because of human activities, and organisms that (in your opinion) would survive without human help. Give reasons for your decision on each organism.

2. Choose some small taxonomic groups (genera or families) that are present in your state or locality. Investigate their distribution in the world as a whole, and construct maps to show this information. Try to explain the distribution shown on your maps; then do library research on the career of a biogeographer.

3. Plan some library research, or correspondence with agencies by mail, to learn how careers in state and national forest services, park commissions, wildlife agencies, and game and fish departments are concerned with (a) numbers of visitors to parks and forests; (b) operation of fish hatcheries; (c) control and management of fires; (d) determination of hunting seasons, or banning of hunting; and (e) control of plant and animal diseases.

4. Explanations of the present geographic ranges of organisms may depend not only on expansion from former ranges but also on reduction of former ranges. What are some of the factors that might decrease an organism's range?

5. The dispersal of starlings in North America is shown in figure 8–47. Investigate other cases of dispersal in North America—gypsy moths, Formosan termites, the fungus of Dutch elm disease.

6. Describe what you think would happen if all human beings left the following places: (a) a farm in Nebraska; (b) a sidewalk in New York; (c) a swimming pool in Seattle, Washington; (d) a landscaped park in Las Vegas, Nevada.

7. Investigate the dispersal and related consequences of the following organisms: in Florida—walking catfish and piranha; in southern California—Xenopus, the African clawed frog.

SUGGESTED READINGS

Elias, T. S. and H. S. Irwin. 1976. Urban Trees. *Scientific American*, November. Relatively few kinds of trees are suited to growth in cities.

Espenshade, E. B., Jr. and J. L. Morrison (eds.). 1982. *Goode's World Atlas*. 16th ed. Rand McNally, Chicago. World maps show distribution of major climatic factors.

Gore, R. 1979. The Desert: An Age-old Challenge Grows. *National Geographic*, November, pp. 586–639.

Guthrie, R. D. and P. A. Zahl. 1972. A Look at Alaska's Tundra. *National Geographic*, March, pp. 293–337.

Kendeigh, S. G. 1974. *Ecology with Special Reference to Animals and Man*. Prentice-Hall, Englewood Cliffs, N. J. Chapters 22–27 describe biomes and their subdivisions.

Fairly advanced.

National Geographic Society. 1979. *National Geographic*, July. An entire issue devoted to the more than 300 U. S. National Parks.

Spurr, S. H. 1979. Silviculture. *Scientific American*, February. Forest productivity can be doubled or tripled by modern management methods.

Whittaker, R. H. 1975. *Communities and Ecosystems*. Macmillan, New York. Discusses biomes, succession, climax, and nutrient circulation.

Zwinger, A. H. and B. E. Willard. 1972. *Land Above the Trees*. Harper & Row, New York. Guide to alpine tundra in the United States. Easy to read, with descriptions of plants and animals in each area.

Careers in Biology: A Florist

Rick Riggs' hobby is also his life's work; he owns a florist shop and greenhouse. Rick was studying biology in college when he started working at a florist shop. Rick received his master's degree in biology, but he became so interested in the business of growing plants that he left the university and bought the shop before finishing work on his Ph.D.

In his shop Rick has many young potted plants. He realizes, however, that it is often hard for a customer to imagine what the young plants will look like when they mature. To help his customers, he has placed full-grown plants next to the young ones, all growing in the right light conditions. People may come in and choose the small inexpensive plants. And they can see that, in time and with proper care, their plants can be tall, healthy, and beautiful.

Rick thinks one of the most rewarding and delightful aspects of his job is to be able to produce a plant from a seed or cutting, watching with satisfaction as it grows to full form. The job requires an understanding of plant physiology, ecology, and horticulture. There's a lot of common sense involved, too.

The Riggs' home is right behind the

Carlye Calvin

Carlye Calvin

B. Rick offers plants in a variety of colors, shapes, and sizes. Many of today's popular houseplants are grown in this section of the greenhouse.

A. A wall of flowers attracts the curious to Rick's backyard garden and then into his shop.

C. Rick has several very uncommon plants. Many of these are only for display, such as this *Dioscorea*, which looks like a large turtle shell.

D. One area of the greenhouse is devoted entirely to cactus plants. This display shows the many types of cacti available.

shop. That makes it easy for Rick, his wife, Carol, and their children to work at the shop. High school students work there part-time, as do college students who are majoring in plant biology.

For their shop Rick and Carol have built an outdoor botanic garden with a beautiful pond and walkways through an herb and vegetable garden, with hanging baskets decorating the area. It just so happens that all this is the Riggs backyard, too.

The Riggs family have found that working together can be enjoyable and profitable—as long as you have "green thumbs."

E. Rick examines an exotic flowering plant from the tropics.

F. John Gonzales left school for a period of time, but he is now a student at a local high school. He earns work-study credits through his work in the greenhouse. John's plans for the future include a career in landscaping.

G. John arranges one of the unique displays in the garden between the Riggs' home and the greenhouse. He helped Rick plant and landscape the garden.

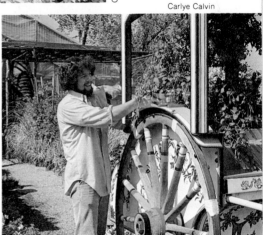

H. Carol Riggs and her daughter, Beth, pick off dead leaves and blossoms from this display of petunias. Customers are attracted to the colorful arrays of plants. They will purchase them and plant them in their yards or window boxes.

Chapter 9

Life in the Water

YOUR GUIDEPOSTS

In this chapter you will have an opportunity to explore these questions in biology:

- How are environmental conditions in water ecosystems different from those on land?
- How can major aquatic ecosystems be distinguished from one another?
- How do aquatic ecosystems affect humans, a terrestrial species?
- How do human activities affect aquatic ecosystems?
- *Adaptations and survival in the water biosphere*

THE HYDROSPHERE

Our planet, when viewed from outer space, is blue with water and water vapor. All this water makes up the **hydrosphere,** just as all the air makes up the atmosphere. The hydrosphere is a vast heat reservoir. It absorbs, stores, and circulates heat that results when radiant energy strikes the earth. It is also a reservoir of chemical elements and compounds. These are continuously being dissolved in water that eventually drains into the

A good atlas may be useful while you study this chapter.

hydrosphere [HY droh sfir; Greek: *hydro*, water, + *sphaira*, sphere]

NOAA

9–1 A part of the hydrosphere.

283

Wide World Photos

9–2 Tuna catch from the ocean off the eastern United States.

In what places have people made the most use of aquatic food resources?

What inland bodies of water are located below sea level?

What inland bodies of water contain large amounts of dissolved minerals?

delta: so called because the deposit of soil at a river mouth is usually triangular, resembling the Greek letter "delta"

oceans. Fossil evidence indicates that the oceans were the original home of life. In short, the hydrosphere is the center of events in the biosphere. Terrestrial happenings are a sideshow.

We are terrestrial organisms. Historically, most human beings have cared little about the hydrosphere. Those who did care were those who skimmed food from the water's edge or used the surface to get from one piece of land to another. However, humans have always lived close to a source of fresh water. Look at the places throughout the world where villages, towns, and cities have developed. They are usually close to a supply of fresh water (creeks, rivers, and lakes). Now, as terrestrial sources of food and material are becoming scarce, scientists have increased their attempts to understand aquatic ecosystems.

Let us begin our study with the distinction between ocean water and inland water. Oceans form the great interconnecting system that surrounds the continents. Tides are clearly evident in these waters. Inland waters are found on the surface of the land. Most are above "sea level" and their water tends to flow downward to the oceans. Oceans usually contain a considerable amount of dissolved minerals. Inland waters usually contain very little. But, again, there are exceptions.

INLAND WATERS

Inland waters are affected in many ways by the surrounding land. But they also have their own environmental characteristics. Puddles in South Dakota, Germany, and Australia contain very similar protists. The Nile delta is surrounded by desert and the Mississippi delta by forest. Yet environmental conditions are similar *within* the slow-moving, warm, muddy waters of both rivers.

Inland-water ecosystems are grouped as standing waters or as flowing waters. As is usual in ecological classification, the boundary between these is not sharp. A pond is an example of standing water. However, many ponds are fed by springs or brooks and many have outlets. Some current of water passes through most ponds. On the other hand, a river is an example of flowing water. Yet in some places a river may have such a slow current that it is difficult to observe.

STANDING WATERS

Standing waters range in size from roadside puddles to the Caspian Sea, over 350,000 km². Puddles may last for only a few days or weeks and ponds may last for a few hundred years. In general, lakes are older than ponds. Standing waters range from very shallow to very deep, from clear to muddy, and from fresh to salty.

A pond. In many parts of the United States, there are no natural ponds, but people have built their own. To understand ponds, it does not matter much whether you study a natural or an artificial one. As an example we will describe a natural pond in the northeastern United States. As you read, try to compare this pond with one you know.

See figure 9–17.

We stand on a hill overlooking the pond. As we walk down the tree-covered slope, mosquitoes start to annoy and "bite." They began their life in the pond. We walk out of the trees into a tangle of low shrubs. As we push our way through willows and alders, the ground becomes wetter. We leave the last shrubs behind us and our feet sink into mud. Before us lies a marsh of sedges and cattails, with shallow water lapping about their stems. Dragonflies—newly emerged from the water—dart about. Frogs sit on driftwood and a water snake slithers through the muddy water. A muskrat interrupts its meal of cattail stems and shuffles away. In wading boots we follow the muskrat through the cattails. At last we see the open water surface. Here and there it is dotted with leaves of water lilies. With our boots in deep mud and with water at our knees we are now in the middle of the pond ecosystem.

See figure 9–4.

emerged [ih MURJD; Latin: *ex,* out of, + *mergere,* to dip]: risen out of (here) water

9–3 A mountain pond in July (Colorado). What are the environmental conditions here and what are their effects?

Haven Kolb

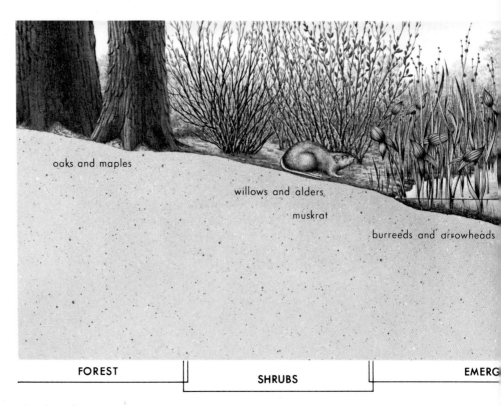

oaks and maples

willows and alders

muskrat

burreeds and arrowheads

FOREST   SHRUBS   EMERG

9—4 Cross section through the edge of a natural pond in the northeastern United States.

In studying any ecosystem, an ecologist first looks for its source of energy. In a pond the most important producers are not the most obvious ones. The large emergent plants such as cattails are conspicuous, but they produce little of the ecosystem's food. Indeed, in some ponds—especially artificial ones—emergent plants may be scarce or absent. We see many plants within the water itself—some floating on the surface, some submerged. Such plants may become so numerous that their thick mass hampers a swimmer. Yet even these are not the most important pond producers.

You may have watched specks of dust drifting in a bright beam of sunlight. In a beam of light shining into a pond, you also can see moving specks that look like dust. But these specks are living organisms. Some are plants, some are protists, and some are animals. All are microscopic or nearly so. Few can swim, but all can stay afloat. They are carried about by the currents in the water. Together all these microscopic organisms are called **plankton.**

Early ecologists began to realize that plankton make up for their small size by their incredible numbers. Careful studies

submerged [sub MURJD; Latin: *sub*, under, + *mergere*]

plankton: from the Greek word for "wanderer"

incredible [in CRED uh bul; Latin: *in*, not, + *credare*, to believe]

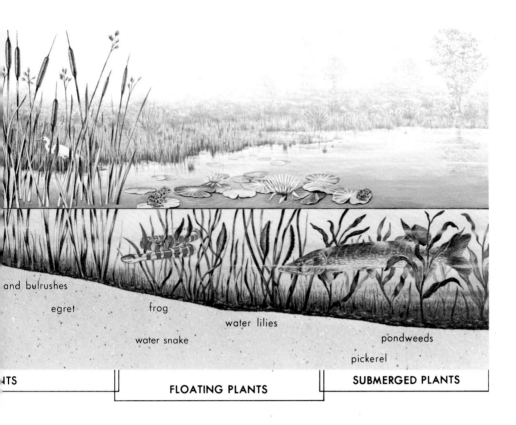

and bulrushes

egret

frog

water snake

water lilies

pondweeds

pickerel

NTS	FLOATING PLANTS	SUBMERGED PLANTS

M. Woodbridge Williams/National Park Service

9-5 Some pond producers.

showed that most food production in all parts of the hydro-sphere—not just in ponds—is the result of photosynthesis by plankton.

phytoplankton
[fyt oh PLANK tun; Greek: *phyton*, a plant, + plankton]

Use the Index and "A Catalog of Living Things," Appendix 3, whenever you need to refresh your memory of organisms.

The plankton producers are collectively called **phyto-plankton.** Many are algae, but some are chlorophyll-bearing protists. Different kinds of phytoplankton vary in abundance from one body of water to another. Diatoms are usually the most numerous, though not the most conspicuous. Green algae may become so abundant in late summer that a pond's whole surface becomes green.

Because most pond producers are microscopic, you might expect the herbivores to be small too. Most of them are, and they are called **zooplankton.** Zooplankton are protists (ciliates

zooplankton [zoh uh PLANK tun]

9-6 Some zooplankton organisms often found in ponds. Can you suggest the phylum and class in which each might be classified?

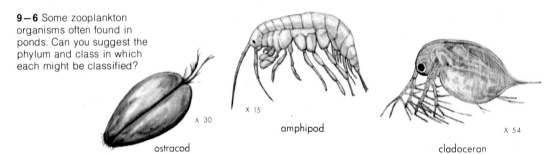

X 30

X 15

X 54

ostracod   amphipod   cladoceran

and flagellates) and animals (rotifers and many tiny crusta-ceans). Some pond herbivores are *not* plankton. For example, young fish are active swimmers, and mussels are macroscopic bottom dwellers. Both are herbivores. Many pond fishes are car-nivores; the larger kinds eat the smaller. Fishes of all sizes eat aquatic insects, many of which are themselves carnivores. Some pond food chains have many links. Most of the macroscopic carnivores stay near the edge of a pond, where the floating plants provide a hiding place. The larger predatory fishes swim throughout the pond.

X 1/3

9-7 A freshwater mussel.

Dead organisms sink, so layers of organic matter build up on pond bottoms. Decomposers such as tubifex worms (anne-lids) burrow in this rich source of energy. As in all ecosystems, however, the most important decomposers are bacteria and fungi.

A pond ecosystem is not sharply bounded by the surface of the water. Insects are usually flying above and around ponds. Many of them hatch from eggs laid in the water and spend most of their lives there. For example, only the last few hours of a mayfly's life are spent out of water when the adults mate in the air. The females lay eggs in the water, and the immature may-flies grow there for a year or more. Frogs live largely on such insects. Water snakes eat fish and frogs. Many kinds of birds

X 10

9-8 A tubifex worm.

and some mammals feed on fish, crayfish, and mussels. Such consumers, though they spend much of their time on land, are truly part of pond ecosystems. Their energy supply can be traced back to phytoplankton.

Lakes. To most people the word "lake" suggests a body of water larger than a pond. To an ecologist a pond is a body of water so shallow that light penetrates to the bottom. A lake, on the other hand, has some depths that are always dark.

The largest of all freshwater lakes is Lake Superior. It covers an area about the size of South Carolina but has a maximum depth of only 410 m. Two very deep lakes are Baikal (1,750 m), in Russia, and Tanganyika (1,449 m), in Africa. Lake Superior is perhaps 10,000 to 20,000 years old. Both Baikal and Tanganyika were formed millions of years ago. Such wide variation in lake size, depth, and age means that conditions for lake life also vary greatly.

Food produced by rooted aquatic plants is even less important in lakes than in ponds. Lake ecosystems depend on phytoplankton. But the phytoplankton of a lake, unlike that of a pond, does not live throughout the lake. It can exist only near the water's surface, where there is enough light for photosynthesis. In deeper lakes light may penetrate to a depth of about 80 m. The depth of light penetration depends on the clearness of the water and the amount of cloudiness in the sky. In deep lakes, therefore, all the food is produced in the upper part of the water.

The existence of aquatic consumers is not limited by light but may be limited by the amount of oxygen in the water. Surface water constantly receives dissolved oxygen from photosynthesis and from the air, particularly through wave action. The oxygen moves slowly downward from the surface, but before going very far most of it is used up by zooplankton. The spread of oxygen into deep water must depend on other factors.

The sun heats the surface water of a lake. The water expands and becomes less dense—lighter. Winds push this surface layer across the lake toward the shore. Here it rolls downward. It does not go down far before it meets colder, denser water. The warm water doubles back across the lake, sliding between the cold water and the warmer surface water. This process carries oxygen from the surface only a short distance downward. The colder, deeper water still remains without oxygen. In the tropics this process goes on all year. It's not surprising, then, that tropical lakes such as Tanganyika have no deep-water aerobic animals.

Outside the tropics, however, another process occurs. As winter approaches, the sun gradually sinks lower in the sky and heats the surface water less. Eventually this water cools to 4°C. At this point the surface water becomes denser than the deeper

mayfly nymph

X 2

X 1

dragonfly nymph

9–9 Many insects occur in water only as nearly wingless, immature forms called nymphs. For adult mayfly and dragonfly, see figure 4–24.

penetrate [PEN uh trayt; Latin: *penitus*, inward]: to pass into something

water beneath it. It then sinks and forces the deep water to the top; a large-scale turnover of the lake water occurs. In this manner oxygen is distributed yearly throughout the lake. So lakes outside the tropics have many animals in their deeper water. Some animals have been found at a depth of 600 m in Lake Baikal.

9–10 Comparison of a lake in the tropics (A) with one in temperate regions (B).

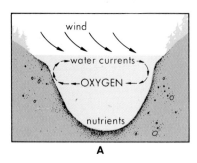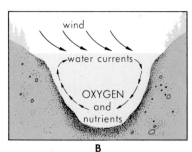

A   B

Although animals are absent from the deeper water of some lakes, anaerobic organisms are probably present on all lake bottoms. There, organic matter that decomposers use as food is plentiful. It continually drifts down from above, as dead organisms in the upper water sink.

If a lake has no outlet, minerals washed in from the surrounding land become concentrated in the water. In arid regions this process is speeded up by the high rate of evaporation. The water may become saturated with minerals. Usually the most abundant is sodium chloride (NaCl), common table salt. The result is an environment unfavorable to almost all organisms. The Great Salt Lake, in Utah, has a high concentration of NaCl in its water. Only brine shrimp, a few species of blue-green algae, and two species of brine flies can survive there. But these are found in great numbers.

See Investigation 2.4.

9–11 Mono Lake, California. The water is so alkaline that only brine shrimp live in it.

Douglas W. James, Jr.

CHECK YOURSELF

A. What is the hydrosphere?
B. How do ecologists divide the earth's waters for study?
C. What are the principal kinds of inland waters?
D. What are plankton organisms?
E. How do phytoplankton affect a pond ecosystem?
F. How is a pond ecosystem linked to surrounding ter-
   restrial ecosystems?
G. How do scientists distinguish between ponds and
   lakes?
H. What limits the depth at which photosynthesis can
   occur in lakes?
I. Why are living animals found deep in Lake Baikal
   but not deep in Lake Tanganyika?

FLOWING WATERS

Some of the water that falls on land runs directly into lakes,
ponds, and streams. Some evaporates. But most of it soaks into
the ground. This ground water reappears in springs, from
which the course to the ocean may be short or long.

What factors might affect the amount of water that sinks into the ground?

From brooks to rivers. Most springs give rise to small brooks.
Such flowing water is usually cool—though some hot springs
do exist. Tumbling through rapids and falls, the water traps
many air bubbles, from which oxygen easily dissolves. Since
cool water can hold relatively large amounts of gases in solution, the water in brooks usually contains much oxygen.

Where might you find hot-water brooks?

In the swift-flowing water of brooks, plankton are absent.

9–12 A brook (Washington). What evidence can you see that this aquatic ecosystem probably has few producers?

P. Steucke/U.S. Forest Service

What are some other reasons why such water lacks plankton?

They are swept away. Producers—green algae, diatoms, and water mosses—grow attached to stones. These producers provide some food and much shelter for aquatic insects. The insects, in turn, are food for small fish. Most of the food supply in a brook ecosystem comes from the land around it. Small terrestrial organisms, such as insects, fall in and are eaten by stream inhabitants. Every rain washes in dead organic matter. Anything not used immediately, however, is washed downstream, so there is very little food for decomposers.

Brooks meet, forming larger streams with wider beds and more water. Here the water usually moves more slowly. Solid substances that have been carried along by the swift brooks are now deposited as sediments. Bits of organic matter, accumulating among the sediments, provide food for decomposers.

sediments [SED uh muntz; Latin: *sedere*, to sit]

As the stream widens, the relative amount of water surface shaded by trees along its banks decreases. Direct sunlight reaches most of the water surface. Increased light increases the rate of photosynthesis, so some phytoplankton organisms may live in this slower-moving water. However, many still are carried downstream. Rooted plants like those in ponds grow in the sediments of a stream bottom. They, too, may be washed away during floods.

Because it contains more producers, a stream supports a larger number of consumers than does a brook. On the bottom are mussels, snails, crayfish, and many immature insects. Dependent on these bottom dwellers are larger consumers such as turtles and fish.

Many streams come together to form a river. Rivers are large bodies of flowing water. As a river approaches the sea, it usually moves more slowly and deposits larger amounts of sediments. Thus, near its mouth a river often builds up land instead

9–13 Part of the delta of the Mississippi River. What major kinds of ecosystems can you see here?

Aero Services Division, Western Geophysical Co. of America

of eroding it. The river banks may actually become higher than the land behind them. During floods a river often breaks through these natural levees. The water left behind is slow to drain away, and it forms a swamp. Many emergent and floating plants grow in these swampy lands. Fruits, seeds, and other parts of these plants are swept into the river during floods. They then contribute to the food supply. But much of the food for consumers in large rivers comes from phytoplankton, which grow well in the unshaded, slow-moving water.

Consumers in rivers are varied and numerous. Zooplankton are food for bigger predators. Mollusks, crustaceans, and fish often grow large. In tropical rivers crocodiles are common. Many terrestrial birds and mammals obtain their food from rivers, just as many do from ponds. And since ancient times many people also have taken advantage of the abundant food in rivers.

Flowing waters as a laboratory. Not all springs give rise to brooks. Some pour forth so much water that large streams flow from them. Many of the short rivers of northwest Florida originated in this way.

The short Florida rivers are fine outdoor laboratories. Each river has lengths with stable conditions of volume, current, chemical composition, and temperature. Ecologists have used several of these rivers in a study of ecological productivity.

Productivity of any community depends on the photosynthetic rate of its producers. This rate can be measured indirectly. Photosynthesizing organisms give off oxygen in a known proportion to the amount of organic substances that they produce. To calculate productivity, biologists first measure the oxygen given off during a measured period of time. Using this number, they can then calculate the amount of organic substance produced through photosynthesis during that same time.

Ecologists measured the amount of oxygen in the water of Rainbow Springs and in the river water at several places downstream (figure 9–14). Such measurements are expressed as "parts per million" (ppm), which is related to percent. (For example, 1 percent is 10,000 ppm, and 1 ppm is 0.0001 percent.) Any increase in the amount of oxygen in the spring water

eroding [ih ROHD ing; Latin *ex*, out, + *rodere*, to gnaw]

levees [LEV eez; Latin: *levare*, to raise]

Many ancient riverside civilizations were agricultural. How did river ecosystems contribute to agriculture?

See figure 3–1.

productivity: here, the amount of organic substance produced per unit of time

Percents are "parts per hundred," which is much too crude for expressing amounts of oxygen dissolved in water.

Rainbow Springs

5.0 km station

8.0 ppm

9.0 ppm

10.5 ppm

7.6 ppm

10.7 ppm

7.35 ppm

9–14 Diagram of Rainbow Springs (Florida) and the river that flows from them.

as it flowed downstream came largely from photosynthesis. Figure 9–14 shows the oxygen content measured at given places along the river. The ecologists also measured the amount of water that flowed past each point per day. With these two pieces of information, the total productivity of the water between its source in the springs and the point of measurement could be calculated. This was expressed as grams of organic substance produced per square meter of stream surface per day. The investigators found an average productivity of 17.5 g/m²/day.

A stream has depth. Why, then, was surface area rather than volume used in calculating productivity?

In further studies the investigators estimated the **biomass** of each major species in the community. Biomass is the total mass of all individuals of a species in a given area. Figure 9–15 shows the result of biomass measurements in the Silver River, another short Florida river. This is one of the many studies on which the energy pyramid in figure 1–20 is based.

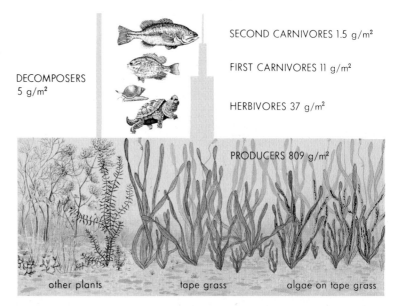

DECOMPOSERS 5 g/m²

SECOND CARNIVORES 1.5 g/m²

FIRST CARNIVORES 11 g/m²

HERBIVORES 37 g/m²

PRODUCERS 809 g/m²

other plants   tape grass   algae on tape grass

9–15 Average biomass measurements from Silver River, Florida. Largemouth bass are top carnivores.

HUMAN INFLUENCE ON INLAND WATERS

Drainage. Shallow ponds, lakes, and marshes are basins where rich organic matter constantly builds up. To grow crops, we need only remove the water from the basins and plow the muck to mix air into it. The crops will thrive.

After the invention of powered machines, humans could easily drain standing inland waters. Throughout the 20th century use of such machinery has reduced the number of natural-water areas in many parts of the United States. This is especially true in the grasslands of Minnesota and the Dakotas. An unfortunate effect of this drainage has been a decrease in duck populations. The grassland ponds and marshes were the main breeding sites for many duck species. When a pond or marsh is drained and turned into a wheat field, the area supplies an increased amount of food for people but no longer supports ducks. This is a clear illustration of one consequence of increasing human population. In the management of farmland and wildlife, as with other resources, choices must be made. These choices are called *trade-offs*. They involve the study of many interacting ecological factors.

Ducks and pond fish can be used as human food as well as wheat. How, then, does drainage increase the food supply?

Artificial ponds and lakes. Although drainage of standing waters has continued, the surface area of inland waters has actually increased during the last 50 years. This has resulted from construction of dams across running waters.

Some dams are built solely to provide a waterfall that will turn electric generators. Most dams, especially in the western states, also form basins in which floodwaters are stored for irrigation and for supplying water to cities. Whatever the purpose, the result is bodies of standing water where once there were streams and land. Such major changes in environment bring about major changes in communities. A large dam may block the passage of fish that swim up rivers to lay their eggs in head-

E. E. Hertzog/U.S. Department of the Interior, Bureau of Reclamation

9—16 Lake Mead, formed by Hoover Dam on the Colorado River. Even if shore slopes are gentle, such reservoirs seldom have emergent vegetation. Can you see why?

catfish. See figure 9–19, far left.

water streams. On the other hand, it may greatly increase the amount of habitat favorable for other species, such as catfish.

Much of the new inland-water area is made up of small ponds that cover only a few thousand square meters. Some artificial ponds are dug merely to provide a supply of water in case of fire. Other ponds supply a summer source of water for range cattle, deer, and game birds. Still others produce fish for food, sport, or both. In such cases the pond owners must understand something about pond ecosystems so they can make favorable habitats for the fish they want.

How might farmers increase the fish crops of their ponds?

9–17 What do you think are the uses of this farm pond?

Haven Kolb

In general, ecosystems in artificial ponds and lakes are simpler—they have fewer species—than those in natural ones. As they become older, however, artificial waters become like natural ones in the same region. As in natural waters, sediments accumulate, reducing the waters' depth. The ultimate fate of most ponds and lakes, natural or artificial, is to be filled slowly and changed from an aquatic ecosystem to a terrestrial ecosystem.

Pollution. One of the first human uses of flowing water was to float boats for transportation. Today boat travel is made easier by machinery used to straighten and deepen rivers. These activities have affected stream ecosystems, principally by simplifying community structure.

People have always used water to flush away unwanted

9-18 Dredging a harbor so ships can dock.

substances. When people come together into towns and cities, their accumulated biological wastes—*sewage*—greatly affect nearby river ecosystems. Sewage is mainly organic substances mixed with water. It increases the growth and reproduction of producers in the water by providing nutrients. If the amount of sewage is large relative to the volume of river water, the producer growth is great. Phytoplankton have short life spans. Phytoplankton die, and decomposers use up the oxygen in the water as they break down the producers' bodies. An anaerobic condition results, which is deadly for all aerobic organisms. However, as the waters of the river flow on, the sewage may be diluted by water from tributary streams. In any case, decomposers eventually use up the sewage materials. River ecosystems once could clean themselves of sewage pollution, as described above. But human populations have increased, and cities have been built closer together. Today a river ecosystem seldom can clean itself up before it receives another load of sewage.

How would this affect consumers?

How is this problem handled?

Human technology produces new kinds of waste substances. Many poisonous substances used to kill insects or weeds on farmlands eventually run into rivers. One well-known example is DDT. It is a chemical poison that was used against agricultural pests, a **pesticide.** Depending on its concentration, DDT is toxic to many organisms.

pesticide [PES tuh syd; Latin: *pestis,* any injurious thing, + *caedere,* to kill]

Clear Lake is 100 miles north of San Francisco. A species of midge, a nonbiting relative of the mosquito, became a pest at Clear Lake. DDD, a pesticide related to DDT, was applied to the lake on three different occasions. The first two applications killed about 99 percent of the midges, but the midge population recovered after each DDD application. Other invertebrates in the lake were killed too. Later birds and fish that fed on the invertebrates of the lake began to die.

Initially, the pesticide was applied in a concentration of only 1 part DDD to 50 million parts water (0.02 ppm). Yet, in

9—19 Diagram of sewage pollution in a stream. (Organisms are not drawn to scale, and distances are greatly decreased.) At the left sewage is attacked by decomposers. The oxygen supply decreases. Aerobic organisms die. Further downstream the amount of sewage decreases. The oxygen supply increases. The phytoplankton and aerobic consumers increase in numbers.

When was the last time a pesticide was used near your home?

the plankton the DDD concentration was 265 times greater—or 5.3 ppm. In small fishes that ate the plankton, the DDD was 500 ppm. In the birds and predatory fishes, concentrations were over 75,000 times greater (1,500 ppm) than that in the lake water. And these predatory fish were game fish caught and eaten by humans.

From factories and mills, alkalis and chromium, lead, and mercury ions have been dumped into bodies of water. All of these are poisonous to some living things. Industrial processes, particularly the generation of electricity, often result in discharge of hot water into rivers. This abruptly changes the abiotic environment and makes it intolerable for many aquatic organisms. The warmer water also may bring about a change in the types of species that can inhabit the area. Nuclear reactors sometimes add small amounts of radioactive substances to streams. These substances accumulate in the bodies of stream organisms, harming them and the organisms that eat them. All of these pollutants may affect the human beings who live beside the waters and often may have to drink them.

CHECK YOURSELF

J. How do abiotic conditions in a brook differ from those in a river?

K. Why is plankton more abundant in rivers than in brooks?

L. Where does biological energy come from in a brook?

M. What kinds of consumers do you find in a river?

N. How do ecologists measure productivity?

O. What usually happens to biomass as you go from one link in a food chain to the next?

P. What benefits do people get from draining inland-water areas? From damming flowing waters?

Q. How may draining and damming be harmful to human interests?

R. What eventually happens to sewage when it is dumped into a river ecosystem?

S. What are the major stream pollutants?

Investigation 9.1   DISSOLVED OXYGEN

INTRODUCTION

The amount of free oxygen (O_2) dissolved in water is an important abiotic environmental factor in all aquatic ecosystems. Oxygen measurements can be used in studying aquatic productivity and, indirectly, aquatic pollution.

Here you are given a procedure for measuring dissolved oxygen. But you must design your own investigation to make use of the procedure. Some suggestions from which you may develop hypotheses are the following:

Aquariums. Amount of oxygen in aquariums with and without (1) artificial light, (2) plants, or (3) aerators. Or amount of oxygen (4) early in the morning and in the afternoon.

Standing water. Amount of oxygen (1) in freshly collected rainwater compared with that in old rainwater puddles, (2) at various depths in a pond or lake, or (3) in a natural pond compared with that in an artificial pond.

Running water. Amount of oxygen (1) in a sewage-polluted stream at various distances from the source of pollution or, (2) in a stream at various times of the year.

PROCEDURE (High Range)

1. Fill the glass-stoppered sample bottle with the water to be tested, by allowing water to overflow into the bottle without trapping any air bubbles.
2. Add the contents of one pillow each of Dissolved Oxygen 1 Reagent Powder and Dissolved Oxygen 2 Reagent Powder. Stopper the bottle carefully so that no air is trapped in the bottle. Grip the bottle and stopper firmly and shake vigorously to mix. A flocculent (soft, flakelike) precipitate will be formed. If O_2 is present, the precipitate will be brownish-orange in color.
3. Allow the sample to stand until the precipitate, or "floc," has settled halfway and

MATERIALS
(per team)

1 Hach Kit (Kit #1469-00) containing:
   1 glass-stoppered sample bottle
   100 Dissolved Oxygen 1 Reagent Pillows
   100 Dissolved Oxygen 2 Reagent Pillows
   100 Dissolved Oxygen 3 Reagent Pillows
   1 plastic measuring tube
   1 square mixing bottle
   1 fingernail clipper for opening reagent pillows
   1 plastic bottle PAO titrant
   Instructions for High and Low
      Range procedures

leaves the upper half of the bottle clear. Then, again shake the bottle and let it stand a second time until the upper half of the bottle is clear.

4. Remove the stopper and add the contents of one pillow of Dissolved Oxygen 3 Reagent Powder. Carefully restopper and shake to mix. The floc will dissolve and a yellow color will develop if oxygen was present. This is the prepared sample.
5. Fill the plastic measuring tube level-full with prepared sample and pour it into the mixing bottle.
6. While swirling the sample to mix, add PAO titrant dropwise, counting each drop, until the sample changes from yellow to colorless. The dropper must be held in a vertical manner. Each drop is equal to 1 mg/liter or 1 ppm dissolved oxygen.

DISCUSSION

(1) How much oxygen did you find in your water samples (in ppm)? (2) Was your hypothesis supported? (3) How does the oxygen content of your sample compare with that of the water samples of other teams? (4) How do you account for the differences (or for the similarities)?

(5) Assuming that the chemical materials were properly prepared, what sources of error may there be in the procedure? (6) What

factors may cause an accurate measurement of oxygen in the sample to be different from the amount of oxygen in the water from which the sample was taken?

OCEANS

Our knowledge of the oceans has grown rather slowly. Humans have been moving about on the ocean surface for quite a while. Until recently, however, our observations were limited to the surface and the shore. It is now possible to observe an ocean from within using instruments that send information from the depths to the surface. Other inventions permit deep diving for direct observation. The popularity of the very large aquariums also has created public interest in the oceans and in the living things found there.

The words "ocean" and "sea" often are not distinguishable in English. However, a sea sometimes means a smaller part of the hydrosphere than an ocean.

ABIOTIC ENVIRONMENT

Salinity. Ocean environments differ in many ways from inland-water environments. Perhaps the principal difference lies in the chemical composition of the water itself. Seawater — the water of the oceans — is about 3.5 percent (or 35 parts per thousand) dissolved minerals. Most inland waters contain only small amounts of dissolved minerals. However, some exceptions, such as Great Salt Lake, contain more minerals than does seawater.

salinity [say LIN ut ee; Latin: *sal*, salt]

What would this be in parts per million?

The minerals dissolved in seawater are mostly salts. And the mineral content of seawater is referred to as *salinity.* Sodium chloride, the most common salt in the ocean, accounts for over 75 percent of the dissolved minerals.

9–20 Average mineral content of seawater. These elements occur as compounds; elemental nitrogen and oxygen dissolved from the air are not included.

9–21 A crystallization pond on the San Francisco Bay. Salt harvested from the pond can be seen on the left.

ELEMENT	SEAWATER (PARTS PER THOUSAND)
Chlorine	18.98
Sodium	10.56
Magnesium	1.27
Sulfur	.88
Calcium	.40
Potassium	.38
Bromine	.065
Carbon	.028
Strontium	.013
Silicon	.003
Fluorine	.001
Aluminum	.0005
Phosphorus	.0001
Iodine	.00005

Salinity varies somewhat at different depths and in different places on the surface. It is greater where evaporation is high
and precipitation is low. For example, in some parts of the Great
Salt Lake the salinity is over 250 parts per thousand. It is lower
where evaporation is low and where much fresh water enters
from rivers.

Evidence from rocks and fossils indicates that the ocean has
had a high salinity for hundreds of millions of years. It seems,
then, that the dissolved substances constantly washed into the
ocean from the land have had only a slight effect on the composition of ocean water. Ocean water represents a steady state.
Substances are continually added to it, but substances also are
continually removed by *marine* organisms. Ocean water is the
environment of marine biota, but it is also a product of their activities. The hydrosphere, like the atmosphere, would undoubtedly have a much different composition if life were absent.

Other abiotic factors. Rapid changes of the atmosphere result in great differences in the climates of terrestrial ecosystems.
Such rapid changes do not occur in the hydrosphere. Even at
the ocean surface, temperature changes between day and night
are very small. Seasonal changes also are small. However, the
average 28°C temperature of surface water at the equator is

What abiotic factors could create
such salinity?

marine [muh REEN; Latin: *mare,*
sea]

From your own experience with
weather, describe some of these
rapid changes.

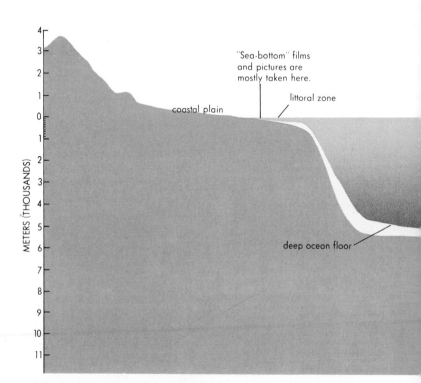

9—22 Diagram of an ocean
in cross section.

very different from an average of −1°C in antarctic and arctic surface waters. At a depth of 200 m, however, the pole-to-equator temperature range is only from 0° to 22°C. At greater depths temperature differences disappear almost entirely.

The amount of light energy available to photosynthetic organisms is greatest at the water surface. The extent to which light penetrates into the water depends on several factors. Two of these are the angle at which light strikes the water's surface and whether the surface is smooth or broken by waves. As light passes through the water, longer wavelengths are absorbed most rapidly. This means that red and yellow disappear first, and blue and violet penetrate farthest. Finally, the rate at which this absorption of light occurs depends on the clearness of the water. The more cloudy the water, the faster is the rate of light absorption.

Ocean currents distribute chemicals that are useful to organisms. Currents also affect water temperatures and salinities at any given place in the ocean. Currents, in turn, are affected by the world pattern of winds and by the earth's rotation.

How can a temperature be below 0°C in *liquid* water?

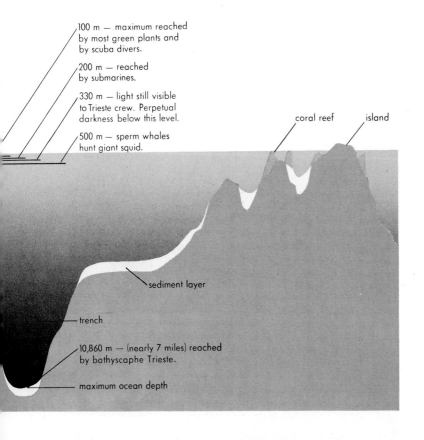

100 m — maximum reached by most green plants and by scuba divers.

200 m — reached by submarines.

330 m — light still visible to Trieste crew. Perpetual darkness below this level.

500 m — sperm whales hunt giant squid.

coral reef   island

sediment layer

trench

10,860 m — (nearly 7 miles) reached by bathyscaphe Trieste.

maximum ocean depth

9–23 Eugenie Clark, marine biologist at the University of Maryland, gathers data during an investigation of sharks.

How does this relate to the location of great ocean fisheries?

OCEAN ECOSYSTEMS

It is possible to recognize and group many marine ecosystems. The term "biome" is not usually used with these ecosystems. We distinguish four major oceanic regions: open ocean, ocean depths, coastal waters, and littoral zone.

Open ocean. The chief producers of the open ocean are diatoms, other microscopic algae, and certain flagellates. The zooplankton depend on these phytoplankton directly. Many food chains are based on these producers, with large consumers being the tuna, sharks, whales, and oceanic birds such as albatrosses.

Many scientists have tried to determine the density of marine plankton populations. Detailed results have come from one study at the marine laboratory at Plymouth, England. The ocean water there contains, at the very least, 4,500,000 phytoplankton organisms in each liter of water! Biologists do not have enough data to give accurate density averages for the ocean as a whole. But they do know that the oceans vary greatly in productivity.

A limiting factor in the ocean, as on land, may be the availability of chemical elements, especially phosphorus and nitrogen. Phytoplankton organisms are continuously using up these elements. Continued growth of phytoplankton, therefore, depends on the resupply of these elements. They may be added from sediments washed from the land or from water welling up from below. Upwelling may occur as a result of seasonal changes, much as does the overturning of lake waters. It may occur when offshore winds move surface water and deep water rises to take its place. Because of upwelling, ocean areas at higher latitudes and close to the land are very productive. The North Sea and the Grand Banks of Newfoundland are examples.

9–24 A plankton net being cast from the *Horizon*, research vessel of the Scripps Institution of Oceanography, California.

These areas of upwelling are very small, however, compared to the entire ocean. Fifty percent of all fish and shellfish harvested from the ocean are taken from 1/10 of 1 percent of its entire surface. On the other hand, ocean regions far from land, especially those in the tropics, have very low productivity. The Sargasso Sea in the Atlantic is an example.

Regardless of the availability of nutrients, phytoplankton need light. All of the photosynthesis of the open ocean occurs in the upper layer of water, where light penetrates beneath the surface. This layer is very thin compared to the total depth of ocean water. Despite the deep penetration of blue light (550 m near Bermuda), phytoplankton are largely limited to the upper 100 m of water.

Ocean depths. For a long time biologists thought that life could not exist in the dark and cold ocean depths because of the tremendous pressure of the water. The first clear evidence that this idea was wrong came in 1858. One of the telegraph cables lying on the bottom of the Mediterranean Sea broke and was hauled up for repair. It was encrusted with bottom-living animals, mostly sponges. Some had grown at depths as great as 2,000 m! Further investigation showed that water pressure has no ill effect on organisms unless they contain spaces filled with air or other gases. Deep-sea organisms lack such spaces, so pressure is exerted equally from both inside and out. In this case, damage due to pressure does not occur.

We terrestrial organisms, however, do have trouble with water pressure because we have internal, air-filled spaces. Without using special diving equipment, we can observe directly only the top few meters of the ocean. In the 19th century the development of diving helmets and air pumps let divers go

U.S. Navy

9–25 A navy photographer-diver films the descent of the *Nemo* during its 500-foot test dive in the Atlantic Ocean. Aboard the *Nemo* are Ed Briggs of Southwest Research Institute and Martin Snoey of the Naval Civil Engineering Laboratory.

deeper and stay down longer. In the 20th century the aqualung gave greater freedom of movement by eliminating the need for an air hose connection to the surface. But neither of these devices enables a diver to descend below 100 m.

In 1935 a heavy steel sphere with thick quartz windows was constructed. It was built to withstand the great pressures of the deep and was lowered into the ocean on a cable. In this sphere scientists descended about 1,000 m in the Atlantic Ocean near Bermuda. For the first time people observed living things directly at such depths. Later the bathyscaphe was designed. This vessel can descend to great depths and come up under its own power. In 1960 a crew in the bathyscaphe *Trieste* descended to the bottom of the Mariana Trench in the Pacific Ocean — 10,860 m below the surface. In doing so, they reached the deepest place in the ocean.

bathyscaphe [BATH ih skaf; Greek: *bathos*, depth, + *skaphe*, boat]

9 – 26 The bathyscaphe *Trieste*.

U.S. Navy

Today scientists use self-propelled, deep-sea research laboratories to study ocean bottoms. These labs can carry several scientists. Some are built so that scientists can live within them for weeks at a time. They never come to the surface during this period. The laboratories also are equipped with mechanical arms that pick up objects and samples for study. This feature is important because these labs dive to deep waters where water pressure would kill divers. A current area of deep-water research is the movement of the earth's crust. Scientists believe that this crust shifts, sometimes causing earthquakes.

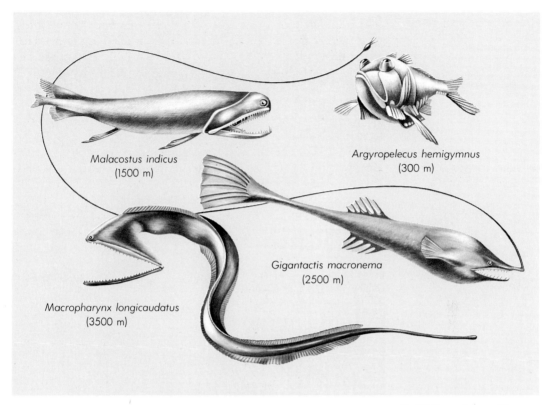

Malacostus indicus
(1500 m)

Argyropelecus hemigymnus
(300 m)

Gigantactis macronema
(2500 m)

Macropharynx longicaudatus
(3500 m)

9–27 Some fishes of the ocean depths and the depths at which they have been caught. All are small; they are shown here × 1.

The ocean depths are special ecosystems that require unusual adaptations in the organisms that survive there. The depths are cold, dark, and quiet. There are no producers. All the biological energy is in organic substances that settle from the water above. The adaptations of organisms to the pressures of the deep also make their ascent to upper levels fatal. So the consumers in the ocean depths form one of the most isolated communities of the biosphere.

In the eternal night of the ocean depths, most animals are either black or dark red and have very sensitive eyes. In the unending darkness of caves and underground streams, however, most are white and blind. In depths of the oceans, many animals produce their own light; they are **bioluminescent.** This ability is not found among animals in the blackness of caves. This may explain the difference in eyes and, perhaps, in color of animals in these two types of ecosystems. The ability to produce light may serve several functions. One species of fish dangles a special luminescent organ in front of its mouth. Apparently this lures unwary victims close enough to be caught and eaten. Deep-sea shrimp escape some predators in clouds of

What other ecosystems contain no producers?

When brought to the surface, fishes caught at great depths often look as if they had exploded. Why?

bioluminescent [by oh loo muh-NES unt]: light-giving from living organisms

9–28 An acorn worm on the ocean bottom (South Pacific, depth about 4,800 m).

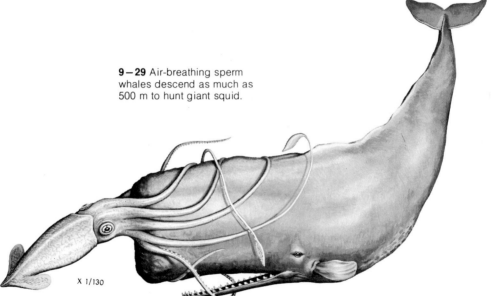

9–29 Air-breathing sperm whales descend as much as 500 m to hunt giant squid.

X 1/130

a luminescent secretion they give off when disturbed. Patterns of light on an animal's body also may serve as marks of recognition in the depths. This would be similar to the color patterns among many organisms in the world of light.

Coastal waters. With few exceptions, oceans are relatively shallow near the continents. These bands of shallow water average less than 200 m in depth. They are widest at the mouths of large rivers and along areas of broad lowlands. Along mountainous coasts, as in California, they may be almost absent.

In these shallow waters some light reaches the bottom. Where there is plenty of light, a luxuriant growth of seaweeds may be found. In middle and higher latitudes the most common and conspicuous ones are brown algae. Among these are kelps,

luxuriant [lug ZHUR ee unt]: rich, abundant

308

9—30 Part of a single brown alga plant. These plants can grow to great lengths, as shown with the help of these three marine biology students.

which may reach a length of 35 m or more. Nevertheless, here, as elsewhere in aquatic ecosystems, phytoplankton are the principal producers.

The physical characteristics of the bottom—sand, rock, or mud—determine the kinds of organisms that live there. Sandy bottoms generally occur where waves or currents wash away the finer particles. Plants are not usually abundant on such unstable bottoms. However, many kinds of animals burrow into the sand, especially crustaceans, mollusks, and annelid worms. Muddy bottoms have even more burrowers, and most of the species are unlike those adapted to sand. Sea cucumbers, clams, and some crabs plow through the mud. On rocky bottoms and coral reefs, many animals attach themselves permanently to one place. Crabs, octopuses, and fishes hide in nooks and crannies among the rocks.

How might your knowledge of plants lead you to predict this fact?

What are some of these?

9—31 Life on a coral reef (Florida keys). Corals, sponges, and reef fishes are conspicuous.

Because they are shallow and close to land, coastal waters offer more opportunity for human use than does the open ocean. From them has come much of the marine food supply of humans. Underwater farming of kelp, fish, crustaceans, and mollusks is a future possibility. It is unlikely, however, that the ocean will supply all the food we will need in the future. With the exception of coastal waters, the ocean is very limited in some of its dissolved nutrients. Rich fertile soils may contain 0.5 percent nitrogen, an important nutrient for growth. The richest ocean water, in comparison, contains only about 0.00005 percent nitrogen.

Some human activities in coastal waters could *decrease* our supply of food. Just as inland waters are convenient places in which to dump wastes, so are coastal waters. Oil-bearing rocks underlie coastal waters in many places. Drilling sometimes results in pollution from escaped oil. Valuable minerals, such as phosphates, may soon be dredged from coastal waters for use on land. This activity could destroy coastal ecosystems, at least for many years.

Why may this be even more of a problem in coastal than in inland waters?

9–32 Black oil drifts away from a wrecked tanker. In this accident, more than 45,000 barrels of oil spilled into the ocean near San Juan, Puerto Rico.

Official U.S. Coast Guard photograph

littoral [LIT uh rul; Latin: *littus*, seashore, coast]

The littoral zone. Everywhere along the margins of the oceans you can see the effects of waves and tides. In the Bay of Fundy (Nova Scotia) the maximum vertical change between high and low tides is 15.4 m. At the other extreme, the average tidal difference in the Mediterranean is only 0.35 m. Wave action, too, varies depending on the place and time. Some shores, such as those of Maine, are pounded by heavy surf. Others, especially in small, protected bays, may be no more exposed to wave action than are shores of small lakes. High and low tides each occur twice a day. The zone between high and low tides—the *littoral* zone—is a difficult environment for life. Twice a day littoral organisms are submerged in salt water and then exposed. They are exposed to air and the bright, hot sun or freezing wind. Between these times the littoral zone is pounded by the advancing or retreating surf.

On rocky coasts life in the littoral region is surprisingly abundant. In cold water different species of brown algae cling to the rocks. They are protected from the drying sun by a jelly-like coating. These tangled algae provide protection and support for other algae, protists, and many animals. In addition, barnacles, chitons, and snails cling firmly to rock or seaweeds. These close up tightly during the periods when they are exposed to air.

Dan Morrill

9−33 Tide pool. On rocky ocean shores many aquatic organisms live during low tides in pools left above the waterline.

On sandy coasts life in the littoral zone is limited to organisms that can burrow in the sand or skitter over it. There are no attached producers, but phytoplankton may be here when the tide is in. The burrowers, such as small crustaceans, eat food particles brought by the high tides. Shorebirds are a link with land ecosystems. They prey on the sand burrowers or forage in the debris left behind by the retreating tide. Land crabs release their young in the water. Sea turtles crawl out on the beach and bury their eggs. We see that terrestrial and marine ecosystems merge.

Wherever ocean meets land there is constant change. In

debris [duh BREE]: rubbish, especially that resulting from destruction

only a few years sediments deposited at the mouths of rivers stretch the land into the ocean. Elsewhere you can observe the ocean pushing back the land as it carves out sandy beaches with its wave action. Such changes have occurred through most of the earth's history.

9—34 California coastline. Wave action helps to form the pattern of rocks and life along the shore.

American Airlines

CHECK YOURSELF

T.   How do marine organisms affect the amount of dissolved substances in ocean water?

U.   Compare variations of temperature in the oceans with those in the atmosphere.

V.   What factors determine the amount and color of light beneath the water surface?

W.   Why do some parts of the oceans have a higher productivity than others?

X.   How do humans explore the depths of the oceans?

Y.   Describe the environment of the ocean depths and the organisms that live there.

Z.   How do coastal ecosystems differ from those of the open ocean?

AA. What human activities affect coastal waters?

BB. Why is the littoral zone a particularly difficult place for organisms to live?

Investigation 9.2   EFFECTS OF SALINITY ON AQUATIC ORGANISMS

INTRODUCTION

If you were to move freshwater organisms into the ocean or ocean organisms into fresh water, they would probably die very quickly. Although salmon migrate from the open ocean into freshwater rivers to reproduce, they first spend several days in water with decreasing salinity. In this way, their bodies adjust gradually to the lower salt concentrations.

Small freshwater ponds become salty as the summer sun evaporates the water. Small aquatic organisms that cannot tolerate the change will either die or go into a dormant stage.

In this investigation you will observe the tolerances of some freshwater organisms to various concentrations of salt solutions. (1) Review the procedure and set up an appropriate hypothesis.

PROCEDURE

1. Take a leaf of elodea from near the tip of the plant. Place the leaf upside down on your microscope slide. Add a drop of fresh water and cover with a cover slip.
2. Using the low power of your microscope, find a cell that you can observe clearly. (Do not move the slide.) (2) Describe the cell contents. Does the cell seem to be completely filled with the cell contents?
3. Add a few drops of 5% salt solution to one side of your cover slip. Draw it under the cover slip by applying a paper towel to the opposite side. (3) Watch your cell and describe what you observe.
4. See if the process is reversible by drawing pure water under the cover slip.
5. Using a medicine dropper, place on a slide a drop of water containing the kind of organisms you have selected to study. Add a cover slip.

MATERIALS
(per pair of students)

living specimens of small
   aquatic organisms
sodium chloride solutions (1%,
   3%, and 5%)
elodea
monocular microscope
3 microscope slides
3 cover slips
medicine dropper
paper towels

6. Using the low power of your microscope, observe the organisms for a few minutes to determine their normal appearance and actions. You can slow down the movement of some kinds of protists by adding a few wisps of cotton or a bit of shredded paper towel to the water.
7. At one edge of the cover slip, place a drop of 1% salt solution. Draw the salt solution under the cover slip as you did in step 3. As the salt solution moves under the cover slip, observe the organisms. Notice particularly changes in movements and shape. Record the percentage of the solution and your observations.
8. Replace the salt solution with water from the original culture in the same way you added the salt solution. (4) What assumption are you making when doing this?
9. Observe the organisms again and record any further changes in movement or shape that you observe.
10. Using a new slide and specimen, repeat the procedure, using 3% salt solution. Repeat with 5%. (5) Which of these is most like ocean water?

DISCUSSION

Individuals of a species usually respond in a variety of ways to an environmental factor. All students who worked with the same organisms should compare their results. (*6*) Did all individuals of the species react in the same way? If not, what differences were noted? (*7*) Did the kind of reaction differ with different salt solutions? Try to explain any differences.

Compare observations of teams that worked on different kinds of organisms. (*8*) Which kind was most tolerant to changes in salt concentration? (*9*) Which kind was least tolerant? (*10*) What kind of aquatic habitat do you think each kind of organism normally inhabits? (*11*) Which of your observations support the hypothesis you set up? (*12*) Do any of your observations weaken your hypothesis? If so, which? (*13*) Taking all your observations into account, restate your hypothesis in the form of a conclusion to the experiment.

FOR FURTHER INVESTIGATION

All the organisms you studied in this investigation are small. Many larger ones (salmon, for example) regularly move from marine water to fresh water (or vice versa), apparently without harm. Others cannot tolerate much change in salinity. Test the salinity tolerance of macroscopic aquatic animals such as crayfish, goldfish, guppies, or snails, using the principles employed in this exercise. If you use a marine species (for example, a clam worm) in your experiments, how should you modify your procedure? (Caution: It is not necessary to kill the animals used in your experiments. Whenever they show signs of discomfort, return them to a more tolerable salinity.)

PROBLEMS

1. Describe a pond in your area. In what ways does it resemble the pond discussed in the text? How does it differ?

2. To answer the following questions about inland waters you do not need further research but only further thought about what you have read in this chapter. (a) How would a cloudy, windy day affect the productivity of phytoplankton? (b) Is a layer of ice on the surface of a lake harmful to fish? Explain. (c) How do the sources of oxygen differ in a brook, a slow-moving river, a pond, and a lake? (d) Would you expect decomposers to be more active on the bottom of a pond or of a lake? Explain. (e) Why is a poisonous substance in a pond—such as a mercury compound—likely to be more concentrated in the flesh of a bass than of a ciliate? (f) Why do household detergents interfere with sewage purification?

3. A program designed to improve the fishing was introduced in a midwestern pond. First, a fish poison was used to kill all the many small fish that were in the pond. Then the pond was restocked with game fish. Instead of large game fish, the new population contained many stunted individuals. Explain.

4. The concentration of hydrogen ions (H^+) and hydroxyl ions (OH^-) is as important in aquatic environments as in soil. Where in North America can you find acid waters? Where can you find basic waters? What differences would you expect to find among the living things in such waters?

5. Differences in the physical characteristics of water and air are important in understanding the contrast between aquatic and terrestrial environments. Consider such questions as these: (a) What land organisms have the most streamlined bodies? With what form of locomotion do you associate this streamlining? (b) What water organisms have the most streamlined bodies? What niches in aquatic ecosystems do these organisms occupy? (c) Why do most plankton organisms have little or no streamlining? (d) How does locomotion by walking on the bottom of the ocean differ from locomotion by walking on land?

6. If you collect 167 snails of a given species from five plots totaling 5 m² and find their total mass is 534 g, what would be the biomass of the snail population?

7. Though 80 to 90 percent of the world's photosynthesis occurs in water, human food comes mostly from the land. Humans might make much greater use of the hydrosphere as a source of food. Consider these questions: (a) What nations at present use the most marine food? (b) What kinds of marine organisms do we eat? (c) How might we make greater use of aquatic producers as food?

8. In the future, more and more career positions will be directly related to freshwater and ocean environments. Physical oceanographers, biological oceanographers, and limnologists are only three of many possible careers. Find out as much as you can about these careers. Report your findings to your class.

9. Though the seas are very large, pollution of marine waters can occur. Investigate the kinds of oceanic pollution and their effects on the marine biota.

10. Estuaries, such as Chesapeake Bay and San Francisco Bay, represent a special kind of aquatic environment. Find out what characteristics distinguish estuarine environments from marine and inland-water environments and how these affect aquatic life.

SUGGESTED READINGS

Amos, W. H. 1970. Teeming Life of a Pond. *National Geographic*, August, pp. 274–298.

Brown, J. E. 1975. *The Sea's Harvest: The Story of Aquaculture*. Dodd, Mead, New York. Readable summary of agriculture in the sea.

Clark E. 1975. Strangest Sea, Red Sea. *National Geographic*, September, pp. 338–343.

Earle, S. A. 1979. Humpbacks: The Gentle Whales. *National Geographic*, January, pp. 2–25.

Goreau, T. F., N. I. Goreau, and T. G. Goreau. 1979. Corals and Coral Reefs. *Scientific American*, August. A look at this rich ecosystem.

Hoover, R. B. 1979. Those Marvelous, Myriad Diatoms. *National Geographic*, June, pp. 871–878.

Lagler, K. F., J. E. Bardach, R. R. Miller, and D. R. May Passino. 1977. *Ichthyology*. John Wiley & Sons, New York. Advanced study of marine and freshwater fish.

Lind, O. T. 1974. *Handbook of Common Methods in Limnology*. C. V. Mosby, St. Louis. Pocket-sized, field-oriented handbook with simple research techniques.

Linehan, E. J. 1979. The Trouble with Dolphins. *National Geographic*, April, pp. 506–541.

Stickney, R. R. 1979. *Principles of Warm Water Aquaculture*. John Wiley & Sons, New York. The commercial raising of freshwater and marine fishes in special ponds.

Chapter **10**

Life in the Past

YOUR GUIDEPOSTS

In this chapter you will have an opportunity to explore these questions in biology:

- What kinds of evidence have scientists used to investigate the past history of life on Earth?
- How have scientists approached the problem of the origin of life on Earth?
- How have ecosystems changed during the history of Earth?
- In what ways can study of the history of life explain the present life on Earth?

EVIDENCE OF THE PAST

WHAT IS A FOSSIL?

An interest in fossils and an understanding of what they are do not always go together. People once thought fossils were merely freakish accidents of nature. Others thought fossils were the result of a great flood. *Geologists* are scientists who study the earth. During the late 18th and early 19th centuries, they concluded that fossils are evidence of organisms that existed during the past. Though fossils often resemble the parts of present-day organisms, most represent species that have long been *extinct.* This view is held by nearly all scientists today.

There are many kinds of fossils. The majority represent the hard parts of organisms. Sometimes these are unchanged — shell, wood, even bone. Usually, however, they have been *petrified.* In this process the organism's organic substances are slowly replaced by minerals carried in water. These minerals may be different from the substances they replace, but the shape of the organism remains.

fossil [Latin: *fossa*, a ditch]. Originally the word meant anything dug up.

geologists [jee OL uh justz; Greek: *gea*, earth, + *logos*, speech, reason]

extinct [ik STINKT]: no longer existing on Earth

petrified [PEH truh fyd; Latin: *petra*, stone, + *facere*, to make]

10—1 Petrified wood.

American Airlines

Fossils also may occur as thin films of carbon. In this case, carbon, found in all organic compounds, is all that remains after the living material has decomposed. Leaves are often preserved in this form. Fossils also may be molds — hollows that are left in rock after the organic material decays. They may be casts — made of mud that fills the molds in the rocks and then hardens. Molds and casts preserve the shape of the dead organism but not the internal detail that petrified objects show. In a very few cases, soft parts of organisms have been preserved. For example, flesh of woolly mammoths has been found frozen in tundra permafrost. And entire insects have been preserved in transparent amber, formed from plant saps and other plant materials.

Any indication of an organism's former presence is considered a fossil. Fossils may be footprints left by animals, burrows of worms, nests of insects, or even hardened dung. Fossilized feces may be particularly valuable. They tell what the animals ate and what type of food was available. The food, in turn, gives clues to what the environment was like. *Paleontologists* are scientists who try to unravel the evidence of the fossil record.

fossil footprints. See figure 10–18.

paleontologists [pay lee un TOL-uh justz; Greek: *palaios*, ancient, + *onta*, beings, + *logos*]

THE GEOLOGICAL RECORD

sedimentary [sed uh MENT uh-ree]

Why do you think fossils would not be expected in volcanic rocks?

Fossils are usually preserved in *sedimentary* rocks. Such rocks were once sediments of sand, mud, or masses of shells. These materials were deposited by water at the bottoms of oceans, lakes, and ponds and in riverbeds. Sand dunes also have been deposited by wind around plant and animal remains. Larger materials were once pushed along by glaciers and left behind by the melting ice. Sediments have always formed where water, wind, and ice erode the landscape in one place and deposit the eroded particles elsewhere.

Smithsonian Institution

10–2 Carbon film: primitive arthropod (British Columbia).　　× 1

American Museum of Natural History

10–3 Soft parts: skin of a baby mammoth found in permafrost (Alaska).　　× 1/6

BSCS photo by Richard R. Tolman; specimen courtesy of Earth Science Materials, Inc.

Smithsonian Institution

10–4 Mold: starfish (New York).　　× 1

10–5 Cast: fern leaves from the Paleozoic era (Pennsylvania).　　× 1/4

strata [STRAYT uh; Latin: *stratum*, a covering]: singular, stratum

What conditions do you think would favor the preservation of organisms as fossils?

The record in the rocks. The *strata* (layers) of sedimentary rocks are usually piled on each other like pages in a book. In general the oldest strata are at the bottom and the newest on top. Geologists now think the oldest rock strata are about four billion years old. But the strata most interesting to paleontologists are those that record the history of living things.

This layered "book of the earth" is not easy to read. For one thing, many of the "pages" are blank. That is, many of the sedimentary strata contain no fossils. Perhaps no organisms existed at the time or place such "blank" strata were formed. Perhaps conditions were not favorable for the preservation of fossils. To reconstruct the whole record, paleontologists must match strata from one place with strata from others as in figure 10–7.

Dead organisms usually are decomposed rapidly and seldom become fossilized. Further, during the history of Earth, the strata have been subjected to breaking, folding, and sliding. Occasionally folding has been so great that older strata have been pushed above younger ones. Sometimes fossils have been eroded from an older stratum and redeposited in a younger one. And, at any one place on the earth's surface, only some of the strata are found. All this makes the fossil history book difficult to interpret.

10–6 The sedimentary strata are orderly along the Colorado River (Utah).

C. Allan Morgan

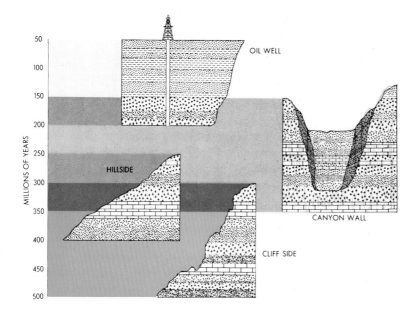

MILLIONS OF YEARS

50
100
150
200
250
300
350
400
450
500

OIL WELL

HILLSIDE

CANYON WALL

CLIFF SIDE

10–7 Geologists fit together strata from different places to construct the "book of the earth."

Geological time scale. Paleontologists have pieced together information from many parts of the world. In this way they have been able to put most of the known rock strata in sequence. Thus they can say that Devonian strata are older than Cretaceous or that Miocene rocks are younger than Eocene (figure 10–8). But how much older or younger are they?

Devonian [dih VOH nee un]

Cretaceous [krih TAY shus]

Miocene [MY uh seen]

Eocene [EE uh seen]

Early attempts to determine the ages of sedimentary rock — and the fossils it contained — were based on measurements of strata thickness. This thickness was divided by the estimated time needed for one meter of sediment to accumulate. It was later determined that sediments do not accumulate at constant rates. This method was, therefore, quite inaccurate.

The most reliable method for dating rocks depends on the presence of *radioactive* chemical elements. For example, uranium is radioactive. Through a series of steps it breaks down to lead at a known rate. Its *half-life* is used to calculate the age of rock. The half-life of uranium is the amount of time it takes half of any amount of uranium to break down to lead — 4.5 billion years. Scientists can remove a sample of rock from a stratum and measure the amount of uranium and lead in it. If they find uranium but no lead (which is highly unlikely), the rock is very new. In other words, the uranium has had no time to break down. If, however, they find equal parts of lead and uranium, the rock is 4.5 billion years old. In this case, half of the uranium has had time to break down to lead.

By measuring the ratios between uranium and lead, we can

radioactive [rayd ee oh AK tiv]: giving off radiations of energy such as X rays (figure 1–19)

uranium [yew RAY nee um]

estimate the ages of rocks that are millions of years old. The measurements are not perfect, but they have provided a time scale that is more accurate than any previous one. Similar calculations have been made using radioactive potassium and rubidium. Radioactive carbon (C^{14}) has been used to date (determine the age of) plant and animal remains. This process is considered accurate in dating remains up to 50,000 years old.

potassium [puh TAS ee um]

rubidium [roo BID ee um]

10–8 The geologic time scale according to the best estimates now available. Pre-Cambrian times indicate only the oldest known rocks discovered and studied, not the total age of the earth.

ERAS	PERIODS	EPOCHS	YEARS SINCE BEGINNING OF PERIOD OR EPOCH
Cenozoic	Quaternary	Recent	10,000
		Pleistocene	2,000,000
	Tertiary	Pliocene	13,000,000
		Miocene	25,000,000
		Oligocene	36,000,000
		Eocene	58,000,000
		Paleocene	63,000,000
Mesozoic	Cretaceous		135,000,000
	Jurassic		180,000,000
	Triassic		230,000,000
Paleozoic	Permian		280,000,000
	Carboniferous		345,000,000
	Devonian		405,000,000
	Silurian		425,000,000
	Ordovician		500,000,000
	Cambrian		600,000,000
Pre-Cambrian			3,600,000,000+

CHECK YOURSELF

A. What are fossils and how are they formed?

B. What do paleontologists do?

C. Why are sedimentary rocks the most important kind of rocks for paleontologists?

D. What difficulties do paleontologists encounter in reading the "book of the earth"?

E. How do geologists determine the age of sedimentary rock?

HISTORY OF LIFE

Interpreting the record of the rocks accurately is difficult. But the record has shown that Earth has had living inhabitants for a long time and that Earth itself has existed for even longer. To biologists fossils are particularly important. They show that basic ecological relationships have endured over long periods of time. Fossils also provide a basis for understanding the geographic distribution of life today. And they are a major source of evidence for the unifying theory of evolution.

theory of evolution. For "theory," see page 70.

ORIGIN OF LIFE

From childhood on, we all ask questions about "where we came from." Biologists are especially curious about the origin of life. The scarcity of fossils in the oldest known rocks suggests that at one time there was no life on this planet. So either life arrived from some other place or it started in some way here on Earth. There are scientific hypotheses that try to explain the mystery of the origin of life. There are also long-established explanations found in almost every religious belief system known.

When scientific evidence is meager, scientists sometimes start with a set of assumptions. Using these, they develop a line of reasoning. This is called *speculation.* It may lead nowhere. It may lead to hypotheses that can be tested. In this section we will present one of the best-supported scientific hypotheses about the origin of life. It is frequently referred to as the "organic soup theory."

speculation [spek yuh LAY shun; Latin: *speculare,* to spy]

Some speculation. Geological evidence suggests that Earth grew very hot after it first formed. Heat speeds up chemical activity. At that time atoms must have been constantly combining and recombining. They must have been forming many kinds of molecules. Geological evidence also indicates that the early atmosphere of Earth included methane, CH_4, instead of present-day carbon dioxide, CO_2. It included ammonia, NH_3, instead of present-day nitrogen, N_2. Some hydrogen, H_2, and much water vapor, H_2O, also were present.

methane [METH ayn]

With the energy of heat and lightning, the gases of the early atmosphere may have combined to form such substances as amino acids. Amino acids are found in all organisms today. Over millions of years, such organic compounds may have accumulated in the very warm oceans, lakes, and pools, forming an "organic soup." Here these simple compounds may have combined to become more complex molecules. Finally, these large, organic molecules may have united somehow to form a very simple kind of reproducing "living thing."

amino [uh MEE noh]. The simplest amino acid is $C_2H_5O_2N$.

simulated [SIM yuh layt ud;
Latin: *similis,* like]: made like
something; molded (see
Investigation 2.2)

Stanley Lloyd Miller: 1930—.
American chemist

Some experiments. A curious investigator might wonder what would happen if a simulated, primitive atmosphere was exposed to an energy source. Stanley Miller, at the University of Chicago, passed electric sparks through ammonia, methane, water, and hydrogen. The electric sparks simulated lightning and the gases were like those on the earth long ago. Nothing else was added. When the substances were analyzed later, it was found that some simple amino acids had been produced.

This experiment has been verified. Other investigators have used ultraviolet light instead of electric sparks. They have obtained the same kind of results. More recently researchers have synthesized organic molecules more complex than amino acids. Some of these complex molecules are involved in carrying characteristics of organisms from one generation to the next.

synthesized [SIN thuh syzd;
Greek: *syn,* together, + *tithenai,* to
place]: constructed by putting two
or more things together

Do these experiments suggest a way in which life might have originated in the distant past? Yes, they do. But it is still a long way from these complex molecules to even the simplest of known organisms.

THE OLDEST FOSSILS

Somewhere, somehow, at some time, life on Earth *did* originate. So let us return to the evidence of fossils. How far back into time does the fossil record extend?

Fossils are fairly abundant in sedimentary deposits of the last 600,000,000 (0.6 billion) years. In deposits older than the Cambrian period, fewer traces of life are found. Recently, however, exploration of remote areas and the study of rock specimens by electron microscopy and other means have revealed the oldest fossils ever found.

Cambrian [KAM bree un]

Fossils of ancient organisms discovered in South African rocks have been dated at 3.1 billion years old! The discoverers named the ancient organisms *Eobacterion isolatum.* These fossils

Eobacterion isolatum [ee oh bak-
TIR ee un eye soh LAY tum]

10−9 Electron micrograph of *Eobacterion isolatum* (*left*) and its imprint (*right*).

were of bacterialike microorganisms. Then, in 1980, a team of 15 biologists from four countries discovered fossil traces of algaelike or bacterialike microorganisms in 3.5 billion-year-old rocks in northwestern Australia. The evidence is both of the fossil cells themselves and of the layers of surface scum they formed, much like "pond scum" today. Well-preserved fossils classified as green and blue-green algae have been collected in central Australia from much later pre-Cambrian limestones dated at 0.7 to 0.9 billion years old.

In still more recent pre-Cambrian rocks are burrows of worms, skeletons of sponges, and shells of marine protozoans. But everywhere the pre-Cambrian fossil record is scanty. One of the reasons for this is that the oldest sedimentary rocks on Earth have undergone changes that have destroyed fossils and modified the rocks.

Suppose that continuing fossil studies indicate the presence of consumers before the presence of producers. How would you explain this?

What is another reason why older fossils are rare?

10−10 A very old animal fossil—probably a worm. The rock in which it was found is more than 0.6 billion years old (South Australia).

M. F. Glaessner, University of Adelaide

CHECK YOURSELF

F. For what biological ideas are fossils important evidence?

G. How were environmental conditions on Earth during its early history probably different from conditions today?

H. What speculation concerns the origin of life on Earth?

I. What experimental evidence supports the *possibility* of such an origin?

J. Which is the first geological period for which fossil evidence is abundant?

K. How far back in time do the oldest probable fossils date?

L. Which organisms of today do the earliest fossils most closely resemble?

ECOSYSTEMS OF THE PAST

Early paleontologists were puzzled because the fossils they found often did not resemble any living thing that they knew. Then, in the middle of the 19th century, the theory of biological evolution linked all the beings of the past and present. From that time on, biologists have been trying to find the ancestors of today's organisms in the fossil record. This task is far from complete. However, a broad outline of the history of organisms has been worked out.

In recent years many paleontologists have begun to study the ecological relationships of organisms of past ages. Let us take a look at some **paleoecosystems.**

paleoecosystems [pay lee oh EE-koh sis tumz; Greek: *palaios*, ancient]

The biosphere in Cambrian time. If this textbook had been written during the Cambrian period, the contents would be very different. The chapter "Life on Land" would be missing. There is no evidence of terrestrial life during the Cambrian.

Although there were no terrestrial ecosystems, marine ecosystems were well developed. There were shallow-water and deep-water organisms—floating, swimming, and bottom-dwelling kinds. The chief marine producers then, as now, probably were microscopic plankton species. Their remains are not abundant, however.

Except for chordates, the major animal phyla known today were present. The most abundant animals of the Cambrian were marine brachiopods and arthropods. Many of the brachiopods were very similar to species living today. But the arthropods were so different that none of them can be placed in modern arthropod classes.

American Museum of Natural History

10−11 An artist's reconstruction of life in a Cambrian sea. How many kinds of organisms can you identify?

Among Cambrian arthropods the ones that left the most abundant fossils were the trilobites. Most trilobites were small−2 to 6 cm long. A few were more than 50 cm long. From Cambrian rocks alone more than 1,000 trilobite species have been described. Most species had two large eyes, but some had no eyes at all. This latter group probably burrowed in the mud of the ocean bottom. Some trilobites were smooth. Others had long, hollow spines over most of the body. These spines may have served as protection against predators, though some paleontologists think they were helpful in floating. In any case, the many different trilobite adaptations suggest that there were many ecological niches in the Cambrian seas.

The trilobites disappeared from the fossil record at the end of the Paleozoic era. Apparently they left no descendants. Many other groups of organisms have a similar history; they were abundant for millions of years and then became extinct. On the

trilobites [TRY luh bytz; Latin: *tri,* three, + *lobus,* lobe]

What reason can you give for this conclusion?

Paleozoic [pay lee uh ZOH ik; Greek: *palaios,* + *zoion,* animal]

era [IR uh]

American Museum of Natural History

10−12 Fossil trilobites (New York). Which of the kinds of fossils (page 319) are these?

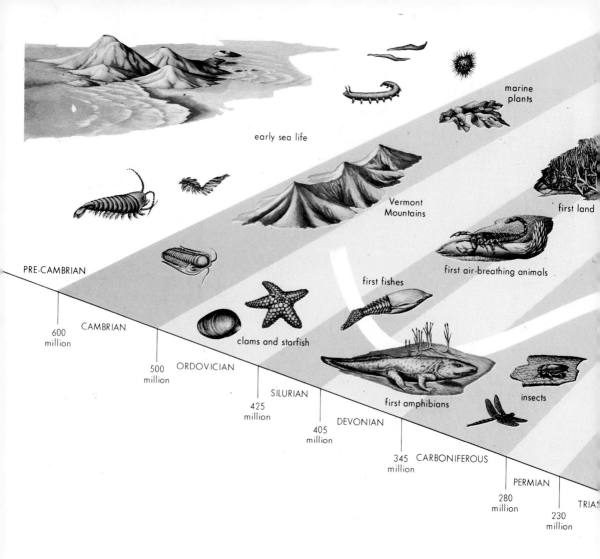

marine
plants

early sea life

Vermont
Mountains

first land

PRE-CAMBRIAN

first air-breathing animals

first fishes

600
million

CAMBRIAN

clams and starfish

500
million

ORDOVICIAN

first amphibians

insects

425
million

SILURIAN

405
million

DEVONIAN

345   CARBONIFEROUS
million

PERMIAN

280
million

TRIA

230
million

10—13 Six hundred million
years of Earth history. On
what kinds of evidence is
this illustration based?

coal-age forests

Appalachian Mountains

pines and
related plants

flowering
plants

Rocky Mountains

ancestors of dinosaurs,
mammals, and birds

birds

DODO

dinosaurs

modern turtles

first mammals

primate

URASSIC

ancestors
of horses

primitive
horses

modern
horses

135
million

CRETACEOUS

63
million

58
million

EOCENE

PALEOCENE

36
million

OLIGOCENE

25
million

MIOCENE

13
million

Today

PLIOCENE

2
million

PLEISTOCENE

☐ Water and swamp
☐ Land

10—14 North America in the Carboniferous period. What kind of evidence did geologists use to draw this map?

Carboniferous [kar buh NIF uh-rus; Latin: *carbo*, coal, + *ferre*, to bear]

other hand, the brachiopods still exist, as do sponges and coelenterates. The present species, however, are different from those that flourished in Cambrian seas.

A Carboniferous ecosystem. There are fossils of freshwater and terrestrial organisms in rocks dated between the Cambrian and Carboniferous periods. By the Carboniferous (coal age) the first forests fringed the shallow seas that covered much of North America at that time. The trees in these forests were mostly relatives of the present-day horsetails, club mosses, and ferns. Strata of the late Carboniferous age contain some gymnosperm fossils. But the most familiar plants of today, the angiosperms, were absent.

Some of the trees had branches. Others had large clumps of leaves at the top of a single stem, as palms do today. When older leaves fell, they left scars in a characteristic pattern on the trunk. The leaves did not fall all at once; the forests were always green.

Beneath the trees was thick undergrowth, mostly of ferns. Stream banks were lined with a dense growth of giant, reedlike plants related to the horsetails. Thick tangles of moss probably covered the ground, but few of these soft and delicate plants have left traces in the fossil record.

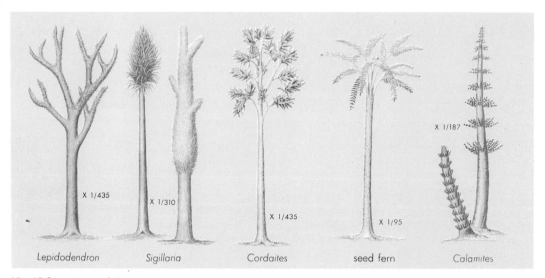

Lepidodendron   Sigillaria   Cordaites   seed fern   Calamites

X 1/435   X 1/310   X 1/435   X 1/95   X 1/187

10—15 Some trees of the coal-age forests: *Lepidodendron* and *Sigillaria* were club mosses. *Cordaites* were primitive gymnosperms. The seed ferns have no living species. *Calamites* were horsetails.

Compare these sizes with those of the trees shown in figure 8–22.

The plants suggest to paleontologists that the climate in which these forests grew was warm and humid. There was probably little or no seasonal change. Compared with tropical forests of today, however, the Carboniferous forests were shallow. The larger trees reached a height of only 30 m and had trunks 2 m in diameter.

Though fossils of Carboniferous decomposers are rare, decay certainly occurred. But the accumulation of great beds of organic remains with much carbon indicates that decay was slow. We now call these compressed and hardened beds coal. In coal itself, remains are usually so altered we cannot see much detail. But in the beds of shale there are many well-preserved fossils. Shale is mud turned to stone. Shale beds lie above and below coal beds. From these fossils we can form an excellent picture of the coal-age forests.

Why? What would have been the result if decay had been rapid?

Insects were numerous. Some predatory ones that darted about in these forests were similar to modern dragonflies. One was the largest insect ever known, with a wingspread of almost 75 cm. Cockroaches were abundant, some nearly 10 cm long.

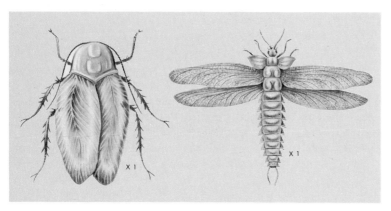

X 1/24

10–16 Insects from the Carboniferous period: a cockroach (*left*) and a possible ancestor of the dragonflies (*right*).

10–17 An artist's drawing (based on fossil bones) of an amphibian of the Carboniferous period.

Except for differences in size, some were almost identical to modern species. But most of the insects belonged to orders now extinct. And some orders familiar today—mayflies, beetles, and mosquitoes—were not present.

Land snails glided over the vegetation. They probably were important herbivores. Scorpions, centipedes, and spiderlike animals were predators. The spiderlike animals had no organs for producing silk, so, unlike those of today, they probably did not make webs.

Why do the paleontologists think that the land snails were herbivores and the scorpions and centipedes were predators?

The only large land animals were amphibians. Of these there were many kinds. Most had four legs, but they could not really stand. Instead they waddled through the muck. Some were snakelike, without legs. None were like present-day frogs. All were probably predators, preying on fishes in the streams and ponds.

A Triassic ecosystem. In the Connecticut Valley of New England are rocks that contain large, three-toed footprints. When

Triassic [try AS ik]

Hugh Spencer

10−18 Fossil footprints in the Connecticut Valley.

these were discovered, many people—including paleontologists—believed they had been made by giant birds. But bone fossils of birds are unknown in the valley. There are many reptile bone fossils, however, and it is now clear that the footprints were made by early dinosaurs. Numerous other fossils help us build up a picture of the ecosystem that occupied the Connecticut Valley late in the Triassic period (about 200 million years ago).

The characteristics of the rocks cause geologists to believe that a slow, winding stream flowed through the valley. They also believe the valley was very dry. The stream carried materials from highlands, which lay on both sides, to a broad, flat plain, where it deposited them. The rocks in the valley show cracks similar to those found today in drying mud. These cracks

luster: shining with reflected light

are filled with material that once was sand or dust. The luster of the rocks suggests they were polished by dry winds. There are a few impressions of large raindrops. This suggests that the valley had a few, sudden, hard showers such as are common in

Figures 8−6, 8−10, and 8−31 show arid regions.

arid regions today.

Narrow bands of coallike rocks indicate that small ponds were present in this arid region. Almost all the fossil plants are from such rocks. There are remains of ferns and horsetails that probably grew around the ponds. Tree fossils, abundant in the coal age, are absent. There are fossil logs of gymnosperms such as cycads, conifers, and ginkgoes, but they were probably brought in from the highlands when the river flooded.

Aquatic insects and several kinds of fishes lived in the

10 – 19 An artist's reconstruction of a streamside scene from the Triassic period. How many of the organisms can you identify?

ponds. There are fossils of lungfish, which could obtain oxygen directly from the air. This suggests that many ponds sometimes dried up, just as do ponds where modern lungfish live. There were also predatory fishes that could not breathe air. This means there must have been some permanent ponds too. Many worm tracks are found in rocks that were once mud along edges of pools.

Reptiles were abundant. Large reptiles, distantly related to modern crocodiles, lived in the ponds. Paleontologists believe they were fish-eaters. The fossil evidence is the many fish bones found inside the reptile skeletons. Scurrying among the horsetails were lizardlike creatures. The structure of their leg

10 – 20 Fossil of a Jurassic fish from the Connecticut Valley. How does it compare with fish of today?

X 1/23

10—21 A Triassic dinosaur.

agile [AJ ul; Latin: *agere,* to act]:
quick and smoothly active

epoch [EP uk]

Geisel [GY zul]

bones suggests they were fast moving. They had small, sharp teeth, which indicates an insect diet. Several species of slender dinosaurs about 2.5 m high roamed the mud flats. It was their tracks that first called attention to this paleoecosystem. Most of the dinosaurs were active and agile carnivores, preying upon smaller reptiles.

An Eocene ecosystem. Let's turn to the Eocene epoch (about 60 million years ago) in the region now called the Geisel Valley of central Germany. Trees of this ancient ecosystem are represented by fossils of stems, leaves, seeds, and even pollen. Among the most common are fossils of sequoia, rubber, palm, fig, and cinnamon. There were many vines. Fossils of mosses and algae are numerous. Among the remains of fungi are some that resemble the living genus *Penicillium.*

Snails are represented by fossils of both land and freshwater species. There are fossils of a number of crayfish. The most common insect fossils are those of beetles, but mayflies and stone flies also are present. Fossil scales from the wings of butterflies provide some of the earliest known evidence of these insects. A fossilized larva of a fly was discovered in the nostril of a fossilized mammal. This evidence shows a kind of parasitism that still exists today.

Thousands of fish skeletons have been found. They represent many modern families, such as those to which bass and salmon belong. Scattered among the fish are remains of frogs and toads in all stages of development, from tadpoles to adults. A study of chemical substances in the preserved frog skin has

10—22 An artist's reconstruction of a scene during the middle Eocene.

made it possible to conclude that the frogs were green. Evidence of color is extremely rare in organisms of the past.

The Geisel Valley beds include fossils of many reptiles. Snakes have been found—some of them so small that they appear to have just hatched. There were long-tailed, tree-climbing lizards, and burrowing lizards, some almost legless. Turtle skeletons are found side by side in shallow depressions. Perhaps death overtook the turtles while they were dormant. The Geisel crocodiles had stubby snouts and limbs well adapted to swimming. Many of their eggs have been discovered, some with the unhatched animals still inside. Bird remains are rare.

Among the fossil mammals in the Geisel Valley is an opossumlike **marsupial.** Skeletons of bats and fragments of their wing membranes, muscles, and hair are preserved. Among rodents are species related to the present-day kangaroo rats of American deserts. All the primate fossils come from species that are relatively small in size, including several kinds of lemurs and tarsiers.

Representing the hoofed mammals are fossils of animals that resembled tapirs and species of the horse family. The carnivores from this deposit are all primitive. Many fossils are of creatures called creodonts. Some of these were large predators strong enough to kill the biggest hoofed mammals of that time. Others were small, weasellike forest dwellers that probably preyed on rodents.

In the Geisel Valley deposits we even have evidence of protists. So perfect is the preservation here that bacteria can be clearly identified in the eye cavities of fish skulls, in fossil frog skin, and in fossil insect muscle. Usually we have to assume the presence of pathogens in ancient ecosystems. In this one we have evidence.

A river floodplain of the Geisel Valley was dotted with many ponds and water holes. Along the river and around the ponds grew a thick forest. On the nearby hills was a grassland. The animal remains crowded around the ancient ponds and water holes indicate a lack of water elsewhere. Evidently there was a hot, dry season. The turtles that were found together apparently died while aestivating. This idea is supported by the fact that some trees in the ecosystem (cinnamon and palm) are known to be intolerant of cold weather. Indeed, the biota was much like that of present tropical regions where wet and dry seasons alternate.

This scene seems much more familiar to us than the ecosystems of the Paleozoic and Mesozoic. But it still is not modern. Most of the families or genera of this ecosystem are familiar, but the species are not.

marsupial [mar SOO pee ul]. This primitive order of mammals is represented today by animals such as kangaroos and opossums. The females carry the young in a pouch on their abdomen.

See "A Catalog of Living Things," Appendix 3.

creodonts [KREE uh dontz; Greek: *kreas*, flesh, + *odous*, tooth]

What additional evidence would you need to show that these protists were indeed pathogens?

10–23 A creodont.

X 1/32

Mesozoic [mez uh ZOH ik]

10–24 An artist's reconstruction of two scenes from the Cenozoic era. The paintings depict the early Pliocene epoch (*above*) and the late Pleistocene epoch (*below*).

Smithsonian Institution

Smithsonian Institution

CHECK YOURSELF

M. What theory links all the opinions of the past to those of the present?

N. In what kind of environment did all the organisms known from Cambrian fossils live?

O. What were trilobites?

P. Compare a forest of Carboniferous time with a forest of today.

Q. What does the presence of coal beds indicate about decomposers?

R. What class of land vertebrates apparently originated between Carboniferous and Triassic times?

S. Why do geologists think that the Connecticut Valley was an arid region in Triassic time?

T. In which vertebrate class are most of the fossils of the Triassic ecosystem placed?

U. What class of land vertebrates apparently originated between Triassic and Eocene times?

V. What evidence is there of ecological relationships between pathogens and hosts in the Geisel Valley ecosystem?

W. In what ways would the biota of the Eocene Geisel Valley seem strange to a person living there today?

Investigation 10.1   COAL BALLS

INTRODUCTION

Usually the remains that make up coal have been so compressed that individual fossils are difficult to distinguish. You will study structures known as "coal balls." In these, the organic matter was invaded at an early stage of decomposition by waters containing calcium carbonate. These waters left a mass of limy substance in which the organic remains were embedded and protected.

PROCEDURE

1. Sprinkle a pinch or two of carborundum powder on the glass plate. With a medicine dropper add a few drops of water. Place the flat surface of the coal-ball slice on the carborundum powder. Grind for about 2 minutes. This exposes a clean layer of organic material. Rinse the ground surface with water.

2. Lay the specimen in a culture dish, ground side up. Flood the surface with the 2% hydrochloric acid solution and allow it to stand for 2 minutes. The surface will turn cloudy with bubbles as the acid reacts with the lime. (*Caution:* Neither acetone nor 2% hydrochloric acid is dangerous *except to eyes*, but both may harm clothes.)

3. Rinse the acid from the surface of the specimen with water. Remove the specimen; empty the culture dish and rinse it with water. Allow the specimen to dry.

4. Prop up the specimen at a slight angle in the culture dish. Flood the surface with acetone.

5. Lower a sheet of cellulose acetate onto the acetone-covered surface, starting at the lower edge of the specimen. Use a rolling motion to spread the acetone evenly and force out air bubbles. Allow about 20 minutes for drying.

6. Take one edge of the sheet between your fingers and slowly peel it from the surface.

7. Tape the peel to a glass slide. Using either

MATERIALS
(per team)

#600 carborundum powder
slice of coal ball
2% hydrochloric acid solution
acetone
microscope
cellulose acetate sheet, a
    little larger than the
    coal-ball specimen
glass plate
glass slide
beaker of water
culture dish
medicine dropper
transparent tape

a dissecting or a compound microscope, scan all parts of the peel. Low power is best for recognizing the forms of fossils that usually are present in a coal ball. Look for leaf and stem outlines and for fossils of spores, seeds, or insect parts. Record your observations in sketches.

8. Using high power, examine details of structure. You should be able to see different kinds of plant cells. Sketch any that you can see. You may be able to identify some of the kinds of cells that you observe by referring to figures 13–4, 13–10, and 13–16, which show the microscopic structure of modern plants.

DISCUSSION

Coal balls were formed during the Carboniferous period. Refer to figure 10–8. (1) How long ago were the fossils from your specimen formed? (2) What organisms did you identify? (3) Compare your slide with another team's. Did you find the same organisms they found? (4) Are your coal-ball individuals related to any present-day organisms? (5) Based on your observations, state your opinion about the amount of structural change that has occurred between present-day organisms and their ancestors.

10−25 Fossil dinosaur eggs. In some cases the bones of the unhatched young have been found within the shells.   × 1/2

Mary Nicol Leakey: 1913—. British paleontologist

Olduvai [OLE duh vy]

THE WORK OF PALEONTOLOGISTS

Collecting facts is the first job in any science. Fossils are the principal facts of paleontology. This makes fossil collecting the basic task for a paleontologist. But important discoveries may come only after months or even years of searching. Fossil digging may turn out to be hot, dusty, and monotonous work. The paleontologist often has to lie on the ground and slowly brush dirt away from a delicate bone or leaf.

Mary Leakey is a paleontologist working in the Olduvai Gorge of Tanzania. She is interested in the evolution of early humans. Leakey spent many months walking in hot, open land before she found her first fossil. Her recent discoveries include fossil jaws and footprints of early human relatives. The age of her finds has been placed at 3.6 million years.

10−26 Mary Leakey measures 3.6-million-year-old footprints of two upright-walking individuals. The footprints were preserved in volcanic mud and ash near Olduvai Gorge.

STUDYING THE EVIDENCE

Even when all the hard parts of an organism are preserved, they are seldom found in perfect condition. They must usually be reassembled and placed in proper relation to each other. To do this well, paleontologists must know how the parts of modern organisms are arranged. They must know the **anatomy** (structure) of modern organisms. Then, to picture fossil organisms as they were in life, paleontologists must imagine the placement of muscles or leaves that have left no trace. Again they are guided by knowledge of the anatomy of modern organisms. Finally, paleontologists may paint the reconstruction — a life-size model based on fossils. The choice of colors is based almost entirely on our knowledge of color in modern organisms.

anatomy [uh NAT uh mee; Greek: *ana*, on, up, + *temnein*, to cut]

In all this work it is possible for different paleontologists to interpret the evidence differently. The farther we go from the basic evidence — the fossils themselves — the greater is the possibility of differing interpretations.

Decisions about classification. Anatomical characteristics are used by taxonomists more often than any other kind. The emphasis is on anatomy because usually no other characteristics are found in fossils. A kinship classification depends heavily on comparison of fossils to organisms now living.

Consider the problem posed by a fossil from the early Mesozoic era, when the first mammals appeared. How can we distinguish a mammal fossil from a reptile fossil of that time? Many characteristics are used to distinguish present-day mammals from reptiles. Mammals have simple jawbones, incisors and molars, hair, and mammary (milk) glands, and are warm-blooded.

10–27 Excavating dinosaur bones at Dinosaur National Monument on the Colorado-Utah border. What information do you think is important enough to be recorded?

C. Allan Morgan

A

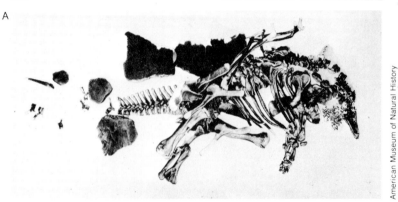

B

10–28 *Stegosaurus*, a late
Mesozoic reptile.   × 1/50
A. Fossil bones laid out as
they were found.
B. Bones of another
specimen, mounted in a
museum.
C. An artist's reconstruction.
D. Another artist's
reconstruction.

C

D

Suppose a fossil shows a jaw and teeth much like those of a present-day mammal. A fossil is not likely to indicate hair, milk glands, or warm-bloodedness. Does the fossil represent a mammal? Could there have been an animal with mammallike jaws and teeth without other mammalian characteristics? Suppose we discover a similar fossil together with an impression of hair. We may speculate that the hair indicates that the animal was warm-blooded. But did it have mammary glands? Is it *fully* a mammal, or is it a mammallike reptile?

Such problems make the work of paleontologists and taxonomists difficult but interesting. If mammals evolved from reptiles, animals must once have existed that showed combinations of reptilian and mammalian characteristics.

X 1/200

10–29 *Brontosaurus*, a reconstruction (*left*) and a fossil skeleton (*below*).

American Museum of Natural History

A principle. From the foregoing examples of paleontologic work, we can see a principle emerging: "The present is the key to the past." Geologists developed this principle about 200 years ago. It means that *unless we have evidence to the contrary,* we interpret the past on the basis of our knowledge of the present. This applies to the structure of organisms, their function, and their development. Indeed, it applies to the whole history of ecosystems.

How was this principle used in describing the paleoecosystems on pages 326–336?

Careers in Biology: Animal Restorations

Have you ever gone on safari in Africa or roamed the snowfields of Northern Canada? Probably not. But you can get a good idea of what you might see on such trips by visiting displays in a natural history museum (**A**).

In large part, the realism of the displays depends on the skills of the taxidermist. Taxidermy is the art of restoring and preserving specimens of vertebrate animals. Many of these preserved animals are used for educational and scientific purposes. Taxidermy combines a knowledge of zoology with the artistry of sculpture.

As a boy growing up in Pittsburgh, Pennsylvania, Joseph Kish was fascinated by mammals and birds. When he graduated from high school, Joe felt a "pressing desire to preserve and continue to enjoy what the hunter throws away." This led him into the field of taxidermy. Joe was a taxidermist at the Denver Museum of Natural History, but he now has his own taxidermy company. Joe's artistic talent, knowledge of biology, and manual skills helped him become successful in this field.

Taxidermists like Joe reconstruct animals from knowledge of the relationship between animal form and function. Before Joe can work on animal hides, he must send them to a tannery to be preserved and softened. When they are returned, they are checked for cuts and tears that must be repaired (**B**). Joe then fastens a hide onto a form that is a perfect model of the animal (**C**). He carefully shapes the skin by hand until it fits exactly to the form (**D**).

Francoise Rice works at the Joe Jonas Jr. taxidermy studio. Francoise was born in Paris, France, where she attended art school. Since 1965 Francoise has been working in taxidermy. Francoise has performed all the tasks involved in

Denver Museum of Natural History

A. From such lifelike displays in museums, people get a vivid picture of animals, plants, and environments in other parts of the world.

B. When the hides are returned from the tannery, they are clean and soft. Francoise examines a zebra hide to determine its condition.

preparing and mounting animal hides. Among other things, she has learned to clean and repair the hides and to fit them to the animal forms.

Francoise now specializes in the finishing work after the hides are mounted (**E**). The natural markings and colors of the hides must be restored exactly as they would be on living animals. Francoise touches up scars and other marks. She brushes away the last bits of dust and fluffs the fur. She also cleans and waxes antlers and horns to preserve their natural beauty. Francoise's finishing work often requires hours of cautious touch-up painting.

When Francoise and Joe have completed their work, the result may be a dainty African Colubus monkey glancing down from a sturdy tree branch. Or it may be a group of wolves that seem to be searching for food. Museum-goers will enjoy and learn from these restorations for many years.

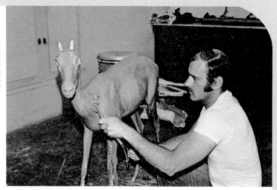

C. Before a hide can be mounted, Joe must build a form that is an accurate copy of the live animal.

D. Fitting the hide to the form takes several days. The hide is carefully shaped around even the smallest curves of the form.

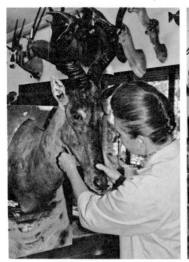

E. Francoise's finishing work includes painting, polishing, and brushing to make the mounts look lifelike.

F. The Joe Jonas Jr. taxidermy studio.

343

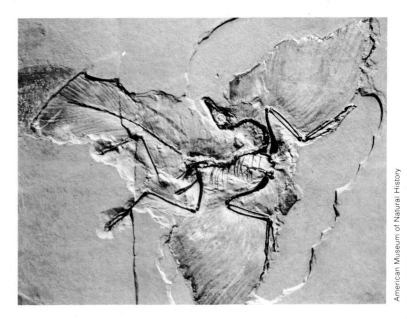

American Museum of Natural History

10–30 *Archaeopteryx,* earliest-known fossil of a bird. Most of the bones are much like those of dinosaurs. What is the evidence that shows it to have been a bird?

SOME PALEONTOLOGIC CONCEPTS

After studying fossils, paleontologists picture for us, in varying detail, the living things and ecosystems of the past. They also develop some concepts that influence the ways in which we think about our world.

Change and stability. No one can examine a large collection of fossils without being impressed by change. This is especially true if the fossils are arranged in chronological order. Changes have occurred in single species of organisms. Whole ecosystems also have changed. Where once there was coal-age swamp in Pennsylvania there is now dry, hilly, oak forest. Such ecosystem changes are further examples of ecological succession. But, instead of successions involving a few years or centuries, these changes involved millions of years.

Many species have died out and left no descendants. Others seem to have merely changed through many generations. Now they are no longer recognizable as the same species. You might suspect that the most advanced forms in one geological period would give rise to the advanced forms in the next. But the fossil record does not support this view. For example, mammals are considered more advanced than reptiles. But reptiles did not become advanced during the Mesozoic and then give rise to mammals in the Cenozoic. On the contrary, the ancestors that gave rise to the reptiles were apparently also the ancestors of the mammals (figure 10–13). Thus, the ancestors of mammals were primitive rather than advanced reptiles.

chronological [kron ul OJ ih kul; Greek: *chronos,* time, + *logos,* speech, reason]: in order of time

What geoecological successions have occurred in the region where you live?

"Advanced forms": If you have forgotten this term, review Investigation 5.2.

Smithsonian Institution

10−31 Fossil casts of brachiopods (New York). × 1

Though the fossil record shows abundant evidence of change, it also provides evidence of great stability. Brachiopods much like those of the Paleozoic seas are found in 20th-century oceans. Many of the fossil ferns and horsetails in Illinois coal beds are like the smaller ferns and horsetails now growing above them. The Triassic lungfish have disappeared from Connecticut, but lungfish still inhabit the lakes of Africa and Australia. And turtles and frogs—only slightly different—survive from the Eocene in Germany.

Extinction. At least 130,000 species of animals are known only from their fossil remains. Perhaps no group of large vertebrates has left so many fossils as have the dinosaurs.

Can you name any?

What caused such extinctions? This problem has been a subject for speculation among paleontologists for a long time. There are many hypotheses. Unfortunately, paleontologic hypotheses are not often testable by experimentation. Perhaps we shall never learn what brought about the extinction of the dinosaurs and other organisms. But as long as there are rocks that have not been opened by the paleontologist's pick, new evidence on this and other problems may be found.

Some paleontologists don't believe all dinosaurs were cold-blooded. Their belief is based on information from fossils, location of the fossil beds, and biomass calculations. Their idea is that some dinosaurs were actually hairy, warm-blooded reptiles. They think that present-day birds descended from these dinosaurs. (See Bakker, "Suggested Readings," p. 354.)

Adaptation. Change in ecosystems depends on the changes of a particular environment. It also depends on the adaptability of the associated organisms. Many structures of organisms seem to be fitted to the ecological niches that the organisms oc-

Marine organisms have probably changed less than land and freshwater ones. If this is true, can you explain why?

cupy. But a structure that adapts an organism to one environment might be a hindrance in a different environment. For instance, if the environment of the North Pole became warmer, the fur coat of the polar bear might become a hindrance.

Throughout the history of life on the earth, the descendants of a small group of organisms have dispersed into a great variety of ecosystems. Their parents may have been adapted originally to a narrow range of ecological conditions. But the descendants in the new ecosystems had slightly different structures. These changes helped adapt them to their new ecosystems.

This process, known as *adaptive radiation,* is well demonstrated by mammals. The few fossils of mammals from the Me-

10–32 Adaptive radiation in the class of mammals. Only the still-living kinds (*outer arc*) are listed in "A Catalog of Living Things," Appendix 3.

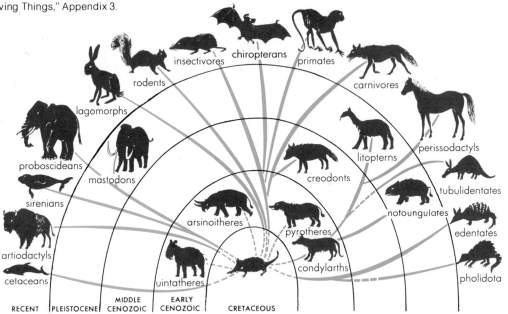

sozoic era indicate that the first were small animals much like present-day shrews. From such ancestors the great variety of Cenozoic mammals developed by adapting to a great variety of ecosystems. Bony fishes probably originated in small, freshwater streams. Their fossil record shows a history of adaptive radiation into the world's aquatic ecosystems. Among plants the angiosperms have adaptively radiated into almost all terrestrial ecosystems.

The fossil record also shows examples of *adaptive convergence.* In such cases, descendants of quite different ancestors have developed similar structures as they adapted to similar ways of life. Compare (figure 10–33) the spiny, leafless euphor-

10–33 Adaptive convergence in plants. A cactus (*left*) and a euphorbia (*right*). Both are in bloom.

bia of the African desert with a cactus of the Mexican desert. Their body forms are similar; yet flower structure shows that euphorbias and cacti are members of two different families.

All animals that burrow are similar in having short appendages or no appendages at all. But these animals may be from very different taxonomic groups—earthworms and caecilians, for example. Another example is the streamlined body of different aquatic predators.

Light on the present from the past. On the whole, fossil evidence favors the hypothesis that each species originated in one place and spread into others. But some species undoubtedly were more widespread at one time than they are today. As a result, there are *discontinuous distributions.*

Sometimes members of the same species are found today in widely separated regions. Consider tapirs, for example. Today tapirs are found in tropical America and Malaysia and nowhere in between. Fossils show that tapirs once existed in Germany and many other regions that are between their present homes. Figure 10–34 illustrates a similar example.

Both camels and llamas are mammals that developed in the Cenozoic era. The map in figure 10–34 shows that both could have dispersed from North America. The narrow sea between North America and Asia has been dry land at various times and has not always been a barrier to terrestrial animals. Distributions of other species that developed in Mesozoic or Paleozoic times, however, cannot be accounted for in the same way.

discontinuous [dis kun TIN yuh-wus]: separated, not connected

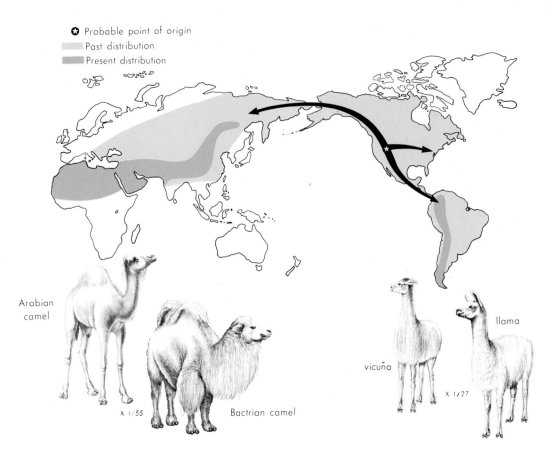

○ Probable point of origin
▨ Past distribution
▨ Present distribution

Arabian camel

Bactrian camel

vicuña

llama

X 1/55

X 1/27

10–34 Past and present distribution of the camel family. How can paleontologists determine the part of the world where the family originated?

Nothofagus [noth uh FAY gus]

Glossopteris [glos SOP tur us]

Continental drift. Figure 10–35 shows a puzzling case. *Nothofagus* is an angiosperm sometimes called southern beech. It is, and apparently always has been, absent from the Northern Hemisphere. A similar pattern of distribution is shown by fossils of *Glossopteris,* a genus of Paleozoic seed ferns, except that they occur also in India and South Africa. Other Paleozoic and early Mesozoic terrestrial organisms have similar patterns of distribution.

These areas are separated by thousands of miles of ocean. The seeds of *Nothofagus* and *Glossopteris* are not adapted to such long-distance travel over the ocean. Then how did the plants and their fossils get to where they are now?

In 1910 a German geologist advanced an idea that the continents have not always been in the positions they now occupy. The idea was that these big land masses might be slowly floating over the hot liquid interior of the earth. More than 40 years later, geologists found great cracks in the middle of the oceans. The cracks seemed to result from the rock separating and moving in opposite directions. To the geologists this was an indication that some continents were moving away from each other.

10–35 Distribution map of extinct *Glossopteris* ferns and living *Nothofagus* trees.

New Guinea

New Caledonia

AUSTRALIA

NEW ZEALAND

Macquarie Island

0   1000
Miles

PACIFIC OCEAN

ANTARCTICA

Heard Island

Kerguelen Island

SOUTH AMERICA

MADAGASCAR

Tristan da Cunha Island

AFRICA

LEGEND

Distribution of *Glossopteris* flora fossils

Distribution of the living plant *Nothofagus*

Many other observations supported a theory of **continental drift.** This is now a part of the theory of **plate tectonics.**

The theory of plate tectonics states that the continents are parts of huge plates that make up the earth's crust. The continents originally may have been joined together near the middle of what is now the Atlantic Ocean. The continents began moving away from the mid-Atlantic ridge near the end of the Paleozoic era. If this theory is correct, then the discontinuous distribution of *Nothofagus* and *Glossopteris* is easily explained. They lived when the southern continents were still parts of a larger continent. Both dispersed easily over much of that vast land mass. When it began to break up, the plants and their fossils were carried to their present positions.

Earlier in the chapter we said, "The present is the key to the past." In the study of discontinuous distribution, we can see that sometimes the reverse is true: The past sheds light on the present. Paleontologists travel far and wide over the earth to seek evidence. To interpret that evidence, they must allow their minds to move freely back and forth between present and past.

tectonics [tek TON iks; Greek: *tektonikos,* a builder or carpenter]

The earth then...

10-36 Continental drift.
These maps show the
positions of the continents
as they began to move away
from each other and as they
are today.

and now

CHECK YOURSELF

X. Why is collecting fossils only the beginning of a paleontologist's work?

Y. If two artists did paintings of an organism known only from fossils, why might the paintings differ?

Z. How would a paleontologist decide whether a particular fossil represented a reptile or a mammal?

AA. What principle guides the interpretation of paleontologic evidence?

BB. How does the fossil record support both the idea of change and the idea of stability in living things?

CC. What problem does the extinction of large groups of organisms—such as the dinosaurs—present to paleontologists?

DD. Contrast the processes of adaptive radiation and adaptive convergence.

EE. How does the fossil record help to explain the discontinuous distribution of tapirs?

FF. How does the fossil record support the geological theory of continental drift?

Investigation 10.2   PALEONTOLOGIC COMPARISON

**MATERIALS
(per student)**

**1 sheet graph paper
pencil**

INTRODUCTION

The first laboratory task of paleontologists
is to remove specimens carefully from surrounding rock. The next task is to describe
the cleaned specimens. This usually involves measuring them. This investigation
shows one of the ways that measurements
are useful in the interpretation of fossils.

Members of the early Eocene genus
Hyracotherium are the oldest known animals of the horse family, Equidae. In rocks
of the late Eocene and of succeeding Cenozoic epochs, fossil remains of this family are
abundant. Paleontologists have classified
the animals represented by these fossils
into 17 genera. They have grouped these
animals by combining many kinds of structural evidence. In this investigation you will
study only one of the many anatomical
characteristics that paleontologists have
used.

In horses the grinding teeth are in the
back of the mouth, separated from the front
teeth by a toothless space. On each side of
each jaw, the grinding teeth (cheek teeth)
consist of 3 premolars and 3 molars (figure
10–38). The span of the cheek teeth has
been measured in many horse fossils. Averages of the data are presented in figure
10–39.

PROCEDURE

1. When plotted on a graph, the data in figure
10–39 suggest certain relationships. Figure 10–40 shows the most convenient
kind of grid. Construct such a grid, making
it as large as possible so that the plotted

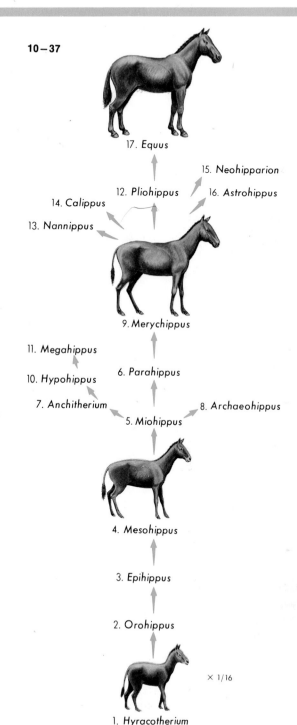

10–37

17. Equus

15. Neohipparion

12. Pliohippus   16. Astrohippus

14. Calippus

13. Nannippus

9. Merychippus

11. Megahippus

10. Hypohippus   6. Parahippus

7. Anchitherium   8. Archaeohippus

5. Miohippus

4. Mesohippus

3. Epihippus

2. Orohippus

× 1/16

1. Hyracotherium

points will not be crowded. On the grid, plot the cheek-teeth span measurements of the 17 Equidae genera. As each point is plotted on the graph, place beside it the number of the genus it represents.

2. Connect the points representing the genera *Hyracotherium, Orohippus, Epihippus, Mesohippus,* and *Miohippus*. (*1*) What seems to have been the trend of evolution in the span of equid cheek teeth during Eocene and Oligocene times? (*2*) Is it possible to connect all the rest of the points with a single line? (*3*) Without drawing any

10 – 38

10 – 39

GENERA OF EQUIDAE	TIME OF EXISTENCE	SPAN OF CHEEK TEETH (in cm)
1. Hyracotherium	Early Eocene	4.3
2. Orohippus	Middle Eocene	4.3
3. Epihippus	Late Eocene	4.7
4. Mesohippus	Early Oligocene	7.2
	Middle Oligocene	7.3
5. Miohippus	Late Oligocene	8.4
	Early Miocene	8.3
6. Parahippus	Early Miocene	10.0
7. Anchitherium	Early Miocene	11.3
8. Archaeohippus	Middle Miocene	6.5
9. Merychippus	Middle Miocene	10.2
	Late Miocene	12.5
10. Hypohippus	Late Miocene	14.2
11. Megahippus	Early Pliocene	21.5
12. Pliohippus	Early Pliocene	15.5
	Middle Pliocene	15.6
13. Nannippus	Early Pliocene	11.0
	Late Pliocene	10.7
14. Calippus	Early Pliocene	9.3
15. Neohipparion	Middle Pliocene	13.1
16. Astrohippus	Middle Pliocene	11.8
	Late Pliocene	11.8
17. Equus	Late Pliocene	18.8
	Pleistocene	17.6

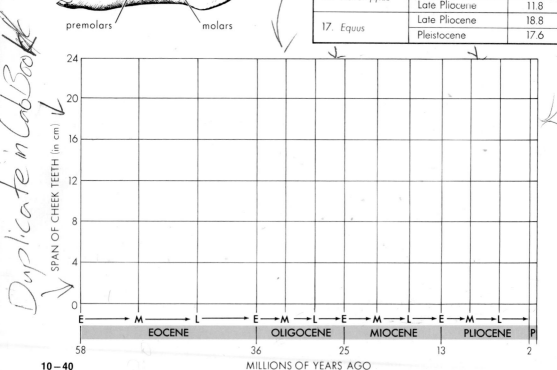

span of cheek teeth

premolars   molars

10 – 40   MILLIONS OF YEARS AGO

lines, describe the general trend of evolution in cheek-teeth span during the Miocene, Pliocene, and Pleistocene.

3. Now you can find out whether the data on this span of the cheek teeth fit other relationships among the equid genera. To do this, draw lines between the plotted points, so that they correspond to the arrows in figure 10–37. For example: Draw a line from the dot for *Miohippus* to that for *Megahippus*, connecting genera 5, 7, 10, and 11. Draw another line from the dot for *Miohippus* to that for *Archaeohippus*, connecting genera 5 and 8. Draw a third line from *Miohippus* to *Equus*, connecting genera 5, 6, 9, 12, and 17. Then draw in the remaining four branches from *Merychippus*, genus 9, as indicated.

DISCUSSION

If data on a single characteristic conflict with relationships worked out from other characteristics, the data will produce a set of crossing lines when graphed. (4) Do the data on

the span of the cheek teeth support the relationships shown in figure 10–37, or do they conflict with those relationships? (5) What was the average change in the span of the cheek teeth per million years from *Hyracotherium* (genus 1) to *Miohippus* (genus 5)? (6) What was the average change per million years from *Miohippus* to *Megahippus* (genus 11)? (7) From *Miohippus* to *Equus* (genus 17)? (8) From these results, what generalization can you make about the rate of evolutionary change within the Equidae?

(9) What evidence do you have that the direction of an evolutionary change can be reversed? (10) From figure 10–37, what would you say was the general trend in the evolution of body size from *Hyracotherium* to *Equus*? (11) How many years passed between the time of the *Hyracotherium* and *Equus* horses? (12) If each horse lived 5 years before it reproduced, how many generations of horses were there between *Hyracotherium* and *Equus*? (13) What does this tell you about the rate of evolution?

PROBLEMS

1. A broad view of the history of life has been developed through study of fossils from all parts of the world. In any one region, such as a state, rocks representing only a few geological time divisions are likely to be found. Obtain a geological time scale indicating the time divisions that are represented in your state and those that are not. Use the map as a guide to places where you may be able to collect fossils yourself.

2. In Greenland and in Antarctica, beds of coal occur. These were formed from abundant plant remains; today the regions are covered with ice caps. How can you account for this evidence of great photosynthetic activity at high latitudes?

3. Investigate the origin of the names given to the geological time intervals that are listed in figure 10–8.

4. In eastern Colorado and western Nebraska extensive deposits of fossils exist in rocks of Oligocene age. Known as the White River deposits, these rocks were formed from silts in which there were streaks of gravel. The plant fossils represent grasses, reeds, hickories, and hackberries. Animal fossils represent freshwater clams, several kinds of freshwater fish, frogs, snakes related to the boas, and several species of large land tortoises; among mammals, saber-toothed cats and species closely related to the modern dogs, members of the camel family, four species

of horses, and several species of rhinoceroses. Some of the rhinos were much like those of the present day. Others had long, slender legs much like those of horses. Others, much like the hippos of today, had heavy bodies with short legs and large feet. Using the evidence given here, describe the ecosystem represented by the White River deposits. Does your interpretation agree with those of other students? How do you support your interpretation where it differs from theirs? What additional evidence would give further support to your interpretation?

5. Fossil skeletons of ichthyosaurs have been discovered with fossil skeletons of small ichthyosaurs inside them. How

would you interpret this situation? What additional evidence would you look for to support your interpretation?

6. Investigate the hypotheses that have been advanced to explain the extinction of the dinosaurs. You may think that one seems more reasonable than the others. If so, explain why you think so.

7. Two groups of hoofed mammals, the litopterns and the notungulates, inhabited South America for a long time. During this time there was no land connection between South and North America. Soon after the Panama land bridge was reestablished in the Pliocene, these animals became extinct. How can you account for this?

SUGGESTED READINGS

Bakker, R. T. 1975. Dinosaur Renaissance. *Scientific American*, April.

Beadle, G. W. 1980. The Ancestry of Corn. *Scientific American*, January. Traces the ancestry of modern corn to a wild grass.

Cloud, P. 1978. *Cosmos, Earth, and Man: A Short History of the Universe.* Yale University Press, New Haven, Conn. Begins with the formation of the solar system, covers the origin and evolution of organisms, and speculates on the future.

Jaber, W. 1978. *Whatever Happened to the Dinosaurs?* Julian Messner, New York. Covers the history, classification, evolution, and extinction of dinosaurs.

Leakey, M. D. 1979. Footprints in the Ashes of Time. *National Geographic*, April, pp. 446–457. The oldest footprints of upright-walking individuals.

Macdougall, J. D. 1976. Fission-Track Dating. *Scientific American*, December. Describes a broad-range dating technique from fission

of small amounts of uranium.

McKerrow, W. S. (ed.). 1978. *The Ecology of Fossils: An Illustrated Guide.* M.I.T. Press, Cambridge, Mass. Traces the changing patterns of forms of life in similar habitats through time. Advanced.

Morris, S. C. and H. B. Wittington. 1979. The Animals of the Burgess Shale. *Scientific American*, July. Describes a Cambrian animal community from fossils in western Canada.

Radninsky, L. 1976. Cerebral Clues. Describes the use of fossil braincases to study animal behavior. *Natural History*, May.

Scientific American. 1979. *Life: Origin and Evolution.* W. H. Freeman, San Francisco. A series of readings from *Scientific American* on the origin of life and the change of organisms through time.

Sclater, J. G. and C. Tapscott. 1979. The History of the Atlantic. *Scientific American*, June. Traces the origin and development of the Atlantic and its role in continental drift.

SECTION FOUR

Within the Individual Organism

WITHIN THE INDIVIDUAL ORGANISM

Individual organisms vary greatly in size. A redwood tree may extend 100 m from root to tip, and a blue whale may weigh 150 metric tons. Near the other extreme, a single bacterium may be only 0.4 μm wide and weigh a small fraction of a milligram. But regardless of their size, we have been treating all of these as equal units. We have considered them as individuals interacting with other individuals and with the abiotic environment.

We have viewed living things somewhat as traffic engineers look at automobiles. These engineers are concerned with the way traffic moves, how collisions upset the movement, and how traffic may be managed. Traffic engineers are not concerned with the way automobile motors and braking systems are constructed, or even with the source of energy that powers automobiles. Mechanics, on the other hand, are concerned with the structure of automobiles — with gears, pistons, and valves. Mechanics are also interested in the way the energy of gasoline is transformed into the motion of turning wheels. Traffic engineers look at automobiles from the outside. Mechanics look at them from the inside.

The two views are not independent, of course. The way a machine is constructed determines what it can do. The same is true of organisms. So the time has now come to shift from the outside view of organisms to the inside view. What activities within an organism produce the activities we have seen from the outside? To understand these internal activities of an organism, we must examine its parts. Is there any basic internal unit from which the parts are constructed? Internal activities imply internal energy. We have seen how energy goes from one organism to another in the biosphere, but what happens to this energy within each organism? We shall consider some of these questions in the following chapters.

The photo on the reverse side of this page is of a jellyfish. Its scientific name is *Cyanea capillata.* The photo was taken underwater near Croker Island, British Columbia. Most jellyfish are transluscent. Many internal organs and structures can be seen. These organisms can be found floating in nearly every ocean in the world.

11

Cells

YOUR GUIDEPOSTS

In this chapter you will have an opportunity to explore these questions in biology:

- How did scientists come to understand the microscopic structure of organisms?

- What principles from physical science help to explain the functions of organisms?

- How do cells duplicate themselves?

- What are some areas of cell biology that still remain unclear?

DISCOVERY OF CELLS

If you examine a fairly large organism, like yourself, you can easily identify a number of parts. Externally you have eyes, arms, and hair. Inside are teeth and tongue. Finally, after a bit of dissection, you find heart, liver, stomach, and other organs. Proceeding with the dissection, you will find smaller and smaller parts.

dissection [dis EK shun; Latin: *dis*, apart, + *secare*, to cut]

By the 16th century, investigation of the structure of the human body had reached the limits of what could be studied with the naked eye. In 1543 Andreas Vesalius published *De Humani Corporis Fabrica (Concerning the Structure of the Human Body)*. Scientists at that time felt this book included all that could be learned about the human body.

Andreas Vesalius [ON dree us vuh SAY lee us]: 1514–1564. Flemish anatomist

Today it seems that Vesalius began, rather than ended, studies in anatomy. As Leeuwenhoek and others applied the microscope to studying life, new features were seen. Scientists could observe the very small parts of humans and other organisms. Robert Hooke, an English scientist, was studying the bark of a Mediterranean oak. In this bark, called cork, he observed neat rows of thick-walled compartments that looked

Robert Hooke: 1635–1703. English physicist and mathematician

357

The word "cell" originally meant a small room.

11–1 One of Hooke's drawings of cork (*Micrographia*, 1665).

Victor Larsen

Jean Baptiste de Lamarck [ZHON bop TEEST duh luh-MARK]: 1744–1829. French naturalist

Matthias Schleiden [muh TEE-us SHLY dun]: 1804–1881

Theodor Schwann [TAY uh dor shvon]: 1810–1882

like honeycomb cells. Hooke called the cork compartments "cells."

The story of Hooke's cells is like the story of Leeuwenhoek's "little animals." (See pages 175–176.) During the next century and a half many others saw cells and "little animals." But no one at that time fully understood either of them.

The cork was dead material. In living materials, however, Hooke found that the cells were filled with a liquid. Attention shifted from the walls of the cells to this liquid inside. In 1809 Jean Baptiste de Lamarck wrote: "Every living body is essentially a mass of cellular tissue in which more or less complex fluids move more or less rapidly."

Scientists slowly came to believe that the cell is the fundamental part of all living organisms. Botanists were the first to accept this idea, because the boundaries of plant cells are easier to see than those of animal cells. By 1839, however, most zoologists also agreed with the generalization. Two Germans, Matthias Schleiden, a botanist, and Theodor Schwann, a zoologist, did much to verify similar cell structure in plants and animals. Schwann wrote, "We have overthrown a great barrier of separation between the animal and vegetable kingdoms."

"Cell" once referred to an empty space. It came to mean a unit of living matter. Leeuwenhoek's "little animals" were thought to be single cells. All other organisms were regarded as

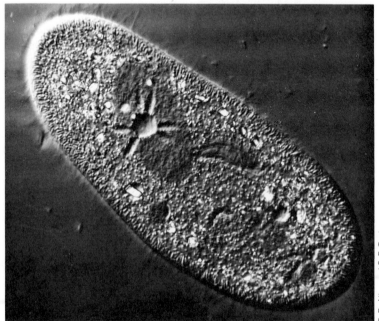

11–2 *Paramecium.* The complex structure of this protist has led some biologists to regard it not as a single cell but as an organism that has lost cellular structure.   × 450

R. D. Allen and S. R. Taub

11–3 Diversity among cells.

A. Red blood cells of a bird.   × 1,200   B. Human white blood cell.   × 11,000

C. A bacterium.   × 6,000   D. Some diatoms.   × 500

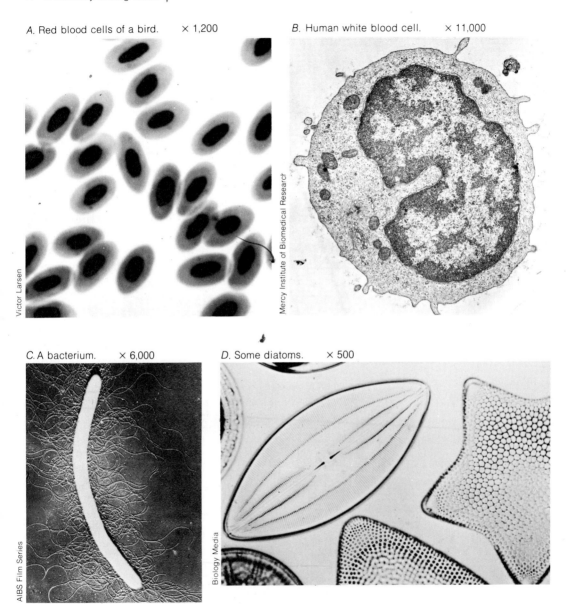

Victor Larsen

Mercy Institute of Biomedical Research

AIBS Film Series

Biology Media

aggregations (groupings) of cells. These groupings, though highly organized, were all made up of single cells.

    Despite the microscope's usefulness, detailed studies of cells had to await another technological development. It was the discovery in the 1850's and 1860's of dyes that make cellular structures more clearly visible. These dyes helped to show that

aggregations [ag rih GAY shunz; Latin: *ad,* to, + *gregare,* to herd]

Cell dyes came to be called stains by microscopists. What stains have you used?

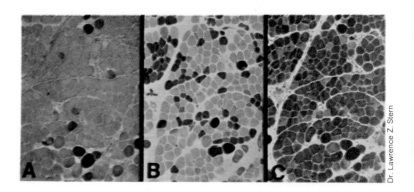

11—4 The use of dyes on these cross sections of human muscle indicates that the patient has a form of muscular dystrophy.

Dr. Lawrence Z. Stern

cells were involved with *every* life process. Cells quickly came to be regarded as the units of structure as well as the units of function.

Investigators soon determined that cells come into being through the division of parent cells. Soon the idea was established that, since the beginning of life, there has been no break in the descent of cells from other cells.

Why is this called a theory rather than a generalization?

Today the **cell theory** may be summarized as three main ideas: (1) Cells are the units of structure in living organisms. (2) Cells are the units of function in living organisms. (3) All new cells come from cells that existed before.

Investigation 11.1   OBSERVING CELLS

INTRODUCTION

Although scientists have not observed *all* kinds of cells, many cells have been described and photographed. In this investigation you will use some of the techniques for observing cells.

PROCEDURE

1. On the inner, concave side of each piece of onion, the **epidermis** (ep uh DUR mus) —skin—is easily peeled off with forceps. Place a small piece of epidermis (much smaller than a cover slip) on a slide. Avoid overlapping or wrinkling it. Add 1 or 2 drops of water and a cover slip.
2. Examine the onion epidermis under low

MATERIALS
(per student or pair of
  students)

several 1-cm² pieces of onion
iodine—potassium-iodide solution (I₂KI)
physiological saline solution
methylene blue solution
elodea leaves
frog blood
frog skin
monocular microscope
microscope slides
cover slips
fine-pointed forceps
scalpel
4 medicine droppers
2 dissecting needles
paper towels
toothpicks

power of your microscope. Look for cell boundaries. Draw a small part of the field of view to show the shapes and arrangements of the cells.

3. Place a drop of iodine stain along one edge of the cover slip. Pull it under the cover slip, using the technique shown in figure A–6 (page 738). Record any changes that occur as the stain spreads across the onion epidermis.

4. Switch to high power and draw a single cell. Include as much detail as you can see. Save your drawing for reference in the next text section, on cell structure.

5. With forceps remove a young leaf from the tip of an elodea plant. Place it upside down on a clean slide. Add a drop of water and a cover slip.

6. Observe the leaf under low power. (1) By slowly turning the fine adjustment back and forth, determine the number of cell layers in the leaf. Switch to high power. Select an "average" cell and focus on it carefully. (2) Is there any evidence that the cell is living? If there is, what is the evidence?

7. Make a drawing of the leaf cell, including as much detail as you can see. Label any parts you can identify. Keep this drawing too for later reference.

8. Using the blunt end of a toothpick, gently scrape the inside surface of your mouth along your cheek. (*Caution: Do not scrape too hard.*) You should obtain a small amount of cloudy material. Rub this material on a clean slide.

9. Add a drop of physiological saline solution. Stir thoroughly with the toothpick.

10. Examine the slide under low power. By carefully using the fine adjustment, try to observe the 3-dimensional shape of the cells. (3) Would you describe them as spherical, disk-shaped, or something else?

11. Add a drop or two of methylene blue and a cover slip. Find several cells, well separated from the others, and draw 1 or 2 of them. Include as much detail as you can see. Label any parts you can identify.

12. Place a drop of diluted frog blood on a clean slide. Add a drop of methylene blue and a cover slip.

13. Examine under low power. Find an area where the cells are neither too crowded nor too scarce. Center it in the field of view. Switch to high power. Draw 1 or 2 cells and label any parts you can identify.

14. Place scrapings from frog skin on a clean slide. Add a drop of physiological saline, a drop of methylene blue, and a cover slip. Using low power, locate cells and then switch to high power. Draw 1 or 2 cells and label any parts you can identify.

DISCUSSION

Construct a chart in your data book. In the first column list all the kinds of cells you observed. Head the other columns with the names of cell parts that you identified. Review your sketches and notes. For each kind of cell examined, place an X beneath the name of each cell structure observed. (4) Does the lack of an X indicate that the structure was not present in the cells observed? Why or why not?

(5) On the basis of your observations, which kind of cell (plant or animal) seems to have more angular, less-rounded shapes? (6) Which has more clearly defined boundaries? (7) What structure may be involved in determining a cell's shape?

CELL STRUCTURE

Study figure 11–5. It shows many cell structures. Some are not found in all cells. The diagram is a guide to the structures, not to a particular kind of cell.

nucleus [NEW klee us; Latin: *nux*, nut]: plural, nuclei [NEW klee-eye]

Nearly every cell contains a ***nucleus,*** and some cells contain more than one. The nucleus is the cell's control center, from which come instructions that keep the cell alive. The nucleus also plays the leading role in cell reproduction. It and other cell structures are surrounded by a semiliquid ***cytoplasm*** rich in proteins and other needed materials.

cytoplasm [SYT uh plaz um; Greek: *kytos*, a vessel, + *plassein*, to form, mold]

11–5 Cell structures. Not all cells contain the same structures.

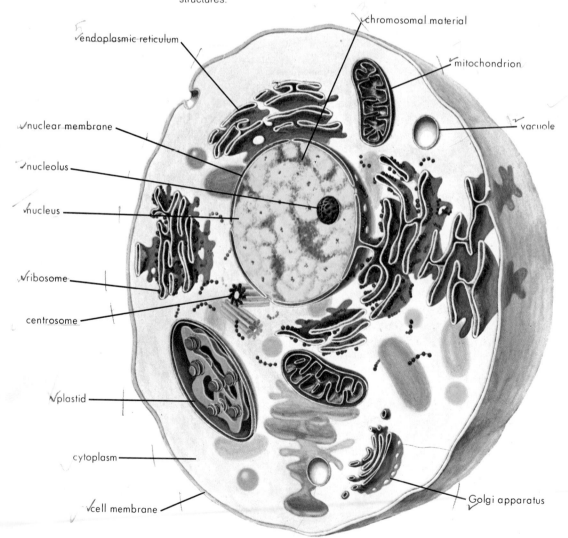

Under a light microscope the nuclei of living cells are often difficult to see. But they are readily visible when stained with certain dyes. Unfortunately, most stains kill cells. However, the phase-contrast microscope, not usually found in school laboratories, allows biologists to see nuclei in unstained living cells.

Within nuclei are one or more small bodies that usually stain more deeply than the nucleus itself. These are the *nucleoli.* They are believed to send instructions for protein synthesis from the nucleus to the cytoplasm. A small structure, the *centrosome,* is found just outside (or, in a few cases, just inside) the nucleus. This structure occurs in almost all animal cells and in most protist cells, but in rather few plant cells. It is involved in the reproduction of the cell.

nucleoli [new KLEE uh lye]: singular, nucleolus

centrosome [SEN truh som; Greek: *kentron,* center, + *soma,* body]

Surrounding the nucleus is the *nuclear membrane.* Chemical investigations show that the nuclear membrane is made up of protein and fatlike substances. It is the boundary between the nucleus and the cytoplasm. Everything going into or out of the nucleus must pass through this membrane. It acts as a filter, allowing some substances to pass through and not others.

The *cell membrane* is the boundary between a cell and its environment. Like the nuclear membrane, this one is composed of protein and fatlike substances. Another similarity is that the cell membrane regulates traffic of materials. Here, of course, the regulation is of materials coming into or going out of the cytoplasm, not the nucleus.

Electron microscopy reveals within a cell a membranous network called the *endoplasmic reticulum* (referred to as ER). This network branches throughout the cytoplasm and appears to connect the cell membrane with the nuclear membrane. Sometimes lining the ER are tiny structures called *ribosomes.*

endoplasmic reticulum [en duh-PLAZ mik rih TIK yuh lum; Greek: *endon,* within, + *plassein;* and Latin: *retum* a net]

ribosomes: [RYE buh somz]

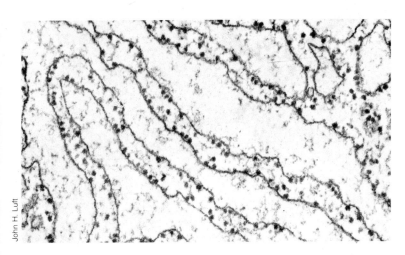

11—6 A portion of endoplasmic reticulum (membrane network) with ribosomes (small black spheres). × 160,000

John H. Luft

These structures are the sites of protein synthesis in the cell. There is evidence that the ER acts as a route for transporting proteins and other materials through the cell. It thus forms a communications network between nucleus and cytoplasm.

Within the cytoplasm are various small structures that are given the general name of **organelles.** **Plastids** are one type of organelle. They can be seen even without stains because they are colored by pigments. Plastids are found in plant and protist cells. Among the variety of plastids, ***chloroplasts*** are of major concern to us. They contain green pigments (chlorophylls) and are involved in photosynthesis.

Mitochondria are another type of organelle. Under a light microscope they appear as very tiny, rod-shaped bodies. Under an electron microscope each mitochondrion shows up as a sausage-shaped body containing parallel infolded layers of membranes. Mitochondria are the powerhouses of the cell. Many important chemical reactions take place inside them. These reactions remove energy from food and make it available for the cell's activities.

organelles [or guh NELZ]: "little organs"

chloroplasts [KLOR uh plastz; Greek: *chloros*, green, + *plassein*]

mitochondria [myt uh KON dree-uh; Greek: *mitos*, thread, + *chondros*, cartilage]: singular, mitochondrion

11—7 Mitochondrion in a cell from a bat.   × 14,700

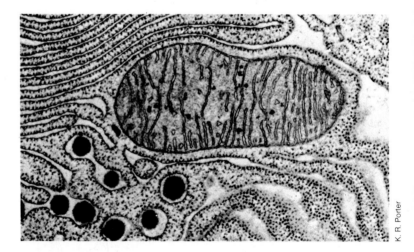

K. R. Porter

lysosomes [LYE suh somz]

Golgi apparatus [GOL jee ap uh-RAT us]

Vacuoles are of several types. For example, ***lysosomes*** are vacuoles that help in the digestion of materials inside a cell.

Until recently the function of the ***Golgi apparatus*** was not known. Within the last few years, however, scientists have been reporting the results of investigations to determine its function. Biologists now describe the Golgi apparatus as a primary site for the packaging of cell secretions. Some also believe that it is involved in the production of large, sugar-based molecules.

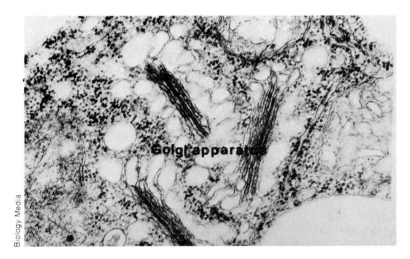

11 – 8 Electron micrograph of Golgi apparatus.   × 4,000

Both animal and plant cells contain *vacuoles.* These are membrane-enclosed, fluid-filled bags. Vacuōles are usually small and few in the cells of animals and protists. In plant cells, however, they are frequently large and numerous. In some protists special vacuoles pump out excess water from the cell. Vacuoles in other organisms are used to store food or pigments.

In addition to their cell membranes, the cells of plants and some protists are surrounded by nonliving cell walls. This is a major difference between plant and animal cells. In a living plant cell the membrane and wall are pressed so closely together that under a light microscope they are frequently difficult to distinguish. Dissolved materials usually pass freely through the cell wall, unlike the cell membrane.

vacuoles [VAK yuh wolz; Latin: *vacuus,* empty]

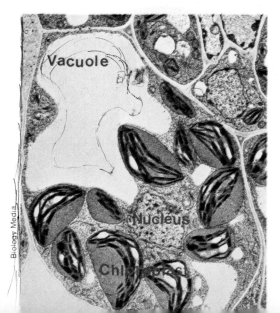

11 – 9 Electron micrograph of a plant cell. Note the cell wall.   × 800

CHECK YOURSELF

A. How has the meaning of the word "cell" changed since Hooke's time?
B. How did the development of staining techniques influence the study of cells?
C. What is the cell theory?
D. What is the function of a nucleus?
E. What is the function of the cell membrane?
F. Name two organelles of the cell and describe their functions.
G. What àre some differences between plant and animal cells?

SOME CELL PHYSIOLOGY

physiology [FIZ ee OL uh jee; Greek: *physis*, nature, + *logos*, speech, reason]

You might own a watch and still not understand how it works. You could never understand how a watch runs without studying its parts. You must investigate a machine's structure to learn how it operates. You have studied some parts of cells — the structure of cells. Now let's look into how a cell runs — how it functions. The study of biological function is called ***physiology.***

metabolism [muh TAB uh liz um; Greek: *metaballein*, to change]

METABOLISM

All activities of organisms require energy. Cells are the basic functional units of organisms. It follows that cells use energy. The organelles that take energy from the materials supplied to the cell, and make it available for cell activities, are the mitochondria. In very active cells, many mitochondria may be present. For example, the tail of a sperm cell, used in swimming to an encounter with an ovum (egg) in fertilization, is packed

11–10 Mitochondria in the tail of a mammalian sperm. × 5,000

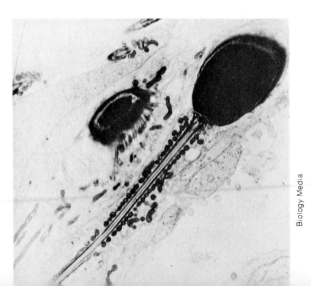

Biology Media

with mitochondria. The mitochondria release chemical energy from food obtained by the cell. Some of this energy is converted to the mechanical energy used in swimming. The sum of all chemical reactions within a cell is called *metabolism.*

To obtain energy for any activity, a cell uses energy-rich food molecules. They are broken down to smaller molecules that are no longer useful for metabolism. However, a cell, like most systems, has a continuing balance of useful and used materials, always in a state of exchange. As the cell carries on its activities, more energy-rich molecules must be brought into the cell, and the useless substances removed. Thus materials continually enter and leave a cell.

molecules [MOL ih kewlz; Latin: *moles*, a mass]

TRANSPORT

A cell, then, is an open system. Materials move into and out of it. Yet there is a definite boundary — the cell membrane — between a cell and its environment. The cell membrane acts as a barrier to keep the living substance inside the cell. But it must also allow certain substances to pass through it. There also are internal membranes — the nuclear membrane, for example — through which substances must pass. Once substances enter the cell, they must move from one part of the cell to another. All this adds up to a complex physiological problem: How do substances move into cells, out of cells, and within cells?

Diffusion. Biologists constantly use concepts developed by physicists and chemists. At this point we need to use the physicists' molecular theory of matter. According to this theory, all matter is made up of tiny particles — molecules and ions. And these are in continuous motion.

diffusion [dif YEW zhun; Latin: *dis*, apart, + *fundere*, to pour]

ions. See page 221.

Do you know any of the evidence on which the molecular theory is based?

If you place a colored, soluble solid called X in a test tube of water, you will see the color gradually spread (diffuse) throughout the water. According to the molecular theory, as substance X dissolves, its molecules begin to move in a random manner. This random movement gradually carries the molecules from a place where they are more abundant to a place where they are less abundant (from a greater concentration to a lesser concentration). This process is called *diffusion.* As the molecules of substance X are diffusing, molecules of the water also are diffusing.

Movement always involves energy. Where do you think the energy for diffusion comes from?

Originally the concentration of water molecules was high where the concentration of substance X was low. Where X was concentrated, the water was not. As the two substances diffuse, therefore, the molecules of water and substance X tend to pass each other as they move to areas of lower concentration. The color (X) and water molecules thus become evenly mixed throughout the test tube.

11–11 Diagram of stages in diffusion. In *D* the particles continue to move; but, because each moves randomly, they remain evenly distributed in the available space.

A   B   C   D

After the solution is completely uniform, collisions and rebounds continue. But, although the molecules move, there is no net change in their distribution.

Cell membranes. The contents of cells are solutions or suspensions of substances in water. And all active cells exist in a water environment. Cells of the human body are no exception. Every one of our living cells is coated with moisture. Therefore, a living cell is a mixture of things in water separated from another mixture of things in water. Cell membranes separate these two mixtures. Everything going into or out of the cell must pass through the cell membrane.

Cells of the outer skin are dead.

Diffusion through membranes. A paper bag will hold potatoes, but it will not hold water very long. A plastic bag holds water, but oxygen passes through the plastic fast enough to keep a goldfish alive in the water. The paper bag is **permeable** to water but not to potatoes. The plastic bag is permeable to oxygen but not to water. Any membrane that is permeable to some substances but not to others is said to be **differentially permeable.**

But not fast enough to keep you alive! You use oxygen more rapidly than a goldfish does.

permeable [PUR mee uh bul; Latin: per, through, + meare, to glide]

Water, carbon dioxide, and oxygen diffuse easily through cell membranes. Some ions of inorganic substances also diffuse easily. But many molecules are too large to diffuse through cell membranes.

The *direction* a substance diffuses is determined by concentration. If concentration of that substance is greater outside the cell than inside it, the direction of diffusion is into the cell. If concentration is greater inside, diffusion is outward.

Assume that the molecules of substance X are too large to diffuse through a cell membrane. Also assume that it is found in high concentration inside a cell but does not occur in the fluid outside that cell. The high and low concentrations of X are separated by the differentially permeable cell membrane. Water can move into or out of the cell, but substance X cannot. Water molecules begin to move through the cell membrane into the cell, because at first there is a lower concentration of water inside the cell than outside. The added water creates pressure on the membrane from the inside. Eventually there may be enough pressure to burst the membrane.

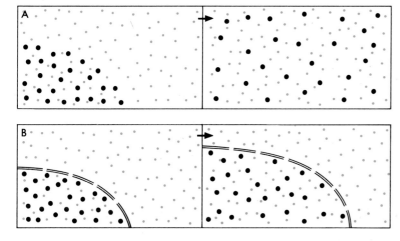

11–12 Diagram of diffusion (A) without a differentially permeable membrane, (B) with such a membrane.

A paramecium lives in a freshwater environment. It contains a high concentration of molecules that cannot diffuse through its cell membrane. Water diffuses into the paramecium because the concentration of the water is higher outside the organism than inside. But the paramecium does not burst from the added water. This is because the excess water accumulates in a vacuole and is periodically "pumped" outside. This, of course, is work – it costs energy.

Review your data from Investigation 9.2. Can you give a fuller explanation of your results?

Active transport. Movements of many substances through cell membranes cannot be explained by diffusion. For example, in most cells the concentration of potassium ions is much greater inside than outside. These ions readily pass through cell membranes by diffusion. Why do they not also leave cells by diffusion?

Actually, there *is* a constant diffusion of potassium ions from cells. Careful study has shown, however, that cells take in potassium ions as fast as some are lost by diffusion. This action is carried out by "ion pumps." The term "ion pumps" refers to the activity that moves ions from a region of *low* concentration *to* one of *high* concentration. This action requires the expenditure of energy – work. Movement of substances from lower to higher concentrations – opposite to the direction of diffusion – is called *active transport.* It occurs through cell membranes and through the membranes of mitochondria and nuclei.

Cyclosis. Diffusion accounts for much of the distribution of substances within cells. In many cells, however, substances also are distributed by motion of the cytoplasm. In plants and protists it is possible to observe with a microscope this "streaming," called *cyclosis.* The exact way in which cyclosis occurs is not known. It is clear, however, that it requires the use of energy, just as active transport does.

cyclosis [sy KLOH sus]

CHECK YOURSELF

H. What is physiology?

I. What is the metabolism of a cell?

J. Why must a cell constantly take in and get rid of substances?

K. How does the molecular theory explain diffusion?

L. Cell membranes are differentially permeable. What does this mean?

M. If water molecules are less concentrated outside a cell membrane than they are inside the membrane, what will be the direction of water diffusion?

N. Why must a paramecium constantly "pump" water out into its environment?

O. What observations by cell physiologists have led to the theory of active transport?

P. Which of the processes by which substances move within cells require the use of energy?

Investigation 11.2   DIFFUSION THROUGH A MEMBRANE

INTRODUCTION

How do things get in and out of cells? In this investigation you will use a model of a cell membrane (cellulose tubing) to observe the movement of water.

PROCEDURE

1. To open the cellulose tubing, first moisten it. Then rub it between your thumb and forefinger. Tie a tight knot about 1 cm from one end of each piece of tubing.

2. Into one tube pour soluble-starch solution to within 5 cm of the top. Pinch the top of the tube together tightly. Rinse the tube under running water to remove any starch from the outside. Fasten the top of the tube tightly with a rubber band not more than 2 cm above the top of the liquid.

3. Place the tube in a beaker of water. Mark the beaker A. Add enough iodine solution to give the water a distinct yellowish color.

MATERIALS
(per team)

15 ml soluble-starch solution
15 ml glucose solution
iodine solution
Tes-tape or piece of Clinitest tablet in test tube
2 lengths of cellulose tubing, 20 cm each
2 beakers, 1,000-ml, with water
glass-marking crayon
2 rubber bands

4. Into the second tube pour glucose solution to within 5 cm of the top.

5. Repeat the procedure given in step 2. Place the tube in a beaker of water. Mark this beaker B.

6. Allow the tubes to stand for about 20 minutes. Dip a piece of Tes-tape into the water in Beaker B (or pour a small quantity of the water into a test tube containing a frag-

11 – 13

iodine solution

cellulose tubing
containing
starch solution

water in beaker

ment of a Clinitest tablet).

7. Record the color of the tape. Observe the tube in Beaker A. Record any changes, including color, that you see in either the tube or the water in the beaker.

8. Let Beakers A and B stand overnight. The next day record any changes observed.

DISCUSSION

(1) On the basis of the chemical test for starch, what must have happened to the iodine molecules in Beaker A? (2) On the basis of the chemical test for glucose, what must have happened to the glucose molecules in Beaker B? (3) From the evidence obtained by allowing the beakers to stand overnight, what other substances must pass through the membrane in Beaker B? (4) Which substance did not pass through a membrane? How do you know that it did not?

Physicists can show that the molecules of any one substance are all about the same size but that the molecules of different substances are different in size. Measurements show that iodine molecules and water molecules are very small, glucose molecules are considerably larger, and starch molecules are very large. (5) On this basis suggest a hypothesis to account for the observations that were made in this investigation. (6) What assumption did you make about the structure of the membrane?

CELL DUPLICATION

The third major idea in the cell theory is that all new cells are produced from cells that already exist. Why and when does one cell become two? Among cells of different kinds there is an enormous variation in size. For example, the volume of the yolk of an ostrich egg (a single cell) is millions of times greater than that of a protist cell. But there is a maximum size a *given kind* of cell can maintain. If a cell is to continue to grow, perhaps it must divide into two since it cannot get any larger.

Whatever the cause, cells do divide. Usually the nucleus and the rest of the cell divide almost simultaneously. Sometimes, however, only the nucleus divides. Such division, if repeated, will give rise to a structure like the hypha of *Rhizopus* (figure 11 – 14). Or the nucleus may divide, with division of the rest of the cell occurring at some later time. This occurs in spore formation by sac fungi.

simultaneously [sy mul TAY nee-uh slee; Latin: *simul*, together with]: refers to two things happening at the same time

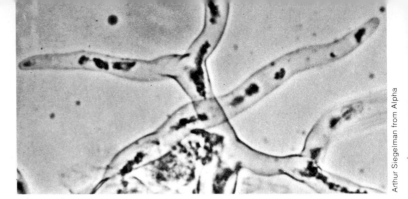

11 – 14 A fungus, *Rhizopus*, containing several nuclei not separated from each other by cell membranes. Is the structure of *Rhizopus* an exception to the cell theory? × 200

mitosis [my TOH sus; Greek: *mitos,* a thread]

duplication [dew plih KAY shun; Latin: *duo,* two, + *plicare,* to fold]

disintegrate [DIS INT uh grayt; Latin: *dis,* apart, + *integer,* whole]

MITOSIS

Division of the nuclear substances is an important part of cell duplication Mature human red blood cells, which have no nuclei, never divide. Instead, they survive a short time (about 110 days) and then disintegrate. On the other hand, cells of blue-green algae divide even though they have no definitely organized nuclei. In most cells, however, there is a definite nucleus. In these, nuclear division, called *mitosis,* occurs before the cells divide.

CELL DIVISION IN ANIMALS

11 – 15 Diagram of mitosis. These six views abbreviate a continuous process. There are no stops and starts between different "stages."

In mitosis of an animal cell, the first observable event is the division of the centrosome. It separates into two parts, which begin to move around the nucleus. (Refer to figure 11 – 15 as you

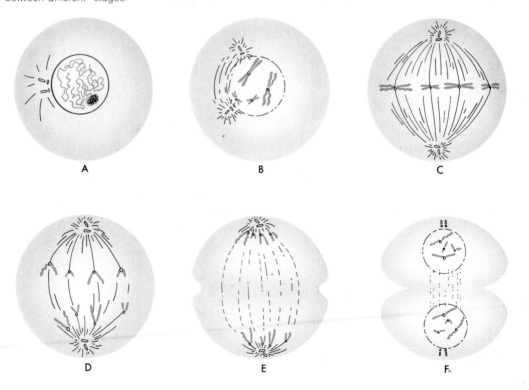

A   B   C

D   E   F.

read on.) Fibers develop around them, radiating from each half centrosome like the spokes of a wheel. As the two centrosome parts continue to move away from each other, the fibers between them lengthen. They form a structure called the **spindle.** While these events are taking place, the nucleolus and nuclear membrane disappear.

In the stained nucleus an observer can now see a set of threadlike parts called **chromosomes.** Close examination shows that each chromosome has two strands. Each strand of a chromosome is called a **chromatid.** The chromatids are attached to each other at a single point, the **centromere.** Gradually the chromosomes become shorter, thicker, and more distinct. Under high magnification it becomes clear that this is due to coiling, just as a long, thin wire can be coiled into a short, thick spring.

chromosomes [KROH muh somz; Greek: *chroma*, color, + *soma*, body]

centromere [SEN truh mir; Greek: *kentron*, center, + *meros*, a part]

When the centrosome halves are on opposite sides of the nucleus, the spindle is complete. The chromosomes are now fully coiled. The positions of the centrosome halves are called the poles of the spindle. The spindle fibers are attached at these poles. We can imagine a plane in the middle of the spindle perpendicular to the fibers. This is the **equatorial plate.** In photographs, cells appear two-dimensional because of high magnification. Therefore, the equatorial plate seems to be a line rather than a plane.

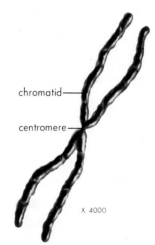

chromatid

centromere

X 4000

11–16 A chromosome before separation of chromatids.

The chromosomes move toward the equatorial plate. Their centromeres become attached to spindle fibers. The centromere of each chromosome now divides, so the paired chromatids separate from one another. Once separated, each chromatid of a pair is called a chromosome. These two new chromosomes move away from the equatorial plate and toward different poles of the spindle. Each centromere leads the way as though pulled by a shortening of the spindle fibers. The rest of the new chromosome trails along. *All* the chromatid pairs in the original single cell divide in the same way. This means that each new cell will have the same number of chromosomes as its parent cell.

Now the fibers of the spindle begin to fade and the chromosomes start to uncoil. At each pole a new nuclear membrane forms around the group of chromosomes, leaving the centrosome outside. A nucleolus develops within each new nuclear membrane. At some time before the next nuclear division occurs, all the chromosomes become double (with two chromatids) again. (Even with modern equipment and techniques, this doubling process still has not been seen.) The formation of new nuclei ends mitosis.

Usually division of the rest of the cell begins as new chromosomes approach the poles. A furrow forms in the equatorial

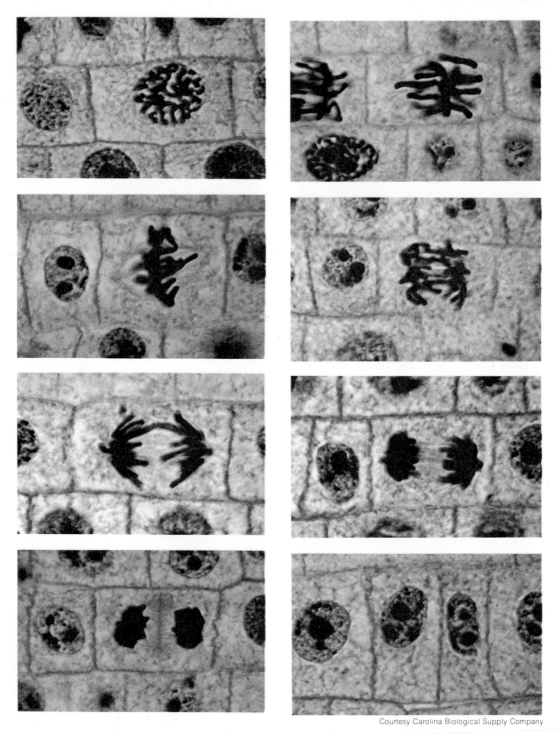

Courtesy Carolina Biological Supply Company

11–17 Dividing cells in onion root tip. The sequence proceeds left to right, top to bottom. How is plant mitosis similar to animal mitosis (figure 11–15)? How are they different?   × 600

plate and deepens until the original cell is cut in two. The mitochondria are distributed more or less equally between the two new cells, because they cluster near the equatorial plate. Unlike the division of the nucleus, however, that of the rest of the cell is not always equal.

SIGNIFICANCE OF MITOSIS

The sequence of events in mitosis appears to be a device that ensures exact, equal division of the nuclear substance. This suggests that the nuclear substance is very important. Research during the past century has supported this idea. Much evidence shows that complex nuclear substances regulate the activities of a cell. The structure and function of a cell are expressions of these activities. Maintaining characteristics from one cell generation to the next depends on the duplication of the chromosomes in the parent cell. Full, identical sets must be transmitted to the offspring cells. Each chromosome of a set is duplicated. The original chromosome and its copy become paired chromatids. Mitosis results in one chromatid of each pair ending up in each new nucleus.

CHECK YOURSELF

Q. How is the spindle formed during animal mitosis?
R. How is the term "chromatid" related to the term "chromosome"?
S. What happens to the new chromosomes at the end of mitosis?
T. In your own words describe the whole process of mitosis.
U. How does the rest of an animal cell usually divide after mitosis of the nucleus?
V. What seems to be the biological importance of mitosis?

Investigation 11.3   MITOSIS AND CELL DIVISION IN PLANTS

INTRODUCTION

If an onion is placed in water and kept in the dark for several days, slender white roots sprout from it and grow into the water. This growth occurs partly by repeated duplication of cells. You might expect, therefore, to see cells in mitosis at the end of a root. And, indeed, you can—with proper procedures—under a microscope. One such procedure can be accomplished within an hour.

PROCEDURE

1. Pour hydrochloric acid-alcohol solution into a Syracuse watch glass to a depth of about 3 mm. (*Caution: Be very careful in working with this solution. Wash immediately in running water if you come in contact with it.*)

2. Using forceps, pick up a root that has been fixed in 70% alcohol. Grasp it by the cut end, not by the pointed end. (*Note: In all later operations handle the root by the cut end only.*)

3. Transfer the root to the watch glass. Allow it to remain in the solution for 5 minutes. This treatment breaks down the material that holds the cells together.

4. Shortly before the 5 minutes are up, pour Carnoy's fluid into a second watch glass to a depth of 3 mm.

5. Using forceps, transfer the root to this second watch glass and allow it to remain there for 3 minutes. This treatment hardens the material that was softened by the acid treatment and reduces the chance of damage to the cells.

6. Using forceps, transfer the root to the center of a clean slide. With a scalpel or razor blade, cut off the tip—the last 2 mm or less of the root. Discard the rest.

7. Immediately add 1 or 2 drops of aceto-orcein solution. Cut the tip into small pieces and allow these to remain in the solution for 5 minutes. This solution stains certain cell structures, including nuclei and chromosomes. Do not let the preparation dry up. If it appears to be doing so, add another drop of solution.

8. Place a clean cover slip over the pieces of root tip. Tap lightly on the cover slip with the eraser of a pencil held vertically. This will separate the cells and spread them out under the cover slip.

9. Fold a cleansing tissue several times so it is the same shape as the slide but slightly larger. Then make a final fold in the tissue, bringing its ends together. Place the

MATERIALS
(per student)

onion roots in 70% alcohol
Carnoy's fluid (with chloroform)
aceto-orcein solution
hydrochloric acid-alcohol solution
prepared slide, long sections
  of onion-root tip
monocular microscope
2 Syracuse watch glasses
fine-pointed forceps
scalpel or razor blade
microscope slide
cover slip
medicine dropper
cleansing tissue

tissue on the table. Insert the part of the slide where the cover slip is located into the final fold. This forms a "sandwich," with several layers of tissue under the slide and several on top of the cover slip.

10. With the "sandwich" resting flat on the table, press down vertically with your thumb on the upper layer of cleansing tissue. This will further spread the cells and flatten them. Be careful to apply pressure without twisting, so that the cover slip is not moved or broken.

11. Carefully remove the slide from the cleansing tissue. You have now made a "squash" preparation.

12. Examine the slide under low power of the microscope. Move the slide so that you can scan the entire area under the cover slip. Look for cells containing nuclei that appear to be made up of distinct threadlike parts. Such cells were undergoing mitosis at the time they were fixed.

13. Locate an area where several cells are in various stages of mitosis. Switch to high power and examine this area carefully. If necessary, adjust the diaphragm of your microscope to increase the clarity of the image.

14. Sketch at least 5 entire cells, each in a different stage of mitosis. Number your drawings in the order in which you think the stages occur during mitosis.

11 – 18 Making a "squash" preparation.

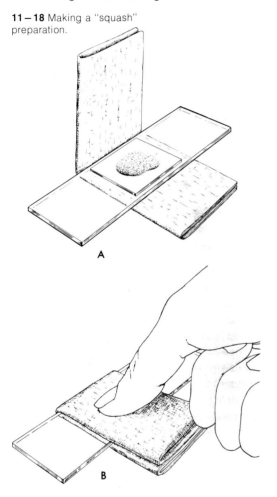

A

B

15. Examine the prepared slide of onion-root-tip sections. Study each section first under low power and then under high power. (1) In what region of the root tip are most of the cells that are undergoing mitosis? (2) How does the shape of cells undergoing mitosis compare with that of cells in other parts of the sections?

16. Study a number of cells in different stages of mitosis, plus several which do not appear to be dividing. (3) Are any structures visible in these cells on the prepared slide that you could not see in the "squash" preparation? If so, draw one or more cells showing them.

17. Refer to the illustrations of dividing animal and plant cells on pages 372 and 374. (4) What differences, if any, can you find in the ways mitosis and cell division occur in animal and plant cells?

FOR FURTHER INVESTIGATION

1. If you were trying to determine the number of chromosomes in cells of a root, would it be better to use "squash" preparations or sections of the root?

2. Suppose you suspected that frequency of mitosis in onion roots varied with the time of day. How would you go about getting data to confirm or refute your suspicion?

3. Do all the events in mitosis take about the same time, or do some of them occur faster than others? Design an experiment to answer this question.

DIFFERENTIATION

After cell division either the offspring cells separate or they remain together. In the first case there are two unicellular individuals where there was one before. Here cell duplication is the same as the reproduction of an individual. If the offspring cells remain together, however, repeated divisions result in a group of connected cells. Multicellular organisms grow in this way. Cells of such organisms may remain approximately alike. For instance, some algae are masses of indefinite size made up of

differentiation [dif uh ren chee-AY shun]

unicellular [yew nih SEL yuh lur; Latin: *unus*, one, + *cella*, cell]

multicellular [mul tih SEL yuh lur; Latin: *multus*, many, + *cella*]

similar cells. On the other hand, the cells of a multicellular organism may become different from each other. In this case different groups of cells are formed in the same individual; each group is made of similar cells. For example, trees have groups of leaf cells, bark cells, and root cells.

A PUZZLE

paradox [PAIR uh doks; Greek: *para*, beyond, + *doxa*, opinion]: an apparently contradictory statement

Buried in the last paragraph is a paradox. We reasoned on page 375 that the process of mitosis ensures that both offspring cells will have *identical characteristics.* Then how can any of the cells in a single organism be different from any other? Every multicellular organism — an oak tree, a cow, a human — develops from a single cell. Yet these adults contain cells of a great many different kinds. This process of developmental change from an immature to a mature form is called *differentiation.*

ingenious: clever, inventive

In the past 70 years many ingenious experiments have provided biologists with information about this puzzle of differentiation. It is now clear that differentiation involves three primary factors. First, it involves selective use of information stored in the chromosomes. Second, it involves ways in which neighboring cells affect each other in the developing organism. Third, factors in the environment are involved. Yet the fundamental question remains unanswered, "How does differentiation occur?"

RESULTS OF DIFFERENTIATION

Differentiation is an orderly process. Cells do not become endlessly different. They usually become different in limited and predictable ways at predictable times. Further, they become different in groups rather than individually. Microscopic examination of a multicellular organism reveals the same basic structural characteristics in all cells of a particular group. In another group in the same organism, all cells may be similar to each other, but different from those in the first group. A group in which all cells have similar structure and function is called a *tissue.*

Some of the money that is available for cancer research goes into studies of cell differentiation. Why?

A tissue might be considered a population of similar cells, just as a species is a population of similar individuals. In both cases one population is surrounded by other populations. In both cases a population has many close and necessary relations with adjacent populations. We can remove a portion of a population of individual organisms — a mouse colony, for example — from its ecosystem. We can keep it in a laboratory. We can also remove a population of similar cells — muscle tissue, perhaps — and cultivate it in a test tube. In such laboratory situations, valuable things can be learned about tissues and about the

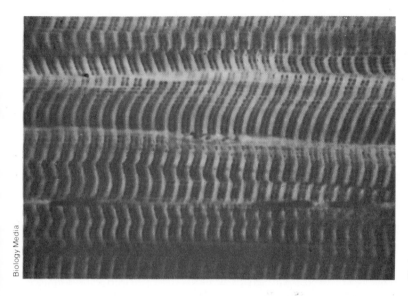

11–19 Muscle tissue.
× 1,000

whole organism. But under natural conditions, neither a mouse colony nor a muscle tissue lives alone.

Some multicellular organisms, such as sponges and some algae, seem to have no organization other than that of tissues. But most organisms have tissues grouped into body parts that function for the whole individual. Such a body part—a leaf or a heart, for example—is called an *organ.* Organs, like tissues, can sometimes be removed from the organism and maintained artificially, but this is not done as often as with tissues.

What things would you have to do in order to maintain a tissue culture?

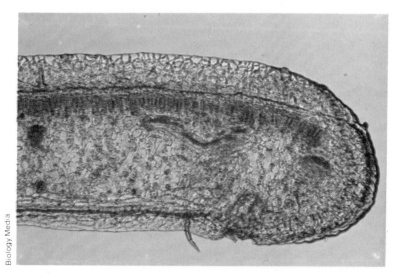

11–20 Cross section of a leaf. What does the green color signify?   × 32

AGING

No individual cell lives forever, but a unicellular organism does not grow old. It can be killed by unfavorable environmental effects (lack of food, buildup of poisonous wastes, or being eaten by other organisms). If it is not killed, a cell simply disappears as a single individual when it divides into two new ones.

In multicellular organisms the situation is more complex. Some cells do not continue to divide, nor are they killed. Instead, they seem to slowly lose their vigor and die. We would say they become old. Why do some cells of multicellular organisms age and die? Do aging and death of such cells result from harmful environmental effects? Or do they result from internal changes that are caused by differentiation?

Perhaps the outer skin cells of vertebrates and those lining the intestine die because of unfavorable environmental conditions. On the other hand, an internal condition—lack of nuclei—may be the cause of the early death of red blood cells of mammals. But the red blood cells of birds, which do contain nuclei, also have a short life span.

There is evidence that physiological changes occur early in the differentiation of some kinds of cells. Some of these changes may be harmful to the metabolic processes. Many biologists now believe the accumulation of such harmful changes may "slow down" a cell. Aging results.

11–21 A process of aging. A snake shedding its skin.

Walker Van Riper, University of Colorado

Some cells grown in tissue culture survive and multiply indefinitely. Cancer cells have this ability. Cultures started many years ago are still being maintained, although the biologists who started the cultures have aged and died. Other cells from differentiated tissues produce a considerable number of cell divisions in tissue culture, then stop. The cultures die. This suggests that the tissues age, like cells in the body. Biologists are continuing to work with such tissues in efforts to find the causes of aging.

Undifferentiated cells show interesting behaviors in tissue culture. Fertilized egg cells start producing new individuals. So do undifferentiated cells from the growth tissue at the tips of plant stems. In the latter case, the new plants have chromosomes identical to the plant from which the stem-tip tissue was taken. They are *clones,* identical in their inherited characteristics to the parent. Clones are common among plants in nature. Strawberries and many grasses that send out runners produce clones as the new plants.

clones [klohnz; Greek: *klōn,* twig]

Can you think of other examples of plant clones in nature?

Cloned animals are much rarer. Only a few lower animals produce clones by putting out buds. Unfertilized eggs that occasionally develop into new animals have only half the number of chromosomes of the parent. You will see why in Chapter 16. These animals are not clones. They are abnormal in every cell nucleus.

Unlike plants, animals do not have stem tips with undifferentiated tissue. So tissue culture clones cannot be produced in the same way. However, frog eggs have had their nuclei removed and replaced by nuclei from muscle cells of the same frog. Most of the eggs died. A few produced clones of the parent frog. They proved that differentiation can be reversed. The muscle cell nuclei gave rise to *all* the kinds of cells in the cloned frogs.

CHECK YOURSELF

W. How does cell differentiation seem to contradict the apparent meaning of mitosis?

X. How are cells related to tissues?

Y. How are tissues related to organs?

Z. How do unicellular and multicellular organisms differ with respect to aging?

AA. What ideas do biologists have about the aging of cells?

BB. . Why is the study of aging important?

CC. How can clones be important in cell research?

Careers in Biology:
A Biological Artist

Jane Larson is a biological artist. She works for a company that develops biology textbooks and other educational materials. Several artists work with Jane to prepare scientific illustrations for books, slide programs, and films on biological subjects. Specialists in many fields of biology help to write the books and prepare the films. Jane enjoys meeting and working with them. As director of an art staff, she must make sure that the drawings and photographs correctly and artistically reflect the ideas of the writers.

Jane's higher education began with nurse's training and art school. Then she attended college and majored in biology. She also studied anthropology and geology. While in college, she worked at the Florida State Museum, where she collected and prepared fossils and did some illustrating. Jane also worked as a scientific illustrator for experts in various biological fields. All this experience now helps her—both as an illustrator and as a supervisor—in a job that demands accuracy in every detail.

Before Jane took her present job, she was a free-lance artist. She loves the Rocky Mountains and spent several years in a small mountain town. Most of her paintings are scenes from contemporary western ranch life, such as branding cattle and moving a herd from summer to winter pasture. She also taught art classes in the junior high and high schools.

Jane has a strong interest in fossils. She collected and preserved fossils of a

B. The shaded areas that emphasize certain lines on a chart are made from overlays, such as the one Jane is preparing.

A. Jane consults with staff members to decide on arrangement and color for a piece of art comparing wing structures of a bird and a butterfly.

giant bison of the Pleistocene. The horns and skull of this huge animal were found in a fossil bed in Florida. Jane also has found fossils of saber-toothed cats in Florida and Colorado.

Many artists like Jane are busy illustrating reports and journal articles prepared by instructors and researchers in universities across the country. Many also work in natural-history museums. They paint and construct the background and scenery for many kinds of displays. These artists may recreate the Alaskan tundra to show off a group of polar bears or a South American hillside for a display of llamas.

Artistic skills are basic to becoming a biological artist. But Jane feels that such a person also must have a knowledge of the biological sciences in order to draw "what is really there, in nature."

Bob Wilson

John Thornton

D. Jane's department must cut and fit the galleys of type onto page layouts. These, together with illustrations, make up the finished pages from which the book is printed.

E. The drawings that appear in a textbook must be accurate. Jane confers with one of the authors to make sure the drawings match the manuscript he has written.

C. The quality of slides from which illustrations will be made is crucial. Here, Jane and a staff member check closely to see that photos are in focus and not scratched.

John Thornton

383

PROBLEMS

1. During the late 19th century most knowledge of detailed cell structure was gained by studying stained dead cells. Some biologists objected to many conclusions drawn from such observation. They argued that the processes of killing, staining, and mounting cells on slides might cause cell structure to appear very different from that in living cells. What kinds of evidence are available today to meet at least some of these objections?

2. Examine various kinds of cells from multicellular organisms, either under the microscope or by means of photomicrographs in books. Discuss the relationships between the structural forms of the different cells and their functions.

3. Working in a police laboratory, you are given a tiny sample of material and asked to identify it as either plant or animal matter. How could you decide which it is?

4. On the basis of your understanding of the diffusion of water, describe what would happen to (a) a marine jellyfish placed in a freshwater stream and (b) a frog placed in ocean water. Some fish (for example, shad and striped bass) annually swim from the ocean into freshwater rivers and back. How are they able to do this?

5. In this chapter mitosis in cells that have single, well-defined nuclei was described. Investigate what is known about what happens to nuclear material (chromatin) during division in (a) a cell that lacks a nucleus (a blue-green alga, for example), and (b) a "cell" with more than one nucleus (*Paramecium*, for example).

6. In unicellular organisms, cells usually separate shortly after division. In some, however, they remain attached, forming colonies. In multicellular organisms they remain attached, but more strongly in some cases than in others. Investigate the ways in which the cells are held together.

SUGGESTED READINGS

Albrecht-Buehler, G. 1978. The Tracks of Moving Cells. *Scientific American*, April. When a moving cell divides, the paths followed by its offspring cells can be mirror images.

Giese, A. C. 1979. *Cell Physiology*. 5th ed. W. B. Saunders, Philadelphia. Covers fundamental cell activities.

Hayflick, L. 1980. The Cell Biology of Human Aging. *Scientific American*, January. Cell cultures reveal the processes that limit the human life span.

Lazarides, E. and J. P. Revel. 1979. The Molecular Basis of Cell Movement. *Scientific American*, May. Various cells incorporate fibers that enable them to move.

Lodish, H. F. and J. E. Rothman. 1979. The Assembly of Cell Membranes. *Scientific American*, January. During cell growth, the differences in cell membranes are preserved.

Maclean, N. 1977. *The Differentiation of Cells*. University Park Press, Baltimore. Explores the mechanism by which cells in a multicellular organism become specialized to perform particular functions in a variety of tissues.

Patterson, P. H., D. D. Potter, and E. J. Furshpan. 1978. The Chemical Differentiation of Nerve Cells. *Scientific American*, July. Covers the development of nerve cells in embryos.

Staehelin, L. A. and B. E. Hull. 1978. Junctions between Living Cells. *Scientific American*, May. The cells of many tissues are linked by specialized structures.

Stephenson, W. K. 1979. *Concepts in Cell Biology*. John Wiley & Sons, New York. A self-instruction text providing an introduction to cell biology.

Chapter **12**

Energy and Life

YOUR GUIDEPOSTS

In this chapter you will have an opportunity to explore these questions in biology:

- What is energy and where does it come from?
- What role does energy play in our lives?
- How is the sun's energy changed to chemical energy in photosynthesis?
- How are the major organic compounds formed?
- How is energy released from food?

Investigation 12.1   **PHOTOSYNTHETIC RATE**

INTRODUCTION

There are several ways that the rate of photosynthesis can be measured. This investigation calls for the use of several sprigs of elodea, a common aquatic plant. You may want to collect and use some other aquatic plant found in your area. If you live near the coast, you may even want to try to measure the photosynthetic rate of seaweed in seawater. After all, most of the photosynthesis on Earth takes place in the ocean.

MATERIALS
(per team)

several sprigs of elodea (or
 other aquatic plant)
erlenmeyer flask, 250-ml
0.5% sodium bicarbonate
   solution, enough to almost
   fill the erlenmeyer flask
ice cubes

battery jar, cutoff glass jug, or
   small aquarium
thermometer
lamp with reflector and 150-watt bulb
watch or clock with second hand
tape
meterstick

For manometer:
ring stand with clamp
glass, U-shaped tube with
   arms 20–25 cm long, inside
   diameter 2–3 mm
colored water with detergent
   to a height of 3–4 cm in each arm
piece of cardboard, 25 × 10
   cm, with a sheet of
   mm-ruled graph paper stapled to it

For stopper:
2-hole stopper to fit flask
2 6-cm pieces glass tubing
2 pieces rubber tubing, 5 cm
   and 15 cm long
1 pinch clamp

PROCEDURE

1. Set up the equipment as shown in figure 12–1.
2. Place the sprigs of elodea in the flask. Fill the flask with the sodium bicarbonate solution to about 3 cm from the top. With the pinch clamp removed, insert the stopper as tightly as possible. Attach the long rubber tubing to the manometer. Place the flask in the battery jar. Place the thermometer in the battery jar and tape it to the rim of the jar.
3. Place the lamp 40 cm from the elodea. Allow the apparatus to stand for 5 to 10 minutes with the lamp on. This will allow the setup to reach equilibrium. Then place the clamp on the short rubber tube.
4. Observe and record the reading of the manometer on the open side of the tube.

Check the temperature occasionally. Add ice as necessary to keep the water bath at room temperature ±2°C.

5. Take manometer readings at 1-minute intervals until the *rate* of increase has stabilized — until 3 consecutive readings are the same. (The liquid will still be moving, but at a constant rate.) Mark this down as the *rate of change per minute*. (1) What is happening in the flask? (2) What kind of material do you think is being produced in the flask to cause the fluid in the manometer to move?
6. Remove the clamp. The colored water in the manometer should return to the same level on each side.
7. Decrease the distance of the lamp from the sprigs to 20 cm. Wait 5 minutes. Replace the clamp. Observe, measure, and record

12–1

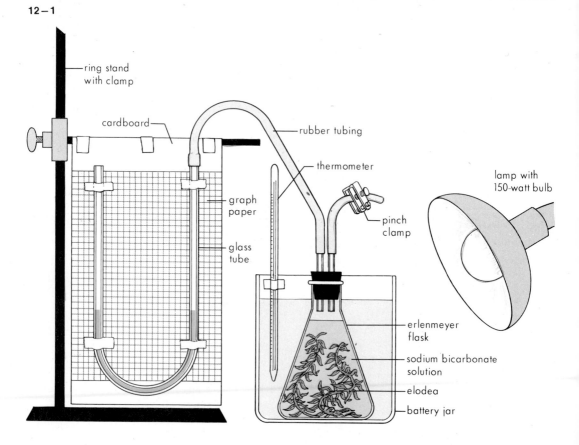

ring stand with clamp

cardboard

rubber tubing

graph paper

thermometer

glass tube

pinch clamp

lamp with 150-watt bulb

erlenmeyer flask

sodium bicarbonate solution

elodea

battery jar

the data as before. Note the rate of change.

8. Decrease the lamp distance to 10 cm. Remove the clamp. Wait 5 minutes; then replace the clamp. Observe, measure, and record the data as before. Note the rate of change.

DISCUSSION

(3) What is the variable in this experiment? Place your data on the chalkboard with the data of other teams. To obtain the class average, add the rates of change at 40 cm for all teams. Then divide the total by the number of teams. Repeat for data obtained at 20 and 10 cm.

Graph the data. Place the distance between lamp and sprigs on the horizontal axis and the average rate of change per minute on the vertical axis. (4) What is the general direction of the slope of the line? (5) What is the relationship between light intensity and photosynthetic rate as indicated by your data?

(6) What other environmental factors may affect photosynthetic rate? (7) In the design of this experiment, which of these factors are controlled? How?

FOR FURTHER INVESTIGATION

Plan and carry out an experiment in which light intensity is held constant and another factor affecting photosynthetic rate is varied.

ENERGY

With a suitable temperature, a source of moisture, and the necessary energy sources, life as we know it might exist anywhere. *Exobiology* is the study of life, if it exists, elsewhere than on Earth. In 1976, two *Viking* space probes landed on Mars and carried out experiments to test for life. The answer was no, but held some uncertainties. In 1979, a *Voyager* space probe photographed Jupiter and its moons. One moon, Europa, is covered with moisture—ice. Another, Io, is far from cold (figure 12–2). Would either support life?

exobiology [EKS oh by OL uhjee; Greek: *exo*, out of, or outside of, + biology]

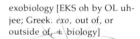

NASA

12–2 *Voyager I* photograph of a volcanic eruption on one of Jupiter's moons, Io. The blue color above the plume was recorded on ultraviolet sensitive film. It would not be visible to the human eye. Earth's history is also rich with volcanic activity.

High Altitude Observatory, National Center for
Atmospheric Research, National Science Foundation

12−3 A total eclipse of the sun. For one brief moment, the moon shades our source of energy — the sun.

ENERGY USED TO MAKE ORDER

You may wish to review pages 17–21.

Living things are extremely complex. Their molecules are arranged into highly organized systems. This is a very unstable situation. All systems tend to move toward a simple, random condition. Think about your room. When it is clean and neat, it is a very organized system. But how long does it stay that way? The tendency is for your room to become disorganized. You must continually use energy to keep it organized.

Like your neat room, a living organism is an organized system. A living frog, for instance, is highly organized. The frog maintains that condition because it eats flies and other organisms with energy in them. The energy from the frog's food keeps the frog together and allows it to grow and reproduce. If the frog dies, however, it becomes disorganized as soil microorganisms use the energy and matter stored in its body cells.

What is the source of energy and raw materials required to keep you in a steady state?

Life processes work toward an organized condition and against randomness. This requires energy, just as it takes energy for you to keep your room clean and neat. No matter how large an organism is, it depends on energy from reactions that take place in its cells. A cell is also a highly organized system. As you might expect, energy is needed to maintain the order of this small system. Cells need and use energy. But what is energy?

ENERGY—THE ABILITY TO DO WORK

All things on the earth can be placed in two groups, matter and energy. Matter is easy to define because we can see it, touch it, and weigh it. Energy is more difficult to understand. It is defined as the ability to do work. Work is *moving* an arm, *riding* a bicycle, *heating* a house, or *building* a skyscraper. Perhaps we also can call *growing* a leaf or a wing "work," since energy is needed in these processes. And, when we consider the cell, there is work involved in *moving* substances within the cell and *building* organic molecules. Energy is needed for these tasks.

Energy comes in many different forms. Light and heat are forms of energy. Other forms are mechanical and chemical energy. Living cells use chemical energy. They do work by using the energy stored in the **chemical bonds** of molecules of food.

Can you name any other forms of energy?

Molecules are formed when atoms are linked together. These links between atoms are the chemical bonds of a molecule. It takes energy for atoms to react. As they form bonds, they may either release or store more energy. Water molecules have had energy *released* from their hydrogen. Food molecules have had energy *stored*. As food molecules are broken down by cells, the energy stored in the chemical bonds is released. The energy can then be used by the cells for their work.

Energy also can be changed from one form to another. Green plants change light energy that they receive from the sun into the chemical energy that they store in their tissues. This chemical energy is then used by organisms.

12–4 Using energy to find more energy. Underground drilling for uranium in Canada.

CHECK YOURSELF

A. What is required to maintain an organized system?
B. What is energy?
C. What kind of energy do living cells use? Where do they get it?

PHOTOSYNTHESIS

Life on Earth continues only because our sun is constantly releasing radiant energy. Some of this energy travels 93 million miles to Earth. Of the radiation intercepted by our planet, 57 percent is absorbed or reflected by clouds or dust in Earth's outer atmosphere. And most of the 43 percent that reaches Earth's surface is lost again into the atmosphere. Only about 1 percent is actually involved in photosynthesis, the process by which green plants and a few other organisms convert sunlight into usable energy.

Almost all living plants and animals depend on photosynthesis for energy and oxygen. Long ago Earth's atmosphere had

12–5 Green leaves receiving sunlight.

Dennis Brokaw

little free oxygen, O_2. With the first photosynthetic organism came the production of free oxygen. Some of this oxygen rose into the atmosphere. With energy from the sun, it recombined to form ozone, O_3. This ozone layer forms a vital shield for living things against harmful radiations from our sun.

ozone [OH zone]

In photosynthesis radiant energy is converted to chemical energy, which is stored in the bonds of organic compounds. In plants some of this stored energy is used in metabolic activities that keep the plant alive. The rest is used for growth and to make tissues of the plant. When eaten by animals, plant tissues support animal metabolism and growth. Photosynthesis also produces free oxygen as a by-product. In fact, it is the primary source of oxygen on the earth.

How does this help to explain the movement of the manometer fluid in Investigation 12.1?

DISCOVERY OF PHOTOSYNTHESIS

Before the 17th century, people believed that plants got most of their substance from soil. This hypothesis was proved incorrect by a simple experiment performed by Jan van Helmont. Van Helmont planted a five-pound willow tree in 200 pounds of soil. The soil was covered so nothing could get in accidentally. Only pure rainwater was given to the plant. At the end of five years, the willow was pulled out and weighed. It had grown to weigh 169 pounds. The soil still weighed over 199 pounds (figure 12–6). Van Helmont concluded that the plant substance

Jan van Helmont: 1577–1640. Belgian philosopher, chemist, and physician

12–6 Van Helmont's experiment.

WILLOW TREE 5 lbs
SOIL 200 lbs

5 YEARS

WILLOW TREE 169 lbs 3 oz
SOIL 199 lbs 2 oz

must have come from the water. This conclusion was logical, considering the limits of the experiment. But this was not the whole story.

In 1772 Joseph Priestley placed a mint shoot in a container of water. A glass jar was placed over both so that air could not enter. To everyone's surprise, the shoot remained alive for several months! In another experiment, a burning candle quickly went out when covered with a similar glass jar. After the candle had burned out, Priestley placed another mint shoot under the same jar. After a few days the candle remained lit for a longer period of time than it had the first time. And, as Priestley said, "The restored air was not at all inconvenient to a mouse which I put into it." However, other investigators were unable to verify Priestley's experiments. Even Priestley could not repeat them.

The reason for this failure became clear in 1779. Jan Ingenhousz showed that plants act as Priestley described only when they are exposed to light. (Apparently Priestley had not done this when he repeated the experiment.) When exposed to light, plants release oxygen as the plants did in Priestley's "restored air." Further experiments showed that only the green tissues of plants release oxygen.

Next it was discovered that plants growing in light absorb carbon dioxide. Following this, in 1804, another scientist showed that the increase in plant mass is greater than the mass of the carbon dioxide taken in. It was concluded that plant growth is due to the intake of both carbon dioxide and water.

By 1845 the main events in photosynthesis were known. Light energy is absorbed and transformed into chemical energy. The chemical energy is stored in compounds formed by plant cells from water and carbon dioxide.

CHLOROPLASTS

Does photosynthesis occur everywhere in a cell or only at certain places? Botanists observed long ago that oxygen is produced only near the chloroplasts of photosynthesizing cells. To demonstrate clearly that photosynthesis occurs only in chloroplasts, it is necessary to remove them from the cell. This was accomplished in the 1930's. It wasn't until 1954, however, that Daniel Arnon was able to show that chloroplasts removed from a cell can indeed carry on the entire process of photosynthesis.

The internal structure of chloroplasts has been seen in electron microscope photos. These show that chloroplasts contain small, disk-shaped bodies. Each of these bodies is made up of a number of flat plates. **Biochemists** have found that each plate is made of chlorophyll, protein, and lipid molecules. The layered structure may allow maximum exposure of chlorophyll mole-

Joseph Priestley: 1733–1804. English clergyman, chemist

Jan Ingenhousz [YON ING un hows]: 1730–1799. Dutch physician and naturalist

12−7 Chloroplasts in cells of a moss.

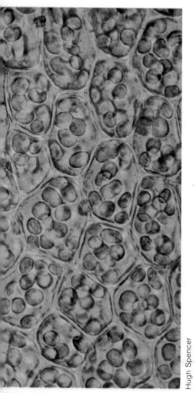

Hugh Spencer

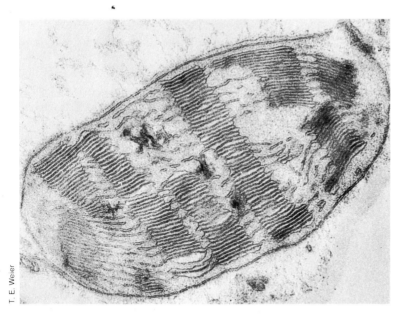

T. E. Weier

Daniel Arnon: 1910—. American plant physiologist, University of California, Berkeley

Biochemists: scientists who study the chemical processes that occur in living organisms

lipid [LIP ud]. See page 401.

12–8 Electron micrograph of a single tobacco chloroplast. × 20,000

cules to light. Or it may bring chlorophyll in contact with the protein layers, where other molecules required for photosynthesis are located.

CHLOROPHYLL AND OTHER PLANT PIGMENTS

The first step in photosynthesis is the absorption of sunlight by green plants. Light energy is trapped by several pigments in plant cells. A pigment is a chemical compound that absorbs only certain wavelengths of light. Other wavelengths are reflected. Green plants, for example, look green because the green plant pigments have absorbed most wavelengths of visible light *except* green. Most of the green light is reflected.

The green plant pigment involved in trapping light is chlorophyll. Five different kinds of chlorophylls are now known. The most common chlorophyll (*a*) is believed to be present in all photosynthetic plants. The other four chlorophylls (*b*, *c*, *d*, and *e*) may be present in different plants in different combinations. In addition, plants may contain other pigments: orange (carotene), yellow (xanthophyll), red (anthocyanin), and brown (tannin). Some of these may work with chlorophyll to trap and absorb various wavelengths of light. Chlorophyll molecules are quite complex. They are produced inside chloroplasts— except in blue-green algae. Very few chloroplasts are formed in the absence of light.

carotene [KER uh teen]
xanthophyll [ZAN thuh fil]
anthocyanin [an thuh SY uh nun]
tannin [TAN un]

Can you demonstrate that a plant requires light for the formation of chlorophylls?

The way colored things absorb light is described by an absorption spectrum. This is a simple graph that shows the per-

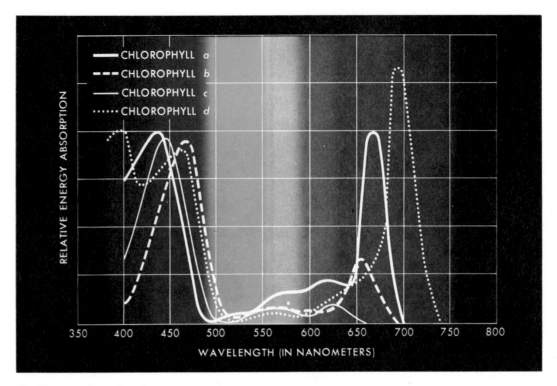

12–9 Energy absorption of visible light by four chlorophylls. (Chlorophyll *e* is not shown.) The background shows the appearance of the wavelengths to our eyes. What wavelengths (colors) do these chlorophylls absorb least?

centage of light absorbed at each wavelength (color). Green plants have very low absorption in the green wavelengths and high absorption in the blue and red. The absorption spectrum of various plant pigments can be seen in figure 12–9.

CHECK YOURSELF

D. What is photosynthesis?

E. In addition to food, what other important substance is produced in photosynthesis?

F. Describe the hypothesis, design, and conclusions of the experiment of Jan van Helmont.

G. Why couldn't Joseph Priestley successfully repeat his mouse, candle, and mint experiment?

H. What is the function of chloroplasts?

I. Chlorophyll is an important plant pigment. What does it do?

J. What is an absorption spectrum?

Investigation 12.2   SEPARATION OF LEAF PIGMENTS

INTRODUCTION

How does a biochemist know that the color of leaves is the result of a mixture of several kinds of pigments? Many methods are used to separate cell substances from the leaves and from each other. Substances such as sugars that are soluble in water are easily separated from substances such as fats that are insoluble in water. But many substances found in organisms are so much alike that the usual methods fail.

In the late 19th century a Russian chemist discovered the principle of chromatography (krom uh TOG ruh fee; Greek: *chroma*, color, + *graphein*, to write). At first this method was used only to separate pigments. By the 1930's, however, chromatography was also being used to separate colorless substances. In the original technique, separation was done on paper. Now it can be done on other materials as well.

Much of the last 50 years' progress in biochemistry has resulted from the use of chromatography.

MATERIALS
(per team)

spinach leaves
ethanol
developing solution (8% acetone, 92% petroleum ether)
several strips of filter or chromatography paper
fine sand
test tube, 25 × 200 mm
cork, to fit into test tube
test tube, 18 × 150 mm
pipette, with a very fine tip
mortar and pestle
test-tube rack
forceps
funnel
funnel support
10 × 10 cm square of cheesecloth
scissors
glass-marking crayon
cleansing tissue
2 pencils
paper clip

PROCEDURE

(*Caution: Because ether is being used, at no time should there be an open flame in the room.*)

1. Using the larger test tube, assemble the apparatus shown in figure 12–10. But do not yet add the developing solution and pigments. Handle the paper carefully with the forceps. Even a small amount of oil from your fingers will affect the results.

2. Adjust the paper in the tube so it does not touch the sides or bottom. Mark on the test tube the level of the *lower* end of the notch.

3. Remove the cork. Remove the paper strip from the hook. Then pour developing solution into the test tube to a depth 5 mm *below* the mark that you made.

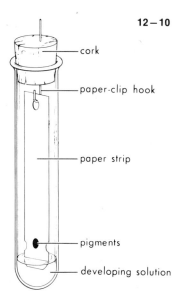

12–10

cork

paper-clip hook

paper strip

pigments

developing solution

4. Place the cork with the hook attached (but without the strip of paper) in the test tube. Place the tube in an upright position in a rack. Support the strip of paper across 2 pencils so that it does not touch the table.
5. Put 2 or 3 spinach leaves, a little sand, and 5 ml of ethanol into a mortar. Grind thoroughly. The ethanol now contains extracted pigments.
6. Place a layer of cheesecloth in a funnel. Add a layer of cleansing tissue.
7. Pour the ethanol into the funnel. Collect the filtrate in the smaller test tube. (*1*) What is the color of the filtrate? (*2*) Is there any evidence that more than one pigment is dissolved in the ethanol?
8. Using a fine-pointed pipette, place a drop of the pigment extract on the paper between the notches. Allow it to dry. Add another drop in the same place, and allow it to dry. Repeat until you have placed at least 4 drops on the paper — one on top of another.
9. When the final drop has dried, remove the cork from the large test tube and hang the strip on the hook.
10. Insert the cork, with the paper strip attached, into the test tube. *Do not allow the pigment spot to touch the developing solution.* If necessary, adjust the length of the hook to avoid this. Be sure the cork is tight.
11. Watch the developing solution rise. When it *almost* reaches the hook, remove the cork from the tube. Take the paper off the hook with the forceps and recork the tube. Hold the paper until it dries.

DISCUSSION

Examine the chromatogram. (*3*) How many bands of color can you see? (*4*) How many bands might be made up of chlorophylls?(*5*) What other colors can you see in the chromatogram? (*6*) Why were you unable to see these colors in the leaf? (*7*) Do you think that all the leaf pigments were soluble in the ethanol? Why or why not? (*8*) Suggest a hypothesis to explain the change of color that often occurs when a leaf dies.

Now consider the process by which the pigments were separated. (*9*) From what point did all the pigments start as the developing solution began to rise? (*10*) When did all the pigments start to move, and when did they all stop? (*11*) In what characteristic, then, must the pigments have differed?

FOR FURTHER INVESTIGATION

1. Why were the pigments studied in this investigation extracted with ethanol? Why was water not used? What liquids besides ethanol can be used to extract these pigments from the leaf?

2. Are there any leaf pigments that are not extracted by ethanol? If so, what are the pigments, and how can they be extracted?

3. What effect does the kind of developer have on the success of chromatography? Try 100% acetone, 100% petroleum ether, 100% alcohol, and different mixtures of any two of these or of all three. Does the nature of the pigments you are trying to separate affect the success of the chromatography? Using some of the developers listed above, try separating other pigments, such as those in ball-point-pen inks.

BIOCHEMISTRY OF PHOTOSYNTHESIS

synthesis [SIN thuh sus]; plural, syntheses [SIN thuh seez]

Photosynthesis is one of the most common reactions going on in living plants. It is the synthesis, or building up, of complex, high-energy, ordered molecules from smaller, simpler molecules, using the sun's energy (figure 12–11). Biochemists have measured the amounts of carbon dioxide (CO_2) and water (H_2O) taken in by chlorophyll-bearing cells in light. They also measured the amounts of oxygen and the energy-rich carbon compound, glucose, that were formed. The formation of glucose and oxygen is summarized as follows:

$$6\ CO_2 + 6\ H_2O \xrightarrow{\text{light energy}} C_6H_{12}O_6 + 6\ O_2$$

(carbon   (water)   (glucose) (oxygen)
dioxide)

Of course, such summary equations merely indicate the major raw materials and some of the finished products. They show nothing of the chemical steps and other substances involved.

Light, carbon dioxide, and water go into a plant; glucose and oxygen are produced. Once the plant has produced glucose, this simple sugar is used as a source of stored energy for the plant. It also is used as raw material for the synthesis of other plant materials.

By 1905 biochemists had obtained evidence that two distinct sets of reactions occur during photosynthesis. One set, the "light reaction," occurs only while a chlorophyll-bearing cell is exposed to light. A second set follows for which light is not required, the "dark reaction." Although light is not *required* for the dark reaction, it can take place in light.

THE SOURCE OF OXYGEN

Oxygen is produced as a by-product of photosynthesis. But where does the oxygen come from? For many years carbon dioxide (CO_2) was thought to be the most likely source. But the problem could not be solved until a way was found to distinguish between oxygen from water (H_2O) and oxygen from CO_2.

Why is oxygen considered a by-product?

Using an instrument called the mass spectrometer, biochemists exposed photosynthesizing plants to CO_2 that contained a heavy form (an isotope) of oxygen atoms. The mass spectrometer showed that all the oxygen (O_2) given off by these plants was the kind usually found in the atmosphere. Other plants were then exposed to ordinary CO_2 but supplied with water containing the heavier isotope of oxygen. With the mass spectrometer the oxygen given off by these plants was identified as the heavier isotope form. Clearly, oxygen came only from the water, not from the carbon dioxide. (The simplified equation at the top of this page does not reflect these details.)

spectrometer [spek TROM ut ur]

isotope [EYE suh tope]

ATP

A significant compound in the energy processes of plant cells, as in all cells, is a substance known as adenosine *triphosphate*,

adenosine triphosphate
[uh DEN uh seen try FOS fayt]

See figure 12–18.

usually abbreviated ATP. Each molecule of ATP includes a main section, symbolized as A. Attached to this section are three identical groups of atoms called phosphates. The chemical bonds linking the phosphates to one another are rich in energy.

Energy is temporarily stored in the ATP bonds. When energy is required by the cell, it is released from ATP by reactions that break one of the bonds and remove the third phosphate group. The remaining molecule, with only two phosphate groups, is called adenosine *di*phosphate, ADP. We can show its formation from ATP as follows:

$$ATP \longrightarrow ADP + P + energy$$

A cell cannot continually use stored ATP as in the above reaction without also rebuilding some ADP back into ATP:

$$energy + ADP + P \longrightarrow ATP$$

In plants this energy comes from the light reaction in photosynthesis. In the light reaction energy from the sun is trapped by the chlorophyll in plants. Some of the energy is stored in ATP. Some of the energy is used to split water molecules, releasing oxygen gas and hydrogen. The hydrogen is picked up by hydrogen-carrier molecules and is held in the plant. The oxygen leaves the plant and enters the atmosphere.

Some biochemists have argued that the formation of carbon compounds should not be considered a part of photosynthesis. How might this viewpoint be defended?

The second stage in photosynthesis, the dark reaction, occurs independently of light. During this reaction carbon dioxide is used in making glucose. The synthesis of glucose involves the transfer of hydrogen, split from water in the light reaction, to carbon dioxide. The energy released from the breaking of ATP bonds is used to make bonds between CO_2 and hydrogen (H). The atoms are combined in a series of reactions. Ultimately glucose is formed.

Melvin Calvin: 1911—. American biochemist at the University of California, Berkeley; winner of the Nobel Prize in 1961

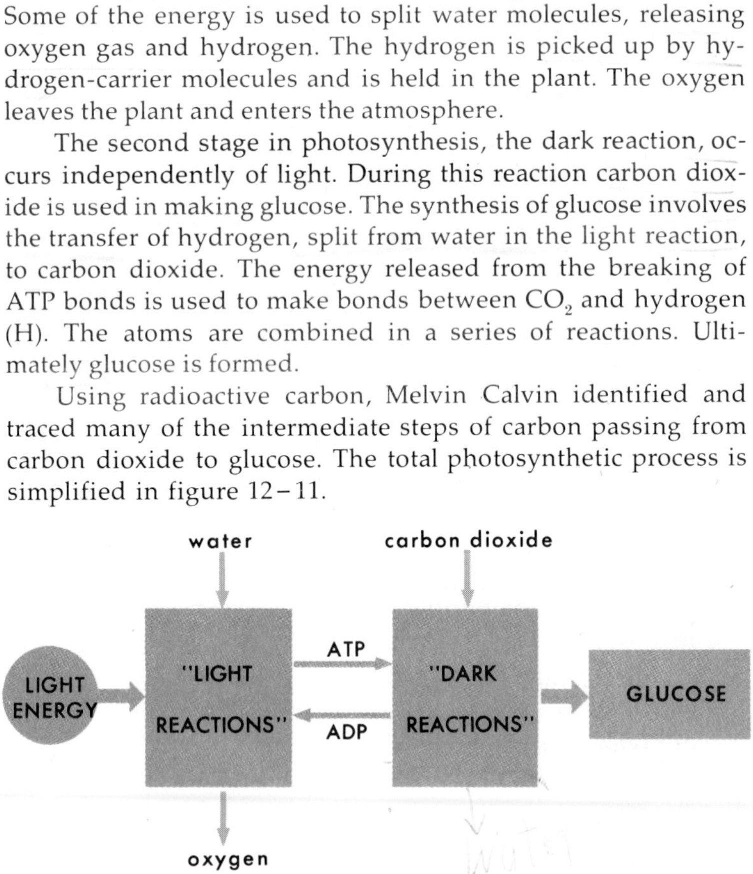

Using radioactive carbon, Melvin Calvin identified and traced many of the intermediate steps of carbon passing from carbon dioxide to glucose. The total photosynthetic process is simplified in figure 12–11.

12–11 Summary of photosynthesis.

FACTORS THAT AFFECT THE RATE OF PHOTOSYNTHESIS

Radiant energy. As you observed in Investigation 12.1, the intensity of radiant energy falling on the chloroplasts of the leaves affects the rate of photosynthesis. The duration of sunshine and the location of a plant on the earth affect its ability to photosynthesize.

Temperature. Some plants are adapted to grow in cold and some in hot climates. Most plants function best between temperatures of 10° and 35°C.

Carbon dioxide. Only about 0.03 percent of the atmosphere is carbon dioxide, and it remains fairly constant. If the concentration of CO_2 is increased artificially, as in a closed greenhouse, the rate of photosynthesis will increase, but only up to a point.

Water. Plants require much more water than that used in photosynthesis. Therefore, water is rarely a limiting factor in photosynthesis. But the amount of water falling as rain or snow frequently determines the *kinds* of plants that grow in a plant community.

Minerals. Plants constantly use soil minerals to build compounds involved in photosynthesis and growth. A lack of proper minerals in soil or water can be a major factor limiting plant growth.

Air pollution. Direct damage to plant leaves by air pollutants has harmed crops in the Los Angeles area during smog episodes. In other field tests, the production of agricultural crops has been significantly reduced by most air pollutants, not affected by others, and increased by only one. However, the one that increased yield damages forest trees and many other plants and kills freshwater fish. It is the sulfur dioxide of acid rain.

These factors all affect the photosynthesis and growth of plants. They become very important to humans involved in providing enough high-quality food for the world's population.

What factors may limit the photosynthetic rate of plants in your area?

CHECK YOURSELF

K. How can plant pigments be separated?
L. What is the general chemical equation for the process of photosynthesis?
M. How have isotopes of chemical elements played a part in the investigation of photosynthesis?
N. How is energy stored in ATP?
O. What major events occur in the light reaction? In the dark reaction?
P. What are some factors that affect photosynthetic rate?

SYNTHESES

Chemical energy is released in cells when large molecules are broken down into smaller ones. You might suppose, therefore, that the *building up* of large molecules from smaller ones — synthesis — would require energy. This is actually the case. A cell grows by adding new molecules to its substance. Most of these molecules must be synthesized. So growth is one of the processes for which a cell requires energy. Directly or indirectly the source of this energy for almost all organisms on the earth is photosynthesis.

Among the chemical compounds in the cell are carbohydrates, fats, and proteins. These are ordinarily thought of as foods. A hungry lion can make use of the carbohydrate, fat, and protein of your cells as food. And you can do the same with the cells of a bean. These substances are present in all cells and, to varying extents, cells can synthesize them.

carbohydrates [kar boh HY drayts]   CARBOHYDRATES

Carbohydrates contain only the elements carbon, hydrogen, and oxygen. Sugars, starches, and cellulose are some examples of carbohydrates.

fructose [FRUK tose]

Glucose and fructose are **simple sugars** — sugars that contain only six carbon atoms. Glucose molecules can be changed into other compounds. The synthesis of many cell substances may be thought of as beginning with glucose.

12–12 Structural formula (*A*) and model (*B*) of a molecule of glucose. In *A*, atoms of oxygen are represented by O, hydrogen by H, and carbon by C. In *B*, atoms are shown as spheres, each kind in a different color. Try to find in the model the atoms shown by symbols in the formula.

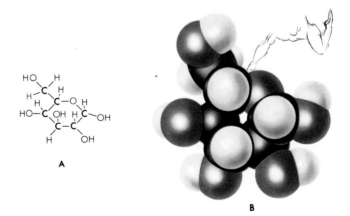

The most familiar sugar is sucrose, table sugar. It has 12 carbon atoms and is formed in a reaction that combines a glucose and a fructose molecule. Sucrose is called a **disaccharide**, because it is built with two simple-sugar units. Larger carbohydrate molecules such as starch and cellulose are formed in syn-

disaccharide [DY SAK uh ryd]: two sugars

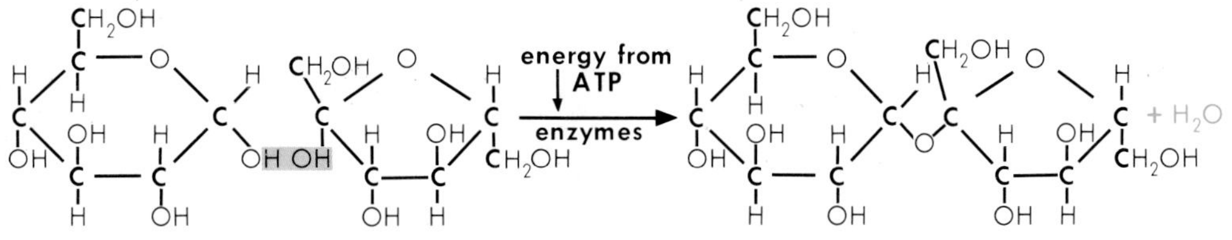

GLUCOSE   FRUCTOSE   SUCROSE

12–13 Formation of sucrose.

thesis reactions where more simple sugars are linked together. When there are many of these sugar units, the carbohydrates are called ***polysaccharides.***

polysaccharides [pol ih SAK-uh rydz]: poly—many, saccharide—sugars

FATS

Like carbohydrates, *fats* are composed of carbon, hydrogen, and oxygen atoms only. But fats always have a greater percentage of hydrogen atoms than do carbohydrates. A certain amount of fat contains more chemical energy than the same amount of carbohydrate. One gram of fat contains over twice as much energy as one gram of carbohydrate.

Fats that are in the liquid state at room temperature (about 20°C) are called "oils."

Fats are synthesized from ***glycerol*** and ***fatty acids.*** Glycerol is an ingredient of candies and cough medicine. In this case, it is called glycerin. Glycerol can be formed in cells from glucose. The simplest fatty acid is acetic acid, the acid in vinegar. Other fatty acids are based on acetic acid. The —COOH group of atoms is characteristic of the molecular structure of the organic acids. We can symbolize any fatty acid as R—COOH (figure 12–14). Here R stands for the rest of the molecule.

In motile organisms food is usually stored as fat rather than carbohydrate. Can you suggest an explanation?

glycerol [GLIS uh rol]

Fats are only one group in a broader chemical grouping, *lipids.* All lipids are formed from organic acids, but not necessarily in combination with glycerol. Many organisms produce lipids that are not fats. An example is a plant wax that is used in floor and automobile polishes.

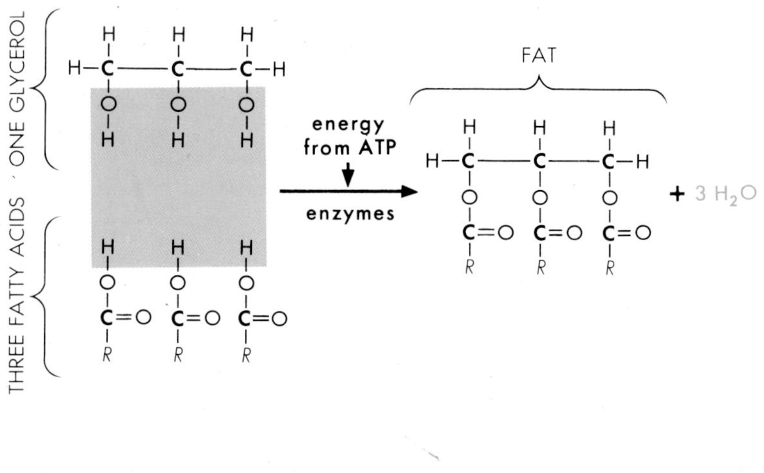

12–14 Formation of a fat.

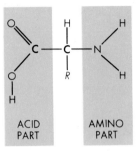

12−15 Basic structure of an amino acid. All amino acids have the parts shown on the green background, but differ with respect to the part *R*.

protein [PROH teen; Greek: *protos*, first]

amino [uh MEE noh]

12−16 Structural formula (*A*) and model (*B*) of a molecule of the simplest amino acid, glycine.

Many animals, however, can change one kind of amino acid to another kind within their bodies. Human cells can transform about 10 amino acids in this manner.

In human nutrition we speak of essential amino acids. What does this mean?

PROTEINS

Molecules of fat are large. Those of polysaccharides are larger. Still larger and more complex than both, however, are **protein** molecules. Ordinarily protein molecules contain thousands of atoms — sometimes tens of thousands. Proteins occur in bewildering variety.

The basic building units of protein molecules are **amino acids.** Amino acids always contain at least four kinds of atoms: carbon, hydrogen, and oxygen, just as in carbohydrates and lipids, and nitrogen. Some also contain sulfur.

Approximately 20 different amino acids occur in proteins. Apparently most green plants and some bacteria can synthesize all of these from inorganic materials. Animals, on the other hand, must obtain amino acids ready-made in their food. We humans need all 20 amino acids for our proteins, but not every kind of food contains all the amino acids. Therefore, we need a balanced diet of protein sources.

The synthesis of proteins involves linking the amino acids together. A long chain of amino acids is a **polypeptide.** Some

12−17 Formation of a tripeptide.

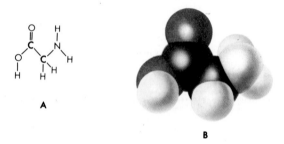

proteins are made of only one polypeptide, but most are made of two or more polypeptides bonded together. In the proteins these chains are coiled and folded and have weak cross bonds between sulfur-bearing amino acids. The three-dimensional structure is important in the proteins' functions.

The number of ways in which 20 different amino acid units can be combined is almost beyond imagination. Think of the English alphabet. We have 26 letters that can be combined in various size groups into an incredible number of combinations. Not all would "make sense," but thousands do. In a similar way the number of possible kinds of protein is tremendous.

NUCLEIC ACIDS

Much of the dark-staining material in the nucleus of a cell is *nucleic acid.* In some cases nucleic acid may make up more than 50 percent of a cell's dry mass.

nucleic [new KLEE ik]

There are two different kinds of nucleic acid: *ribonucleic acid* (RNA) and *deoxyribonucleic acid* (DNA). Both are made up of individual units called *nucleotides.* Nucleotides are made up of a phosphate group, a five-carbon sugar, and a base. The base may be one of five different kinds made up of carbon and nitrogen. RNA nucleotides contain *ribose*, a five-carbon sugar. DNA nucleotides contain *deoxyribose*, another five-carbon sugar that differs from ribose in having one less atom of oxygen.

ribonucleic [RY boh new KLEE ik]

deoxyribonucleic [DEE ok sih ry-boh new KLEE ik]

nucleotides [NEW klee uh tydz]

ribose [RY bose]

deoxyribose [dee ok sih RY bose]

Ribonucleic acid is found throughout cells. It is involved in the synthesis of proteins. In most cells deoxyribonucleic acid occurs mainly in nuclei. But in cells of blue-green algae, which have no organized nucleus, it is distributed throughout. DNA is a main part of chromosomes. It is the memory center of the cell. It has the information that keeps the cell and organism alive. It also contains information that carries the characteristics of an organism from one generation to the next.

ADENINE   RIBOSE   PHOSPHATE

12–18 Structural formula of a nucleotide. Adenine is one of the bases. Addition of a phosphate group would make this ADP. Addition of two phosphate groups would make it ATP.

CHECK YOURSELF

Q. Why does the synthesis of carbohydrates, proteins, and fats require the input of energy?

R. What are the building units of carbohydrates? Of proteins? Of fats? Of nucleic acids?

S. Why do we need a balanced diet of proteins?

Investigation 12.3   **FOOD ENERGY**

INTRODUCTION

Living organisms require both organic and inorganic compounds. But their energy requirements are provided by organic foods. Foods are compounds that contain carbon, hydrogen, oxygen, and often other elements as well. Chemically foods are somewhat like the fuels burned in furnaces and automobiles. Indeed, wood, coal, oil, and natural gas are carbon compounds derived from dead cells. They serve as fuels because they contain chemical energy. During the chemical reactions of burning, this energy is rapidly released in the form of heat and light.

All foods contain energy. How much energy? Do equal amounts of different foods contain the same amount of energy? In this investigation you will use a calorimeter (figure 12–19) to measure energy in food.

This energy will be measured in calories. Recall that a calorie is the amount of heat required to raise the temperature of 1 ml (1 g) of water 1°C. Calorie values of foods in diet charts are listed in kilocalories (1,000 calories). They are abbreviated as "C" or "kcal." Accepted caloric values for some common foods will be given to you later by your teacher.

You will measure the difference in temperature (ΔT) of a measured volume of water. The temperature change is caused by the absorption of the heat given off by the burning of a known mass of food.

MATERIALS
(per team)

For calorimeter

soft-drink cans
tin snips
hammer and nail
heat-resistant test tube to
   hold 15 ml
cork
cork pad or piece of plexiglass
straight pin or needle
thermometer (10°–110°C)

For testing food

lard or suet
peanuts, walnuts, or other
   combustible foods
balance
graduated cylinder, 100-ml
safety matches

PROCEDURE

1. Construct the calorimeter, using figure 12–19 as a guide. (Caution: Can edges may be sharp.)

2. Weigh out 0.2 g of the food to be tested. Place the food on the pin held up by the cork.

3. Place 15 ml water in the test tube and record the initial temperature of the water (T_i). Remove the thermometer.

4. Ignite the food to be tested and immediately place it under the test tube inside the calorimeter. Try to "catch" as much of the heat as possible.

12–19 A calorimeter.

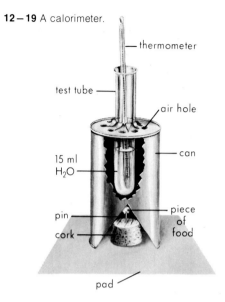

thermometer

test tube

air hole

15 ml
H₂O

can

pin

cork

piece
of
food

pad

5. Burn the food completely. Immediately measure the temperature of the water. If the food is not burned completely, ignite it again, record the new initial temperature, and add the new temperature change to the previous one. Record your data.

6. Repeat each test twice more with the same type of food. Change the water in the tube each time. Allow the tube to cool off before putting more water into it. (*Caution: Do not touch the tubes or the calorimeter while they are hot.*)

7. For each of the 3 trials, calculate the number of calories produced (c) per gram. To do this, multiply the increase in water temperature (ΔT) by 15, the number of ml of H₂O. Next divide this number by the number of grams of food burned. This will give you the calories produced per gram of food. To convert this into kilocalories, *divide* this number by 1,000.

The kilocalories listed in most diet charts are per 100 g, per ounce, per cup, or per serving. To compare your results, you may need to convert to common units.

DISCUSSION

(*1*) How do your data (adjusted for 100 g) compare with the values for 100 g of the same or similar food listed by your teacher? (*2*) How do you account for any differences? (*3*) If the same amount of each food you tested were completely used in the cells of the human body, what would you expect the energy release to be?

(*4*) Which of the foods you tested seems to be the best energy source? (*5*) Why might some foods with fewer calories be better energy sources than other foods with more calories? (*6*) What was the original source of energy in all of the foods tested?

HOW IS ENERGY RELEASED FROM FOOD?

How is the energy of a peanut you eat (left over from Investigation 12.3) released in your body? First it must be broken down chemically into molecules that are small enough to pass into your cells. This is what your digestive system does. Once inside the cells these smaller molecules are also broken down chemically. The energy stored in their bonds can then be released and used by your cells.

The chemical energy stored in food molecules is released when chemical reactions occur in your body cells. But these chemical reactions are quite different from what happened when you burned food in a calorimeter. In cells chemical reactions occur at much lower temperatures. The reactions are controlled, and little energy is released as heat and light.

How can energy-releasing chemical reactions occur at the low temperatures in cells? Chemists have discovered certain substances that greatly speed up chemical reactions without themselves being used up in the reactions. For instance, a cube of sugar heated over a flame will melt and char, but it will not burn. But, if a little ash is added, the sugar cube will burst into flames. The ash does not change, nor is it used up when the sugar burns. The ash speeds up the reaction; it acts as a *catalyst.*

catalyst [KAT ul ust; Greek: *kata,* down, + *lyein,* to loosen]

In cell chemistry, too, catalysts accelerate reactions. Cell catalysts, however, are not simple substances like the minerals in ash. They are organic compounds made by living cells. They differ greatly from inorganic catalysts like ash, and they have a special name, *enzymes.* Enzymes are complex proteins manufactured by cells. Each type of enzyme catalyzes a single, different chemical reaction. Like other catalysts, enzymes speed up reactions but are not used up in the reaction. They are needed in very small amounts, because the same enzyme molecule can complete the same reaction thousands of times in a single minute.

enzymes [EN zymz; Greek: *en,* in, + *zyme,* a material to raise bread dough]

Most chemical reactions going on in living organisms are controlled by enzymes. Most of the reactions fall into two groups. One group is involved with the breakdown of complex molecules to simpler ones. Examples are the reactions that take place in the digestive systems of organisms. Most of these reactions are called *hydrolysis* reactions because water is involved as the molecules are broken down. The other group of reactions builds large complex molecules from simple ones. These are called synthesis reactions.

hydrolysis [hy DROL uh sus]: water-splitting

The substance that interacts with the enzyme is called the *substrate.* Substrates are what go into the chemical reaction that is catalyzed by enzymes. In the case of hydrolysis, the substrate may be a single, large molecule that joins to the enzyme and then is split into smaller molecules. In synthesis two or more small molecules join with an enzyme and are themselves joined together. The *enzyme-substrate complex* is a *temporary* union while the reaction is going on. The enzyme never remains joined to the substrate after the reaction. Note that the enzyme is not changed and can catalyze another reaction of the same kind with similar substrate molecules.

substrate [SUB strayt]

The shape and chemical makeup of an enzyme molecule determines which substrate it will react with. Enzyme and substrate must fit together, somewhat like a lock and key. Only a specific enzyme can react with a certain substrate. Heating changes the shape of an enzyme so it will not react with its specific substrate.

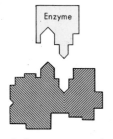

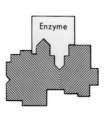

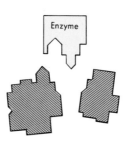

12–20 An enzyme-substrate complex in a hydrolysis reaction (*above*) and a synthesis reaction (*below*).

A. Enzyme approaches substrate molecule.

B. Enzyme structure fits specific portion of molecule.

C. Enzyme leaves after molecule has been split. Enzyme repeats action many times.

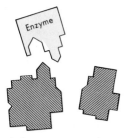

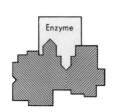

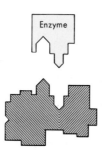

A. Enzyme approaches substrate molecules.

B. Enzyme unites molecules.

C. Enzyme leaves after molecules are united. Enzyme repeats action many times.

CHECK YOURSELF

T. Why can food be considered a fuel?

U. What is a calorie?

V. What is the difference between the release of energy in burning and the release of energy in cells?

W. List several characteristics and actions of enzymes.

X. What is an enzyme-substrate complex?

Investigation 12.4   A STUDY OF BIOCHEMICAL REACTIONS

INTRODUCTION

Hydrogen peroxide (H_2O_2) is a highly active chemical, often used for bleaching. It is sold as a 3% solution in water. Within cells, hydrogen peroxide is formed continually as a by-product of biochemical processes. Be-cause H_2O_2 is toxic (poisonous) to cells, it would soon kill them if not immediately removed or broken down.

In this investigation you will observe the activity of two substances, both of which break down hydrogen peroxide. One of

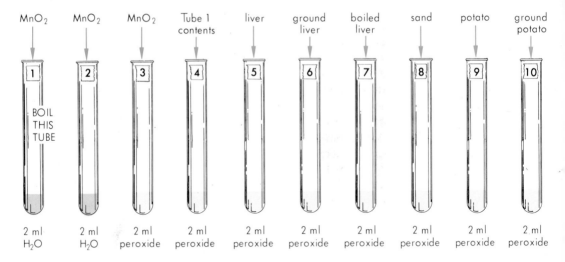

these is manganese dioxide, an inorganic catalyst. The other is an enzyme, catalase, an organic compound.

PROCEDURE

1. Arrange the test tubes in the rack and number them from *1* to *10*. Pour 2 ml water into each of Tubes 1 and 2.
2. Pour 2 ml hydrogen peroxide (H_2O_2) solution into each of the other tubes. *After each of the following steps, record your observations.* Compare observations on different tubes frequently.
3. Into Tube 1 sprinkle a small amount (about half a scalpel bladeful) of manganese dioxide powder (MnO_2).
4. Repeat for Tubes 2 and 3.
5. Place Tube 1 in boiling water for a few minutes. Then pour its contents into Tube 4.
6. Using forceps, select a small piece of fresh liver and drop it into Tube 5.
7. Place another piece of fresh liver (the same size) into a mortar. Add a little fine sand and grind the liver. Transfer the resulting mixture to Tube 6. Wash the mortar thoroughly.
8. Place a 3rd piece of liver in boiling water for a few minutes. Drop the boiled liver into Tube 7.

MATERIALS
(per team)

3 pieces fresh liver, each
   about 6 mm in diameter
fresh potato
100 ml 3% hydrogen peroxide solution
manganese dioxide powder
fine sand
10 test tubes, 13 × 100 mm
graduated cylinder, 10-ml
beaker
scalpel
forceps
test-tube rack
mortar and pestle
hot plate
glass-marking crayon

9. Into Tube 8 sprinkle the same amount of sand as of the manganese dioxide used in Tubes 1, 2, and 3.
10. Using the scalpel, cut 2 cubes of fresh potato, each the size of the liver used. Place 1 potato cube in Tube 9.
11. Grind the other potato cube in the mortar with sand. Place the potato-sand mixture in Tube 10.

DISCUSSION

   (*1*) What was the purpose of Tube 2? (*2*)

Do you have any evidence that manganese dioxide catalyzes the breakdown of hydrogen peroxide instead of reacting with it? (*3*) What additional steps in the procedure would be needed to confirm this?

Biochemists have obtained experimental evidence that manganese dioxide is indeed a catalyst in this reaction. Consider the formula of hydrogen peroxide and the kind of reaction you observed in Tube 3. (*4*) What are the most likely products of the breakdown of hydrogen peroxide? (*5*) How might you confirm your answer?

(*6*) What caused the reaction when you put the liver into Tubes 5 and 6? (*7*) How do you explain the difference in activity resulting from the whole piece of liver and from the ground liver? (*8*) Why is Tube 8 necessary for this explanation? (*9*) How do you explain the difference in activity resulting from fresh and boiled liver?

Suppose that someone compared Tubes 3 and 5 and concluded that liver contains manganese dioxide. (*10*) What evidence do you have either for or against this conclusion? (Consider the reaction in Tube 4.)

(*11*) What additional information do the results from Tubes 9 and 10 provide?

CELLULAR RESPIRATION

Biochemists refer to the main energy-releasing process as *cellular respiration.* This is a series of cellular chemical reactions that occur in both plant and animal cells. This may be a little confusing, because "respiration" is often used to mean breathing. Breathing is certainly a part of the energy-releasing process. Through breathing, you and many other land animals get oxygen from the air into the blood. Oxygen in the blood is transported close to every cell, where it is available for use in cellular respiration.

During cellular respiration, the chemical energy in foods is released in several reactions controlled by enzymes. The energy is stored as ATP. The main part of this process takes place in mitochondria. Each mitochondrion contains all the enzyme "machinery" for the respiration process.

Why do you think mitochondria are called the "powerhouses" of a cell?

During burning, the chemical energy of fuels is released as light and heat. The chemical energy in foods is stored in ATP. During cellular respiration, this chemical energy may then be transformed into motion. The movement of a muscle may be involved. Or, the movement of molecules or ions by active transport may be involved. The energy from cellular respiration also may be used to form new chemical compounds. To a very small extent, some may be changed into light (as in fireflies). Some heat is released, but this energy is lost as far as cell processes are concerned.

Although lost for cell processes, how may this heat be of advantage to a warm-blooded animal?

AEROBIC BREAKDOWN OF GLUCOSE

Glucose is one of the principal carbon compounds broken down to release energy in cellular respiration. As glucose is broken down, the energy stored in its chemical bonds is released for use in the cell. Most foods do not contain glucose, but do con-

Fats are another energy-rich food used in respiration. Even amino acids from proteins are occasionally broken down directly when they are in excess supply or are damaged.

tain other energy-rich carbon compounds. After the foods are eaten, they are broken down. The complex carbon compounds in these foods often are converted to glucose in the cells. These glucose molecules can then be used in respiration.

The glucose molecules are broken down and some of their energy is stored in ATP molecules. In the course of ATP formation, hydrogen is removed from the glucose molecules. The hydrogen combines with oxygen in the air we breathe to form water. The chemical energy stored in the bonds of glucose molecules is transferred to the ATP molecules. Their energy is then used in most of the cell's activities. After the energy is released from the glucose molecule and the hydrogen is taken away, the carbon and oxygen atoms remain. These are released as carbon dioxide when we exhale.

12–22.Breakdown of glucose to supply a cell's energy.

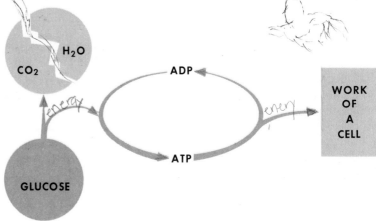

aerobic: see page 229.

During the process of aerobic cellular respiration, 36 molecules of ATP energy are formed from each molecule of glucose. The general equation for cellular respiration, in the presence of plenty of oxygen, is as follows:

$$36\ ADP + 36\ P + C_6H_{12}O_6 + 6\ O_2 \xrightarrow{\text{enzyme}}$$
$$\text{(glucose)} \qquad 36\ ATP + 6\ CO_2 + 6\ H_2O$$
$$\text{(carbon} $$
$$\text{dioxide)}$$

fermentation [fur mun TAY shun]   FERMENTATION

Without oxygen, the breakdown of glucose is inefficient. Very little usable energy is produced—not enough to keep us alive. What happens if a cell does not have enough oxygen for the normal process of cellular respiration? In our own bodies, for example, when we run we use a lot of energy. When this happens, we breathe faster to increase the oxygen supply in our bodies. But we may use energy faster than oxygen can be supplied to our cells. The cells are then in an anaerobic condition. In this case glucose is only partially broken down through *fer-*

mentation. Here ATP is still formed, but at a much slower rate. Also formed is a product called lactic acid. As this builds up under anaerobic conditions, muscle fatigue results. When you stop running, you continue to breathe deeply. You return to your normal breathing rate when your oxygen supply catches up with your cells' demands.

Fermentation is a general term for anaerobic energy release. Figure 12–23 shows that aerobic cellular respiration traps in ATP about 1.5 kcal of the 3.8 kcal in a gram of glucose—about 40 percent of the possible energy. Recall that 36 ATP molecules are formed through aerobic respiration of one glucose molecule. By contrast, fermentation produces only two ATP molecules per glucose molecule. So in fermentation only about $2/36 \times 40$ percent, or 2.2 percent, of the total glucose energy is trapped in ATP.

In anaerobic conditions animals form lactic acid in fermentation. On the other hand, plants form alcohol. The general equation for this kind of fermentation of glucose is as follows:

$$2 \text{ ADP} + 2 \text{ P} + C_6H_{12}O_6 \xrightarrow{\text{enzyme}} 2 \text{ ATP} + 2 \text{ CO}_2 + 2 \text{ C}_2H_5OH$$

(glucose) (carbon dioxide) (alcohol)

Wineries make use of this process. They use yeast cells to ferment grapes to wine. Bakers also use yeast to produce small bubbles of carbon dioxide, which cause bread to rise. Both of these processes use the waste products of fermentation from the living yeast cells.

The cells of most animals can survive for a short time on the limited amount of energy released by fermentation. Eventually oxygen is necessary for the more efficient aerobic respiration. However, some organisms exist entirely by the fermentation process. For example, *Clostridium tetani*, the bacterium that causes lockjaw, does. Others, such as yeast, can exist very well anaerobically. But, if oxygen is available, they switch to the more efficient aerobic method.

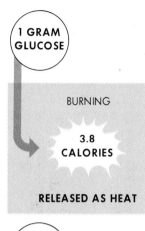

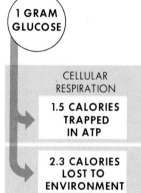

12–23 Does the amount of energy obtained from food depend upon the way it is released?

Clostridium tetani [klos TRID.ee-um TET uh ñee]

Would you expect *Clostridium* cells to have mitochondria? Why or why not?

CHECK YOURSELF

Y. Where does cellular respiration take place?

Z. What role does glucose play in cellular respiration?

AA. What chemical compound is stored, and provides energy for most cellular activity?

BB. Write out the general chemical equation for the process of aerobic cellular respiration.

CC. What is fermentation?

DD. Compare the amounts of energy trapped by aerobic cellular respiration and by fermentation.

PROBLEMS

1. A hundred years ago the carbon dioxide in the atmosphere was measured at 0.0283 percent. Today the level is 0.0330 percent. What human activities during the last 100 years may have contributed to this increase? What are some possible future consequences if this trend continues?

2. Many botanists today are searching for plants that synthesize fuel-related carbon compounds. Part of our energy needs could be met by growing these plants commercially. What other types of useful compounds are produced by plants? Find out about all the new careers involved. Report your findings to the class.

3. Calculate the surface area and volume of ten spheres having diameters of 1 mm, 2 mm, 3 mm, and so on to 10 mm. Plot the two sets of results on the same grid. Allow the vertical axis to represent both mm² and mm³. Keeping in mind the requirements of all living cells for energy and materials from which energy is released, comment on the meaning of your graph. What are the biological consequences of a cell growing to a large size?

4. You may have seen some fats and cooking oils referred to as "polyunsaturated." Find out what this means in chemical terms.

5. Proteins in the cells of a wheat plant differ from the proteins in your cells. How can the differences be explained? What must happen when you use wheat as a nutrient for the formation of your proteins?

6. Experiments with photosynthesizing vascular plants have shown that when they are grown in an atmosphere without oxygen they take up carbon dioxide at 1.5 times the rate in natural atmosphere, which is about 20 percent oxygen. (a) What does this indicate about the relationship between photosynthesis and cellular respiration? (b) How might this relationship affect the composition of the earth's atmosphere?

7. Many botanists believe that the concentration of carbon dioxide in the air was much greater during the Carboniferous period, when most of the large coal deposits were being formed, than it is at present. What might be the basis for their belief?

8. Gather whatever information you can find about conditions on the surfaces of Mars and Venus. Then, using your knowledge of cell metabolism, comment on the possibility of life existing on these planets. What life-supporting equipment would probably be desirable for astronauts planning trips to these planets?

SUGGESTED READINGS

BSCS. 1975. *Life's Energy.* Collegiate Minicourse. W. B. Saunders, Philadelphia.

Dickerson, R. E. 1980. Cytochrome C and the Evolution of Energy Metabolism. *Scientific American*, March. The basis for metabolism in modern organisms can be traced to bacteria, used in research on the origin of cell respiration.

Gore, R. 1980. What Voyager Saw: Jupiter's Dazzling Realm. *National Geographic*, January, pp. 2–29.

Hinkle, P. C. and R. E. McCarty. 1978. How Cells Make ATP. *Scientific American*, March. Shows how light or oxidation produces the fuel of cells.

Koshland, D. E. 1973. Protein Shapes and Biological Control. *Scientific American*, April.

Lechtman, M. D., B. Roohk, and R. J. Egan. 1979. *The Games Cells Play: Basic Concepts of Cellular Metabolism.* Benjamin-Cummings, Menlo Park, Calif. Provides the needed chemical background for studying cells.

Chapter 13

Functioning Plants

YOUR GUIDEPOSTS

In this chapter you will have an opportunity to explore these questions in biology:

- How is the structure of plants related to the life functions that they perform?
- In what ways are land plants adapted to the terrestrial environment?
- How does growth in plants differ from that in animals?

PLANTS AS ORGANISMS

As producers, plants are of primary importance to other organisms in the web of life. But plants carry on many activities other than photosynthesis. Like other living things they use nutrients, grow, and reproduce. They also have structural diversity of cells, tissues, and organs.

About 80 percent of the photosynthesis on the earth occurs in the seas — mostly in single-celled plants and protists. In many parts of the world, wild algae are harvested for food, agar, and fertilizer. In Japan and China, kelp is grown in vast "sea gardens." Kelp is rich in inorganic salts and it contains several vitamins.

Then why are oceans sometimes compared to deserts?

But humans are land animals, and in most parts of the world we have made little use of the seas' productivity. By and large we obtain our food, directly or indirectly, from land plants. Moreover, we are most familiar with terrestrial organisms. It seems reasonable, therefore, to use the familiar land plants — the tracheophytes, or vascular plants — as the chief examples in the discussion of how plants function.

VASCULAR PLANTS

We may begin our study by taking a look at a potted house-plant—perhaps a geranium. Unlike most animals, such a plant lives in two very different environments at the same time. One environment is the air, and the other is the soil.

The part above ground—the shoot—is made up of stems, leaves, and, perhaps, flowers and fruits. It is surrounded by air, which provides almost no support against gravity. If you leave your geranium outside, wind, rain, sleet, or snow may batter it. The shoot must withstand all types of weather if it is to remain whole and upright.

saturated [SACH ur ayt ud; Latin: *satur*, full]: with a relative humidity of 100 percent. (See Investigation 3.2.)

Loss of water from a plant to the atmosphere occurs continually. This happens because the air usually is not saturated with water, and water diffuses from the plant into the air. In addition, a plant shoot has a large surface in contact with the air. So water is readily lost from the shoot. But, being in air, the shoot has an abundant oxygen supply and a steady supply of carbon dioxide. Depending on where your geranium and all other plants grow, they may receive varying intensities of light.

The roots' environment—the soil—is quite different. Soil is dense, often moist, and little light penetrates it. Support for the plant is firm, and here water is usually absorbed rather than lost.

13−1 A tree in two environments—above and below the soil.

Gordon E. Uno

This simplified view of a vascular plant and its environment runs into difficulties. There are some roots that live above ground and some stems that live underground. This generalization, however, is helpful to an overall understanding of plant structures and functions.

LEAVES

Most botanists consider leaves as organs. To call a leaf an "organ" may seem somewhat strange. In the human body, organs are usually one or two of a kind. For instance, your liver and eyes are organs. A large land plant, however, may have thousands of leaves. A leaf is composed of different tissues, each of which performs some general function in the life of an organism. Therefore, leaves are considered organs. For any particular species, the leaf shape is usually distinctive and constant enough to be useful in identification.

What are some tracheophytes that lack leaves?

See Investigation 5.1.

X 1/2

A leaf may or may not have a petiole connecting the blade to the plant stem. In the needle leaves of many conifers, there is neither blade nor petiole. In a *simple leaf* the blade is in one piece. In a *compound leaf* the blade is divided into separate leaflets. Whatever their form, the primary function of most leaves is photosynthesis. Some leaves, however, are so modified that they do not function in photosynthesis—spines of cactus, for example.

13–2 Variation in leaves taken from a single white poplar tree. No two leaves on any one plant are exactly alike. Shapes and sizes vary according to many factors including age of the plant and amount of sunlight received.

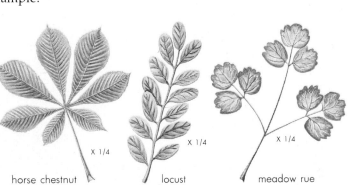

X 1/4

X 1/4

X 1/4

horse chestnut   locust   meadow rue

13–3 In these compound leaves each blade is divided into separate parts. What other plants with compound leaves can you name?

Figure 13–4 shows the cellular structure of a leaf blade. Several different tissues can be distinguished. With your knowledge of photosynthesis, you might set up some hypotheses about the functions of these tissues. As cells in a multicellular organism differentiate in structure, they usually acquire special functions. In other words, they become *specialized.*

Upon what generalization should your hypotheses be based?

13–4 A portion of a leaf blade. Colors are diagrammatic only.

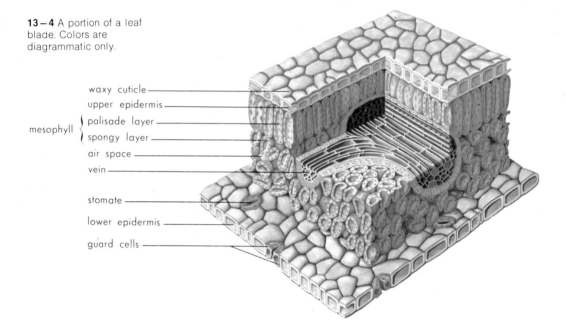

waxy cuticle

upper epidermis

mesophyll { palisade layer

spongy layer

air space

vein

stomate

lower epidermis

guard cells

mesophyll [MEZ uh fil; Greek: *meso*, middle, + *phyllon*, a leaf]

Photosynthesis occurs in the *mesophyll* cells (palisade and spongy tissues) which contain chloroplasts. The epidermis covers the leaf but allows light to pass through. Both of the raw materials of photosynthesis, H_2O and CO_2, are present in air. The amount of water vapor in the air varies a great deal. But, unless it is raining, water molecules are not as abundant in the air as in living leaf cells. Thus, according to the principle of diffusion, leaves should lose H_2O to the air.

The amount of CO_2 in the air normally does not vary much. But, depending on rates of respiration and photosynthesis, the amount of CO_2 does vary within chlorophyll-bearing cells. Therefore, CO_2 might either be given off or taken in by them. An exchange of gases between inner-leaf cells and the air is suggested by the many slitlike openings – *stomates* – in the epidermis. The stomates lead from the outside of a leaf through the leaf's surface and into the air spaces of the mesophyll. Gas exchange between inner-leaf cells and the air occurs through the stomates.

stomates [Greek: *stoma*, mouth]

Look at the tubular vein in figure 13–4. Water comes to the leaf from other parts of the plant by way of veins. Air contains less water than cells do. As air moves among mesophyll cells, water diffuses from these cells into the air, and the plant loses water. The drier the air, the more rapidly the water is lost.

Air enters and leaves through the stomates. Each stomate is surrounded by a pair of specialized cells called **guard cells.** The inner walls of the guard cells are thick. When the guard cells fill with water, they bend outward. As they bend, the stomate opens and air flows into and out of the leaf. When the water volume decreases, the stomates close and the air flow slows down.

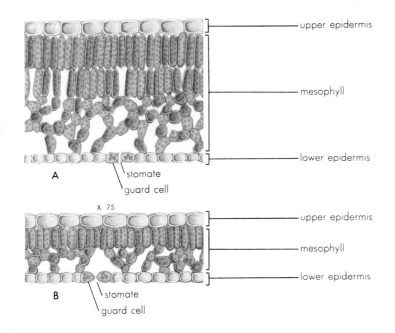

A

X 75

B

— upper epidermis

— mesophyll

— lower epidermis

stomate
guard cell

— upper epidermis

— mesophyll

— lower epidermis

stomate
guard cell

13–5 Leaves vary internally as well as externally. Sections through two leaves from one plant: (A) A leaf that was exposed to full sun. (B) A leaf that was shaded most of the day. How many structural differences can you see?

Experiments have shown that the bending of guard cells is related to the concentration of CO_2 dissolved in the cell. Evidence indicates that, as photosynthesis proceeds, the CO_2 level drops and the guard cells open. Botanists still have much to learn about how stomates work.

What other metabolic process in guard cells affects their supply of CO_2?

Land plants lose much water through the stomates of their leaves. They also lose some water through the epidermal cells of the whole shoot. Water loss from plants, through both stomates and epidermal cells, is called **transpiration.** This loss is greatly reduced, however, by the **cuticle.** The cuticle is a waxy layer that covers the epidermal cells. It is very thin in some cases, as on lettuce leaves, and rather thick in others, as on pine leaves and the shoots of cacti.

transpiration [Latin: *trans*, across, + *spirare*, to breathe]

cuticle [KYEWT ih kul; Latin: *cutis*, skin]

13–6 These are leaves of a carnivorous pitcher plant (*Darlingtonia californica*). The leaves are tubular with an opening just below the hood. Insects are attracted by nectar beneath the hood and fall into the leaf. Unable to escape, they are digested by bacteria and their nutrients are then absorbed by the leaf.

Douglas W. James, Jr.

CHECK YOURSELF

A. In what ways do the usual environments of a plant root and of a plant shoot differ?
B. On what basis can we call a leaf a plant organ?
C. In what ways do the external parts of leaves vary?
D. What characteristics of the internal structure of a leaf relate to photosynthesis?
E. What are the principal substances that pass into and out of plants through the leaves?
F. How do stomates function?
G. What is transpiration?

Investigation 13.1   GAS EXCHANGE AND PHOTOSYNTHESIS

INTRODUCTION

Following the principles of diffusion, carbon dioxide would normally flow into a leaf during the day and oxygen would flow out as photosynthesis proceeds. In this investigation, you will disrupt the normal gas exchange process and observe the effects.

PROCEDURE

A. Number of stomates

1. Tear a leaf at an angle while holding the lower surface upward. The tearing action should peel off a portion of the lower epidermis. It will appear as a narrow, colorless zone extending beyond the green part of the leaf.

2. Using a razor blade, cut off a small piece of this epidermis. Immediately place it in a drop of water on a slide. Add a cover slip. Do not allow the fragment to dry out.

3. Using the low-power objective of your microscope, locate some stomates. Then switch to the high-power objective. Make a sketch to show the shape of a stomate, its guard cells, and a few adjacent cells in the epidermis.

4. Count the number of stomates in 10 high-power fields of the microscope and average them. (Refer to Appendix 2 to calculate the diameter of the high-power field. Use this figure to calculate the area of the leaf observed under the microscope.) Calculate the average number of stomates per mm² of leaf surface.

5. In the same manner, count the stomates on the upper epidermis of the same leaf. Examine as many other kinds of leaves as possible. Compare the number of stomates per mm² on the upper and lower surfaces of each kind of leaf.

B. Light and photosynthesis

1. Select 2 healthy plants of the same species. Place one where it will receive no light. Place the other where it will be exposed to sunlight.

2. After 3 days remove a leaf from each plant. Place a small notch in the margin of the illuminated one.

3. Immediately drop the leaves into a beaker of boiling water.

4. When they are limp, transfer the leaves to a beaker half full of alcohol. Place this beaker in an electrically heated water bath. (*Caution: Never heat alcohol over an open flame or permit its vapor to come into contact with an open flame.*)

5. Heated alcohol extracts chlorophyll from leaves. It also makes them brittle, because most of their water is removed. As soon as the leaves are no longer green, use forceps to take them out of the alcohol. Then drop the leaves into a beaker of water at room temperature. After a minute or so, they will become quite soft.

6. Spread each leaf out in a petri dish and cover it with iodine solution.

7. Allow the iodine solution to act on the leaves for several minutes. Then remove both leaves. Rinse them in water, and spread them out in petri dishes of water placed on a piece of white paper. Record the color of each leaf.

MATERIALS
(per team)

For Part A

fresh leaves, several kinds
razor blade
microscope
microscope slide
cover slip
forceps
medicine dropper

For Part B

2 potted plants
alcohol (95%)
iodine solution
xylene
3 beakers, 400-ml
beaker, 1,000-ml
4 petri dishes
forceps
scissors
hot plate
water, at room temperature
petroleum jelly
paper towel
absorbent cotton
white paper

8. Select 4 similar leaves on the plant that has been kept in the dark. *Do not remove them from the plant.* Thoroughly coat the upper surface of one of these leaves with petroleum jelly. (A layer of petroleum jelly, though transparent, is a highly effective barrier across which many gases cannot pass.) Cut 1 notch in this leaf's margin.

9. Coat a 2nd leaf on its lower surface and cut 2 notches in its margin.

10. Coat a 3rd leaf on both upper and lower surfaces and cut 3 notches in its margin.

11. Do not coat the 4th leaf, but cut 4 notches in its margin. Place the plant where it will be exposed to sunlight.

12. After 3 days remove all 4 leaves and place them on paper towels. Remove the petroleum jelly by gently rubbing the leaves with absorbent cotton saturated with xylene.

13. Following the procedure used before,

perform the iodine test on each leaf. Compare the color reactions of the 4 leaves, and record your observations.

DISCUSSION

(*1*) How did the number of stomates per mm² in different areas of the same side of a piece of leaf epidermis compare? On opposite sides? (*2*) Did the stomates vary in the amount they were open? How can you explain this? (*3*) What would you do to assure a reliable comparison of the number of stomates per mm² for 2 species of plants?

(*4*) What do your data suggest about the distribution of stomates in leaves of your species of plant? (*5*) What assumption must you make in drawing this conclusion?

(*6*) What was the purpose of the 1st set of iodine tests? (*7*) If you use this test as an indication of photosynthetic activity, what assumption are you making?

(*8*) What is the purpose of the leaf that is marked with 4 notches?

(*9*) In which of the leaves coated with petroleum jelly did photosynthetic activity appear to have been greatest? (*10*) In which of the leaves did photosynthetic activity appear to have been least? Do your data support your hypothesis?

FOR FURTHER INVESTIGATION

Compare the number of stomates and their locations on leaves of 2 different species. Select one species that usually grows in full sunlight and one that grows in shade.

ROOTS

Terrestrial tracheophytes lose water mostly through their leaves. Except for epiphytes, all terrestrial plants obtain water from the soil through their roots. Along with the water, they absorb dissolved minerals. Roots have three additional functions: anchorage, food storage, and the transportation of water and minerals. Transportation will be discussed in connection with stems, which share this function.

Anchorage. Anyone who has pulled weeds in a garden knows that the roots of a plant anchor it firmly in the soil. In some species there are many thin and, often, short roots coming from the bottom of the plant. This is a *fibrous-root* system. It

13–7 Two kinds of root systems.

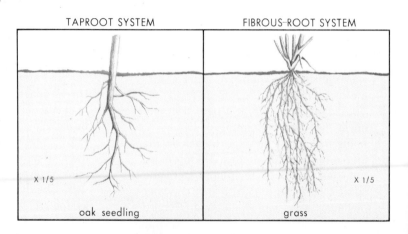

TAPROOT SYSTEM   FIBROUS-ROOT SYSTEM

X 1/5   X 1/5

oak seedling   grass

13—8 In some plants, such as this banyan tree in Florida, roots sprout from stems. Then they grow downward and penetrate into the soil.

is characteristic of plants such as corn, beans, and clover, for example. In other species the plant is anchored by a long, tapering root with slender, short, side branches. This is a *taproot* system, found in dandelions, mesquite, and carrots.

To what ecological conditions do you think each of these kinds of root systems is adapted?

If a plant is pulled up, most of its root system remains in the soil. But, if the soil is gently washed away by a stream of water, the smaller branch roots are not damaged. In this way the root system can be seen more completely. When its roots were carefully exposed, a rye plant 60 cm tall was estimated to have a root system with a total length of 480 km. The roots of this one plant had a total surface area of more than 600 m² — twice that of a tennis court!

Absorption. If radish seeds are germinated on moist paper in a petri dish, the young roots can be seen easily. The tip of a young root is pointed and bare. Just behind the tip is a fuzzy white region. As the root grows, this fuzzy zone seems to remain just behind the root tip.

13—9 A radish seedling. What part of the plant was first to emerge from the seed coat?   × 9

This zone looks fuzzy because it has many *root hairs.* Each root hair is a thin-walled extension of a single epidermal cell. The central part of a root-hair cell is occupied by a large vacuole filled with water and dissolved substances. Root hairs penetrate the spaces between soil particles and come in contact with soil water. Water and many other substances required by a plant flow into these root hairs.

Substances dissolved in soil water are seldom as concentrated as they are in the vacuole of a root hair. Because cell membranes are differentially permeable, many substances inside root-hair cells cannot pass out through the membranes. Under such conditions more water diffuses into the cell.

Thus, we can explain how the two materials required for photosynthesis get into land plants. Carbon dioxide enters chiefly through leaf cells by way of the stomates. Water enters a plant chiefly through the root hairs.

Review pages 367–369.

13–10 The terminal portion of a root. Colors are diagrammatic only.

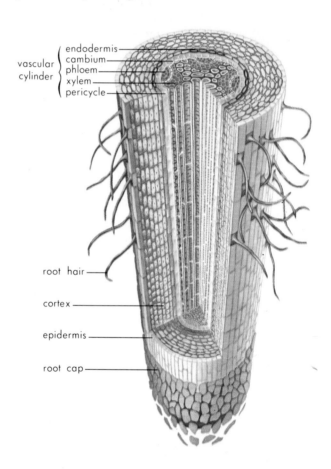

vascular cylinder {
endodermis
cambium
phloem
xylem
pericycle

root hair

cortex

epidermis

root cap

In addition to CO_2 and H_2O, a plant requires mineral nutrients. The elements needed enter with soil water as dissolved ions or compounds. Roots take in nitrogen, for example, in the form of ammonium or nitrate ions. These mineral nutrients are continually being used in the synthetic activities of a plant. They are usually less concentrated inside root-hair cells than in

Recall the roles of plants in the nitrogen cycle, figure 7–27.

the surrounding water, and they pass into the root hairs by diffusion.

Some substances needed by a plant may be more concentrated in root-hair cells than in soil water. Under these circumstances, absorption of minerals involves active transport as well as diffusion. Experiments have shown that plants can absorb substances that exist in very low concentrations in soil water. When dissolved substances are moved in a direction opposite to that of diffusion, cell respiration speeds up.

Water and mineral nutrients usually enter a plant through root-hair cells. On their inner sides these special epidermal cells are in contact with other root cells (figure 13–11). Absorbed substances move deeper into the root by diffusion or active transport from one layer of cells to another. Eventually, these substances reach the conducting cells. In these cells, the substances move to the stem and leaves.

Why is a speeding up of cell respiration in a root-hair cell an indication of active transport?

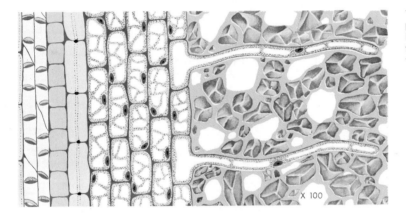

13–11 Root hairs penetrating into soil. On the left are conducting tissues of the root. Soil is shown as in figure 7–18.

Fibrous-root systems are relatively close to the soil surface. This means that rainwater does not have to penetrate the soil very deeply before it can be absorbed. Rainwater must penetrate soil further to be absorbed by a taproot system since the root hairs are deeper in the ground. On the other hand, taproots can use water sources that are deep in the soil.

Storage. The *cortex* of a young root may be shed as the root grows older, or it may form part of the bark around the older root. Sometimes a plant stores food in the cortex. Sometimes food is stored in modified conducting cells. Food usually is stored as starch, but sometimes as sugar. Carrots, radishes, and turnips are examples of storage roots.

What plant stores so much sugar in its root that we use it as a sugar source?

13–12 When large quantities of food are stored, both taproots (*left*) and fibrous roots (*right*) may be thickened.

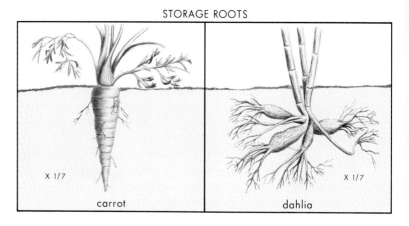

STORAGE ROOTS

X 1/7   carrot   dahlia   X 1/7

CHECK YOURSELF

H. What are the principal functions of a root?
I. How do fibrous-root and taproot systems differ?
J. Through what root structures does a plant take in most of its water and nutrients?
K. Describe the movement of water into a root.
L. What evidence indicates that absorption of substances from the soil involves more than simple diffusion?

STEMS

Can you name a plant that appears to have no stem?

The plant stem is usually the principal part of the shoot. It is the connection between the leaves and the roots. Botanists distinguish between a root and a stem by the arrangement of their tissues and by how they originate in embryos within seeds. The easiest way to make the distinction is to look for buds. Buds are found on stems, but not on roots. Each bud is a miniature shoot consisting of a short stem, tiny leaves, and sometimes flowers. The "eyes" of a white potato are really buds. The potato, therefore, is an underground stem. A sweet potato has no buds; it is a root. Most stems, however, grow above ground, supporting leaves and reproductive organs in light and air.

Macroscopic structure. Stems differ greatly in structure. Let us use a woody twig from a deciduous tree to discuss stem structure. Such a twig, when the leaves have fallen, usually has conspicuous buds. Growth from a terminal (tip) bud lengthens the twig. Growth from a lateral (side) bud starts a new branch. A bud may or may not be covered with protective scales (modified leaves). If present, scales fall off when growth starts in the spring.

terminal [Latin: *terminare,* to end, limit]

lateral [Latin: *latus,* a side]

Lenticels are small openings in the bark. Air diffuses into

lenticels [LENT uh selz]

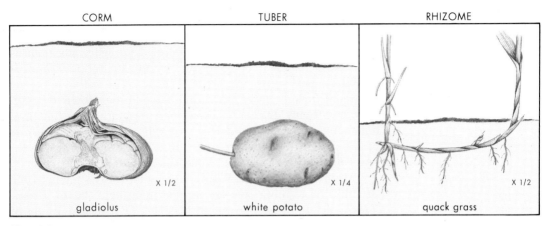

CORM

gladiolus

X 1/2

TUBER

white potato

X 1/4

RHIZOME

quack grass

X 1/2

13-13 Structural adaptations of underground stems. What do you think is the principal function of each kind?

13-14 An opening hickory bud.

Lynwood M. Chace

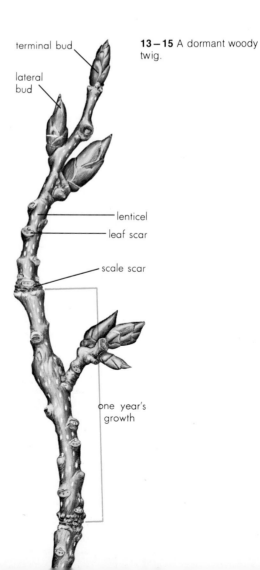

terminal bud

lateral bud

lenticel

leaf scar

scale scar

one year's growth

13-15 A dormant woody twig.

and out of the living cells through lenticels. Only the tissues of the inner bark and the outer part of the wood are alive. The rest of the wood and bark is composed of dead cell walls such as Hooke saw in cork. In cross section, wood usually shows annual growth rings.

Plant liquids move up through wood and down through bark. Eventually, the center wood loses its conducting function. It is then called *heartwood.* Heartwood may serve to support the upper parts of a tree, but some trees stand erect and live for years after much of the heartwood has rotted away.

Microscopic structure. Figure 13–16 shows the microscopic structure of a young stem in three dimensions. This is a stem from a dicot. By examining thin slices of different kinds of stems with a microscope, you can find — as with roots and leaves — that there are many variations. Much of the information about plant cellular structure has been studied by anatomists such as Katherine Esau. She has documented this information in her book, *The Anatomy of Seed Plants* (page 442).

Pith usually is present in young stems, but older plants in most species have none. The *cambium* tissue consists of cells

13–16 A young stem. Colors are diagrammatic only.

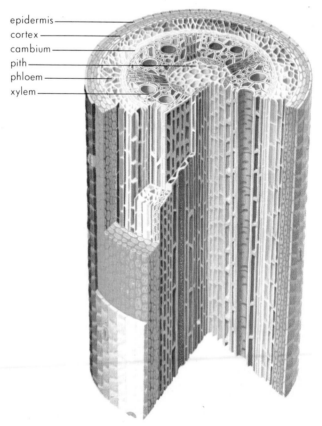

epidermis
cortex
cambium
pith
phloem
xylem

that divide and form other plant tissues. It lies just inside the bark. When a cambium cell divides into two new cells, one of these cells becomes a conducting or supporting cell. The other cell remains a part of the cambium tissue and divides again. *Xylem* cells are continually being formed at the inner surface of the cambium. Most of the stem eventually consists of xylem. *Phloem* is continually being formed at the outer surface of the

cambium [KAM bee um; Latin: *cambiare*, to exchange]

xylem [ZY lum; Greek: *xylon*, wood]

phloem [FLOH em; Greek: *phloos*, bark of a tree]

13–17 Section of a woody stem. How old was this tree? How many rings of heartwood are there? What separates bark from wood?

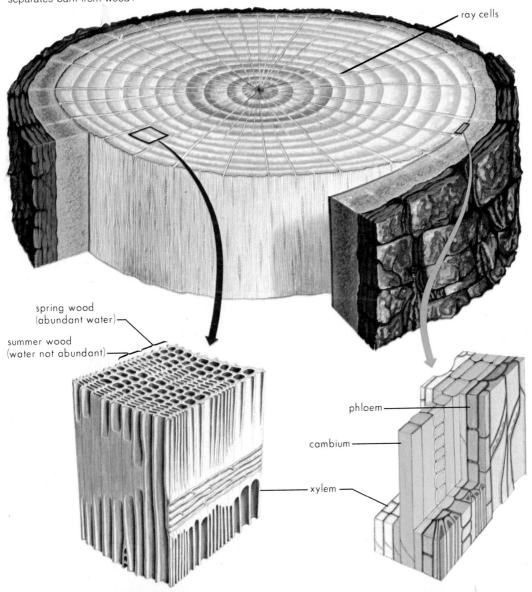

ray cells

spring wood (abundant water)

summer wood (water not abundant)

phloem

cambium

xylem

The fibers of some plant stems are commercially valuable. What is an example?

tracheids [TRAY kee udz; Greek: *tracheia*, windpipe]

Xylem is colored red in figures 13–4, 13–10, and 13–16.

nucleated: having a nucleus

cambium. Xylem and phloem are primarily vascular tissues, but they also contain *fiber* cells that strengthen the stem.

In some plants the xylem is made of **tracheids.** These are long cells with thick walls. Tracheids grow to their full size and then die. Thin areas in the walls of these dead cells are called *pits.* In most cases a pit in the upper end of one tracheid is closely paired with a pit in the lower, overlapping end of another tracheid. Through these pits, water and dissolved materials pass upward from one tracheid into another. Xylem also may consist of *vessels.* Each vessel is made of several long, thick-walled cells. These cells have no end walls — they are small tubes. Several are joined end to end to form one vessel that extends through the stem. As in tracheids, the living substance of these cells dies and disappears. Water and minerals move up the plant through tracheid cells or through vessels. In some plants the xylem contains both.

Food produced by photosynthesizing leaf cells is transported throughout the plant in the phloem. *Sieve cells* in the phloem form tubes. As each sieve cell develops, many small holes form in both end walls. These holes interconnect the cells. As a cell matures, its nucleus disintegrates. Located beside each sieve-tube cell is a smaller, nucleated *companion cell.* These cells are believed to regulate the sieve-tube cells.

13–18 Fibrovascular bundle in a cross section of a sunflower stem. In the bundle the dark outer region is composed of fiber tissue (*A*); next within is conductive phloem (*B*); and inside that, xylem (*C*).   × 290

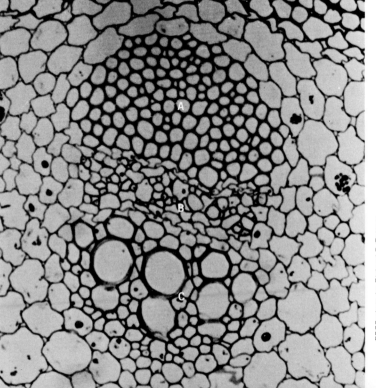

BSCS photo by Richard R. Tolman

American Forest Institute

13-19 A graduate student is using an increment borer to take a core of wood from a tree. The core can then be analyzed for growth rings without killing the tree. Forestry and horticulture personnel can tell much about a forest or an orchard by examining the growth rings.

13-20 Cells from conducting tissues of tracheophytes.

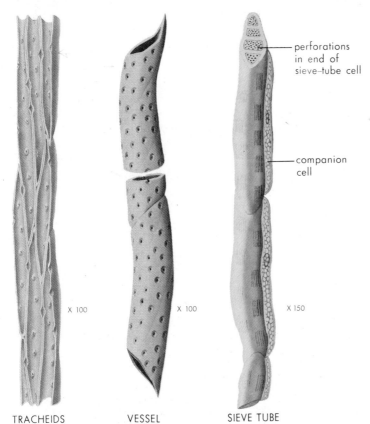

perforations in end of sieve-tube cell

companion cell

X 100   X 100   X 150

TRACHEIDS   VESSEL   SIEVE TUBE

13—21 These tall redwood trees in California tower 100 m over the car below.

adhere [ad HIR; Latin: *ad,* to, + *haerere,* to stick]

cohesion [koh HEE zhun; Latin: *cum,* with, together, + *haerere*]

13—22 An experiment on the rise of liquids in stems.

CONDUCTION

Imagine that you are standing with a long soda straw on top of a three-story building. The straw reaches down into a bottle of root beer on the ground. No matter how hard you try, you cannot suck the root beer up from the bottle. You could not do this even with a vacuum pump.

How, then, do water and dissolved materials move up the xylem? In the tallest trees, water moves up for over 100 m. Many experiments have shown that water from roots rises through root xylem to stem xylem to the xylem in the veins of leaves. This movement is *against* the force of gravity. Let us consider a theory to explain this movement.

Under certain conditions water can be pulled up a tube in a continuous column. One condition is that the tube must have a very small diameter. A second condition is that the tube must be made of a material to which water molecules will adhere. These conditions exist in the xylem tubes of plants. In addition, there is an attraction of water molecules for adjoining water molecules — *cohesion.* As a result of the cohesion of water molecules, an unbroken column of water is maintained in each xylem tube. As a result, when water molecules are lost by transpiration from the upper end of the column, in the leaves, a pull results. The pull is transmitted through the length of the column. In this way water from the roots moves up the plant to the leaves.

Some experimental results, however, do not fit this theory. If the shoot of a well-watered grapevine is cut off and a vertical glass tube is sealed to the rooted stump, fluid rises in the tube. In this situation one condition assumed in the transpiration-cohesion theory is lacking. There is no transpiration. Here it seems that the fluid rises because it is pushed from below rather than pulled from above. This push has been called *root pressure.* Measurements of the force of root pressure have indicated that water might be pushed to a height of 90 m under some conditions.

In spite of these measurements, however, plant physiologists doubt that root pressure is an important factor in the rise of liquids in plants. For one thing, not all plants develop root pressure when their shoots are cut. Some plants that do not are tall trees. And, in plants that develop root pressure, the pressure is lowest in the summer. This is when the largest volume of water is being transported. As yet no botanist has fully explained where the force of root pressure comes from.

You might think the downward movement of photosynthetic products (food) in the phloem is easily explained. Gravity alone might be the cause. But the sieve cells of the phloem are not just empty tubes. They contain living cytoplasm through which liquids must pass. Of course, substances could diffuse through cytoplasm. However, the rate at which the fluid moves through phloem is thousands of times faster than diffusion could account for. And in many cases the direction of movement is from a lesser to a greater concentration— *opposite* to that of diffusion. Some kind of active transport may be involved.

Materials in solution move up or down the stems of plants through the xylem and the phloem. Water, minerals, and food also move sideways through the *ray cells.* Figure 13–17 shows how these ray cells are arranged in relation to the xylem and phloem. Pits in the walls of the ray cells communicate with pores in both the xylem and phloem. Water and minerals are supplied to the phloem. Food material is supplied to dividing cambium cells as they enlarge to form plant tissue.

Conduction of liquids is the main function of stems. But, in most plants, stems also perform other functions. Some stems carry on photosynthesis. In most herbs photosynthesis occurs in chlorophyll-bearing cells just beneath the stem epidermis. Even in woody plants young twigs contain photosynthetic tissues. In most terrestrial plants mature stems are not involved in photosynthesis. However, they make food production possible by conducting water to photosynthetic tissue and by supporting leaves where they may be exposed to sunlight. In many plants, stems also serve as storage organs. Sugarcane plants store sucrose in their stems. Large quantities of water and food are stored in most cactus stems.

X 1/10

13–23 Bark and cambium were removed from a strip around the trunk of this tree a year before the top was cut off. Can you explain this result?

What are some kinds of plants that carry on most of their photosynthesis in mature stems?

Can you give an example of a stem that seems to have a storage function but no conduction or support functions?

13–24 Storage stem of a South African plant. In this environment what do you think might be the chief substance stored?

Robert J. Rodin

CHECK YOURSELF

M. What is the easiest way to distinguish a stem from a root?

N. How does growth from a terminal bud differ from growth from a lateral bud?

O. What is the function of lenticels?

P. What is the main function of cambium tissue?

Q. What are the principal differences between xylem and phloem?

R. Using your own words, explain the theory of conduction.

S. Why is root pressure unsatisfactory as a complete explanation for the rise of liquids in stems?

T. How does conduction occur through phloem tissue?

U. Summarize the functions that plant stems perform.

Investigation 13.2   WATER AND TURGOR PRESSURE

INTRODUCTION

Some plants maintain a position above ground, resisting the forces of gravity, wind, rain, and snow, because of the rigidity (firmness) of the plant body. This is true in woody plants in which much of the body consists of nonliving thickened cell walls.

In herbs many cell walls are thin and structurally weak. Their support depends on **turgor pressure.** This is the pressure that the contents of individual cells exert against their walls. Turgor pressure varies as the volume of the cell contents changes as a result of water being taken in or lost. In such plants, maintaining position is directly related to maintaining shape, which depends on turgor pressure. Turgor pressure, in turn, depends on the water relationships of individual cells.

Read the procedure. (1) Then state a hypothesis appropriate to the design of the experiment.

PROCEDURE

1. Using the knife, cut off one end of a potato, perpendicular to its long axis. Then make another cut parallel to the first one about 7 cm from it. Discard the end pieces.
2. Place one cut surface on top of the cardboard square on the laboratory table. Cut a core of tissue by forcing the cork borer down through the potato, with a twisting motion. Then, using the rod, force the core out of the borer into the bottom half of a petri dish. Repeat this coring procedure 3 more times.
3. Place the cores in petri dishes. Line up the dishes and label them *0.0 M, 0.2 M, 0.4 M, 0.6 M.* (M = **molar.**) A molar solution (1.0 M) of sucrose contains 342 g of this sugar per liter.
4. Weigh and record the mass of each core.

MATERIALS
(per team)

white potato, large
sucrose solutions, 0.2 M, 0.4
  M, 0.6 M, 75 ml of each
4 petri dishes, 100 × 20 mm
beaker, 250-ml
balance
knife, with 12-cm blade
cork borer, 1-cm diameter,
  with rod
metric scale, graduated in ml
heavy cardboard, 15-cm
  square
glass-marking crayon
paper towels
graph paper
refrigerator
metric ruler
distilled water

Measure and record the length of each core. Determine the rigidity of each core by holding it at each end between your fingertips and *gently* bending it. (2) Are there any marked differences in rigidity among the cores? If so, record them. Replace each core in its dish.
5. Now add to Dish 0.0 M enough water to cover the core. Add to each of the other 3 dishes enough of the appropriate sucrose solutions to cover the cores.
6. After 30 minutes remove the core from Dish 0.0 M. Dry it gently by rolling it between 2 pieces of paper towel and lightly pressing each end on the paper. Repeat for each of the other cores.
7. Determine whether there has been any change in rigidity among the cores. If so, devise a system to describe the differences and record them.
8. Return each core to its dish. Then place the dishes in a refrigerator.
9. After 24 hours remove the dishes from the refrigerator. Repeat the drying procedure for each core and immediately

determine and record rigidity, mass, and length.

10. Calculate the differences, if any, between initial and final mass and initial and final lengths of each core. Record these, using a + sign to indicate increase and a − sign to indicate decrease.

11. Graph these differences, using a grid as shown in figure 13–25.

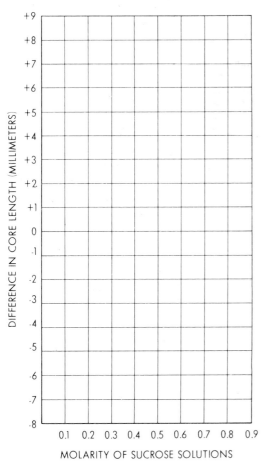

MOLARITY OF SUCROSE SOLUTIONS

DISCUSSION

Review the discussion of diffusion in Chapter 11, pages 367–369, and in Investigation 11.2. Cell membranes of potato are highly permeable to water and highly impermeable to sucrose molecules. The thin cell walls are highly permeable to both. The walls of these cells can be stretched or contracted only to a limited extent. Their shape when contracted, however, can be readily changed. (3) On what basis can you explain differences in rigidity, if any, among the cores placed in various concentrations of sucrose? For each of the cores, compare the rigidity change, if any, after 30 minutes. (4) Which core showed the greatest change in rigidity? (5) Which showed the least change?

(6) Is there any relationship between your observations on rigidity and differences between initial and final lengths of the cores? If so, explain. (7) Between initial and final mass? If so, explain.

(8) Do your data support the hypothesis you stated at the beginning of this investigation? (9) What is the relationship between water content and rigidity of plant structures that have thin-walled cells?

FOR FURTHER INVESTIGATION

1. Using the same experimental approach, investigate the effects of sucrose solutions having concentrations of 0.8 M and 1.0 M. Compare data obtained with those derived from your original experiment.

2. Investigate the effects on elodea leaves of sucrose solutions of the same range of concentrations as used in this investigation. Mount detached leaves on a microscope slide in the sugar solution, and add a cover slip. Observe this first under low power and then under high power for 5 minutes.

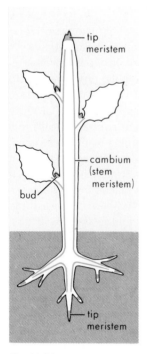

13–26 Diagram showing location of principal meristems.

meristem [MER uh stem; Greek: *meristos,* divided]. Note that there is no relation to the word "stem."

These leaves can increase in length even after most of the blade has been cut off by a grazing animal or a lawn mower.

GROWTH

Mammals, birds, and insects have definite limits to growth. Many other animals and all multicellular plants continue to grow throughout their lives—usually at a decreasing rate. But there is a fundamental difference between growth in animals and growth in multicellular plants. Most kinds of animal cells retain the ability to duplicate even after they differentiate. In vascular plants, however, cells that have differentiated do not duplicate.

Meristems. Each cell of xylem, phloem, and mesophyll tissues is formed from *meristem* tissue. The cambium is one type of meristem tissue. A meristem is undifferentiated tissue that continues mitosis and cell division as long as the plant lives. Meristematic tissue is found in many places of a living plant.

In roots a meristem is located just behind the *root cap,* the protective cells covering a root tip (figure 13–10). Part of this meristem forms root-cap cells at the tip. These cells do not accumulate. They are rubbed off as the root pushes through the soil. This meristem also forms cells that differentiate into specialized root tissues. These tissues become a permanent part of the root.

As the stem of a plant grows longer, the tissue at its tip remains meristematic. Small masses of meristem also are left behind. From these, branches and leaves develop. Each branch has a meristem at its tip. In most leaves, however, all the cells differentiate into the leaf tissues (including xylem, phloem, and mesophyll) at an early stage in leaf formation. In late summer deciduous woody plants develop tiny, but fully formed, leaves inside a bud. In spring the new leaves expand mostly by the enlargement of the small cells in the bud. Leaves of grasses and some other plants are an exception. These leaves grow continually from a meristem at the base of the leaf.

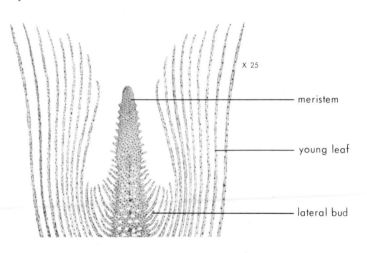

X 25

— meristem

— young leaf

— lateral bud

13–27 Tip of an elodea shoot.

Not all the cells left behind along a growing root or stem branch off or differentiate. The cambium in vascular plants, except in monocots, remains around the entire length of each stem and root. From the cambium new xylem and phloem are formed. This increases the diameter of the stems and roots. Cambium remains as a boundary between the central core of wood (xylem) and the bark (phloem). Bark can usually be peeled from a tree trunk rather easily, because the walls of cambium cells are thin and easily broken (figure 13–17).

Investigation 13.3   ROOT GROWTH

INTRODUCTION

In this investigation, you will observe the growth patterns of corn seedlings just a few days after they have germinated. Are all parts of the root involved in growth? Do any parts of the root grow faster than others?

PROCEDURE

1. Place a piece of filter paper in the bottom of each of 2 petri dishes marked with your team's symbol. Add distilled water to dampen the paper. Pour off any excess water.
2. Select 4 seedlings. Using a Magic Marker with a fine tip, carefully mark the shortest root with a straight, very narrow line exactly 2 mm from the tip. (You don't have to mark the entire circumference of the root.) Be careful not to crush or damage the root. Draw as many lines as possible, 2 mm apart, behind this first mark. Repeat for the other 3 roots. All roots should have the same number of marks.
3. Measure the distance from the tip to the last mark. This is the initial root length.
4. Carefully place your 4 marked seedlings on the moist filter paper in one of the petri dishes. Place them so that the markings are visible.
5. Mark the remaining 8 seedlings as fol-

MATERIALS
(per team)

2 petri dishes
4 pieces filter paper (to fit petri dishes)
12 germinated corn seeds
glass-marking crayon
Magic Marker with fine tip
distilled water
razor blade
8 cardboard tags
metric ruler

lows: Using the Magic Marker, place a dot 5 mm from the tip of each root. Be sure to handle the roots carefully, and don't let them dry out.

6. Using a razor blade, cut off 1 mm of the tip of 2 corn seedling roots; cut off 3 mm of the roots of 2 others; cut off 5 mm of 2 others. Leave the remaining 2 seedlings untreated.
7. Label each seedling as to the amount of root cut off. To do this, use a small cardboard tag tied to each seedling. Place all of these seedlings in the other petri dish.
8. Cover the seedlings in both dishes with a piece of filter paper. Add water to moisten them. Press down lightly to insure that the paper is firmly placed in the dishes. Then pour off any excess

water. Place the dishes away from direct sunlight and heat. Do not let the paper dry out during the experiment.

9. After 24 hours, uncover the first seedlings you prepared. Examine each seedling. Measure the distance between the tip of the root and the last mark. Measure the distances between each of the lines, in order, from the tip to the base. Record your measurements.

10. Note the appearance of all the lines. (1) Are all the lines as clear as they were yesterday?

11. Discard these seedlings, and clean or discard the dishes.

DISCUSSION

Add together the lengths of all 4 roots, from tip to last mark. Divide by 4. Subtract from this length the initial root length in step 3. (2) What is this average amount of growth for each seedling?

(3) In your roots, did growth occur at the tip, at the base, or all along the root? (4) How much growth occurred between the tip of the root and the first mark? (5) Between the last 2 marks? (6) How do you explain the smears or wider marks at or near the tip of the roots? (7) On the basis of these results, what do you predict will be the results of cutting off the root tips?

PROCEDURE

12. After 2 days, examine the roots in the other petri dish. Measure and record the distance from the original 5-mm mark to the tip of the root for each seedling.

13. Discard the seedlings and clean or discard the dish.

DISCUSSION

Add the measurements for the 2 seedlings that were not cut and determine the average. (8) Has there been any growth in these 2 seedlings? (9) Prepare a bar graph of the class data showing the amount of growth of the roots cut at 1 mm, 3 mm, and 5 mm. Compare with the growth of the uncut roots.

(10) How important is the tip for growth of the root? (11) What information do these observations give you that the earlier observations did not? (12) Predict what would happen if you grew these roots for a longer period of time.

FOR FURTHER INVESTIGATION

1. Is the growth pattern of peas or beans the same as that of corn? Germinate some of these seeds and conduct the same experiment as you did on corn.

2. Design and carry out an experiment to measure the growth rate of a leaf of a common houseplant.

phototropism [foh TAH truh pizum; Greek: *photos*, light, + *tropos*, turning]

Charles Darwin: 1809–1882. English naturalist, author of *The Origin of Species*

Chemical control of growth. For a long time it has been known that most green plants grow toward light. This response is often called **phototropism.** It is easily observed in plants growing on windowsills, where the most intense light comes from one side. A century ago Charles Darwin investigated this response. From previous studies he knew that several zones could be distinguished in a developing plant stem. At the tip is the meristem. Just behind it is a *zone of elongation* in which the newly formed cells grow longer. Behind this is a zone in which the cells become differentiated.

13 – 28 Most of the branches on these trees point in one direction. Do you think this is due to phototropism?

Darwin observed that bending toward light does not occur at the very tip. It occurs in the zone of elongation, a few millimeters behind the tip. He experimented with seedlings of grasses and oats. These seedlings have a closed tubular structure called a **coleoptile** within which the first leaves develop. Darwin placed tiny caps over the tips of the coleoptiles. No light could penetrate the caps. None of the seedlings bent. Darwin concluded that "when seedlings are freely exposed to a lateral light some influence is transmitted from the upper to the lower part, causing the latter to bend."

coleoptile [koh lee OP tul; Greek: *koleos*, sheath, + *ptilon*, feather]

Further investigation by others suggested that a chemical moved from the tip to the zone of elongation. Oat seedlings were placed in a container that provided light from only one side. The coleoptile tips of some were cut off and others were left intact. The intact seedlings bent toward the light source. The tipless seedlings grew straight up. Gelatin was used to fasten the cutoff tips back on to the tipless coleoptiles. These seedlings began to bend toward light just as the intact plants did. It was concluded that the chemical that caused the bending passed from the tip through the gelatin into the coleoptile below. (See figure 13–29, A and B.)

intact [in TAKT; Latin: *in*, not, + *tangere*, to touch]: here, whole, uncut

How does the chemical substance cause the bending toward the light? To investigate this question, thin pieces of mica were inserted *halfway* through oat coleoptiles, just behind the tips. It was assumed that the chemical substance could not pass through mica as it had through gelatin. When the seedlings were placed so that the mica was toward the light source, they bent toward it. When they were placed with the mica away from the light, they did not bend. These results indicated that some substance produced in the tip moved down the coleoptile on the side *away from* the light. This substance caused the cells on that side to lengthen, forcing the plant to bend toward the light. (See figure 13–29, C and D.)

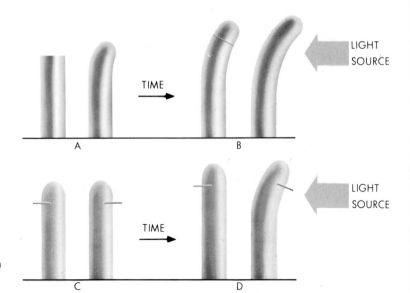

13—29 Two experiments with grass seedlings and light.

In another experiment, tips of oat coleoptiles were cut off and placed on thin layers of agar. The tips were removed from the agar and discarded. The agar was then cut into blocks. Each small agar block was placed on the *edge* of a seedling stump. *Without* exposure to light, the seedling bent. It always bent away from the side on which the piece of agar was placed. Evidently the substance in the tip had first diffused into the agar and then from the agar into the coleoptile.

13—30 An experiment with seedling tips and agar.

LAYER OF AGAR
WITH SEEDLING TIPS

TIPS REMOVED AND AGAR
CUT INTO SMALL BLOCKS

Leaves pulled out
to support agar block

AGAR BLOCK ATTACHED
TO TIP OF SEEDLING

Because the substance produced in the seedling tip stimulated increased elongation, it has been referred to as a growth substance. It was named **auxin.** Scientists later found that there were several kinds of natural auxins. Some of these are effective in very tiny amounts.

auxin [OK sun; Greek: *auxein,* to increase, grow]

Many artificial chemical substances have similar effects. One, called 2,4-D, stimulates growth when used in small quantities. In larger quantities, however, it may kill many kinds of

How might a growth substance kill a plant when present in large quantities?

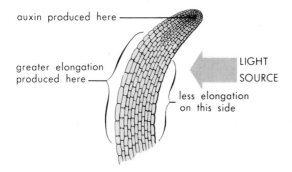

auxin produced here —————

greater elongation
produced here ————

less elongation
on this side

LIGHT
SOURCE

13—31 Differential
elongation of cells on
opposite sides of a shoot
produces bending.

plants. Since, at the concentrations generally used, it does not affect members of the grass family, it is used to control weeds in lawns and grain fields.

There are other naturally occurring growth substances. Many years ago Japanese rice farmers noticed that rice plants sometimes grow gigantically tall and then fall over and die. Japanese botanists found that these *bakanae* ("silly seedlings") are infected with a fungus. They studied the disease and discovered that growth substances (called *gibberellins*) are formed by the fungus. Gibberellins bring about the strange growth of rice. It is now known that some vascular plants and algae also produce gibberellins. When treated with gibberellins, many kinds of plants grow to double or triple their normal height. Many species, however, are only slightly affected by such treatment. The study of gibberellins and their many effects is an active field of botanical research.

bakanae [bok ah nah ee]

gibberellins [jib ur EL inz; named after the fungi in which they were first found, the genus *Gibberella*]

13—32 The top row of holly cuttings was treated with an auxin. The bottom row was not treated. How might this growth substance be used commercially?

USDA

See Chapter 5 and Appendix 3 for illustrations of nonvascular plants.

NONVASCULAR PLANTS

The majority of multicellular plants are tracheophytes. However, mosses, many algae, and most fungi are also multicellular. They carry on the same basic functions as tracheophytes — absorption of nutrients, transportation of dissolved substances, storage of food, and growth. These plants, however, lack vascular tissues.

Many mosses appear to have roots, stems, and leaves. Microscopically, however, none of these parts resembles the roots, stems, and leaves of tracheophytes. Botanists use the terms "root," "stem," and "leaf" to indicate organs with vascular tissues. These words, therefore, should not be used in describing mosses.

More important than the names of the structures, however, is the effect that the lack of vascular tissues has on the physiology of these plants. A few mosses live in water, but most are land plants, getting their water from soil. Because they lack vascular tissues that carry water upward, they do not grow higher than 40 cm. They reach such heights only in environments with a high humidity and where transpiration rates are very low. Many mosses become dormant when the water supply is low. Such species survive in some very dry places, such as in deserts and small crevices in rocks. There they grow actively only during a few days after each rain.

13 – 33 Liverworts — nonvascular plants.

G. E. Johnson

Multicellular algae also lack vascular systems. Because they live in water, however, this does not hinder their growth. Indeed, some brown algae reach a length of 45 m, which is far longer than most middle-latitude deciduous trees are tall. Such seaweeds are only a few centimeters thick. This means that none of their cells are far from the surrounding water and its minerals.

See figure 9–30.

All algae carry on photosynthesis. Many contain chlorophylls that are different from those of the tracheophytes and mosses. But the biochemistry of photosynthesis seems to be similar. Most groups of algae have a useful classification characteristic — the kind of food they store. Although most plants store food mainly as starch, algae store it as other polysaccharides or as oils.

What can you predict about the height of fungal stalks above ground level?

Fungi also lack conducting tissues. But the lack of chlorophyll is a more distinctive characteristic in their physiology. Fungi, like animals and many protists, are consumers. They obtain their energy from food that they get from the environment. Unlike animals, however, they seldom need to take in such molecules as amino acids. Like other plants, they are able to synthesize most of the organic substances they require from the food they take in.

CHECK YOURSELF

V.   How does growth in plants and animals differ?

W.   Where are meristems located in vascular plants?

X.   Why is bark usually easy to peel from a woody stem?

Y.   What is phototropism?

Z.   How did Darwin study phototropism?

AA. Describe an experiment to demonstrate that shoot-tip tissue produces a substance causing elongation of stem cells.

BB. In what way do gibberellins resemble auxins?

CC. What seems to be the principal reason that mosses never grow very tall?

DD. How can some algae grow to very great lengths without vascular systems?

EE. How do fungi metabolically resemble both animals and plants?

PROBLEMS

1. Water-lily plants are rooted in mud at the bottom of ponds, but their leaves float on the water surface. How might the cellular structure of the roots, stems, and leaves of water lilies differ from that in terrestrial tracheophytes?

2. A few species of tracheophytes do not carry on photosynthesis. In what ways might you expect their roots, stems, and leaves to differ from those of the photosynthetic tracheophytes?

3. How is the gas exchange between an underground root and its environment different from the gas exchange between a leaf (in sunlight) and its environment?

4. During the growing season farmers spend considerable time cultivating their crops—loosening the soil between plants. What advantage does this have for the crop plants?

5. Ten years ago a farmer built a fence 1.5 m high and attached one end of it to a tree that was 7 m high. Now the tree has grown to a height of 14 m. How far above the ground is the attached end of the fence? Explain.

6. The following questions concern lateral growth in woody stems: (a) How is an annual ring formed in the wood of a tree? (b) Within a given biome, how would the annual ring formed in a wet year differ from one formed in a dry year? (c) Sometimes two rings are formed in one year. How might this happen? (d) What is the science of dendrochronology and how is it used? (e) What happens to phloem as the trunk of a tree increases in diameter? (f) Would you expect to find annual rings in the bark of a tree?

7. Investigate careers related to vascular plants. How many careers can you identify that are based on vascular plants? Report your findings to the class.

8. In a middle-latitude biome a pine and an apple tree are growing side by side. Compare amounts of water lost by these two trees throughout the year.

SUGGESTED READINGS

Esau, K. 1977. *The Anatomy of Seed Plants*. 2nd ed. John Wiley & Sons, New York. A basic introductory text including the relation between structure and function.

Fogg, G. E. 1975. *Growth of Plants*. Penguin Books, New York. Though growth is the focus of attention, all phases of plant physiology are discussed. Somewhat advanced.

Galston, A. W., P. J. Davies, R. L. Satter. 1980. *The Life of the Green Plant*. 3rd ed. Prentice-Hall, Englewood Cliffs, N. J. The basic structure and function of higher-level green plants.

Heslop-Harrison, Y. 1978. Carnivorous Plants. *Scientific American*, February. Plants that add to their nutrients from animal sources may help meet soil deficiencies.

Lee, Addison. 1963. *Plant Growth and Development*. A BSCS Laboratory Block. D. C. Heath, Lexington, Mass.

Rahn, J. E. 1978. *Watch It Grow, Watch It Change*. Atheneum, New York. Describes changes in plants over a single growing season.

Schery, R. W. 1972. *Plants for Man*. 2nd ed. Prentice-Hall, Englewood Cliffs, N. J.

Street, H. E. and H. Opik. 1976. *The Physiology of Flowering Plants*. 2nd ed. University Park Press, Baltimore. Growth and development. Intended primarily as an introductory botany text.

Chapter 14

Functioning Animals

YOUR GUIDEPOSTS

In this chapter you will have an opportunity to explore these questions in biology:

- How do animals get their energy?
- How do the carbon dioxide—oxygen exchange systems of animals differ from those of plants?
- How do animals get rid of metabolic wastes?
- How do animals regulate their internal environment in a constantly changing external environment?
- How do muscles and bones enable humans to move?

Investigation 14.1   ANIMAL STRUCTURE AND FUNCTION

MATERIALS
(per class)

2 aquariums, each at least 60 cm long,
   containing water to a depth of 10 cm
refrigerator

(per team)

For Procedure A

live frog
60 cm gauze bandage

For Procedure B

pithed frog
sodium chloride crystals
warm sugar solution (0.2% sucrose)
saline solution (0.7% sodium chloride)
petri dish
pipette
medicine dropper

monocular microscope
microscope slide
2 forceps
scalpel
dissecting pan
distilled water
scissors
watch with second hand
glass-marking crayon
paper towels
plastic bag
rubber band
10 pins

For Procedure C

frog (from Procedure B)
dissecting pan
10 pins
forceps
hand lens
scissors

INTRODUCTION

No one species can fully illustrate animal structure and function. But frogs have some advantages. They are vertebrates — enough like ourselves to throw some light on our own structure and function. Yet they are sufficiently unlike us to provide some important contrasts.

PROCEDURE A

1. Moisten the top of the table where you will place the frog. A piece of gauze bandage has been tied to one of the frog's legs. Tie the loose end of the gauze to a table leg or some other fixed object. Sit quietly and allow the frog to become accustomed to its surroundings. If you remain quiet, you will increase your chances for making accurate observations.

2. Compare the frog's body with your own. Think of your body as having a head, neck, trunk, and 4 appendages — arms and legs. (1) Are any of these lacking in the frog? If so, which? Consider a cat, a cow, or a lizard. (2) What other body structure is present in these but absent in both the frog and you? (3) What kind of symmetry does the frog's body have? What kind does your body have?

3. (4) How do the frog's eyes differ from yours? Its ears are located behind and below its eyes. Its eardrums are stretched across the ear openings. (5) How do your ears differ from the frog's? (6) How does the frog's skin differ from yours?

4. Each of your upper appendages consists of an upper arm, forearm, wrist, hand, and fingers. Each of your lower appendages consists of a thigh, shank, ankle, foot, and toes. (7) Are any of these parts lacking in the appendages of the frog? If so, which? (8) In what ways do the *terminal* parts (those that are farthest from the trunk) of the frog's appendages differ from yours?

5. Using the eraser end of a pencil, *gently* prod the frog until it jumps. (9) What is the function of each pair of appendages in jumping? You can leap somewhat as the frog does, but the frog cannot stand erect as you do. (10) By examining the structure of the frog's legs and trunk, give evidence to support the preceding statement.

6. You must watch very carefully to see how the frog breathes. First locate its nostrils. (Ducts lead from them to its mouth.) Then, without touching the frog, watch the floor of its mouth. When the floor is lowered, the mouth cavity enlarges. (11) Where does the air that fills the enlarged mouth cavity come in? Observe the motion of the nostrils. (12) How does this motion relate to that of the floor of the mouth? (13) As the floor of the mouth is raised, where must the air in the mouth cavity go? (14) When you breathe, where does the principal motion occur? (15) Can you breathe with your mouth open? Can the frog?

7. Remove the gauze bandage from the frog's leg. Place the frog in the water at one end of a large aquarium. Watch it swim. (16) How does it use its toes in swimming? (17) What structures are associated with the toes in swimming? (18) Are these structures present on the fingers? Try to get the frog to float. (19) What is the position of its eyes, ears, and nostrils with respect to the surface of the water? Hold the frog underwater for 1 minute. This will not hurt the frog. (20) Do you observe any breathing movements? Try to explain. (21) While the frog is underwater, do you see any eye structure that you lack? If so, describe it. Return the frog to the container designated by your teacher.

PROCEDURE B

1. Each team will receive a frog in which the brain and spinal cord have been destroyed — a **pithed** frog. Such an animal has no sense of feeling. However, its tissues remain active for a number of hours. Thus you can observe several functions.

2. Place the frog on the dissecting pan, ventral side up. Fasten it to the wax in the pan by inserting pins through the ends of the appendages and into the wax. The frog's skin is attached quite loosely to its muscles. With forceps, hold the skin free from the muscles of the ventral body wall. Use scissors to make a small crosswise cut through the skin at the midline of the abdomen (figure 14–1A). Insert one tip of the scissors into this opening, and cut anteriorly (toward the head) along the midline of the body to the throat region. Then cut posteriorly along the midline as far as possible (figure 14–1B).

3. Cut laterally from the ends of the incision you just made (figure 14–1C). Two flaps of skin can now be opened and pinned to the sides (figure 14–1D). Use a scalpel to separate the skin from the body wall.

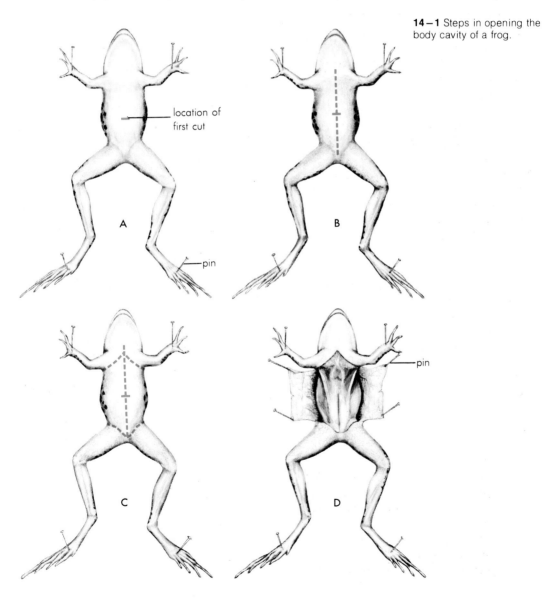

14–1 Steps in opening the body cavity of a frog.

location of first cut

pin

A

B

pin

C

D

4. Open the muscular body wall, following the procedure you used to open the skin. The organs of the body cavity lie just inside the body wall. Lift the body wall from the organs beneath. Insert only the *tip* of your scissors when cutting. As you cut anteriorly, you will run into the breastbone. In opening the body wall laterally, you may need to remove about 8 mm of the breastbone. Some effort may be required to open the body wall at the anterior end.

5. Observe the heart beating. (*22*) How many times does it contract per minute? Carefully slit the thin, transparent membrane that surrounds the heart. (*23*) Do the contractions travel in any particular direction?

6. Open the mouth. Locate a slitlike opening in the floor of the mouth. Insert one end of a pipette into the opening. Blow *gently* on the other end of the pipette. If you have located the correct opening, the lungs will become inflated. (*24*) Describe their appearance.

7. Female frogs may contain so many eggs that it is difficult to see the organs in the posterior part of the body. In this case, use forceps to pick the eggs out carefully. Attached to the egg masses are white, coiled tubes through which the eggs pass when they are laid. Remove these also.

8. Sprinkle a few crystals of NaCl along the surface of the intestine. Observe for at least 2 minutes. (*25*) Describe any movements of the intestine.

9. Using scissors, snip across the small intestine about 1.5 cm from the stomach and the same distance from the large intestine. Free the small intestine from the *mesentery*—the membrane that holds it in place. Drop the intestine into a petri dish containing distilled water. (*26*) Describe any reaction.

10. Cut off a piece of the intestine about 5 mm long. Slit the piece open and spread it out, inner side up, on a slide. Add a drop or two of warm sugar solution. Observe (without a cover slip) under low power of a monocular microscope. Note the small projections on the inner wall of the intestine. (*27*) Describe their activity.

11. Remove the pins from the frog. Close the body wall and the skin over the body cavity. Wrap the frog in a paper towel that has been dipped in saline solution. Mark a plastic bag with your team symbol. Place the frog in the bag. Fasten the bag with a rubber band, and store in a refrigerator.

PROCEDURE C

1. Remove the frog from the plastic bag and paper towel. Pin it to the dissecting pan, as in Procedure B.

2. Just posterior to the heart is the reddish-brown liver. (*28*) How many sections does it have? On the frog's right side the liver covers the **gall bladder.** Using forceps, raise the liver and find the gall bladder. (*29*) What color is it?

3. On the left side the liver partially covers the stomach. The diameter of the stomach depends on the amount of food it contains. (*30*) Toward which side does the stomach curve from anterior to posterior end? At its posterior end the stomach leads into the small intestine. These 2 portions of the alimentary canal (digestive tract) join together. At this point a narrow constriction, the **pyloric valve,** is visible. Between the inner edge of the curved stomach and the first loop of the intestine is the long, light-colored **pancreas.** Nearby, within the mesentery, is a dark organ, the **spleen.** (*31*) What is its shape?

4. After you have located these organs, remove the stomach. Using scissors, slit the stomach along its outer curve and spread it open. Observe the inner surface with a hand lens. (*32*) Describe this surface.

5. You have already removed most of the small intestine. Now push the mesentery

and the remaining organs aside and look for the kidneys. They are reddish-brown and attached to the back. (33) Describe their shape. Using a hand lens, locate the thin tube that leads from the posterior end of each kidney. (34) To what does it lead?

6. Dispose of your frog as directed by your teacher.

DISCUSSION

(35) On the basis of this investigation and your understanding of your own body, write a brief comparison of the structures and functions of a frog and a human.

FOR FURTHER INVESTIGATION

1. Divide a group of live frogs into two sets, each containing the same number of individuals. Weigh and mark each frog. Leave one set overnight in a container with a small amount of water. Leave the other overnight in a container without water. The next day weigh all frogs again. Compare the data from the sets of frogs. Suggest an explanation.

2. Prepare one of the dead frogs as a skeleton. First, using scalpel and forceps, remove as much flesh as possible. This may be difficult because many of the bones are small and delicate. Be careful not to cut through the small ones in the appendages and the thin ones in the head. Second, gently simmer the roughed-out skeleton for about 30 minutes in a little water with some soap powder. Do not let the water evaporate completely. Third, using a scalpel and a stiff-bristled toothbrush, gently scrape the remaining flesh from the bones. Finally, using thin wire, assemble the bones in their natural relationship to one another. Attach them to a piece of stiff cardboard.

ACQUIRING ENERGY AND MATERIALS

All animals spend a great deal of time either eating or hunting for things to eat. They are all consumers. As they eat food, animals obtain energy, minerals, vitamins, and water.

An animal's organs can be grouped according to their functions. These groups of organs with related activities are *systems*. In this chapter we will study the main systems of animals.

14−2 Praying mantis eating a grasshopper.

Harold R. Hungerford

nutrition [noo TRISH un; Latin: *nutrire*, to suckle, nourish]

See figure 6–11.

ingestion [in JES chun; Latin: *in*, in, + *gerere*, to carry]

Can you think of a land animal that waits for its prey to come by?

NUTRITION

The processes by which animals obtain, distribute, and use nutrients are known collectively as **nutrition.** Nutrition can be considered under three headings: ingestion, digestion, and absorption.

Ingestion. A microscopic particle of food might be overlooked by many animals, but to a sponge it is a meal. Sponges have no special organs for getting food. Indeed, they have no organs at all; their bodies are merely collections of cells. Many sponge cells have a single flagellum. As the flagella wave, they keep a current of water moving through the sponge. When a food particle comes by, a cell may engulf it and draw it into a vacuole, just as an ameba does. This process of taking food particles into some body cavity is called **ingestion.** It is a characteristic of animals. Although no plants ingest their food, some protists do.

Some other aquatic animals also ingest nutrients as sponges do. Most aquatic and land animals, however, actively pursue their food. And in many cases this food source is not microscopic.

Most animals have some means of capturing their food. One way predators get food is by poisoning their prey. For example, the tentacles of a coelenterate have stinging capsules. Each capsule contains a long, coiled, hollow thread with barbs near its base. When a food organism brushes one of the tentacles, the thread is shot out with such force that it pierces the

14–3 The long, sticky tongue of an anteater is an organ of ingestion. How do you think it works?

New York Zoological Society

14—4 A sea anemone with its tentacles waving in the ocean.

body of the victim. A paralyzing poison is injected into the prey. It is then drawn into the coelenterate's body cavity by the tentacles.

paralyzing [PAIR uh lyz ing]: causing to lose the power of movement

A leech has another way of obtaining food. It attaches itself to its victim by means of a posterior sucker. It makes a wound with its three-toothed jaw, and sucks the victim's blood. Many arthropods also use liquid nutrients as a food source.

What other animals that you know poison their prey?

Among vertebrates, jaws, beaks, and teeth are structures that aid ingestion. There are many adaptations of these structures. For example, a snake can unhook its lower jaw from its upper jaw. The two can then be moved independently. These adaptations permit a snake to swallow a prey that is larger than its own head.

What liquid-sucking arthropods do you know?

Digestion. Ingested food enters a digestive cavity inside an animal's body. Digestive cavities are of three main kinds: vacuoles within individual cells; sacs; and tubular alimentary canals.

digestion [dy JES chun; Latin: *dis*, apart, + *gerere*]

Only relatively small molecules can pass through cell membranes. But most nutrient particles that animals ingest are not molecular size. Even the microscopic particles that sponges take in are much too large to pass directly into cells. Food that is ingested by animals must be broken down into small molecules. The processes of this breakdown are known collectively as *digestion.*

Breakdown of large pieces of food into smaller ones is the first step in digestion. It is the physical part of digestion. Most mammals have teeth that cut or grind food into smaller pieces. But in many animals, movements of the digestive cavity break down food. The gizzard of a bird, for example, is a specialized part of the stomach that grinds up food. Some birds swallow

gizzard [GIZ urd]

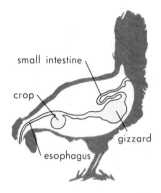

14–5 Alimentary canal of a bird. Food is swallowed without being chewed and is stored temporarily in the crop.

Although the metabolic processes are almost the reverse of each other, less energy is released in digestion than was required in the synthesis of the food particle.

lysosomes. See page 364.

14–6 Kinds of digestive cavities: (A) Intracellular (vacuole) in a cell of a sponge. (B) Extracellular with one opening (sac) in a hydra. (C) Extracellular with two openings (alimentary canal) in a roundworm.

sand and small pebbles. These increase the effectiveness of the birds' gizzards. In some animals the physical part of digestion is unimportant. For example, a snake may swallow a whole rat. The snake then lies quietly for as long as a week while chemical digestion of the rat proceeds.

Physical digestion, such as chewing, increases the surface area of the food. Increased surface area means that the second part of digestion—the chemical part—can take place more quickly. Here enzymes take over the breakdown of food. The chemical part of digestion is almost the reverse of the synthetic processes described in Chapter 12. It is similar in all animals.

In sponges and to some extent in coelenterates and flatworms, chemical digestion takes place in a vacuole inside a cell. This is *intracellular* digestion. The vacuole is formed when a food particle is surrounded by a section of cell membrane. But a cell membrane is made up of the same substances that make up foods—for example, fats (lipids) and proteins. Why isn't the cell itself digested? Saclike bodies called lysosomes contain the digestive enzymes. Lysosomes are not digested by the enzymes. A lysosome fuses with a vacuole. Chemical digestion occurs within this new structure. Small molecules produced by chemical digestion pass out of the vacuole into the cell's cytoplasm. Only then can the nutrients be used by the cell.

In most animals digestion takes place in an *extracellular* space—enzymes are secreted *from* cells into a digestive cavity. There is great variation in the form and complexity of digestive systems. In the digestive sac of a coelenterate, some of the cells lining the cavity secrete enzymes. Some cells have flagella that move foods through the cavity. But in these organisms there are no *tissues* with digestive functions. In the simple alimentary canal of a roundworm, all digestive enzymes are produced by cells in the lining. In most animals with alimentary

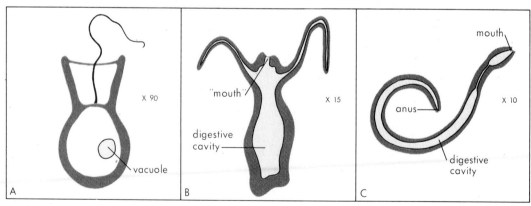

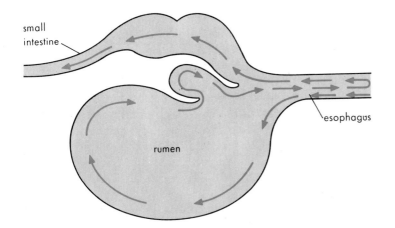

14–7 The complex stomach of a cow. Food is swallowed without being chewed and is stored in the rumen. Later it is brought back into the mouth for chewing. Bacteria in the other parts of the stomach carry on cellulose digestion, for which a cow has no enzymes. What ecological relationship exists between cow and bacteria?

canals, however, there are specialized digestive tissues called glands. Some herbivorous vertebrates, such as cows, have special digestive chambers that contain cellulose-digesting microorganisms. Vertebrates have no cellulose-digesting enzymes themselves, but they can use compounds produced by these microorganisms.

Absorption. The process by which small food molecules pass from an alimentary canal into an animal's cells is **absorption.** The rate of absorption depends on the surface area of the canal's lining. The greater the surface area, the faster is the rate. The lining of the alimentary canal has many folds. Folding is a common adaptation by which surface area is increased. The lining of the alimentary canal in mammals has many small fingerlike extensions called *villi.* These increase internal surface area by as much as a hundred times.

Where did you observe such folding?

villi [VIL eye; Latin: tufts of hair]; singular, villus

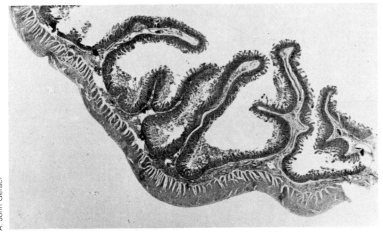

14–8 Portion of a small intestine. You can see small villi on the surfaces of the folds of the inner side.   × 8

A. John Geraci

saliva [suh LY vuh]; salivary
[SAL uh ver ee]

Digestion in humans. Now let us examine in some detail the digestive system of a complex animal—you. Digestion begins in your mouth. Physical digestion begins as your teeth break up large pieces of food. Saliva, secreted by three pairs of salivary glands, flows into your mouth. There it moistens the food and begins to change it chemically. However, food is usually not in the mouth long enough for much chemical digestion to occur there. Your tongue keeps the food between your teeth during chewing. It then pushes chewed food to the back of your mouth. There, muscular contractions carry the food into the *esophagus,* a tube through which the food passes into the stomach.

esophagus [ih SOF uh gus; Greek: *oisein*, to carry, + *phagein*, to eat]

gastric [GAS trik; Greek: *gaster*, stomach]

In the stomach muscular contractions continue physical digestion. They also mix in **gastric juice,** secreted by gastric glands in the stomach wall. Gastric juice is mostly water. The contents of the stomach, therefore, soon become like a cream soup. Gastric juice also contains hydrochloric acid. This causes

14–9 Digestive system of a human. The appendix, attached to the large intestine, is a sac that has no known function.

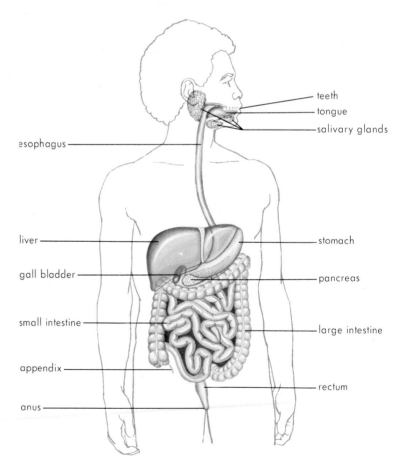

a low pH (acid) in the stomach. Digestive enzymes in the stomach require a low pH to catalyze the breakdown of protein molecules.

The pyloric valve is a circular layer of muscle in the alimentary canal wall between the stomach and the small intestine. Contraction of the pyloric valve holds partially digested food — now called *chyme* — in the stomach for about five hours. The pyloric valve relaxes occasionally, permitting some chyme to pass into the small intestine. There, three more digestive juices are added. These have a high pH (basic), and they neutralize the hydrochloric acid of the chyme. This is important because the enzymes of the small intestine require a neutral medium.

One of the three juices added in the small intestine is *bile.* Bile is secreted by the liver and stored in the gall bladder. Human bile contains no digestive enzymes. It is very alkaline and breaks large globules of fat into fine droplets. This speeds up the chemical digestion of fats into fatty acids and glycerol. *Pancreatic juice* is secreted by the pancreas. It has enzymes that catalyze carbohydrate, protein, and fat digestion. *Intestinal juice,* secreted by glands in the wall of the small intestine, has other enzymes. Most chemical digestion occurs in the upper part of the small intestine.

In the lower part of the intestine, almost all absorption of nutrients occurs. Amino acids and simple sugars are, respec-

pH: Where have you already met this term?

chyme [KYM; Greek: *chymos,* juice]

Can you explain why vomit sometimes tastes sour and sometimes bitter?

pancreatic [pan kree AT ik; Greek: *pan,* all, + *creas,* flesh]

SECRETION	ENZYME	SUBSTANCES ACTED UPON	PRODUCT
saliva	amylase	starch	maltose
gastric juice	pepsin	some protein	polypeptides
pancreatic juice	amylases	starch	maltose
	lipase	fats	glycerol and fatty acids
	pancreatic proteases	protein	polypeptides and amino acids
intestinal juice	disaccharidases	sucrose, maltose, lactose	simple sugars
	peptidases	polypeptides	amino acids

14–10 Summary of major enzymes of chemical digestion in mammals. Products absorbed are shown in boldface italic type. In what connection were these substances discussed in Chapter 12?

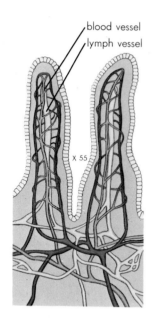

blood vessel
lymph vessel

X 55

14–11 Diagram of two villi. Refer back to figure 14 – 8.

lymph [LIMF]. See page 466.

feces [FEE seez]

anus [AY nus]

tively, the end products of protein and carbohydrate digestion. They are absorbed by diffusion or active transport through the villi into the blood. Some fat molecules pass into the lymph vessels of the villi. Most of the fatty acids and glycerol recombine during absorption to form fat. The fat then passes into the lymph vessels. Very small amounts of fatty acids are absorbed into either the lymph or the blood.

Normally digestion and absorption are completed in four to seven hours. Substances left in the small intestine then pass into the large intestine. Most of the water is absorbed here. Undigested foods, indigestible substances, mucus, dead cells from the digestive tube lining, and bacteria make up the *feces.* The feces leave the digestive tube through the *anus.*

CHECK YOURSELF

A. Why is eating an important animal activity?
B. How do the various food-getting devices of animals illustrate structural diversity?
C. Distinguish between ingestion and digestion.
D. Distinguish between physical digestion and chemical digestion.
E. How is chemical digestion related to the chemical syntheses carried on by cells?
F. In what ways do digestive cavities differ among animals?
G. What role does your tongue play in digestion?
H. What changes occur in the pH of the human digestive system as food passes through it?
I. In what part of the human digestive system does most of the chemical digestion occur?
J. Where does most of the absorption of digested foods occur?
K. Why are feces normally semisolid though chyme in the small intestine is semiliquid?

Investigation 14.2   **ACTION OF A DIGESTIVE ENZYME**

INTRODUCTION

In Chapter 12 the discussion of enzymes centered on those involved in energy release and in syntheses. Now you will study an enzyme that acts in digestion. You will study salivary amylase. Because this enzyme is secreted into the mouth cavity, it is easily available for study.

PROCEDURE A

Your teacher will demonstrate the action of maltose, a disaccharide, on warm Benedict's solution.

1. Crush a piece of cracker (9 cm²) into a test tube. Add warm water to a depth of 5 cm. Shake and pour into a funnel lined with filter paper.
2. Collect **filtrate** (the liquid that seeps through the filter paper) to a depth of 1 cm in a 2nd test tube.
3. Collect filtrate to a depth of 2 cm in a 3rd test tube.
4. Test the filtrate in the 2nd test tube for starch. Test the filtrate in the 3rd tube for maltose.
5. Have one team member chew a piece of paraffin and collect a few milliliters of saliva in a 4th test tube. Test the saliva for maltose. If the test is positive, have another student try.
6. A student who has no maltose in his or her saliva should then chew a piece of cracker (9 cm²) thoroughly for 2 or 3 minutes. Deposit the cracker and saliva mixture into a funnel lined with filter paper. Add 5 ml warm water (37°C) and collect 3 ml of the filtrate in a test tube. Test the filtrate for maltose. *(1)* Considering the procedure used, what conclusion can you draw from a negative test? From a positive test?

PROCEDURE B

In Procedure A the enzyme action occurred *in vivo* (Latin: in a live condition). It occurred in its normal situation in the mouth. To test the action of the enzyme under laboratory conditions, it is convenient to work *in vitro* (Latin: in glass — that is, in a test tube, beaker, etc.).

1. Using paraffin, collect saliva from a student whose saliva gives a negative result with Benedict's solution. Label 7 test tubes *1* through *7*. Add saliva to each tube to a depth of 2 cm. Using a wide-range pH test paper, determine the pH of the saliva in

MATERIALS
(per team)

For Procedure A

unsweetened cracker
iodine–potassium-iodide solution
Benedict's solution
5 test tubes
test-tube holder
thermometer (−10° to +110°C)
funnel and support
bunsen burner
2 sheets filter paper
paraffin

For Procedure B

starch solution
Benedict's solution
hydrochloric acid solutions, pH 6 and pH 3
sodium hydroxide solutions, pH 8 and pH 11
pH test paper
7 test tubes
glass rod
test-tube holder
7 beakers
bunsen burner
thermometers (−10° to +110°C)
ring stand
paraffin
ice
medicine dropper

each tube. It should be the same in all 7 tubes.

2. Add 5 drops of starch solution to Tube 1. Shake. Place the test tube in a beaker containing water at 37°C. Leave it there 10 minutes. Remove and test for maltose.
3. Add 5 drops of starch solution to Tube 2. Shake. Immediately place the test tube in a beaker of boiling water. Leave it there 10 minutes. Remove and test for maltose.
4. Add 5 drops of starch solution to Tube 3. Shake. Immediately place the test tube in a beaker of crushed ice. Leave it there 10 minutes. Remove and test for maltose.
5. To Tube 4 add a volume of pH 6 hydrochloric acid equal to the volume of saliva. *(Be careful when using the hydrochloric acid.)* Mix by rolling the tube between the palms

of your hands. Add 5 drops of starch solution and again mix. Place the tube in a beaker of water at 37°C. Leave it there 10 minutes. Remove and test for maltose.

6. To Tube 5 add an equal volume of pH 3 hydrochloric acid solution. Mix. Add 5 drops of starch solution and again mix. Place the tube in a beaker of water at 37°C. Leave it there 10 minutes. Then remove and test for maltose.

7. To Tube 6 add an equal volume of pH 8 sodium hydroxide solution. (*Be careful when using the sodium hydroxide.*) Mix. Add 5 drops of starch solution and again mix. Place the tube in a beaker of water at 37°C. Leave it there 10 minutes. Remove and test for maltose.

8. To Tube 7 add an equal volume of pH 11 sodium hydroxide. Mix. Add 5 drops of starch solution and again mix. Place the tube in a beaker of water at 37°C. Leave it

there 10 minutes. Then remove and test for maltose.

DISCUSSION

If the work has been divided among teams, assemble the data on the chalkboard. (2) At what temperature and pH did the enzyme act *in vivo* (in the mouth)? (3) Under which of the experimental temperature conditions did the enzyme act *in vitro* (in the tubes)? (4) At which experimental pH did the enzyme act? (5) Use the data to make a general statement about the effect of temperature variation on the action of the enzyme. (6) Use the data to make a general statement about the effect of pH variation on the action of the enzyme. (7) Would you expect enzymes inside a cell to be more or less sensitive to variations in temperature and pH than are enzymes outside a cell? Why?

OBTAINING OXYGEN

Animal cells may release energy by anaerobic methods, but they can do so only for short periods. They depend on aerobic cellular respiration. Animals, therefore, must live where there is oxygen. They also must be able to transport oxygen to all their cells. And they must be able to rid themselves of carbon dioxide, the waste product of respiration.

In very small animals—such as rotifers and some plankton—intake of oxygen and release of carbon dioxide occur entirely through the body surface. The body surface is large compared with the volume of living substance. This means that the surface area is large enough to allow sufficient amounts of oxygen to enter the organism. As body size increases, however, the ratio of surface area to volume becomes smaller. In general, large animals do not have large enough body surfaces to allow sufficient gas exchange. Thus, they must have organs that increase the surface area through which respiration can occur.

In aquatic animals such organs are usually feathery or platelike structures called **gills.** These may be waved through the water, or water may pass over them as the animal moves. In

Why is movement important?

crayfish

marine annelid

bony fish

14—12 Gills in three aquatic animals. The body of the marine annelid is enclosed in a mud tube. Only its gills are exposed.

either case dissolved oxygen diffuses in and carbon dioxide diffuses out through the gill cells. Gills are remarkably similar in a wide variety of animals.

In terrestrial animals the cell surfaces through which gases diffuse must be kept moist, because the cells are living. Water can diffuse through any surface that respiratory gases can. Therefore, these animals lose a great deal of water through their respiratory organs. For this reason, terrestrial animals that breathe through gills (sow bugs, for example) must live in places where air is moist — that is, where evaporation is slow. This is also true of land animals that take in oxygen through their body surfaces (slugs, earthworms, and salamanders, for example).

Many terrestrial animals live where the air is dry. They need an extensive surface *inside* the body where air can be kept moist. There are two principal ways of meeting this requirement. In insects and some other arthropods, a complicated system of air tubes extends to all parts of the body. The tubes carry oxygen directly to most cells. Body movements help move air through the tube system. In air-breathing vertebrates air passes into lungs. Lungs are divided into such a large number of tiny air sacs that they appear spongy. Through the enormous moist surface area provided by these sacs, respiratory gases diffuse.

Again let us take humans as an example. The **diaphragm** is a muscular wall that separates the body cavity into two parts. As the diaphragm moves down and your ribs move up and out, the chest cavity enlarges. This lowers the pressure in the lungs so that air outside your body is pushed inward. As it passes through your nostrils and nasal cavities, it is warmed and moistened. When you eat, food from your mouth and air from your

Is this important for aquatic animals? Consider the gills of a fish living in fresh water.

Do you know of any terrestrial vertebrate that normally has only one lung?

Why can you "see your breath' on a cold day?

diaphragm [DY uh fram; Greek: *dia*, through, + *phragma*, fence]

Why is this method of breathing impossible for a frog?

pharynx [FAR ingks; Greek: the throat]

epiglottis [ep uh GLOT is; Greek: *epi*, upon, + *glotta*, tongue]

14 – 13 Movements of breathing in humans.

nasal cavities pass into the ***pharynx.*** The opening to the lungs is protected by a flap of tissue called the ***epiglottis.*** It is usually open, admitting air. It closes when food passes by on the way to the esophagus.

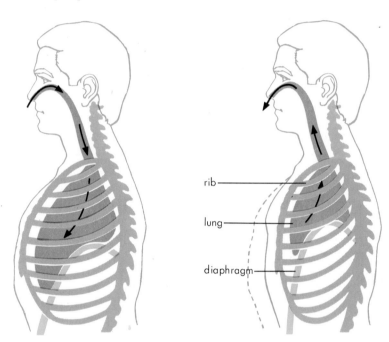

14 – 14 The breathing system of humans.

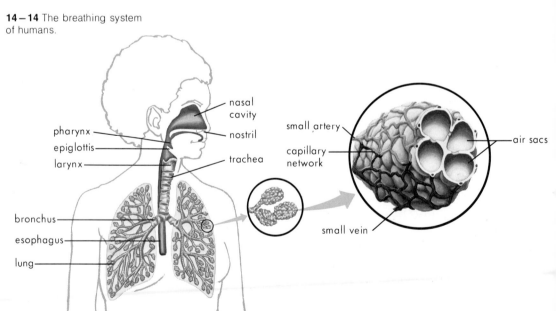

The *trachea* is the air passage that extends through the neck ventral to the esophagus. In the upper chest it divides into two *bronchi.* Each bronchus leads to a lung, where it branches and rebranches. The smallest divisions end in almost microscopic air sacs. The walls of these sacs are very thin and have a dense network of tiny blood vessels. Respiratory gases diffuse into and out of the blood through the thin membranes of the tiny blood vessels and air sacs. Oxygen passes from the air sacs into the blood. Carbon dioxide passes from the blood into the air sacs.

trachea [TRAY kee uh; Latin: *tracheia,* windpipe]

bronchi [BRONG ky; Greek: *bronchos,* windpipe]; singular, bronchus

CHECK YOURSELF

L. What are the principal gases exchanged with the environment by the breathing systems of animals?
M. Why does a very small aquatic animal require no breathing system?
N. What is the essential characteristic of a gill?
O. Why does a terrestrial animal lose water through its breathing surfaces?
P. How is air moved into human lungs?
Q. What is the function of the epiglottis?

TRANSPORTING SUBSTANCES

An early milestone in biology was the discovery that blood circulates. This happened early in the 17th century through the research of William Harvey. As a physician, Harvey was interested in human physiology. Harvey wrote a book, *On the Motion of the Heart and Blood.* In it, he wrote:

> I have also observed, that almost all animals have truly a heart, not the larger creatures only, and those that have red blood but the smaller and seemingly bloodless ones also, such as slugs, snails, scallops, shrimps, crabs, crayfish, and many others; nay even in wasps, hornets and flies. I have with the aid of a magnifying glass, and at the upper part of what is called the tail, both seen the heart pulsating myself, and shown it to many others.

pulsating: moving rhythmically, beating

Harvey apparently had not observed other animals that have much simpler transport systems. Some lack not only hearts but even a circulating fluid.

SIMPLE TRANSPORT SYSTEMS

cyclosis. See page 369.

In a single-celled organism, cyclosis is an adequate transportation system. In some multicellular organisms, such as sponges
and coelenterates, almost every cell has part of its surface exposed to the environment. Each cell can obtain its own oxygen
and get rid of its own wastes. Though not all cells in these animals take in food, no cell is very far from those that do. In these
cases diffusion and active transport are sufficient for moving
substances into cells.

A similar situation exists in free-living flatworms. In
roundworms, however, there is a fluid-filled body cavity surrounding the digestive tube. As the roundworm wriggles, the
fluid is squeezed about from one place to another. In this way
substances dissolved in the fluid are carried to and from the
body cells.

CIRCULATORY SYSTEMS

It is also referred to as a vascular
system. Why?

Most animals that have a body fluid also have a system of tubes
through which the fluid flows — a circulatory system. Muscular
pumps (hearts) propel the fluid (blood) through tubes (vessels).
The direction of flow is controlled by *valves* inside the tubes.
The basic function of a circulatory system is always the same. It
is to transport materials throughout an organism's body. Where
blood flows slowly and where membranes are thin, substances
move to or from the blood by diffusion or active transport. The
blood then moves rather rapidly through the vessels to another
place. There it again flows slowly, in contact with thin membranes. Substances again move to or from the vessels of the
system.

Invertebrate systems. In arthropods and most mollusks blood
is pumped through blood vessels that empty into body spaces.
Through these spaces the blood moves about sluggishly, in
contact with the tissues. Eventually it gets back into another
set of vessels. These carry it back to the pumping point. Such an
incomplete vascular system is called an *open circulatory system.*

You can easily see the movement
of blood in the dorsal vessel of an
earthworm.

Annelids, on the other hand, have a *closed circulatory
system.* In this system blood flows within vessels through all
of its course. An earthworm has a system with five pairs of
hearts and a complicated set of finely branched vessels. These
vessels eventually empty into a large dorsal vessel. This dorsal
vessel then returns the blood to the hearts. Valves in this vessel
keep the blood flowing in only one direction through the
system.

Vertebrate systems. In vertebrates circulation also occurs in
a closed system. A single, muscular heart with two or more
chambers pumps blood through the system. There are three

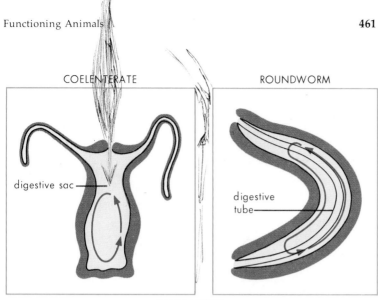

14 – 15 Diagrams of fluid transport in four invertebrate animals.

COELENTERATE

digestive sac

ROUNDWORM

digestive tube

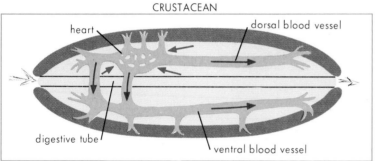

CRUSTACEAN

heart

dorsal blood vessel

digestive tube

ventral blood vessel

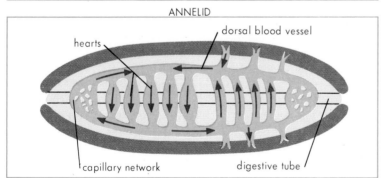

ANNELID

dorsal blood vessel

hearts

capillary network

digestive tube

kinds of vessels. ***Arteries*** have rather thick, muscular walls and carry blood *away* from the heart. ***Veins*** have relatively thin walls with little muscle. They carry blood *toward* the heart.

By ingenious experiments, Harvey showed that blood leaves a vertebrate heart through arteries and returns to the heart through veins. Therefore, he reasoned that blood circulates. But Harvey never actually saw blood passing from arteries to veins, because the use of microscopes was not yet widespread. Later in the century, another scientist first observed

arteries [Latin: *arteria*, windpipe or blood vessel] (Ancient anatomists could not determine whether vessels in dissected animals had contained air or blood.)

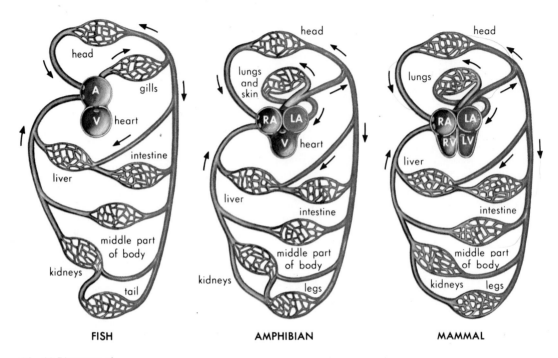

FISH   **AMPHIBIAN**   **MAMMAL**

14 – 16 Diagrams of circulation in three vertebrate classes. Red indicates oxygenated blood. Blue indicates deoxygenated blood. A = atrium. V = ventricle.

atrium [AY tree um; Latin: central court of a Roman house]; plural, atria

capillaries, the third kind of vessel. They are very thin-walled, and connect arteries and veins. This observation confirmed Harvey's reasoning about circulation.

In all mammals and birds the heart is a double pump. It has right and left sides, and each side is connected with its own set of veins and arteries. In mammals the right side receives blood from almost all parts of the body and sends it to the lungs. The left side receives purified blood from the lungs and returns it to all other parts of the body. Each side has two chambers. One, an *atrium,* receives incoming blood. When the heart muscle relaxes, this blood passes into another chamber, a ventricle. When the heart contracts, the muscular wall of the ventricle gives the blood a strong push. This forces together the tissue flaps between the two chambers. They act as valves that prevent backflow into the atrium. The blood is then forced out of the heart through an artery.

Arteries and veins also have valves. When blood is pumped from the heart, the flaps in an artery are forced against the artery wall. Blood can then flow through the vessel away from the heart. When the ventricles relax between heartbeats, back pressure of the blood forces the flaps away from the artery wall. They block the artery so that blood cannot flow back toward the heart. In veins, similar valves allow blood to flow only *toward* the heart.

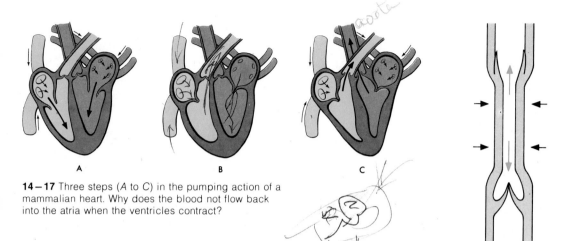

14–17 Three steps (*A* to *C*) in the pumping action of a mammalian heart. Why does the blood not flow back into the atria when the ventricles contract?

Capillary walls are only one cell thick. As blood flows through the capillaries, substances move from the blood through the thin walls into the body tissues. Other substances move from the tissues into the blood at the same time.

BLOOD

In many marine animals there is little difference between body fluids and the seawater environment. But in land animals body fluids are mixtures of substances in water, and the environment is a mixture of gases. In general, organisms with circulatory systems have blood that is different from the fluids in their environments. Different animal groups may also have different types of blood. Some bloods are red; others are greenish, brownish, or colorless. Some contain cells; others do not. All bloods, however, are made up mostly of water in which many substances are dissolved or suspended.

Plasma. When you watch your blood flow from a small cut, it looks like a uniform red liquid. When you examine a thin layer of it under a microscope, you see many faintly red cells. But other cells show up when the blood is stained. Using a centrifuge, all these blood cells can be concentrated. A clear yellowish liquid called *plasma* is obtained.

About 91 percent of human plasma is water. The rest is substances dissolved or suspended in the water. About 8 percent of these are proteins. Close to 0.9 percent are minerals, especially ions of calcium, potassium, sodium, and phosphate. There are also small amounts of amino acids, simple sugars, and metabolic wastes.

Among the many blood proteins are the antibodies, which protect against infections. Recent research has shown that closely related species of animals have many blood proteins in

14–18 Movement of blood in veins is brought about by pressure from adjacent muscles. Compression forces blood in both directions, but valves prevent blood from flowing backward – away from the heart.

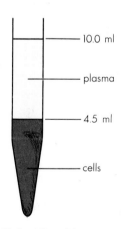

14–19 Centrifuged human blood. In a centrifuge, liquids that contain tiny solid particles (as does blood) are placed in tubes. The tubes are whirled rapidly in a circle. This action separates the particles from the liquid. What percentage of the sample was plasma?

plasma [Greek: *plassein,* to form or mold]

common. However, even individuals within a species differ slightly from each other in their proteins.

Cells. Human blood contains **red blood cells** and **white blood cells. Hemoglobin** is an iron-containing, red pigment in human red blood cells. It gives our blood the ability to carry oxygen. When oxygen is abundant around a red blood cell (as it is in lung capillaries), it combines with the hemoglobin in the cell. Bright red *oxyhemoglobin* is formed. Oxygen in this form is carried to other cells for use in respiration. When oxygen is scarce (as it is in active muscle tissue), oxygen is released from the oxyhemoglobin. Dull red hemoglobin is left. The red blood cells return to the lungs to pick up more oxygen. In the condition called anemia there is either an abnormally low number of red cells or a low hemoglobin content per cell. Anemic people usually are very tired.

hemoglobin [HEE muh gloh bun]

anemia [uh NEE mee uh; Greek: *an*, without, + *haima*, blood]. Why is an anemic individual less active than a normal one?

A human spleen is not shaped like a frog spleen, but generally the function is similar in all vertebrates.

Human red cells live only 110 to 120 days. Then they are removed from circulation and destroyed in the liver and spleen. The liver salvages iron ions from these cells. Cells in bone marrow use these ions to make new red cells.

White cells have no hemoglobin and are therefore colorless. Unlike red cells, they do not merely float along in the plasma. A white cell can move about like an ameba. It can slip through the thin walls of capillaries and wander about among the cells of muscle and other tissues. There are several kinds of white cells. They differ in size, function, and reaction to stains. Primarily, however, white cells destroy particles, such as pathogenic organisms, that invade your body. Some do this by engulfing and digesting the particles as an ameba does. Others synthesize antibodies. Some white cells also seem to aid in the repair of wounds.

14–20 A comparison of some characteristics of blood "elements." This is a term used by those who wish to emphasize that platelets are only fragments of cells.

ELEMENT	DIAMETER (in μm)	NUMBER (per mm^3)	MAIN FUNCTION
red blood cells	7-8	4,500,000-5,500,000	oxygen transport
white blood cells	9-12	7,000-10,000	defense against microorganisms
platelets	2-4	300,000 (much variation)	blood-clotting

Clotting. Normally, when a vertebrate animal suffers a small wound, the blood at the surface *clots*—hardens. But, if the blood is gently drawn into an open, paraffin-lined vessel, it does not clot. Therefore, exposure to air alone cannot be the cause of clotting. Clotting illustrates what research sometimes reveals about the complexity of apparently simple biological processes.

Clotting begins with *platelets*. Platelets are colorless blood cells. Usually, they are disk-shaped. Like red blood cells, they do not have nuclei. Their life span is about four days. Whenever they are exposed to a rough surface, platelets tend to stick to it and then to break up. Because the lining of blood vessels is smooth, they do not stick to it. When platelets break up on a rough surface, they release a substance called thromboplastin. This substance brings about a change in prothrombin, one of the plasma proteins. This reaction does not occur unless calcium is present—as it always is in normal blood. During the reaction prothrombin is converted to thrombin. Thrombin then acts to convert fibrinogen, another blood protein, into fibrin. Fibrin is an insoluble substance that forms threads within the plasma. Blood cells are trapped in this network of fibrin threads, thus building up a clot.

platelets [PLAYT luts; Greek: *playtus*, broad, flat]

thromboplastin [throm boh-PLAS tun; Greek: *thrombos*, a lump, clot, + *plassein*]

prothrombin [proh THROM bun; Greek: *pro*, before, + *thrombos*]

fibrinogen [fy BRIN uh jun; Latin: *fibra*, fiber, + *genitus*, born]

14−21 Scanning electron micrograph of a red blood cell caught in threads of fibrin.   × 10,250

Emil Bernstein and Ella Kairinen

LYMPH

The water and minerals of plasma easily pass through capillary walls to body tissues. Little of the plasma protein does so, however. White cells also may escape from the closed vascular system; red cells do not. Thus the fluid that bathes tissue cells, though somewhat like blood, is nearly colorless and is lower in protein content.

Some of this fluid may ooze back into the blood capillaries. But most of it collects in a set of vessels different from those in which blood is carried. Here it is called **lymph.** These vessels join to form larger vessels. Contractions of the muscles that surround the vessels move the lymph along. In the walls of the small intestine, lymph vessels in the villi absorb fats. Many of the metabolic wastes of cells also pass into the lymph. Thus it has a higher fat content and a higher waste content than does blood.

At many points the vessels of the lymph system divide into tiny twisted passages. As a result, the lymph flows slowly through them. Here pathogenic organisms and other foreign materials that have entered the body are engulfed by white blood cells. The lymph system thus is a defense system.

Have you ever had "swollen glands" in your armpits or neck during a severe cold? On the basis of this paragraph, explain this condition.

Eventually all vessels join, forming a duct that carries the lymph to the region of the left shoulder. There it is emptied into a blood vein. The fluids that left the blood at the capillaries are returned to the blood as it enters the heart.

CHECK YOURSELF

R.   What kinds of animals are able to survive without circulatory systems?
S.   What is a circulatory system and what is its function?
T.   Distinguish between open and closed circulatory systems.
U.   What are the differences among arteries, veins, and capillaries?
V.   Explain how our four-chambered heart functions.
W.   How is blood in mammals kept flowing in one direction?
X.   How does human blood plasma differ from whole blood?
Y.   What substances are contained in human plasma?
Z.   How is oxygen carried in human blood?
AA. What is anemia?
BB. How do white blood cells differ from red blood cells?

CC. Draw a diagram to show how blood clots.
DD. In what ways does lymph differ from blood?
EE. Why is the lymph system considered a defense
   system?

Investigation 14.3   A HEART AT WORK

INTRODUCTION

Crustaceans of the genus *Daphnia* are
abundant in small bodies of fresh water.
Individuals are just large enough to be seen
with the naked eye. But when magnified
even 20 times, many of the internal organs—including the heart—can be seen
through the body wall. Before you begin
this investigation, become familiar with the
appearance of the animals. Look carefully
for the beating heart. Do not confuse its
motion with that of the legs, which also
move rhythmically.

   Read through the procedure. (*1*) State a
hypothesis that is appropriate to it.

PROCEDURE

1. Check the temperature of the water in
   which the *Daphnia* are living. It should be
   at room temperature before you begin.
2. With a medicine dropper, transfer one

MATERIALS
(per team)

6 to 8 *Daphnia,* in a small beaker
  of aquarium water
thermometer (−10° to +110°C)
medicine dropper
microscope slide with depression
stereomicroscope
watch with second hand
beaker large enough to hold *Daphnia* beaker
crushed ice
hot water
graph paper, 1 sheet per student
paper towels

Daphnia to the depression in the slide.
3. Soak up excess water with a piece of paper towel. By limiting the amount of water,
   you increase the likelihood that the animal
   will lie on its side, the position in which
   heart action can best be seen.
4. Team members should take turns at keep-

14−22 Daphnia.   × 60

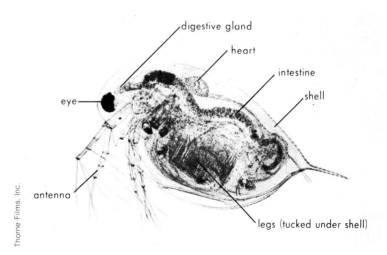

digestive gland
heart
intestine
shell
eye
antenna
legs (tucked under shell)

Thorne Films, Inc.

ing time with the watch and observing the specimen's heartbeats through the stereomicroscope. It may be difficult to count as rapidly as the heart beats. If so, try tapping a pencil on a piece of paper at the speed of the heartbeat. Then count the pencil dots.

5. When the observer is ready, the timer says "Go!" At the end of 15 seconds, the timer says "Stop!" Multiply the count by 4 to obtain the number of heartbeats per minute.
6. Make at least 3 timed counts. Return the *Daphnia* to the beaker.
7. Place the beaker of *Daphnia* in a larger beaker of water and crushed ice. Stir the water in the *Daphnia* beaker *gently* with the thermometer. When the water reaches the temperature assigned to your team, quickly transfer a *Daphnia* to a slide. Make at least 3 counts as quickly as possible.
8. As soon as the *Daphnia* is removed from the beaker, members of the team who are not timing or counting should remove the *Daphnia* beaker from the large beaker. Pour out the ice water from the larger beaker and put in hot water (50° – 70°C). (*Caution: Allow the beaker to warm slightly before pouring hot water into it.*)
9. Place the *Daphnia* beaker in the larger beaker again. Stir the water in the *Daphnia* beaker *gently* with the thermometer. By the time the water temperature rises to the 2nd point assigned to your team, counting at the lower temperature should be finished. Quickly transfer a *Daphnia* to the slide. Make at least 3 counts as quickly as possible.

DISCUSSION

Consider the heartbeat data obtained from *Daphnia* at room temperature. (2) Why were several counts made by each team? (3) What factors might account for the variability in these data?

Assemble on the chalkboard the room temperature data from all teams. (4) Calculate the average rate of heartbeat at different temperatures. If 2 or more teams obtained data at the same temperature, calculate the average for that temperature. Graph the data, placing rate of heartbeat on the vertical axis and temperature on the horizontal axis.

(5) On the basis of your graph, make a general statement about the effects of variation in environmental temperature on the rate of heartbeat in *Daphnia*. (6) Does your graph support your hypothesis? Explain. (7) Would you expect similar effects of temperature on the heartbeat rate of a frog? Of a dog? Explain.

FOR FURTHER INVESTIGATION

1. Young pond snails have thin shells through which the heart can be seen, just as in *Daphnia*. Make a study of snail heartbeat for comparison with that of *Daphnia*. Try to account for any differences you observe.

2. The easily observed heart of *Daphnia* can lead to some understanding of the way in which drugs affect heartbeat rate. Investigate the effects of alcohol (about 5%) and of a stimulant (such as dexedrine sulfate) on *Daphnia* heartbeat. Caffeine and epinephrine may also be used.

REMOVING SUBSTANCES

excretion [ik SKREE shun; Latin: *ex*, out of, + *cernere*, to sift]

secretion [see KREE shun; Latin: *se*, aside, + *cernere*]

Waste substances are removed from cells by a process called *excretion.* But if a substance leaving a cell is useful to the organism, the process is called **secretion.** Because carbon dioxide is a metabolic *waste* formed in every living animal cell, it is an excretion. Gastric juice, which passes out of cells that line the stomach, is a secretion. Substances in gastric juice are useful in digesting food.

Let us consider what we mean by "wastes." Some products of metabolism are poisonous. These are clearly wastes. One example is ammonia, which is formed in the breakdown of proteins. Some substances, however, are toxic only if large amounts accumulate. For example, sodium chloride, which is a normal cell substance, is toxic in large amounts. Ordinarily this salt constantly diffuses into cells from their environments. Only by continuous excretion can the normal proportion of sodium chloride be maintained in cells. In general, then, any substance can be called a waste if an organism has too much of it.

Both secretion and excretion involve the passage of substances through cell membranes. This may occur by diffusion. Frequently, however, a substance is more abundant outside a cell than inside. Then energy is required to "pump" the substance out of the cell by active transport. Otherwise, diffusion would carry these substances *into* the cell.

Once a substance has passed outward through a cell membrane, it has been excreted or secreted. In multicellular animals, however, it still may be inside their bodies. For example, liquid from certain cells above the eyes of many terrestrial vertebrates enters into ducts. These ducts force the liquid onto the surface of the eyeballs. The liquid in these tear ducts is no longer in cells, but it is still within the body — at least in the usual sense. The process by which substances are forced out of body cavities is called **elimination.** Elimination can be from small cavities, such as tear ducts, or large ones, such as digestive tubes.

> Can you show how this definition of "waste" involves circular reasoning?

> elimination [Latin: *ex*, out of, + *limen*, threshold]

EXCRETIONS

In small aquatic animals wastes may simply diffuse out through cell membranes. Sponges and coelenterates — though not always small — also excrete wastes directly through their body surfaces. This can happen because all their cells are close to a water environment. Most animals, however, have special devices for ridding their bodies of wastes.

Water. Through cellular respiration, animal cells constantly produce water. What happens to this water depends on the kind of environment in which an animal lives. Consider a jellyfish in the ocean. Its cells contain a mixture of substances in water. Outside the cell membranes is another mixture — the salty seawater. But the concentration of water molecules inside and outside the jellyfish normally are almost equal. As fast as metabolic water is produced, it diffuses into the environment. This is true of many other marine invertebrates as well.

Now consider a planarian in a freshwater stream. There are very few dissolved substances in fresh water, and the concentration of water molecules is high. But in a planarian's cells the concentration of dissolved substances is high and the water concentration is low. Therefore, water is always diffusing *into* a planarian. Metabolic water is constantly added to this excess. We might expect that water would build up inside a cell and increase its volume. Eventually, the cell might burst unless water was somehow expelled from it. In one experiment, drugs that interfered with the active transport within planarians were given to them. Their cells soon began to burst because of excess water. For freshwater animals, then, excretion of water by active transport is necessary for survival.

Terrestrial animals are in a similar situation. You, for example, take in a great deal of fresh water. Your cells also produce water by metabolism. As a land animal you are always in danger of drying out, but sometimes people can also swell up with excess water. In the condition called edema this swelling occurs, as water collects in body tissues.

edema [ih DEE muh; Greek: *oidēma*, swelling]

Animals maintain water balance within their cells through a variety of structures. In planarians this function is performed by a system of *flame cells.* They are spread throughout the body and are connected by tubules. Each flame cell has cilia that project into a tubule. Wastes enter the flame cell. The waving action of the cilia moves fluid and wastes through the tubule. Many tubules join and eventually empty wastes into the environment through a pore. In this system there are many flame cells and many pores.

To early microscopists, the action of cilia resembled the flickering of a candle flame.

tubule [TEW bewl; Latin: *tubulus,* little tube]

14 – 23 Excretory structure in a planarian.

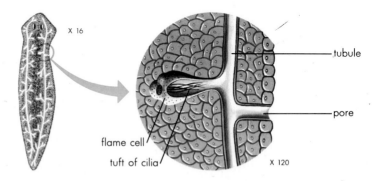

X 16

tubule

pore

flame cell

tuft of cilia

X 120

Most annelids (including earthworms), mollusks, and crustaceans have a different excretory system. In most of these animals the functional unit is a tubule leading from the body cavity to the outside. Again, there are many tubules. Wastes enter the tubules from the body cavity. Around each tubule there is a network of capillaries. In many cases more wastes from these capillaries are added to the wastes already in the tubule. At the same time, useful materials are absorbed back into the blood or body fluid. Each tubule leads to the outside where the wastes are emptied. In vertebrates somewhat similar tubules are found in the kidneys.

Nitrogenous wastes. Excretory organs have developed chiefly as water-regulating devices. In most animals, however, they also regulate the excretion of wastes, especially those with nitrogen.

Amino acids contain nitrogen and are used by cells to build proteins. But an animal often takes in more amino acids than it can use. Some proteins in an animal are constantly broken down into amino acids. Unlike carbohydrates and fats, amino acids and proteins cannot be stored in large amounts. Therefore, there is usually a surplus of amino acids. This surplus cannot be used for energy until the amino group ($-NH_2$) is removed from each amino acid.

During what part of your life do you think amino acid requirements might be greatest?

In vertebrates, amino groups are removed mainly in the liver. Ammonia (NH_3) is formed in the process. It is quite toxic but also quite soluble. If a large supply of water is available, the ammonia can be carried out of the body in solution. In one experiment a freshwater fish was placed through a tight-fitting hole in a rubber partition. Its anterior end (with gills) was on one side. Its posterior end (with the opening from the kidneys) was on the other. Ammonia built up in the water on the anterior end of the fish. In such fish, then, nitrogenous wastes are excreted through the gills.

Marg and Bill Staley

14–24 Nitrogenous wastes of these brown pelicans paint the rocks white. In some places where many sea birds gather, the wastes are collected and used as fertilizer.

uric [YEUR ik; Greek: *ouron*, urine]

urea [yew REE uh]

In other vertebrates the kidneys are the main route for excretion of nitrogenous wastes. But in birds, reptiles, and insects, amino groups are excreted as **uric acid.** Uric acid is almost insoluble and is excreted with only a small loss of water. In most adult amphibians and mammals, amino groups are converted to a waste called **urea.** Unlike uric acid, urea is soluble. It diffuses into the blood, from which it is removed by the kidneys. It is then excreted in solution.

14 – 25 Urea. *(A)* Structural formula. *(B)* Model. How many molecules of urea must a mammal excrete to rid itself of the same amount of nitrogen as does a fish excreting 100 molecules of ammonia?

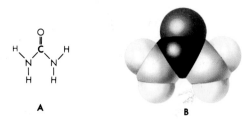

A   B

Other substances. Sodium chloride is one of many salts usually excreted. Salts enter the body faster than they are needed, especially in marine and land vertebrates. For those on land, kidneys are the chief excretory organs for salt as well as nitrogenous wastes. But humans also excrete salt in tears. Many seabirds take in much salt water. They have special salt-excreting glands in their nostrils.

Do you think that human beings could drink seawater if their tear glands produced saltier tears? Why or why not?

Water, some nitrogenous wastes, and salts are excreted through your sweat glands. The remains of dead red blood cells are excreted through your liver. Almost all the carbon dioxide produced during cellular respiration is excreted through your lungs. There is, then, no one organ that performs all excretory functions in your body. Nevertheless, loss of function in both kidneys is always fatal.

fatal: causing death. But in humans death from kidney failure can be prevented by two procedures. What are they?

HUMAN KIDNEY FUNCTION

A human kidney requires energy for three main functions. The first is filtration of blood. This occurs through a *glomerulus,* a ball of capillaries surrounded by the expanded end of a tubule. Each kidney contains many thousand glomeruli. Blood pressure forces some of the blood's fluid through the thin vessel walls. This fluid (filtrate) contains no blood cells or proteins. Otherwise, it has the same composition as blood. The filtrate collects in the tubules. As it moves down the tubules, useful substances such as sugar, amino acids, some salts, and much water are reabsorbed by cells in the walls of the tubules. These substances

glomerulus [gluh MER yuh lus; Latin: little ball]; plural, glomeruli [gluh MER yuh lye]

blood pressure: represents energy expended by the ventricle in pumping blood

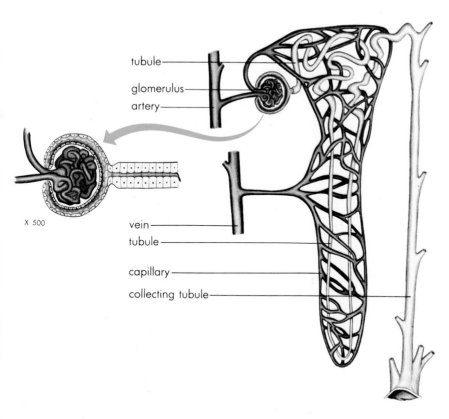

tubule——

glomerulus——

artery——

X 500

vein——

tubule——

capillary——

collecting tubule——

14 – 26 Diagram of an excretory unit in a human kidney.
Each kidney contains thousands of such units.

are then transferred back to the blood in capillaries that surround the tubules. Urea and other wastes are left behind. These
are gradually converted to *urine* by removal of useful materials
and concentration of wastes. Urine constantly trickles from each
kidney through a *ureter* (tube) to the *urinary bladder.* It is
eliminated from the urinary bladder through a tube called
the *urethra.*

ureter [YEUR uh tur]

urethra [yew REE thruh]

    If wastes were not concentrated in urine before being elim-
inated, we would lose tremendous amounts of water every day.
A healthy pair of human kidneys filters 135 to 150 liters of fluid
every 24 hours. During the same period, only about 1.5 liters of
urine are eliminated from the bladder. In other words, about 1
percent of the fluid filtered by the kidneys is eliminated. Without reabsorption of water by the kidneys, we would need to
drink almost a bathtub of water a day!

Kidneys are often described as
homeostatic organs. Explain this.

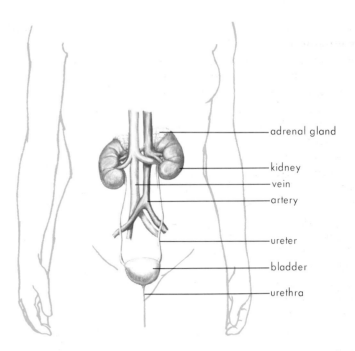

adrenal gland

kidney

vein

artery

ureter

bladder

urethra

14–27 Urinary system in a human. Adrenal glands are attached to the kidneys but are not a part of this system.

CHECK YOURSELF

FF. Distinguish among excretion, secretion, and elimination.

GG. What is meant by a "waste" in an animal?

HH. What are the main kinds of excreted substances?

II. Give one reason why the liver can be considered a part of the excretory system of a vertebrate.

JJ. Describe how urine is formed.

MAINTAINING THE INTERNAL ENVIRONMENT

To any one cell within a multicellular organism, all the other cells are outside. They are part of that one cell's environment. This environment is then external to the cell. But it is internal to the multicellular organism as a whole. Thus we have the paradoxical but useful idea of an *internal environment*. The internal environment of one cell includes neighboring cells as well as body fluids. These fluids are to a cell what the seawater is to a sea animal. They are the source of its requirements and the place to which its wastes are returned.

One of the major concepts in this book is homeostasis — a swinging balance held within limits by different mechanisms. We can observe homeostasis inside an organism as well as in an ecosystem. In freshwater and land animals the primary function of homeostatic mechanisms is to regulate body fluids. These mechanisms maintain a stable fluid environment for each cell, as stable as seawater is for a marine organism.

Consider, for example, the homeostatic regulation of glucose in human blood. After a large meal, digestion forms a large amount of glucose in your small intestine. This is absorbed into your blood, but it does not stay there long. Figure 14–16 shows that blood (and glucose) travels from the capillaries in your digestive system directly to those in your liver. Here glucose in excess of 0.1 percent of the solution is removed. It is changed to the polysaccharide **glycogen,** which is then stored in your liver cells. When your meal contains many carbohydrates, a very large amount of glucose may be produced. Your liver cannot take in all the excess. In this case, glucose is excreted through your kidneys.

glycogen [GLY kuh jun; Greek: *glykys,* sweet, + *genea,* birth]

Now suppose you exercise, perhaps doing gymnastic exercises or swimming. Muscle cells use a great deal of glucose as an energy source. Glucose comes from the environment of your muscle cells — from your body fluids. Reduction of glucose in your body fluids leads to reduction of glucose in your blood. Under these circumstances, glycogen in your liver is changed to glucose, which enters the blood. In this way your liver and your circulatory and excretory systems provide homeostatic mechanisms. They maintain and regulate a glucose supply in the internal environment of your cells.

Review pages 69–70.

14–28 Shirley Babashoff winning an 800-meter, freestyle event. Describe the homeostatic regulation of glucose in her blood.

Wide World Photos

coordination [koh ord un AY-shun; Latin: *cum*, with, + *ordinare*, to arrange]: adjustment of one part of a system to other parts

Homeostasis results from the coordination of all the parts of a living system. This coordination requires communication among the cells inside an organism. In most animals this communication is by chemicals that travel through body fluids or by specialized nerve cells. Chemical and nervous communication act together, but it is convenient to separate them for discussion.

CHEMICAL COORDINATION

Knowledge of the chemical system of coordination has increased greatly within the last century. Just as knowledge of microscopic organisms depended on the development of microscopes, so knowledge of chemical systems has depended on the development of chemistry.

hormones [Greek: *hormaein*, to stimulate]

Hormones. In all multicellular organisms some cells secrete chemicals that influence the growth, development, or behavior of other cells. We discussed one of these—auxin—in Chapter 13. In general, such substances are called *hormones.* As yet, little is known about hormones in most animal phyla. Hormones have been studied chiefly in mollusks, arthropods, and chordates.

Hormones may be secreted by individual cells scattered among other cells of an animal's body. But usually the secreting cells are grouped into tissues or into distinct organs—glands. Glands that secrete tears, sweat, and saliva empty their products into a tubule or duct. Those that secrete hormones empty their secretions directly into the circulatory system. The hormones are then carried in blood. Because these *endocrine,* or

endocrine [EN duh krun; Greek: *endon*, within, + *krinein*, to separate]

ductless, glands interact with each other, we can say that there is an endocrine system. This is true even though its parts are scattered throughout an animal's body.

Endocrine glands of vertebrates. Most vertebrates have similar hormones. However, the same hormone may have different functions in animals of different vertebrate classes. For example, the hormone that causes the mammary glands of mammals to secrete milk causes hens to incubate their eggs.

What experimental procedure could be used to demonstrate this?

You have hormones that cause changes in skin color in certain fishes and amphibians. But your skin does not contain special color cells that would let you match the colors of your surroundings. Within a vertebrate class, however, a particular hormone has the same effects in most species. The discussion that follows applies mainly to mammals.

hypothalamus [hy poh THAL uh-mus; Greek: *hypo*, below, + *thalamos*, chamber (here, a part of the brain)]

The *hypothalamus* is in the ventral part of the brain and is a part of the nervous system. But it has special cells that produce hormones. These hormones pass through vessels or are released

pituitary [puh TEW uh ter ee]

by neurons into the *pituitary gland* just below the brain. They

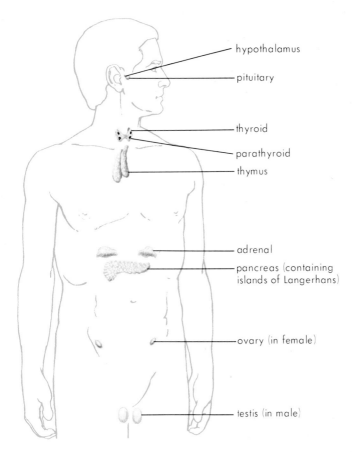

hypothalamus

pituitary

thyroid

parathyroid

thymus

adrenal

pancreas (containing islands of Langerhans)

ovary (in female)

testis (in male)

14–29 Location of the principal endocrine glands in a human body.

cause the pituitary gland to release its own hormones. The pituitary hormones, in turn, control the rate at which other endocrine glands function. Thus the hypothalamus is a major link between the nervous and endocrine systems. The pituitary also secretes several hormones that regulate blood pressure and urine flow.

All vertebrates have *thyroid glands.* The thyroid hormone (thyroxin) regulates the rate of cellular respiration. Too little of the hormone brings about an increase in weight, since food is stored rather than used in energy release. Other effects are slow movement, sleepiness, and lowered body temperature. Too much thyroid hormone increases the rate of cellular respiration. So very little food is stored. The individual loses weight, has an excess of energy, and is very active.

Parathyroid glands are present in all vertebrates except fishes. In mammals only, they are embedded in the thyroid glands. Parathyroid hormone controls calcium metabolism. Calcium plays a part in the contraction of muscles. If the parathy-

thyroid [Greek: *thyreos*, a shield, + *eidos*, form]

parathyroid [pair uh THY roid; Greek: *para*, beside, + thyroid]

14–30 A patient with an enlarged thyroid gland that is secreting an excess of thyroxin. One of the symptoms of this condition is seen in the eyes (*left*). Same patient after treatment (*right*).

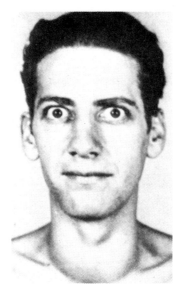

Lisser, H., and Escamilla, R. F.: *Atlas of Clinical Endocrinology*, 1962, The C. V. Mosby Co.; courtesy Dr. W. A. Reilly, Dir., Radioisotope Unit, VA Hosp., San Francisco

What other functions might be affected by the control of calcium metabolism?

insulin [IN suh lun]

adrenal [uh DREEN ul; Latin: *ad*, to, at, + *renes*, kidneys]. Note their position in figure 14 – 27.

epinephrine [EP uh NEF run]; also known as adrenalin. Fish have a similar hormone but no adrenal glands.

ovaries, testes [TES teez]. See page 552.

roid glands are injured or removed, death results because of interference with muscle contraction.

Embedded in the pancreas (figure 14–29) are bits of endocrine tissue that produce *insulin.* This hormone controls the metabolism of glucose. A lack of insulin results in a lack of cellular energy. Glucose is not metabolized and is excreted in the urine.

Adrenal glands are found in amphibians, reptiles, birds, and mammals. The best-known adrenal hormone is *epinephrine.* It raises blood pressure and speeds up heartbeat. It also increases the rate of blood clotting and raises the percentage of glucose in the blood. All these effects increase an individual's chances of survival when faced with an emergency.

During the development of an individual, adrenal glands are formed from two different tissues. The part of an adrenal gland that secretes epinephrine develops from nerve tissue. Most of the rest develops from tissue that also gives rise to the reproductive system. Hormones from this latter part affect many functions. Among these are the following: depositing of fats, protein synthesis, glucose formation from amino acids, and salt excretion. Obviously, adrenal glands are of vital importance to an organism's functioning.

Ovaries and testes are organs in which reproductive cells are formed. Embedded in both are endocrine cells. Hormones from these cells control an individual's sexual development. The reproductive hormones will be discussed in Chapter 16.

Sometimes included in the endocrine system are small glands in the walls of the intestine, just below the pyloric valve. When food passes through the pyloric valve, these glands produce *secretin.* This hormone travels through the blood to the pancreas, where it stimulates production of pancreatic juice.

secretin [sih KREET un]. This was the first substance to be called a hormone—in 1902.

Other kinds of chemical coordination. Many substances that cannot be called hormones aid in coordination of physiological processes. No biologist, for example, would call carbon dioxide a hormone. It is a waste product—an excretion rather than a secretion. But CO_2 in the blood plays a part in determining the rate of breathing. An increased CO_2 concentration stimulates nerves to speed up the breathing motions in your chest. This chemical control of breathing operates whether you are conscious or not.

There is a large group of hormonelike compounds derived from fatty acids—the *prostaglandins.* Prostaglandins lower blood pressure, cause smooth muscle to contract, and regulate many processes in cells and tissues. They appear to be synthesized in cells and tissues throughout the body. As researchers discover more about prostaglandins, these substances will become featured in our understanding of hormones.

prostaglandins [pros tuh-GLAN dunz]

NERVOUS COORDINATION

The control of breathing shows how closely nervous and chemical coordination are associated. In general, however, rapid adjustments in animals are brought about by nervous systems.

Kinds of nervous systems. Sponges have no nervous systems. Indeed, they have nothing that we can call nerve cells. Plants and protists have no nerve cells either, but like sponges they still adjust to changes in their environment. They react to *stimuli.*

stimuli [STIM yuh LYE]; singular, stimulus

Coelenterates have nerve cells. Some of these cells are specialized to receive only certain stimuli. The nerve cells are connected in a network that permits some coordinated responses, such as in digestion.

Flatworms also have nerve networks. But a flatworm has a centralized system of two cords that extend along the length of its body. At the anterior end is a large mass of nerve tissue, a *ganglion.* A ganglion is a center where nerve impulses are exchanged. Flatworms also have cells specialized for receiving stimuli. The eyespots of planarians are examples. These eyespots cannot form images, but they can detect the direction and intensity of light.

ganglion [GANG lee un]

Annelids have well-developed nervous systems. A main nerve cord extends along the ventral side of the body. Many ganglia occur along the nerve cord. A large ganglion, sometimes

14–31 Nervous systems in five diverse kinds of animals

COELENTERATE

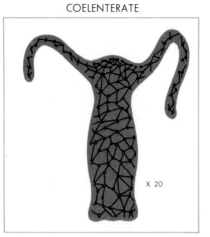

FLATWORM

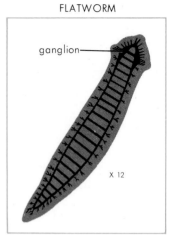

ANNELID

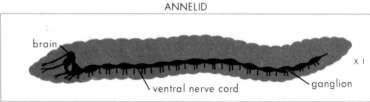

CRUSTACEAN

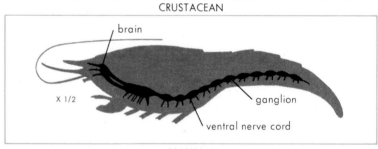

MAMMAL

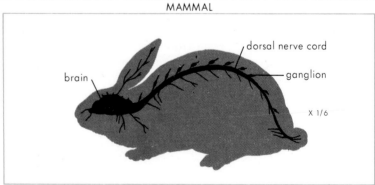

Recall Investigation 4.3. You may be able to devise some experiments to test an earthworm's ability to detect various kinds of stimuli. called a brain, is found at the anterior end of the body. Although earthworms have no obvious sense organs, they can detect many stimuli. Other annelids have specialized sense organs, including eyes.

Among mollusks and arthropods there is a great variety of nervous systems. All are basically of the annelid type. However, they are more numerous and varied than those of annelids.

A dorsal, tubular **nerve cord** is a distinctive characteristic of the chordate phylum. In vertebrate chordates an anterior enlargement of this nerve cord — the brain — dominates all the rest of the nervous system.

Nerve cells. The basic structure in all nervous systems is a **neuron,** a nerve cell. Each neuron has an enlarged region, the **cell body,** which contains the nucleus. From the cell body extend one or more long projections called **nerve fibers.** Neurons do not occur singly. The nerves that are visible in a dissected vertebrate are *bundles* of fibers. In humans the fibers of some neurons are almost a meter long. The cell bodies of neurons are mostly in the brain or in the spinal cord.

Neurons transmit **nerve impulses.** These are short in duration — usually a few ten-thousandths of a second. Physiologists do not completely understand just what a nerve impulse is. It is not an electric current even though electrical changes occur along a neuron during the transmission of an impulse. For one thing, nerve impulses travel more slowly than electrical currents.

In mammals three kinds of neurons can be distinguished by their functions. **Sensory neurons** receive impulses from a **receptor** such as the part of the eye that reacts to light. They then transmit these nerve impulses to another type of neuron. Motor neurons carry the impulses to an **effector** — that is, to a

How many kinds of sense organs can you find in a grasshopper? In a crayfish?

neuron [NEW ron; Greek: nerve]

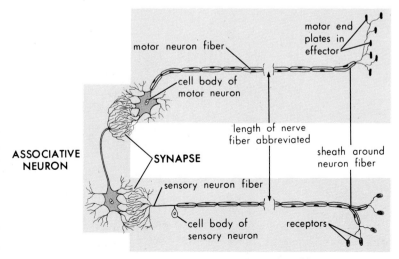

MOTOR NEURON

14 — 32 Kinds of neurons.

motor neuron fiber

motor end plates in effector

cell body of motor neuron

length of nerve fiber abbreviated

ASSOCIATIVE NEURON

SYNAPSE

sheath around neuron fiber

sensory neuron fiber

cell body of sensory neuron

receptors

SENSORY NEURON

synapse [SIN aps; Greek: *syn*, with, + *apsis*, a fastening]

14–33 Brains of animals in five vertebrate classes. Olfactory bulbs are related to odor. Optic lobes are related to sight. The pituitary is not part of the brain. From these examples, what generalizations about brains in vertebrates can you make? Note carefully the size comparisons.

muscle or a gland. The effector gives a special response to the impulse, such as movement or secretion. **Associative neurons** transmit impulses from one neuron to another.

Neurons do not directly touch each other. When an impulse reaches the end of a neuron, a chemical that starts an impulse in the next neuron is released. A **synapse** is the very narrow space between two neurons through which this chemical passes. Transmission across a synapse takes place only in one direction. Therefore neurons conduct impulses only in one direction.

Nerves and internal coordination. The activities that you can control are coordinated by your **central nervous system.** This system is made up of your brain, spinal cord, and the nerves that lead directly into and out of them. Thinking, reading, and speaking are functions that involve the **cerebrum** of your brain. The coordination of muscles involves your **cerebellum.** Your

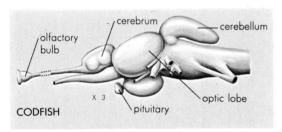

CODFISH

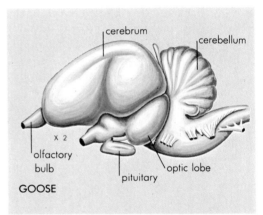

GOOSE

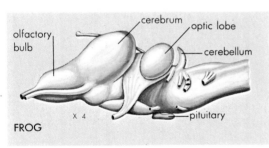

FROG

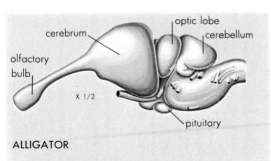

ALLIGATOR

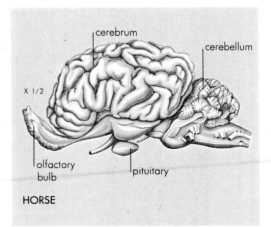

HORSE

central nervous system also coordinates some activities that you can control in part but do not usually think about. An example is your rate of breathing.

Much activity in your nervous system happens without your being aware of it. Some of this is controlled by your central nervous system. But most of this activity is under the control of your **autonomic nervous system.** This system, in turn, is controlled through your hypothalamus. Examples of this activity are reabsorption of water in your kidneys, your stomach movements, and secretion of bile by your liver. Your autonomic system consists of interconnecting neurons that coordinate activities of your internal environment.

One basic functional unit of the nervous system is the **reflex.** It is an automatic, unconscious response. Consider

Consider speaking: What you say is cerebral, but saying it is cerebellar. Explain.

autonomic [awt uh NOM ik; Greek: *autos,* self, + *nomos,* law]

14—34 Diagram of a reflex. The bending of the leg involves neurons in leg and spinal cord only. *Feeling* involves the brain, but this is not necessary for the reflex.

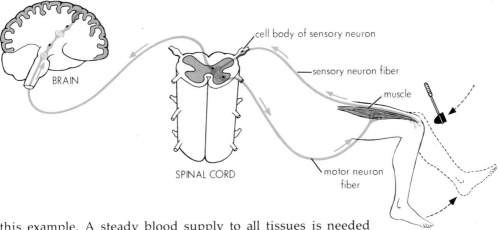

cell body of sensory neuron

sensory neuron fiber

muscle

BRAIN

SPINAL CORD

motor neuron fiber

this example. A steady blood supply to all tissues is needed to maintain a favorable internal environment. Suppose that, after sitting on the sidelines for the first quarter, you are put into a basketball game. The sudden muscular activity forces blood into the right atrium of your heart much faster than it is being pumped out. This happens because, for the moment, your heart continues to beat at the normal rate. The extra blood stretches the walls of the atrium. Within the atrial walls are sensory neurons. They are stimulated by the stretching, and impulses pass through their fibers to your brain. These impulses then trigger other impulses in motor neurons that go to your heart. Its contractions then speed up.

Describe what happens when you go out of the game to the bench.

CHECK YOURSELF

KK. What is the internal environment of an animal?

LL. Describe the homeostatic regulation of glucose in human blood.

MM. What are hormones?

NN. How do endocrine glands differ from other glands?

OO. What are the principal glands of a mammalian endocrine system?

PP. What is the result of an overactive or inactive thyroid gland?

QQ. Give an example of nonhormone chemical coordination.

RR. Compare the nervous system of a vertebrate with that of a flatworm.

SS. Describe a nerve cell.

TT. How do sensory neurons differ from motor neurons?

UU. What is a synapse?

VV. Describe the functioning of the autonomic nervous system.

WW. What is a reflex?

ADJUSTMENT TO EXTERNAL ENVIRONMENT

Ability to move is one of the most obvious characteristics of animals. It is also one of the main ways animals adjust to their external environments. Of course, not all animals move rapidly. In fact some, such as oysters and sponges, remain anchored like a plant for most of their lives. However, we are concerned with any motion that helps an individual adjust to stimuli from its environment.

Senses. A runner's heart beats faster than normal at the lineup for a race. But the endings of the sensory nerves are in the walls of the heart. They cannot receive direct stimulation from the sights and sounds outside. Usually we do not think of internal sensory neurons when we speak of the senses. We consider only those that receive stimuli directly from the external environment. The runner as a whole organism hears the whistle, the crowd, and the coach. As a whole organism, the runner reacts to these stimuli.

Ability to receive and to react to stimuli from the environment is one of the basic characteristics of living things. This ability is developed to different degrees in different organisms. In most animals different kinds of stimuli are detected by specialized receptors. In humans, for example, receptors in the skin of the fingertips are sensitive to pressure but not to light. Only receptors in the eyes are light sensitive. But *they* are not sensitive to sound waves.

BSCS photo by Richard R. Tolman

14−35 A blind person reads a book printed in Braille. This is possible because touch receptors in the fingers are sensitive to pressure.

In most animals some receptors are concentrated in special organs. You are well acquainted with your principal ones—eyes, ears, nose. Other kinds of receptors, such as those sensitive to pressure and heat, are distributed widely in your skin.

No organism has specialized receptors for all the stimuli in the environment. Many cave-dwelling animals have no receptors for light. You have no receptors for the electromagnetic waves that carry radio and television signals. Lack of ability to detect light is ordinarily no handicap to cave animals. However, if a cave animal leaves its cave, its inability to see might mean disaster. You use instruments like television that change electromagnetic waves to sound and light waves. For these you *do* have receptors. But you can suffer from nuclear radiation without being aware of your exposure unless you have an instrument to detect it.

Can you give any explanation for the lack of these receptors?

Muscles. In animals, motion usually involves muscle cells. Sponges again are an exception. They have no muscle cells, although individual cells are capable of movement. Their larvae swim by means of cilia, just as many protists do.

Coelenterates have some specialized cells that allow the animals to move their tentacles. Flatworms have cells organized into definite muscle tissues. But locomotion is still accomplished largely by cilia. In all other animal phyla, muscle tissues are organized into bundles (muscles). The muscles are controlled by nervous systems.

There are two general types of muscle tissue, striated and smooth. **Striated muscle** is best developed in arthropods and vertebrates. It moves the skeleton and, in general, contracts more rapidly than smooth muscle. In arthropods and vertebrates, **smooth muscle** is found in the walls of blood vessels, of various ducts, and of the alimentary canal. Smooth muscle is usually involved in the regulation of the internal environment. Striated muscle, on the other hand, is usually involved in adjustments to the external environment.

striated [STRY ayt ud; Latin: *stria*, a furrow]

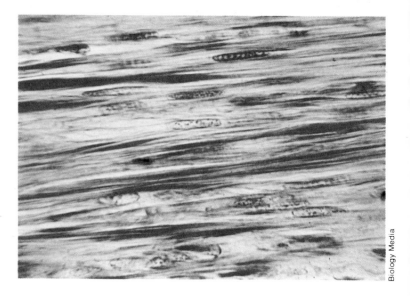

14 – 36 A stained preparation of vertebrate smooth muscle tissue × 1,000. Refer to figure 11 – 19 (page 379) for a picture of striated muscle tissue.

Biology Media

The chemistry of muscular contraction is an active field of investigation. In some recent experiments proteins were extracted from muscle, and an artificial fiber was made from them. This fiber was placed in a water bath. When ATP was added, the fiber contracted. Moreover, tests showed that the ATP was changed to ADP during contraction. This and other experiments indicate three things: (1) Proteins make up the contraction apparatus of muscles. (2) Certain of the proteins in muscle

14–37 Mitsuo Tsukahara using striated muscle in his arms to win a still-rings event.

tissue are enzymes that release the chemical energy needed for contraction. (3) The energy for this action comes from ATP.

Even when an animal appears to be at rest, its muscles are not completely relaxed. The muscles of a healthy organism are always in a state of partial contraction that is called *muscle tone.* This produces the firmness that can be felt even in "relaxed" muscles.

Skeletons. The skeleton of a sponge consists of small, rigid parts scattered through the soft, living tissues. These parts support the softer tissues. The stony skeletons built up by corals support the animals and also protect them from predators. In mollusks the skeletons (shells) are chiefly protective.

Support and protection are functions of arthropod and chordate skeletons. But, in these phyla, skeletons also function in the movements of the animals, particularly in locomotion. Of course, a skeleton is not necessary for movement. An earthworm wiggles and moves along very well without a skeleton. In our own bodies, muscles that have no connection to our bones move food along the alimentary canal.

chitin: any substance structurally similar to polysaccharide but containing nitrogen

Arthropod skeletons are external, with the muscles attached to the inner surfaces. These exoskeletons are composed of chitin, which is flexible when thin. In many arthropods, calcium compounds, deposited along with the chitin, make the exoskeleton hard and strong. It is all one piece, but it is rigid only in sections. Thin flexible chitin joints allow bending.

Vertebrate skeletons are internal structures. Muscles are attached to them. Skeletons consist of one or both of two kinds of tissue: cartilage and bone. The hardness of bone is, in part, a result of calcium and magnesium compounds. Both cartilage and bone contain cells that secrete these compounds. Thus the skeleton can grow as the animal grows. Though the skeleton begins as cartilage, most of it is gradually replaced by bone. At your age this process is well advanced. But it will never be completed — the tip of your nose and the external parts of your ears will never become hard bone.

What function does the skeleton in ears and nose have? What function does the skull have?

Skeletal movement. The parts of a vertebrate or arthropod skeleton act together as levers. Muscles supply the force to move these parts, and joints act as fulcrums. A muscle attached to a bone is like a rope attached to a wagon. With a rope you can pull a wagon, but you cannot push it. If you want to move the wagon back to its original position, you must attach a rope to the other end and again pull it. Muscles act in the same way — in pairs. While sitting, you raise and straighten your leg by contracting one set of muscles. Gravity will pull your leg back to a bent position. But if you stand and bend your knee, you use another set of muscles. These muscles work opposite to the ones you used to straighten your leg. All your skeletal movements are performed by contracting opposing sets of muscles.

14—38 Relation of muscles to skeletons. Why are two muscles shown in each example?

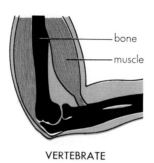

bone
muscle

VERTEBRATE

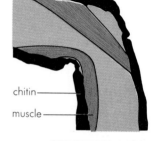

chitin
muscle

ARTHROPOD

Careers in Biology: The Human Body– Performance and Treatment

Performances by athletes, gymnasts, and dancers exhibit the strength, agility, and graceful movement of which the human body is capable. But it needs constant care to keep it running smoothly. All of us need to get adequate sleep, and we must eat well-balanced, nutritional meals. Regular exercise also is important. Many careers involve the athletic performance or professional care of the human body.

Physical-education instructors and gymnastics coaches, like Dick Foxal, understand the anatomy and physiology of the human body. Dick's interest in how the human body functions began in high school when he was on the wrestling team. He took biology courses in high school and in college. Dick knows which

Ron McDuffie/Atoz Images

A. A tennis instructor demonstrates the correct way to grip the racket.

Robert Wilson

B. Runners speed toward the finish line in a 100-meter dash.

C. Dick offers suggestions to improve a student's performance on the parallel bars.

D. The students in Dick's classes work hard to learn the graceful techniques of a gymnast.

muscles are used in each gymnastic routine (**C**). He also knows what exercises will strengthen certain muscles. Dick advises his gymnasts to eat the right foods in order to perform well. He shares his awareness of the abilities and limitations of the human body with his gymnastics students (**D**). His training probably prevents injuries to these performers as they run, jump, swim, or practice their gymnastic routines.

Sometimes a human body fails to function properly or is accidentally damaged. Then a medical team must be called upon. Steve Humphrey and Elizabeth Spinuzzi are nurses in a small hospital. They often work in the emergency room. They must think and act quickly as each new patient is brought in for treatment. They must be ready, for example, to attend to a woman who was thrown from a horse. She may have a broken back. After a doctor has tested her ability to move and respond to

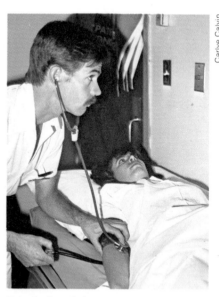

E. In the hospital emergency ward, Steve checks the vital signs of a young woman who was injured when she was thrown from a horse.

touch, Steve checks blood pressure, pulse, respiration, and temperature (**E**).

The next emergency is a woman who has had a heart attack. Liz assists the doctor by administering oxygen and by checking the woman's vital signs — blood pressure and so on (**F**). One of the most important parts of a nurse's work is reassuring friends and relatives of sick or injured persons that everything possible is being done to help the patient.

Many patients are treated even before they reach the hospital. Emergency medical technicians (EMT's) arrive at the scene of an automobile accident and give emergency first-aid treatment to the injured (**G**). They know how to stop bleeding and how to protect fractured bones until a doctor can set them. If an injured person is having trouble breathing, an EMT will provide oxygen. EMT's are especially trained in techniques of placing an injured person on a stretcher so that injuries are not made worse by the movement. Sometimes EMT's must deal with cases of severe shock after accidents. Or the ambulance that accompanies them may be carrying the victim of a heart attack or a diabetic suffering from insulin shock. At such times, the EMT's call the hospital on the radio-telephone in the ambulance and receive instructions to administer drugs or give a transfusion of blood plasma.

Coaches and athletic instructors take pride in training us to use our bodies skillfully and efficiently. But we do not always take good care of ourselves, and sometimes we take chances. The experts who care for sick and injured people know their work is an essential, often life-saving, enterprise.

Carlye Calvin

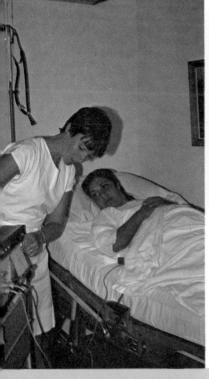

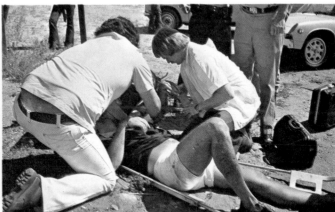

G. Emergency medical technicians must evaluate the injuries and quickly give the proper first-aid treatment.

F. Liz checks the heartbeat of a patient.

PHYSIOLOGICAL REGULATION

To summarize our understanding of animal physiology, consider one case of homeostasis. It is the regulation of body temperature in warm-blooded animals. Like all chemical reactions, those of metabolism are influenced by changes in temperature. They slow down at low temperatures and speed up at high temperatures. Therefore, warm-bloodedness is an advantage. Warm-bloodedness permits an animal to be active when environmental temperatures are low.

Can you think of some disadvantages of being warm-blooded?

In warm-blooded animals — birds and mammals — the temperature of the skin and the tissues just beneath it may fluctuate. It is only internal body temperature that is constant. This can occur only if the rate of heat loss is the same as that of heat production. Receptors that respond to temperature changes are necessary to keep body temperature unchanged. Inside the hypothalamus are receptors that detect changes in blood temperature. The hypothalamus, with its mixture of nervous and endocrine functions, is the regulator in temperature control.

What does a warm-blooded animal do when the environmental temperature becomes *cooler* than its body temperature? The first adjustments are usually those that conserve heat. Impulses pass along neurons of the autonomic nervous system, constricting the small arteries in the skin. This reduces the flow of blood to the skin. In turn, this reduces the amount of heat lost through the skin.

What happens to the coloration of your lips when you become cold?

At the same time, other impulses along the autonomic nervous system contract the small muscles that control the position of each hair or feather. This erects the individual hairs, thus increasing the amount of air space between them. And this improves the insulation provided by fur or feathers.

You have the skin muscles but very little of the hair. How, then, does this nerve action affect you?

If these actions are insufficient, the rate of heat production can be increased. For example, an involuntary increase in muscle activity — shivering — helps to increase the metabolic rate in cells. This increases the release of energy from food. Much of the released energy is lost from cells in the form of heat. But this heat energy is useful to the organism in maintaining a constant body temperature.

In addition to making these internal adjustments, most birds and mammals behave in ways that conserve heat. When cold, a cat curls up in a ball and covers its nose with its tail. This reduces the amount of surface exposed to the cold air. The cat also covers an uninsulated surface, its nose, through which heat loss is very rapid. This action also leads the warm air from the lungs under and around the body. A bird tucks its legs up under its feathers and puts its head under its wing. Many birds thus cut their heat losses in half.

BSCS by Jane Larson

14-39 A cold-blooded animal (lizard) rests on a rock in the hot sun. This behavior increases its body temperature.

What happens when environmental temperature becomes *warmer* than body temperature? At such time maintenance of a constant body temperature requires a reduction of heat production, an increase of heat loss, or both. Again nerve impulses from the hypothalamus activate the mechanisms. The walls of the small arteries in the skin relax, and more blood circulates to the surface of the body. Thus more heat is lost. In some mammals, such as humans and horses, the activity of sweat glands increases. This provides more water on the skin. Evaporation of water always requires heat, and heat for the evaporation of sweat comes from the body. Dogs have sweat glands only in their footpads. But a dog can increase the rate of heat loss by increasing the flow of air over the moist surfaces of the upper part of its respiratory system—by panting.

Heat production through metabolism is reduced by inactivity. In hot weather many mammals and birds are quite inactive during the warmer part of a day. They seek the coolness of shade, where heat can be lost more rapidly. Bathing, wading, or standing in water also increases heat loss. This is because water conducts heat from an animal's body much more rapidly than does air.

What happens to the coloration of your skin when you become hot?

Thus many homeostatic mechanisms are involved in regulating the body temperature in warm-blooded animals. We would find equally extensive mechanisms if we were to examine any other aspect of internal regulation. Some examples are the maintenance of water content of the body, glycogen content of the liver, and salt content of the blood.

14−40 What does the position of the cat probably indicate about the environmental temperature?

CHECK YOURSELF

XX. What kinds of information do vertebrates obtain through their receptors?

YY. Give two examples of animals that move by means other than muscles.

ZZ. Distinguish between striated and smooth muscle.

Aa. What are two principal functions of animal skeletons?

Bb. How do skeletons differ in vertebrates and arthropods?

Cc. Why must skeletal muscles occur in pairs?

Dd. Describe how muscular, skeletal, nervous, and chemical systems all interact in a warm-blooded vertebrate to regulate internal temperature in cold environmental temperatures.

Investigation 14.4   YOUR CHEMICAL SENSES

INTRODUCTION

Many animals have nerve endings that
are sensitive to chemical substances.
Arthropods have such receptors in their
antennae and feet. Vertebrates have them
in their mouths and nasal passages where
the senses of taste and smell are found.

The study of these senses in nonhuman
animals is complicated by a lack of communication. Humans can at least give
descriptions of particular stimuli. But even
then there are difficulties in interpreting
such reports. So a complete understanding
of sense organs — even in humans — is not
easy.

PROCEDURE A

During this procedure you will locate the
taste receptors on your tongue for 4 kinds of
chemical substances.

14–41

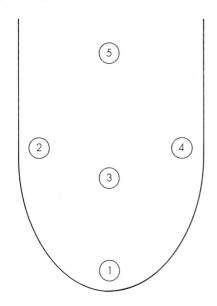

MATERIALS
For Procedure A
(per team of 2)

2 ml 10% salt solution
2 ml 5% sucrose solution
2 ml 1% acetic acid solution
2 ml 0.1% quinine sulfate solution
Syracuse watch glass
2 beakers, filled with water
4 cotton swabs
waste jar for every 6 students

For Procedure B
(per team of 3)

solutions of orange juice, milk,
  onion juice, 2% vinegar,
  sugar, dill-pickle juice — any
  3 or all 6
handkerchief (for blindfold)
3 to 6 paper cups

Student A: Pour about 2 ml of 10% salt
solution into a watch glass.

Student B: Make a copy of figure 14–41
and label it *Salt*.

Student A: Dip an applicator (a cotton
swab) into the solution. Drain excess solution
from the applicator. Touch the applicator to
the tongue of Student B at the point marked
1 in figure 14–41.

Student B: At Point 1 in your drawing,
place a minus sign (−) if you sense no taste
of salt. Place a plus sign (+) if you sense a
mild taste of salt, and a double plus (++) if
you sense a strong taste of salt.

Student A: As soon as Student B has recorded the sensation, touch the applicator to
B's tongue at Point 2.

Student B: Record your sensation.

Students A and B: Continue until sensation has been recorded at all 5 points on the
tongue.

Student B: Rinse your mouth with water.

Student A: Break the applicator. Discard

it. Pour the salt solution from the watch glass into the waste jar. Rinse the watch glass.

Student B: Pour about 2 ml of 5% sucrose solution into the watch glass.

Student A: Make a copy of figure 14–41. Label it *Sweet*.

Student B: Dip an applicator into the sucrose solution and drain off excess. Touch the applicator to the tongue of Student A at Point 1.

Student A: Record your sensation.

Students A and B: Continue until sensation has been recorded at all 5 points.

Student A: Rinse your mouth with water.

Student B: Break the applicator and discard it. Pour the sucrose solution from the watch glass into the waste jar. Rinse the watch glass.

Student A: Pour about 2 ml of 1% acetic acid solution into the watch glass.

Student B: Make another copy of figure 14–41 and label it *Sour*.

Student A: Dip a new applicator into the acid solution and proceed to test Student B, following the procedure described above.

Student B: Record your sensation.

Students A and B: Following the same procedure for changing solutions and students, test the effects of a 0.1% solution of quinine sulfate. Label the diagram *Bitter*.

PROCEDURE B

During this procedure you will investigate the relationship between taste and smell. It is important that the student being tested not know what the substance is.

Student B: Blindfold Student A. Obtain a paper cup, labeled *A*, containing a few ml of Test Solution 1.

Student C: In your data book, copy the chart shown in figure 14–42. Enter a "1" in the first space under the heading "Solution Presented."

Student A: *Holding your nose tightly*, sip the solution. Report its taste, and try to identify the substance in the solution.

SUBJECT	SOLUTION PRESENTED	NOSE CLOSED		NOSE OPEN	
		Taste	Identity	Taste	Identity

14–42

Student C: Record these reports on the chart.

Student A: Without holding your nose, sip the same solution. Again report its taste, and try to identify the substance.

Student C: Record these reports.

Students A, B, and C: Repeat the procedure, with Student B as the subject. Student C obtains Test Solution 2, and Student A records the reports. When tests with Solution 2 are completed, repeat the procedure, with Student C as the subject. Student A obtains Test Solution 3 and Student B becomes the recorder. If time permits a 2nd round of testing, use Solutions 4, 5, and 6.

DISCUSSION

On the chalkboard make 4 large diagrams, as in figure 14–41. Label them *Salt, Sweet, Sour,* and *Bitter*. Assemble all the data obtained in Procedure A. At each test point on the diagrams, record the total number of minus, plus, and double-plus responses. (1) What are some of the possible causes for variability in the data? (2) Which kinds of variability are the result of "errors of observation"? Which kinds are the result of physiological variability?

On the chalkboard list the solutions (1, 2, 3, etc.) used in Procedure B. Tally separately the tastes reported with nose closed and with nose open. Also tally the identifications of solutions. (3) Are the kinds of tastes reported with nose open more varied than those reported with nose closed? Less varied? Neither? (4) Are the identifications made with nose open more accurate than those made with nose closed? Less accurate? Neither? (5) What assumption is involved in holding the nose closed?

(6) Do the data from Procedure A support the hypothesis that receptors of the 4 kinds of taste are equally distributed on the surface of the tongue? Explain. (7) If the data fail to support this hypothesis, where on the tongue is each kind of taste receptor located?

(8) On the basis of the data from Procedure B, write a brief statement relating the sense of taste to the sense of smell.

FOR FURTHER INVESTIGATION

1. Hold a bottle containing oil of cloves about 1.5 cm from your nose and vigorously and continuously inhale, exhaling through your mouth. How much time passes before you can no longer clearly detect the smell of cloves? You now have "olfactory fatigue." Immediately smell peppermint oil. Can you detect its odor?

2. Stick your tongue out and keep it out during the following procedure. Dry your tongue with a piece of gauze or paper towel. Place a few crystals of sugar on your tongue and note the time. How much time passes before you can taste the sugar? Rinse your mouth with water. Again stick your tongue out, but do not dry it before placing sugar crystals on it. How much time passes before you can taste the sugar? Rinse your mouth with water. Try the same procedure with salt crystals. Again measure the time. What conclusion can you draw from your results?

PROBLEMS

1. How might you proceed experimentally to show the following? (a) Secretin causes the pancreas to secrete digestive enzymes. (b) Diabetes mellitus is caused by lack of insulin. (c) Hormones secreted by the pituitary gland affect thyroid and adrenal glands.

2. Antibodies from horse blood can produce some kinds of immunity in humans (Chapter 7). Insulin from a cow pancreas can be used in treating human diabetes. Why cannot whole blood of horses and cows be transfused to humans?

3. We have implied that excretion is a biological process essential to maintain life in *all* organisms. Yet we did not discuss the process in Chapter 13. And it is seldom mentioned in botany textbooks. Explain.

4. Blood transports many substances dissolved in plasma. It can be shown, however, that in mammals less than 10 percent of the carbon dioxide in the blood is dissolved in plasma. How is the remainder of the CO_2 transported?

5. Describe the route followed by a molecule of oxygen as it moves from the air of your external environment to a mitochondrion in one of your muscle cells.

6. A thyroxin molecule contains four atoms of iodine. What effects would an iodine-free diet have on a mammal?

7. Hemoglobin acts as a respiratory pigment in animals of several phyla, but there are other such pigments in the animal kingdom. Investigate this matter, considering the following questions: (a) Do all respiratory pigments act in the same way? (b) What are the chemical similarities and differences among respiratory pigments? (c) Do respiratory pigments provide any clues to the evolutionary relationships

among animal phyla?

8. A temporary reddening of the skin surface is sometimes called a "flush" and sometimes a "blush." The first term is often used in cases of fever. The second is usually used to describe a reaction to some situation in the external environment. Is the body mechanism the same in both cases? If it is, how does it operate? If it is not, what are the differences?

9. You eat a lettuce and cheese sand-

wich. Describe what happens to the sandwich from the moment you take the first bite until its remains are passed from your anus. First you must decide what classes of substances are in the sandwich.

10. In some cases of slow blood clotting, physicians prescribe calcium compounds. Explain. In other cases they prescribe vitamin K. What part does this vitamin play in the clotting process?

SUGGESTED READINGS

Binkley, S. 1979. A Timekeeping Enzyme in the Pineal Gland. *Scientific American*, April. Chemical activity appears to be a clock mechanism in at least some animals.

Geller, J. 1978. *Inner Space: The Wonder of You*. Richards Rosen, New York. A readable text covering metabolism, nutrition, digestion, respiration, circulation, and excretion. Deals with controversy surrounding health-related issues.

Perutz, M. F. 1978. Hemoglobin Structure and Respiratory Transport. *Scientific American*, December. A "lever" system in the hemoglobin molecule enables it to take up oxygen and then release it.

Regan, D. 1979. Electrical Responses Evoked from the Human Brain. *Scientific American*, December. Clues to brain function provided by voltage changes recorded during the performance of specific tasks.

Schmidt-Nielson, K. 1978. *Animal Physiology:*

Adaptation and Environment. 2nd ed. Cambridge University Press, New York. Explanations of many vertebrate mechanisms, including desert adaptations.

Schwartz, J. H. 1980. The Transport of Substances in Nerve Cells. *Scientific American*, April. The role of the axon in regulating impulses between the cell body and the nerve endings.

Scientific American. 1974. *Vertebrate Structures and Function*. W. H. Freeman, San Francisco. A collection of 40 papers providing a resume of current thought on the interrelationship of structure and function.

Wilson, J. A. 1979. *Principles of Animal Physiology*. 2nd ed. Macmillan, New York. Covers the basics of animal function.

Wilson, R. 1979. *How the Body Works*. Larousse, New York. A well-illustrated and readable text on human physiology.

15

Behavior

YOUR GUIDEPOSTS

In this chapter you will have an opportunity to explore these questions in biology:

- What is behavior? What kinds of organisms show it?
- With what life process is plant behavior usually associated?
- What are some kinds of animal behavior? What examples can you cite from your own experience?
- How does learning compare with innate patterns of animal behavior?

Investigation 15.1   TROPISMS

MATERIALS
(per team)

For Part A

4 soaked corn grains
petri dish
cotton
scissors
heavy blotting paper
cellophane tape
glass-marking crayon

For Part B

4 flowerpots, about 8 cm in diameter
4 cardboard boxes, at least 5 cm
  higher than the flowerpots
40 radish seeds
soil
red and blue cellophane
scissors
cellophane tape

For Part C

4 shoots of *Zebrina*, about 20
  cm long
4 test tubes, 18 × 150 mm
4 1-hole stoppers, to fit test tubes
4 burette clamps
ring stand
melted paraffin, in a beaker
small brush
glass-marking crayon

INTRODUCTION

This investigation consists of three separate investigations. Each part will be conducted by some teams in each class.

   (1) Before you begin the part your team will conduct, read through all the procedures and form a hypothesis for each part.

All members of the class should observe the results and participate in a discussion of the outcome of each part.

PROCEDURE

Part A

1. Place 4 soaked corn grains in the bottom half of a petri dish. Arrange them cotyledon side down, as shown in figure 15–1.

15–1

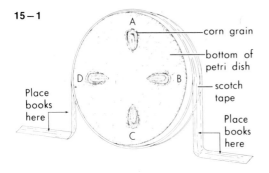

2. Fill the spaces between the corn grains with wads of cotton to a depth slightly greater than the thickness of the grains.
3. Cut a piece of blotting paper slightly larger than the bottom of the petri dish. Fit it snugly over the grains and the cotton.
4. Hold the dish on its edge and observe the grains through the bottom. If they do not stay in place, repack with more cotton.
5. When the grains are secure in the dish, wet the blotting paper thoroughly. Seal the two halves of the petri dish together with cellophane tape.
6. Place the dish on edge in dim light.
7. Rotate the dish until one of the grains is at the top. With the glass-marking crayon, write an *A* on the dish beside the topmost grain. Then, proceeding clockwise, label the other grains *B*, *C*, and *D*.
8. Fasten the dish with a long strip of tape, as shown in figure 15–1. (If further support is needed, stack books on top of the tape, against the edges of the dish.) Do not

change the position of the dish.
9. When the grains begin to germinate, make sketches daily for 5 days, showing the directions in which the root and the shoot grow from each grain.

Part B

1. Turn the 4 cardboard boxes upside down. Number them 1 to 4. Label each with your team symbol.
2. Cut a rectangular hole in one side of each of 3 boxes. (Use the dimensions shown in figure 15–2.)

15–2

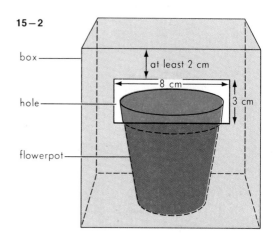

3. Tape a strip of red cellophane over the hole in Box 1. Tape a strip of blue cellophane over the hole in Box 2. Leave the hole in Box 3 uncovered. Do not cut a hole in Box 4.
4. Using a pencil, number 4 flowerpots 1 to 4. Label each with your team symbol. Fill the pots to 1 cm below the top with soil.
5. In each pot, plant 10 radish seeds about 0.5 cm deep and 2 cm apart. Press the soil down firmly over the seeds, and water the pots. Place them in a location that receives strong light but not direct sunlight.
6. Cover each pot with the box bearing its number. Turn the boxes so the sides with the holes face the light.

7. Once each day remove the boxes and water the pots. (*Do not move the pots; replace the boxes in the same position.*)
8. When most of the radish seedlings have been aboveground for 2 or 3 days, record the direction of stem growth in each pot — upright, curved slightly, or curved greatly. If curved, record in what direction with respect to the hole in the box.

Part C

1. Fill 4 test tubes with water. Insert a 1-hole stopper firmly into each tube.
2. Remove all leaves within 8 cm of the cut ends of 4 *Zebrina* shoots.
3. Push the cut end of each shoot through a stopper until about 5 cm of it is in water.
4. Seal tubes, stoppers, and shoots by applying melted paraffin with a brush. (*Caution: Avoid spilling hot paraffin on your skin.*)
5. Using a glass-marking crayon, label the tubes *A, B, C,* and *D*.
6. Attach a burette clamp to each tube. Fasten the tubes to a ring stand as shown in figure 15–3.
7. Place this assembly in a location that receives bright light from one side.
8. Observe the shoots daily for about a week. Record your observations.

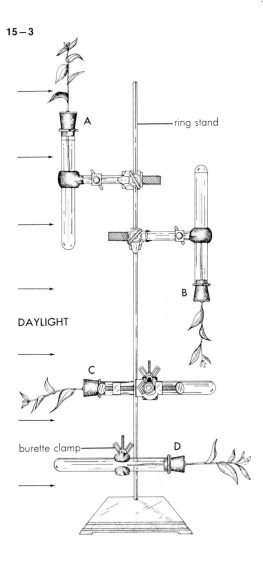

15–3

ring stand

DAYLIGHT

burette clamp

DISCUSSION

Part A

(2) From which end of the grains did the roots grow? (3) From which end did the shoots grow? (4) Did the roots of all grains eventually turn in one direction? If so, what was the direction? (5) Did the shoots of all 4 grains eventually turn in one direction? (6) To what stimulus did the roots and shoots seem to be responding? Were the responses **positive** (toward the stimulus), or **negative** (away from the stimulus)?

Part B

(7) In which pot were the stems most nearly perpendicular? (8) Were all the stems curved in one direction in any pot? (9) If so, in which pot and in what direction? If not, in what direction did *most* of the stems curve? (10) To what stimulus do you think the stems responded? (11) What effect, if any, did the red and blue cellophane have on the direction of stem growth?

Part C

(12) Did any shoots grow without bending? If so, which ones? (13) Did any shoots

bend as they grew? If so, which ones bent? (*14*) If you noticed any bending, in what direction did it occur in each case? (*15*) To what stimulus did the shoots seem to respond?

(*16*) For each of the hypotheses that you formed at the beginning of the investigation, state a conclusion based on the data from this investigation.

FOR FURTHER INVESTIGATION

Will centrifugal force overcome the response of plant parts to gravity? To test this idea, mount the setup used in Part A on the turntable of a phonograph. Refer to R. G. Beidleman, 1966, *Dynamic Equilibrium*, Patterns of Life Series, BSCS, TIB Department, Boulder, Colo., pp. 44 – 48.

WHAT IS BEHAVIOR?

stimulus; plural, stimuli: In the study of behavior, a stimulus is something within an organism or in its environment that causes that organism to react.

response: anything an organism does in reaction to a stimulus

behavior: movement, communication, or other directly *observable* responses—singly or in a pattern—by any organism in reaction to one or more stimuli

All living organisms are continually *doing* something. They respond to **stimuli** from their environment. Not all these **responses** are called **behavior.** When light is directed to a green plant, the plant begins to split water molecules in photosynthesis. This physiological reaction is not considered behavior. However, if the plant is left exposed to light from one side, the leaves and tip of the plant begin to turn toward the light. This is considered behavior. A cat lies in the sun; muscles move its latest meal through its intestines. This is not what biologists consider behavior. A bird chirps or calls nearby. Unless the cat is deaf, the receptors of its ears react, sending impulses to the brain. This also is not—or is not yet—behavior. However, the cat opens its drooping eyelids, raises its ears, and twitches its tail. This is behavior.

15 – 4 The cat's behavior tells an observer that it is aware of the bird's presence.

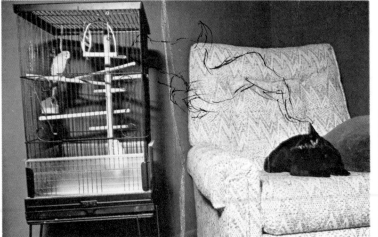

BSCS photo by Richard R. Tolman

BEHAVIOR IN ORGANISMS WITHOUT NERVOUS SYSTEMS

The ability to respond to stimuli, **irritability,** seems to be one of the fundamental characteristics of living substance. Even the simplest organism can respond to changes in its environment. A slime mold engulfs food particles but flows around inorganic particles. It responds differently to objects in its environment, just as you respond differently to a doughnut and a rubber band.

irritability [ir ut uh BIL ut ee]

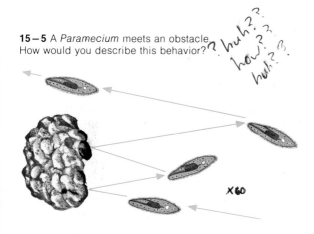

15–5 A *Paramecium* meets an obstacle. How would you describe this behavior?

15–6 *Vorticella.* An individual in feeding position (*left*); same individual after a light touch (*right*).

Vorticella [vor tih SEL uh]

If a ciliate of the genus *Vorticella* is touched lightly, it usually contracts its stalk. If a *Vorticella* is touched repeatedly, it responds in a variety of ways. It may bend away, it may reverse the direction in which its cilia are beating, it may contract, or it may swim away. But these behaviors occur in protists, which have no receptors, brain, or muscles.

Sometimes, these simple behaviors involve movement away from (negative) or toward (positive) a stimulus in the environment. They are related to factors such as light, temperature, humidity, gravity, or touch. These simple behaviors are called **taxes** when they occur in animals or protists. Taxes direct the whole organism away from unfavorable conditions or toward more favorable conditions. A *Euglena*, for example, is positively phototactic. Near its anterior end is a spot of pigment sensitive to light. As *Euglena* swims, its body rotates so that the pigment spot detects the direction of illumination. Somehow this information is transmitted to the flagellum, which then directs the organism toward the light.

taxes [TAK seez; Greek: *tassein,* to arrange]; singular, taxis [TAK sus]

In plants, similar responses are called **tropisms.** Tropisms involve parts of a plant, such as leaves, stems, or roots. In mosses and vascular plants most behavior is closely associated with

tropisms [TROH piz umz]

A — Reaction to a drop of 0.5% salt
    solution.

B — Reaction to a drop of weak
    acetic acid.

15—7 Behavior of small populations of *Paramecium* in response to five environmental stimuli. Using the terms in the text, describe the behavior in each case.

C — Reaction to a piece of filter
    paper.

D — Reactions to a bubble of air
    and a bubble of CO_2.

growth. Though tropisms are a somewhat fixed kind of behavior, they are not entirely invariable. The responses sometimes vary if the intensity of the stimulus changes. Bermuda grass, for example, is positively phototropic to weak light but negatively phototropic to strong light. Thus this grass grows well unless it receives too much sunlight.

15—8 Leaves of a plant (*Mimosa*) as they normally appear (*above*) and a short time after being touched (*below*). How do you think an organism without muscles can perform this response?

BSCS photos by Carlye Calvin

STUDYING ANIMAL BEHAVIOR

OBSERVATION AND EXPERIMENT

We all see the behavior of our pets and of other animals, though few of us notice the behavior of plants or protists. But merely *watching* something is not necessarily scientific observation. And, because behavior is action, observing it is especially difficult. Motion pictures help and have provided a method of verification, which is essential in science.

In the laboratory a biologist can learn much about what an organism *can* do. But laboratory experiments cannot tell us for certain what an organism *will* do in its natural setting. ***Ethologists*** are biologists who study animal behavior. They try, whenever possible, to test hypotheses by making observations under controlled conditions. Controlled experiments can be performed in laboratories, but in field experiments the control of conditions is more difficult.

15–9 Dr. Anne Bekoff taking notes in the field on behavior of Adelie penguins at Cape Crozier, Ross Island, Antarctica.

ethologists [ee THOL uh justs; Greek: *ethos*, character, habit, + *logos*, speech, reason]

15–10 Dr. Richard Boolootian records the sounds of elephant seals on San Nicholas Island off the coast of California.

Scientists who study human behavior are called ***psychologists.*** They do many of their experiments in laboratories. But experimental study of human behavior is difficult, so psychologists also study other organisms. Psychologists and ethologists sometimes disagree about their conclusions and concepts. With increases of knowledge, however, differences in viewpoint are lessening.

psychologists [sy KOL uh justs; Greek: *psyche*, spirit, soul, + *logos*]

INTERPRETATION

At times all biologists have difficulties drawing conclusions from their data and fitting their conclusions together with those of other investigators. This is the job of interpretation — giving meaning to observations. Behavioral scientists have some special problems.

Consider a laboratory experiment. We place on the side of a frog's body some substance that we think is unpleasant. Immediately the frog's hind foot rubs at the spot where the substance was placed. Aha! we think, the frog doesn't like the substance and is trying to rub it off. But how do we know that the frog isn't trying to rub it *in* because it likes the substance? Interpretation of this behavior becomes even more perplexing if we destroy the frog's brain. The frog continues to bring its hind foot up to rub at its side. Can we use either "liking" or "not liking" to interpret the behavior of a frog without a brain?

In observing behavior, we tend to put ourselves in the organism's place. We explain its behavior in human terms. We may say that a barking dog is "angry," that a purring cat is "contented," or even that the roots of a cactus are "searching" for water. This is **anthropomorphism,** the interpretation of the behavior of other organisms as if they were human. But we don't know that other organisms have any of these human emotions. Therefore, ethologists do not use such explanations. Instead, they look for physiological, genetic, or environmental explanations.

anthropomorphism [an thruh-puh MOR fiz um; Greek: *anthropos*, human, + *morphe*, form]

PERCEPTION

Take a walk with a dog along a street. You may notice a few odors from automobile exhaust or from freshly cut grass. But the dog goes sniffing along from one odor to the next. And most of these are completely unnoticed by you. You have great difficulty imagining the ability of a bloodhound to follow the "scent trail" of an animal or a human that passed by an hour or a day before. Humans live in a world that is primarily visual. What we perceive in our environment — our **perception** of it — is made up mostly of colors, shapes, and movements. Dogs lack color vision, and they do not distinguish shapes nearly as well as we do. But dogs hear sounds that we do not; dog whistles will call dogs home though we hear nothing.

perception [pur SEP chun; Latin: *per*, through, + *capere*, to grasp]

Why do dogs often howl when musical instruments such as violins and flutes are played?

If it is difficult to understand the perceptual world of a dog, a familiar mammal, how much more difficult it is to understand the world of a bird, fish, bee, or octopus. Yet, if we are going to understand an organism's behavior, we must know what it perceives in its environment. We must determine what kinds of receptors it has and how sensitive they are. Biologists often use instruments that can translate things humans cannot perceive into things we can. Flowers that look white to us may have patterns of color to a bee. Bees can see ultraviolet light, which is invisible to human eyes. We can "see" what the bee sees only in photographs taken by ultraviolet light.

15–11 Marsh marigolds. Photographed on film that records light much as we see it (*left*). Photographed on film that records ultraviolet light as bees see it (*right*).

CHECK YOURSELF

A. What is behavior?

B. What is irritability?

C. Distinguish a tropism from a taxis.

D. How does perception differ in different kinds of animals? What difficulties does this present for a behavioral scientist?

E. Why is anthropomorphism not useful in interpreting the behavior of animals? What other explanations do ethologists look for?

BEHAVIOR IN ORGANISMS WITH NERVOUS SYSTEMS

Animal behavior involves the whole individual and is directed toward the organism's external environment. It involves what an animal does (movement) and what it is (physiology). It also is affected by where the animal lives (environment). In addition, the stimulus that triggers a response may come from the animal's internal environment (for example, hunger) or its external environment (for example, a predator).

Except for the sponges, all animals have nerve cells that are differentiated. Organisms that have nerve cells also have muscle cells that bring about movement. Animals with the simplest nervous systems have the simplest behaviors.

INNATE BEHAVIOR

Planaria (see figure 4–32) are frequently found in wet, dark habitats under stones. If you remove one of these stones, the planaria's habitat becomes exposed to light. The planaria's response to this increase in light intensity is an increase in movement. They wander from side to side as well as moving forward. Eventually they come upon another dark spot and the response stops.

When a male moth emerges from its cocoon and detects the odor produced by a female of its species, it flies upwind toward the source of the odor. The first time that a tree squirrel sees a nut, it tries to bury the nut. The squirrel will do this even if it has never seen another squirrel do so. A young squirrel may even try to bury the nut in the floor of a cage. Young spiders weave webs as well constructed as those of older spiders.

innate [in AYT; Latin: *in*, in, + *natus*, born]

These are examples of **innate** behavior. Behavior is considered to be innate if it occurs in response to a particular stimulus the first time an individual is exposed to that stimulus. Innate behavior is thought to be the result of something that is inherited.

15–12 Feeding is the primary behavior in nestlings. These young spoonbills respond to the parent's presence in the nest with their raised bills.

Caulion Singletary

To test for innate behavior, ethologists hatch animals in isolation. Whatever these animals do, they do without following another animal's example. With mammals it is perhaps impossible to determine what behavior is innate. There is always some chance of learning from the mother. Mother birds even communicate with their unhatched chicks. So a convincing test of innate behavior is difficult to achieve for many vertebrates.

An animal frequently reacts more or less automatically to a stimulus. The stimulus may come from the abiotic environment or from a plant or another animal. Each species has characteristic responses. But some of these responses may not appear until long after birth or hatching. Sometimes a response switches from one stimulus to another. This may happen, for example, if one food supply runs out and a similar food is available. It may become stronger or fade away, depending on the experience of the individual. The physical appearance of one member of a species may cause mating behavior, feeding behavior, or aggressive behavior in another member. And some behaviors occur in response to gravity, light intensity, or other abiotic factors.

aggressive [uh GRES iv]: being the first to attack

Investigation 15.2 PLANARIAN BEHAVIOR

INTRODUCTION

Planaria are common, free-living flatworms that live in fresh water. They have a simple nervous system consisting of 2 cerebral ganglia and a "ladder-type" nerve cord (see figure 14–31). The responses of planaria are often referred to as taxes.

Read through the procedure and write a hypothesis you think it was designed to test.

PROCEDURE

1. With the medicine dropper, remove one planarian from the culture bottle. Quickly and gently release the water containing the animal into the test tube. (The planarian may fasten itself to the medicine dropper. If it does so, insert the dissecting needle through the open end of the dropper and gently prod the animal loose. At the same time, squirt the water slowly from the dropper.)

2. Add dechlorinated water to the test tube until it is nearly full. Insert the stopper. When the stopper is inserted, it should displace some of the water. This elimi-

MATERIALS
(per team)

planarian *(Dugesia tigrini)*
dechlorinated water
2 microscope slides
test tube, 13 × 100 mm
cork stopper to fit test tube
test-tube rack or small bottle
square of aluminum foil, 12 × 12 cm
medicine dropper
dissecting needle
glass-marking crayon
sheet of white paper

nates the possibility of an air bubble in the tube. Draw a line at the midpoint of the test tube. Hold the test tube horizontally until the flatworm has moved near the center of the tube.

3. Place the test tube, cork end *up*, in the test-tube rack or small bottle. It should be illuminated evenly from all sides. (1) Why is this necessary? Observe the planarian for 10 minutes. Record how much time it spends in each half of the tube.

4. Hold the test tube horizontally until the

flatworm has moved near the center of the tube.

5. Place the test tube, cork end *down,* in the rack or bottle. Again, observe and time the reaction of the planarian. (2) To what environmental factor do you think the animal is responding? Is its response negative or positive?

6. Again, hold the test tube horizontally until the flatworm has moved near the center of the tube. Lay the tube on a sheet of white paper on a flat surface. (If the tube is not level, stack 1 or 2 microscope slides under the low end.)

7. Observe the planarian for 10 minutes. Record how much time it spends in each end of the tube. Be sure the test tube is evenly lighted with diffuse room light along its entire length.

8. Form a cap of the aluminum foil to fit over the rounded end, covering about 1/2 of the test tube.

9. Wait until the planarian is near the middle of the tube and is headed for the corked end. Then slip the aluminum-foil cap over the rounded end of the tube.

10. For another 10 minutes record the time the planarian spends in each end of the tube. (3) What is the stimulus for this response? Is the response negative or positive?

DISCUSSION

(4) Can you use your results of this investigation to describe the behavior of all planaria? Why or why not?

Compare the results of all teams in your class. (5) Did all of the planaria behave similarly? (6) What might be the advantage of these behaviors for the planaria?

RESPONSE TO CHEMICALS

Response to odors or certain chemicals can be observed in many animals. Snakes have very sensitive receptors for odor. A king cobra in one zoo would eat nothing but other large snakes. To stretch the food budget, the zookeeper skinned indigo snakes and stuffed the skins with other kinds of food. The cobra ate these stuffed skins. Experiments indicate that the cobra ate them because the skins retained the odor of the indigo snakes.

King snakes are not harmed by the bite of a rattlesnake. Sometimes they can kill and eat a rattler. When a rattler encoun-

15—13 What behavior is shown by this rattlesnake? What could be the stimulus? Explain your answer.

Judd Cooney

ters another animal, it rattles and then attacks. When a rattler meets a king snake, however, it does not rattle or attack. Instead, it hides its head and hits at the king snake with a loop of its body. This variation in behavior is a response to the particular smell of the king snake.

PATTERNS

In the behavior of a newly emerged male moth, many muscles work together to produce flight. The behavior of a squirrel burying a nut is more complex. Different muscles must be used in digging, pushing the nut into a hole, and then covering it. Moreover, these actions must be performed in a certain order. The construction of a spiderweb also requires a very complex behavior pattern. Yet the existing evidence indicates that all of these behaviors are innate. Such complex behavior patterns are sometimes called *fixed-action patterns*. But the behavior is not invariable. It depends on the animal's physiology as well as on a stimulus. A sick squirrel or one that is tired may pay no attention to a nut.

Many ethologists are interested in the stimuli that start the chains of physiological reactions in behavior patterns. They have found that the required stimulus is often very simple. Such a stimulus—called a *releaser*—acts like a key that unlocks the whole physiological sequence. Like a key, a releaser is spe-

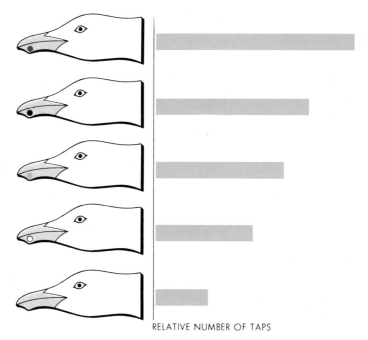

RELATIVE NUMBER OF TAPS

15–14 Herring-gull nestlings tap at a red spot on the bill of the parent; the parent then feeds them. An ethologist presented different cardboard models (*left*) to newly hatched chicks and recorded the results (*right*). Can you draw any conclusion about this behavior?

cific. Only a particular releaser starts a particular behavior pattern. And the releaser and the behavior pattern may be specific to one species.

Much of the behavior of invertebrates can be classed as innate. But this, of course, does not *explain* behavior. Physiologists explore the nervous and hormonal mechanisms that control such behavior. Ethologists analyze such behavior experimentally by varying stimuli and by interrupting the sequence of steps in the complete behavior.

CHECK YOURSELF

F. What is innate behavior?
G. How do ethologists test for innate behavior?
H. Describe a negative taxis. A positive one.
I. Name some complex behavior patterns that seem to be innate.
J. What is a releaser stimulus?

BEHAVIOR PATTERNS

Many biologists are interested in how behavior functions in the survival of individuals and of species. Behaviors, however, are so varied that they are difficult to classify. Some behavior is associated with responses to factors in the abiotic environment — heat, humidity, salinity, for example. Some is associated with food-getting, escape from enemies, or reproduction. Instead of attempting to glance briefly at many parts of behavioral science, we will concentrate on a few, leaving others for you to explore if you wish. (See "Suggested Readings," page 532.)

CYCLES

Perhaps you have observed that many activities of plants and animals do not occur continuously. Rather, they seem to occur at certain times each day. Many birds sing mostly at sunrise. Flowers of some plants open in the morning and close at night. Those of other species open in the evening. Most moths fly at night and rest in the daytime, but most butterflies behave in just the opposite way.

Are these daily cycles of activity the result of alternating daylight and darkness? In 1729 a French scientist took plants deep into a mine. For several days (while the plants were still healthy) their leaf movements were similar to those that took place under natural conditions of day and night. These observations strongly indicated that something within the plant, not something in the environment, was causing the movements.

As has happened so often in history, scientists of the time failed to recognize the importance of these observations. It was 200 years later that a German botanist showed that in many organisms—plants, animals, and protists—some behaviors occur periodically. These behaviors happen without regard to changes of light and dark. They also have a kind of innate rhythm of behavior.

More recently a white-crowned sparrow was kept under constant conditions of continuous light and uniform temperature. Its feeding activity was observed. In each 24-hour period (a natural day) the bird began to eat about one hour earlier. Its cycle of feeding behavior was about 23 hours. Similar experiments have been done with a large variety of organisms in many activities. Among these were observations of leaf movements in plants; cell division in some protists; changes in human body temperature; and time of activity in birds, mammals, and insects. Almost all of these occurred in approximately 24-hour cycles. Such cycles are referred to as *circadian rhythms.*

Circadian rhythms are innate. But under environmental conditions that provide a light-dark cycle, the rhythms conform to the cycle. The innate mechanism is reset each day by stimuli from the environment. For example, a white-crowned sparrow, in a natural environment, has a 24-hour feeding cycle. Although details differ among species, in most organisms circadian rhythms are readjusted to fit new light-dark cycles in a few days.

The problem of adjustment is quite important to humans who fly from one continent to another. Consider a jet traveler who flies from San Francisco to London. At first the traveler's circadian rhythm ("biological clock") tends to retain San Francisco time. It may take a day or two for this individual's biological clock to be "reset" according to the local light-dark cycle.

Recently, researchers have begun to study the possibility that animals also have *circannual rhythms.* Ground squirrels were kept in a windowless room that was lighted 12 hours each day, all year. Plenty of food and water was provided at all times, and the temperature was kept constant at 0°C. Without clues from the environment, the squirrels nevertheless went into hibernation, on schedule, in the fall. They stopped eating, and their body temperatures dropped to near 1°C. At the usual time—the following April—their body temperatures rose, and they began eating. Still without receiving any information from their environment about weather or daylength, they hibernated again in September.

15—15 White-crowned sparrow. (× 1/4) This species breeds in the northwestern part of North America and in winter may be found throughout much of the United States.

Are all of these activities behaviors?

circadian [sur KAD ee un; Latin: *circum*, around, + *dies*, day]

Would readjustment of the "biological clock" be necessary on a trip from New York to Santiago, Chile?

circannual [sur KAN yuh wul; Latin: *circum*, + *annualis*, yearly]

15–16 In its natural habitat, a ground squirrel burrows underground and builds a nest of grass, hair, and other materials. It curls up like a ball during hibernation. Can you think of any ways in which this curled-up position might be an advantage to the squirrel?

Migrating birds have two homes. They live in one place during winter but spend summers in another. Some warblers, for example, breed in Europe during spring but migrate to Africa for fall and winter. Some newly hatched warblers were taken to Africa in the spring. Others were kept in Europe. Some birds in each group were kept indoors and some were kept outdoors. Even in these diverse geographic and climatic conditions, *all* the birds showed migratory behavior at nearly the same time.

A circannual clock may serve several purposes. A hibernator for instance, begins depositing body fat *before* cold weather arrives. Such an internal clock may account for changes in behaviors that occur prior to the mating season, cold weather, or an annual dry season or period of food shortage. Birds wintering near the equator fly back to their breeding place in the temperate zone at the same time each year. The climate and daylength at the equator change very little throughout the year. An internal circannual clock could be the explanation for this behavior.

The circannual clock, however, is never set at exactly 365 days. Clues from the environment seem to reset the rhythm each year. No doubt, variations in light and temperature are involved in regulating circannual rhythms, as they regulate circadian rhythms. In addition, the rhythms probably depend on more subtle factors that are as yet unknown.

The search for internal clocks, circadian and circannual, has barely begun. One group of physiologists is trying to locate the clock in the brain of a fruit fly. A few studies suggest that some physiological and behavioral activity in humans operates on annual cycles. Much more research must be done before anyone can state conclusively that humans do, indeed, have circannual as well as circadian rhythms.

TERRITORIALITY

Some species of animals will defend small areas against other members of their species. This type of behavior is called **territoriality.** The study of territoriality is a meeting place for many kinds of biologists. Both nervous and endocrine systems are involved in the physiology of territorial behavior. The interactions of individuals are of interest to ethologists. The function of territoriality in a community structure and in the homeostasis of ecosystems greatly concerns ecologists.

territoriality [ter uh tor ee AL ut-ee; Latin: *terra*, land]

Gordon S. Smith

15–17 In herring gulls, only the immediate vicinity of the nest is defended. This territorial dispute does not affect birds nesting only a few meters away.

Many studies of territoriality have been made. Most of the early studies were made on birds. One of the first questions investigated concerned differences between summer and winter behaviors. Experiments with captive birds and investigations in the field have resulted in some progress toward understanding these differences.

In late winter the days become longer. The lengthening hours of daylight somehow affect the hypothalamus of male white-crowned sparrows. This causes the anterior pituitary to release hormones that cause gradual growth and development of the testes. Other hormones increase the birds' appetites. Excess calories are stored as fat. Similar changes in hormones and glands occur in the females. Soon the birds begin their nocturnal migratory flight northward.

By the time the birds reach the breeding ground, the testes of the males are producing sex hormones. One effect of these hormones (together with the sight of the breeding area) is to cause territorial behavior. The response of one male to another is completely different from his response a few weeks earlier in the wintering flock. As spring dissolves into summer, the days cease to lengthen. The anterior pituitary of the white-crowned sparrow no longer releases hormones that affect the testes. The testes stop producing male sex hormones. In the absence of these hormones, the territorial response to other males disappears. The males assemble with females and young in flocks that move southward.

The breeding ground of black-headed gulls is among the grassy sand dunes along the northern European seas. These birds nest in groups on the ground. Males arrive at the breeding site first, in early spring. Each male takes up a position in the dunes and defends a small area from intruders. It repeatedly gives a loud call, stretching its body forward. The response of a calling male to another male that enters the territory is a series of **displays.** The male whose territory has been entered stretches its neck up, holding its beak ready to slash downward. If this display is unsuccessful, the bird may point its beak directly at the intruder, holding its body parallel to the ground. Then the defending bird may hold this position and charge at the intruder. Such displays are usually successful, and the defending bird retains his territory.

displays: characteristic behavior patterns that act as visual stimuli

When the females arrive at the breeding site, they are attracted by the loud calling of the males. Further displays between males and females establish breeding pairs. Each pair settles in a nesting spot, which they defend vigorously.

Territorial behavior is a response to environmental stimuli and to physiological changes that occur in these birds. It also may be a response to stimuli from other members of the same species. To find out what these intraspecific stimuli were, an ethologist placed a robin model on a branch in an area occupied by brightly colored, English robins. The birds paid no attention to the stuffed robin during the winter. But in the spring the model bird was attacked by pairs of robins that were building nests nearby. Over a period of several days, the ethologist removed parts of the robin model. The birds continued to respond to it, even when nothing remained but a bunch of red and white breast feathers. Apparently this bright bunch of feathers triggers the territorial response in nesting English robins.

X 1/3

15 – 18 During the nesting season, a male English robin raises his head and puffs out his breast when he encounters another male. Here an ethologist has placed a tuft of breast feathers in a tree. Without anthropomorphism, can you explain the response of the bird?

You may have noticed that several kinds of birds live in a park or cemetery, or along a tree-lined street, near your home. The territories of birds not only have length and width; they also have depth. Different species of birds establish their nests at different levels in the trees. Thus two or three pairs of birds of different species may peacefully occupy one large tree, but two or three pairs of the same species may not.

Territories are places where animals mate, nest, and feed. So territorial defense is important to the survival of animals. An animal in familiar surroundings has a better chance of avoiding predators. Also, offspring are more likely to survive in the security of a defended territory. Most often a territory is defended by males, but sometimes by females. Sometimes mated pairs defend a territory, as did the English robins. At other times a whole population may participate in this defense. Territorial behavior may limit the number of mating pairs. After territories are established, little fighting usually occurs. The animals' energies are used for food-gathering and rearing of young.

You can observe territorial behavior in many species. Territorial behavior has been reported in mammals, reptiles, amphibians, fish, and even some invertebrate animals.

Can you describe observations of your own that indicate any kind of territoriality in humans?

COMMUNICATION

Any activity of one organism that causes a reaction in another can be regarded as *communication.* In this broad and basic sense, communication must occur in all ecological relationships — among plants and protists as well as among animals.

15–19 Long observation led one investigator to interpret the positions of wolves' tails in this way. Have you observed similar tail positions in dogs? Do you think they communicate the same meanings?

Submissive attitude   Normal position   Self-confidence   Confident threat

Most biologists, however, use the term in a narrower sense, though they do not always agree on the limits. In this discussion, communication is restricted to animals.

To be of value for communication, each kind of stimulus must have a "meaning." A biologist can find out what this meaning is only by observing what organisms do when the stimulus is given. Anything that can be sensed by another organism—any kind of stimulus—may serve for communication. Sounds, scents, and sights are the most common stimuli.

Repeatedly, when a male white-crowned sparrow sings, biologists observe that most other males avoid the vicinity of the singer and that females may approach him. In this case the stimulus caused one response in males and another in females.

ornithologists [or nuh THOL uh-justs]

Ornithologists are scientists who study birds. They have studied, recorded, and analyzed the sounds birds make. Expert bird-watchers can identify many birds by their sounds. The most easily recognized song is usually the territorial call of the males. But ornithologists have learned that birds make a variety of sounds in a variety of situations. And they have seen other birds react to sound emitted by one of their own species. Suppose a bird is caught by your neighbor's cat. It emits a distress cry. In response to this sound, other birds in the area may fly away. One scientist used the recorded shrieks of alarm of a starling to rid a small town of its large population of starlings. The sound was replayed through a sound-amplifying truck. The truck was driven through the town, and the starlings left. They did not return.

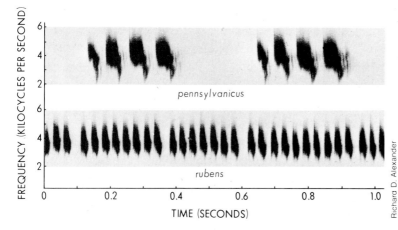

Richard D. Alexander

15–20 "Songs" of two species of field crickets: *Gryllus pennsylvanicus* (above) and *G. rubens* (below). Ethologists can transform air vibrations into visible form. In this way, they can compare animal sounds.

Some chemical substances produced by animals are sex attractants. Others are repellents. Some mark territories, and some identify an animal's offspring. Chemicals involved in animal communication are called **pheromones.** By leaving their scents at various places, some mammals mark the limits of their territories. When ants find a food source, glands in their abdomens release a pheromone. The ants thus leave a scent as they return to the anthill. Other ants are attracted to the scent. They follow it and find the food. When the food supply is exhausted, returning ants do not leave a scent trail.

pheromones [FER uh monz]

A male gypsy moth is attracted to a female even in a dense forest. The male senses the sex attractant given off by a female some distance away. The attractant draws the male to the female, and they mate. The skin of a wounded minnow gives off a pheromone that is a repellent. If one minnow in a group is attacked by a predator, the other minnows swim away.

Humans have a poor sense of smell compared to many other animals. But we use sight and sound extensively for communication. Most animals that have sight use it for communication. Usually visual stimuli consist of movements. Often movements are made more conspicuous by some structure of the body. A startled white-tailed deer raises its tail. The white underside of the tail flashes conspicuously in contrast to the dark upper side. The rest of the herd may respond by fleeing.

Many visual displays have been observed in a wide variety of animals. Birds and most mammals have territorial and mating displays. In fireflies patterns of light pulses attract males and females. Each species of firefly exhibits its own pattern. In some species of spiders males bring females something to eat

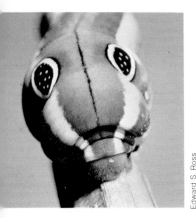

Edward S. Ross

15–21 Hornworm, a caterpillar that has false "eyes."   × 3

before mating. This food may save the male's life, because otherwise the larger female would eat the male.

In humans visual communication takes the form of facial expressions. Or, it may be in the way the arms and legs are held or how the body moves.

Often the response to a visual stimulus occurs in another species, such as a predator. Many predators will attack only prey that moves. For example, when hognose snakes or North American opossums stay motionless, the visual stimulus of movement is not given. Thus predators usually do not attack.

Some caterpillars have spots that from a distance look like large eyes. (The caterpillars' true eyes are very small.) Food-seeking birds respond to these large "eyes" by staying away from the caterpillars. Some species are the same color as their surroundings. Many insects and small animals look like a blade of grass, a piece of bark, or a patch of dirt. Thus their predators may not see them.

SOCIAL BEHAVIOR

Fish schools. Many species of fishes move about in compact groups. Such a *school* is usually made up of fish not only of the same species but also of the same size. At any particular instant, all individuals in the school swim in one direction. When one fish changes direction, all do.

15–22 A school of mackerel. Can you think of any ways in which this behavior might be an advantage to the fish?

Douglas P. Wilson

Many species that behave in this way have sleek bodies that glitter as they move. A school's movements seem to be controlled in part by visual releasers; fish that cannot see do not school. In other cases, touch receptors along the sides of a fish may receive stimuli that keep it at a certain distance from the other fish.

Insect societies. If you look through the animal kingdom for something like human societies, you may find the greatest similarities when you observe certain insects. Among ants, bees, and termites, many individuals carry out special tasks and seem to work together closely for the good of the group. Within a species we find individuals that specialize in different kinds of work. Some are food collectors, or fighters, or even living "food bins." Others are "baby-sitters" for ant eggs and larvae. Some species cultivate fungi for food. Some wage war and make slaves. Some construct complicated housing projects. You can easily see the anthropomorphism here.

Humans have long been interested in the behavior of honeybees. They are one of the few kinds of insects we have domesticated. So the use of anthropomorphic language has been especially common in describing the activities of bees. But bee societies are very different from those of humans. For one thing, the inhabitants of a beehive are really one gigantic family. All are offspring of the queen. All the workers are sisters; all the drones are brothers. Modern human societies, of course, consist of many families.

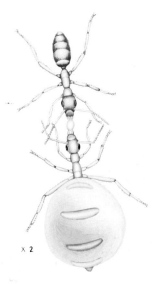

× 2

15–23 In some ant species specialized workers serve as storage bins for food. What environmental conditions might favor such behavior?

worker   drone   queen

15–24 Honeybees. Each of these kinds of individuals has specialized behavior. Drones are males; workers are nonreproductive females; queens are egg-layers.   × 2

Furthermore, repeated experiments show that highly organized insect societies are based on innate behavior. A fungus-cultivating ant goes through the necessary actions automatically. Each generation of people, on the other hand, has to learn how to care for crops.

15—25 A high degree of social behavior is required in these ants that cultivate a fungus on bits of leaves (Panama).

Neal A. Weber

15—26 Some species of ants feed on a substance secreted by aphids. They care for the aphids much as humans care for cows. Why, then, are the behaviors of humans and of ants not comparable?

John Kohout from Root Resources

Clarence R. Carpenter: 1905—. American psychologist and anthropologist

red howler. See page 761.

persistent [pur SIS tunt]: occurring again and again

Primate societies. Primates are usually placed in the taxonomic order with humans. In the study of primate behavior there has been an unusual degree of coordination between investigations in the laboratory and in the field.

One of the first field studies was made by C. R. Carpenter, who spent almost a year observing howler monkeys on Barro Colorado Island. Carpenter was especially interested in social organization. He found that there were about 400 howlers on the island. They were organized into 23 clans (groups) that varied in size from 4 to 35 individuals. The clans were strictly territorial. When two clans came near each other along a territorial border, vigorous howling started. The vocal battle continued until one band or the other retreated. There were a few solitary males. When these tried to join a clan, they were shouted off. In one instance, however, Carpenter saw one lone male who, after persistent attempts over several weeks, was finally accepted into a clan.

Carpenter could not find that the clans had specific leaders. A male was usually in the lead when a clan moved, but
sometimes it would be one male, sometimes another. No instance of fighting within a clan was observed. Among other
kinds of monkeys, particularly Indian rhesus monkeys and
African baboons, there is some evidence that one of the males
is the recognized leader. Other observers, however, have noted
that leadership changes frequently. Shirley Strum observed
baboons for several months at Kekopey Ranch in Kenya. She
noted that male baboons even move from one troop to another.

Having been successful with his earlier studies, Carpenter
turned to gibbons, which are not monkeys but apes. This group
of animals, the pongids, are structurally and physiologically
most like humans. Other biologists have studied other apes —
orangutans, chimpanzees, and gorillas. Jane Goodall has made
many studies of chimpanzees near Lake Tanganyika in Africa.
The results of all these studies show varied social behavior.

Orangutans spend more time in trees and less time on the
ground than do other apes, making study difficult at close
quarters. Nevertheless, social relationships among them —
including between adolescents — have been confirmed. Gibbons have small family groups consisting of male and female
with their young. Gorilla bands contain several adult males and
females dominated by one older male that rules the band.
Chimpanzees also live in groups of several adults and young.

A dominant male in a troop of gorillas or chimpanzees retains his leadership role by means of dominance displays. Actual fighting rarely occurs. One male simply outperforms another. He thumps the ground more firmly, beats the brush with a
bigger branch, or hoots more loudly. After the encounter, one
male is dominant and the other exhibits submissive behavior.
Once dominance is established, the relationship of the two
males usually remains peaceful.

Chicago Zoological Society

15 – 27 Dominance display
in a male baboon.

Are studies of primate social organization of any help to
psychologists who are trying to understand the social organization of humans? Our social organizations vary greatly today
and apparently have varied in the past. Moreover, our use of
language and symbols makes our societies vastly more complex
than any other primate society. Therefore, even though facts are
becoming more abundant, statements concerning the social
behavior of both humans and apes are still opinions rather than
conclusions. But primate behavior continues to fascinate. If you
visit the primate house in a zoo and watch what occurs on *both*
sides of the bars, you will find that not only biologists are
interested in primate behavior.

CHECK YOURSELF

K. What are circadian rhythms? Circannual rhythms?
L. What kinds of territorial behavior have been observed in animals?
M. How can a biologist determine the "meaning" of a communication stimulus?
N. What kinds of stimuli occur in communication between animals?
O. What are pheromones?
P. What kinds of behavior can be recognized in a school of fish?
Q. Biologists regard insect societies as only superficially like human societies. Why?
R. Why are studies of the social behavior of other primates difficult to apply to an understanding of human behavior?

X 1/4

15–28 Chaffinch. This is a European species that has been used in behavior studies.

precisely [prih SYS lee; Latin: *prae*, before, + *caedere*, to cut]: sharply defined, not vague

LEARNING

The nut-burying behavior of a squirrel seems to be innate. So, too, is nut opening. A young squirrel opens a nut satisfactorily. But, as the squirrel becomes older and more experienced, its efficiency at opening nuts increases greatly. Chaffinches reared from hatching in soundproof rooms develop a song pattern basically like that of wild chaffinches. But their songs never include *all* the notes of the wild song. When the birds hear the wild song, however, they learn it. Evidently a basic song pattern is innate, but something is added to the innate behavior during the life of the birds. In both squirrels and birds *learning* occurs.

Learning is not easy to describe precisely. It depends on the experiences of an individual. Usually it brings about a lasting change in behavior. We must say a "lasting" rather than a "permanent" change in behavior, because forgetting occurs in learned behavior—as we all know!

There is another difficulty in describing learning. Some kinds of lasting changes in behavior occur simply as a part of development. When a tadpole's legs develop, its tail disappears. The resulting change from tail swimming to leg swimming is clearly associated with a change in structure. In other cases, it is extremely difficult to determine whether changes in behavior depend on learning or merely on structural development. Is experience—learning—necessary before a child can climb stairs? An experiment was tried with identical twins—twins with exactly the same genotype. The rate of development should be about the same in such twins. At an early age one twin was allowed much practice on stairs. The other was kept on flat surfaces and had no experience with stairs. Yet, when the second was finally allowed to climb stairs, her performance was about as good as that of her experienced twin.

Most learning requires more than a single experience. In the 1930's, however, Konrad Lorenz discovered a kind of learning that depends on just one experience. This kind of learning is called *imprinting.* Geese follow the first moving object they see after hatching. Normally this is their mother. But geese hatched in an incubator first saw Dr. Lorenz. Afterward they behaved toward him as though he were the female goose. He was imprinted in the experience of the goslings as the stimulus to follow.

Konrad Lorenz [LOR enz]: 1903—. Austrian biologist and one of the first ethologists

15–29 Konrad Lorenz and some of his imprinted geese.

Nina Leen

Imprinting resembles the action of a releaser, but the particular stimulus is not recognized innately — it must be learned. In imprinting, however, the learning is the result of just one experience. And that experience must come at a particular time in the early development of the individual. Often the *first* moving object that a young bird or fish sees will later release responses that normally are caused by the presence of a parent. This is particularly true if the object also gives appropriate sounds — quacking, in the case of ducks. Imprinting is a very simple kind of learning, closely related to innate behavior.

Imprinting was discovered by an ethologist. **Conditioning** was discovered much earlier by a physiologist. Ivan P. Pavlov was interested in the physiology of mammalian nervous systems. He began to study the reflex involved in the production of saliva in dogs. He soon found that the odor or sight of meat was sufficient to start salivation. Pavlov wondered whether other stimuli would produce the salivation response. Just before presenting meat to a dog, he rang a bell. He repeated this procedure many times with the same dog. Before long the dog began to secrete saliva as soon as the bell was rung, before the meat was presented. Eventually the dog would salivate merely at the ringing of the bell, without the stimulus of seeing or smelling the meat. This kind of learning — the transfer of a response from one stimulus to another — is called conditioning.

Pavlov extended his research in many directions. He showed that the substitute stimulus must come *before* the original stimulus if the response is to be transferred. He also showed that the shorter the time interval between the two stimuli, the quicker the response becomes associated with the substitute stimulus. Biologists have extended Pavlov's principles to other animals, including humans.

In conditioning, the learner is passive. More complicated kinds of learning experiments require movement by the learner. Animals make many kinds of movements. **Trial-and-error learning** begins when an animal associates certain movements with favorable or unfavorable results.

B. F. Skinner devised a box for investigating trial-and-error learning. A bar in the box releases a pellet of food when pressed. A hungry rat, placed in the box, moves about at random. Sooner or later it strikes the bar. Before long most of the rats that were tested associated pressing the bar with food. This device has been used to investigate many questions about learning. For example, what happens if the food pellet is not released after the rat has learned to obtain it by pressing the bar? What happens if the pellet is released sometimes but not always? If you are curious, refer to Scott's *Animal Behavior* (page 532).

Ivan P. Pavlov [ih VON POV lof]: 1849–1936. Russian physiologist

B. F. Skinner: 1904—. American psychologist

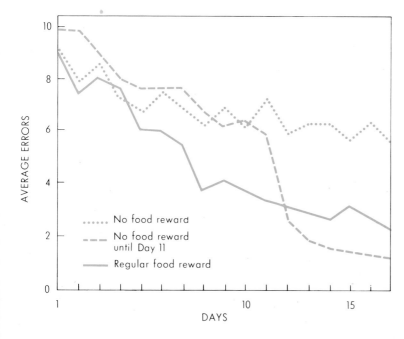

15–30 A learning experiment. Three groups of rats were tested daily in a maze. The route through the maze forked 14 times, and none of the choices could be repeated. The number of errors in choice was counted for each rat, and an average obtained for each group. How do you interpret the results?

Legend in figure:
...... No food reward
– – – No food reward until Day 11
——— Regular food reward

By means of a maze, biologists can observe learning in planaria and other animals that are capable of locomotion. A maze is a route with one or more choices of turns leading to a goal that is favorable or unfavorable to the planarian. The simplest form is the T-maze. How can we know that learning has occurred in a maze? With a T-maze we expect that, by chance, 50 percent of a planarian's turns will be to the right and 50 percent to the left. Assume a T-maze in which a turn to the right is rewarded by food. If, after several trials, the planarian turns to the right 90 percent of the time, we might conclude that learning has taken place.

There is a wide diversity in learning abilities among different kinds of animals. Thus far, in all experiments with sponges, coelenterates, and echinoderms, it seems possible to explain their behaviors without assuming that learning has occurred. But in planaria a simple kind of learning does occur. For example, unlike the other animals mentioned, a planarian has an anterior end and a posterior end, with a simple nervous system. There may be something about such a structure that favors the learning process. But, even in organisms with well-developed nervous systems, very little learning may occur. Many kinds of beetles, if put on a tabletop, will crawl to the edge and fall off. No matter how many times this happens, they never learn to avoid the edge of the table.

Compare the beetle's behavior with that of the frog and the "unpleasant" substance (page 506). What assumption is made about the beetle's "desires"?

On the other hand, learning occurs frequently in vertebrates. For example, along the coast of Florida, gulls feed on a variety of things. They have learned to follow ships to pick up food scraps thrown overboard. The laughing gulls on Siesta Key are fed by visitors to the beaches in the area. They learn to take food from a picnicker's hand or to pick up scraps tossed on the ground.

The territorial behavior in some of these birds seems to happen in response to the sight of a person carrying a bag or bundle (that might contain food). A gull establishes a territory around such a person. Each gull defends its person-territory with several threat displays and a long warning call. The territorial behavior is innate. The appearance of this behavior in response to a person carrying a bundle involves learning.

If it is difficult to describe what we mean by learning, it is even more difficult to describe **reasoning.** Perhaps it is best described in an example. The raccoon in figure 15–31 cannot quite reach the food by going directly toward it. First it must go back around Stake B. Given enough time, almost any active animal accomplishes the task by trial and error. Raccoons learn quickly in this way. But the test of reasoning hinges on what the animal does on the *first* exposure to the problem.

15–31 A problem.

Put in the raccoon's place, what would you do? You would immediately "size up the situation." You would walk back around Stake B and reach the food. Raccoons do not do this. In this situation chimpanzees and most monkeys behave as you would. Many primates apparently do not see A, B, C, and the rope as separate items. Rather, they see them as parts of a whole situation. The meaning is in the situation, not in the items. This behavior is often described as resulting from *insight.*

In another kind of experiment, an animal is allowed to watch the experimenter place food under one of two identical cups. After a delay, the animal is released to find the food. (Of course, odor must be controlled in such an experiment.) Animals such as rats, cats, and dogs fix their attention on the cup covering the food and go directly to it. But, if their attention is temporarily diverted, they do no better than would be expected on the basis of chance. Most primates, however, do not seem to fix their attention on the cup under which the food is placed. Even if they are removed from the situation and then brought back later, they still go immediately to the correct cup. Does the nonhuman primate mind form some lasting image, such as "food under right-hand cup"? If so, this behavior closely approaches the language-based behavior of humans.

Nonprimates apparently do not have insight. Some, such as raccoons, learn quickly. Even an octopus can learn to go around barriers. Often observations of wild animals reveal behaviors that seem to demonstrate insight. But such behavior may be merely the result of past experience.

CHECK YOURSELF

S. What evidence shows that much behavior results from both innate behavior patterns and learning?
T. What difficulties are involved in defining "learning"?
U. How does imprinting differ from other kinds of learning?
V. What do we mean by conditioning?
W. In what way is trial-and-error learning studied?
X. What is insight?

Investigation 15.3   CONDITIONING

MATERIALS
(per team)

For Part A

10–12 sow bugs or pill bugs
slice of carrot or potato
piece of sponge, 2 cm³
mixture of moist soil and leaf litter
coffee can, with plastic lid
glass or metal tray, about 20 × 30 cm
2 laboratory desk lamps
blotting paper, about 20 × 15 cm
8-penny nail
masking tape

For Part B

4 sow bugs or pill bugs
small piece of carrot or potato
mixture of moist soil and leaf litter
4 small vials, with plastic lids
box, about 10 × 15 × 2 cm, all
    plastic or with plastic cover
2 laboratory desk lamps
forceps
scissors
cardboard, about 12 × 12 cm
glass-marking crayon
masking tape
paper towel

INTRODUCTION

Sow bugs and pill bugs are crustaceans — relatives of crabs and shrimp. Unlike most crustaceans, they are terrestrial. However, they breathe by gills as do other crustaceans. They are found in many biomes, though different species may be found in different places. Any species may be used for this investigation.

PROCEDURE

Part A

1. Pour a mixture of moist soil and leaf litter into a coffee can until it is 2/3 full. Place a few dead leaves on the surface. Then add a small piece of moistened sponge and a slice (about 2 × 5 × 1 cm) of carrot or potato.
2. Put in 10 to 12 sow bugs or pill bugs. Using a nail, punch 6 to 8 holes in the plastic lid. Place the lid on the container. Keep the sponge moist and replace the carrot or potato slice every few days.
3. In subdued light, place all the sow bugs in the center of a large tray. (1) Do the animals remain together? If not, do they wander about aimlessly, or do they move in one direction?
4. Remove the animals gently. Place some moist blotting paper at one end of the tray so that half the bottom is dry and the other half is covered by the moist paper. Place all the animals in the center of the dry end of the tray. Observe the animals for several minutes. (2) Do the animals respond to the moisture? Is the response negative or positive? (3) If some animals move to the moist end, do they climb on top of the blotter or move underneath it? (4) When individuals move, do they move faster in the dry half or in the moist half of the tray? Why do you think this happens?
5. If some animals move under the blotter, wait about 5 minutes and then pick the blotter up. Observe the distribution of animals on its underside. (5) Are they

uniformly distributed, or are they clustered in groups? Make notes of any other behavior that you observe.
6. Set two lamps of equal intensity about 50 cm apart. Place one of the animals equidistant from the two lamps and about 20 cm from the imaginary line connecting them. (6) If the animal moves, sketch its route in relation to the two lamps. Repeat this several times.
7. Now cover the animal's right eye with a tiny piece of masking tape. Repeat the procedure. Again sketch the route in several trials. (7) Is there any consistent difference in the routes under the two conditions? (8) To what stimulus is the animal responding? Is its response negative or positive?

Part B

1. Mark 4 vials A, B, C, and D; add your team symbol to each.
2. Place a mixture of moist soil and leaf litter in each vial until it is about half full. Add a spiraled strip of moist paper towel and a small piece of potato or carrot.
3. Place one sow bug or pill bug into each vial. Perforate the lids and cover the vials.
4. Using a plastic-topped cardboard (or all-plastic) box, prepare a T-maze as shown in figure 15–32. Use strips of cardboard for the inner walls. Hold them in place with masking tape. Cut one hole in the box wall at the base of the T and one at

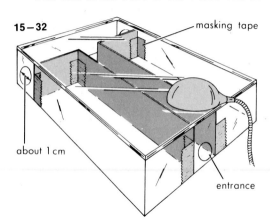

15–32

masking tape

about 1 cm

entrance

the end of each T arm. Place a lamp directly above the T base but do not turn it on.

5. Place Animal A in the entrance of the maze and cover the hole with masking tape. Turn on the lamp. (9) How does the animal react? When the animal reaches the crossarm of the T, it usually will turn in one direction or the other. Note the direction. When it reaches the end of a T arm, remove it immediately and repeat the "test run." Make a total of 5 "test runs." Record the direction of turn each time. Return the animal to its vial.

6. Follow the same procedure with Animals B, C, and D.

7. While you are working with the latter animals, Animal A is "resting." Now make 5 more "trial runs" with each animal, in the same order.

8. Next day repeat the whole procedure. You now have the results of 20 trials for each animal. Tabulate the results for each animal. Record on its vial L (for consistent left-turner), R (for consistent right-turner), or B (for an animal that turns either left or right without any consistency).

9. You are now ready to train your animals. Use only the L and R animals. Start with any one of them. Place a lamp at the end of the T arm down which it consistently turned. Do not turn the lamp on yet.

10. Place the animal in the maze as before (turn on the lamp above the beginning of the T base). When the animal reaches the end of the T base, turn on the light at the end of the T arm. (10) What is the animal's reaction? Remove the animal from the maze and replace it in its vial.

11. Carry out this procedure with each individual. Always place the lamp at the end of the T arm the individual consistently turned into during the "trial runs."

12. Go back to the 1st individual and repeat the procedure. Continue until each individual has been given 10 runs.

13. Repeat the whole training procedure each day for at least 3 days. When training has been completed, test each individual in the maze 20 times *without using a light*. Record the direction in which each animal turned.

DISCUSSION

Part A

(*11*) Can the behavior of your animals with respect to moisture be related to their survival? If so, how? (*12*) Can the behavior of your animals with respect to light be related to their survival? If so, how? In Chapter 4 a term was used to describe a structure that seemed to fit an organism to its environment. (*13*) What term can you use to describe the behavior you observed in this investigation?

Review the discussion of levels of behavior. (*14*) Which term best fits the observed behavior? (*15*) What information would increase your confidence in your decision?

Part B

(*16*) What kind of learning was this procedure designed to produce? (*17*) Did you obtain any evidence of learning in the animals with which you worked? If so, what was the evidence? (*18*) If you obtained evidence of learning in the species, did all individuals learn equally well? (*19*) Do you think that individual differences in their ability to learn would have any effect on a population of the animals?

FOR FURTHER INVESTIGATION

In Chapter 8 it was pointed out that a biologist investigating tolerances has difficulty separating the effects of one factor from the effects of another. In Part A of this investigation you encountered the same problem with respect to stimuli. Criticize the procedure and then try to design one that would better separate effects of the stimuli involved.

PROBLEMS

1. The following are examples of behaviors that have been called instinctive: (*a*) the web-building of spiders, (*b*) the nest-building of birds, (*c*) the comb-building of bees, and (*d*) the dam-building of beavers. How might it be possible to obtain evidence showing to what extent these activities are innate and to what extent they are learned?

2. Make a list of animals from a number of phyla and arrange it in order of the care given the young—from least to most. List the same animals in order of numbers of young produced—from most to least. Explain any relationships you can find between the two lists.

3. Biologists have found evidence of organization even in apparently simple groupings of animals—for example, in herds of domestic cattle. What is a social hierarchy? How is it formed? How is it maintained? What is the effect on the hierarchy of introducing new individuals into the group? What effect do hormones have on hierarchical behavior?

4. Of what importance are behavioral studies to people in these careers?

beekeeper	National Park ecologist
endocrinologist	nature photographer
entomologist	pesticide manufacturer
horticulturalist	wildlife conservation officer

SUGGESTED READINGS

Galdikas, B. M. F. 1980. Living with the Great Orange Apes. *National Geographic*, June, pp. 830–853. Orangutans, as well as chimpanzees and gorillas, can learn to communicate with humans by signing.

Goodall, J. 1979. Life and Death at Gombe. *National Geographic*, May, pp. 592–621. An update on the author's earlier, famous behavioral studies of chimpanzees.

Krebs, J. R. and N. B. Davies (eds.). 1978. *Behavioral Ecology*. Sinauer Associates, Sunderland, Mass. A text emphasizing the relationship between behavior and the environment. Available also in paperback.

Menzel, R. and J. Erber. 1978. Learning and Memory in Bees. *Scientific American*, July. Bees can learn not only where food is but also learn, and retain the learning, about the color and odor of the food flower.

Patent, D. H. 1978. *Animal and Plant Mimicry*. Holiday House, New York. A wealth of examples of the role mimicry plays in behavior.

Patterson, F. P. 1978. Conversations with a Gorilla. *National Geographic*, October, pp. 438–465.

Price, E. O. and A. W. Stokes. 1975. *Animal Behavior in Laboratory and Field*. 2nd ed.

W. H. Freeman, San Francisco. Paperback. Useful collection of investigations. First section includes methods of data gathering.

Scientific American. 1979. *Hormones and Reproductive Behavior*. W. H. Freeman, San Francisco. A collection of papers from *Scientific American* dealing with the influence of the sex hormones on behavior.

Scott, J. P. 1972. *Animal Behavior*. 2nd ed. University of Chicago Press, Chicago. Originally published in 1958 by Doubleday, but still a good introduction. Available in paperback.

Strum, S. C. 1975. Life with the "Pumphouse Gang." *National Geographic*, May, pp. 673–691. New insights into baboon behavior.

Tinbergen, N. 1973. *The Animal in Its World*. Harvard University Press, Cambridge, Mass. An excellent sourcebook for students of animal behavior.

Vogel, S. 1978. Organisms That Capture Currents. *Scientific American*, August. Organisms as diverse as sponges and prairie dogs harness water currents and wind for their own purposes.

Würsig, B. 1979. Dolphins. *Scientific American*, March. The question of how intelligent these mammals are is still open.

SECTION FIVE

Continuity
of the Biosphere

CONTINUITY OF THE BIOSPHERE

We have been looking into organisms. We have been concerned with the way in which a living individual is constructed. We have studied the internal chemical and physical processes that distinguish living from nonliving matter. Much current research centers on problems of this "inner" biology—anatomy, physiology, biophysics, biochemistry. What biologists learn about such matters is of importance to all of us. But its importance becomes evident only when internal processes show up in external actions—behavior. So even in Section Four we had to return to the whole organism, maintaining its internal environment against changes in the external environment.

Individual organisms exist in populations. Through natality and mortality individuals come and go, but populations of organisms exist for ages. And, as we saw in Chapter 10, the evidence from fossils indicates that the biosphere itself has endured for three and a half billion years or more. Thus there is continuity in the biosphere. But there is also change. Again the fossil record is the evidence. It indicates that change has been slow and, in general, orderly. In other words, there is homeostasis between populations of organisms and their abiotic environment.

How do populations achieve continuity? How are individuals replaced? How are characteristics maintained generation after generation? And how do characteristics *change* over many generations, so that ecosystems of today are recognizably different from those of past ages? These are some of the questions we shall consider in Section Five.

To start the discussion, we shall have a look again at cell units, at "inner" biology. But we shall soon return to individual units.

How do you think continuity is represented in the section opening photograph of snowy egrets?

Chapter 16

Reproduction

YOUR GUIDEPOSTS

In this chapter you will have an opportunity to explore these questions in biology:

- Why is reproduction essential?
- How does reproduction relate to other biological functions?
- In which organisms do asexual and sexual reproduction occur?
- How are methods of reproduction related to the environment in which organisms live?
- How do the embryos of organisms develop?

WHY REPRODUCTION?

Living things die. An organism may be eaten by a predator or killed by parasites. It may starve or be destroyed by natural events. It may be frozen in a blizzard, boiled in lava, or crushed in an avalanche. Very few organisms die of old age.

Since individuals die, new ones must continually be formed. One possibility is that nonliving substances somehow come alive spontaneously. Another is that new organisms may be formed from existing individual living things. The first possibility is referred to as spontaneous generation. The second is called **reproduction.** Reproduction is the process by which organisms give rise to offspring. The experiments of Redi and Pasteur discredited the theory of spontaneous generation. Reproduction, then, is the only way to account for the appearance of new individuals.

Recall Investigation 6.2.

For a species, reproduction solves the problem of death. For an individual, there is no biological solution to death. And for an *individual*, there is no need for reproduction. Reproduction, therefore, is somewhat different from the life processes discontinuity [kont un OO uh tee]: the state or quality of being continuous

cussed in Section Four. Reproduction concerns, not the maintenance of individuals, but the continuity of species.

KINDS OF REPRODUCTION

ASEXUAL REPRODUCTION

Why is asexual reproduction of a plant desirable if you want to be sure that the offspring will have certain desirable characteristics that the parent possesses—for example, flavor in apples or flower color in tulips?

We can say that, when new individuals are produced by a *single* parent, the process—with a few exceptions—is ***asexual.*** Most organisms that reproduce asexually also have other methods. But in "imperfect" fungi only asexual reproduction is known.

Vegetative reproduction. In spring, potato farmers in Maine and Idaho prepare for planting. They cut potatoes into pieces, each with an "eye" (actually, a bud). After planting, the bud grows into a leafy shoot. The shoot at first uses food stored in the piece of potato. Roots sprout, and before long a new plant is formed. From one potato, therefore, have come many new individuals. This is one example, from plants, of ***cloning.***

cloning [KLOHN ing]: asexual reproduction of offspring that are identical to the parent in their characteristics

16–1 Vegetative reproduction of a strawberry. The younger plant on the left is a clone that will eventually lose its connection with the parent plant.   × 1/4

For branches taking root, see figure 13–32.

16–2 Vegetative reproduction of *Bryophyllum*. Tiny new plants, clones, develop in notches of the leaf.

In plants a bud or a branch may take root, or a piece of root may sprout a stem. In either case, a whole new plant may be formed. Many plants reproduce in this way without human assistance. When a new plant grows from a part of another plant, the process is called ***vegetative reproduction.***

Because starfish eat oysters, it was once a common practice to chop up starfish that were caught. The starfish arms were tossed back into the water. But each arm that was attached to a part of the center portion grew into a whole new starfish. The practice of chopping up the starfish actually increased their number! However, starfish do not break up into separate pieces on their own. In other words, they do not reproduce vegetatively. In fact, few animals do. Some freshwater annelids are the exceptions. They reproduce by simply breaking in half. Then the anterior piece grows a new posterior section, and vice versa.

Vegetative reproduction is possible because some multicellular organisms have the ability to replace lost parts. This is the process of **regeneration.** It is one aspect of the general growth process. You have the ability to regenerate lost pieces of skin. In starfish this ability is developed to an extreme degree. A small part, separated from one individual, can grow into an independent new individual.

X 3

16−3 Cloning by a hydra. This process is also called budding.

Human chromosomes, though not human beings, are being cloned today in new medical experiments to investigate hereditary defects these chromosomes sometimes transmit. Many plants, and a few animals, reproduce by cloning. Virtually no higher animals reproduce by cloning.

Fission. Among single-celled organisms such as diatoms, many green algae, and most protists, reproduction is often just a matter of cell division. Two offspring are formed, and the parent loses its identity in the process. This kind of reproduction is called *fission.* Some organisms apparently always reproduce by fission. Others may alternate between fission and another form of reproduction.

fission [FISH un; Latin: *findere,* to split, cleave]

Fission usually involves the process of mitosis. Among ciliates, bacteria, and blue-green algae there are, however, exceptions. It was long thought that bacteria had no organized nuclear material. Now the electron microscope has revealed a struc-

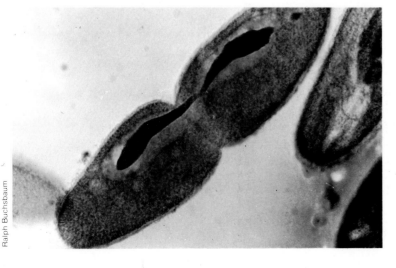

16−4 Fission of a paramecium as seen in a stained specimen. This is another example of cloning.   × 600

Ralph Buchsbaum

ture that is similar to a nucleus. Studies of heredity indicate that each bacterium has a single chromosome. However, mitosis (at least as described in Chapter 11) does not occur. In the blue-green algae nothing resembling a nucleus has been demonstrated thus far.

Reproduction by spores. Vegetative reproduction produces a new individual from an outgrowth of nonreproductive tissues. In fission, also, there is no special reproductive structure. But in most multicellular organisms (and some unicellular ones) there are specialized reproductive parts.

In many algae and some fungi, special reproductive structures are formed. A common term for these structures is *spore case*. But many specific names are used for this, depending on the organism that produces it. Many spores are produced inside the spore case by repeated mitotic divisions. When the spore case breaks open, the spores are released. Spores may be carried long distances by air or water. If spores reach a favorable environment, they germinate to produce new organisms. Spore formation is common in plants and protists but not animals.

16–5 Spore cases on the underside of a fern leaf. Each brown spot is a collection of many tiny spore cases. Each spore case contains many fern spores. Fern spores, unlike those of many algae and some fungi, are part of a sexual reproductive cycle. × 1

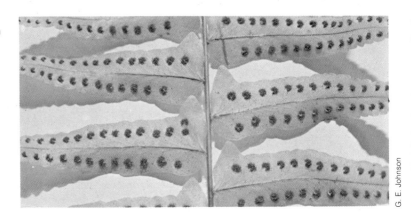

G. E. Johnson

CHECK YOURSELF

A. From the viewpoint of an individual organism, how does reproduction differ from other life processes?

B. How does vegetative reproduction occur among plants?

C. In what way is vegetative reproduction related to regeneration?

D. What is fission? In what groups of organisms does it occur most frequently?

E. What is a spore case?

Investigation 16.1   VEGETATIVE REPRODUCTION

INTRODUCTION

Coleus is a plant that usually does not reproduce vegetatively. However, gardeners
often cause it to do so. In this investigation
you will explore the conditions in which
vegetative reproduction occurs.

PROCEDURE

1. Place a large stone or a piece of broken
   pot over the drainage hole in the flowerpot. Pour sand into the pot to within 2 cm
   of the rim. Place the pot in a saucer or
   shallow pan.
2. Water the sand thoroughly. Pour excess
   water from the saucer.
3. Using a pencil, divide the surface of the
   sand into quarter sections. Mark 4 pot
   labels *A, B, C,* and *D.* Place one along the
   outer edge of each section (see figure
   16 – 6).

16 – 6

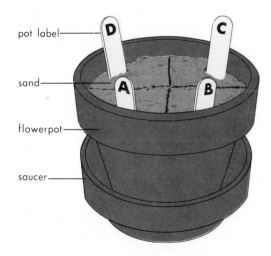

pot label

sand

flowerpot

saucer

4. Using a scalpel, take 4 cuttings from the
   coleus plant. Three of these (A, B, C)
   must each have 3 pairs of leaves and a
   terminal bud. The 4th cutting (D) must be
   at least 5 cm long. It must be taken from

MATERIALS
(per team)

live coleus plant
shallow flowerpot, 15- to 20-cm
  diameter
stone or piece of broken pot
enough sand to fill flowerpot
saucer or shallow pan
4 pot labels
scalpel
plastic bag
string

between pairs of leaves. If possible, obtain D and one of the other cuttings from
the same branch.

5. From Cutting A remove the bottom pair of
   leaves. With a pencil, make a hole in the
   sand in the center of Section A. Insert
   Cutting A into the hole so that the lower
   pair of leaves is just above the sand. Press
   the sand together around the cutting.
6. From Cutting B remove the tip of the
   branch and all but the uppermost pair of
   leaves. Make a hole in the center of Section B, and plant as you did Cutting A.
7. Prepare Cutting C just as you did B. Plant
   it in Section C. Then remove its remaining pair of leaves.
8. Place Cutting D so that at least 5 mm project above the level of the sand.
9. Cover the cuttings with a plastic bag.
   Fasten the bag's open end around the rim
   of the pot with a string.
10. Set the pots containing the coleus plant
    and the cuttings in a place where they will
    receive abundant light. Add water to the
    saucer whenever necessary.
11. After about 3 weeks, examine the plant
    from which the cuttings were taken. *(1)*
    What, if anything, has happened at the
    points where cuttings were removed?
12. Remove the plastic cover from the pot

containing the cuttings and examine them. (2) Which ones seem to be alive? In each case, what is the evidence for your decision?

13. Loosen the sand and remove Cutting A. (3) Have roots developed? If so, at what points on the cutting? (4) What, if anything, has happened to the cut surface? (5) What, if anything, has happened to the tip of the cutting?

14. Loosen the sand and remove Cutting B. (6) Have roots developed? If so, at what points? (7) What, if anything, has happened to the end that was in the sand? (8) What, if anything, has happened to the exposed end?

15. Loosen the sand and remove Cutting C. (9) Have roots developed? If so, at what points? (10) What, if anything, has happened to the end that was in the sand? (11) What, if anything, has happened to the exposed end?

16. Loosen the sand around Cutting D. (12) Have roots developed? If so, at what points? (13) What, if anything, has happened to the end that was in the sand?

(14) What, if anything, has happened to the exposed end?

DISCUSSION

First consider only the plant from which the cuttings were taken. (15) What evidence do you have that coleus has the ability to regenerate parts lost by injury?

Now consider the evidence from the cuttings. (16) To what extent might the accidental breaking up of a coleus plant (by a hailstorm, for example) result in the reproduction of coleus plants?

FOR FURTHER INVESTIGATION

1. Use this procedure to investigate and compare the abilities of other plant species to reproduce vegetatively. Plants such as tomato, household geranium, begonia, bean, pepper, marigold, and zinnia can be used.

2. Is regeneration in planarians related to their asexual reproduction? For experiments see F. Moog, *Animal Growth and Development,* a BSCS Laboratory Block, D. C. Heath, Lexington, Mass.

SEXUAL REPRODUCTION

The main point in **sexual** reproduction is quite simple. In sexual reproduction a new individual begins with the union of two cells. These cells unite in a process called **fertilization.** The consequences of fertilization are great. They affect heredity, the mechanisms of evolution, and the behavior of organisms.

gametes [guh MEETS; Greek: *gamos,* marriage]

Gametes and zygotes. Only specialized cells called **gametes** can unite in fertilization. In most cases gametes are specialized in function and look different from other cells. Furthermore, the two gametes of any uniting pair are usually different from each other. One kind, the **sperm** cell, is usually small. It carries very little reserve food and is motile. The other kind, the **ovum** (egg cell), is usually larger. It carries a reserve food supply and is

Note that the plural of sperm is sperm and the plural of ovum is ova.

nonmotile. The differences between sperm and ova are the basis for defining sexes. An organism (or any part of an organism) that produces ova is called *female.* An organism (or any part) that produces sperm is called *male.*

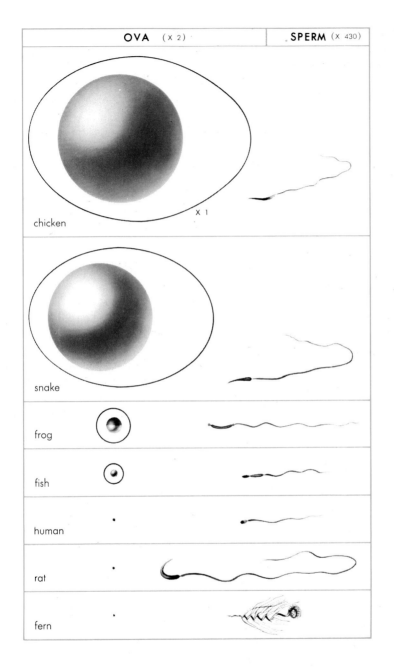

OVA (x 2)	SPERM (x 430)
chicken	x 1
snake	
frog	
fish	
human	
rat	
fern	

16—7 Comparison of some ova (eggs) and sperm. Notice the very different magnifications. In chicken, snake, frog, and fish, the ova are surrounded by other materials (*shown in outline*).

In some organisms there is no visible difference between the uniting gametes. There are, however, some biochemical or chromosomal differences. For example, in one common kind of mold the hyphae that unite in sexual reproduction are not just any two hyphae. They must be from two different varieties

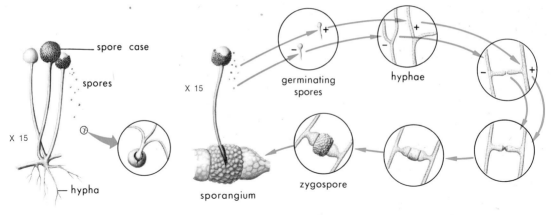

ASEXUAL REPRODUCTION   **SEXUAL REPRODUCTION**

16–8 Comparison of asexual and sexual reproduction in black bread mold, *Rhizopus nigricans*.

(strains). However, because the two strains look alike, they cannot be called male and female. They are simply referred to as minus (–) and plus (+).

zygote [ZY gote; Greek: *zygon*, yoke]

A cell produced by the union of two gametes—by fertilization—is a ***zygote.*** After zygote formation there are many paths of development. In a unicellular organism a zygote is itself a complete new individual. But in a multicellular organism a zy-

16–9 In the algal genus *Ulothrix* gametes have flagella. Are these sperm cells?

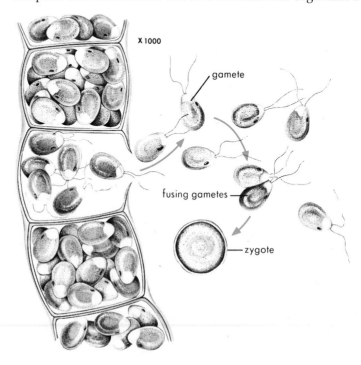

gote is only a beginning. From this beginning, a new individual grows by repeated mitotic cell divisions. But these divisions may not occur immediately. In some species, a zygote produces a thick covering that is resistant to heat and drying. In this form it may remain dormant for months or even years. In other species, a zygote grows into an embryo, which then becomes dormant. In still other species, a zygote grows to adulthood without pause, though embryo and other stages can be recognized.

Chromosome numbers. By 1890 cell biologists had shown that cells contain definite numbers of chromosomes. Counting chromosomes is a difficult job, but chromosome number has now been determined for many species. For example, in corn the number is 20; in houseflies, 12; and in humans, 46. At some step in the life cycle of a sexually reproducing organism, the number of chromosomes *must* be reduced to make up for their doubling at fertilization.

How and when does this reduction occur? Most of the solution to this problem was worked out just before the beginning of the 20th century. Answers to the "how" part of the question are similar for all sexually reproducing organisms. The number of chromosomes is reduced through a process called **meiosis.** But the answers to the "when" part vary a great deal.

meiosis [my OH sus; Greek: *meioun*, to make smaller]

Meiosis. The process of meiosis consists of two nuclear divisions that occur in special cells in sexually reproducing organisms. As you read the following description, refer often to figure 16–10 on the next page.

Review mitosis, pages 372–374.

A spindle forms first. Then chromosomes become visible as slender threads. Close observation reveals that each chromosome has doubled. Each chromosome now consists of two threads — two chromatids. The chromatids are held together by a centromere. Each chromosome pairs with its **homologue,** another chromosome that looks just like it. These two chromosomes join at their centromeres. Since each chromosome has two chromatids, the chromosome pair has four chromatids. The chromatids shorten and thicken. Then the two centromeres of the chromosome pair start moving toward opposite poles. One chromosome of each pair is carried to opposite poles. As a result, half of the chromosomes gather at each pole.

homologue [HOH muh log; Greek: *homos*, the same, + *logos*, speech]

The cell may now begin to divide. The chromosomes, however, do not fade from view as they do at the end of mitosis. Instead, another division immediately begins in each chromosome group. This division is much like a mitotic division. The chromosomes gather at the equator of each new spindle. Each chromosome still has two chromatids. The centromeres divide. The chromatids (now chromosomes) begin to move to opposite poles of the spindle. New nuclei are formed, and the rest

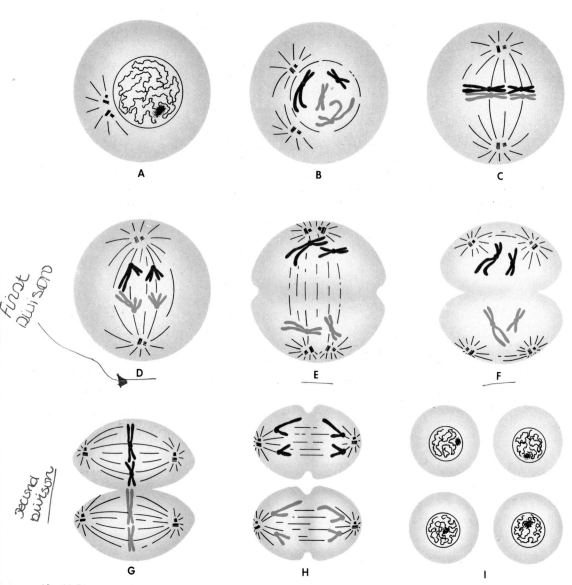

A

B

C

First division

D

E

F

Second division

G

H

I

16–10 Diagrammatic representation of meiosis. In this case, what is the diploid number of chromosomes?

2N

diploid [DIP loid; Greek: *diploos*, double, + *eidos*, form, shape]

haploid

monoploid [MON uh ploid; Greek: *monos*, single, + *eidos*]. A synonym is "haploid" [Greek: *haploos*, single, simple]

of the cell divides. The result of the whole process is four new nuclei. Each has half the number of chromosomes that the original cell had. The number of chromosomes before meiosis is called the **diploid** number. The number after meiosis is called the **monoploid** number. The monoploid number is half the diploid number. Gametes contain the monoploid number for a particular species. Union of gametes at fertilization restores the diploid number.

To simplify our description, we left out one important feature of the first meiotic division. Figure 16–11 shows that when chromosomes are paired, the chromatids may twist around each other. Two of the four chromatid strands join in much the same way as the two halves of a zipper. At that time the two chromatids may actually exchange parts. We cannot see precisely what is happening to the four chromatids in the photograph. Two possibilities are shown in the drawings beside the photograph. Which is the correct interpretation? The answer must await evidence presented in Chapter 17. At present we can only say that this complex pairing pattern is necessary to place the chromosomes properly on the spindle. Then, one chromosome of each pair can move to each pole.

The numbers of chromosomes mentioned on page 543, paragraph 2, are diploid. What is the monoploid number of each of these organisms?

16–11 Photograph of two homologous chromosomes during meiosis (A).   × 500 Drawings of two possible interpretations (B and C).

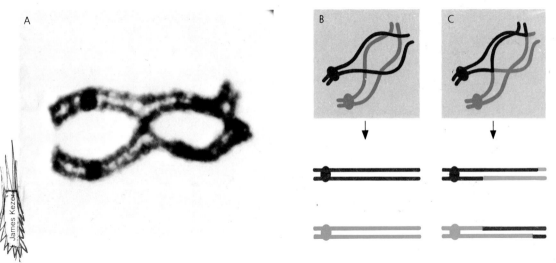

A

B

C

James Kezer

CHECK YOURSELF

F. What is the basic event in the process of sexual reproduction?

G. How may gametes be distinguished from other cells?

H. What is the biological distinction between the terms "male" and "female"?

I. How is a zygote formed?

J. Why is meiosis an important event in reproduction?

K. In what ways does meiosis differ from mitosis?

Investigation 16.2   A MODEL OF MEIOSIS

INTRODUCTION

Many biological events are easier to understand when they are explained by models. In this investigation you will duplicate the nuclear events of meiosis, using a model.

PROCEDURE

1. Cut 2 of the pipe cleaners in half. Set them aside.
2. String the pipe cleaners with beads to make 8 strands as follows:

   red beads: 2 strands of 8 beads
                        2 strands of 10 beads
   blue beads: 2 strands of 8 beads
                        2 strands of 10 beads

   Each of the strands of beads represents a chromatid.
3. Use the short pieces of pipe cleaner to represent centromeres. With one piece, fasten 2 similar chromatids together to form 1 chromosome. Form the 3 other chromosomes in the same manner.

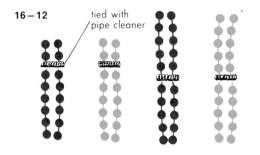

16–12   tied with / pipe cleaner

4. Draw a spindle on a large sheet of wrapping paper. Make it large enough to contain the chromosomes you have made. Assume that the early events of the 1st division have already occurred. In other words, the spindle and chromatids have been formed, and the nuclear membrane has disappeared.
5. Pair the 2 short chromosomes. Pair the 2 long ones. Assume that 1 chromosome of

MATERIALS
(per team)

36 red beads
36 blue beads
10 pipe cleaners
scissors
piece of wrapping paper
crayon

each pair (the red one) was derived from this organism's male parent. Its homologue (the blue chromosome) came from the female parent.

6. Arrange the 2 chromosome pairs along the equator of the spindle. Show the overlapping of chromatids by overlapping the beads of each homologous pair.
7. To show the possible exchange of chromatid parts (figure 16–11), exchange beads from 1 chromosome with an equal number of beads from its homologue. The colors make the exchange visible throughout the rest of the investigation.
8. Begin to move chromosomes of each homologous pair toward opposite poles of the spindle. Move them by grasping the centromeres and pulling. (Note that either 2 red or 2 blue chromosomes *or* 1 red and 1 blue chromosome can move to each pole.)
9. Draw 2 more spindles. Center these spindles on the poles of the 1st division. Their axes should be perpendicular to the axis of the 1st. The model is now ready for the 2nd division of meiosis.
10. Place the chromosomes along the equators of the 2 new spindles. Unfasten the centromere of each chromosome. Grasp each chromatid at the centromere. Pull the chromatids to opposite poles of their spindles. If there are 4 members on your team, all the chromatids can be made to move at once, as they do in a living cell.

11. Reassemble the chromosomes as they are shown in figure 16–12. Use the other side of your piece of wrapping paper and repeat the process of meiosis without referring to the directions printed here.

DISCUSSION

(1) How would a mitosis model differ from this one? (2) What are some advantages of using a model to visualize a process? (3) What are some disadvantages?

REPRODUCTION AMONG PLANTS

Thus far we have been considering basic similarities in the reproductive processes of all organisms. But there are also some well-defined differences among organisms. These differences are most conspicuous in multicellular plants and in animals.

CHARACTERISTICS

In the plant kingdom asexual methods of reproduction are more frequent than in the animal kingdom. But sexual reproduction is equally frequent in both kingdoms. Some algae and fungi grow vegetatively most of the year. They form zygotes chiefly under *unfavorable* environmental conditions—such as the approach of winter.

In bryophytes and tracheophytes (and in many fungi and the red and brown algae) there is a regular *alternation of generations.* One generation of these plants is monoploid, and the next, after fusion of gametes, is diploid. Alternation of generations is not easy to observe in flowering plants, however, because the sexual generation is microscopic.

In plants the gametes may be alike and motile (figure 16–9). Or they may be alike and nonmotile. But more often than not the two gametes are different.

What might be the adaptive advantage of sexual reproduction at the onset of unfavorable environmental conditions?

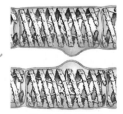 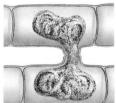 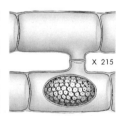

X 215

BEGINNING OF CONJUGATION   UNION OF GAMETES   ZYGOTE FORMED

16–13 Nonmotile gametes develop from undifferentiated cells in the algal genus *Spirogyra.* This kind of sexual process is referred to as conjugation.

One major difference between sexual reproduction in plants and in animals is the timing of meiosis. In animals meiosis occurs during the formation of gametes. In plants meiosis occurs much earlier.

EXAMPLES

Several times in this chapter we have referred to reproductive processes of fungi and algae. Now we shall look at mosses and flowering plants.

A moss. In looking at the life cycle of a moss (figure 16–14), we may start with spores. If a spore reaches a favorable environment—usually a moist soil surface—its wall bursts open. The cell within begins to divide by mitosis. A set of long green threads is formed. From these threads arises the familiar moss plant. It has a stalk, tiny leaflike structures, and rootlike threads that absorb water and nutrients.

At the tips of such plants, reproductive structures are formed. *Antheridia* are sperm-producing structures. *Archegonia* are ovum-producing structures. In some species a single plant produces both kinds of gametes. In others the sexes are separate. During wet weather, sperm swim to an ovum. Fertilization occurs in an archegonium.

A zygote is formed. It begins to divide immediately and

antheridia [an thuh RID ee uh; Greek: *anthos*, flower, + *idion*, little]

archegonia [ar kih GOH nee uh; Greek: *archos*, first, chief, + *gonos*, offspring]

How might the fact that the sexes are on separate plants affect the gametes produced?

16–14 Reproductive cycle of a moss. Parts are drawn to different scales. The small ellipse shows relative duration in the life cycle of gametophyte and sporophyte generations. Compare with figure 16–18.

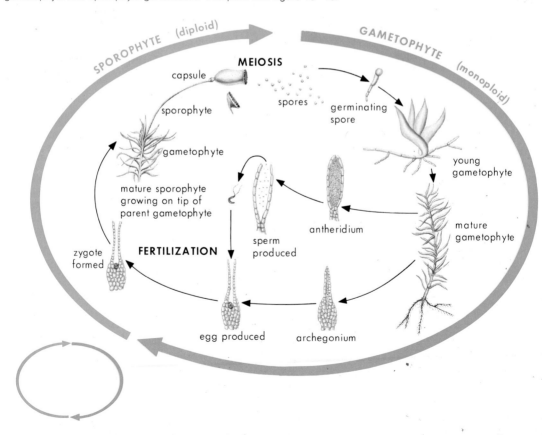

grows into an embryo. The embryo eventually grows out of the archegonium and may become taller than its parent. It often forms chlorophyll and produces its own food. But it *must* obtain water and dissolved minerals from its parent, to which it remains attached. Eventually a spore case develops at its tip. Within this case meiosis occurs. Cells with the monoploid number of chromosomes are formed, and they soon develop into spores. This completes the cycle.

Two points are useful for comparing this life cycle with cycles of other plants. First, fertilization requires a liquid in which the sperm may swim. In terrestrial mosses it can occur only when there is rain or dew. Second, the cycle involves two generations. The first generation begins with the spore. Since spores are formed by meiosis, the moss plant that develops directly from a spore must be composed entirely of monoploid cells. This monoploid organism is called a **gametophyte** because it produces gametes. When two gametes unite, a diploid zygote is formed; and the second generation begins. The plant that develops from the zygote is called a **sporophyte** because it bears spores.

gametophyte [guh MEET uh fyt]

sporophyte [SPOH ruh fyt]

An angiosperm. Think of the pistils and stamens of an angiosperm flower. They are the reproductive structures of an angiosperm and are both highly modified leaves that produce spores. The pistils produce the larger spores. The stamens produce the smaller ones. We can call the pistil a female structure and the stamen a male structure.

In most angiosperms, male and female structures occur in the same flower. In some — the oak family, for example — they occur in separate *flowers* on the same individual plant. In a few angiosperms, such as holly, *plants* are either entirely male or entirely female. The male plant bears flowers with stamens but no pistils. The female plant, on the other hand, has flowers with pistils but no stamens.

Why is it impossible to call a buttercup plant (see figure 5–7) either male or female?

Meiosis occurs in cells within the pistil. But the spores do not separate from the sporophyte as they do in mosses. Instead, spores grow inside the pistil of the flower. Each grows into a gametophyte that has only a few cells. This, with some enclosing tissues, is called an **ovule.** Within one cell of the ovule, several nuclei form. One of these nuclei is the egg nucleus. Pistils of some species contain only one ovule each. Other species have many ovules per pistil.

How does this statement relate to the explanation of "male" and "female" given on page 540?

In the tip of the stamen, many small spores are produced by meiosis. Each spore divides into two cells. Then the spore wall around them thickens. The result is a **pollen grain.** Stamens of some species each contain thousands of pollen grains.

What structures in angiosperms might correspond to antheridia and archegonia?

If fertilization is to occur, a pollen grain must be transport-

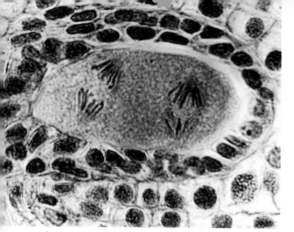

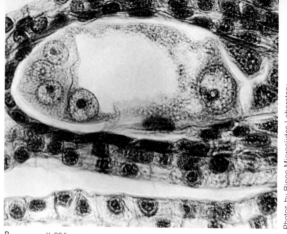

A   X 225   B   X 225

16-15 Female gametophyte of an angiosperm (a lily). (*A*) Meiosis in the developing ovule. (*B*) Mature ovule ready to be fertilized; the egg nucleus is one of those on the left.

16 – 16 Male gametophyte of an angiosperm.

pollen grain

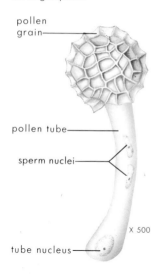

pollen tube

sperm nuclei

X 500

tube nucleus

A pollen tube may be surprisingly long—for example, in corn as long as the silk.

Like angiosperms, gymnosperms are not dependent on water for fertilization.

triploid [TRIP loid; Latin: *triplus*, threefold, + Greek: *eidos*, form]

In what ways may seed dormancy be of adaptive value?

ed from a stamen to a pistil of a flower of the same species. This transfer is called **pollination.** Because most flowers have both stamens and pistils, pollination might seem to be an easy matter. The pollen would simply fall from the stamen onto the pistil of the same flower. Such self-pollination does occur, but in many plants various devices prevent it. Pollen also may be transported from one flower to another by wind. Many angiosperms, however, are pollinated by animals, mainly insects. When pollen is transferred from a flower of one plant to a flower of another, the process is called cross-pollination.

On the pistil there is usually a sticky area to which pollen grains adhere. Each pollen grain grows a **pollen tube,** which penetrates the pistil. The pollen grain, together with its tube, is the male gametophyte. It produces two sperm nuclei, which are carried along in the pollen tube as it grows (figure 16 – 16). Thus angiosperms are not dependent on water for fertilization:

Eventually a pollen tube reaches an ovule. One of the sperm nuclei unites with the egg nucleus, forming a zygote. The second sperm nucleus unites with a fusion "nucleus" in the ovule. A fusion nucleus has a diploid number of chromosomes. Thus, when an angiosperm fusion nucleus is fertilized by a sperm, a triploid nucleus is formed. This nucleus divides to form a mass of food-storing cells, the **endosperm.**

The zygote grows into an embryo. Unlike an embryo of mosses, an angiosperm embryo becomes dormant. With its endosperm and a coat formed from ovule tissues, it is a seed. The pistil, often with other parts of the flower, develops into a fruit around the seed. There may be many seeds in a fruit. Each seed began its development when one ovule in the pistil was fertilized by a sperm nucleus from one pollen grain. The life cycle of a flowering plant is similar to that of a moss in two ways. First, meiosis occurs just before spore formation. Second, there is an alternation of generations. There are, however,

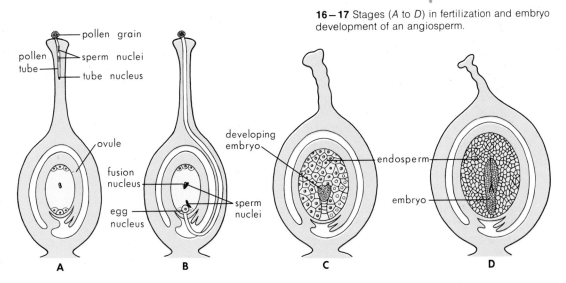

16–17 Stages (*A* to *D*) in fertilization and embryo development of an angiosperm.

several differences. Water is not necessary for fertilization, as it is in mosses. In addition, the gametophytes are much smaller than the sporophytes. In fact, the gametophytes of flowering plants do not constitute separate plants as in mosses.

16–18 Reproductive cycle of an angiosperm. The parts are drawn to different scales. The small ellipse shows relative duration in the life cycle of gametophyte and sporophyte generations.

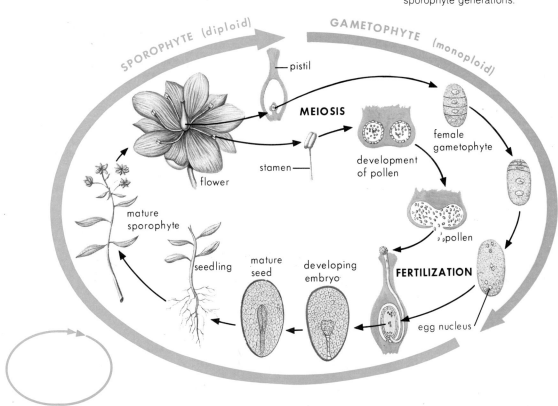

CHECK YOURSELF

L. What is an "alternation of generations"?
M. How does the timing of meiosis differ in animals and in plants?
N. What are the functions of antheridia and archegonia?
O. What environmental condition is necessary for fertilization to occur in mosses?
P. What are the essential male and female parts of a flowering plant?
Q. What is pollination?
R. What is the difference between self-pollination and cross-pollination?
S. Describe fertilization in an angiosperm after pollination.
T. What characteristics of the life cycle in mosses and in angiosperms are similar?
U. What characteristics of the life cycle are different?

REPRODUCTION AMONG ANIMALS

CHARACTERISTICS

Reproduction is primarily sexual in the animal kingdom. Even in species that have asexual methods, as do many coelenterates, sexual reproduction takes place frequently. In animals, alternation of monoploid with diploid generations is unknown. In coelenterates there is an alternation of a sexual generation with an asexual generation, but both are diploid. Furthermore, gametes in animals are always of two kinds, and meiosis occurs just before or during gamete formation.

Gamete formation. In all animals except sponges, meiosis and gamete formation occur in structures called **gonads.** Gonads that produce ova are **ovaries.** Those that produce sperm cells are **testes.** The two kinds of gonads are usually distinct. In American oysters, however, gonads produce ova during one year and sperm during the following year. When the gonads produce ova, the oyster is female. When they produce sperm, it is male.

gonads [GOH nadz; Greek: *gonos,* offspring]

In animals meiosis is accompanied by divisions of the whole cell. In the testes each of the resulting four cells becomes a sperm. There is no growth between the two meiotic divisions. As a result, only a small amount of cell substance surrounds the nucleus of each sperm. Most of the cell is a tail by which the sperm swims. The sperm's head consists mainly of the nucleus.

In the formation of ova, the cell substance is distributed somewhat differently during meiosis. In the first meiotic divi-

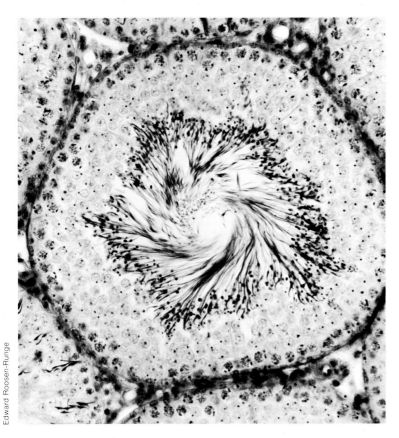

Edward Roosen-Runge

16 – 19 Photomicrograph of a section through a rat testis. Sperm cells are formed in the walls of tubules. Cells between tubules secrete hormones.   × 375

sion, almost all of it goes to one cell. One large and one small cell are formed. In the second meiotic division, the large cell again divides into one large and one small cell. The first small cell then becomes two small cells. The end result is one large cell and three small ones. The one large cell has almost all of the original cell's substance. It becomes an ovum. The three others usually die.

In many species, ova increase in size after they are formed. But there is enormous variation in their size when fully developed. For an idea of this variation, refer to figure 16–7. A chicken ovum (the yolk of the egg) is many times larger than a human ovum. This may seem surprising in view of the difference in size between a newly hatched chick and a newborn baby.

Sex in animals. In most adult animals, an individual has either ovaries or testes, not both. Often this difference in the gonads is accompanied by differences in related characteristics — secondary sexual characteristics. These may be differences in appearance, voice, and behavior.

Both ovary and testis tissue are present in the early stages of many embryos.

X 1/15

male   female

DEER

X 1/3

female

male

CHICKEN

male   X 1/7

female

SALMON

X 1/3

male

female

MOTH

16 – 20 Some secondary sexual characteristics in animals.

hermaphrodite [hur MAF ruh dyt; Greek: Hermes, a god, + Aphrodite, a goddess]. This word is not used by botanists, but essentially the same condition is very frequent among angiosperms. Can you give examples?

striped bass. See figure 16–26.

In some animals an individual has both ovaries and testes. This is true of earthworms. It is also true of many other annelids, most flatworms, and some crustaceans. An animal that has both ovaries and testes is called a **hermaphrodite.** Even among vertebrates, hermaphroditic individuals occasionally occur. However, they are not normal in any vertebrate species.

Fertilization. Sperm cells swim, and this requires a liquid. Animals that live in water can release eggs and sperm directly into their environment. This is *external* fertilization. But sperm contain only a very small amount of stored food. Hence, they can survive only a short time after being released from the male parent. Obviously, then, if a sperm is to unite with an egg, both must be released at approximately the same time and place.

Consider the striped bass that annually swim up all the large rivers of the Atlantic coast and some of the Pacific. The trip upriver brings the fish into shallow pools. Here females lay eggs and males deposit sperm at the same time. What factors bring male and female bass to the same place at the same time,

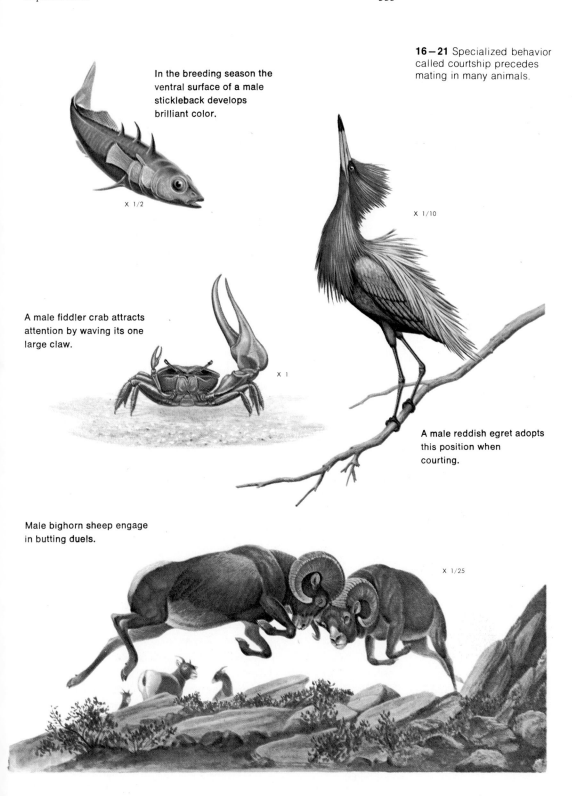

In the breeding season the ventral surface of a male stickleback develops brilliant color.

x 1/2

16—21 Specialized behavior called courtship precedes mating in many animals.

x 1/10

A male fiddler crab attracts attention by waving its one large claw.

x 1

A male reddish egret adopts this position when courting.

Male bighorn sheep engage in butting **duels.**

x 1/25

with eggs and sperm ready to be released? This is a question that involves study of hormones, behavior, and environmental factors. Biologists have investigated these matters in detail but do not yet have completely satisfactory answers.

In many phyla fertilization is *internal.* In this case the male places sperm directly into the body of the female. There the sperm swim through part of the female's reproductive tract. The two gametes meet at some point between the ovary and the opening to the environment. Internal fertilization is not necessary for aquatic animals, but it does occur among many crustaceans and all cartilaginous fishes.

Among terrestrial animals internal fertilization is necessary because sperm cannot swim through air. But there is still the matter of timing. If, when sperm arrive, the ova have not yet reached a proper stage of development, fertilization usually will not occur, because sperm are short-lived. There are exceptions to this, however. For example, in some insects sperm are stored in a special sac after they have been deposited in the female's reproductive system. There they remain alive, and are released as eggs are laid. In bees this is sometimes several years later! Human females have no special storage sac for sperm. However, sperm may live five to six days after being released in the female.

16–22 From March to July, always a day or two after full moon, grunions come to the beaches of southern California, where their eggs are laid and fertilized. What may time this meeting of the sexes?   × 1/3

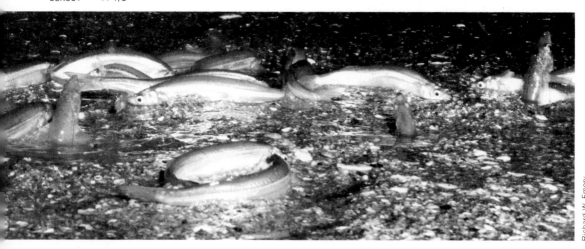

Richard W. Emery

parthenogenesis [par thuh noh-JEN uh sus; Greek: *parthenos,* maiden, + *genesis,* origin]

Parthenogenesis. In some animals, and under certain conditions, an ovum may develop into a new individual without fertilization by a sperm. Such reproduction by ***parthenogenesis*** occurs, for example, among aphids. During summer, many generations of aphids are produced in this manner. But there is a problem here. Recall that gametes are monoploid and that fertilization restores the diploid number of chromosomes. What happens when there are successive generations without fertilization?

Research has revealed several answers to this question. Meiosis in the female may be bypassed. Or, after meiosis, two of the four ova produced may unite inside the ovary. Another answer is that, after the first meiotic division, the surrounding cell may fail to divide. In all three cases a diploid ovum results. Therefore, offspring are diploid *without* fertilization. In some species of bees and ants, individuals produced by parthenogenesis are indeed monoploid as expected. These individuals are always male.

Do you consider parthenogenesis a sexual method of reproduction? Why or why not?

CHECK YOURSELF

V. In the animal kingdom, is reproduction primarily sexual or asexual? Is there an alternation of generations?

W. Distinguish among the terms "gonad," "ovary," and "testis."

X. How does the formation of sperm in animals differ from the formation of ova?

Y. What do we mean when we say that an animal is hermaphroditic?

Z. Why is it usually important that sperm be released near ova in time and place?

AA. Under what circumstances is internal fertilization necessary?

BB. With respect to parentage, how does parthenogenesis differ from the usual methods of sexual reproduction?

CC. How may the diploid chromosome number be retained during parthenogenesis?

EXAMPLES

In multicellular organisms fertilization is merely the *beginning* of reproduction. The zygote then develops into an embryo. The embryo develops further until it becomes an individual capable of maintaining itself. Only at this point has reproduction been accomplished. *Embryology* is, therefore, a part of the study of reproduction.

embryology [em bree OL uh jee]: the study of the formation and development of embryos

Hydra. Through much of the year, hydras reproduce asexually by budding. But under certain conditions they produce ovaries and testes. Most species are then hermaphroditic. The testis is a cone-shaped bump on the outer body wall. Sperm are released from it through a small pore at its tip. The ovary is a large round structure also on the outer body wall. Only one ovum is formed in each ovary. At maturity the ovum bursts the ovary wall but remains attached to the parent hydra.

How many parents may a sexually reproduced hydra have?

If an ovum is fertilized, the zygote divides by mitosis into two cells of equal size. Each of these divides, forming four cells; the four form eight, and so on. This division process is called *cleavage.* As the number of cells increases, a hollow ball, the *blastula,* is formed. Further divisions of the blastula fill the hollow space with cells. Thus the embryo includes an outer layer of cells and an inner mass of cells.

blastula [BLAS chuh luh]

16 – 23 Stages in the embryology of a hydra.

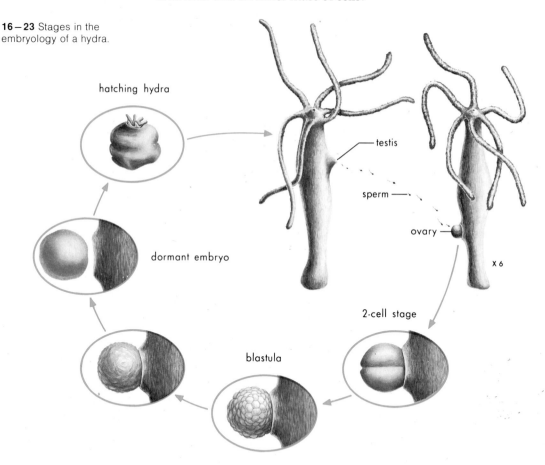

hatching hydra

testis

sperm

ovary

x 6

dormant embryo

2-cell stage

blastula

At this point the hydra embryo separates from the parent and sinks to the bottom of the pond. There it remains in a dormant condition, protected by a thick wall secreted by its outer cells. Eventually the protective wall breaks and the embryo grows longer. The body of a hydra has only two layers of cells:

an **ectoderm** (outer) and an **endoderm** (inner). These two layers develop from the two groups of cells in the early embryo. A hollow space forms inside the inner cells. Tentacles develop at one end of the embryo, and in their midst a mouth appears. Development of the new hydra is now complete.

Earthworm. Earthworms are hermaphroditic. But the ova in an individual are not fertilized by sperm of the same individual. Tubes from the ovaries lead to the surface of one segment. Those from the testes lead to the surface of an adjoining segment. Fertilization is internal. When two earthworms **copulate** (mate), sperm of one individual are deposited in a special sac of the other. Likewise, sperm from the second worm are deposited in the first. Later, ova move from the ovary and pass the sperm-storage sac. Sperm are released, and the ova are fertilized.

ectoderm [EK tuh durm; Greek: *ektos*, outside, + *derma*, skin]

endoderm [EN duh durm; Greek: *endon*, within, + *derma*]

copulate [KOP yuh layt; Latin: *copulare*, to unite, couple]

How many parents does an earthworm have?

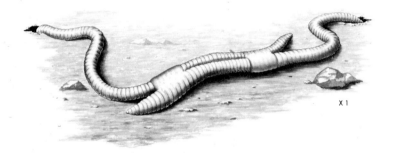

X 1

16—24 Earthworms copulating. The thickened bands aid in the transfer of sperm and later secrete a protective coating around the developing embryos.

Earthworm zygotes are enclosed in a tough case secreted by the parent. Cleavage occurs inside this case. The first cells formed are not of equal size. As a result, the cells of the blastula have a spiral arrangement. This is characteristic in many animal phyla, but not in echinoderms or chordates.

An earthworm embryo also differs from a hydra embryo in having a third layer of cells, a **mesoderm,** between the other two. From each of the three layers, the organ systems of the body are derived. An earthworm embryo requires two to three weeks for development. After this it escapes from its case as a small copy of the adult.

Striped bass. In striped bass fertilization occurs externally. Within a few hours after fertilization, two or more cell divisions occur. The divisions are just about equal, but they do not involve the whole zygote. As figure 16—26 shows, new cells are formed only on the top. The **yolk** (food supply) remains undivided and nourishes the embryo. Another difference from hydra or earthworm development is the presence of a fluid-filled membrane that surrounds the ovum. Thus, the embryo develops in a somewhat protected environment.

16—25 Section through a gastrula (stage following the blastula) of an earthworm embryo.

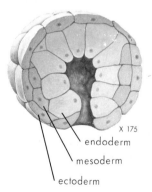

X 175

endoderm

mesoderm

ectoderm

mesoderm [MEZ uh durm; Greek: *mesos*, middle, + *derma*]. This layer develops in the embryos of most animals except for sponges and coelenterates.

16 – 26 Stages in the embryonic development of a striped bass.

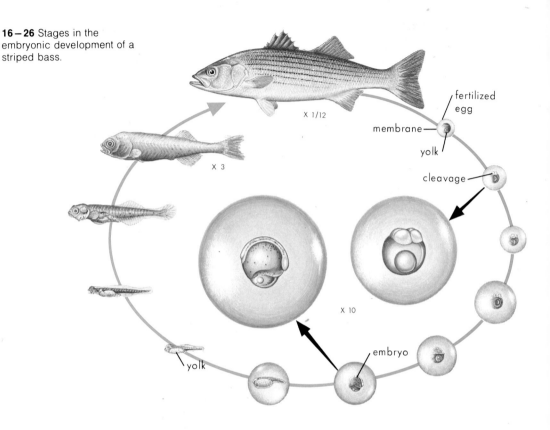

X 1/12

X 3

fertilized egg

membrane —

yolk

cleavage —

X 10

embryo

yolk

Three cell layers — ectoderm, mesoderm, and endoderm — are formed early in development. Within 36 hours an embryo that looks like a tadpole is visible on top of the yolk. Twelve hours later this tiny, undeveloped organism has hatched through the membrane enclosing it and is wriggling about in the water. But the hatchling is not a fully developed fish. It has no mouth, and for many days it lives on the food supply in its yolk. In about a month the hatchling has developed into a complete young fish.

Chicken. A female chicken has only one ovary. A tube called an *oviduct* leads from the ovary to the outside. During copulation *semen* is deposited in the oviduct. Semen is a fluid that males secrete and in which the sperm swim. The sperm swim up the oviduct. Fertilization occurs in the oviduct's upper end. Then, as the zygote descends, glands in the oviduct wall secrete a shell around the zygote and its yolk. Meanwhile, cleavage occurs. When the egg is laid, the embryo already consists of a few cells on the surface of the yolk. Further development of the embryo occurs as the egg is incubated by the body heat of the parent.

oviduct [OH vuh dukt; Latin: *ovum*, egg, + *ducere*, to lead]

semen [SEE mun; Latin: *semen*, seed]

CHECK YOURSELF

DD. What is cleavage?

EE. Compare blastula formation in hydras and earthworms.

FF. From what three embryonic cell layers do the organs of most animals' bodies develop?

GG. What term is applied to the process by which sperm are transferred to a female in earthworms?

HH. In what ways does development of a striped bass embryo differ from that of a hydra?

II. Where do most animal embryos obtain their food during early development?

JJ. What is semen?

KK. In chickens how do sperm cells reach an ovum?

Investigation 16.3   CHICK EMBRYOLOGY

MATERIALS
(per team)

For Part A

unincubated, fertilized chicken egg
finger bowl
stereomicroscope

For Part B

chicken egg, incubated 48 to
  52 hours
physiological saline solution
petri dish
medicine dropper
forceps
finger bowl
stereomicroscope or hand lens
monocular microscope
thermometer (−10° to +110°C)
egg incubator
watch with second hand
scissors (fine-pointed)
filter paper
paper towels

For Part C

chicken egg, incubated 5 to 6 days
stereomicroscope or hand lens

finger bowl
forceps
medicine dropper
scissors (fine-pointed)
egg incubator
thermometer (−10° to +110°C)
paper towels

For Part D

chicken eggs, incubated 10,
  14, 18, or 21 days
physiological saline solution
hand lens
finger bowl
forceps
thermometer (−10° to +110°C)
scissors (fine-pointed)
egg incubator

PROCEDURE

A. Unincubated egg

1. Crack a fresh, fertilized chicken egg crosswise. Use both hands to hold the egg, with one thumb on each side of the crack. Carefully pull apart the two ends. Let the

contents drop gently into a finger bowl.

2. Observe the **albumen** ("white"), which is made up largely of protein and water. (*1*) Where is it most dense?

3. The embryo appears as a white area on the surface of the yolk. (*2*) Describe its appearance under the stereomicroscope.

4. Examine the inside of the shell and the membrane that lines it. (*3*) At which end of the egg is the membrane not closely attached to the shell? (*4*) What occupies this space between membrane and shell? (*5*) List in order the structures added around the ovum as it passes down the hen's oviduct. (*6*) Suggest a function for each of the structures.

B. Two-day embryo

Figure 16–27 shows a chick embryo after 33 hours of incubation at 38°C. At this stage the embryo is still so thin that the parts shown in the drawing can be observed only if stained. **Somites** are blocks of tissue from which vertebrae and muscles develop. Refer to this fig-

ure as you observe the embryo.

1. Crumple one or two paper towels into a finger bowl. Hollow out a space in the center to support an egg.

2. Obtain an egg that has been incubated 48 to 52 hours. Before removing it from the incubator, mark a *T* on the top of the egg. Carry the egg to your work space, holding the marked side up. Keep that side up and place the egg in the hollow of the paper.

3. Hold the egg gently but firmly. Follow the steps shown in figure 16–28. If you have not rotated the egg since taking it from the incubator, the embryo should be on the top of the yolk. If it is not, push the yolk gently with the medicine dropper until the embryo is on top. Be very careful not to break the yolk.

4. The yolk sac encloses the yolk. When the embryo is exposed, you can see the extent of the sac by noting the blood vessels on the surface of the yolk. (*7*) About what percentage of the yolk is now covered by the yolk sac? (*8*) What do you think is the function of the yolk sac?

5. Using a stereomicroscope or hand lens, examine the embryo. Locate the heart by

16–27 Chick embryo after 33 hours of incubation. At this stage, the yolk sac is about 1 cm in diameter and is growing along its edge.

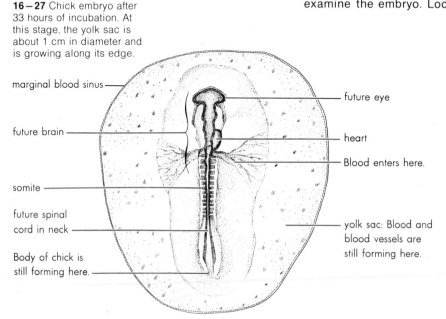

marginal blood sinus

future brain

somite

future spinal cord in neck

Body of chick is still forming here.

future eye

heart

Blood enters here.

yolk sac: Blood and blood vessels are still forming here.

A. Carefully insert point of scissors at x, barely penetrating the shell, and slowly clip the shell completely around the egg.

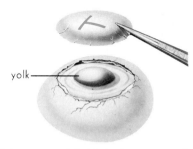

yolk

B. With forceps carefully lift the loose piece of shell and discard.

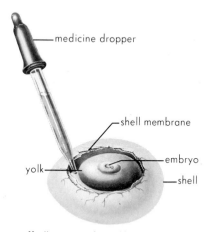

medicine dropper

shell membrane

embryo

yolk

shell

C. Draw off albumen with medicine dropper until yolk is not covered.

D. Remove more of the white and shell until only one half of the egg shell remains.

16 – 28 Steps in exposing a chick embryo in an early stage of development.

looking for pulsating movement. (*9*) How fast is the heart beating (pulsations per minute)?

6. Further observation will be easier if you remove the embryo from the yolk. To do this, follow the steps shown in figure 16 – 29. Before placing the filter-paper ring on the yolk, make sure that none of the albumen is on the surface of the embryo. If it is, repeat step C, figure 16 – 28.

7. The saline solution may become cloudy after you have transferred the embryo to the petri dish. If this happens, draw off the saline with a clean medicine dropper. Replace it with fresh, warm saline.

8. Place the petri dish on the stage of a monocular microscope. Observe under low power. (*10*) Which of the structures shown in figure 16 – 27 can you see? (*11*) Compare the general shape of the embryo with that of the 33-hour embryo. Most of the large mass of tissue near the heart will become brain. This part of the embryo may have a membrane over it. This is the developing **amnion.** It will become a complete sac enclosing the embryo. You may be able to see an ear opening, which was not visible in the 33-hour embryo.

9. Examine the heart carefully. (*12*) Can you trace the path of the blood to and from the heart? If so, describe it.

C. Five-day embryo

1. Using the technique shown in figure 16 – 28, open an egg that has been incubated 5 days. (Caution: The yolk is quite watery at this stage. Some of the delicate membranes are close to the shell. Therefore, insert *only the tips* of the scissors beneath the shell.)

2. Compare the amnion in this embryo with the one in the 2-day embryo. (*13*) Describe any differences.

16—29 Steps in removing a chick embryo from the yolk.

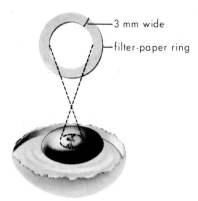

— 3 mm wide

— filter-paper ring

A. Measure diameter of marginal blood sinus. On filter paper, draw a ring that has inner diameter slightly less than diameter of marginal blood sinus. Cut out ring and place over edges of sinus.

B. Grasp ring and edge of membrane. Clip membrane all the way around ring. Slowly lift ring, membrane, and embryo away from yolk.

C. Place ring, membrane, and embryo in petri dish containing physiological saline solution (3 mm deep) at 38°C.

3. Gently probe the surface of the amnion with a blunt pencil. (*14*) Is anything besides the embryo inside? If so, what?

4. Next to the amnion and attached to it by a stalk is a bladderlike membrane covered with blood vessels. This is the **allantois.** Through it the embryo obtains oxygen and excretes carbon dioxide.

5. Observe the number of blood vessels on the surface of the yolk. (*15*) Approximately what percentage of the yolk is now covered by the yolk sac?

6. Using forceps and scissors, carefully cut away the amnion, exposing the embryo. (*16*) Compare the size of the eyes with the size of the head. This size relationship is a characteristic of bird embryos in contrast to mammalian embryos.

7. Look for the parts that will become the appendages. (*17*) How is it possible to distinguish wings from legs at this stage? (*18*) Describe any other differences you can see between a 2-day and a 5-day chick.

D. Later stages of development

1. Different teams will open eggs incubated 10, 14, 18, and 21 days. To open these eggs, use the technique shown in figure 16—30. Try not to break any membranes.

2. When the shell has been removed, you will notice that it is lined with a continuous membrane containing blood vessels. This is the **chorioallantoic membrane.** It is formed when the allantois is extended and united with another embryonic membrane, the **chorion.** (*19*) What substances, then, probably pass through the chorioallantoic membrane?

3. Using scissors and forceps, carefully remove the chorioallantoic membrane. (*20*) Can you find the yolk sac? How is it connected to the embryo? (*21*) How is the food in the yolk transported to the embryo?

4. Remove the amnion from around the embryo. (*22*) Note all features that indicate the organism is a bird.

A. Crack the large end of the egg with scissors or scalpel handle. Use forceps to pick away the shell. Try not to break the shell membrane.

B. After part of the shell has been removed, put the egg in a finger bowl of physiological saline (at 38°C) and pick off the rest of the shell.

16–30 Steps in exposing a chick embryo in a late stage of development.

5. After each team has studied its embryo, exchange embryos until all teams have seen each stage of development. (23) Note (with the day of incubation) features you were unable to see in your own embryo.

DISCUSSION

(24) List all the structures you have observed in the order of their first appearance during development.

Using the observations you made in this investigation, consider the following questions. What characteristics of a chicken egg are adaptations that enable it to develop on land? If the egg developed inside the hen instead of outside, what structures would be less important? What explanations can you give for the early development of heart, blood, and blood vessels?

(25) Write a summary statement on chick-embryo development that includes your thinking on these questions.

FOR FURTHER INVESTIGATION

What effect would incubation at higher or lower temperatures have on the development of a chick embryo? Experiment to test your hypotheses.

Mammals. Monotremes are the only mammals that lay eggs. In all others the fertilized ova remain inside the female parent. Embryos grow in the female's *uterus.* This is a thick-walled part of the tubes that lead from the ovaries to the outside.

Most animals reproduce only at certain times of the year. Many reproduce only once a year. Among domesticated animals such seasonal reproduction is less clearly marked than in wild ones. But even dogs and cattle breed more frequently at some seasons than at others. Primates, however, tend toward continuous breeding. Apes and humans reproduce during all months of the year.

The seasonal reproductive cycle usually affects both sexes. In addition, female mammals have a shorter cycle of reproduc-

monotremes [MON uh treemz]. A duck-billed platypus is an example.

uterus [YEWT uh rus]. In nontechnical language this is called the womb.

16—31 The birth of a foal. The head and right front leg of the young horse are the first parts of the body to emerge.

estrous [ES trus]

Review the discussion of these systems in Chapter 14.

tive activity — the ***estrous cycle.*** A physiological cycle such as this implies controls. Perhaps we might look to the nervous and endocrine systems for such controls.

Past research indicated that the pituitary gland plays an important part in control of the estrous cycle. In experiments with adult female rats, pituitary glands were removed. Development of ova in the ovaries stopped. Thickening of the uterine lining, a usual event in the cycle, failed to occur. These results raised questions. Does the pituitary directly influence only the ovaries, which then influence the uterus? Or does the pituitary directly influence only the uterus, which in turn influences the ovaries? And, if removal of the pituitary gland stops the functioning of ovaries and uterus, why are they not continuously active when the pituitary is present?

intact [in TAKT]: here, entire or with nothing missing

Other experiments provided some answers to these questions. Rat ovaries were removed, leaving both the uterus and pituitary intact. The uterine lining failed to thicken. Apparently, then, function of the uterus depends on the ovaries. But we know from the previous experiments that uterine function also depends on the pituitary. In still another set of experiments, both pituitaries and ovaries were removed. Then the rats were injected with hormones from ovaries of other rats. Thickening of the uterine lining followed. Physiologists concluded that pituitary hormones influence the ovaries and that ovarian hormones influence the uterus.

More recent research shows that the hypothalamus, a region of the brain adjacent to the pituitary, helps to con-

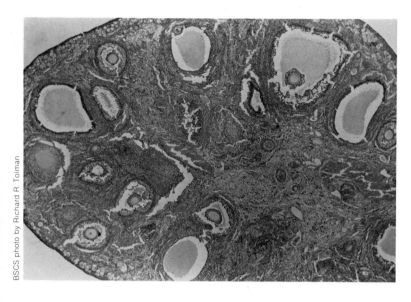

BSCS photo by Richard R. Tolman

16–32 Cross section of a rat ovary, showing numerous follicles. Can you locate an ovum in a follicle? × 26

trol the pituitary. **Releasing hormones** that are produced by the hypothalamus have been identified. Some releasing hormones are secreted directly into the pituitary. Others travel from the hypothalamus to the pituitary by way of the bloodstream. Among the latter are releasing hormones that stimulate the pituitary to secrete the hormones that influence the ovaries. Many other functions of the body, including those of the uterus, are influenced by both the hypothalamus and the pituitary.

Humans. Human females do not have an annual reproductive cycle. They do, however, have a short-term (monthly) cycle. It differs from that in other mammals and has another name—the **menstrual cycle.**

Let us begin a description of hormonal and tissue changes in a female at the time when the lining of the uterus is thin. The hypothalamus secretes follicle-stimulating-hormone-releasing hormone (FSHRH), which stimulates the pituitary to secrete follicle stimulating hormone (FSH). FSH causes development of a **follicle** in an ovary. A follicle is a jacket of cells that surrounds an ovum. Inside the follicle an ovum develops. Usually only one ovum develops in each cycle.

Ovum and follicle enlarge and move to the surface of the ovary. The follicle begins to secrete the hormone estrogen. Estrogen does three things. It causes thickening of the uterine lining. It causes the hypothalamus to influence the pituitary to stop producing FSH. It also stimulates the hypothalamus to secrete luteinizing-hormone-releasing hormone (LHRH). LHRH stimulates the pituitary to secrete large amounts of luteinizing hormone (LH). LH then brings about **ovulation.**

menstrual [MEN struh wul; Latin: *mensis,* month (because the average length of the cycle is 28 days, the lunar month)]. Do you think this length is coincidental?

follicle [FOL ih kul]

estrogen [ES truh jun]

luteinizing [LOOT ee un eyz ing]

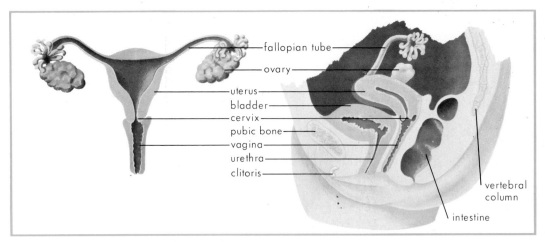

fallopian tube
ovary
uterus
bladder
cervix
pubic bone
vagina
urethra
clitoris
vertebral column
intestine

16–33 The human female reproductive system. The principal organs and their positions are shown in a frontal view (*left*) and in a sectional view (*right*).

ovulation [ov yuh LAY shun]

fallopian [fuh LOH pee un]

corpus luteum [KOR pus LOOT-ee um]

progesterone [proh JES tuh rone]

vagina [vuh JY nuh]

menstruation [men struh WAY-shun]

scrotum [SKROHT um]

During ovulation the ovum bursts from the follicle and enters the adjacent *fallopian tube.* After ovulation the follicle becomes a body called the *corpus luteum.* This secretes two hormones, estrogen and progesterone. Progesterone greatly speeds the growth of glands and blood vessels in the uterine lining. This causes the lining to become still thicker.

What happens if the ovum is not fertilized? When the follicle bursts at ovulation, its production of estrogen declines. This means there is no longer estrogen in the blood stimulating the hypothalamus to stimulate the pituitary to produce LH. Without LH, the corpus luteum stops making progesterone. And, with no more progesterone, the thick lining of the uterus breaks down. Blood and the material from the uterine lining are discharged through the *vagina.* This process is called *menstruation.* Meanwhile, decline of estrogen and progesterone in the blood affects the nervous system. This, in turn, stimulates the hypothalamus to secrete FSHRH. The FSHRH stimulates the pituitary to secrete FSH again. A new cycle begins. The entire cycle is summarized in figure 16–34.

But what happens if the ovum *is* fertilized? This requires the presence of sperm, so we turn to the male reproductive system.

In human males, millions of sperm are produced continuously in coiled tubules in the two testes (called testicles). The testicles lie outside the body wall in a sac of skin, the *scrotum.* From the testicles, sperm pass through ducts that lead up into the body cavity. Along the way secretions produced by three sets of glands are added to the sperm. Semen is formed. The semen is stored in a pouch near the three sets of glands.

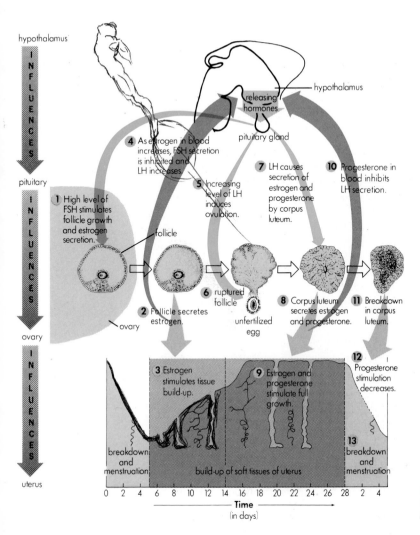

16 – 34 Hormonal changes in the human female reproductive cycle.

As a result of sexual stimuli, veins in the **penis** contract, slowing the flow of blood. Consequently, blood accumulates in the spongy tissue of the penis. This causes stiffening of the penis so that it is able to penetrate the vagina. A similar accumulation of blood occurs in the **clitoris** of the female. Upon further stimulation semen is ejaculated into the female. The sperm swim from the vagina through the uterus and into the fallopian tubes. If an ovum is present, fertilization occurs.

Under the influence of the hypothalamus, the pituitary of a male produces both FSH and LH at an almost constant rate. Thus there is no cycle in the reproductive organs of a human male. LH stimulates endocrine cells in the testicles to produce testosterone. Testosterone is a hormone that increases

penis [PEE nus]

testosterone [tuh STOS tuh rone]

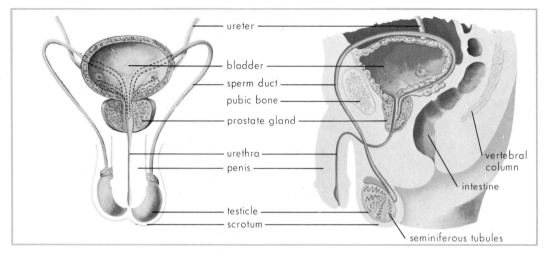

ureter
bladder
sperm duct
pubic bone
prostate gland
urethra
penis
testicle
scrotum

vertebral column
intestine
seminiferous tubules

16–35 The human male reproductive system. The principal organs and their positions are shown in a frontal view (*left*) and in a sectional view (*right*). The duct from each testicle unites with the urethra that leads through the penis.

16–36 Human ovum surrounded by sperm. In fertilization only one sperm cell penetrates the membrane of an ovum. × 500

16–37 Female hormonal relationships during the early part of pregnancy.

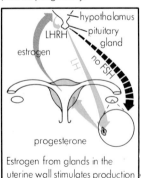

hypothalamus
pituitary gland
LHRH
estrogen
LH
no FSH
progesterone

Estrogen from glands in the uterine wall stimulates production of a hormone which maintains the uterine lining.

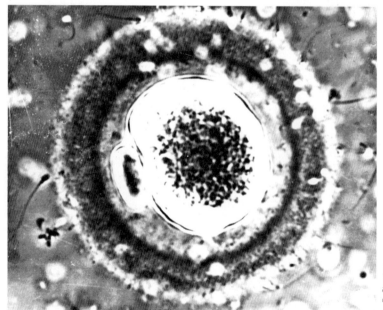

L. B. Shettles

the male's secondary sex characteristics. It is related to growth of the beard and deepening of the voice. FSH stimulates production of sperm.

Now we can return to the female. If an ovum is fertilized, the menstrual cycle is interrupted. The zygote moves along the oviduct. When it reaches the uterus, it becomes embedded in the soft, spongy lining. ***Pregnancy*** begins. The embedded embryo causes glands in the uterine wall to produce estrogen.

Uterine estrogen functions just as does estrogen produced by the follicle. It prevents production of FSHRH and FSH. It also stimulates production of LHRH by the hypothalamus and LH by the pituitary gland. LH, in turn, causes the corpus luteum to continue to produce progesterone. The progesterone maintains the thick lining of the uterus. As long as progesterone is produced, the lining remains intact, pregnancy is maintained, and no new ova develop in the ovaries.

Very early in pregnancy, embryonic membranes form. A chorion develops against the uterine wall. Together the chorion and an outgrowth of the uterine wall form the *placenta.* An allantois grows out from the embryo. Its blood vessels connect the embryo with the placenta through the *umbilical cord.* The placenta eventually lines much of the uterus. The placenta and umbilical cord together provide the bridge to the parent. Through this bridge the embryo receives food and oxygen and discharges carbon dioxide and some other wastes. An amnion develops around a human embryo, just as it does around a chick. It is filled with liquid and protects the embryo from physical injury. The embryo, now in its later stages of development, is called a *fetus.*

Hormonal control continues during pregnancy. The developing chorion, for example, secretes a hormone that stimulates the corpus luteum to continue secreting progesterone. This

pregnancy [PREG nun see]: having offspring developing in the uterus

placenta [pluh SENT uh]

umbilical [um BIL ih kul]

In marsupial mammals placentas do not form fully. How might this affect the development of marsupial embryos?

fetus [FEET us]

16–38 Developing fetus in uterus and diagrammatic section through a placenta. The circulations of embryo and mother are separate but close to each other. Blood of the embryo passes through networks of capillaries that are surrounded by small pools of maternal blood.

chorion
amnion
placenta
umbilical cord
uterus
fetus
amniotic cavity
umbilical vein
umbilical arteries

uterus (tissue of mother)

exchange of materials between fetus and mother

maintains the uterine lining until the placenta begins to secrete both estrogen and progesterone. Eventually the placenta secretes enough hormones to maintain pregnancy even if the ovaries are removed. However, many factors may upset this hormonal control. An accident to the mother may injure the fetus even though it is protected by the uterus and amnion. In such cases, the fetus may be ejected prematurely from the uterus, an event called spontaneous abortion.

ejected [ih JEK tud]: thrown or pushed out

spontaneous abortion [spon TAY-nee us uh BOR shun]

By the ninth month (280 days) of human pregnancy, an unborn baby's head is usually turned downward. Birth begins when muscle layers in the wall of the uterus start to contract and relax. At first the contractions move the baby slowly toward the vagina. At this stage the amnion usually breaks, and its fluid contents are released. Contractions in the muscles of the uterus become stronger and more frequent. Finally, the baby, still attached to the placenta by the umbilical cord, is pushed out through the vagina. Muscular contractions of the uterus continue, pushing out the placenta, commonly called the "afterbirth."

Late in pregnancy the mammary glands of the mother undergo changes that prepare them for producing milk after the baby is born. If the baby does not feed from its mother's breasts, the glands soon stop secreting milk. Usually when milk secretion stops, menstruation begins again.

B

16–39 Stages in the development of a human embryo.
(A) 6 1/2 weeks. × 6
(B) 16 weeks. × 3/4

A

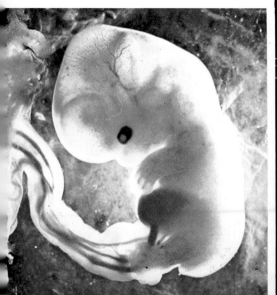

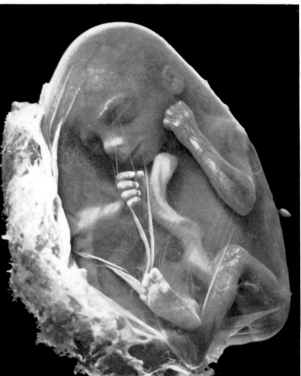

Photos by Lennart Nilsson, A CHILD IS BORN © 1977 Delacort Press, New York

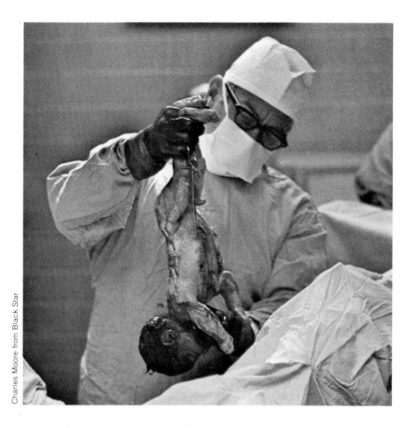

16–40 The process of human birth.

CHECK YOURSELF

LL. How does the reproductive season vary among animals?

MM. What evidence suggests that the hypothalamus and the pituitary gland play important roles in the estrous cycle?

NN. What series of hormonal events brings about ovulation in human females?

OO. When an ovum is not fertilized, what series of events brings about menstruation in a human female?

PP. Where does fertilization occur?

QQ. What is the function of testosterone?

RR. How is the thick lining of a uterus maintained during pregnancy?

SS. What is the relationship between the umbilical cord and the placenta?

TT. What is the average length of human pregnancy?

UU. How does birth occur?

VV. What is the "afterbirth"?

PROBLEMS

1. What experimental procedures could be used to show that progesterone in a particular mammalian species is secreted by the placenta?

2. Testes of vertebrates develop in the body cavity. In human males, if they do not descend into the scrotum, they produce no live sperm. In some mammals with seasonal breeding, they descend into the scrotum only during the breeding season. During the nonbreeding season they are in the body cavity and produce no sperm cells. If temperatures around the scrotum of an experimental animal are kept the same as the internal body temperature, sperm either are not produced or are weak. Yet the testes of birds never leave the body cavity, and birds have a higher internal temperature than most mammals. Can you explain these data?

3. What are the advantages to humans of propagating plants by rooting portions of an older plant instead of planting seeds? What is the relation of grafting to this propagation by cuttings?

4. Sexuality is usually discussed in terms of "male" and "female." But we have seen that these terms are not always meaningful—as in some molds. In some protists the situation becomes even more complicated. Investigate "mating types" in the genus *Paramecium* and try to explain the situation as a special case of sexuality.

5. Investigate the ways in which self-pollination is prevented among gymnosperms and angiosperms. Are there, on the other hand, plants in which self-pollination always occurs? Can you see any advantages to a plant species either in self-pollination or in cross-pollination?

6. From your understanding of plant reproduction, explain each of the following: (a) Seeds will not develop in yuccas unless a certain small species of moth lives in the area. (b) Berries do not develop on holly trees unless two trees are planted together. Even then berries do not develop on both and may not develop on either. (c) In 1839 a single individual of the plant species *Alchornea ilicifolia*, bearing only pistillate flowers, produced abundant seeds in the Kew Gardens, near London. The nearest male plant in the species was in Australia. (d) Some kinds of flowers open only at night. (e) Orchardists often keep apiaries as a sideline. (f) Pea plants, even when grown in an insect-free greenhouse, produce seeds. (g) At the request of local alfalfa growers, many highways in the American West have signs reading "Slow: Low-flying Bees."

7. Is human reproduction lacking in seasonality? Record by months the birthdays of the members of your biology class and of as many other classes as possible. If you can obtain the data from all the students in your school, you will have a fairly satisfactory sample. Present the data in the form of a bar graph—one bar for each month. What does the graph indicate about the question?

SUGGESTED READINGS

Arehart-Treichel, J. 1976. Human Reproduction and Aging. *Science News*, November 6, p. 297.

Jenkins, M. M. 1975. *Embryos and How They Develop*. Holiday House, New York. Discusses how reproduction occurs and how life develops in organisms—from single-celled ones to humans.

Keller, D. E. 1972. *Sex and the Single Cell*. Pegasus, Indianapolis. Informative; easy to read.

Martin, R. D. 1975. Strategies of Reproduction. *Natural History*, November.

Parker, S. 1979. *Life Before Birth: the Story of the First Nine Months*. Cambridge University Press, New York. Human reproduction from inception to birth.

Chapter 17

Heredity

YOUR GUIDEPOSTS

In this chapter you will have an opportunity to explore these questions in biology:

- How are characteristics passed from one generation to the next?
- How does knowledge of the processes of heredity increase our understanding of ourselves?
- How do new hereditary characteristics arise?
- How are the principles of scientific investigation applied to the history of the study of heredity?

INHERITANCE

One of the early biological ideas developed by humans was that a child resembles its parents and grandparents in many ways. Even today no biological idea is of more interest to expecting parents.

17–1 Offspring resemble their parents.

BSCS by David S. Galusha

People also have had interests in the transmission of characteristics from one generation to another—in ***inheritance.*** They try to increase desired characteristics in domestic plants and animals. For example, wool-growers send sheep that produce poor wool to market as mutton. They select the best wool producers as the parents of their future flocks. Corn-growers save ears with the largest and most numerous grains. These are used as the seed for the next crop. In many cases, such selective breeding has produced the desired characteristics.

We have long known that many characteristics are inherited. But only in the past century have we begun to understand *how* they are inherited.

In 1910 a Chicago physician examined a young black man who was suffering from a number of ailments. The patient had muscular aches, swollen joints, dizziness, and shortness of breath. Among the red cells in a blood sample from this patient were many with a nucleus. This was not normal, but it is a situation typical of persons with anemia. Many other blood cells from this patient were thin, long, and sickle-shaped. This was the first description of what is now known as *sickle-cell anemia.*

Seven years later a physician in St. Louis treated a young black woman who had symptoms similar to those of the man in Chicago. This physician also took a blood sample and found red cells that looked normal. They changed to the sickle shape, however, when they were kept sealed on a slide for a day.

A sample of blood was taken from the young woman's father. The father's red blood cells appeared nonsickling. But, after a day on a sealed slide, they also became sickle-shaped. Not as many of the father's cells sickled as did the daughter's. Nor were the father's cells so sickled in shape. Today we would say that the father had the sickle-cell *trait.* The daughter, on the other hand, like the young man in Chicago, had sickle-

17–2 (A) Red blood cells of a person who does not have the sickle-cell trait or sickle-cell anemia. (B) Cells of a person who has the sickle trait. (C) Cells of a person who has sickle-cell anemia.

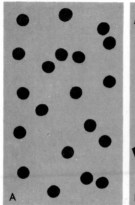

cell anemia. The symptoms of sickle-cell anemia vary greatly from person to person. Some people are severely affected; others show only minor symptoms. Sickle-cell *trait* is not a disease. Under normal circumstances it produces no symptoms.

FAMILY DATA

In the example of sickle-cell anemia, two people in the same family had similar rare characteristics. In such cases a biologist may hypothesize that the characteristics are in some way related to each other. With this idea in mind, medical biologists began to search out new cases of the sickle-cell problem. They particularly wanted to examine blood samples of whole families whenever a case was discovered. During the past half-century medical studies have revealed many families in which some members have shown sickle cells.

Data from such studies can be put in the form of a family chart called a *pedigree.* Figure 17–3 shows pedigrees of three families in which sickle-cell anemia occurs. You can see that any person who has sickle cells has at least one parent with sickle cells. Furthermore, any person who has sickle-cell *anemia* has parents both of whom have sickle cells. On the other hand, parents with the sickle-cell *trait* may have children without sickle cells.

pedigree [PED uh gree; Latin: *pes,* foot, + *grus,* a crane]: (from the branching lines of such a chart)

17–3 Pedigrees of red blood cells in three families. Squares = males; circles = females; crosses = deaths. Children listed with oldest on left. For red-blood cell symbols, see figure 17–2.

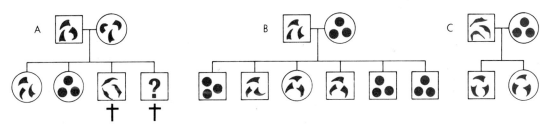

These observations lead us to believe that sickle-cell anemia is a hereditary condition. But such observations do not tell us how inheritance occurs. We need to pool data from many families. To understand these data we need to know something about *probability.*

pool: to sum, put together

The mathematics of probability was originally developed by people interested in gambling – in games of chance. "Chance" describes any situation in which there are so many factors affecting the outcome that we can never hope to determine one cause. The expression "choosing at random" means choosing by chance.

There is one basic question in probability: How often should we expect a particular event to occur in a given number of events? Of course, gamblers would like to know exactly when, for example, the ace of spades will appear in a deck of cards. But the best that mathematicians can do for either gamblers or scientists is to tell them what expectation will least often bring disappointment. In the language of the gamblers, this is giving the best "odds."

The simplest way to express probability is by means of fractions. When a coin is tossed into the air, it may come down either heads or tails. The number of possibilities is the denominator of the fraction — in this example, 2. What is the probability that a coin will come up heads when you toss it? In this question you are looking for one specific event, the appearance of the head of a tossed coin. This is the numerator of this particular fraction: 1. Thus the probability that a coin will land heads up is 1/2. (We also can write this as 0.5 or 50%.)

Investigation 17.1   PROBABILITY

INTRODUCTION

What is the probability that you will draw a spade from a shuffled deck of cards? There are 52 cards in the deck—52 possibilities. Of these, 13 cards are spades. Therefore, the probability of choosing 1 spade from this deck is 13/52 (or 1/4, or 0.25, or 25%). What is the probability that you will draw the ace of diamonds? Again there are 52 possibilities, but this time there is only one way to meet the conditions of the question. The probability is 1/52.

PROCEDURE

Student A: Prepare a scoresheet with 2 columns. Label 1 column *H* ("heads"). Label the other *T* ("tails").

Student B: Toss a penny 10 times. Toss it into a cardboard box to prevent the coin from rolling away.

Student A: Use a slash mark(/) to indicate the result of each toss. Tally it in the appropriate column on the scoresheet. After the 10th toss, draw a line across the 2 columns and pass the sheet to Student B. Take the

MATERIALS
(per pair of students)

2 pennies (1 shiny, 1 dull)
cardboard box

penny and make 10 tosses.

Student B: Tally the results of Student A's tosses. Draw a line across the scoresheet.

Students A and B: Continue reversing the roles until the results of 100 (10 series of 10) tosses have been tallied.

Student A: Prepare a scoresheet with 4 columns: *Both H, Both T, Dull H/Shiny T,* and *Dull T/Shiny H.* (H = heads; T = tails.)

Student B: Obtain 2 pennies—1 dull and 1 shiny. Toss both pennies together 20 times.

Student A: Tally each result in the appropriate column of the scoresheet.

Students A and B: Reverse roles once (resulting in a total of 40 tosses).

DISCUSSION

(*1*) How many heads does probability lead you to expect in a series of 10 tosses of the penny? How many did you actually observe?

Deviation is a measure of the difference between expected and observed results. It is *not* the difference itself. It is the ratio of the difference between expected and observed results to the total number of observations. To calculate deviation, first determine the difference between the number of heads you expected and the number of heads you observed. Then determine the difference between the number of tails you expected and the number of tails you observed. Add these two numbers together. Divide the sum by the total number of tosses. This will give you the deviation. Thus:

$$\text{deviation} = \frac{\left(\begin{array}{c}\text{difference between}\\ \text{heads expected and}\\ \text{heads observed}\end{array}\right) + \left(\begin{array}{c}\text{difference between}\\ \text{tails expected and}\\ \text{tails observed}\end{array}\right)}{\text{number of tosses}}$$

Calculate the deviation for each of the 10 sets of 10 tosses. Then calculate the deviation for your team's total (100 tosses). Add the data of all teams in your class. Calculate the class deviation. If your school has more than one biology class, combine the data of all classes. Calculate the deviation for all classes. (2) How does increasing the number of tosses affect the average size of the deviation? You have just worked out an important principle of probability.

On the chalkboard record the data on tossing 2 pennies together. Total each column of the chart. (3) In how many columns do data concerning heads of a dull penny appear? (4) In what fraction of the total number of tosses did heads of dull pennies occur? (5) In how many columns do data concerning heads of a shiny penny occur? (6) In what fraction of the total number of tosses did heads of the shiny pennies occur? (7) In how many columns do heads of *both* dull and shiny pennies appear? (8) In what fraction of the total number of tosses did heads of *both* pennies appear at the same time? (9) To which of the following is this fraction closest: to the sum, the difference, or the product of the 2 fractions for heads on 1 penny at a time? You have just worked out a second important principle. It is the relationship between the probabilities of separate events and the probability of a combination of events. (10) What is this relationship?

ANALYZING FAMILY DATA

What do pooled family data show us about sickle-cell anemia? We can pool the data from many families in which neither parent has sickle cells. In this case, none of the children have sickle cells.

Parents		*Offspring*
no sickle cells × no sickle cells	⟶	100% no sickle cells

Another study was made of several families in which one parent had the sickle-cell *trait*. The other parent of each couple did not have sickle cells. A total of 66 children were born to these parents. Thirty had the sickle-cell trait and 36 did not have sickle cells. This is close to 50 percent for both groups.

Parents		*Offspring*
no sickle cells × sickle-cell trait	⟶	50% no sickle cells: 50% sickle-cell trait

In another study of pooled family data, *both* parents had the sickle-cell trait. Among the children of these parents, 146 did not have sickle cells, 273 had the sickle-cell trait, and 154 children died from sickle-cell anemia. The best simple ratio that fits these data is 1:2:1.

Parents
sickle-cell trait ×
sickle-cell trait   ⟶

Offspring
25% no sickle cells:50% sickle-cell trait:25% sickle-cell anemia

17−4 Children expected from the marriage of two persons both of whom have the sickle-cell trait. The symbol for the nonsickle-cell gene is **Hb**^A. The symbol for the sickle-cell gene is **Hb**^S.

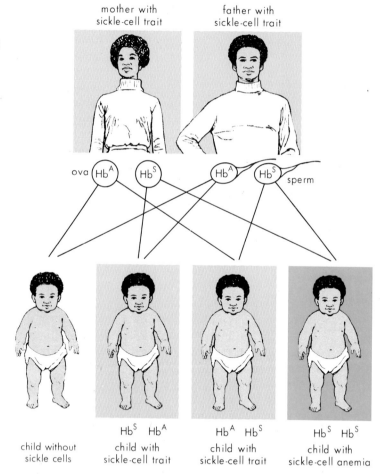

From these studies it appears that parents without sickle cells transmit something that causes their children's red cells not to sickle. Geneticists refer to these "somethings" as **genes.** Persons with the sickle-cell trait seem to carry genes of two kinds—in equal proportions (figure 17−4). Therefore, a parent with the sickle-cell trait sometimes transmits the gene for nonsickling red cells. At other times a parent with the sickle-cell trait transmits the gene that causes some of his or her children to have sickled red cells.

If one parent has the sickle-cell trait and the other has no sickle cells, the probability is that they will produce children in a 1:1 ratio of sickle-cell trait to no sickle cells. Each child with the sickle-cell trait must receive from the "sickle-cell" parent a gene that causes sickle cells. From the other parent the child must receive a gene for nonsickling red cells.

Why do we not assume two (or more) genes for sickle-cell from each parent?

If this reasoning is true, then what types of offspring would you expect from the marriage of two persons with the sickle-cell trait? Because gametes are the only physical bridge between parent and offspring, genes must be carried in gametes. Therefore, one way to represent your expectation is shown in figure 17–4. The diagram shows that you would expect a ratio of one child without sickle cells to two children with sickle-cell trait to one with sickle-cell anemia. The data shown at the top of page 580 support this reasoning.

CHECK YOURSELF

A. How do red blood cells of people with sickle-cell anemia differ from nonsickling red blood cells?
B. What differences exist between a person who has the sickle-cell trait and one who has sickle-cell anemia?
C. What is a pedigree?
D. What evidence indicates that sickle-cell anemia is a hereditary condition?
E. What is probability?
F. What is the probability of choosing one heart from a deck of cards?
G. Does the deviation increase or decrease with an increase in the number of repeated events?
H. How do you determine the probability that two tossed coins will land heads up?

GENETICS

genetics [juh NET iks; Greek: *gignesthai*, to be born]: the branch of biology that deals with heredity

You have now studied some data about a human characteristic that seems to be inherited. A century and a half ago, an Austrian monk, Gregor Mendel, suggested how inheritance occurs in pea plants. Mendel was trained in mathematics as well as in biology—a combination most unusual for that time. He planned experiments that differed in four important respects from those of other scientists.

Mendel limited each study to a *single* characteristic and kept accurate records on pedigrees of all experimental plants. He then pooled the results of many identical matings. Finally, Mendel applied probability to the results. His work is the basis on which the field of **genetics** has developed.

Mendel worked with seven **traits** (characteristics) that occurred in several varieties of garden peas. He studied one trait at a time. Each trait occurred in two forms (figure 17–5). The selected varieties were **true-breeding**. That is, for many generations the plants of each variety showed only one of the two forms of any single trait.

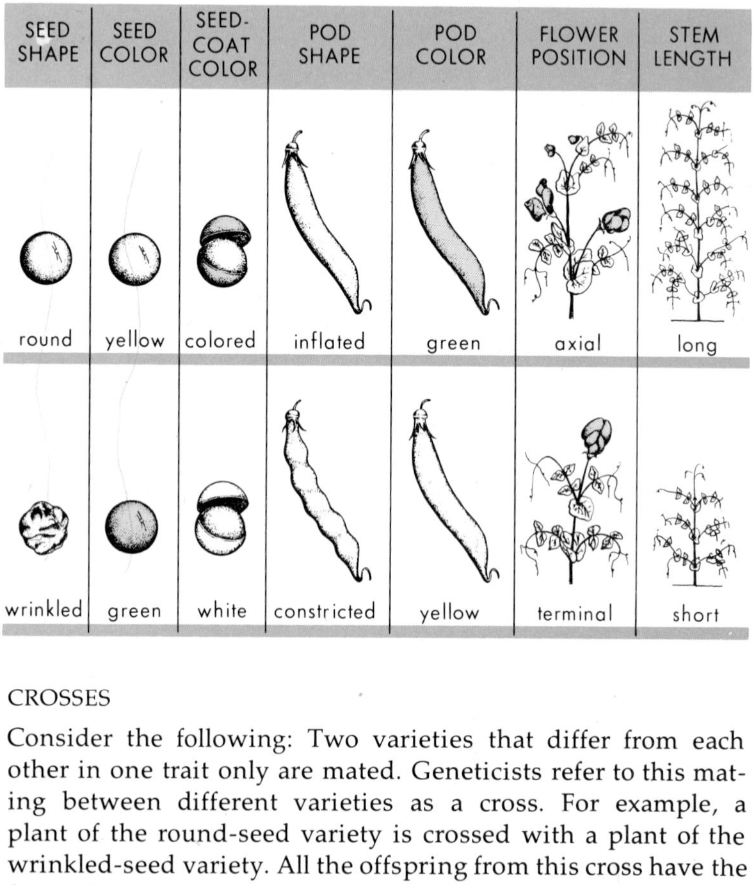

17–5 The seven traits of garden peas studied by Mendel.

SEED SHAPE	SEED COLOR	SEED-COAT COLOR	POD SHAPE	POD COLOR	FLOWER POSITION	STEM LENGTH
round	yellow	colored	inflated	green	axial	long
wrinkled	green	white	constricted	yellow	terminal	short

CROSSES

Consider the following: Two varieties that differ from each other in one trait only are mated. Geneticists refer to this mating between different varieties as a cross. For example, a plant of the round-seed variety is crossed with a plant of the wrinkled-seed variety. All the offspring from this cross have the form of the trait shown by only one parent. In our example, they all have round seeds.

The original, true-breeding parent plants are called the P_1 (parent) generation. Their **hybrid** (not true-breeding) offspring are known as the F_1, or first filial, generation. Continuing with our example, F_1 plants are allowed to fertilize themselves (self-

hybrid. This word has a special meaning in the study of heredity. The more common meaning is "offspring of parents belonging to different species," as on pages 107–108.

filial [FIL ee ul; Latin: *filius*, son]

pollination) or each other. They produce the F_2 (second filial) generation. In the F_2 generation both forms of the parental trait are present. Some plants have round seeds and some have wrinkled seeds. The trait that disappeared in the F_1 generation (wrinkled seeds) reappears in the F_2 generation!

All the F_1 hybrid plants, in this example, have the form of the trait shown by just one of the two parent plants. This is the **dominant** form. The form that seems to disappear in the F_1 generation but reappears in the F_2 plants is the **recessive** form.

Mendel accumulated the F_2 data shown in figure 17−6 by conducting crosses such as those described above. In each case the dominant form appears in about three-fourths of the plants. The recessive form appears in one-fourth of the plants. The ratios are very nearly 3:1 (or 3/4:1/4). Are all of the F_2 individuals that show the dominant form true-breeding? If F_2 plants that have the dominant form of a trait are allowed to self-pollinate, they show a 1:2 ratio of true-breeding to non-true-breeding. Therefore, the ratio among the F_2 plants can be re-written as 1:2:1. Or, in fractions, 1/4 of all F_2 plants are true-breeding dominants, 2/4 are non-true-breeding dominants, and 1/4 are recessive.

17−6 Mendel's data from self-pollination of his F_1 plants.

	P_1 CROSS	F_1 PLANTS	F_2 PLANTS	ACTUAL RATIO
1.	round X wrinkled seeds	all round	5,474 round 1,850 wrinkled 7,324 total	2.96:1
2.	yellow X green seeds	all yellow	6,022 yellow 2,001 green 8,023 total	3.01:1
3.	colored X white seed coats	all colored	705 colored 224 white 929 total	3.15:1
4.	inflated X constricted pods	all inflated	882 inflated 299 constricted 1,181 total	2.95:1
5.	green X yellow pods	all green	428 green 152 yellow 580 total	2.82:1
6.	axial X terminal flowers	all axial	651 axial 207 terminal 858 total	3.14:1
7.	long X short stems	all long	787 long 277 short 1,064 total	2.84:1

Mendel concluded that parent plants transmit through their gametes "elements" that control the development of certain traits. We have learned that these "elements" are genes. Even though a recessive gene cannot be detected in the F_1 generation, it must be present because it reappears in the F_2 generation. And when the recessive form reappears, it precisely resembles the original recessive form. (Wrinkled F_2 seeds, for example, are no more or less wrinkled than the P_1 seeds.) Apparently genes occur in pairs. Genes of each pair must *segregate* (separate) during gamete formation. As a result, each gamete carries only one gene of each pair. Your reasoning about sickle-cell anemia implied the same thing.

alleles [uh LEE ulz; Greek: *allelon*, of one another]

Refer to figure 17−7. The symbols **R** and **r** are used to represent the different forms (*alleles*) of a single gene. They represent alleles of the gene that determines the shape of pea seeds. **R** represents the dominant allele (round seeds), and **r** represents the recessive allele (wrinkled seeds). In a plant that is true-breeding, both alleles of a gene pair are the same. True-breeding plants with round seeds have two **R** alleles. True-breeding plants with wrinkled seeds have two **r** alleles. The true-breeding plants with round seeds produce only gametes with one **R** allele (plus many genes for other traits). Plants with wrinkled seeds produce only gametes with an **r** allele.

When true-breeding, round-seed (**RR**) plants are crossed with true-breeding, wrinkled-seed (**rr**) plants, all the resulting

17−7 One of Mendel's crosses. An example of gene transmission from one generation to the next. Note that the genes of a pair segregate during gamete formation.

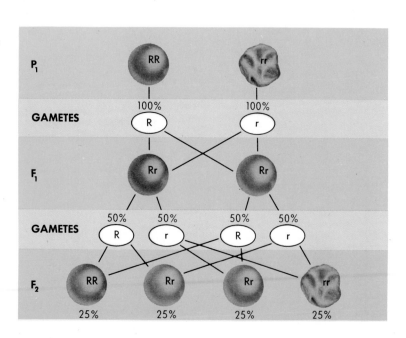

zygotes have both alleles (**Rr**). All of these F_1 plants produce round seeds. Apparently only one dominant allele (**R**) is needed in a pair of genes to direct the plant to form round seeds.

When plants of the F_1 generation form gametes, half of the gametes will get the **R** allele and the other half will get the **r** allele. Then if gametes unite at random during fertilization, the ratio of individuals that show the dominant to those that show the recessive in the F_2 generation is 3:1.

Refer back to Investigation 17.1, item 9.

Using our knowledge of probability, could we have predicted this ratio? Let us assume that F_1 (**Rr**) plants produce equal numbers of gametes with an **R** or an **r** allele. The chance of a gamete having an **R** is 1/2. And there is an equal chance that any gamete will unite with any other gamete. What is the probability that an **R** gamete will unite with another **R** gamete? ($1/2 \times 1/2 = 1/4$.) The same is true for the uniting of two **r** gametes. We should expect 1/4 of all new individuals to have two **R**'s and to have round seeds. We should expect another 1/4 to have two **r**'s and wrinkled seeds.

What is the probability that an **R** gamete will unite with an **r** gamete? The probability of a male producing an **R** gamete is 1/2. The probability of a female producing an **r** gamete is also 1/2. So, $1/2 \times 1/2 = 1/4$. However, the male in this case can also produce an **r** gamete and the female can produce an **R** gamete. Thus, $1/2 \times 1/2 = 1/4$. Since there are two ways an **Rr** individual can be formed, you add the two probabilities together. Thus, $1/4 + 1/4 = 1/2$. One half of all individuals can be expected to have **Rr**. Recall that 1/4 of all new individuals are expected to have two **R**'s and 1/4 to have two **r**'s. This gives a 3:1 ratio of dominant to recessive individuals (25% **RR,** 50% **Rr**'s, and 25% **rr**).

But the ratio 3:1 concerns the appearance of the seeds — their **phenotypes.** If we consider their genes as shown by the symbols — their **genotypes** — the ratio is 1:2:1 (25% **RR,** 25% **Rr** + 25% **Rr,** 25% **rr**). We refer to genotypes made up of the same alleles (**RR** and **rr,** for example) as being **homozygous.** Those made up of two different alleles (**Rr,** for example) are **heterozygous.** Thus, in a cross between two heterozygotes, half of the offspring will be homozygous for one allele or the other. The other half will be heterozygous.

phenotypes [FEE nuh typs; Greek: *phainein,* to show]

genotypes [JEE nuh typs]

homozygous [hoh muh ZY gus; Greek: *homos,* the same, + *zygon,* a yoke]

heterozygous [het uh roh ZY gus; Greek: *heteros,* the other, + *zygon*]. Heterozygous individuals are referred to as heterozygotes.

DIHYBRID CROSSES

It is possible to consider two traits at the same time — a **dihybrid cross.** Plants that are true-breeding for both round seed shape and yellow seed color are crossed with plants that are true-breeding for both wrinkled seed shape and green color.

dihybrid [dy HY brud; Greek: *dis,* twice, + hybrid]

The round and yellow traits are dominant to the wrinkled and green. What combinations of shape and color will appear in the offspring? In what ratios? In the F_1 generation of true-breeding pea plants, all the offspring have the same phenotype. The seeds are both round and yellow. This can be expected, since these are the dominant forms of the two traits (figure 17−8). But the F_2 generation produces the following offspring:

round, yellow	301
round, green	99
wrinkled, yellow	99
wrinkled, green	30
	529

17−8 A dihybrid cross.
R = gene for round seed.
r = gene for wrinkled seed.
Y = gene for yellow seed.
y = gene for green seed.

The closest simple ratio for these numbers is 9:3:3:1. How can these results be explained?

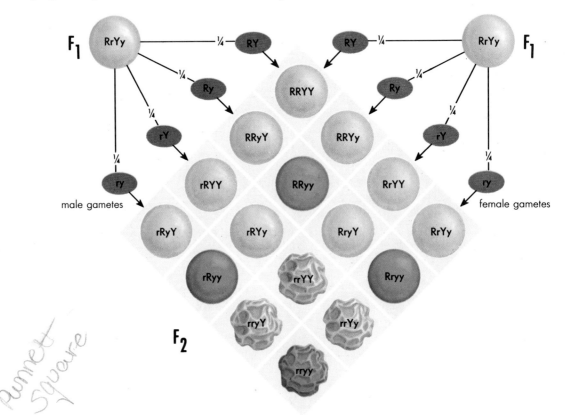

The genotypes of the true-breeding P_1 generation were **RRYY** for the "round, yellow" and **rryy** for the "wrinkled, green." All the F_1 individuals must have had the genotype **RrYy**. We can assume that alleles **R** and **r** segregated into gametes independently of the alleles **Y** and **y**. Four types of male gametes (1/4 **RY**, 1/4 **Ry**, 1/4 **rY**, 1/4 **ry**) are formed. The same four types of female gametes also are formed. If we assume that the gametes unite at random, the expected outcome is that shown in figure 17–8. The expectations shown in the figure can be combined as follows:

Compare the formation of gametes with your penny-tossing experiment on pages 578–579.

Fraction	Genotype	Phenotype	Fraction
1/16	**RRYY**	round, yellow ⎫	
2/16	**RrYY**	round, yellow ⎬ 9/16	
2/16	**RRYy**	round, yellow ⎪	
4/16	**RrYy**	round, yellow ⎭	
1/16	**RRyy**	round, green ⎫ 3/16	
2/16	**Rryy**	round, green ⎭	
1/16	**rrYY**	wrinkled, yellow ⎫ 3/16	
2/16	**rrYy**	wrinkled, yellow ⎭	
1/16	**rryy**	wrinkled, green 1/16	

The phenotype fractions, expressed as a ratio, are 9:3:3:1.

What is the ratio for each individual trait?

CONCLUSIONS

Three major principles can be drawn from this discussion:

1. The principle of dominance. When the alleles of a gene pair for a particular trait are different, the effect of one is observed (dominant). The effect of the other one remains hidden (recessive).

Was this true of sickle-cell anemia? Of course, Mendel did not know about that.

2. The principle of segregation. Genes controlling a particular trait are separated during gamete formation. Therefore, each gamete carries only one allele of each gene pair.

3. The principle of independent assortment. When two traits are studied in the same cross, the genes for one trait assort independently of the genes for the other.

CHECK YOURSELF

I.   Who was Gregor Mendel?
J.   What does "true-breeding" mean?
K. Describe an experiment designed to distinguish dominant and recessive forms of a trait.
L.   What is a gene?
M. If you say two genes are alleles, what do you mean?
N. Using sickle-cell anemia as an example, explain the difference between "genotype" and "phenotype." Between a homozygous and a heterozygous individual.
O. What is a dihybrid cross?
P.   What are three major principles Mendel discovered?

Investigation 17.2   SEEDLING PHENOTYPES

INTRODUCTION

One variety of pea produces short vines and another produces tall vines. A little observation shows, however, that the size of plants is affected by the kind of soil in which the plants grow. Scientists can control this variable by growing all test plants in the same soil. But we may still raise these questions: To what extent is the phenotype of an organism the result of its genotype? And, to what extent is the phenotype influenced by its environment?

PROCEDURE

1. Cut 8 disks of paper toweling to fit snugly in the bottom of a petri dish. With a pencil, write a large *A* on one disk and a large *B* on another. Place the *A* disk on top of 3 others in one petri dish. Place the *B* disk on top of 3 others in another petri dish.
2. Pour water into each dish. When the paper is thoroughly soaked, pour off the excess water.
3. Sprinkle 30 tobacco seeds into each dish. Using forceps, arrange the seeds so that each is at least twice its own length from any other. Be sure that the *A* and *B* remain visible.
4. Cover the dishes and label with your team symbol. Put both dishes in a warm place that receives strong light but not in direct sunlight.
5. Cover the *B* dishes of all teams with a box that will keep them in darkness.
6. Check the dishes each day. If the paper begins to dry out, add water with a medicine dropper.
7. When at least 1/2 the seeds have germinated (sprouted), examine them with a hand lens.
8. Each young tobacco plant has a colorless root and 2 tiny leaves, the cotyledons (figure 17–9). Usually the root appears first,

MATERIALS
(per team)

60 tobacco seeds
2 petri dishes
beaker filled with water
2 forceps
medicine dropper
hand lens
glass-marking crayon
scissors
paper towels
box (1 per class—large
   enough to cover half the
   dishes used by the class)

17–9 Stages in the germination of a tobacco seed.

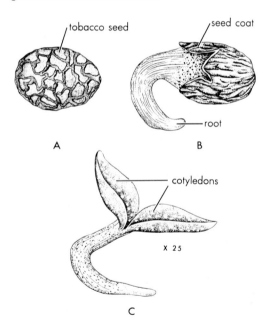

but in this experiment you are concerned only with the cotyledons. Some seedlings have green cotyledons and some have cream-colored, or yellowish, ones. Count the number of each kind in each dish. At least 2 members of the team should make counts. Recount if there is disagreement.

Using a form like that in figure 17–10, record the counts opposite "Day 1."

17–10

DAY	DISH A			DISH B		
	Green	Yellow	% Yellow	Green	Yellow	% Yellow
1						
2						
3						
4						

9. Replace the lids. Return the dishes to the assigned location, covering the *B* dishes as before.
10. On Day 2 make another count. Record the counts.
11. Calculate the percentage of yellow seedlings. To do this, divide the number of seedlings with yellow cotyledons by the total number of germinated seeds. Make this calculation for each dish.
12. Return the dishes to the assigned location, but this time do not cover the *B* dishes. Allow all dishes to remain exposed to light.
13. On Day 3 count the seedlings again. Record the counts and return the dishes to their assigned place. Allow all dishes to remain exposed to the light.
14. On Day 4 make final counts and calculate the percentage of seedlings with yellow cotyledons in each dish.

DISCUSSION

From the data obtained on Day 2, compare the percentages of yellow seedlings in Dishes A and B. (*1*) In what ways are they different? (*2*) What experimental variable may be associated with this difference? (*3*) Can this variable be considered the cause of yellow color in tobacco seedlings? Why or why not?

Compare the percentage of yellow seedlings in Dish B on Day 2 with the percentage on Day 4. (*4*) What change occurred? (*5*) What experimental variable is associated with this change? (*6*) Can this variable be considered the cause of yellow coloration in tobacco seedlings? Why or why not? (*7*) How can you account for the difference among the seedlings in Dish A?

(*8*) Do any data support the statement, "Yellow color of tobacco seedlings is caused by environment"? If so, which data? (*9*) Do any data support the statement, "Yellow color of tobacco seedlings is caused by heredity"? If so, which data? (*10*) Try to formulate a statement that accounts for all the data.

THE CHROMOSOME THEORY

Mendel's work, published in 1865, lay neglected until early in the 20th century. Few biologists understood the mathematics of his work. Between 1865 and 1900, however, much progress was made in the study of cells. As a result of certain staining techniques, chromosomes were discovered. Details of mitosis and meiosis were outlined.

Geneticists concluded that the links between sexually reproducing parents and offspring are sperm and ova. These reproductive cells must, therefore, contain the genes. Sperm and ova must contribute equally to the heredity of the offspring. They resemble one another only in their nuclei. It may be concluded, therefore, that nuclear material controls heredity.

17—11 All the chromosomes of a normal human female. To make this chart, a photomicrograph of a cell in mitosis was taken. Then the picture was cut apart and the chromosomes rearranged in pairs.

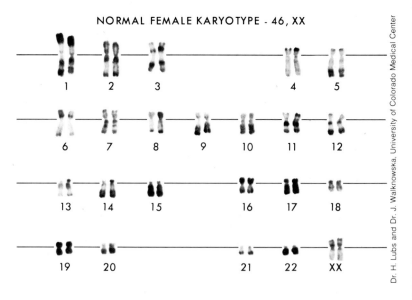

NORMAL FEMALE KARYOTYPE - 46, XX

1 2 3 4 5

6 7 8 9 10 11 12

13 14 15 16 17 18

19 20 21 22 XX

Dr. H. Lubs and Dr. J. Walknowska, University of Colorado Medical Center

Chromosomes are nuclear material, and they appear in both mitosis and meiosis. After meiosis the number of chromosomes in each sperm or ovum is half that found in other cells of the same organism. Thus, one allele of each gene pair is present in each gamete. Each sperm or ovum has a monoploid set of chromosomes. The union between the two reestablishes in the new individual the diploid set of chromosomes. Each chromosome is copied once before meiosis. One of the two meiotic cell divisions, unlike mitosis, separates the chromosomes of each pair. The other separates each chromosome from its new duplicate. The result is monoploid gametes.

During meiosis each pair of chromosomes separates independently. Let us assume one monoploid chromosome from the male parent is A and the homologous chromosome from the female is A'. Another pair consists of B (from the male) and B' (from the female). In meiosis, A does not always go to the pole that B goes to. Nor does A' always end up with B'. Instead, there may be at the poles AB, A'B, AB', or A'B'—and with equal frequency. This is a result of independent assortment.

In summary, then, genes must be small particles located in chromosomes. This is the *chromosome theory of heredity.* The surest way to test a theory is to use it as the basis of a prediction. If the new data do not support the theory, it must be revised or discarded. If a theory continues to account for new data as they appear, it becomes more convincing. But what kind of evidence could be gathered to support the chromosome theory of heredity?

NUMBERS OF GENES AND CHROMOSOMES

If there were just one gene pair on each chromosome pair, the number of traits under genetic control would be limited to the number of chromosome pairs. Some organisms have only two or three pairs of chromosomes, and humans have only 23 pairs. Yet an organism has many inheritable traits. Thus many different genes must be located on each chromosome. Geneticists use the word **linkage** to describe the groups of genes for different traits that are located together on the same chromosome.

If genes for two different traits are carried on the same pair of chromosomes, we would predict they would not assort independently. Instead the genes would always occur together. The phenotype ratio would be the same as it would be for a single trait.

SEX IN THE FRUIT FLY

The study of heredity was placed on a new basis when T. H. Morgan began experiments with a fruit fly, *Drosophila melanogaster*. These insects have only four pairs of chromosomes. Three of the four pairs are identical in both males and females (figure 17–12). In males the fourth pair consists of a rod-shaped chromosome, called X, and a hook-shaped one, called Y. In females the fourth pair consists of two X's.

Thus, females can contribute, from the fourth chromosome pair, only an X to each gamete. Males can contribute either an X or a Y. Sex appears to be a clearly visible trait in these cells. It can be associated with the like or unlike chromosome pair — usually called the **sex chromosomes.** Here was visible evidence that an inherited trait (sex) is determined by something involving chromosomes.

SEX-LINKAGE

In *Drosophila melanogaster* the eyes are normally red. While examining thousands of flies bred in the laboratory, Morgan found one male that had white eyes. When he crossed this male with a normal red-eyed female, the resulting F$_1$ generation consisted entirely of red-eyed flies. Next, Morgan allowed the members of the F$_1$ generation to mate. Among the F$_2$ offspring the ratio was 3 red-eyed flies to every white-eyed fly. This was expected. But *all* the white-eyed flies were males; none were females. Here was a trait related in some way to sex — a **sex-linked trait.**

Since the Y chromosome differs from the X chromosome in appearance, we might assume that it also differs in whatever genes (if any) it carries. Suppose, then, we hypothesize that a

x   y

MALE

x   x

FEMALE

17–12 Chromosomes of *Drosophila melanogaster* arranged in pairs.

Drosophila melanogaster [droh SOF uh luh MEL uh noh-gas tur]

Construct a diagram for the inheritance of sex that corresponds to the diagram in figure 17–4.

Is white-eye dominant or recessive?

Why not hypothesize the
opposite?

gene for red eye color is located in the X chromosome but that
no gene for eye color is carried in the Y chromosome. What
might we expect in a breeding experiment?

Let **R** stand for the normal dominant red-eye gene. Let **r**
represent the recessive white-eye gene. Since we have hypothesized that these genes occur only on the X chromosome, we can
write X^R, X^r, and Y for the three kinds of chromosomes. The
genotype of the original white-eyed male must have been X^rY.
That of the normal red-eyed, true-breeding female must have
been X^RX^R. With these symbols, figure 17–13 shows the result

17–13 Inheritance of the
white-eye trait in *Drosophila*.
Compare this with the results
of one of Mendel's crosses
diagramed in figure 17–7.

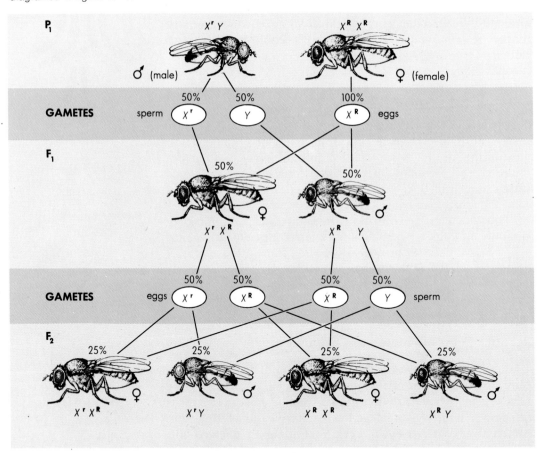

to be expected according to our hypothesis. The evidence supports our hypothesis that the gene for eye color is only on the X
chromosome, not on the Y.

chi-square [ky square]

CHI-SQUARE

To test their hypotheses, scientists make predictions and then
design experiments to verify those predictions. Is the difference

between observed and expected results *significant?* In other words, is the difference greater than would be expected by chance alone? This is a question that every scientist faces repeatedly. Scientists believe that if the difference is significant it is not due to chance alone.

Consider an example. A biologist crossed two kinds of tomato plants. The hypothesis was that half the offspring would have green leaves and half would have yellow leaves. (In certain kinds of tomatoes, this is a reasonable expectation.) One experiment involved 1,240 seedlings. Of these, 671 had green leaves and 569 had yellow leaves. The expected numbers from a total of 1,240 are 620 of each kind. Is this a minor difference—a matter of chance? Or is it significant? Should the biologist suspect that there is something wrong with the hypothesis or with the conditions of the experiment?

In Investigation 17.1 you learned one way to express deviation. A more precise way is called **chi-square**. It is symbolized by the Greek letter *chi* and the square sign, thus: χ^2. Chi-square is found as follows. For each class of objects, obtain the difference between the number expected and the number observed. Square this difference. Divide by the expected number. Finally, add all the quotients together. The sum is the value of χ^2.

In mathematical form this is:

$$\chi^2 = \Sigma \frac{(O - E)^2}{E}.$$

Σ means "the sum of," $O =$ observed number, and $E =$ expected number. In our example of tomato leaves, the difference for the first class of objects, green-leaved plants, is $671 - 620$, or 51. Squaring this, we get 2,601. Dividing by the expected number, 620, we get the quotient 4.2. The difference for the other class of objects, yellow-leaved plants, is $569 - 620$, or -51. Squaring this, we get 2,601. Dividing by 620, we get 4.2. Added together, the two quotients come to 8.4, the value of χ^2.

17–14 Table of chi-square values.

χ^2 for four classes	.115	.352	.584	2.366	3.665	6.251	7.815	11.341
χ^2 for three classes	.020	.103	.211	1.386	2.408	4.605	5.991	9.210
χ^2 for two classes	.0002	.004	.016	.455	1.074	2.706	3.841	6.635
Times in 100 that chance alone might give χ^2 this large or larger.	99	95	90	50	30	10	5	1

But what does this value mean? Mathematicians have provided the information needed to judge whether a χ^2 value represents a difference that occurs by chance alone. A table prepared from the equation shows how often (in 100 cases) a given value of χ^2 is expected to arise by chance alone.

For two classes of objects, the χ^2 value of 8.4 goes beyond the table. There is less than one chance in 100 that the difference between the observed and expected numbers of tomato plants could have been caused by chance alone. In this case the difference is said to be significant. The difference probably did not occur by chance but may be due to real differences among the experimental plants.

In our example using tomato plants, further experimentation showed that the difference from the expected numbers occurred because the yellow-leaved plants were less sturdy than the green-leaved plants. Therefore, fewer of their seeds germinated and lived.

When more than two classes occur among the results of an experiment, it is necessary to use other lines in the χ^2 table. For example, to test the significance of the 9:3:3:1 ratio of a dihybrid cross, χ^2 for four classes is needed.

CHECK YOURSELF

Q. How do scientists test their theories?
R. Why must we conclude that each chromosome contains genes for more than one trait?
S. How do the "sex chromosomes" differ from other chromosome pairs in fruit flies?
T. What is a sex-linked trait?
U. How did the inheritance of white eye color in fruit flies link the inheritance of a particular trait with a particular chromosome?
V. For what purpose is the chi-square test used?

Investigation 17.3   INHERITANCE IN FRUIT FLIES

INTRODUCTION

Before using fruit flies in experiments, you must understand their life cycle. Also, you should practice techniques for handling them, and learn to distinguish males from females.

The eggs are usually laid on the surface of food. They hatch into tiny wormlike creatures (larvae) in about 24 hours. Larvae eat almost continually. In a laboratory culture, you can easily see their black mouthparts moving back and forth in the medium. Mature larvae usually climb up the side of the culture bottle or onto a paper strip in the bottle. There they become **pupae** (singular, pupa). During this stage the pupae appear to be inactive. They are, however, changing into adult flies. When the adults emerge from the pupal cases, they are fragile and light in color. But within a few hours the body color darkens and wings expand. Females will mate about 12 hours after emerging from the pupae. During mating they store many sperm. Fertilization occurs later, when the eggs are laid.

PROCEDURE

A. Examining fruit flies

The W culture contains flies with the form of the trait that is normal in wild populations. It is referred to as the **wild-type** trait. The L culture contains flies with a form that appears in laboratory populations. To determine the difference, compare the flies in the two cultures when they are quiet.

1. Refer to figure 17–15 as you perform the following procedure for etherizing flies. (*Caution: Do not use ether in a room where there is an open flame.*)
   a. Place a finger beneath the neck of the funnel of the etherizer. Pour several drops of ethyl ether on the string at the upper end of the neck. Avoid using too much ether. Its vapor will anesthe-

MATERIALS
(per team)

etherizer (figure 17–15)
ethyl ether, in dropping bottle
examination plate
small water-color brush
stereomicroscope
morgue (figure 17–15C)
glass-marking crayon

For Part A

culture of wild-type (W) flies
culture of laboratory-type (L) flies

For Part B

culture of W flies
culture of L flies
2 culture vials containing
   fresh medium

For Part C

culture vial containing
   offspring of P_1 cross

For Part D

culture of either W or L flies
culture of F_1 flies
culture vial containing fresh medium

tize the flies. Liquid ether will kill them. When the ether trickles down the neck and reaches your finger, place the funnel in the etherizer glass.

17–15 Anesthetizing fruit flies.

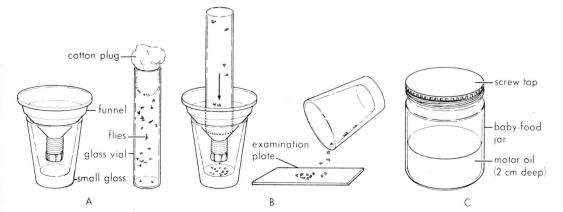

cotton plug

funnel

flies

glass vial

small glass

A

examination plate

B

screw top

baby-food jar

motor oil (2 cm deep)

C

b. Gently but rapidly tap against your knee the bottom of the vial containing the flies. This forces the flies to the bottom of the vial. Quickly remove the cotton plug. Invert the vial, and place it firmly in the funnel.

c. Hold vial, funnel, and glass firmly together. Tap the bottom of the glass against your hand or knee. This dislodges the flies into the glass.

d. The flies should be quiet within a few seconds. As soon as the last fly stops moving, remove the funnel. Empty the flies onto the examination plate. (Caution: Flies left in the etherizer more than a minute may die.)

e. Use a small brush to move the flies about on the examination plate. Move them gently; they are easily injured. Flies resume activity in about 5 minutes. They may be re-etherized if necessary. Place flies that are accidentally killed into the morgue.

2. Using the demonstrated procedure, examine the flies in the W culture. Note differences between males and females (figure 17–16).

3. Examine the flies in the L culture. Record the trait in which these flies differ from the W flies. What are the two forms in which the trait occurs?

B. The P₁ mating

1. Use cultures from which all adults were removed about 8 hours ago. These females will not have mated. (1) Why is this necessary?

2. Etherize the flies in the culture.

3. Pick out 2 or 3 females. Do not select flies having a very pale color or incompletely expanded wings. These have too recently emerged and are easily injured.

4. Using a brush, transfer the selected females into a culture vial that contains a supply of fresh food. Return the other flies to the original vial.

17–16 Comparison of male and female fruit flies.

5. Now etherize the flies in the other vial (the W culture if your females are from the L culture, the L culture if they are from the W culture).

6. Select 2 or 3 male flies. Place them in the new culture vial with the female flies. Return the remaining flies to the original vial.

7. On the new culture vial mark the date, the cross (sex and form of trait in each parent), and your team symbol.

8. After 7 or 8 days, remove the parent flies and place them in the morgue.

C. The F₁ generation

1. About 10 or 12 days after the mating, adult flies of the F₁ generation should begin to emerge. Etherize them and examine each for the trait you are studying. Place them in the morgue after you are through. For each fly make a tally mark on a chart similar to the one in figure 17–17.

17–17

Date of Mating _____

Date Parents Removed _____

P₁ ♂ _____ X ♀ _____

Generation _____

DATE	WILD-TYPE	MUTANT
↕	↕	↕
Total		

2. Each day examine the adult flies that appeared during the previous 24 hours. Discard them and tally the counts. Do not count beyond the 9th day after the emergence of the first F₁ flies. (Otherwise, you might run into some individuals of the F₂ generation.) (2) With respect to the trait you are studying, how many phenotypes occur among the P₁ flies? Examine your data from the F₁ generation. (3) How many phenotypes occur among the F₁ flies? (4) What Mendelian principle is illustrated by the results of this cross?

D. The testcross mating

1. In a testcross, recessive individuals are mated with individuals of unknown genotypes. From your F₁ results, identify the recessive phenotype. Ask your teacher for a culture of parent (true-breeding) flies with this phenotype.

2. Using the procedure described for the P₁ mating, make a cross between these flies and those of the F₁ generation. (Your teacher will designate from which culture you should take females and males.)

3. Mark the new culture vial with the date, the phenotype and sex of the adult flies, and your team symbol.

4. After 7 or 8 days, remove the adult flies and place them in the morgue.

5. When adults begin to emerge, make daily counts. Record the results on a chart like the one used before.

DISCUSSION

In the data from the F₁ generation, compare results obtained by teams that used wild-type females in the P₁ mating. (5) Is the number of F₁ phenotypes the same in both cases? If not, try to explain the difference. (6) With respect to the trait you are studying, how many phenotypes occur among the testcross flies? (7) On the basis of your team's data, calculate the percentage of individuals showing each phenotype in the testcross generation. (8) Now combine the data that all the teams have gathered and calculate class percentages.

Here are some questions that may help you develop a hypothesis appropriate to the procedure you have used. Flies of both the W and L parental cultures were true-breeding. (9) With respect to the trait you are studying, what types of gametes do you expect males and females of each kind to produce? In what ratio? (10) What, then, should be the genotype of the F₁ males? (11) What types of sperm should these F₁ males produce? In what ratio? (12) On the basis of this reasoning, what ratio of phenotypes do you expect in the generation resulting from the testcross? Your answer is your hypothesis for the testcross.

(13) Are the percentages of flies in your testcross generation close enough to those predicted to give you confidence that your hypotheses may be correct? Use the combined data of all teams to calculate chi-square for the testcross generation of fruit flies.

(14) Are the data significantly different from the numbers expected on the basis of your hypothesis? (15) If the difference is not significant, what conclusion can you make?

(*16*) If the difference is significant, how might you explain it?

You may have found, as dozens of geneticists have, that your hypothesis is supported by your data. The ratio of phenotypes in the testcross offspring is the same as the ratio of gamete types produced by F$_1$ males. The testcross method enables a geneticist to measure the ratio of differing gametes—which could not be done visually with even the most powerful microscope. Just to check your understanding: (*17*) Which of the testcross phenotypes is true-breeding? (*18*) Why not both?

FOR FURTHER INVESTIGATION

Once you have learned the techniques of handling fruit flies and have used chi-square to test the significance of breeding results, you can carry on many genetic experiments. Here are some questions you can investigate: (*a*) What phenotype ratios would you expect in the F$_2$ generation of your experimental crosses? (*b*) What ratio would you expect if, after they have had an opportunity to mate, you put 6 or 8 of the homozygous-recessive females from the testcross offspring into a fresh culture vial (with no males) and allowed them to produce offspring?

FURTHER DEVELOPMENTS

By 1915 Morgan's fruit flies had become the center of genetic research. But heredity in maize (corn), guinea pigs, mice, and many other organisms was also being investigated. From this research came many data that did not always agree with the three major principles Mendel first discovered.

CODOMINANCE

In all Mendel's experiments, one allele was dominant over the other. A pea plant with a genotype **YY** (homozygous yellow-

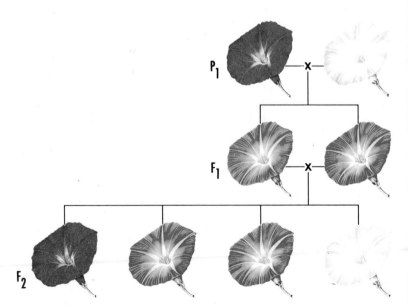

17—18 Inheritance of flower color in morning glories. An example of codominance.

seeded) may *look like* a **Yy** individual (heterozygous yellow-seeded). But today many cases are known in which *neither* allele dominates the other; they are codominant. Three phenotypes result. Hybrid organisms show an intermediate degree of the trait. Their phenotype is different from that of both the homozygous parents. The two alleles for nonsickling cells and sickle cells are of this sort (figure 17–4).

RECOMBINATION

Early in the 20th century, cases contrary to the principle of independent assortment were found. Consider the following situation. In *Drosophila melanogaster* the genes for gray body color and normal wings are dominant and are on the same chromosome. The recessive alleles are for black body color and vestigial wings. Flies homozygous for gray body and normal wings were crossed with flies with the two recessive traits. All the F_1 flies had gray bodies and normal wings. In a testcross, the F_1 progeny were then mated with black-bodied, vestigial-winged flies. The results were:

Gray body, normal wings	241 flies
Black body, vestigial wings	252 flies
Gray body, vestigial wings	51 flies
Black body, normal wings	56 flies

This ratio is not 3:1, as you would expect, since the two genes are on the same chromosome. What could the answer be?

A solution to this problem lies in the crossing-over that sometimes occurs during meiosis (page 545). Suppose we are studying two traits—one of which is determined by alleles **A** (dominant) and **a** (recessive). The others are alleles **B** (dominant) and **b** (recessive). Suppose, further, that the genes for these two traits are on the *same* chromosome. The ***locus*** (position) of **A** (or **a**) is near the middle of the chromosome. The locus of **B** (or **b**) is at the end. Figure 17–19 shows what happens if crossing-over occurs between the **A** and **B** loci in 36 percent of the cells during meiosis. Without crossing-over, 50 percent of the gametes would have **A** linked with **B**. Fifty percent would have **a** linked with **b**. In this example, only 41 percent of the gametes have the first linkage (**AB**) and 41 percent the second (**ab**). Nine percent have **A** on the same chromosome with **b**, and 9 percent have **a** linked with **B**. The new linkages are called ***recombinations.*** If F_2 zygotes are formed from such gametes, the two dominant traits are not always associated—nor are the two recessive traits. Instead, some zygotes are recombinants of dominant and recessive genes—**Ab** or **aB**—producing two new dihybrid phenotypes.

locus [LOH kus; Latin: a place]: plural, loci [LOH sy]

Assuming that figure 17–19 illustrates meiosis in a *Drosophila* female, what sort of male would you use in a mating to reveal the frequency of recombination?

17-19 Genetic effect of crossing-over in *Drosophila*. Crossing-over during meiosis does not occur with most chromosomes. Those pictured here are only the chromosomes in which crossing-over does take place. Note that only the combinations **AB** and **ab** occur before meiosis. Crossing-over between **A and B** results in the recombinations **Ab** and **aB** in the gametes. What is the ratio of gametes carrying **Ab** and **aB** to *all* gametes in which crossing-over occurred?

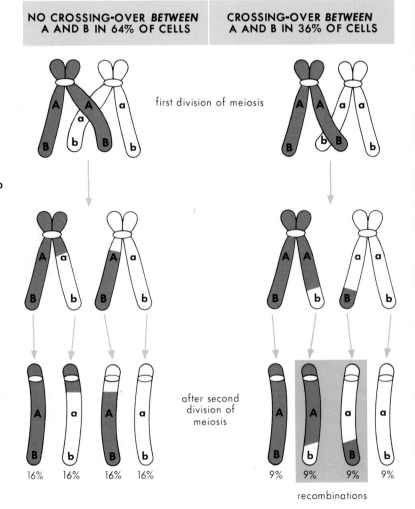

Can you explain why this is so?

In our example, **A** would be the allele for gray body and **a** the allele for black body. **B** would be the allele for normal wings and **b** the allele for vestigial wings. The chance that crossing-over will occur between two given loci depends on the distance between them. It is unlikely that crossing-over will occur between genes at two loci that are very close together. We say the genes at these loci are closely linked. In general, then, the greater the observed number of recombinants, the farther apart we infer the loci are on the chromosome. Using the proportions of recombinations between different pairs of linked loci, a continuous linkage map can be constructed (figure 17-20).

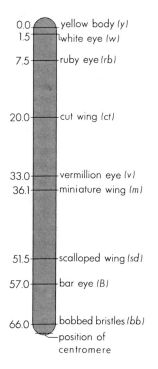

17 – 20 Gene loci on one of the chromosomes of *Drosophila*. The numbers at the left are determined by the percentage of recombinations observed in experimental breeding. They indicate, for example, that recombinations between **ct** and **v** are about 13 percent; between **v** and **m**, 3 percent; and between **ct** and **m**, 16 percent—the sum of 13 percent and 3 percent.

MULTIPLE ALLELES

With codominance and just two kinds of alleles, one gene locus can yield three phenotypes. Cases of more than three phenotypes can result from multiple alleles. Normally, an *individual* has only two of these alleles for any trait—one gene from its male parent, the other from its female parent.

A good example of multiple alleles is the inheritance of certain blood characteristics in humans. In some cases, blood from one person can be transfused safely to another person. In other cases, it cannot. A system was worked out for distinguishing the kinds of human blood that were important in transfusions. These were designated Type A, Type B, Type AB, and Type O. Together they constitute the "ABO" system.

The "ABO" types are determined by three alleles available for one locus: I^A, I^B, i. Allele I^A causes the formation of blood factor A. Allele I^B causes the formation of factor B. Allele i does not cause either factor to form. The table shows the genotypes that are responsible for the various phenotypes:

Genotype	Blood Type (Phenotype)
$I^A I^A$ or $I^A i$	A
$I^B I^B$ or $I^B i$	B
$I^A I^B$	AB
ii	O

What does this chart show about the dominance relationships of these alleles?

X 1/10

CC or Cc^{ch} or Cc^h or Cc   c^{ch}c^{ch} or c^{ch}c^h or c^{ch}c   c^{h}c^h or c^{h}c   cc

17 – 21 Four coat-color phenotypes in domestic rabbits. From left to right: normal("wild type"), chinchilla, Himalayan, white. Genotypes are shown beneath each animal. Explain the dominance relationships of the genes.

CONTINUOUS VARIABILITY

A continuous variable in genetics shows differences among all individuals. It does not have only two, or only a few, phenotypes. Suppose for example, that you plotted on a graph the heights of all the tenth graders in your school. Between the shortest and tallest person there would be many other people that cover the whole range of height. This kind of trait is different from one such as sickle-cell hemoglobin, which is either present or absent. That kind of trait is called discontinuous or discrete. Such traits are generally controlled by a single pair of genes.

Even multiple alleles cannot account for many characteristics that vary continuously. Continuous variability is explained by polygenic inheritance. This is the interaction of multiple genes with a large number of possible environmental variables. (Note that the concept of multiple genes is not the same as that of multiple alleles.) Geneticists believe that most human traits are determined by polygenic inheritance. The importance of environment in such inheritance is obvious. There are many debates about which is more important in the development of some human traits—genes or environment. Generally such arguments are fruitless, since an individual needs both to develop any characteristic fully.

Some disorders such as cleft lip and spina bifida are polygenic. They are caused by a number of genes interacting with certain environmental factors in the mother's uterus during pregnancy. The probability of transmission of polygenic traits cannot be predicted as precisely as for single gene traits, such as sickle-cell hemoglobin.

polygenic [pol ih JEN ik]: affected by many genes that are not alleles at a single locus

What evidence can you cite to illustrate that the environment influences how heredity is expressed in humans?

cleft lip: a genetic disorder in which the upper lip is divided, usually at the middle

spina bifida [spy nuh BIF uh-duh]: a genetic disorder in which the vertebrae are divided, exposing the spinal cord

NONDISJUNCTION

Meiosis is a remarkably exact process. But it is not perfect. Rarely, chromosomes of a pair do not separate during meiotic divisions. Instead both go to one pole of the spindle—an event called ***nondisjunction.*** When this occurs, there is no chromosome of that pair at the other pole. Humans normally have 23 pairs of chromosomes. When nondisjunction occurs, one of the gametes has 24 chromosomes and the other has only 22. If these gametes are fertilized, abnormal zygotes are formed. They would have either 45 or 47 chromosomes. This does happen — though not commonly.

Occasionally the abnormal zygote survives and grows. In one case, the individual has a total of 47 chromosomes in each cell. This is accompanied by a phenotype abnormality called Down sydrome. Such an individual has a characteristic facial appearance and a mental deficiency.

In addition to Down syndrome, other kinds of nondisjunction effects are known in humans. Nondisjunction occurs in other organisms too. In fact, it was actually first described in fruit flies.

J. L. H. Down: 1828–1896. British physician

syndrome [SIN drome; Greek: *syn*, with, + *dramein*, to run]: a group of symptoms that occur together

How does nondisjunction provide evidence supporting the chromosome theory?

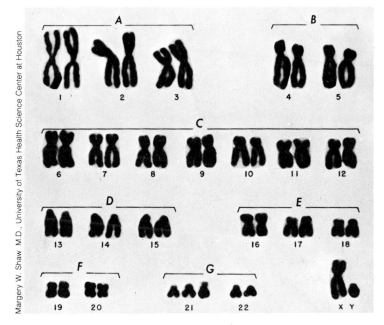

17—22 Chromosomes in Down syndrome. Was this a female or a male? Compare with figure 17–11.

17—23 A child showing characteristic facial features of Down syndrome.

mutations [myew TAY shunz;
Latin: *mutare*, to change]

MUTATIONS

The basic fact of heredity is that offspring resemble their ancestors. But the fossil evidence outlined in Chapter 10 clearly shows that there have been enormous changes in organisms through geological time. Therefore, new heritable traits must have appeared in the past. These newly appearing traits are called **mutations.** The white-eyed male that Morgan found among his flies was almost certainly the result of a mutation.

According to the chromosome theory of heredity, mutations should result from changes in chromosomes. We might, then, look for visible changes in the chromosomes and associate them with the appearance of a new trait. Mutations of this sort are called chromosomal mutations.

Often, however, mutations occur without any visible change in the chromosomes. These are due to chemical changes in genes. Such mutations are called gene mutations. For example, a gene that normally controls the formation of red pigment in a flower might change. The result could be purple pigment or no pigment at all.

Genes are quite stable. Each gene usually replicates exactly for hundreds of cell generations. A human gamete, for instance, carries thousands of different genes. And an individual may produce millions of gametes. Thus even if there is a low mutation rate overall, there may be several mutations carried in each gamete. Most of these, however, will have little effect, since mutations are usually to recessive alleles. It has been calculated that there may be one new mutation per ten gametes. The rate is known to vary somewhat at different loci.

Mutation rates can be increased by changes in certain environmental factors. Within the range of temperature that a given organism can tolerate, the higher the temperature, the greater is the mutation rate. Mutation rates also can be increased by the action of certain chemicals. And they can be greatly increased by high-energy radiations, such as X rays and the beta and gamma rays of nuclear radiation.

CHECK YOURSELF

W.   What are the stages of development in *Drosophila?*
X.   If neither allele of a pair dominates the other, how many phenotypes can occur?
Y.   In the F_2 generation of a dihybrid cross, the ratio of phenotypes often is neither 9:3:3:1 nor 3:1. Why?
Z.   On what does the chance of crossing-over depend?

AA. Use human blood types to explain how multiple alleles can lead to more than three phenotypes.
BB. How can the inheritance of traits that show great variability in phenotypes be explained?
CC. If nondisjunction occurred during meiosis, what result is visible in the set of chromosomes of a zygote?
DD. What is Down syndrome?
EE. What is a mutation?
FF. Distinguish between chromosomal and gene mutations.
GG. What factors in the environment affect the rate of mutation?

THE GENETIC CODE

WHAT A GENE DOES

Experiments led to the theory that heredity is controlled by genes in the nucleus of a cell. Further experiments showed that genes must be located in chromosomes. How does a gene cause a pea plant to develop round rather than wrinkled seeds? How do genes work?

Experiments with a mold, *Neurospora crassa*, provided the first clear evidence of how genes act. This mold can be grown easily in a test tube. It is grown on a medium of a dilute solution of minerals, some table sugar, and a single vitamin. Hyphae of the mold grow beneath the surface of the medium. Then tufts of pink or orange spore-bearing threads grow upward through the surface.

A mature mold plant is made up of a wide range of pro-

Neurospora crassa [nyoo ROS-puh ruh KRAS uh]

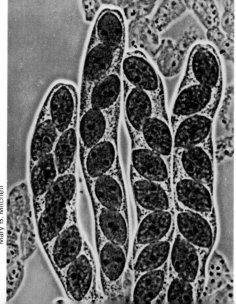

Mary B. Mitchell

17–24 *Neurospora crassa*, a sac fungus. Eight spores in each sac can easily be seen. × 750

teins, carbohydrates, lipids, vitamins, nucleic acids, and pigments. In a test tube, the mold must produce all these complex chemical compounds from the simple raw materials in the medium. These materials must be put together in just a certain way that will make the new mold plant resemble its parents.

George W. Beadle: 1903—. American geneticist

Edward L. Tatum: 1909–1975. American biochemist

In the early 1940's G. W. Beadle and E. L. Tatum treated spores of *Neurospora* with X rays. They placed them on the simple medium that had supported the parents' growth. Many of the treated spores could not grow. Apparently, the X rays had caused some kind of mutation. The two investigators formed a hypothesis. They said that a mutant spore failed to grow because it was unable to make some substance for itself from the materials in the medium. They devised a complete medium, which contained many vitamins and all the amino acids known to be required for protein synthesis. When more spores treated by X ray were placed on this complete medium, almost all grew. These results supported the hypothesis.

17–25 Procedure used by Beadle and Tatum. In this case the *Neurospora* spore has lost the ability to synthesize Substance C.

Which substance in the complete medium could not be made by the mutant? Figure 17–25 shows the procedure Beadle and Tatum used to investigate this question. They found that

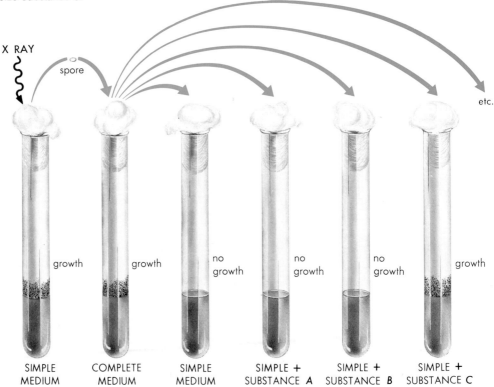

X RAY

spore

etc.

growth — SIMPLE MEDIUM

growth — COMPLETE MEDIUM

no growth — SIMPLE MEDIUM

no growth — SIMPLE + SUBSTANCE **A**

no growth — SIMPLE + SUBSTANCE **B**

growth — SIMPLE + SUBSTANCE **C**

the production of almost every substance normally synthesized by *Neurospora* can be blocked by mutations caused by X rays.

How can the synthesis of a substance be blocked? You have seen that syntheses are controlled by enzymes. Beadle and Tatum suggested that each mutant failed to synthesize a growth substance because it lacked a specific enzyme. If the mutant was unable to make the enzyme, it was unable to make the substance necessary for growth. But, if the missing substance was added to the growth medium, the mutants were able to grow.

Each missing growth substance was linked to a missing enzyme. Each missing enzyme was linked to a single gene mutation. If a gene mutates, the offspring possessing this mutation might have a different, and unfavorable, characteristic from their parents.

GENES AND DNA

Enzymes are proteins. Genes somehow direct the construction of enzymes. Geneticists had much evidence to show that genes are located in chromosomes. They also knew that chromosomes contain much DNA (deoxyribonucleic acid). In fact, it is restricted largely to chromosomes. But chromosomes also contain protein, so geneticists were not sure whether the DNA or the chromosomal protein directs enzyme production.

Experiments were conducted to determine whether DNA or protein is the genetic substance. One was carried out with a pneumonia bacterium. Dead cells of one type of this organism (called X cells) can transform living cells of a second type, Y, into X. Because dead cells can do this, it is possible to take them apart and find out which part causes the transformation. Proteins were separated from dead bacterial cells. The proteins were unable to transform living cells. The remaining DNA could, however. DNA was, therefore, the active substance that transformed Y cells into X cells.

More evidence was obtained from bacteriophages. They have a core of DNA surrounded by a protein coat. Experiments in which the protein was labeled with radioactive sulfur showed that the coats do not penetrate bacterial walls. Labeling the DNA with radioactive phosphorus showed that DNA does penetrate the bacterial walls. Once inside a bacterial cell, this DNA takes over the cell's physiological machinery. New bacteriophage particles are made. They are just like the original ones—complete with new protein coats. So DNA is capable of performing the function of genes. DNA could carry characteristics (in this case, viral characteristics) from one generation to the next.

Recall that bacteriophages are viruses that attack bacteria.

Why was sulfur labeled in protein and phosphorus in DNA?

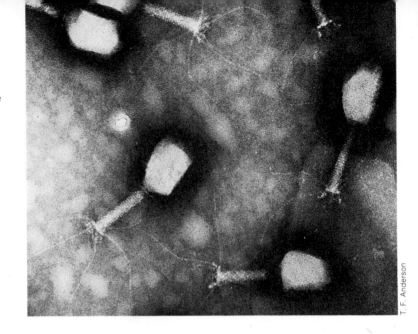

17–26 Bacteriophages. The large "head" is filled with DNA. Each tail has prongs by which the particle attaches itself to the bacterium.   × 120,000

James D. Watson: 1928—. American biochemist

F. H. C. Crick: 1916—. English biophysicist

M. H. F. Wilkins: 1916—. English biophysicist

Rosalind Franklin: 1916–1958. English biophysicist

thymine [THY meen]; guanine [GWAH neen]; adenine [AD un een]; cytosine [SYT uh-seen].

17–27 Diagram of a small part of a DNA molecule.

Structure of DNA. Many biologists were reluctant to give up the idea that genes were proteins, since proteins are much more complex than DNA. Most doubts were removed in 1953 by J. D. Watson and F. H. C. Crick. They were using data collected by M. H. F. Wilkins and Rosalind Franklin. Watson and Crick proposed a structure for DNA that helped geneticists to imagine how it could act as a gene. They described a DNA molecule as a long, twisted, double-stranded structure (like a twisted ladder). The two strands are made of four kinds of nucleotides. The four nucleotides each have a different nitrogenous base—thymine, guanine, adenine, or cytosine. The sugar-phosphate parts of the nucleotides are joined to each other to form the sides of the "ladder." A nitrogenous base from one strand pairs with another base from the other strand. In this way, they form the "rungs" of the ladder (figure 17–27).

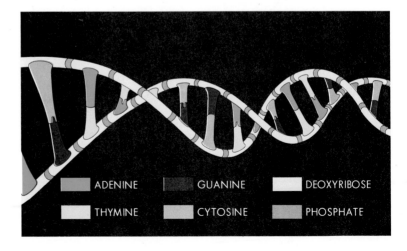

| ADENINE | GUANINE | DEOXYRIBOSE |
| THYMINE | CYTOSINE | PHOSPHATE |

Furthermore, because of the structure of the bases, only thymine can pair with adenine. Only cytosine can pair with guanine. These base pairs can occur all along the length of a DNA molecule. But the chemical bonds that hold the base pairs together are weak. If they are broken, two separate DNA strands result. Then a duplicate of the missing strand can be made on each strand. Two identical strands of DNA result, which are exactly like the original DNA molecule (figure 17–28).

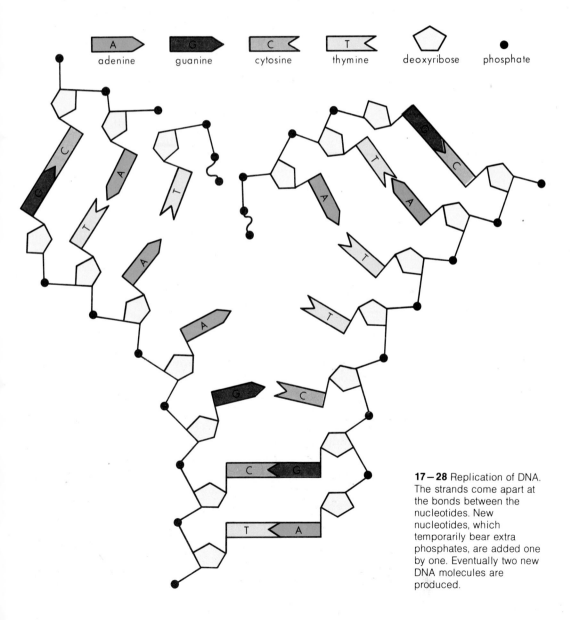

17–28 Replication of DNA. The strands come apart at the bonds between the nucleotides. New nucleotides, which temporarily bear extra phosphates, are added one by one. Eventually two new DNA molecules are produced.

Function of DNA. How could DNA molecules function as genes? We know that genes direct the building of proteins. We also know that proteins are made up of amino acids. Could each base in a DNA strand correspond to an amino acid? But there are 20 different amino acids—and only four kinds of bases. Could two bases together correspond to an amino acid? Not quite, because there can be only 16 combinations of four different bases. So geneticists hypothesized that a combination of three adjacent bases on a DNA strand correspond to each amino acid. Such triplet bases can be thought of as a kind of code for amino acids.

What are the 16 combinations?

What principle would prevent them from hypothesizing more than three?

Chromosomes with their DNA are in a cell's nucleus. But many experiments showed that ribosomes are the sites of protein synthesis. Ribosomes are outside the nucleus (figures 11–5 and 11–6). How can genes direct protein synthesis outside the nucleus from their position inside it?

RNA is the second kind of nucleic acid. It is found both outside and inside nuclei. It is very much like DNA except that its sugar is ribose instead of deoxyribose. Also, the base, uracil, is substituted in RNA for the thymine found in DNA. In most organisms, RNA is synthesized by copying a DNA strand. Then it separates from the DNA strand and passes through the nuclear membrane.

uracil [YOOR uh sil]

Three distinct kinds of RNA are found in cells. One kind, together with proteins, makes up ribosomes. It is called ribosomal RNA (rRNA). A second, long-stranded kind is called messenger RNA (mRNA). The mRNA carries instructions for protein synthesis from DNA in the nucleus to the ribosomes. The instructions are in the form of the triplet bases along the length of mRNA. The third type of RNA is short and is called transfer RNA (tRNA). It transfers amino acids to the ribosomes, where the amino acids are added to a growing protein chain. Each tRNA molecule first picks up a specific amino acid. The tRNA molecules then carry the amino acids to the ribosomes. Here the tRNA molecules "read" the triplet codes on the mRNA. The order of the codes on the mRNA specifies the order for assembling amino acids to make a particular protein.

As this understanding of protein synthesis was being worked out, other investigators were trying to find out which base triplet codes for which amino acid. By the end of the 1960's, biochemists had discovered the amino acids that can be specified by most of the possible nucleotide triplets.

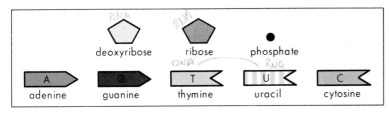

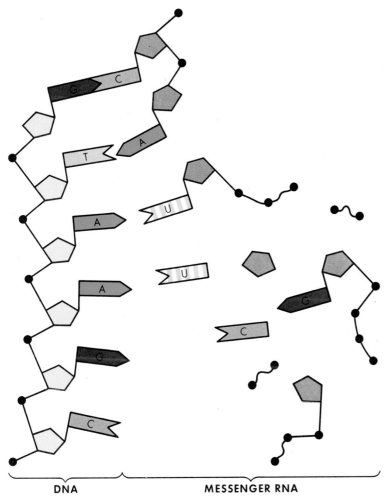

17—29 Formation of part of a strand of mRNA on one strand of a DNA molecule.

DNA   MESSENGER RNA

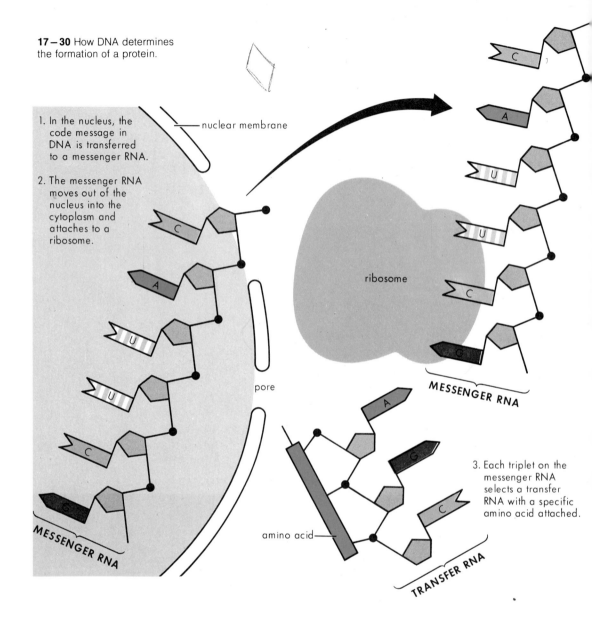

17—30 How DNA determines the formation of a protein.

1. In the nucleus, the code message in DNA is transferred to a messenger RNA.

2. The messenger RNA moves out of the nucleus into the cytoplasm and attaches to a ribosome.

nuclear membrane

ribosome

MESSENGER RNA

pore

3. Each triplet on the messenger RNA selects a transfer RNA with a specific amino acid attached.

amino acid

MESSENGER RNA

TRANSFER RNA

CHECK YOURSELF

HH. Describe the work of Beadle and Tatum.

II. Why did this research turn the interest of geneticists to proteins?

JJ. How did research on pneumonia bacteria provide evidence that DNA rather than protein is the genetic substance?

4. The ribosome moves along the messenger RNA
   as it "reads" the code. The amino acids are
   joined to each other in the order coded.
   A protein molecule is formed.

5. After delivering its amino acid,
   transfer RNA can pick up another
   amino acid molecule.

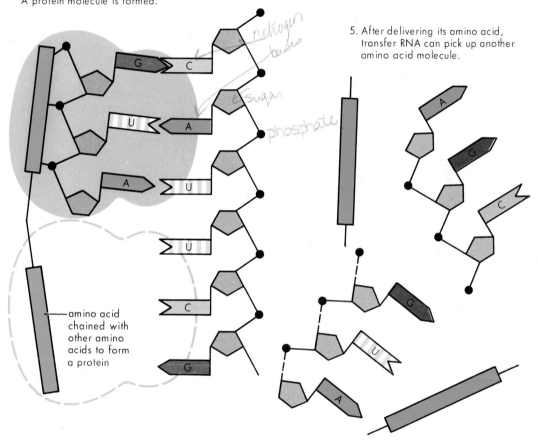

nitrogen bases

sugar

phosphate

amino acid
chained with
other amino
acids to form
a protein

KK. How did research with bacteriophages confirm
    this finding?
LL. Describe a DNA molecule.
MM. How is a strand of DNA accurately replicated?
NN. Why are *three* adjacent bases in a DNA molecule
    needed to specify one amino acid in a protein
    molecule?
OO. How does messenger RNA differ from transfer
    RNA in function?

Investigation 17.4   GENE MUTATION

INTRODUCTION

We know that the structure of DNA molecules is related to the structure of protein molecules. Now it is possible for you to understand more clearly what is meant by gene mutations. You can most easily arrive at such understanding by working out some hypothetical examples.

PROCEDURE

1. Assume that figure 17–31 represents a part of a DNA molecule. The whole molecule is much longer, and the strands of deoxyribose and phosphate groups have been omitted. The key to the bases is:

    a = adenine   c = cytosine
    t = thymine   g = guanine

17–32 An incomplete chart of codons.

RNA CODON	AMINO ACID
aag	lysine
auc	isoleucine
aug	methionine
cau	histidine
cga	arginine
gaa	glutamic acid
gga	glycine
guc	valine
uac	tyrosine
uca	serine
uga	none
uua	leucine

17–31

—t—t—a—c—a—t—c—g—a—a—a—g—g—t—c—a—t—g—a—t—c—
—a—a—t—g—t—a—g—c—t—t—t—c—c—a—g—t—a—c—t—a—g—

2. Assume that the lower strand is the one from which a messenger RNA strand will be copied. (1) Using paper and pencil, write the sequence of bases in an mRNA strand that would be formed on the DNA strand. (Remember that in RNA, uracil — symbolized by u — replaces thymine.)

3. Reading from left to right, divide your sequence of mRNA bases into code triplets (codons — pronunciation, KOH donz). (2) Then, using figure 17–32, construct the protein segment — the chain of amino acids — that is specified by your sequence of mRNA codons.

    The dictionary of RNA codons provided here does not include all the amino acids. Even if it did, you would find that there are many more possible codons than there are

amino acids. (There is more than one codon for some of the amino acids.)

4. Assume that by X-radiation a geneticist destroys and thus removes the left-most base pair of the DNA molecule shown in figure 17–31. (3) To discover the effect of this kind of mutation, construct the new mRNA chain indicated by the remaining letters, starting at the new base on the left.

5. (4) Again using the chart, construct the chain of amino acids specified by the complete codons of the new mRNA. (5) What has happened to the codon on the right end? The codon that does not appear in the chart specifies arginine. Thus a single amino acid can be specified by more than one codon. (6) Does the deletion in the DNA molecule change the resulting

protein? If so, in what way? One codon (uga) in the altered mRNA does not specify an amino acid. Codons of this sort specify the ends of protein molecules.

6. Assume that X-radiation deleted the 1st 3 base pairs on the left instead of just the 1st one. (7) Would this kind of deletion have more or less effect on an amino acid sequence than deletion of a single base pair? Explain.

7. Occasionally, errors in DNA replication occur—apparently without environmental causes. For example, at rare intervals adenine pairs with cytosine instead of thymine. The consequence of this error is as follows:

After 2 replications, one of the 4 DNA molecules has the base pair
$$\begin{matrix} \text{-g-} \\ : \\ \text{-c-} \end{matrix}$$
, while the others have the original
$$\begin{matrix} \text{-a-} \\ : \\ \text{-t-} \end{matrix}$$
. An error of this sort, if it had occurred in the DNA molecule diagramed at the beginning of this investigation, would substitute c for t at some point in the DNA strand.

8. Assume such a substitution occurs at the 3rd base pair from the right. (8) Show how this changes the mRNA. (9) Show how it changes the amino acid chain.

9. One of the changes known to occur in this way involves the substitution of glycine for glutamic acid at one site within the protein molecule. (10) What error in the normal DNA molecule would account for this mutational change?

DISCUSSION

Studies of amino acid sequences in hemoglobins show that there is only one difference between nonsickling **Hb^A** and sickle-cell **Hb^S** hemoglobins. This is the substitution of one amino acid (valine) for another (glutamic acid). This occurs in a polypeptide chain 146 amino acids long! (11) According to the codon chart in figure 17–32, how many changes in base pairs would be necessary to specify this substitution in amino acids?

Because there are 4 codons for valine (guu, guc, gua, gug) and 2 for glutamic acid (gaa, gag), the change can be made by a mutation in only one base pair. (12) What are the possibilities for such a change? (13) Which possibility is more likely: that the mutation involves changes at two base pairs simultaneously or a change at just one pair? From such a small difference in genotype arise the great differences in phenotype between persons who have and those who do not have sickle-cell anemia!

17–33

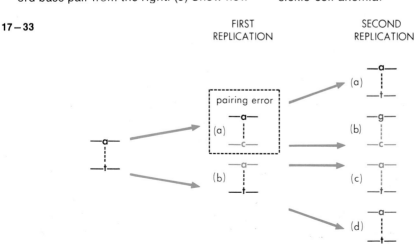

FIRST REPLICATION

SECOND REPLICATION

GENES AND SICKLE CELLS

Now we can return to sickle-cell, the human trait with which we began this discussion of genetics. In some way, red blood cells that sickle differ from nonsickling red blood cells. About one-third of each red blood cell is hemoglobin, and hemoglobin is protein. Therefore, you might hypothesize that the difference in the red cells is a result of a difference in their proteins.

Linus Pauling: 1901—. American chemist

In 1949, Linus Pauling and colleagues found that all the hemoglobin in a person suffering from sickle-cell anemia *is* different from that of a person with nonsickling cells. Pauling also tested hemoglobin from persons with the sickle-cell trait. Persons with the sickle-cell trait were found to have both non-sickling *and* sickle-cell hemoglobin.

The kind of hemoglobin in red blood cells depends on the kind of genes a person has. If someone has only nonsickling hemoglobin, that person must have *only* genes that direct the formation of that protein. Therefore, the person must be homozygous for it. We can write this genotype Hb^AHb^A. The hemoglobin of a person who has sickle-cell anemia must all be of that type. This person is also homozygous, with a genotype Hb^SHb^S. People with the sickle-cell *trait* have both kinds of hemoglobin. Therefore, they have one gene for nonsickling and one for sickle-cell hemoglobin. They are heterozygous, genotype Hb^AHb^S.

GENETICS TODAY AND TOMORROW

It is now clear that long DNA molecules (in chromosomes) are subdivided into regions (genes) that correspond to individual proteins. DNA can replicate in an exact way and can carry "information." Put very simply, this means that there is a *genetic* difference between a pine tree and a worm, or between you and your neighbor. It is the sum of the differences in the DNA molecules they (or you) contain that makes each individual unique.

Current knowledge is being applied to research on genetic disorders. Sickle-cell anemia is just one of these. Thalassemia is a genetic disorder that resembles sickle-cell anemia. Tay-Sachs, which is marked by an early degeneration of the nervous system, results from a genetically determined abnormal protein, an enzyme. It occurs most frequently among Jewish people of eastern European descent. It results in blindness, severe mental retardation, and death at about age three. Down syndrome represents a group of chromosomal abnormalities. Cystic fibrosis, a respiratory disorder, and albinism are genetic disorders. Cystic fibrosis affects mainly Caucasians. PKU is an enzyme deficiency that leads to severe mental retardation. A fairly simple and inexpensive test was discovered in 1961 that could determine if infants a few days old had PKU. Although the screening process shows some false positives (infants that appear to have PKU but do not), many PKU infants have been detected, treated, and can live normal lives if kept on a special diet. In some cases, living cells from within the amniotic sac of an unborn fetus are removed by a process called amniocentesis. Biochemical and chromosomal tests can reveal whether the fetus has a serious genetic disorder. Such disorders often cause physically and mentally handicapped children. With some disorders, the children do not live very long. If such a disorder is present, the parents — after consultation with their doctor — must decide if the pregnancy is to be maintained or terminated by an induced abortion.

Biochemists now can break long strands of DNA into shorter segments. These segments can be rearranged and connected to one another in whatever combination the biochemist wants. This technique is called gene-splicing. Such reconstructed molecules can be introduced into cells of the bacterium *Escherichia coli*. The *E. coli* then makes proteins for which the short DNA segments code. Human insulin has been produced by *E. coli* with gene-splicing techniques. Using human insulin instead of cattle or pig insulin will eliminate many side effects suffered by persons with diabetes. Geneticists also hope to use these artificially constructed gene combinations to cure some human genetic disorders. If normal genes could be inserted into a patient's body cells, they might produce enzymes that the patient needs. These enzymes would then function properly in cellular metabolism. These same techniques also might solve some problems in plant and animal breeding.

CHECK YOURSELF

PP. How do the amino acid sequences of nonsickling and sickle-cell hemoglobin differ?

QQ. How do the genotypes of people with sickle-cell anemia differ from those with the sickle-cell trait in regard to their hemoglobin?

RR. Name three genetic disorders and tell how they affect people.

SS. How can genetic characteristics of an unborn fetus be determined?

TT. What are some ways in which genetic knowledge may contribute to improving conditions for humans in the future?

Careers in Biology: A Genetic Counselor

Marie-Louise Lubs is a geneticist, a researcher, and a genetic counselor. She was born and raised in Sweden and went to college there. Though Marie-Louise majored in chemistry at the university, her real interest was genetics. She earned her second degree in this field and became an instructor of genetics. At the same time, she did research on various projects, including the inheritance of heart diseases and the relationship of these diseases to smoking.

Marie-Louise presented the results of some of her research on the inheritance of allergies at an international meeting in Chicago. There she met another geneticist whom she later married. Marie-Louise and her husband decided to stay in the United States. One of her first projects here was a study of the occurrence of birth defects and cancer (such as leukemia) in the children of parents who had been exposed to radiation.

Dr. Lubs has continued her study of inheritable disorders. She was surprised to discover how few parents in this country know that many disorders, such as hemophilia and many forms of muscular dystrophy, are inherited.

As a genetic counselor, Marie-Louise explains to potential parents the risks involved with genetic disorders. She begins working with a couple who plan to have a child by tracing the history of a genetic disorder in the families of the man and the woman. She then can determine the chances of that couple's

A. Dr. Marie-Louise Lubs confers with a technician in her genetics laboratory.

B. When a genetic disorder such as Tay-Sachs is known to have occurred in a family, young couples must face the possibility that their children could be affected. A large part of Dr. Lubs' job is counseling such couples about their chances of having a child with a genetic disorder.

C. An important step in genetics research is tracing the occurrence of a disorder throughout a family's history. Here, Dr. Lubs examines the "pedigree" of an inherited disorder as it occurred in one family.

John Thornton

having a child affected by the disorder. She gives them information to help them decide whether or not to have children. She also tries to diagnose genetic disorders in newborn babies, so they can receive immediate care.

Marie-Louise is pleased that so many families have benefited from her counseling. She plans to continue her research and expand her studies to include other disorders that may have a genetic basis. Her research into the history of families with genetic disorders may help find new means of diagnosis and treatment.

D. Babies affected by a genetic disorder may require special care. The newborn baby Marie-Louise is examining is in an intensive-care incubator.

John Thornton

PROBLEMS

1. The polled (hornless) trait in cattle is dominant. The horned trait is recessive. A certain polled bull is mated to three cows. Cow A, which is horned, gives birth to a polled calf. Cow B, also horned, produces a horned calf. Cow C, which is polled, produces a horned calf. What are the genotypes of the four parents?

2. In shorthorn cattle, when a red bull (**RR**) is crossed with a white cow (**rr**), the offspring are roan (intermingled red and white hairs). How could a rancher establish a herd of roan cattle?

3. In sheep, white coat is dominant. Black is recessive. Occasionally, a black sheep appears in a flock. Black wool is worthless. How could a farmer eliminate the genes for black coat from the flock?

4. In summer squash, white fruit color is dominant. Yellow is recessive. A squash plant that is homozygous for white is crossed with a homozygous yellow one. Predict the appearance of the F_1 generation. Of the F_2. Of the offspring of a cross between an F_1 individual and a homozygous white individual.

5. The storage roots of radishes may be long, round, or oval. In a series of experiments, crosses between long and oval produced 159 long and 156 oval. Crosses between round and oval produced 199 round and 203 oval. Crosses between long and round produced 576 oval. Crosses between oval and oval produced 121 long, 243 oval, and 119 round. Show how root shape is inherited in radishes.

6. In tomatoes, red fruit color is dominant to yellow. Round-shaped fruit is dominant to pear-shaped fruit. Tall vine is dominant to dwarf vine. If you cross a pure-breeding tall plant bearing red, round fruit with a pure-breeding dwarf plant bearing yellow, pear-shaped fruit, predict the appearance of the F_1 generation. Assuming that the gene loci controlling the three traits are in three different pairs of chromosomes, what are the possible genotypes in the F_2 generation? What are the expected ratios of the phenotypes?

7. What are the possible blood types of children in the following families?
   a. Type A mother, Type A father
   b. Type A mother, Type O father
   c. Type B mother, Type AB father
   d. Type AB mother, Type AB father
   e. Type A mother, Type B father

8. Before Mendel, the chief theory of heredity was "blood-line inheritance." According to this theory, the parents' traits are blended in the offspring, just as two liquids blend when mixed together. Mendel's theory rested on the idea that traits are transmitted by particles (genes) and do not blend. Give evidence in support of the older theory. Then show how the results of Mendel's experiments fail to fit that theory.

9. How would you go about improving the characteristics of the seedless orange?

10. At the present time, there is no such thing as an all-blue tulip. The first one found will be quite valuable. How might a tulip breeder increase the chances of finding a blue tulip?

11. The Himalayan coat pattern in domestic rabbits is influenced by environment. Find out what factor is involved and as much as you can about how it works. Then write a comparison between this case and your results from Investigation 17.2.

12. How does proof in science differ from proof in mathematics?

13. A die (singular of "dice") has six sides. What is the probability that an even number will come up on one throw of a die?

14. If base pairs in DNA molecules can consist only of adenine-thymine or of

cytosine-guanine, what must be the ratio of the amount of adenine to thymine? Of the amount of cytosine to guanine? Of adenine to cytosine?

15. The pedigree in figure 17–34 shows the descendants of Mohan, a white tiger captured in India. Assuming that whiteness in tigers is a single-locus trait, is it recessive or dominant? What evidence supports your answer?

17–34

GENEALOGY OF CAPTIVE WHITE TIGERS

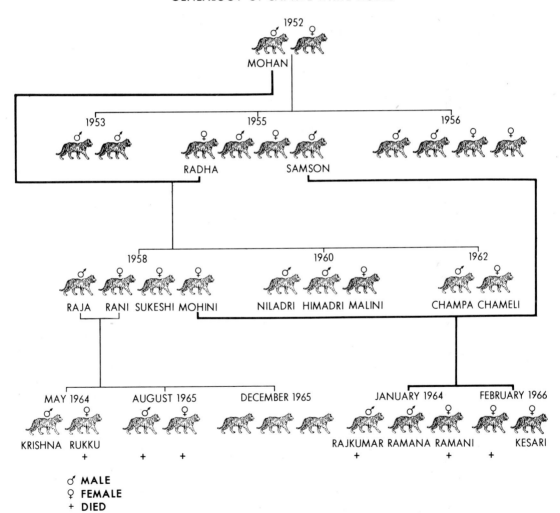

MOHAN

RADHA   SAMSON

RAJA RANI SUKESHI MOHINI   NILADRI HIMADRI MALINI   CHAMPA CHAMELI

MAY 1964   AUGUST 1965   DECEMBER 1965   JANUARY 1964   FEBRUARY 1966

KRISHNA RUKKU   RAJKUMAR RAMANA RAMANI   KESARI

♂ MALE
♀ FEMALE
+ DIED

National Zoological Park Washington, D.C. April 1, 1966

Smithsonian Institution

SUGGESTED READINGS

Cohen, S. N. and J. A. Shapiro. 1980. Transposable Genetic Elements. *Scientific American*, February. Rings of genes can be shifted among plasmids, viruses, and chromosomes of living cells.

Crow, J. F. 1979. Genes That Violate Mendel's Rules. *Scientific American*, February. Some genes can favor their own transmission to fertilized gametes, violating the laws of chance.

McKusick, V. A. 1971. The Mapping of Human Chromosones. *Scientific American*, April.

Reisfeld, R. A. and B. D. Kahan. 1972. Markers of Biological Individuality. *Scientific American*, June.

Sayre, A. 1978. *Rosalind Franklin and DNA.* W. W. Norton, New York. True story of a scientist's efforts in discovering the nature of DNA.

Scientific American. 1978. *Recombinant DNA: Readings from Scientific American.* W. H. Freeman, San Francisco. Contains 13 *Scientific American* reprints on gene-splicing.

Sutton, H. E. 1980. *An Introduction to Human Genetics.* 3rd ed. W. B. Saunders, Philadelphia. Surveys the entire field of human genetics, emphasizing how human genetic conditions are analyzed.

Chapter 18

Evolution

YOUR GUIDEPOSTS

In this chapter you will have an opportunity to explore these questions in biology:

- What is the theory of evolution?
- Who was Charles Darwin, and what role did he play in the advancement of science?
- What are the sources of change in hereditary characteristics?
- How are new species formed?
- How is an organism's fitness related to where it lives?

CHARLES DARWIN AND EVOLUTION

The Galápagos Islands are a bleak volcanic archipelago. They straddle the equator in the Pacific Ocean 1,000 kilometers west of Ecuador. Their shores are fringed by broken black lava rocks. Marine lizards crowd the shores and huge tree cacti guard the arid hills of each island.

Galápagos [guh LOP uh gus; Spanish: tortoise]

archipelago [ar kuh PEL uh goh; Greek: *archos*, chief, + *pelagos*, sea]: a group of islands

18−1 Cactus forest on Santa Fé Island, Galápagos.

Robert I. Bowman

X 1/40

18–2 Galápagos tortoise.

X 1/4

18–3 Galápagos mockingbird.

18–4 (*continued on opposite page*) The Galápagos finches—or, today, "Darwin's finches." Which part of the body varies most?

Late in 1835 a British exploring vessel, HMS *Beagle*, landed at the Galápagos. Among the first ashore was the ship's naturalist, Charles Darwin. This young Englishman had already spent nearly four years in scientific exploration of South American lands and waters. Darwin was fascinated by the harsh landscape of the islands. For three weeks he roamed them, observing and collecting animals and plants. Many things aroused his curiosity, including the giant tortoises. Darwin rode one of these at the alarming speed of "360 yards an hour." He also became curious about the mockingbirds. They seemed to be different on each island. But nothing made a more lasting impression than a group of small, dull-colored finches.

In general these birds reminded Darwin of finches he had seen in Ecuador. But what diversity there was among these in the Galápagos! Finches ordinarily are seed-eaters. And some of the Galápagos finches did eat seeds. But others fed on the fleshy parts of cacti. There was even one kind that held a cactus spine in its beak as a tool to extract insects from under the bark of tree cacti. This was especially interesting, since Darwin noticed that there were no woodpeckers on the islands. Every habitat seemed to contain finches. There were big and little finches. Some finches lived on the ground and some lived in trees. There were seed-eaters, fruit-eaters, insect-eaters, and even a "woodpecker" finch!

In his notebook Darwin jotted down observations. In his mind he recorded vivid pictures of the island scenes. There in the Galápagos he began to form new ideas. But not for 23 years would the world hear of these ideas—and never would it be the same again!

X 1/2

X 1/2

18−4 (*continued*) One of the finches (*above right in drawing and below in photo*) uses sharp cactus spines to dig insects out of tree bark.

Roger Perry

THE RELUCTANT SCIENTIST

Charles Darwin was enthusiastic about things he enjoyed. He liked to read, enjoyed travel, and collected everything he could get his hands on. But he did not set out to be a scientist. His attempt to follow in his father's footsteps by studying medicine was a failure. He found both the medical lectures and the lecturers dull. Furthermore, he became sick at the two operations he attended. With the idea of becoming a minister, Darwin went to Cambridge University. At Cambridge he was befriended by several teachers.

A special friend who was a botanist arranged for Darwin to receive an exciting offer. A British naval expedition was setting out to survey the coast of South America. There was room for an unpaid naturalist, who would observe and collect plants, animals, and geological specimens. Charles' father vehemently objected to the invitation—an unpaid naturalist, indeed! Nevertheless, on December 27, 1831, at the age of 22, Darwin put to sea from Plymouth aboard the *Beagle*.

THEORIES FORMING

Five years later, having sailed entirely around the world, the *Beagle* again docked in England. There, as he prepared his official report, Darwin relived the sights and sounds of the trip. He began to see patterns among the questions hastily jotted down during the voyage.

The tremendous variety of life seemed to require some explanation. Those odd finches on the Galápagos, for example — all were so similar. Yet each had some peculiar characteristic of its own. And there were geological problems — for instance, the origin of islands in the open ocean. Could there be any connection between the biological and geological problems? Darwin took Sir Charles Lyell's book *Principles of Geology* with him on his voyage. Lyell had already gathered evidence showing that the rocks of the earth are subject to change. Darwin had checked this evidence throughout South America. If rocks, islands, and continents could change, might not time also bring about changes in living things?

Indeed, domesticated animals and plants have changed in the relatively short time that humans have been breeding them.

Sir Charles Lyell [LY ul]: 1797–1875. British geologist

18 – 5 The red jungle fowl, a bird of Southeast Asia, is thought to be the species from which the many breeds of domestic chickens have been developed. Which of the breeds shown seems to retain the greatest number of the wild bird's traits?

How have such changes occurred? Darwin began to collect examples of variation among domesticated animals and plants. He went directly to the sources of information — to farmers and animal breeders. And he did experiments of his own as well.

At the same time, Darwin dug deeper into the knowledge of geology. He checked the evidence that showed many changes in a series of fossils taken from older to younger rocks. Could the older fossils be the ancestors of the more recent forms? Darwin found much evidence that made him think so. In part, the way present-day plants and animals are distributed could be linked to the past distribution of their possible ancestors. So Darwin sifted through reports of expeditions that had charted the distribution of organisms.

The structures of organisms that are now living might hold clues to the structures of their ancestors. Then, too, learning how modern organisms develop might reveal something about how their ancestors had changed. So Darwin, though he had little training in laboratory biology, took up the study of anatomy and embryology.

As the years went by, from a hill of hypotheses a mountain of facts arose. All pointed to the conclusion that individuals within species vary. From these variations great changes in species have occurred. Still lacking, however, was a guiding principle. To produce populations adapted to their environment (as species populations are), variations must take some direction. Or, if all sorts of variations occur, then some of them must be preserved and others not. What directs change?

If Darwin had known only the peaceful English countryside, he might never have answered this question. But still fresh in his mind was the teeming life of the Brazilian rain forest. In a variety of ways, the rich plant life of the tropical forest seemed to struggle upward toward the light. After noticing this, Darwin began to detect in all kinds of habitats the struggle among individuals to obtain the necessities of life. Moreover, not long after he returned to England, Darwin read Malthus' book *An Essay on the Principle of Population.* Malthus had concluded that humans tend to produce more offspring than they can support. If this were true of all organisms, wouldn't there be a struggle for existence among them? Under such circumstances, wouldn't the offspring best fitted for survival be the ones most likely to grow up and produce offspring like themselves? So it seemed to Darwin.

Malthus. See page 46.

The breeder of domestic animals selects as parents for the next generation those individuals that have certain desired characteristics. In a like manner, Darwin thought, there is a struggle for existence in nature. This struggle might remove

18−6 Comparative embryology of some vertebrates. Zygotes are shown on the left, adults on the right, and comparable embryological stages between. (Drawings are not on the same scale.) The similarity between early stages in the development of many different animals helped convince Darwin that all forms of life shared common ancestors.

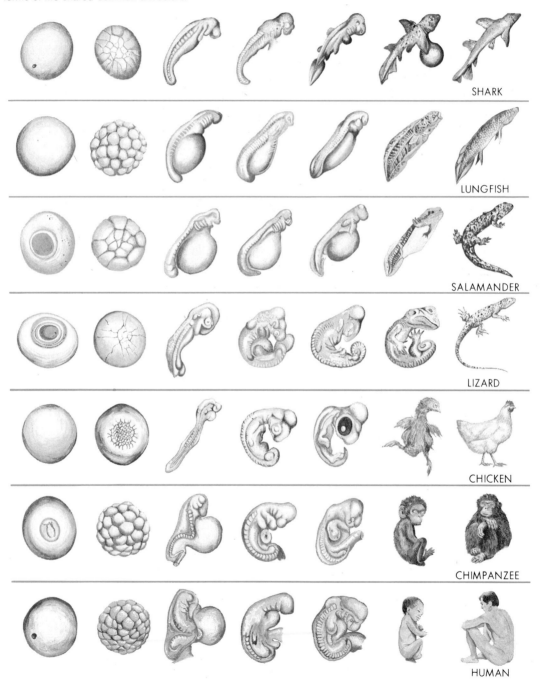

SHARK

LUNGFISH

SALAMANDER

LIZARD

CHICKEN

CHIMPANZEE

HUMAN

from each generation the individuals poorly fitted to live in their environment. Only the more fit would be left to produce the next generation. *Natural selection*, then, might explain how populations arise with characteristics that meet the demands of new environments.

18—7 Under domestication, species of the genus *Cucurbita* have developed a wide range of fruit forms. Working with domesticated *Cucurbita* nearly a century ago, a French botanist proposed the biological definition of "species."

Victor Larsen

CHECK YOURSELF

A. How did Charles Darwin become a biologist?

B. What questions did Darwin ask after his voyage on the *Beagle?*

C. What kinds of evidence did Darwin gather to develop his theories?

D. How did the ideas of Malthus influence Darwin's thinking?

THE THEORIES PUBLISHED

It is one thing to convince yourself. It is something else to convince your fellow scientists and the public. As patiently as he gathered evidence supporting his idea of natural selection, Darwin also gathered objections to it. He examined contrary evidence. He worked over flaws in reasoning. He tried alternative methods of explaining the facts. Nearly a quarter of a century passed.

Then, quite unexpectedly, he received a scientific paper from a young man who had been exploring in Malaya. The ex-

Alfred Russell Wallace:
1823–1913. British naturalist

identical [eye DENT ih kul;
Latin: *idem,* the same]: alike
in all respects

Linnaean [luh NEE un]. From its
name, what do you think may
have been the interests of this
society?

How true is that?

Lamarck. See page 358.

plorer, A. R. Wallace, asked Darwin to read it. He asked that, if Darwin found the paper "sufficiently novel and interesting," he send it on to Lyell for comment. Imagine Darwin's surprise when he discovered that Wallace had worked out ideas almost identical to his own. Darwin felt that he could not now, in fairness to Wallace, publish his own ideas. But a few of Darwin's friends persuaded him to summarize his theories and make a joint presentation with Wallace. So, on July 1, 1858, both papers were presented at a meeting of the Linnaean Society of London. Neither Wallace nor Darwin was present, however.

The next year Darwin assembled his accumulated studies in a book, *The Origin of Species by Means of Natural Selection.* In it he proposed two theories. First was the theory that the species of today are modified descendants of those that populated the earth in bygone ages. This was the **theory of organic evolution.** Actually, the idea was far from new. It had been held by some of the ancient Greeks. During the previous century it had been used to explain the fossil evidence that was beginning to accumulate. But Darwin was the first to present such an enormous body of carefully sifted evidence to support this theory. Within a decade many of the biologists of the world were convinced that this theory was as "true" as any theory can be. Darwin's second theory attempted to explain by what processes evolution could occur. This **theory of natural selection** became widely, but not universally, accepted by biologists of Darwin's time.

In 1809 Jean de Lamarck had published a theory of his own. His theory was that a change could be made in an individual by its experiences in its environment. This was known to be true. For example, among humans, athletes had long been known to develop larger muscles. Among livestock, better fed animals grew larger than less well fed ones. But Lamarck's theory went further, stipulating that such acquired characteristics could be passed on to offspring. No evidence existed for this part of the theory. Lamarck believed that an animal which browsed on twigs and leaves of trees would stretch its neck to reach food. As a result of the stretching, the next generation would be born with longer necks. In this manner, said Lamarck, giraffes could have developed from short-necked ancestors somewhat similar to antelopes.

Darwin tried to reject this idea. He believed that variation is a basic characteristic of living things and that all kinds of variations occur. He thought that ancestors of giraffes included both short-necked and long-necked individuals. Over a long period more long-necked individuals survived because they were better able to reach food. On the average, they produced a larger percentage of the offspring. Therefore, the average neck length of giraffes increased. But Darwin was still troubled. What made the variations occur in the first place? And how are variations transmitted from one generation to the next?

Darwin was never able to answer these last questions. Apparently he never ran across the work of Mendel.

THE PROCESS OF EVOLVING

All the evidence Darwin presented in support of his theory of natural selection was indirect. No one could live long enough to observe directly what most biologists believe are the processes of evolution. At least it seemed so to Darwin and to biologists for more than half a century after him. They were wrong.

AN EXAMPLE

Consider the case of *Biston betularia*, the peppered moth. It is a common inhabitant of English woodlands. To a casual observer all peppered moths look alike. But, if you examine a large number of them carefully, you find—as in all populations—many individual differences. A few have shorter antennae than most. Some have longer legs. The most noticeable difference, however, is in color. Some individuals are light and others dark.

For a long time collecting moths has been a popular hobby in Britain. Thus, many specimens collected over the last two centuries and from all parts of the country are available for study. Biologists find that the variations among moths caught in 1850 are mainly the same as those among moths collected a

Biston betularia [BIS tun bet-yew LAY ree uh]

18–8 The basis for natural selection in the peppered moth (*Biston betularia*). Dark and light forms on a tree covered with light-colored lichens (*left*). The two forms of the moth on a tree blackened by soot (*right*). Which moth in each photo is most likely to be eaten by predators?

Gordon E. Uno

hundred years later. But there is one startling difference. Among moths collected in 1950, there are more dark than light ones. In 1850 there were many more light than dark moths.

However, if biologists examine only rural southern England moths from 1950, they find a ratio of light to dark like that of 1850. It is when they examine collections from the heavily industrialized Midlands of England that they find very few light moths. Why should light moths predominate in one region and dark moths elsewhere? And why should dark moths have been rarer in the past than now?

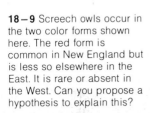

Before reading further, can you state a hypothesis of your own?

The biologists who investigated this matter developed a hypothesis that they proceeded to test. In the Midlands they placed both light and dark moths on smoke-blackened tree trunks. The moths were placed in the position they normally take during their daytime rest. The biologists soon observed that birds ate more light than dark moths. Both light and dark moths were then placed on trees common to southern England—soot-free and encrusted with white lichens. Here the birds ate more dark than light moths.

What can we conclude from the experiments? In the industrialized Midlands the tree trunks became covered with black soot. Dark moths survive predation better than white ones on these trees. Moth coloration is controlled genetically. During the last century, therefore, Darwin's natural selection favored the moths most protectively colored in the new environment. Meanwhile, white moths survive successfully in rural areas, where tree trunks are not sooty.

18−9 Screech owls occur in the two color forms shown here. The red form is common in New England but is less so elsewhere in the East. It is rare or absent in the West. Can you propose a hypothesis to explain this?

Lynwood M. Chace

CHARACTERISTICS OF THE EVOLUTIONARY PROCESS

Comparing the populations before and after industrialization, we can note three main points.

First: An evolutionary event involves a change in a population. *Individuals* do not undergo evolutionary changes during their lifetimes. The makeup of the population does change—over a long period of time. The frequency of different kinds of individuals in the population changes. Some dark individuals occurred in the 1850 moth population, but they were much more frequent in the 1950 population.

Second: An evolutionary event involves few characteristics at any one time. Organisms are systems of complex interactions. The change in frequency of dark moths may have brought about some less obvious changes in other moth characteristics. But, when we consider all characteristics, very few changed in frequency. This is due to a stability factor in the characteristics of populations.

Third: An evolutionary event involves a change in a particular direction. There must, therefore, be some foundation for change to work on—some "raw material." In the 1850 population there were both white and dark moths. This coloring is hereditary. Thus, an evolutionary event, such as the increase in frequency of dark moths, first requires genetic variations as its raw material. There are many hereditary variations in the moths of a century ago. But only one, the dark color, became the foundation for a change in the population. In other words, an evolutionary event does not involve *all* the raw materials available. Evolution is a selective change. Environmental factors (the soot and the birds, in our example) guide the selection.

Frequencies can be expressed as fractions, ratios, or percentages. In what investigation did you deal with frequencies?

18–10 What evolutionary processes explain the results of this experiment?

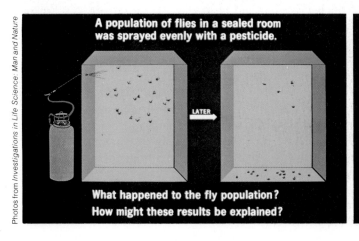

A population of flies in a sealed room was sprayed evenly with a pesticide.

LATER

What happened to the fly population? How might these results be explained?

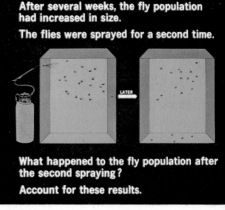

After several weeks, the fly population had increased in size.

The flies were sprayed for a second time.

LATER

What happened to the fly population after the second spraying?

Account for these results.

Photos from *Investigations in Life Science: Man and Nature*

CHECK YOURSELF

E. What event influenced the publication of Darwin's theories?

F. Which of Darwin's theories merely restated an old idea?

G. How did Lamarck theorize that changes between generations could occur?

H. How did Darwin's ideas differ from those of Lamarck?

I. What has been the foundation for natural selection in the peppered moth? On what evidence is this conclusion based?

J. Why can a single individual organism not indicate an evolutionary change?

K. What are the characteristics of the evolutionary process?

Investigation 18.1   GENETIC STABILITY

INTRODUCTION

We have seen how natural selection works to change the frequency of characteristics in a population. In this investigation you will study a population existing through time with no selective forces acting on it.

Evidence for genetic stability was found when mitosis and meiosis were linked with the inheritance of characteristics. Since these processes are so precise, it seems that organisms must conserve genetic characteristics through many generations.

PROCEDURE

Consider a hypothetical species of squirrel. Assume that among the variations in this hypothetical species are two hereditary hair types. One type is straight, and the other is curly. Assume that the trait is determined by a single pair of alleles. Straight (**S**) is dominant over curly (**s**). Finally, assume that the species population consists of 1,000 squirrels,

with equal numbers of males and females. Among the 500 squirrels of each sex, 250 are homozygous straight-haired (**SS**), and 250 are homozygous curly-haired (**ss**).

Use the symbols ♂ for male and ♀ for female. (*1*) Identify all the possible phenotype matings in this hypothetical population. (*2*) List all the possible kinds of matings in terms of genotypes — for example, **SS** × **ss**. (*3*) Beside each kind of mating write all the kinds of genotypes that occur among the offspring. (*4*) Does any cross produce more than one kind of offspring?

Assume that the offspring generation also consists of 1,000 squirrels. Assume also that each kind of mating you listed for item *2* contributes equally to this population. (*5*) What is the expected ratio of straight-haired squirrels to curly-haired squirrels in the offspring? (*6*) Is this phenotype ratio the same as that in the 1st generation?

The frequency of any particular characteristic within a group is expressed as a fraction. Thus, in a group of 100 marbles containing 20 red and 80 blue ones, the frequency of red marbles is 20/100, or 1/5, or 20%, or 0.2. The frequency of blue marbles is 80/100, or 4/5, or 80%, or 0.8. Regardless of how the fractions are written, their sum must always equal 1:

$$20/100 + 80/100 = 100/100 = 1$$
$$1/5 + 4/5 = 5/5 = 1$$
$$20\% + 80\% = 100\% = 1$$
$$0.2 + 0.8 = 1.0$$

In this example, suppose each marble is a gamete and gametes unite at random. Recall that the probability of two separate events occurring at the same time is the product of their individual probabilities. Thus, the frequency of genotype red-red in the next generation would be $0.2 \times 0.2 = 0.04$. The frequency of blue-blue would be $0.8 \times 0.8 = 0.64$. What would be the frequency of the red-blue genotype? We know that the total of the frequencies of the genotypes must equal 1.0. Therefore, $1.0 - .04 - .64 = .32$. This means that in the next generation of 100 individuals, we expect 32 to be heterozygotes.

Now consider the two genes **S** and **s**. (7) What were their frequencies (expressed as decimal fractions) in the original squirrel population? (8) What are their frequencies in the offspring generation? (9) How do the gene frequencies in the original population compare with those in the offspring generation?

Now make the same calculations for a 3rd generation. You could do this by mating every genotype with every other genotype in proportion to their frequencies. But you can obtain the same result by using the gene-pool method. Write the frequencies of all the kinds of gametes in the 2nd generation (in this case, the frequencies of genes in item 8). Then assume random combination of these gametes. The frequency of **S** plus the frequency of **s** represents the total sperm population. (Likewise, the frequency of **S** plus the frequency of **s** represents the total egg popu-

lation.) By algebraic multiplication of these frequencies, you can obtain the frequencies of the 3rd-generation genotypes just as you did with the red and blue marbles above.

Use the gene-pool method to answer the following questions: (10) What are the frequencies of the genotypes in the 3rd generation? (11) Assuming that the 3rd-generation population is again 1,000, what are the frequencies of **S** and **s** in the 3rd generation? (12) Is the phenotype ratio the same as in the 2nd generation? (13) Are gene frequencies the same as those in the 2nd generation?

Retaining all other assumptions, change the original population to 400 homozygous straight-haired squirrels and 600 homozygous curly-haired squirrels. Each group contains males and females in equal numbers. (14) What are the frequencies of the two genes among males in the population? (15) Among females? (16) By algebraic multiplication determine the frequencies of genotypes among the offspring. (17) What are the frequencies of the two genes in the offspring population? (18) Calculate the frequencies of the genes in a 3rd generation.

DISCUSSION

(19) In a single sentence try to state a conclusion concerning gene frequencies in populations.

If you have been successful in formulating your sentence, you have stated the basic idea of the **Hardy-Weinberg principle.** G. H. Hardy was an English mathematician, and W. R. Weinberg was a German physician. In 1908 they independently worked out the effects of random mating in successive generations on the frequencies of alleles in a population. You have just done the same thing.

You may have noticed that in many ways the hypothetical population differs from real ones. Nevertheless, the Hardy-Weinberg principle is important for biologists because it is the basis of hypothetical stability from which to measure real change.

THE CHANGE FACTOR

In our example of evolution, frequency of black moths could not have changed if there had been no black moths to begin with. Evolution could not occur without genetic differences among individuals in a population — without variations. Darwin easily found variations among the individuals of many species. He asked where the variations came from, but he could give no answer.

18–11 Variation within a population. In almost all populations — plant or animal — there are genetic differences among the individuals. Just consider the students in your class.

Gordon E. Uno

Review page 604.

An answer came from 20th-century genetics: mutation is the ultimate source of variation. The sickle-cell gene in humans originated by mutation. Some of the characteristics of the peas studied by Mendel originated by mutation.

Errors occur only rarely during DNA replication. However, each of us has thousands of gene loci at which mutations can occur. Even with low mutation rates, we are likely to carry some mutant genes. Most of these mutations do not cause problems. Many mutations that are *potentially* harmful will not have any effect, because they are recessive. Unless two gametes with the same recessive gene unite, the mutation will not appear in the offspring. Thus, a homozygous recessive may suffer from a harmful mutation, but a heterozygote will not. (Of course the homozygous dominant will not suffer either since it has no recessive genes.) The mutation can, therefore, remain in a population in the heterozygotes and in any homozygous recessives that do not die from the harmful effects of the mutation.

Once mutant genes have accumulated within populations, new combinations of them can be formed. This can happen through independent assortment and crossing-over. The number of combinations increases much more rapidly than the number of mutant genes themselves. If only gene **A** is found in a population, then there is only one genotype, **AA,** and one phenotype possible for all offspring. Suppose one gene **A** mutates to gene **a,** as in figure 18–12. Then two alleles at one gene

18–12 How mutation and recombination produce a wide variety of individuals.

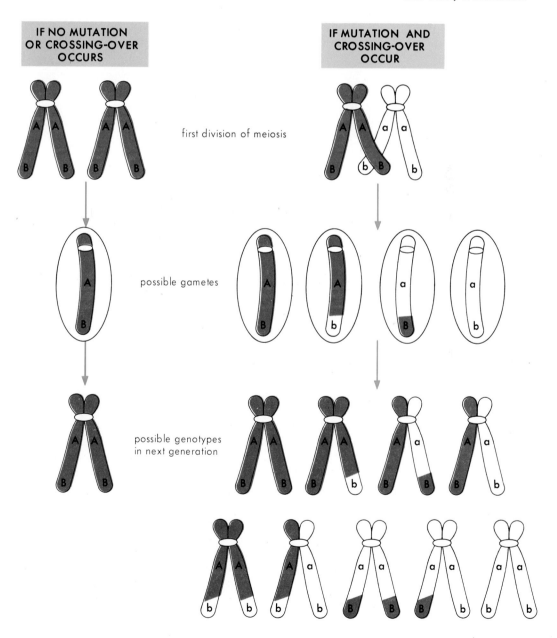

IF NO MUTATION OR CROSSING-OVER OCCURS

IF MUTATION AND CROSSING-OVER OCCUR

first division of meiosis

possible gametes

possible genotypes in next generation

locus, **A** and **a,** produce three possible genotypes: **AA, Aa,** and **aa.** Now consider two mutations, one at each of two loci of the *same* chromosome. Suppose **a** and **b** are the mutations of genes **A** and **B.** Then suppose genes **A** and **B** are on one chromosome and **a** and **b** are on the other. If there is no crossing-over, then only three genotypes are possible: **AABB, AaBb,** and **aabb.** If, however, crossing-over and independent assortment take place, there are nine possible genotypes in the offspring population. These nine genotypes are possible only if recombination takes place. Thus, recombination can yield a wide variety of individuals from relatively few mutations.

Summing up: Mutation supplies the raw material for evolution. Recombination casts mutations into new combinations. But there is no evidence that mutation occurs to supply a needed or desirable change. It just causes change — any change.

THE GUIDING FACTOR

Mutation is a random process. Fossils are the evidence for evolution in the past. They clearly show that the changes in living things during geological time *have not* been random. On the contrary, the combinations of traits that we find in living things both past and present are in most cases well organized and well coordinated.

How can such order come from the chaos of random mutations? The theory devised to answer this question is the most important accomplishment of Charles Darwin. His theory of natural selection supplied reasonable, natural causes as the guiding factor of evolution. The theory was worked out on the basis of evidence then available to naturalists. The more recent evidence from 20th-century genetics (*Drosophila* studies, for example) has supported it.

Let us summarize the theory of natural selection. First, in every species there are many hereditary variations. Indeed, very few individuals of any species are exactly alike genetically. Second, in most cases reproduction operates so that offspring are more numerous than the parents that produce them. If, in any species, all offspring grew up to become parents, after a few generations the population would be greater than could be supported. Third, it is clear that this increase in numbers is checked. The net population of a species does not continue to increase sharply over long periods of time. This means that many members of each generation fail to reproduce. Usually they die from one cause or another before reaching the age of reproduction.

Which ones die? There must be a kind of competition

What are these genotypes? How many genotypes will two different alleles at each of three loci produce?

Does this statement apply to organisms that reproduce asexually? Explain.

chaos [KAY os; Greek: *khaos,* empty space]: total disorder

Review Investigation 2.2.

among individuals within each species — **intraspecific** competition. This competition is for food, light, water, and other environmental factors important to their survival. This intraspecific competition takes place among individuals that are slightly different from one another. Often it is inheritable (genetic) differences that determine which individuals survive and which do not.

In any particular environment there are individuals with characteristics that improve their ability to survive. On the average, they reach reproductive age more often than do individuals lacking such characteristics. In each generation, then, we should expect a slight increase in the proportion of individuals having high *viability.* Viability is having many characteristics favorable for survival. That is what Darwin called "survival of the fittest."

viability [vy uh BIL ut ee; Latin: *vivere,* to live, + ability]

Now let us see how the theory of natural selection worked in the case of the peppered moths. On the light-barked trees, before the area was industrialized, birds ate more dark moths than light ones. So dark moths remained very rare in the population. But, after industry moved in, the dark moths in the sooty woods were eaten less often than the light ones. This was because their darker color made them better fit to withstand predation in the new environment. So more dark moths survived to have dark offspring than did light ones to have light offspring. Therefore, after many generations the ratio of dark moths to light ones in the population increased. Eventually the light moths became rare. Dark moths — fittest in the new environment — became common.

In the 1950's the British Parliament passed a clean-air act. Factories were forced to switch from sooty coal to less smoky fuels. This law has led to a marked decrease in the amount of soot in the air. In the 1970's English scientists checked the moth numbers again. They reported a small, but significant, increase in the frequency of the light-colored moths in industrial England. Refer to the Bishop and Cook article ("Suggested Readings," page 658).

Note that fitness is an ecological characteristic of an organism. It is the interaction of a particular organism and a particular environment. Blackness of the moths does not fit them to live everywhere — only in places where tree trunks are dark. Consider another example. In most environments the possession of wings is obviously an advantage to a fly. But in the southern Indian Ocean, far from any other land, is an island swept all year by savage winds. Flies are present there, but none have wings. It is easy to imagine what would happen to any mutant winged fly on that island.

Many flightless land birds live on islands, but some do not. Look up some examples and try to explain their survival as species.

Marg and Bill Staley

Judd Cooney

18–13 The snowshoe hare (*left*) has a nearly white coat in winter, although it is brown in summer. The coat of the cottontail rabbit (*right*) changes little from summer to winter. Which species is likely to escape predators better in Georgia? In Ontario?   × 1/8

Do you think nearsightedness was an advantage or a disadvantage to individual survival in a primitive hunting tribe?

Not every characteristic of every organism is adaptive. Natural selection can act only on whole organisms. Genes of poor adaptive value may be closely linked to those of high adaptive value. If such is the case, selection can sort out poorly adaptive genes only after recombination has separated them from highly adaptive ones.

Now one more important point. Superior ability to survive—viability—is not the only factor in natural selection. Equally important is superior *fertility* — the ability to produce offspring. High viability and high fertility do not always go together. The most fertile individuals in a population are not always the biggest, the strongest, or even the healthiest ones. Differences in viability and differences in fertility add up to differences in reproduction. On the average, populations whose members produce the most offspring capable of living to maturity tend to survive and increase in numbers.

18–14 Quail (*left*) produce a large brood. Golden eagles (*right*) produce one or two offspring a year. What might you hypothesize about the mortality of the young in these two species?

Photos from Denver Museum of Natural History

CHECK YOURSELF

L. What is the Hardy-Weinberg principle? From your study of the hypothetical squirrel population, try to state the assumptions on which this principle is based.

M. What are the bases for the change factor in evolution?

N. What is the reasoning that leads to the theory of natural selection?

O. Why must environment, as well as an organism's characteristics, be considered in describing fitness?

P. How can you explain the continued existence of unfavorable characteristics in a population?

Q. Why must fertility, as well as viability, be taken into account when studying the natural selection in a population?

Investigation 18.2   SICKLE CELLS AND EVOLUTION

INTRODUCTION

Before beginning work on this investigation, review the genetics of sickle-cell anemia in Chapter 17 (pages 576–581 and 616).

PROCEDURE

The **Hb**^{S} gene brings about the formation of hemoglobin associated with sickle-cell anemia. It is rare in most human populations. In some parts of Africa, however, the sickle-cell trait (genotype **Hb**^{A}**Hb**^{S}) is found in as much as 40% (0.4) of the population. (1) In such a population, what is the probability that any two heterozygous individuals will marry? (2) What percentage of their offspring may be expected to be homozygous for the sickle-cell gene? (3) On the average, then, which would you expect to leave more offspring— individuals with the sickle-cell trait or individuals with normal red blood cells? (4) How many sickle-cell genes are lost from the gene pool when a child with sickle-cell anemia

dies? (5) What effect would you expect the death of children with sickle-cell anemia to have on the frequency of the sickle-cell gene in any population? You have described an evolutionary change in terms of modern genetics. (6) How would Darwin have described this situation?

Actually, there is no evidence that the frequency of the gene for sickle-cell is becoming less in African populations. Therefore, a biological problem arises. How can the frequency of the gene for sickle-cell be maintained at such a high level when selection works so strongly against the gene?

You know that a scientist begins an attack on such a problem by devising hypotheses. These are explanations that can be tested by making observations or carrying out experiments. Biologists have developed at least 3 hypotheses to account for the high frequency of the sickle-cell gene in African populations. One is based on mutation rates.

A 2nd is based on fertility and a 3rd on resistance to disease. (7) Using these clues, devise 3 hypotheses to explain the persistently high frequency of the sickle-cell gene in African populations. *Write these down before reading further.*

The rate at which sickle-cell genes are lost from the gene pool is about 100 times the average mutation rate of gene Hb^A to Hb^S.

In addition, geographically, mutation rates vary only slightly. (8) Does this information support or weaken your 1st hypothesis? Explain your answer.

At present there is no evidence that individuals with the sickle-cell trait produce more children than do those with normal red blood cells. (9) Does this information support or weaken your 2nd hypothesis? Explain your answer.

As data on sickle-cell anemia were collected, the frequencies of the sickle-cell trait in various populations were plotted on maps. It became clear that the gene is most common in a belt extending across central Africa. In the same region malaria and hookworm disease are common. Consider your knowledge of these two diseases and of the part of the body affected by sickle-cell anemia. (10) Which of the two diseases, if either, would you think more likely to be associated with sickle-cell anemia? The foregoing question—and its answer—provides new information for your 3rd hypothesis. (11) How might you now word it?

To test this hypothesis, an investigator examined the blood of 290 children of an East African population. Both malaria and sickle-cell anemia were common in this population. The results are given in figure 18–15. (12) Calculate the percentage of SC's (persons with either the sickle-cell trait or sickle-cell anemia) who also have malaria. Find the percentage of NSC's (persons without the trait or anemia) who have malaria.

You can use the chi-square (χ^2) test to determine whether the difference between

	With Malaria	Without Malaria	Total
SC's	12	31	43
NSC's	113	134	247
Total	125	165	290

18–15

SC's and NSC's, with respect to malaria, is significant. But the calculations are somewhat more complex than those in Investigation 17.3. You must consider 4 combinations: (a) SC's with malaria, (b) SC's without malaria, (c) NSC's with malaria, and (d) NSC's without malaria.

First obtain the expected values for each of the 4 combinations. Multiply the totals in the far-right column by a ratio obtained from the totals in the 3rd line. For SC's with malaria, this is 125/290 × 43. For SC's without malaria, this is 165/290 × 43, etc. (13) Calculate the chi-square. In the table on page 593 use the χ^2 for 2 classes. (14) Based on the chi-square results, do these data tend to support or weaken the hypothesis?

To test the hypothesis further, 30 volunteers were inoculated with malaria parasites. The volunteers were men of approximately the same age and physical condition. A blood test at the beginning of the experiment showed that none had malaria parasites. Of the 30, 15 had the sickle-cell trait and 15 had normal red blood cells. Two of the SC's and 14 of the NSC's developed malaria. (15) Apply the chi-square test to see whether the difference between the SC's and the NSC's, with respect to malaria infection, is significant. (16) Does the result tend to support the hypothesis in item 11?

About 22 percent of the ancestors of American blacks had sickle-cell trait or anemia. (17) Would genetic mixture of American blacks with the population of European ancestry and with the American Indian population have caused this frequency to increase? To decrease? Or to remain the same?

In the United States, humans have almost completely eliminated the vector of malaria, the *Anopheles* mosquito. (*18*) Do heterozygotes of sickle-cell still have a survival advantage over homozygotes in this country? Recall that an individual homozygous for sickle-cell often dies before reaching reproductive age. Consider your answer to item *18*. (*19*) What might you predict to happen to the frequency of the **Hb**^{S} gene in the United States?

DISCUSSION

(*20*) How does sickle-cell illustrate the factors in the evolutionary process? (*21*) How does this investigation show that evolution involves interaction between the genetic makeup of an organism *and* its environment? Hereditary traits (and the genes that determine them) are sometimes described as "beneficial" or "good" and "harmful" or "bad." (*22*) Keeping in mind the ideas in this investigation, comment on the use of such terms.

SPECIATION

speciation [spee shee AY shun]

Darwin called his book *The Origin of Species.* But, so far in our description of evolution, no species have originated — there has been no *speciation.* Mutation and natural selection have merely changed the ratios of different kinds of individuals in a population. At the end of a century, most of the peppered moths in industrial England were dark-colored. There were, however, some light-colored ones with which they could interbreed. In rural England a large percentage of light moths interbred with the few dark ones. We cannot say, then, that any new species has developed. No population has become reproductively isolated from other populations. That is, no peppered moth population has developed that cannot interbreed with individuals from other populations. How can *reproductive isolation* of a population develop?

Recall the biological definition of "species," pages 107–109.

ISOLATION IN TIME

Perhaps the most complete fossil record of any evolutionary line is that of the horse family. The oldest fossils that definitely show characteristics of the family came from the Eocene. This animal was scarcely larger than a dog. It had a short muzzle and low-crowned teeth. It probably browsed on bushes. It had four toes on each front foot and three on each hind foot. Each toe had a tiny hoof. A modern horse has a long muzzle, with a wide gap between the front and rear teeth. Its teeth are high-crowned, with ridges of resistant enamel. This is a fine adaptation for grazing on coarse, dry grasses. On each foot it has only one toe, which ends in a large hoof. There are many other differences between the Eocene horses and modern horses.

See Investigation 10.2.

muzzle: the projecting nose and jaws of an animal

18–16 Some characteristics in five genera of the horse family. For relationships of these genera to others, see Investigation 10.2.

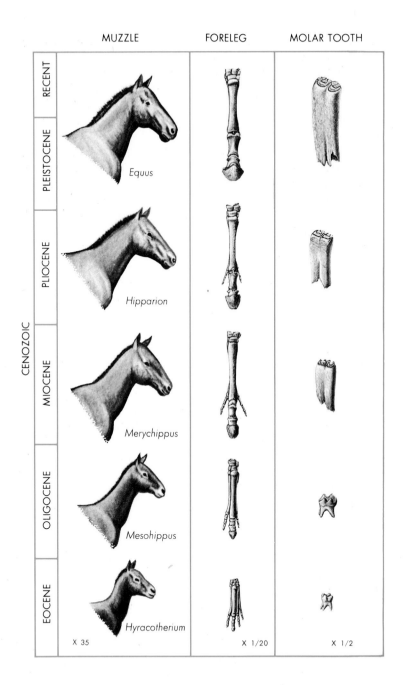

The fossil record shows that all these differences resulted from a series of many gradual changes. Each change that became established through natural selection must have been very slight. Only when many such changes accumulated did they result in detectable differences. A later population may have become so different that it could not have interbred with the earlier one, even if the two had existed at the same time.

How can this long sequence of horses be divided into species? We cannot try to breed the extinct species of the family with the modern ones — horse, donkey, and zebra. Nor can we breed the extinct ones with each other. Yet the skeletal differences among many of the extinct populations are much greater than the differences among horse, donkey, and zebra. When differences among extinct populations are large, most paleontologists agree to call the populations different species. These slight changes accumulated over a long period of time — 58 million years. *Millions* of generations were involved in the changes from the ancient to the modern horse.

ISOLATION IN SPACE

Islands. The finches of the Galápagos interested Darwin. They were similar to each other and to the finches of the distant mainland of Ecuador. Yet they had many *different* kinds of beaks.

See figure 18–4.

It is easy to suppose that a few Ecuadorian finches might have been carried by storms from the mainland to the Galápagos. The islands are so close to each other that local storms may have carried birds from one island to another. Yet they are far enough apart to make interbreeding between finch populations on different islands a rare event. Therefore, mutations and gene recombinations in one population are not readily carried to other islands. The different island environments also select different traits from the traits that do occur. So the isolated populations have taken separate ecological and genetic paths for hundreds of years.

For aquatic organisms, what might maintain isolated populations in the way islands do for terrestrial organisms?

18–17 Some of the species of honeycreepers (Hawaii). Why doesn't this arrangement illustrate the same idea as the arrangement of horses in figure 18–16? What ideas does it suggest to you?

Kauai akialoa

iiwi

apapane

Kauai creeper

akepa

palila

Maui parrotbill

X 1/2

The gene pools of the isolated populations now differ greatly. In some cases the differences are so great that gametes from one population cannot fertilize gametes from another. In other cases the difference in genotype might not be so great. However, the phenotype differences—in mating calls and in courtship behavior—might prevent interbreeding. Even if interbreeding were successful, the hybrid offspring might have less viability and fertility than either parent. In any case, isolation on separate islands resulted in accumulated differences among the finches. These differences have produced species different from the one (or few) that originally colonized the islands.

Eight hundred kilometers northeast of the Galápagos lies a single island, Cocos. It serves as a kind of control for the long "Galápagos experiment." It has but one species of Darwin's finches. And this species is unlike those of either Ecuador or the Galápagos.

Variation on continents. It is difficult to believe that evolution of new species has taken place only on islands. Is there any basis for isolation on continents? Many species have wide geographic ranges. And characteristics often vary among populations of the same species in different parts of the range. The variation may be in the frequency with which a characteristic occurs. Or it may be in both the frequency and the intensity of the characteristic. In some cases, there is a continuous increase or decrease in the variation as we move through the range. This variation is called a *cline.*

cline [Greek: *klinein*, to slope]

Hamsters, natives of Eurasia, are often found in school biology laboratories. Domesticated hamsters come in many colors. In most of their natural geographic range, however, wild

18–18 Cline in the frequency of the I^B gene (see page 601) in the human population of western Asia and Europe.

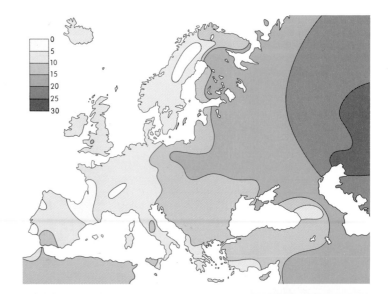

0
5
10
15
20
25
30

hamsters have two color phases, agouti and black. In southern Russia the frequencies of the two colors are known from trapping records, since hamster pelts are economically important there. Figure 18–19 summarizes these records. As you can see, the frequency of black hamsters decreases as you go from the center toward the edges of the hamsters' range.

agouti [uh GOOT ee]: a hair color in which each hair has bands of yellow, black, or brown pigment; frequent in wild mammals

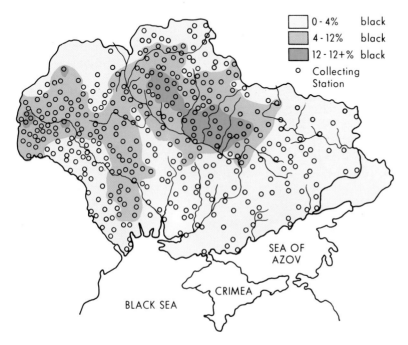

▨ 0 - 4%	black
▨ 4 - 12%	black
▨ 12 - 12+%	black
○	Collecting Station

SEA OF AZOV

CRIMEA

BLACK SEA

18–19 Distribution of two forms of hamsters in southern Russia.

X 1/4

A cline in the intensity of a characteristic is found in the California yarrow (*Achillea millefolium*). In general, yarrow plants in the Central Valley of California are much taller than

Achillea millefolium [ak uh LEE uh mil uh FOLE ee um]: a common white-flowered herb

18–20 Cline in the height of yarrow plants.

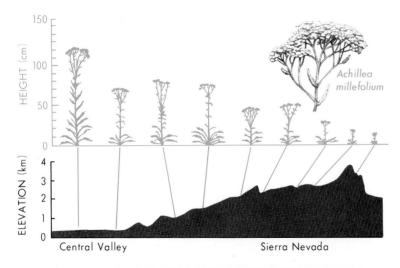

Achillea millefolium

Central Valley   Sierra Nevada

those on the mountain peaks of the Sierra Nevada. Between these two locations the stem length in yarrow plants gradually decreases as you go higher into the mountains.

A cline is not always gradual. This is shown by a characteristic of the black-racer snake, *Coluber constrictor.* Along the Atlantic coast there is a variation in the number of white scales on the ventral surfaces of the snakes' heads. In the New York population the average number of white scales is low. In Florida populations it is high. But the cline is not even. From central Florida to Georgia the decline in the number of white ventral scales is steep. But the change northward from Georgia is slight.

Coluber constrictor [KOL yuh-bur kun STRIK tur]

18–21 Cline in a trait of the black racer (*Coluber constrictor*). The areas from which population samples were taken are shown in color. The graph shows the average number of white scales in specimens from each population.

New York

X 1/4

South Carolina

Florida

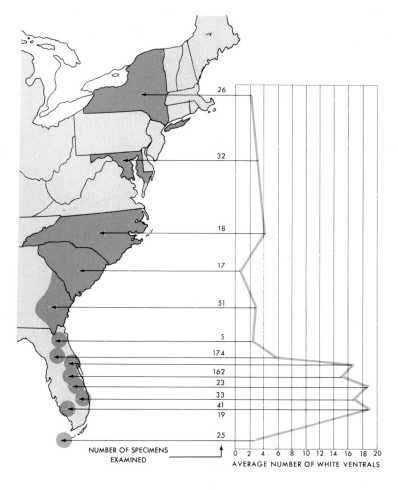

NUMBER OF SPECIMENS EXAMINED

AVERAGE NUMBER OF WHITE VENTRALS

Subspecies into species? Within the large range of a widespread species there may be clines in many traits. The clines do not necessarily coincide in location, direction, or intensity. If they do, however, a species is divided into **subspecies.** It is impossible to draw lines on a map that show boundaries be-

coincide [koh in SYD]: to occupy the same place

tween subspecies because all adjacent populations can inter-breed. As a result, there are no completely separate gene pools.

Figure 18–22 shows the distribution of some of the sub-species of the black racer in the eastern United States. Consider the facts of geographical variation recorded on the map. Suppose that the sea were to invade the Mississippi and Ohio val-leys, as it has in the distant past. Suppose this flood destroyed all the populations of *Coluber constrictor* between the areas in which *flaviventris* and *constrictor* are found. At first the two subspecies would still be capable of interbreeding. But the wa-ter barrier between them would prevent it. Consequently, new mutations that occurred in *flaviventris* or in *constrictor* could not be exchanged. Different mutations could accumulate over a long period of time in each subspecies. Might not the two even-tually lose the ability to interbreed? Would they become sepa-rate species? Maybe. But let us examine some further evidence.

flaviventris [flay vee VEN trus]. Subspecies are represented by trinomials. Thus the black-snake subspecies in the northern part of the Middle West is called *Coluber constrictor flaviventris.*

18–22 Distribution of subspecies of *Coluber constrictor* in a part of eastern North America.

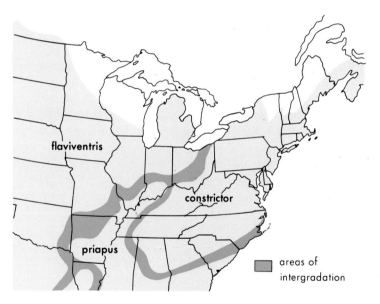

areas of intergradation

X 1/4

18–23 Lazuli bunting (male).

Indigo buntings (*Passerina cyanea*) are small birds that breed throughout the eastern United States. Lazuli buntings (*Passerina lazuli*) breed over much of the western United States. Both nest in bushes and small trees. Between these two regions lie the Great Plains. By placing the two species of buntings in the same genus, taxonomists have indicated that they consider these two species to be closely related. At one time there may have been a single bunting species. It could have spread through a continuous forest that probably once grew across the United States. The treeless plains developed as the climate be-came unsuitable for the growth of trees. The plains, in turn,

Passerina cyanea [pas uh REEN-uh see AY nee uh]

lazuli [LAZ yuh lee]

were a habitat unsuitable for buntings. This change would have separated the eastern and western bunting populations. During this separation, visible genetic differences could have arisen — especially in the males.

Humans have now transformed the prairies and plains. Patches of trees and shrubs surround hundreds of farmhouses and line miles of streets in towns. Indigo buntings have spread westward from the deciduous forest. Lazuli buntings have spread eastward from the mountains. The case of the buntings is much like that of the black-racer snakes. In both there is a reunion of two populations that have acquired genetic differences through *geographical isolation.* What is the result? In many places lazuli buntings mate with indigo buntings. The hybrid offspring seem to be fertile. But their fertility and their viability may not be as high as those of the parent species. There is as yet no evidence that *P. cyanea* and *P. lazuli* are merging.

On the basis of this evidence, do *you* consider these populations to be separate species?

CHECK YOURSELF

R. What seems to be the explanation for the high frequency of the sickle-cell gene in central-African populations?

S. If we are to recognize that speciation has occurred, what must happen to a population of organisms?

T. How is time a factor in the process of forming new species?

U. How might a small population of one species, carried to an archipelago, develop into a number of separate species?

V. What is meant by a cline?

W. What is the relationship between clines and subspecies?

X. What events may bring about geographical isolation between subspecies?

Y. How might geographical isolation of subspecies on a continent lead to speciation?

Investigation 18.3   **A STEP IN SPECIATION**

INTRODUCTION

The small salamanders of the genus *Ensatina* are strictly terrestrial. They even lay their eggs on land. Nevertheless, these sala-

MATERIALS
(per student)

outline map of California
colored pencils

manders need a rather moist environment and do not thrive in arid regions. In California *Ensatina eschscholtzii* (en suh TY-nuh es SHOLT zee eye) has been studied by R. S. Stebbins of the University of California (Berkeley). This investigation is based on his work.

PROCEDURE A

Imagine that you are working with Stebbins' salamander specimens, some of which are pictured in figure 18–24. In the following list, the parentheses after each subspecies name contain a number and a color. The number is the total of individuals that Stebbins had

18–24 Specimens of the salamander species *Ensatina eschscholtzii.*

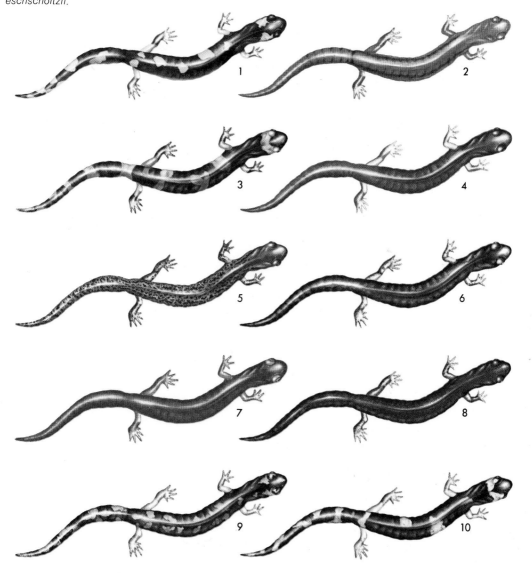

available for his study. The color is for you to use in designating the subspecies. Following this is a list of collection areas. They are indicated by a code that fits the map of California in figure 18–25. For example 32/R means that one or more *E. e. croceator* specimens were collected at the intersection of Line 32 and Line R.

1. *croceator* (15; brown): 32/R, 32/S, 30/T, 31/T
2. *eschscholtzii* (203; red): 30/M, 32/O, 34/S, 35/V, 36/W, 35/Z, 38/Y, 40/Z
3. *klauberi* (48; blue): 36/Z, 38/a, 40/a, 39/a
4. *oregonensis* (373; pink): 9/B, 7/E, 6/E, 13/C, 10/C, 7/D, 15/D
5. *picta* (230; yellow): 2/B, 2/C, 3/C, 4/C
6. *platensis* (120; green): 8/J, 10/J, 11/M, 13/M,

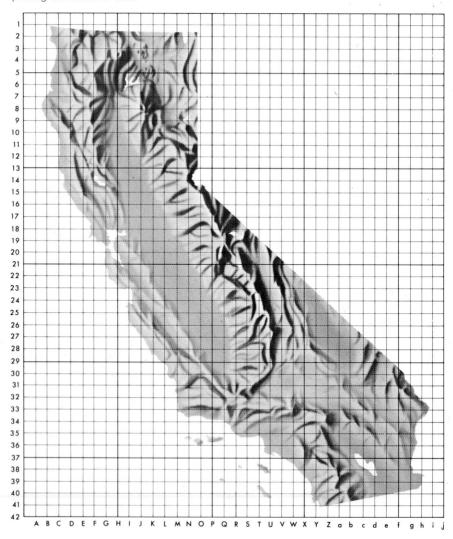

18–25 Map of California, with the grid to be used in plotting distributional data.

15/M, 15/O, 17/M, 15/P, 20/Q, 24/S, 21/R, 25/T, 26/U

7. *xanthoptica* (271; orange): 17/G, 17/F, 19/H, 19/O, 20/I, 20/J, 21/I

Plot each collection area by making a small *X* mark on an outline map that has a grid like the one in the figure. Write with pencils of different colors to indicate the different populations.

DISCUSSION

You now have a distribution map of the sub-species of *Ensatina eschscholtzii* in Califor-nia. (*1*) Is the species uniformly distributed throughout California? Use your knowledge of the species' ecological requirements to offer an explanation for its distribution. Now consider the physiography of California (fig-ure 18–25). (*2*) Does the species seem more characteristic of mountain areas or of large valley areas? (*3*) Do you expect any order in distribution of subspecies? Why or why not?

Examine the pictures in figure 18–24. Note that some subspecies have yellow or orange spots and bands on a black body. Some have fairly plain, brown-orange bodies. One has small orange spots on a black back-ground. There are other differences as well. For example, some of them have white feet. Now refer to your distribution map. (*4*) Does there appear to be any order to the way these color patterns occur in California? For exam-ple, do the spotted forms occur only along the coast? Do spotted forms occur in the north and unspotted ones in the south? Sub-species *eschscholtzii* and *klauberi* are very different from each other. (*5*) What relation-ship is there between their distributions?

PROCEDURE B

You may wonder whether there might not be salamanders in some of the areas for which you have no records. You may also wonder whether there might be additional subspecies for which you have no specimens. A biologist faced with these questions would leave the laboratory and go into the field to collect more specimens. Imagine that you do so, too, and return with the following additional data:

eschscholtzii (16; red): 36/Z, 41/Z, 33/M, 34/W, 34/U

klauberi (23; blue): 40/b, 40/Z, 36/a

Unidentified population #8 (44; black and green): 4/1, 5/H, 7/H, 7/F, 6/J, 9/F

Unidentified population #9 (13; black and red): 28/T, 27/T, 26/T, 28/S, 29/T

Unidentified population #11 (131; black and blue): 23/J, 24/K, 24/I, 29/M, 25/J, 25/I

Unidentified population #12 (31; black and yellow): 6/C, 7/C, 6/B

Mark with a *0* the following places that were searched for *Ensatina* without success:

11/I, 14/I, 17/K, 19/K, 22/N, 26/Q, 5/M, 32/U, 32/a, 35/f.

Specimens of #8 and #9 are shown in figure 18–24. There are no illustrations for #11 and #12.

DISCUSSION

According to Stebbins, the unidentified pop-ulations are not additional subspecies. (*6*) What, then, is the probable genetic relation-ship of Populations #8, #9, and #11 to the subspecies already plotted on the map? (*7*) On this basis, describe or make a colored drawing of the appearance you would expect specimens of Population #11 to have. (*8*) Why is it unlikely that you would ever find in-dividuals combining characteristics of *picta* and *xanthoptica*?

Now consider *eschscholtzii* and *klauberi*. Look at the distribution of the original collec-tions. (*9*) What reasons were there for trying to collect additional specimens from extreme southwestern California? (*10*) How do the results of the additional collections differ from the results in other places where two different populations approach each other?

Bear in mind the biological definition of a species and also the appearance and distribution of the named populations of *Ensatina*. *(11)* Which one of these populations could best be considered a species separate from *E. eschscholtzii*? This population was indeed once considered by biologists to be a separate species.

Now imagine that, while examining another museum collection, you find the specimen shown in figure 18–24, #10. Compare its characteristics, especially the spotting pattern, with those of the named populations. Also consider the distribution of these populations. *(12)* Between which two is this specimen most likely a hybrid? On your map draw a line along which you might expect to collect other specimens like this one.

(13) In a brief paragraph explain why Stebbins concluded that there is but one species of *Ensatina* in California.

Suppose that the mild volcanic activity that now occurs in northern California should become violent and completely destroy all the salamanders of that region. *(14)* How would this event affect the concept of species in *Ensatina*?

FOR FURTHER INVESTIGATION

Problem: What accounts for the one record of *xanthoptica* in the Sierras, whereas the rest of the subspecies occurs along the coast?

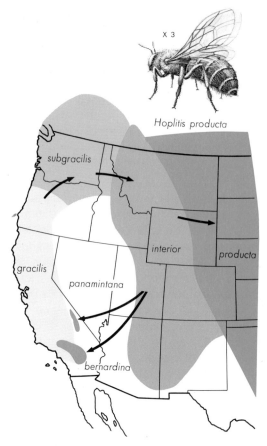

18–26 Ranges of the subspecies of *Hoplitis producta* (a bee). The subspecies *panaminta* and *bernardina* do not interbreed with *gracilis*. Arrows show the way in which the species probably spread from an origin in California. How does this relate to the case of *Ensatina*?

OTHER KINDS OF ISOLATION

Perhaps geographic isolation is always necessary to get populations started toward the formation of new species. Many biologists think so. But other factors can contribute to permanent reproductive isolation.

In Michigan there are two populations of the deer mouse (*Peromyscus maniculatus*). One of these inhabits the shoreline of the Great Lakes. The other lives in wooded areas. Between shore and woods is a zone of meadowland that both populations avoid. Individuals from the two populations rarely meet.

X 1/3

18–27 Deer mouse.

Peromyscus maniculatus [per uh-MIS kus muh nik yuh LAH tus]

However, there is a good reason to suppose that, if they did meet, they could still interbreed. In this case, the two populations are isolated because they live in different habitats — *ecological isolation.*

Pacific salmon spend most of their lives in the ocean. When they mature, they enter rivers and swim upstream toward the headwaters. Each individual swims toward the small stream where it was hatched. When the salmon reach the headwaters, they breed and then die. Because of this behavior, the new generation in each stream obtains its genes from a preceding generation of the same stream. As a result, salmon that have been living together for years in the ocean are not really an interbreeding population. They are genetically separated by *behavioral isolation.*

How might an adult salmon recognize the stream in which it hatched?

But the salmon population of each small stream is not considered a separate species. Can you explain the reasoning of taxonomists in this case?

Tom Walker/Tom Stack & Associates

18–28 Spawning red salmon in a creek. The salmon seek out quiet, smooth, gravel-bottomed streambeds in which to deposit their eggs. Their usual silvery color turns to red as they begin to spawn.

THE OUTCOME OF ISOLATION

Looking at the organisms now living around us, we see many degrees of reproductive isolation — many stages in the evolution of species. Anything that hinders the free exchange of genes (interbreeding) between populations sets the stage for speciation. Geographical, ecological, or behavioral isolation may fail. Old barriers may fall and mating may resume between individuals of different populations. But the more complete the isolation and the longer it continues, the greater the genetic differences between populations will become. We can predict, therefore, that genetic differences will become so great that interbreeding will not be possible.

Where did you read of an example of this?

Sperm of a duck do not survive in the reproductive system of a female chicken. Pollen grains from one plant species often burst and die when placed on the pistil of a different species. Sperm and eggs may meet but fail to unite. They may unite but the zygote or young embryo may die. A hybrid may live but be very weak or sterile. Finally, a hybrid may survive and mate but produce no living offspring. In all of these cases, gene flow between populations has ceased. The gene pools of the two populations are separated. Speciation is complete.

ABRUPT ORIGIN OF NEW SPECIES

We have seen that the process of evolution can be observed directly. But must not speciation—reaching complete reproductive isolation—require a very long time? Not always.

Sometimes, especially in plants, meiosis is so abnormal that gametes are formed with two whole sets of chromosomes. The gametes of these plants are diploid. If one of these diploid gametes is fertilized by a normal monoploid gamete, the new individual has three sets of chromosomes—it is triploid. Occasionally, even higher numbers of chromosome sets may occur. The general term for this situation is **polyploidy.**

triploid [TRIP loid; Latin: *triplus,* threefold, + Greek: *eidos,* form]

polyploidy [POL ih ploid ee; Greek: *polys,* many, + *eidos*]

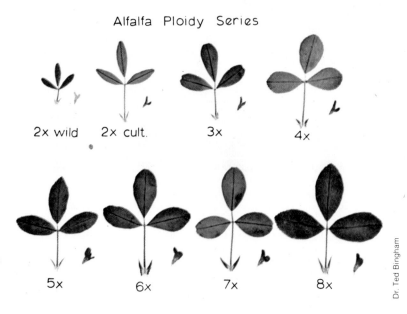

Alfalfa Ploidy Series

18–29 Effects of increasing ploidy on leaves and flowers of alfalfa. (2X = diploid, 3X = triploid, etc.; cult. = cultivated.)

Dr. Ted Bingham

An Asiatic species of cotton has a monoploid number of 13. When it is crossed with a wild American species of cotton (monoploid number also 13), the hybrid is sterile. This sterility occurs because the 13 chromosomes from the two parents fail to pair during meiosis. Apparently they are very different from each other. Chromosome doubling can, however, occur in the hybrids. Each resulting cell then has two sets of chromosomes from each of the parent species—a total of four sets (tetraploid).

tetraploid [TEH truh ploid; Greek: *tettares,* four-parted, + *eidos*]

In such cells each chromosome from the Asiatic cotton has an identical chromosome with which to pair. The same is true with each chromosome from the American cotton. Therefore, normal meiosis can occur. Each gamete formed then receives a complete set of the Asiatic *and* a complete set of the American chromosomes. By self-fertilization, these gametes can again produce a tetraploid plant. And such a hybrid is completely self-fertile.

If the tetraploid hybrid is crossed with either ancestral species, only sterile offspring are produced. Possibly this happens because a diploid gamete uniting with a monoploid gamete produces a triploid. In a triploid individual, how can chromosomes pair during meiosis, in forming new gametes? Thus, a new tetraploid species—reproductively isolated from its parents—may arise suddenly, in only two generations. In this case speciation can be directly observed.

Not all triploid plants are sterile (see figure 18–29). What happens in the gametes during meiosis is still being investigated.

The cultivated cottons and wheats of today are all polyploids that have come into existence in this way. Many of these originated naturally, as have polyploids in many wild species. But now plant breeders can increase the frequency of polyploidy by the use of chemicals. In a sense, then, they can create new species at will.

Look through seed and nursery catalogs for examples of polyploid plants.

CHECK YOURSELF

Z. In addition to geographical isolation, what other kinds of isolation may lead toward speciation?

AA. If geographic, ecological, and behavioral isolation barriers fall, what might prevent two populations from interbreeding?

BB. How can the process of polyploidy produce new species suddenly?

PROBLEMS

1. Sexually reproducing organisms are most likely to adapt rapidly to changing environments. Self-fertilization and parthenogenesis reduce the adaptability of populations. Explain these statements, using your knowledge of both reproductive and evolutionary mechanisms.

2. How do you explain that the variability in a domesticated species is greater than that in the same species, or a similar one, in the wild? (For example, dogs *versus* wolves; chickens *versus* red jungle fowl; pigeons *versus* rock doves.)

3. *Polydactyly* (more than the normal number of fingers and toes) is caused by several different genes. One is dominant, yet the phenotype is rare in humans. Type O blood results from a recessive gene. Yet in some populations of North American Indians, as many as 97 percent of the individuals may have Type O blood. Explain these two situations.

4. Look back at the question in the caption to figure 8–16. Do you recall how

you answered the question? Would you answer it differently now?

5. It is sometimes said that an organism that has only asexual reproductive methods (domesticated bananas, for example) has reached the "end of the evolutionary road." To what extent do you think this expression is true?

6. In many species of birds, populations living at higher latitudes lay more eggs per clutch than do those living at lower latitudes. Would you expect the former gradually to replace the latter? Why or why not?

7. What effects may modern medicine have on the future of the evolution of humans? The facts needed for investigating this problem are found in biological science, but the interpretation of the facts lies outside the realm of verifiable conclusions. It is necessary, therefore, to distinguish carefully between the facts and your interpretation of them.

8. In Cambrian rocks, brachiopods have been found that are indistinguishable from the modern *Lingula* (page 752). Modern cockroaches are very similar to those of the Carboniferous period. Turtles of the genus *Caretta* occur in Cretaceous rocks and in the modern seas. Yet, during these same long years, other organisms have changed greatly. How can you explain such great differences in the rate of evolution among species?

9. You are collecting grasshoppers in the vicinity of a canyon. The canyon is 80 km long and averages 800 m deep, but in several places it is only about 300 m from rim to rim. Along one rim of the canyon, most of the grasshoppers have yellow wings. Along the opposite rim, most have orange wings. How can you account for this difference? Where would be the most likely place to look for grasshoppers that have intermediate wing color?

10. Deep-sea animals and cave animals both live in lightless environments. Few, if any, deep-sea animals are blind, and a great many are luminescent. (See Chapter 9.) Few, if any, cave animals are luminescent, and most are blind. Try to explain these facts from an evolutionary viewpoint.

SUGGESTED READINGS

Bishop, J. A. and L. M. Cook. 1975. Moths, Melanism and Clean Air. *Scientific American*, January.

Darwin, C. 1975. *The Origin of Species.* Edited by Philip Appleman. Paperback reprint. W. W. Norton, New York.

Moore, R. 1969. *Evolution.* Time-Life Books, New York. Many striking pictures and text that stresses history rather than explanation. Fairly easy.

Patterson, C. 1978. *Evolution.* Cornell University Press, New York. An introductory text that is both concise and broad ranging. Covers classical topics through molecular evolution and sociobiology.

Scientific American. 1978. *Evolution.* W. H. Freeman, San Francisco. A reprint of the September, 1978, issue of *Scientific American*, exclusively devoted to evolution.

Shapiro, I. 1977. *Darwin and the Enchanted Isles.* Coward, McCann and Geoghegan, New York. A small, elementary book about Darwin, the voyage of the *Beagle*, and the Galápagos Islands.

Sheppard, P. M. 1975. *Natural Selection and Heredity.* 4th ed. Halsted Press, New York. Available also in paperback from Humanities Press, Atlantic Highlands, N. J. Clearly relates genetic principles to evolutionary processes. Advanced.

Humans
and the Biosphere

HUMANS AND THE BIOSPHERE

Some ideas have tied together all the words, pictures, and investigations of the preceding five sections. Through all the facts, hypotheses, and theories have run some unifying thoughts:

Each organism — you and every other — continually interacts with its environment. Individual organisms, interacting with each other and with their abiotic environments, form ecosystems. Conditions in ecosystems, in communities, in populations, and within individuals fluctuate. But the tendency everywhere in the biosphere is toward a balanced state. A balanced state is achieved through the homeostatic functioning of each organism, and this is dependent on its structure. But the structure of each organism has meaning only in relation to its functioning.

Function depends on the experiences of an organism in its environment and on its heredity. Through the mechanisms of heredity, one generation of organisms is linked to the next. Thus, all organisms of the present have a continuity with organisms of the past. But none is entirely the same in structure and function as its ancestors. Living things have changed through time and are changing today.

These ideas are the result of a long history of observation, experimentation, and thought. And they are continually changed by new knowledge. Ideas exist only in human minds. So any kind of activity that involves ideas — any kind of study — involves human beings. Yet humans belong to a species. They function as a unit of the biosphere and have a part in all of its processes.

You as a human being, then, have a double role in a biology course. You are both the observer and the observed. You began your biology course as an observer of human biological problems. In the pages that followed, the biology of the human species was not neglected, but neither was it emphasized. In Section Six you will devote some special attention to human biology — your biology.

Chapter 19

A Biological View of Humans

YOUR GUIDEPOSTS

In this chapter you will have an opportunity to explore these questions in biology:

- How are humans like all other mammals?
- How are humans different from all other animals?
- What is the fossil evidence in the history of humans?
- In what ways do humans differ from each other?

THE HUMAN SPECIES

Human beings belong to the animal kingdom. If you cut one open, you find that the organs — heart, intestines, liver, lungs — differ little from those of dogs, cats, or monkeys. You also are able to study human nervous or endocrine systems, respiration, digestion, reproduction, or muscle contraction. Again you will find chemical and physical processes similar to those found in many other animals.

19 – 1 Humans doing something other animals do. In what other ways are you like other animals?

BSCS photo by Richard R. Tolman

Judd Cooney

Obviously humans are vertebrates. Among the vertebrates they are mammals. Mammals have hair, and nurse their young with milk. To be sure, humans have a small amount of hair, but some mammals have even less — whales, for instance. Humans are unique among mammals in their striding, bipedal locomotion. This is a pattern of walking that even kangaroos, although bipedal, do not have. You can obtain some understanding of other important human characteristics by studying a skeleton.

bipedal [by PED ul; Latin: *bis*, twice, + *pedes*, feet]

Investigation 19.1   A STUDY OF SKELETONS

INTRODUCTION

Vertebrate skeletons are composed of two major divisions. One is the **axial** skeleton, and the other is the **appendicular** skeleton. The axial skeleton consists of the skull and the column of vertebrae arranged along the long axis of the body. It includes the ribs, which are attached to certain of the vertebrae. The appendicular skeleton consists of the shoulder and hip girdles. Attached to the girdles are the bones in the appendages.

In this investigation you will compare a human skeleton with that of a four-footed mammal.

PROCEDURE

In this procedure you will make observations on both cat and human skeletons. When you are directed to examine a part of the skeleton, examine that part in both animals.

Begin with the axial skeleton. Examine the general outline of the skull. (*1*) Which occupies the greater volume — the brain case or the bones of the face? (*2*) With respect to the rest of the skull, are the eye sockets directed forward, downward, backward, sideward, or upward? (*3*) What change in the facial bones of the cat would bring its eye sockets into the human position?

Viewing the skeleton from the side, hold a ruler along the axis of the vertebrae in the upper part of the neck. (*4*) In which skeleton

MATERIALS
(per class)

mounted human skeleton
mounted cat skeleton
2 rulers

is the axis of the vertebrae closer to the vertical midline of the skull? Holding the 1st ruler in position, place another ruler along the base of the teeth. (*5*) In which skeleton is the angle formed by the rulers closer to a right angle? The **articulation** (jointing) of the skull with the 1st vertebra occurs around the **foramen magnum** ("big opening"). Through the foramen magnum the spinal cord connects with the brain. (*6*) In which skeleton is the foramen magnum closer to the posterior end of the skull? If you look closely, you will notice roughened areas and ridges on the bones. These mark places where muscles were attached. Examine the back of the skull. (*7*) In which skeleton is there a greater area (in proportion to skull size) for muscle attachment?

Examine the vertebral column. (*8*) Which skeleton has the greater number of vertebrae? (*9*) In what portion of the column does the number of vertebrae differ? (*10*) In general, which skeleton (in proportion to its size) has the thicker vertebrae? (*11*) How do the vertebrae in the region of the hip girdle differ in the human and the cat? Observe the vertebral column from the side. (*12*) Ignoring the vertebrae of the neck and tail, in which skeleton does the vertebral column form a single arch?

Now consider the appendicular skeleton. The posterior legs are attached to the **pelvis.** This is a set of bones that, in adults, have grown together. (*13*) In proportion to its size, which skeleton has the heavier pelvis? (*14*) Is the pelvis articulated with the vertebral column, or are the 2 structures fused together?

The forelegs, or arms, in humans, are attached to an anterior girdle. This girdle is made up of 2 broad, flat **scapulas** (shoulder blades), 2 collarbones, and a **sternum** (breastbone). (*15*) In which skeleton are the bones of this girdle more closely associated? (*16*) How are these bones attached to the vertebral column? (*17*) With respect to their attachment to each other, how do the bones of the anterior girdle differ from those of the pelvis?

Compare the bones of the human hand with the bones of one of the cat's front feet. (*18*) In which skeleton are the bones of the **digits** (fingers and toes) longer in proportion to the total length of the appendage? (*19*) In which skeleton is the inside digit articulated in such a way that it is **opposable** to (can be pressed against) the other digits?

Compare the cat's posterior appendages with the human's. (*20*) In which skeleton is the knee joint in normal standing position closer to a 180° angle? Consider each leg to be made up of upper leg, lower leg, and foot (including toes). (*21*) What fraction of the length of the upper leg does the length of the foot equal? (*22*) Which animal normally stands on its toes, with its heels raised from the ground?

DISCUSSION

The following questions may help you interpret your observations and organize your thoughts.

(*23*) What nonskeletal human characteristic is implied by your answer to item *1*? Items *2* and *3* are related to a visual charac-

teristic found in many primates. (*24*) What is that characteristic? Observations reported in items *4* to *7* are concerned with structural adaptations that support a relatively heavy head in an upright position. Assume that the structure of distant human ancestors was somewhat like that of the cat. (*25*) What mutations in that structure would have been changes favorable to the development of a large brain? Of upright posture?

(*26*) In a cat, where is most of the weight of the anterior part of the body supported? (*27*) Where is the anterior weight supported in a human? (*28*) How do items *10* to *13* relate to items *26* and *27*?

(*29*) Judging from the structure of its anterior girdle, do you think a cat could easily support its weight on its forelegs? (*30*) Can a human being? Of course, persons moving in an upright position do not need to support their weight on their arms. But they have the same kind of strong anterior girdle that many primates use in moving about through trees. (*31*) How is this structural characteristic an advantage to humans, who walk upright on the ground?

(*32*) How is the position of the legs in a person who is poised to start a race similar to the normal position of the posterior appendages in a cat? (*33*) What advantage does this position have for athlete and cat? Try to stand 5 minutes in this position. (*34*) What disadvantage does it have for us?

(*35*) In a paragraph, summarize characteristics of the human skeletal system that are related to the upright posture of humans.

FOR FURTHER INVESTIGATION

Aristotle described humans as "featherless bipeds." The adjective was necessary because birds also are entirely bipedal. (Aristotle, of course, knew nothing of dinosaurs, some of which were bipeds, or of kangaroos.) Using a mounted skeleton of a pigeon or a chicken, make a comparison with the human skeleton.

PRIMATE INHERITANCE

People, monkeys, and apes are very similar in the details of their anatomy. They are therefore grouped together in the order Primates. Most primates are arboreal and possess structures and behaviors that relate to the arboreal way of life. This life is dangerous and demanding, and mistakes are likely to be fatal. Therefore, natural selection of adaptations to this life must be severe.

19—2 Steps in the locomotion of a gibbon. What adaptations does this animal have for arboreal life?

X 1/25

The digits of primates are well developed and give the animal a powerful grasp. Nails support the grasping fingertips. Epidermal ridges—which are what produce fingerprints in humans—help prevent slipping from tree limbs. In addition to being powerful, the digits are very sensitive. They can easily tell if a surface is crumbly or slippery.

Why is this an advantage for an arboreal animal?

The eyes of primates are directed forward instead of to the side, as in most mammals. Both eyes view the same object from slightly different angles. This allows the brain to perceive the object in three dimensions so accurate distance judgments can be made. The brains of most primates are exceptionally large compared with those of all other mammals except cetaceans. Primates have a sense of color that is lacking in most mammals.

Bearing one young at a time is the rule among primates, though twins are not unusual. An active arboreal animal cannot carry many offspring. To feed these young, a female primate has only two mammary glands. Young primates, unlike young horses or jackrabbits, are given much maternal care for a long time. Primate young cannot afford to learn all of their activities by trial and error.

19−3 A potto, primitive primate. What primate characteristics can you see?

Primates tend to be omnivorous. They consume many different fruits, seeds, insects, eggs, and young birds. They gather their food in social groups. They often communicate by vocal signals.

omnivorous [om NIV uh rus; Latin: *omnis*, all, + *vorare*, to eat]

HUMAN CHARACTERISTICS

People share some characteristics with all other primates. Some of these characteristics are similar to those of primates that are adapted to life in trees. Others are like those of larger

19−4 Arm positions and shoulder muscles appear similar for humans and many other primates. But human hip and leg structure is today unique. Our upright-walking stance has been shared only by hominids of the past. (See figure 10−26.)

anthropologists [an thruh POL-
uh justs; Greek: *anthropos*,
human, + *logos*]: scientists who
study humans

Refer to figure 4–9 as you read
this section.

primates that live mostly on the ground. ***Anthropologists*** find it
difficult to describe clearly the *biological* differences that distinguish human beings from other primates. The following discussion describes a few distinguishing characteristics.

Structure. The outstanding structural distinction of humans
is their upright position. In this position they stand, walk,
and run on their hind legs. This ability involves many anatomical modifications. Human legs are longer than human arms.
Knees are locked for striding. Feet have high arches, and big
toes are in line with the other toes. A human foot is well adapted for walking or running but not for grasping.

The upright position leaves human hands free. Our hands
can manipulate complex objects such as tools and musical and
writing instruments. While sitting, other primates also have
great skill in handling objects. But they cannot carry objects easily because they use all four appendages in locomotion.

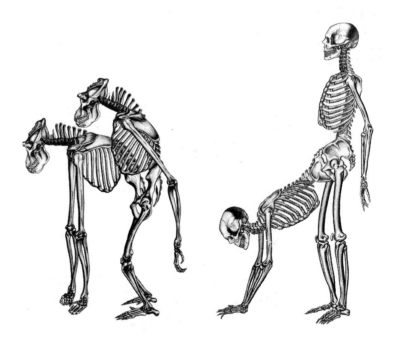

19 — 5 Skeletal proportions
and postures of gorilla and
human.

The upright position is also related to the pivoting of the
head on the top of the spinal column. This allows humans to
look straight ahead when they are standing. Also, in this position the large human brain is supported by the spinal column.

Humans have very large brains. In modern humans the
volume of the brain cases is 1,200 to 1,500 cc. The volume of a
chimpanzee's brain is 350 to 450 cc. There is, however, no exact
relation between brain size and intelligence. Individuals with

the largest brains are not necessarily the brightest. But the large human brain certainly reflects a great ability to learn.

Another difference between humans and lower primates is the shape of the head. The human head has a vertical face and a less projected jaw. There is a distinct chin and a prominent nose with an elongated tip. Also, the lips have an external mucous membrane. Canine teeth in humans are no more prominent than the other teeth. The small canine teeth permit the molars to grind plant material with a circular motion. The large canines of other primates restrict the jaws to a simple crushing motion that requires great jaw strength.

Another important characteristic is the distribution of hair on the human body. This varies somewhat in different human populations. Most human individuals have long hair on the head; males of some populations have heavy beards. Over the rest of the body there are varying amounts of visible body hair. Humans are actually as hairy as apes, but most of our hairs are so small and light that they are difficult to see. At the bases of all four appendages are special patches of hair. There is still much speculation about the adaptive meaning of this hair distribution.

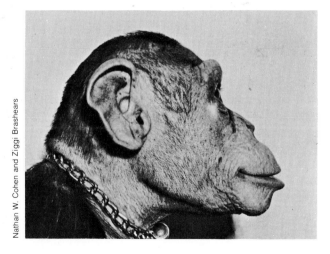

Nathan W. Cohen and Ziggi Brashears

19–6 Facial features of a chimpanzee.

Physiology. Physiologically, humans are not very different from other mammals, especially other primates. Humans, however, have no definite breeding season. Their reproductive activity can occur at any time of the year, unlike reproduction of most other mammals. Because of the artificial shelters in which humans live, their offspring can be protected from harsh weather in any season.

Why is this an advantage in medical research?

In most organisms the physiological processes weaken at the onset of old age. This weakening provides an opportunity for predators or parasites to eliminate an individual. It is difficult to determine the natural life span of most organisms from specimens held in captivity. This is because animals in zoos and aquariums lead protected lives. Some data on possible length of life have been obtained, however. Only the large tortoises are known to live longer than humans. The *average* life span of humans is probably longer than that of any other animal. It seems that this results only partly from better care and protection. In addition, human physiology is adjusted to a long existence.

But what about plants?

Is there a physiological limit to the human life span? If you think so, can you find any information about it?

19–7 Two long-living organisms. The tortoise may live more than 100 years, while the bristlecone pine may live 4,000 years or longer.

Denver Museum of Natural History

Gordon E. Uno

People need a long time to grow up. This is true no matter how we define "growing up." Many animals are independent from the time of hatching or birth. Most mammals other than humans require at least a few weeks or months before they can care for themselves. In the meantime they must be nourished by the mother's milk. Among the great apes, for example, the young need perhaps two years to become independent. A human child depends *completely* on adults for six to nine years. Partial care (even in primitive societies) is necessary for some time after that.

Humans reach reproductive age at about 14 years. The apes reach this age at about 10 years. Most other mammals—even those with long life spans—are able to reproduce at a much earlier age. Full skeletal development in humans is reached in about 22 years; in the apes, in about 12 years.

Behavior. Physiological characteristics help to define human beings as clearly as do structural characteristics. Behavioral characteristics, however, are also important. As an individual, a person is often helpless—despite a large brain. Imagine the plight of a person alone in the forests of Europe during one of the ice ages. He or she probably would not have survived long. Normally, however, people are not alone; they are social animals. Of course, there are other social animals. But insect societies are not really comparable to those of humans. And societies in other mammalian species, even in the apes, are not as highly organized as even the simplest human societies.

But there are cases in which a human has survived for a long period of time alone. Can you explain one?

See page 521.

19−8 A primitive family group of the present— Bushmen of southwestern Africa. Social behavior is important to survival in their harsh, arid environment.

Laurence K. Marshall

Much that is characteristic of human societies can be traced to the long period of growing up. During this period of dependency on parents, children are woven into the social group. Also during this time, the experience of one generation is passed to the next. Thus the same discoveries need not be made anew by each generation. In this way, knowledge accumulates within the group.

The transfer of knowledge depends on communication among individuals. Human beings may communicate by gestures. These are, however, usually just a substitute for language, or are used for emphasis. Human language is more complicated than other forms of communication. Language sets us apart from other animals. It is much more than just a system of cries and calls. Language depends on unusual capabilities of the human brain and the human vocal cords. Yet, we have

Chimpanzees and gorillas cannot speak words in human languages because of their vocal cords. To find out how well they can communicate with humans in sign language, look into Problem 3 at the end of this chapter.

How might you try to investigate the origin of speech?

no knowledge of how or when speech began. The languages of "primitive" people living today throw little light on the early stages of language development. Many such languages are more complex than our own. But there can be no doubt that talking is an important part of human social behavior.

19—9 Deaf people communicate using a language of finger and hand signs.

Investigation 19.2   HUMAN BLOOD GROUPS

INTRODUCTION

The substances that are the basis for the human ABO blood groups (page 601) are a human physiological characteristic. As with other such characteristics, this one is not clear-cut. Blood of apes contains substances that are chemically similar to those in human blood.

The major problem in blood transfusion is the clumping of red blood cells. Clumps of red cells cannot pass through capillaries, and these tiny blood vessels become clogged. If many capillaries are clogged, the circulatory system is blocked. Death may result.

MATERIALS
(per team)

anti-A serum
anti-B serum
70% isopropyl alcohol
monocular microscope
2 forceps
glass-marking crayon

(per student)

microscope slide
disposable sterile lancet
several cotton balls
sheet unlined white paper
2 toothpicks

In the ABO system of blood types, there are two **antigens** (which are proteins) that occur on red blood cells. These are called "A" and "B." Two **antibodies** called "anti-A" and "anti-B" are found in the plasma. The clumping of the red blood cells results from a reaction between an antigen and an antibody. The blood of different people contains different combinations of these two substances. The following combinations occur: People with A on their red cells have anti-B in their plasma. Those with B on the red cells have anti-A in the plasma. Those with *both* A and B on the red cells have no antibodies in the plasma. Individuals with *neither* A nor B on the red cells have both anti-A and anti-B in the plasma.

PROCEDURE

1. With the glass-marking crayon, draw a line across the short axis of a microscope slide, dividing it in half. In the upper left corner of the left half, write *A*. In the upper right corner of the right half, write *B*. Place the slide on the sheet of paper.
2. Wash your hands thoroughly. Using forceps, dip a ball of cotton in alcohol. Scrub the tip of a finger (on your left hand if you are right-handed, on your right hand if you are left-handed). Allow the alcohol to dry.
3. Use a sterile, disposable lancet to make a small puncture in the tip of your finger. (*Caution: A quick, light, but firm thrust is all that is necessary.*) Wipe off the 1st drop of blood with a dry ball of cotton. Place a small drop of blood in the middle of each half of the slide by touching your finger to the slide. Cover the puncture with a ball of cotton soaked in alcohol, but continue working. (Hold the cotton in place with the thumb of the same hand for 5 minutes.)
4. Immediately place a drop of anti-A serum on the drop of blood on the *A* half of the slide. (Serum is plasma from which fibrinogen has been removed.)
5. Use a toothpick to mix blood and serum.

Be careful to mix them within a very small area. Break the toothpick and discard it.
6. Place a drop of anti-B serum on the drop of blood on the *B* half of the slide. Use a 2nd toothpick to mix this blood and serum. Break the toothpick and discard it.
7. Compare the reaction on each side of the slide with those shown in figure 19–10. Check your observations by examining the slide under low power of a microscope.

DISCUSSION

Clumping on:	Blood type is:
Side A only	A
Side B only	B
both sides	AB
neither side	O

(*1*) What is your blood type? (*Note: There are a number of factors that may produce errors in this test. Only the results obtained by an experienced technician are satisfactory for medical purposes.*)

On the chalkboard tally the blood types of everyone in your class. Other classes will do the same. Total the tallies of all classes and calculate the percentage of each type. (*2*) Why are individual errors in blood typing not likely to have much effect on the percentages of blood types when the data from all classes are combined? (*3*) In your student population, which type occurs most frequently? (*4*) Least frequently?

(*5*) Name the red-cell and plasma substances in your blood. Large numbers of "foreign" red blood cells are introduced in blood transfusions. But the introduced plasma is quickly diluted in the plasma of the recipient (the person who receives blood). (*6*) Describe what would happen to your circulation if you were given a transfusion of Type A. (*7*) Of Type B. (*8*) Of Type AB. (*9*) Of Type O. (*10*) Describe what would happen to the circulation of individuals of each type if you were the **donor** (the person who gives blood).

(*11*) With respect to blood types, can your biology classes be considered a random

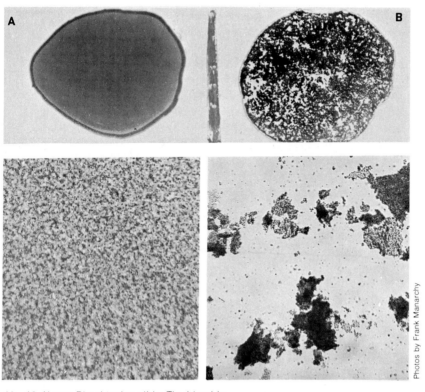

Photos by Frank Manarchy

19–10 *Above:* Blood-typing slide. The blood is Type B. *Below:* The same samples as seen with a microscope.   × 650

	A	B	AB	O
London, England	43	8	1	48
Paris, France	42	12	6	40
Berlin, Germany	43	14	6	37
Montana (American Indian)	76	0	0	24
Republic of Zaire, Africa	30	29	10	31
Peking, China	25	34	10	31
Tokyo, Japan	38	22	10	30

sample of the population of your community? Explain. Regardless of your answer to item *11*, assume that the percentages derived from the pooled class data represent the percentage in your community. Compare them with the percentages in the following samples:

(*12*) Explain similarities and differences between your percentages and these.

unique [yew NEEK; Latin: *unus,* one]: unlike any other

HUMANS ARE UNIQUE

Our species has all the basic characteristics of living things. There are few structural and physiological characteristics that clearly separate us from other existing species. Yet it is quite obvious that in some ways, such as communication by means of language, we are very different from every other living thing. We are unique.

This uniqueness is based on behavior and accomplishment. It lies in the human way of life, in our culture. The word "culture" is used by anthropologists to cover all human knowledge. Culture describes all the human ways of doing things that are passed from one generation to another by teaching and learning. Our uniqueness comes from the vast bank of information that our species has built up and shared among its members through the years.

Physiologically, we are animals. It is not easy, however, to separate the animal from the cultural human. In fact, the separation is impossible. Everything we do is affected by our culture. We eat, for example, because, as animals, we have to have food. But whether we eat oysters, rice, ham, grasshoppers, potatoes, or spaghetti depends on our cultural attitudes toward these things. The physical aspect of humans has modified human culture. On the other hand, human cultures have modified human biology and evolution, as well. In the study of humans then, there is a broad overlap between the biological and the social sciences.

CHECK YOURSELF

A. On what bases do taxonomists classify humans as a mammalian species?
B. What structural characteristics of primates are related to an arboreal habitat?
C. How does human anatomy differ from that of apes?
D. Why is a breeding season not a necessary adaptation for humans?
E. How does the life span of humans compare with that of other organisms?
F. How is the slow development of a human being related to culture?
G. In what ways are humans different from all other animals?

HOMINID HISTORY

When Charles Darwin published *The Descent of Man* in 1871, no science of paleontology existed. At least one fossil primate skull was known, but remained unidentified. Nothing found with this heavy-boned skull indicated the creature's way of life. It was only a mysterious skull, unearthed in 1856 in the Neander Valley of Germany. Small wonder that Darwin's book was highly speculative. And small wonder that people confused a modern primate family—apes, the Pongidae—with the unknown primitive ancestors suddenly being discussed by readers of Darwin's latest book.

hominid [HOM uh nid]: classified in the same taxonomic family with humans

Pongidae [PON juh dee]

Hominidae [hoh MIN uh dee]

The family Hominidae and the family Pongidae are separate. Humans are the only living species in the Hominidae. This entire taxonomic family has been set aside for human beings and whatever upright-walking primates are discovered from fossils. Fossil skulls along with backbones and hip girdles are enough to make this determination. But to go further and say that an upright-walking species known from fossils was *human* requires more than this. Here paleontologists are helped by anthropologists. Any evidence found with the fossils is carefully noted. The evidence that anthropologists seek is:

1. broken or intact stone tools
2. collections of bones from food animals (indicating that food killed elsewhere was brought to a home site and shared)
3. charcoal from campfires
4. carvings or art on cliff and cave walls
5. graves (indicating a burial custom)

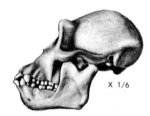

19–11 Skull of *Dryopithecus*, a Miocene primate.

Do you agree with these guidelines for determining whether fossil primates were human? Why or why not?

The older the fossils, usually the less the evidence found with them. Crude stone tools alone do not necessarily indicate humans. Several modern primates other than humans occasionally use stones as battering tools. Numbers 1 and 2 in evidence together are classified *tentatively* as human. No other animals are known to share food other than with their own offspring — at least not usually. Numbers 1 and 2 in evidence along with any *one* of Numbers 3, 4, or 5 are accepted as definite human evidence.

Dryopithecus [dry oh PITH uh-kus]

Among the oldest fossil primates known, from Miocene times, are those of the genus *Dryopithecus*. Fossil evidence from two continents is still scanty, but indicates that these individuals probably did not walk upright. They may or may not have been ancestral to any or all of the modern primates — we simply do not know.

Ramapithecus [RAH muh pith-uh kus]

Somewhat later, in the early Pliocene, *Ramapithecus* fossils are known. There are interesting differences between *Ramapithecus* and *Dryopithecus*, suggesting a possible line of primate descent. But, this hypothesis awaits more fossil evidence.

Eugène Dubois [dew BWAH]: 1858–1940. Dutch physician and paleontologist

In 1887 Eugene Dubois was looking for fossils in Java. Rich fossil beds were known there, and Dubois was looking particularly for human fossils. As it turns out, he found them. But his fossil discovery proved to be older than he had hoped. A number of crude stone tools but nothing else occurred with the fossils. Dubois was cautious and did not use the genus name *Homo* (human). Instead he named the fossils *Pithecanthropus erectus*.

Homo [HOH moh]

Pithecanthropus erectus [pith-uh KAN thruh pus ih REK tus]

Raymond Dart was an anatomy professor in South Africa. One day in 1924 he began studying some of the fossil-bearing rocks from a quarry near Johannesburg. There were pieces of a skull in one rock. Dart carefully removed the pieces and put them together. The completed skull, in some respects, looked like that of a five- or six-year-old child. Dart named the fossil find *Australopithecus africanus*. After four years of work, he succeeded in separating the jaws so that the teeth were fully revealed. They were remarkably like those of a human child. Dart also studied the position of the foramen magnum, the hole where brain and spinal cord met. From this evidence he felt certain the creature had held its head upright as humans do.

In 1929 hominid fossil remains were discovered in China. During the next 12 years parts of more than 40 individuals were dug up from a cave floor near Peking. Many stone tools chipped like a chisel on one edge were with the fossils. The fossils themselves were remarkably like Dubois' discovery. Over the next 50 years similar finds have been made on every continent except the Americas, Australia, and Antarctica. Evidence of food-sharing as well as tools is widespread. The fossils range in age from 200,000 years to 1,500,000 years or more. With the most recent, charcoal in tended fire pits has been found.

Meanwhile, the *Australopithecus* finds also have been expanded. Mature individuals of *A. africanus* have been unearthed. Bones of the hip girdle and upper legs confirm what Dart only suspected from the fossil child's foramen magnum. *A. africanus* stood and walked upright. These hominids also used crude tools. Moreover, a second species of *Australopithecus* emerged. Larger than *A. africanus*, it is also distinguished by a bony ridge running from front to back on top of the skull. Both of these species appear to have lived in Africa more than 2,000,000 years ago, and to have become extinct more than 1,000,000 years ago. The species of larger individuals, *Australopithecus robustus*, also walked upright and used crude tools.

Louis and Mary Leakey, their son Richard, and Don C. Johanson, working together and separately, have enlarged still more upon each of these fossil histories. The Leakeys have found the oldest fossil skull known of the Java and Peking types, but in East Africa. They have also found more individuals of both *Australopithecus* species. They have worked at Olduvai gorge in Tanzania, and near the shores of Lake Rudolph and Lake Turkana. Near Lake Rudolph they found a skull, and part of another, that are the oldest human-appearing skulls known. The almost complete skull (No. 1470) is more then 2,200,000 years old. But it was not found with tools, bones of shared food, or other cultural evidence that indicates it was human. Identification must await future discoveries. Johanson, working in Ethiopia, has found a whole fossil group of homi-

19–12 A pebble tool. Such crude instruments have been found with the remains of *Homo erectus* (page 676). Is the use of tools a distinctively human characteristic?

Smithsonian Institution

19–13 Skull of *Australopithecus*. Hominid fossils are usually fragments. Note the restored parts of this one.

Australopithecus africanus [ostray loh PITH uh kus af rih-KAH nus]

Australopithecus robustus [roh-BUS tus]

Louis S. B. Leakey: 1903–1972. British (born in Kenya) paleontologist

Mary Leakey. See page 338.

Richard E. F. Leakey: 1944—. Director, National Museums of Kenya

Don C. Johanson: 1943—. American paleontologist

Olduvai [OLE duh vy]

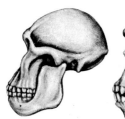
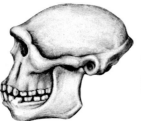
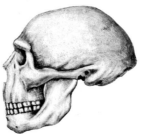
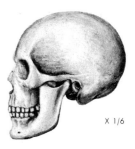

X 1/6

Australopithecus   *Homo erectus*   *Homo sapiens neanderthalenis*   *Homo sapiens sapiens*

19–14 Reconstructions of some hominid skulls. Can you see any characteristics that might distinguish *Homo* from *Australopithecus*? That might distinguish *Homo sapiens* from *H. erectus*?

Homo erectus [HOH moh ih-REK tus]

Homo sapiens [SAP ee unz]

subspecies. See pages 648–650.

Homo sapiens neanderthalensis [nee and ur thawl EN sis]

19–15 Artist's reconstruction of heads of some hominids. The reconstructions begin with fossil skulls (*above*). The methods used are those by which victims of homicides are given facial reconstructions for identification, when only skeletal remains have been found.

nids dated at 3,000,000 years old. These fossils are still being studied.

THE GENUS *HOMO*

Using the guidelines on page 674, paleontologists and anthropologists have concluded that a human species, *Homo erectus*, lived in Java, China, Africa, Europe, and the Near East from 1,500,000 to a few hundred thousand years ago. In Africa these people coexisted and probably competed with two similar species that were more closely related to humans than to apes — *A. robustus* and *A. africanus*. Only *Homo erectus* used fire, and this was only toward the end of its occupancy of Earth. Apparently our species, *Homo sapiens*, was descended from *H. erectus*.

The 1856 Neander Valley skull is more recent than *Homo erectus*. Additional fossil discoveries have associated these Neanderthal people with all five of the guidelines on page 674. They lived in the open, in caves, and in skin tents, throughout Europe and the Near East. Today they are classified in our own species, as the subspecies *Homo sapiens neanderthalenis*. They became prominent as *Homo erectus* gave way to *Homo sapiens* at some time between 150,000 and 200,000 years ago. Remains of mixed bouquets of flowers have been found on their graves.

X 1/6

Australopithecus   *Homo erectus*   *Homo sapiens neanderthalensis*   *Homo sapiens sapiens*

MODERN HUMANS

Much remains to be discovered about Neanderthal peoples, especially their sometimes heavy bony structure. At the beginning of their occupancy of Europe and the Near East, they coexisted with *Homo erectus*. At the end, some 100,000 years later, they coexisted with our own subspecies, *Homo sapiens sapiens*, the Cro-Magnon peoples. Thus the Neanderthals bridged ancient and modern humans.

Cro-Magnon [kroh MAG nun]: after the Cro-Magnon cave, in France, where remains were discovered

Cro-Magnons and Neanderthals both had brains of larger average size than our own. The Cro-Magnons also looked like us. They lived in the same places Neanderthals did, from 25,000 to 50,000 years ago. They made beautiful cave paintings in full color. They engraved delicate designs on bone and ivory tools. They flaked artistically beautiful stone tools. Only the discovery of agriculture and metal tools distinguished later peoples from the Cro-Magnons.

The prehistoric time span characterized by the use of tools such as these is called the Stone Age.

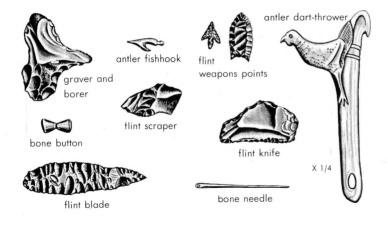

graver and borer

antler fishhook

flint weapons points

antler dart-thrower

bone button

flint scraper

flint knife

X 1/4

flint blade

bone needle

19–16 Some drawings of actual tools of primitive (Stone Age) *Homo sapiens sapiens* of North America. The people who made these tools lived somewhat later than Cro-Magnons.

CHECK YOURSELF

H. Why are the living apes (the Pongidae) inappropriate to consider as human ancestors?
I. What evidence would be necessary to classify skull 1470 and similar finds as human?
J. On what evidence did Dart base the conclusion that *Australopithecus africanus* was a hominid?
K. What have the Leakeys contributed to the study of human ancestry?
L. What are the apparent relationships of the fossils from Java and China (Peking) to each other and to modern humans?
M. How did Neanderthals differ from modern humans?
N. How are Cro-Magnons similar to existing humans?

VARIETIES OF MODERN HUMANS

All living hominids form a single biological species, *Homo sapiens*. There is much evidence that the most diverse varieties can and do interbreed and produce fertile offspring. Yet populations of the human species differ considerably in appearance. For example, there is a great range in size. The tall people of the upper Nile River average 1.78 m in height, while Pygmies of the Congo forest average only 1.42 m in height. Skin color ranges from very dark to very pale. There are wide differences in the texture and distribution of visible hair on the body. The shape of the skull and facial features, such as nose and lips, also differs.

19–17 A young Masai tribesman of Kenya, Africa. The Masai are all very tall. These people live near the upper Nile River.

Manert Kennedy

BSCS photo

19–18 *Above:* The Mongoloid eye fold. *Below:* An eye without the fold.

People wander about extensively. Thus gene flow among human populations has been much greater than among populations of other organisms. However, mass migrations of humans have occurred mostly during the last 500 years. Before then there was a rough correlation between geographical areas of the world and variations in certain human characteristics. In other words, human varieties showed geographical patterns, just as do varieties of other organisms.

Originally Europe and western Asia were inhabited by rather light-skinned people with thin lips. The males had heavy beards and abundant body hair. Head hair was either straight or wavy. In eastern Asia the human population had yellowish or yellow-brown skin. These people had brown eyes; very little facial and body hair; straight, black head hair; and a fold in the upper eyelid (figure 19–18). In Africa, south of the Sahara, the common traits were dark skins, very curly head hair, relatively thick lips, and wide noses. In Australia the native people were somewhat similar to Europeans. Their head hair was curly, and the males had thick beards and abundant body hair. Their skin, however, was generally quite dark. In America the original population was similar in some ways to that of eastern Asia, but the eye fold was less developed.

From these sets of traits, some anthropologists have recognized five human varieties. They are the Caucasoid, Mongoloid, Negroid, Australoid, and (sometimes) Amerind populations. But wide transition zones link each (except the Australoid) to the others. Further, many subdivisions can be

Caucasoid [KAW kuh soid; Caucasus, a mountain range in southeastern Europe, + Greek: *eidos*, form]
Mongoloid [MON guh loid; Mongolia, a region in central Asia, + *eidos*]
Negroid [NEE groid; Spanish and Portuguese: *negro*, black, + *eidos*]
Australoid [AWS truh loid; Australia, + *eidos*]
Amerind [AM uh rind]

19–19 Examples of variation in some physical characteristics among humans.

Photos from BSCS by Carlye Calvin

Bill Farrell

Photos from BSCS by Carlye Calvin

made within each of these groups. Some anthropologists have named as many as 30 human varieties.

The classification of human populations into five varieties correlates well with geographical distribution. This does not, however, necessarily mean that the characteristics of populations are adaptations to a region or a climate. From northern Europe southward into equatorial Africa, there is a cline of skin pigmentation, from very light to nearly black. Is this because dark skin allows body heat to escape, while light skin does not? Is it that unpigmented skin allows the formation of adequate vitamin D in the cloudy north-European climate? Does pigmented skin reduce the chance that too much vitamin D will be produced by the skin of Africans? Is it that dark skin protects against cancer in equatorial sunlight, while no such protection is required in northern regions? Or might it be a combination of two or more of these? In the Americas, Indian populations inhabit an area as large as that spanning Europe to Africa. But there is remarkably little change in skin color throughout this large range. It is obviously easier to ask questions about the complexities of human characteristics than it is to answer them. What can definitely be said is that all existing human varieties have been successful in coping with the environments they have encountered. If they had not been successful, they would not exist today.

There are many curious facts of distribution. One is the similar-looking Pygmy people in Africa and in the Philippine Islands.

vitamin D: a substance required for bone formation. Some can be synthesized by action of ultraviolet light on substances in skin. Too much can be injurious.

Does this necessarily mean that any one, or all, will cope with future environments? Explain.

CHECK YOURSELF

O. Why do biologists say that all existing humans are a single species population?
P. What characteristics are used in attempts to distinguish varieties of *Homo sapiens?*
Q. How does the simple classification of human populations correlate with ancient geographical distribution?
R. What biological explanations can be given for the pole-to-equator cline in skin coloration from northern European to African human populations?

Investigation 19.3   BIOLOGICAL DISTANCE

INTRODUCTION

Anthropologists use gene frequencies as a basis for classifying human populations. They refer to the degree of similarity in the gene frequencies of two or more populations as *biological distance.* The more similar the gene frequencies of two populations, the less the biological distance between them.

Conversely, the less similar the gene frequencies, the greater the biological distance.

An American biochemical anthropologist proposed a human classification system based on frequencies of the genes that determine blood types. There are several advantages to using blood types for this purpose. First, the ways in which the blood-type genes are inherited are well known (page 601). Second, the blood type of an individual does not change with age or with changes in environment. Third, natural selection does not seem to cause any rapid changes in the frequencies of blood-type genes. Therefore, present frequencies indicate to some extent how human populations have mixed with one another in the past. Fourth, blood types are rather easy to determine from blood samples taken for various medical purposes. So, data for a large number of individuals representing many human populations are readily available for study.

In this investigation you will consider the following questions: To what extent are three selected North American populations genetically related to each other? How do the migrations of human populations affect gene frequencies? How can the mixing rate of two different populations be calculated?

PROCEDURE

The 4 blood types, A, B, AB, and O, are determined by allelic genes, I^A, I^B, and i. Figure 19–20 shows the frequencies of the 3 alleles in an Eskimo population inhabiting Barrow, Alaska; in the Indian population of British

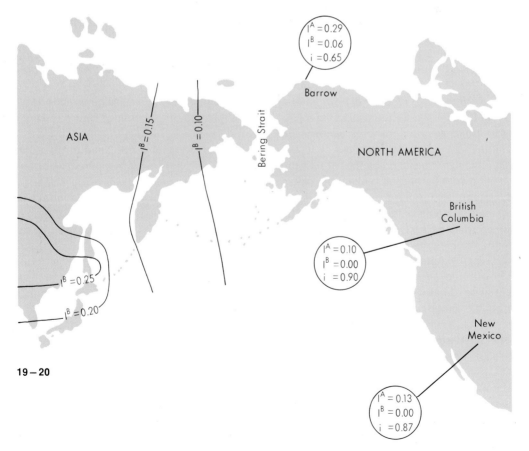

19–20

Columbia, Canada; and in the Navajo population of New Mexico. These gene frequencies have been calculated from the blood-type frequencies found in samples of the populations. (1) Do you think these three human populations should be classified as one variety or as three? Explain your answer.

Examine the data. (2) On the basis of the I^A gene frequencies, which two populations are most alike? (3) On the basis of the I^B frequencies, which two are most alike? (4) On the basis of the i frequencies, which two are most alike? (5) Would you now classify these three populations in a single human variety? Explain your answer.

Look again at figure 19–20. It shows the frequency of the I^B gene in Asia. (6) As you move westward and southward into Asia from the Bering Strait, what happens to the frequency of the I^B gene? (7) As you move eastward and southward in North America from the Bering Strait, what happens to the frequency of the I^B gene?

Over much of central Asia, the frequency of I^B is 0.25 to 0.30. Westward from central Asia into Europe, the frequency declines (figure 18–18). Several hypotheses account for this situation, but we shall consider only one. Briefly, this hypothesis states that at first the population of Asia had all 3 alleles. It states that Europe and America were populated from central Asia. The hypothesis also assumes that the first emigrant populations from the Asian homeland either lacked the I^B gene or lost it along the way.

How could an interbreeding population lose a gene? Loss by selection seems highly improbable. Blood types apparently have neither selective advantages nor disadvantages. The Hardy-Weinberg principle (pages 634–635) states that gene frequencies remain constant. That is true if, in large interbreeding populations, neither mutation nor natural selection occurs. But what about small populations—the kind very probably involved in early human migrations?

Consider a hypothetical human population with ABO blood-type genes distributed in the following frequencies: 25% I^A, 10% I^B, and 65% i. Suppose it is a very small population of only 50 persons per generation. Of course, each individual has 2 genes for blood type. According to the Hardy-Weinberg principle, then, we should expect to find among the 50 children of one generation 25 I^A, 10 I^B, and 65 i genes. Yet, from your experience in penny-flipping and genetics experiments, you know that you don't always get exactly what is expected on the basis of probability. In penny-flipping, you expect to get heads as often as tails. But if you flip a penny only 10 times, you might obtain 9 heads and 1 tail—or even all heads or all tails.

You might find similar results in a small population of people. Instead of getting expected results, you might find that purely by chance there were 28 I^A, 4 I^B, and 68 i genes. If this occurred, what should we expect in the next generation? We would expect a repetition of the new frequencies—28 I^A, 4 I^B, and 68 i. Of course, in a third generation the frequencies might by chance return toward the original ones. But they might result in a further reduction of the I^B gene in the population. This might even happen several times, until the I^B gene disappears from the population. Then it could never return unless reintroduced by mutation or by immigration of I^B genes in individuals coming from some other population.

This process of change in gene frequency is called **genetic drift.** Thus, the first small populations of *Homo sapiens* to reach Europe and America may have had genes I^A and i only. (8) What blood types could they have had? According to the hypothesis, other populations emigrating from central Asia later reintroduced the I^B gene into American and European populations through interbreeding. Consider the difficulties of primitive travel. (9) Where would you expect these later emigrant populations to be most numerous? Least numerous?

Consider the I^B gene frequencies. (10) Which of the North American populations shown in figure 19–20 probably has had the most recent genetic contact with populations of Asia? The frequency of the I^B gene is 0.00 in the Basque population of southwestern France. (11) On the basis of the I^B gene only, what can you say about the biological distance between the Basques, the natives of central Asia, and the Navajos? (12) Does this mean that the Basques and the Navajos represent one variety? Why, or why not?

Now, for a study of the *rate* of gene flow from one population to another. Two populations with the following characteristics are needed: Both populations must be large. They must differ markedly in the frequencies of alleles at one or more loci. The traits determined by these genes must be easily and precisely identifiable. And, of course, the populations must interbreed. All of these characteristics are found in the Caucasian (Caucasoid) and black (Negroid) populations that have come into North America during recent centuries.

The genetic trait best suited for this study involves another blood characteristic. In 1940, in a series of experiments, the blood of rhesus monkeys was injected into rabbits. Material from the blood of these rabbits caused the red blood cells of some people to clump. Such persons are said to be "Rh positive." ("Rh" for "rhesus monkey.") Persons whose red blood cells do not clump are "Rh negative." Further study showed that the Rh blood types are genetically more complex than the ABO types. Among the genes involved is one that has been symbolized **RH^O** This gene can easily be identified, and its frequency differs greatly in the two populations that you are considering.

In black populations of Africa, the frequency of the **RH^O** gene is about 0.60. In Caucasian populations of Europe, it is about 0.03. In the American black population, it is about 0.44.

(13) What is the difference between the frequencies of the **Rh^O** gene in the African and European populations? (14) In the African and American black populations? The amount of mixing between the Caucasian and black populations in North America may be expressed as a percentage. (15) To do so, divide your answer to item 14 by your answer to item 13. Multiply by 100.

The year 1625 may be taken as the beginning of the genetic mixing between Caucasian and black populations in America. The frequency of the **Rh^O** gene among the American black population was obtained from data gathered about 1950. (16) Assuming an average generation length of 25 years, how many generations of mixing could have occurred? (17) On the basis of this number of generations, what was the average amount of mixing per generation?

From calculations like this—crude though they may be—anthropologists can estimate the biological distance between populations, the routes of human migration, and the rates at which genetic differences among populations change. And from these studies anthropologists can deduce some aspects of the biological history of humans.

PROBLEMS

1. In which of the following activities would a human most likely excel over all other species of animals?

running
swimming
throwing a ball
shooting a bow

high jumping
distance jumping
climbing a rope
hitting a tennis ball

Summarize the ways in which human physical achievement is superior to that of other animal species.

2. Why are tropical forests poor sources of fossil evidence? Consider both the conditions for fossilization and the conditions for finding fossils.

3. Language is considered an important part of human social behavior. Several researchers have claimed that chimpanzees can also learn to communicate with symbols. Check the *Readers' Guide to Periodical Literature* for articles on this subject. What evidence do researchers present to indicate that chimpanzees can use language as humans do? What additional evidence is needed? Try to design experiments to test for the missing evidence.

4. Assume that pre-humans resembled *Homo sapiens* in lacking a breeding season. How would their social organization differ from that of a wolf pack in which there is a definite breeding season?

5. Make a list of human characteristics that have been used to describe varieties of humans. Which of the characteristics in your list are best suited for describing these varieties as subspecies of humans? Why are blood groups particularly useful in describing subspecies of humans? Why

are characteristics of skull shape less useful? Which of the two is easier to use in studying subspecies of humans from past geological time? (See "Suggested Readings" below.)

6. On September 23, 1789, 9 Englishmen and 17 Tahitians left Tahiti and sailed to Pitcairn. Pitcairn is an isolated, uninhabited island in the South Pacific. For 24 years they and their descendants had no visitors. Since then, their contacts with the rest of the world have been few. The effects of this isolation on both biological and social evolution are described in H. L. Shapiro, 1976, *The Heritage of the Bounty*, rev. ed., AMS Press, New York. Can you find any evidence of random genetic drift among the Pitcairn Islanders?

7. Consider the factors that bring about death among people in modern urban and suburban environments. Include factors that kill individuals before, during, and after the age of reproduction. Consider also factors that reduce health or impair development, and factors that reduce fertility or the survival rate of offspring. Speculate on the possibility that these factors could cause changes in characteristics of future human populations.

SUGGESTED READINGS

Asimov, I. 1979. *How Did We Find Out About Our Human Roots?* Walker, New York. A readable account of the development of our current knowledge of human history.

Cavalli-Sforza, L. L. and W. F. Bodmer. 1978. *The Genetics of Human Populations.* 2nd ed. W. H. Freeman, San Francisco. A leading reference on human population genetics.

Edey, M. A. 1972. *The Missing Link.* Time-Life Books, New York. A well-illustrated review of primate history and genetic relationships.

Howell, F. C. 1973. *Early Man.* Time-Life Books, New York. A well-illustrated review of human ancestors.

Leakey, R. E. and R. Lewin. 1977. *Origins: What New Discoveries Reveal About the Emergence of Our Species and Its Possible Future.* E. P. Dutton, New York. Despite a cumbersome title, an interestingly written, up-to-date review of human fossil evidence.

Patterson, F. 1978. Conversations with a Gorilla. *National Geographic*, October, pp. 438–465.

Chapter 20

Humans in the Web of Life

YOUR GUIDEPOSTS

In this chapter you will have an opportunity to explore these questions in biology:

- What were some ecological relationships of primitive humans?

- Do these ecological relationships differ for present-day humans?

- What limits the population of the earth?

- What are the main biological problems facing us today?

- How can we attempt to solve these problems?

THE WEB OF LIFE: A SUMMARY

Many chapters ago your study of biology began with a rabbit and a raspberry bush. From that beginning you learned about the contrasting roles played by plants and animals in the maintenance of life on the earth. Plants capture energy from sunlight and transform it into chemical energy. Animals eat plants or other animals and convert chemical energy into heat. Eventually the chemical wastes (CO_2 and H_2O) produced by all organisms are again converted by plants into energy-rich molecules.

Chemical energy follows a network of feeding patterns in the biosphere. This network is the web of life. Ultimately it links together every organism on Earth. Microorganisms, rabbits, raspberry bushes, and human beings are all tied together.

The web of life, the flow of energy, and the cycles of chemi-

20-1 Humans in the web of life.

cals have persisted through the past two or three billion years. During this time, the characters in the web of life have undergone many changes. Mammals have largely replaced reptiles as the great herbivores and carnivores. Reptiles earlier had replaced amphibians. Before amphibians, life did not exist on land, only in the seas. But even there food webs existed.

Two evolutionary changes are of major significance. The first of these is the origin of green plants. Before green plants arose, life was confined to the water—safe from the lethal ultraviolet rays in sunlight. Once green plants appeared, there existed a mechanism for using sunlight to build complex molecules and also for producing oxygen. Oxygen absorbs ultraviolet rays. As oxygen accumulated in the atmosphere, life on land became possible. The presence of oxygen permitted the development of cellular respiration as it exists today (Chapter 12).

The second major event was the origin of *Homo sapiens*, of human beings. The remainder of this chapter will be devoted to a discussion of the role humans play in the web of life. This discussion should make clear why the origin of humans also must be regarded as a major evolutionary event. The discussion will involve the human population, the role of the human intellect, and the consequences of our use of natural resources and power.

ECOLOGICAL HISTORY OF *HOMO SAPIENS*

HUNTING AND GATHERING

When Cro-Magnon women and men appeared about 25,000 years ago, they were hunters and food-gatherers. They were particularly efficient predators because they used tools, were intelligent, and formed social organizations. The human niche in a biotic community was not unlike that of wolves. For instance, human tribes could find food in a variety of communities, just as do wolf packs. However, any one tribe (like any one pack of wolves) was probably part of a single community — because of territorial behavior.

Cro-Magnon beings. See page 677.

20–2 A few food-gathering cultures still exist. Here, a person is fishing in the Northern Territory of Australia.

Tom Stack and Associates

Though early humans ate meat, they frequently gathered berries, fruits, and nuts, and dug up roots. Among today's few remaining hunting and food-gathering tribes, about 5 km² of land are needed to support each person. Based on this figure for land need, the total human population 25,000 years ago must have been small. It also must have been scattered in widely separated groups.

The estimated population of the earth at that time is five to ten million. See *Scientific American*, September, 1974, p. 41.

Early humans were undoubtedly hosts for many kinds of parasites. Because the human population was scattered, however, conditions were not favorable for the spread of contagious diseases from one person to another. The most common diseases were probably those involving pathogens with alternate hosts. Yellow-fever virus, for example, can live in both people and monkeys. The virus is passed between them through forest mosquitoes. Thus, if monkeys are numerous, people can be infected no matter how scattered their population may be.

Primitive hominids were gatherers of many plants, predators on some animals, and sometimes prey to other animals. Hominid ecological relationships changed little for perhaps a million years. Indeed, in some remote parts of the world they continued unchanged well into the 20th century.

Do you know of any hunting-and-gathering people of the present day?

AGRICULTURE

At least 15,000 years ago hunters formed a mutualistic relationship with species of the genus *Canis*. From this relationship came what is probably the earliest domesticated organism — the dog. With the help of dogs in hunting and perhaps with the invention of nets for fishing, some human groups began to form permanent settlements.

A by-product of settled life — the garbage dump — must have appeared almost at once. Wild plants were gathered for food and were brought into the settlement. People may have noticed how a discarded portion of a wild plant sometimes grew into a mature plant on their dumps. They may then have dug up favorite wild plants and transferred them to their settlement. At any rate, sometime before 10,000 B.C. people began to cultivate plants. That is, people assisted the growth of plants and harvested their products. This was the beginning of the *Agricultural Revolution.*

In what other way might wild plants appear on dumps?

What kind of ecological relationship is this?

The principle ecological result of the long period known as the Agricultural Revolution was a shift of humans' role in the biosphere. Humans had been merely *members* of a biotic community. Now they became *makers* of biotic communities. From a biological point of view, agriculture is the art of managing ecosystems. The principal aim of agriculture is to establish the simplest possible community composed of one crop (plant or animal) and humans. A wheat field should contain only wheat, which is directly used by humans. A pasture should contain only plants that are edible by consumers useful to humans, such as cows or horses. These simple communities are unstable, however. A *single* parasite species can wipe out an entire agricultural community.

Remains of domesticated animals are found only in agricultural communities. Except for dogs, remains of domesticated animals are never found with the remains of hunters. Perhaps during times of drought, wild herbivores invaded fields and gardens. Such animals could be captured, penned up,

V-DIA Scala

20–3 A primitive digging-stick agriculture can affect the biosphere only slightly (southeastern Asia).

and, later, used for food. Raising the young that were born to the captured animals must have happened eventually. Thus, domestication of cattle, sheep, and goats may have begun.

Well after the beginning of the Agricultural Revolution, some primitive farmers discovered that not only could animals be eaten—some could be put to work. Of course such animals had to be fed. But, directed by humans, the animals' energy allowed a farmer to grow far more food than the animals ate. An-

This discovery apparently was never fully made in ancient America. What domesticated animals did American Indians have, and how were they used?

20−4 Animal-powered agriculture. Plowing rice fields with water buffalo in India. Compare its effects on the biosphere with the effects of the kinds of agriculture shown in figure 20−18.

Manert Kennedy

What do you think may have been a source of mechanical energy used even earlier by humans?

other niche was formed in what we may call the "community of domesticated organisms." Humans thus took a long step in *applying energy other than that of their own muscles to the modification of their environment.*

Agriculture demanded a foresight much greater than that needed for hunting. Farmers had to adjust their activities to the changing seasons. They had to store products between harvests. They had to be willing to work without immediate reward. However, agriculture also provided increased leisure time. During planting, cultivating, and harvesting, a primitive farmer worked longer hours than a primitive hunter. But once the harvest was in and the surplus had been stored, there was usually a period of weeks or months when farmers did not need to worry about their next meal. A hunter, on the other hand, had no such leisure time.

Stored agricultural products, in greater quantities than needed by farm families, also supported ancient craftspeople. They gathered with farmers in primitive urban centers. The Agricultural Revolution thus permitted the formation of large groups of people. As a result, the development of *culture* was encouraged.

INDUSTRY

What physical characteristic enables humans to make more use of tools than do other animals?

Even the most primitive *Homo sapiens* were skillful in tool manufacture. The Agricultural Revolution, however, brought about an increased demand for tools of many new kinds.

Stone was originally the basic material used by toolmakers. In many parts of the world, people discovered how to use metal. Smelting of metals required large amounts of heat. Fuels became important for use in the industry of toolmaking as well as for warmth and for cooking food. Humans began to look at all the things in their environment as resources—things that they could turn to their own use.

But all kinds of resources are not found in all places. Flint was an especially desirable kind of stone for toolmaking. Even in the Stone Age, it was traded from one group of hunters that had the stone to another that did not. Resources (such as flint) from distant lands increased the size of each human group's ecosystem. To tie the widespread human ecosystems together, trading became a necessary occupation. Tin from Britain was sent to the eastern Mediterranean 3,000 years ago. In America, Indians in Alabama obtained copper from near Lake Superior long before Europeans arrived.

Villages grew into towns of artisans and traders. Food for the townspeople came through trade with nearby farmers. Crowding encouraged the spread of contagious diseases. Many of the biological wastes of the townspeople were scattered on fields and in water. Microorganisms and parasitic worms found their way easily from one person to another.

artisan: a person trained in some special skill of the hands

Why could most foods not be traded as distantly as metals?

20–5 Today, townspeople throughout the world obtain their food from both nearby and distant farmers. They may buy the food or trade goods or services for it.

Tom Moen

The *Industrial Revolution* is said to have begun in the 18th century. It was a revolution in the sense that for the first time humans applied energy to *reshape* ecosystems. Humans had long used the energy of animal muscle, the energy of wind and water, and the simple heat energy of fire. But it was the discovery of ways to channel heat energy through machinery that allowed humans to change the environment in a revolutionary way. In the 1940's humans succeeded in using for the first time a source of energy that is independent of the sun—atomic (nuclear) energy. And our search for new sources and uses of energy continues today.

ENERGY AND POWER: SOME NUMBERS

Modern society is built on energy. Energy runs the factories and the farms. Energy transports farm produce and manufactured goods. Energy is used to obtain more energy. For instance, nearly one-third of the energy obtained from coal is used for mining more coal.

20−6 An electric-powered truck loaded with coal rolls through the mine.

Consolidation Coal Co.

What is the source of this energy? Originally it was the sun. That is, the energy in coal, oil, and natural gas is chemical energy that was stored by green plants nearly 300 million years ago. These plants were not completely decomposed. Over many centuries, their remains (which still contained some of the plants' energy) were formed into fossil fuels. These fuels are now being consumed within the United States at a rate of 500 billion kg of coal, 5 billion barrels of oil, and 590 trillion cubic meters of natural gas per year. The Alaskan oilfields are believed to contain 10 billion barrels of oil. This amount would meet the total energy demands of the United States for just one year! About 85 percent of all our energy comes from fossil fuels. And usually this energy can be used only once.

demands. As used by economists, this means what a person is willing to pay for.

Marathon Oil Co.

20 – 7 An oil well off the coast of Louisiana. Every year our natural resources are more difficult to obtain.

A second source of energy is water. Indirectly, the sun's energy is the source of this waterpower. Sunlight causes evaporation of water from the oceans, lakes, and rivers. This water later falls as rain or snow to fill the rivers and reservoirs that drive the hydroelectric power plants. At present less than 5 percent of all energy used in the United States comes from natural and artificial waterfalls. The total amount of hydroelectric power will not increase much in the next few years. Nearly all the rivers that can be used for generating hydroelectric power have already been dammed.

Nuclear energy is the only major type of energy whose source is not the radiant energy of the sun. At the present time, about 7 percent of the total electrical energy generated in the United States comes from nuclear power plants. In these power plants atoms of radioactive materials are split, releasing huge amounts of energy. Because our supply of fossil fuels is dwindling so fast, the importance of nuclear energy may increase in the future.

Can you name any other power resources?

Sacramento Municipal Utility District

20 – 8 The Rancho Seco Nuclear Generating Station (California). What advantages and disadvantages does this have compared with a steam-power plant?

A modern industrial society needs a continuous supply of energy. In Chapter 12 you learned that energy is required to create order. Without the continuous input of energy, disorder grows, molecules become randomized. Through the use of huge quantities of energy, modern societies maintain a complex, highly organized structure. If these societies are to be maintained and enlarged, larger sources of energy must be found.

How have *your* demands for power increased in the past two years?

20 – 9 A solar-powered home. Sunlight pours through the glass panels in the roof. The sun's energy is used to generate electricity that can be stored in batteries until needed.

Grumman Corp.

THE DEMAND FOR RESOURCES

power: force that can be put to work

Energy provides the power for an industrialized society. Raw materials provide for its structure. Some of the demands for coal, oil, and natural gas were mentioned earlier. To appreciate the magnitude of our demand for resources other than fuels, consider this brief list of metals used in the United States in 1976.

Copper	1,500,000,000 kg
Lead	500,000,000 kg
Nickel	18,000,000 kg
Iron	80,000,000,000 kg
Aluminum	4,500,000,000 kg
Uranium	10,000,000 kg
Zinc	450,000,000 kg

bauxite [BAWK syt]: the ore from which aluminum is extracted

Energy is required to get pure metal. For example, every kilogram of aluminum extracted from bauxite requires from 13 to 18 kilowatt-hours of electrical power. The production of 4.5 billion kg of aluminum alone obviously requires a huge amount of electricity.

The United States has about 5 percent of the world's population. Yet our citizens consume about *40* percent of the world's resources. Americans have a longer average life span and greater resource-consumption rate than most other people on the earth. Because of this, one American uses about the same amount of resources as 25 people in India.

20 – 10 City of New York at night. How much energy does your city or town use every day?

Resources are frequently classified as *renewable* and *nonrenewable.* Renewable resources are those that can be continuously replaced such as living things, air, water, and soil. Wood and lumber are renewable resources because they are obtained from living organisms. On the other hand, the fossil fuels that we burn cannot be used again as fuels. Even though the carbon remains in the atmosphere or is picked up again by plants the carbon cycle is too long for any possible management. So, such substances as fossil fuels are classed as nonrenewable resources.

What are some other nonrenewable resources that are important to an industrial culture?

20 – 11 Wasting a resource that is difficult to renew (New Jersey).

Erich Schmidt from Alpha

USDA – Soil Conservation Service

Careers in Biology:
A Wildlife Conservation Officer

She rides the mountain trails on a horse (**A**) and hikes through the sage and pines. She watches for foxes, coyotes, bighorn sheep, deer, and elk on the tops of rugged ridges. Grouse scatter as she walks along a trail—and for Susan Smith, it's all in a day's work.

Susan is a wildlife conservation officer with the Colorado Game and Fish Department. Her district covers about 1,500 square kilometers surrounding the town of Vail, in the Rocky Mountains (**B**).

Susan's days are busy, and not all of her work is fun. In addition to patroling her district, Susan conducts hunter-safety courses for young people and keeps the local license agents aware of the latest regulations. Law enforcement is a big part of Susan's job, especially during the hunting season. "There are hunters all over," she explains, "and they're not all doing the right thing." In the summer she hikes to some of the high mountain lakes and creeks (**D**).

Manert Kennedy
Manert Kennedy

A. Susan takes good care of her horse. She often rides it through the difficult terrain of her conservation district.

B. To cover the 1,500 square kilometers of her district, Susan drives her truck, rides on horseback, or hikes. Often she starts out in the truck but ends up on foot because of the terrain.

C. Along mountainous highways, motorists often see "deer crossing" signs. Whether a driver wasn't paying attention or the deer was in a state of panic and confusion, the result was the same—death.

D. Part of Susan's job is stocking mountain streams with trout.

E. Susan has to distribute game maps to stores. She must also haul building materials to sites where fences and live traps are being constructed.

There, she stocks streams and lakes with various species of trout.

Game management is another important part of Susan's job. During late winter and spring, she tries to determine the kinds, numbers, and sex ratios of the wild animals in her district (**C and F**). From her counts, Susan makes recommendations about how many permits should be issued and how long the hunting season should be in the fall. "We have to have hunting," she points out, "because so many predators have been driven away." In this area, building developments have disturbed or destroyed much of the natural habitat available to wildlife.

Susan is pleased that more people are becoming concerned about the natural environment and endangered species. She has been able to influence decisions about development in her district. For example, county governments agreed with her suggestion that light industry should not be built on land that is winter range for elk herds (**G**).

Susan's educational background is in zoology and wildlife biology. Her experience in hiking, backpacking, camping, and riding horses has been of great value in her work. She feels that anyone who is planning a career in wildlife conservation, national parks or sanctuaries, fisheries, or other fields related to the environment needs a knowledge of "all-around basic biology." Susan's natural love of the out-of-doors inspired her to seek a job in conservation.

F. Susan sets a live trap to catch and band deer. Banding makes it possible to study the sizes and movements of deer populations.

G. To prepare a winter grazing area for deer and elk, Susan digs ditches to divert a mountain stream into a meadow.

All organisms, as you learned in Chapter 2, produce more progeny than can survive. Because many progeny will die unless space and nutrients are supplied to them, we can—with care—harvest the adults for our own use. The young then will take the place of the adults.

Harvesting requires care, however, because of several problems. If we harvest too many, the resource—passenger pigeons, tuna fish, whales, or trees—will, in time, become extinct. Passenger pigeons, for example, became extinct in 1914 when the last one died in a Cincinnati, Ohio, zoo. The species had been overhunted by market hunters.

Overharvesting is a great temptation, and humans interested in financial profit are faced with a dilemma. Careful harvesting of a resource, such as commercial fish in a lake, means that only a small percentage of the adults can be taken. This percentage, however, can be taken year after year, virtually "forever." In this manner a financial profit can be gained every year. If, however, the entire population of fish were to be harvested in a single year, a very large profit may be earned—but only once. In the long run, careful conservation will result in a greater total profit, but one that is spread over a period of many years.

American Forest Institute

20–12 Block harvesting of Douglas firs (Oregon). The bare areas are quickly reseeded by the surrounding forest. Compare this with cutting of large areas (clear cutting), as shown in the upper right photograph, page 725.

Another problem we must face in harvesting is the recycling time required for some renewable resources. For example, trees such as redwoods require a very long time for the renewal process. Use of such a slowly recycling resource can be considered overharvesting, and its classification as renewable is somewhat misleading.

20–13 Another method of harvesting timber: selective logging (Michigan). Though 40 percent of the timber volume was removed here, the forest community was only slightly disturbed.

THE NECESSITIES OF LIFE

Human beings, like other living things, have certain basic needs. We all need food, water, and oxygen. To get these in a modern society requires energy and natural resources. Food is transported into large cities. Water for drinking, washing, and irrigation often is piped for thousands of kilometers. In some places local industries must take action to keep the oxygen supply clean and breathable. They use dust and soot collectors, and scrubbers in their smokestacks to remove noxious gases. Thus, the business of living is becoming expensive.

20–14 A water-treatment plant in New Jersey. Our technology allows us to treat and recycle water once used by humans. In this way water is renewed for human use.

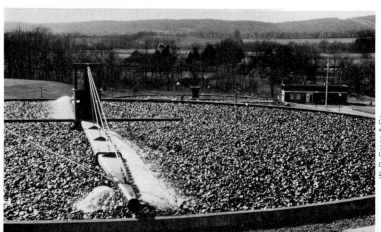

CHECK YOURSELF

A. Why was the evolution of green plants of significance?

B. What was the ecological niche of humans in a hunting-and-gathering culture?

C. What change in methods used by humans to obtain their biological energy first greatly changed their ecological niche?

D. What further discovery greatly increased human ability to cultivate fields?

E. Why was the rate at which culture developed probably greater in agricultural villages than in hunting camps?

F. How did the geographically unequal distribution of resources broaden the extent of human ecosystems?

G. What are the three main types of energy used in the United States?

H. How does the resource-use rate of Americans compare with that of other people?

I. Why must resources such as coal and oil be considered nonrenewable?

DEMANDS OF LARGE POPULATIONS

The number of people on the earth is increasing at a tremendous rate. Before the Industrial Revolution even the largest and most famous cities were scarcely more than what we would now call big towns. London, Paris, Vienna, Rome—each had fewer than 100,000 people. In 1650 all of England had only 4,000,000 people—almost half the present population of London alone.

Demographers are scientists who study the size, density, and distribution of human populations. They estimate that the number of individual *Homo sapiens* alive today is equal to 10 percent of the total number that have *ever* lived. You are presently one of more than 4,500,000,000 living human beings! We are not only numerous; we are also big. The 4.5 billion (4.5×10^9) of us require a large portion of the food consumed by all animal species.

Approximately 330,000 babies are born every day. About 130,000 people die every day. Since there is neither world immigration nor world emigration, the population of the earth increases annually by 73,000,000 persons. This is more people than now live in California, New York, Texas, and Illinois *together*.

demographers [dih MOG ruh-furz; Greek: *demos*, the people, + *graphein*, to write]

See figure 2–32.

Can you estimate the biomass of the living human population?

20–15 How many people can Earth's supplies of energy and matter support?

Increase of population is not something happening only in *other* countries. In 1979 the population of the United States was about 219,484,000. This was an increase of 39.5 million since 1960. Though birthrate is declining, the population increase continues.

Demographers have estimated that the average annual rate of population growth for the world was about 0.2 percent until a few hundred years ago. The growth rate began to rise sharply during the 18th and 19th centuries. In 1980 the growth rate was estimated at about 1.8 percent. If this growth rate continues, the present world population of 4.5 billion could reach 9 billion by the year 2020. This is a *doubling time* of only 40 years.

What would the doubling time be if the growth rate was 3.5 percent? 7 percent? 1 percent?

What has happened to the human species? The basis for the present world growth of human population is simply this: Natality exceeds mortality. Mortality was high in the early history of *Homo sapiens*. We, like primitive humans, still die—but we die later in life and from different causes. Long ago humans freed themselves from most of the dangers of predation. Now we have almost freed ourselves from pathogens. This freedom, however, is not enjoyed equally in all parts of the world.

What effect does postponing death to older ages have on a population?

Only a century has passed since Pasteur, Koch, and others discovered the causes of infection. In that time, great progress has been made in the control of infectious diseases, particularly those dangerous to infants. As a result, fewer individuals die in infancy now than before. In 1900, 162 out of every 1,000 infants born in the United States died in their first year of life. By 1978 this figure had been lowered to 13.6 out of every 1,000.

Figure 20–16 shows how the causes of death have changed in the United States. In 1900 the leading causes of death were influenza, pneumonia, tuberculosis, and diarrhea—all infections. By 1978 they were heart disease, cancer, and cerebral hemorrhage. None of these three are infections and all are chiefly diseases of the elderly. Diseases such as typhoid, diphtheria, and smallpox have practically disappeared.

diarrhea [dy uh REE uh; Greek: *dia*, through, + *rheein*, to flow]

hemorrhage [HEM uh rij; Greek: *haima*, blood, + *rhegnynai*, to burst]

NUMBERS OF DEATHS CAUSED BY:	1900	1910	1920	1930	1940	1950	1960	1968	1978
INFECTIOUS DISEASES									
influenzas and pneumonias	203	162	208	103	70	31	37	37	26.7
tuberculosis (all forms)	202	160	114	72	46	22	6	3	1.3
diarrheas and intestinal diseases	133	117	54	26	10	5	4	2	0.8
diphtheria	43	21	26	5	1	0.3	0.0	0.0	0.0
typhoid and paratyphoid fevers	36	26	8	5	1	0.0	0.0	0.0	0.0
syphilis	12	14	16	16	14	5	2	0.3	0.1
measles	12	12	9	3	0.5	0.3	0.2	0.0	0.0
whooping cough	12	11	12	5	2	0.7	0.1	0.0	0.0
scarlet fever	10	12	5	2	0.5	0.0	0.0	0.0	0.0
malaria	8	2	4	3	1	0.0	0.0	0.0	0.0
erysipelas	5	4	3	2	0.0	0.0	0.0	0.0	0.0
smallpox	2	0.4	0.6	0.1	0.0	0.0	0.0	0.0	0.0
NONINFECTIOUS DISEASES									
heart diseases	132	159	159	206	293	300	366	373	441.3
cerebral hemorrhages and thrombosis	72	76	82	81	91	100	107	106	179.1
cancer (all forms)	63	76	83	97	120	140	151	160	181.6
bronchitis	46	23	13	4	3	2	3	3	1.9
cirrhosis of liver	13	14	7	7	9	7	11	15	13.7
appendicitis	10	11	13	15	10	2	1	0.7	0.1
diabetes mellitus	10	15	16	19	27	16	17	19	18
kidney diseases	89	99	89	91	82	21	11	5	3.7
senility	—	26	14	10	8	13	12	13	14
congenital malformations	92	88	85	61	12	13	10	8	5.9
OTHER									
suicide and homicide	14	22	17	25	21	18	15	18	22.3
accidents	72	84	70	78	70	61	52	58	49.5
miscellaneous	479	264	202	196	186	205	139	143	132
all causes	1770	1498	1310	1132	1078	962	944	966	882.3

20–16 Causes of death in the United States (per 100,000 people).

Much of the decrease in fatal infectious disease has come about through the discovery of drugs and antibiotics. These chemical agents are effective against bacteria and other protists. Equally important in reducing infectious disease are sanitation and public-health practices that prevent the spread of pathogens. But not all infectious-disease problems have been solved. In many species of pathogens, individuals that are resistant to chemical agents now occur. The most susceptible pathogenic individuals have been killed. The more resistant ones, however, have survived and have multiplied, producing new resistant populations. This is an excellent example of natural selection.

A similar problem exists in the control of vector diseases. In the past, for example, we have controlled malaria by killing

susceptible [suh SEP tuh bul; Latin: *sub*, under, + *capere*, to take]: easily affected by mosquitoes with poisonous sprays. Through natural selection, however, most species of mosquitoes are developing resistance to many of these substances.

There are still many medical problems remaining, but one point is clear. Our increased ability to prevent disease has resulted in a decrease in mortality. This decrease in death rate has been greatest in the industrial countries. But we can easily transport medicines and teach sanitation methods. Increasing medical cooperation between countries is reducing mortality everywhere.

In Ceylon (now Sri Lanka) in 1947 there was an intensive campaign to control malaria. The annual death rate dropped abruptly from 20 people per 1,000 to 13 per 1,000. During the same period the birthrate increased slightly, from 38.4 people per 1,000 in 1946 to 40.2 in 1948. In 1962 the introduction of a measles preventative reduced by half the infant death rate in Upper Volta, Africa. Elsewhere, especially in industrialized nations, natality has declined. But in very few places has the decline in natality been as large as the decline in mortality.

Human population growth in the biosphere has been compared with the growth of a cancerous tissue in an organism. Cancerous tissue escapes growth controls and multiplies at the expense of normal tissues. Likewise, people are multiplying at the expense of the rest of the biosphere. There is a frightening possibility that we, with our increasing numbers, may multiply our way to destruction.

A comparison of figure 2–32 with your graph from Investigation 2.2 indicates a *possible* future. To project future population sizes, demographers have used methods similar to yours, and the *present* rates of mortality and natality. They have calculated that by 2560 A.D. there could be one person for every 5 m² of land surface on the earth—including forest, desert, tundra, and farmland. But a sharp population decline would probably come long before this time. Most demographers therefore think this projection will not be fulfilled.

SPACE FOR FOOD

Malthus considered food supply to be the limiting factor for the human population. At times in the past it certainly has been. At some time in the future, unless the population of people on the earth stabilizes for other reasons, the food supply will be limiting again.

At the moment, to most of us famine seems remote. Within industrialized nations, scientific methods have been applied to agriculture, and machinery has replaced laborers and animals. Both have greatly increased food production. In these nations

Photos by DeKalb AgResearch, Inc.

20–17 Geneticists have contributed greatly to the increase of food production. In two strains of corn (*left*) that have been inbred for several generations, many undesirable, recessive traits are homozygous. Crossing these strains makes the traits heterozygous, and the hybrid (*right*) is greatly improved.

famine is unknown and starvation is rare. In many of them, total agricultural output has increased even faster than has the population.

However, this is true only if we restrict our view to the food supply of present-day industrialized countries. In many places — as in much of Asia, Africa, and South America — the number of people to be fed is increasing much more rapidly than is the amount of food with which to feed them. An inactive person, well insulated from the cold, uses about 2,000 Calories per day. In many places an *average* of only 1,800 Calories per day per person is consumed — many individuals get far less. Much of the world lives under near-famine conditions. On the average, the daily intake of a person in the United States, on the other hand, is over 3,000 Calories.

But the number of Calories is not the only factor we need to consider in judging the nutrition of food. Even 3,000 Calories, if obtained entirely from corn bread or rice, do not nourish a person. Food is not only the source of energy but also of chemical substances. And humans require some specific substances. Vitamins and, particularly, certain amino acids that are rare in plant proteins are needed. Animal proteins have these amino acids in abundance, but animal protein is expensive. It is expensive in money and in energy. To give an American 3,000 Calories of food that supplies all required vitamins and amino acids, a farmer must raise 11,000 Calories in plant substance. Most of this goes to feed animals being raised for meat.

The number of persons living today is so large that each one has only one-half hectare of farmland available for growing his or her share of food. As the population increases, the amount of farmland per person will decrease. Most farmland in the United States is very productive. But high productivity can

hectare: 100 m²

20 – 18 Wheat harvesting (Nebraska). How does the energy used in this kind of agriculture differ in its ecological effects from that shown in figure 20 – 4?

The energy we invest in agriculture goes chiefly for the manufacture of fertilizers and pesticides and for transportation.

Why do new food-production methods depend on industrialization?

be sustained only by enormous inputs of energy. The energy invested in our highly mechanized agriculture exceeds the energy obtained in meat, cereals, and fruit. If available energy dwindles, this form of agriculture will decline as well.

SPACE FOR HOUSING

As we said in Chapter 15, many animals establish territories in which they live. For example, birds may establish territories that serve for both nesting and feeding.

Human beings also require space for living. For food production this space amounts to one-half hectare each. People who live in cities do not see their food territories. As long as food arrives regularly, however, someone must be tending this half hectare properly.

20 – 19 Often the search for open recreational space is in vain. Beaches are as crowded as are cities and suburbs (Waikiki Beach, Hawaii).

People require other space for living: a place for beds, tables, and chairs. The space demanded per family is increasing dramatically. Many city dwellers who once lived in apartments have moved into rural and suburban areas. Each house in these areas occupies about one-eighth hectare. Four houses occupy one-half hectare, an area capable of providing food for one person. In recent years, 400 hectares have been lost to new housing each year on Long Island, New York, alone.

The conflict between housing space and agricultural space is a genuine one. Real estate developers often prefer to build new housing on farmland because it is already cleared of trees and rocks. Very little housing is erected on rocky, unproductive land. Consequently, suburban housing often occupies land that once produced farm crops.

20–20 Human activities now change whole landscapes. A mixed forest-grassland begins to give way to new development.

SPACE FOR TRANSPORTATION AND INDUSTRY

The modern American landscape has been shaped largely by the private automobile. Widespread suburbs are possible only because each suburban family has one, and very often two, cars. Railroads once were the leading movers of food and manufactured goods. Today, however, they cannot deliver their cargo to widely scattered homes and shopping plazas. Trucks have become the means by which manufactured articles are shipped from factories to consumers.

The shift from urban to suburban living has caused a demand for a large, complex, highway system. This system requires space. Beneath the highways alone is enough farmland to feed a half-million people.

A second consequence of the population shift has been the shift of light industry out of the cities and into suburban areas. Most of these low rambling factories also are built on what was once productive farmland. These industries also must be served by highway transportation.

20–21 Many people use the mass-transportation facilities of a city instead of using their own cars.

Peter Gridley from Alpha

BIRTH CONTROL

The need for space becomes a problem only when there are many people who require the space. If available space is limited and a population grows, the carrying capacity for that species will soon be reached. When this happens, many individuals will suffer. Birth control has been used throughout human history to prevent local populations from reaching local carrying capacities. Many procedures and beliefs have been used to help control pregnancies. One is *abstinence* from sexual activity. Another is the *separation* of men and women for long periods of time. *Taboos* concerning menstruation and post-childbirth "cleanliness" lowered the birthrate in some cases. Finally, numerous *potions* and other natural substances were used to prevent pregnancies. Only by such practices could island populations, for example, maintain their productivity and still remain below the carrying capacities of their land.

abstinence [AB stuh nunts]: the act of doing without something voluntarily

taboos: things strongly forbidden by custom or religion

Sexual activity is a normal physical function that is distinct from reproduction. But it often leads to reproduction. Many people wish to, or must, limit the size of their families. Some wish to out of concern for the size of the world's population. Others must for medical or financial reasons. These people have sought modern, efficient means for preventing unwanted pregnancies.

Devices that prevent sperm cells from reaching ova in the oviduct can prevent fertilization. They are made of rubber and are designed for both the male (condom) and the female (diaphragm). Both are inexpensive and effective. The condom has the added advantage of providing *partial* protection against the transmission of the microorganisms that cause syphilis, gonorrhea, herpes, and other venereal diseases.

devices: things that have been designed to achieve some purpose

condom [KUN dum]

diaphragm [DY uh fram]

The intrauterine device (IUD) is a wire and plastic coil that is placed within a woman's uterus. It prevents the implantation of fertilized eggs in the uterine wall. Once inserted it can remain in place for considerable periods of time. These devices, however, have irritated or punctured the uterine wall in a small proportion of their users.

Biological knowledge of female reproductive cycles has led to the development of hormone-containing pills. These are probably the most widely used of all birth-control devices. One commonly used pill contains a mixture of progesterone and estrogen that imitates a pregnant woman's hormonal condition. This condition suppresses ovulation. Pregnancy is thus prevented. Unfortunately, interference with normal hormonal cycles may have serious effects on the health of some women who take these pills. Looking for more effective, less dangerous, chemical control of ovulation is still a very active area of research. The possibility of discovering a pill for men is included in this search.

effective [ih FEK tiv; Latin: *ex*, out, + *facere*, to make]: having a desired result

An existing birth-control technique for men is a process called a vasectomy. In this very simple operation the sperm-conducting tubes are cut or tied off. Following the first few ejaculations after a vasectomy, no sperm are released during intercourse. In women, the oviducts can be cut or tied off. This is called a tubal ligation. Both methods prevent pregnancy.

vasectomy [vuh SEK tuh mee; Latin: *vas*, vessel, + Greek: *ek*, out, + *tomos*, a cutting]

Perhaps the oldest of all techniques aimed at avoiding pregnancy is the "rhythm" method. Ovulation occurs about midway between menstrual periods. If intercourse is avoided for several days around this mid-period, sperm are less likely to encounter the ovum. Unfortunately, the human menstrual cycle is variable, and the rhythm method is the least reliable of all commonly used birth-control techniques.

Birth can be controlled by deliberate premature termination of pregnancy—induced abortion. This is done after the developing embryo has been implanted in the uterine wall. Induced abortion has been used to control population size, as in post–World War II Japan. An abortion, like any other surgical operation, places the pregnant woman in some (even though slight) danger. No surgery is entirely risk-free. Also, at least in most Western nations, more convenient and less traumatic procedures are available.

CHECK YOURSELF

J.   What is happening at present to the size of the human population in the world as a whole? In the United States?

K.   What does "doubling time" mean? What is the doubling time for the world's population?

L.   What changes have occurred in the principal causes of death in the United States during the 20th century?

M.   How does natural selection act as a factor in the control of infectious diseases today?

N.   How is the action of human organisms in the biosphere similar to the action of cancer cells in tissues?

O.   Why can't human food supply be considered only in terms of Calories?

P.   How is sexual activity different from reproduction?

Q.   What means are available at present to prevent pregnancy even though intercourse occurs?

HUMAN IMPACT ON THE BIOSPHERE

As we human beings have built cities and moved to suburbs, many of us have lost our sense of kinship with other humans and with natural ecosystems. In urban surroundings we find it difficult to realize that we are a part of the biosphere—*in* the web of life. After a year's study of biology, let us see if the questions encountered at the beginning of this course (review Investigation 1.1) mean more than they did then.

20–22 Humans simplifying an ecosystem.

Caterpillar Tractor Co.

SIMPLIFIED ECOSYSTEMS

Producing large crops with modern agricultual techniques requires much energy. To use machinery efficiently, single crops are planted over large fields. Thus ecosystems are simplified.

In such large, simplified, artificial ecosystems the effects of natural homeostatic mechanisms are reduced or eliminated. A field of corn or cabbage offers a splendid opportunity for consumers that eat these plants. (These consumers are *pests* to our way of thinking.) For example, the larvae of cabbage butterflies feed only on cabbage and a few closely related plants. Under natural conditions these butterflies must search through scattered vegetation to find appropriate plants on which to lay their eggs. In a cabbage field, however, they need spend no time in searching. All the plants are suitable. Such conditions are ideal for the multiplication of cabbage butterflies. The same principle applies to pathogens that cause plant diseases.

To control these pests and pathogens, many poisons have been used. The poisons, however, may destroy the natural predators of the pests. This increases the need for more poisons. Further, the pest organisms often develop new resistant varieties. So new kinds of poisons are required. The cycle is then repeated.

In general, then, high yield of human food per hectare is achieved only by use of many resources and at hidden ecological costs.

20—23 Cabbage butterflies and their larvae.

How does the term "pest" compare with the term "weed"?

Why might predator species be destroyed by poisons before the pests on which they prey?

See figure 18–10, page 633.

BIOCIDES IN THE FOOD WEB

Insecticides, herbicides, and other pesticides can be lumped under the term "biocides." Each year in the United States 400 million kg of biocides are produced. (An average of 0.5 kg per km^2 of insecticides alone are sprayed on nearly 2 million km^2 of United States cropland.) What is the fate of these 400 million kg of poison? Where do they go?

DDT can serve as an example. Other insecticides are known to behave similarly, as we have seen before with DDD (page 297). Marshes occupying the north shore of Long Island were sprayed with DDT to control mosquitoes. Later plankton and algae were found to have about 0.1 ppm (parts per million) of DDT in their tissues. The small fish, clams, and snails that ate these microorganisms had levels of DDT two to five times higher—about 0.4 ppm. Within organisms occupying the next level in the food web—eels, flukes, and minnows—the levels of DDT reached about 1.5 ppm. Among the species of the next level—ospreys, herons, and gulls—the levels of DDT reached 10 to 20 ppm. The concentration of DDT in the tissues of organisms increased nearly 200 times in moving up the food web. Some human beings, in keeping with their position in the web of life, contain some 15 ppm of DDT.

The DDT gets concentrated into fewer individuals in going up the food web. This is because a single consumer eats a large number of organisms at the next lower level in the food web. The greater the DDT concentration, the greater the physiological effects. Ospreys and pelicans are affected drastically by DDT. At one point, some populations became nearly extinct. Because of the DDT, these birds were not able to make normal, fertile eggs. No one expected that DDT and other such poisons would affect organisms far from the area of the spraying program. Today it is understood that persistent poisons will have precisely this effect.

Many newer pesticides, such as carbaryl, break down very rapidly and are not persistent.

ENDANGERED SPECIES

As human beings expand their activities, they occupy more land for their homes, automobiles, and industries. Their influence spreads over larger areas. This process destroys the habitats of many other species.

The smog of Los Angeles is killing trees of many species over wide areas in southern California. The needles of ponderosa pines gradually turn brown. Palm trees bear only a small tuft of fronds at their tops. Eucalyptus trees do not thrive.

In past decades butterflies were common, colorful natural displays. Now, in many regions of the country, they have become rare. Only one or two individuals may be seen per day rather than the profusion of species that once flitted everywhere. Cabbage butterflies are an exception. Despite attacks on them by DDT-spraying farmers, these butterflies are still common.

Drainage programs undertaken at one place prove to have profound effects on communities 50 to 80 km away. The Everglades represent such a delicate area. The ecology of the entire region depends on a slowly moving sheet of water that flows from north to south down imperceptible slopes. Drainage ditches constructed at the northern edge of the swamp have decreased the flow of water over the entire area. Many alligator holes, which helped to contain fires in the Everglades, have dried up. Fires are now more frequent in this national park.

Slopes are imperceptible because the average elevation in the Everglades is about 6 m.

For certain organisms, changes made in the environment by humans have been disastrous. On the average, one species of mammal has disappeared from the earth every year since 1900. Zoologists have compiled a list of 600 species of mammals that now seem in danger of extinction. Botanists list hundreds of plant species that are endangered in the United States alone. Extinction, of course, is nothing new. But industrialized nations

Hawaii oo

X 1/3

X 1/8

passenger pigeon

X 1/15

great auk

X 1/8

Carolina paroquet

X 1/10

dodo

X 1/34

white-tailed gnu

X 1/18

European lynx

X 1/34

Père David's deer

20–24 Some animals that have been completely or nearly exterminated through the activities of humans.

continue to alter entire ecosystems, and the rate of extinction is increasing rapidly.

What difference does it make that passenger pigeons and dodo birds have disappeared from the earth? Or that whooping cranes may disappear tomorrow? Cro-Magnon beings were probably quite satisfied when the last cave bear was killed. And there is certainly no place for brontosauruses in the vicinity of New York City. It may be difficult to argue a case for *every* threatened species, but there are good biological arguments against extinction in general. One of these arises from genetics. As long as wild populations exist, a vast resource of genetic characteristics remains available. But the extinction of each wild population erases its gene pool forever.

Another argument arises from the ecological principle that instability is a characteristic of simplified ecosystems. Although new species are evolving, speciation is usually a very slow process compared with the rate at which humans are capable of extinguishing species. So each time a species becomes extinct, the simplification of the world ecosystem is carried one step further. And the difficulty of maintaining a stable biosphere becomes greater.

Why usually?

X 1/14

20–25 Whooping cranes are the tallest of North American birds. Efforts to save this endangered species have received wide publicity.

CHECK YOURSELF

R. Why are large fields of single crops planted?
S. What problems arise in simplified, agricultural ecosystems?
T. What are "biocides"?
U. What difficulties have developed in the use of biocides such as DDT?
V. How have humans endangered the survival of other species?
W. What are the biological arguments for protecting species near extinction?

IMPACT OF HUMAN WAYS ON HUMAN BEINGS

Four hundred years ago an Indian on Cape Cod might have used the shell of a clam to make a hoe for cultivating corn. Or the Indian might have tossed it on the heap that had grown through the years around the camp. Thus the shell could be a resource for technology or a waste to be discarded. Four thousand years ago, Chinese farmers carefully collected human feces and spread these as fertilizer on their fields. Today American cities spend millions of dollars to rid themselves of human feces. These waste materials contain matter and energy that could be recycled and are, therefore, an unused resource.

pollutant. Recall the basic meaning of pollution from page 96.

All organisms produce substances that they discard into their environments. These wastes may accumulate to such an extent that they become harmful. They are then called pollutants. For example, wastes from seabirds that nest in colonies may kill surrounding vegetation. Humans discard not merely their biological wastes but a great variety of things that result from technology. The combination of the great number of humans and — in many parts of the world — their highly developed technology produces tremendous amounts of polluting wastes.

There are many kinds of wastes. These include sewage, garbage, plastic and glass containers, automobile-exhaust gases, chemicals from industry and agriculture, silt, smoke, radioactive substances, and even hot water. All have one basic effect: they make our environment less favorable to live in. Each acts in its own way. Each must be studied separately. But most of them interact with others, so the study of pollution, like all ecological studies, is complex.

BSCS photo by Robert Judy

20 – 26 Oil or gasoline spills can ruin miles of beaches or rivers. Each year thousands of birds such as this redhead duck are killed by oil or gasoline pollution.

SEWAGE, GARBAGE, AND JUNK

Sewage is made up of biological wastes that usually are flushed away in water. This water also contains soaps and detergents that have been used in washing. The disposal of sewage raises two major problems. Disease microorganisms, which usually are present in sewage, will be spread if the sewage is not treated to remove them. And the high organic content of sewage encourages the growth of decomposers. The decomposers, in turn, use up dissolved oxygen. The oxygen supply may become so low in a highly polluted river or lake that nearly all animal life dies.

detergents [dih TUR junts; Latin: *de,* from, + *tergere,* to wipe]: cleaning substances — usually, other than soaps

20 — 27 Garbage ready to be towed to sea for dumping (New York City).

Henry Monroe from DPI

Garbage once meant wastes from slaughterhouses. Later it included solid organic wastes, such as discarded foods from kitchens. Now it often refers to solid household wastes of all kinds, particularly containers — paper, metal cans and wrappers, plastics, and glass. Some wastes are quickly decomposable (biodegradable) such as lettuce leaves. Many, however, are slowly decomposable, such as paper. Others are almost indestructible, such as cans, plastics, and glass. In cities many metric tons of this mixture must be removed each day. And each day the problem of where to put it becomes greater Other solid wastes — junk — must also be removed. Junk includes items such as old mattresses, broken furniture, and worn-out refrigerators.

20 — 28 Accumulation of wastes in our environment. The problem of where to put our garbage is increasing.

Manert Kennedy

WASTES FROM FUELS

The burning of fossil fuels — coal and oil — has greatly increased the rate at which carbon dioxide is added to the atmosphere. Photosynthetic organisms have not used all of this CO_2. As a result, atmospheric CO_2 has increased about 20 percent in this century. CO_2 traps infrared radiation — heat rays — reducing the rate at which it escapes from Earth. On the other hand, CO_2 interferes only slightly with radiant energy arriving from the sun. The mean world temperature has increased by 1.6°C since 1900. Some ecologists feel that this increase may be explained by the increase of atmospheric CO_2.

What other processes add CO_2 to the atmosphere?

But effects of atmospheric pollution are not this simple. Offsetting the upward trend of mean world temperature in the early part of the century has been a *decline* of 0.3°C in the years since 1940. This too can be traced to pollution. Besides CO_2, burning fuels release into the atmosphere many tiny particles. These are often visible at first as smoke. These particles reflect solar radiation, which reduces the amount of energy that reaches the earth's surface. Thus, wastes from fuels have widespread effects on the biosphere.

Fossil fuels are not entirely compounds of carbon, oxygen, and hydrogen. They contain other elements also. And burning is not always complete. As a result, many kinds of gases besides CO_2 and water vapor are produced. Some of these are particularly noticeable in the waste gases from automobile engines. Among them are carbon monoxide and oxides of sulfur and nitrogen. All are harmful to most kinds of living things. Under certain atmospheric conditions these gases, together with solid

How does carbon monoxide affect a person?

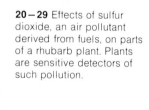

20–29 Effects of sulfur dioxide, an air pollutant derived from fuels, on parts of a rhubarb plant. Plants are sensitive detectors of such pollution.

USDA

particles and water vapor, accumulate in the air. Such an accumulation is called **smog.** It is especially likely to occur near large cities, where automobile traffic is heavy and wastes from burning other fuels are added to those from gasoline.

We humans have problems of fuel wastes—just as we have sewage and garbage problems. This is because there are so many of us and because we depend on a technology that uses such a vast amount of resources. Reducing air pollution *rates* has not improved conditions because it is offset by industrial and transportation growth.

What efforts have been made to reduce air pollution in your region during recent years?

RADIOACTIVE WASTES

In what other way may nuclear energy be used?

Nuclear energy is converted to electrical energy in power plants. Nuclear-power plants produce neither smoke nor chemically injurious gases. But they do produce radioactive wastes. Each year such a plant produces up to 80 million curies of radioactive wastes that pose a biological problem.

A substance giving off 1 curie, if placed in the middle of a football field, would make the whole field unsafe for a person—even for a few seconds.

Nuclear-power-plant accidents, such as the one that happened on Three Mile Island, can also release radioactivity. Such accidents are a constant concern. But the safety technology is continually being improved.

20 – 30 Radiation damage to a forest ecosystem (Brookhaven, New York). Organisms in an experimental forest are exposed to radioactive cesium-137 for 20 hours each day. Another forest in the area is used as a control.

The radioactive half-life of many of these wastes is thousands of years. They must, therefore, be kept away from living things for many generations. Where can they be put? At present they are stored in abandoned salt mines. This plan is less than perfect, because they could contaminate underground water. In addition, they might escape during accidents as they are transported from power plants, or in natural catastrophes involving the mines.

Can you suggest any other ways to dispose of these wastes?

TOXIC METALS

Solid metals make up a large percentage of garbage and junk. But many metallic elements are discarded as ions or as parts of complex molecules that are carried in air and water. Some of these substances — such as mercury, lead, zinc, and cadmium — are toxic to living things.

20–31 Recycling cans saves one of our limited resources — metal. It also helps to reduce the amount of garbage that must be placed somewhere.

Elemental mercury is sometimes dumped into rivers and lakes by industries. Certain bacteria are able to change elemental mercury to organic mercury compounds that are toxic. These are soluble in water. Taken in by aquatic producers, the toxic substances move through food webs. Other toxic mercury substances are used by farmers to prevent the destruction of seeds by fungi. These substances enter food webs through water run-off from agricultural fields.

Lead compounds improve the burning qualities of gasoline. These compounds get into the air by way of automobile-exhaust gases. Lead also enters the biosphere from industrial processes and from some kinds of paint. In experimental animals, lead compounds have affected brain development. There is also direct evidence that similar effects occur in children.

Can you suggest ways pollution by toxic metals might be reduced?

DRUG USE AND THE DANGERS

Over the past several thousand years, humans have discovered hundreds of substances that affect our physiology — *drugs.* Some drugs — penicillin, for example — are used because they interfere with the physiology of parasitic organisms. They help a host overcome a disease that the parasites cause. Other drugs change the physiology of the host itself. Many of these do so by affecting nerve endings. Particularly valuable are the drugs that physicians use in treating human nervous disorders.

In human nervous systems neurons shuttle messages back and forth. Messages usually are passed from one neuron to another across synapses. Chemicals secreted by synaptical nerve endings determine whether a neuron will "fire" and pass the message along. *Serotonin* inhibits neuron firing, while *norepinephrine* encourages it. Both chemicals are destroyed rapidly after they are formed. Their action, therefore, depends on constant production by the nerve endings.

Neuron firing will increase if the synthesis of serotonin is stopped. It also will increase if serotonin is destroyed as fast as it is formed or if the receptor sites for serotonin on the motor neurons are blocked. In these cases, the muscle attached to the motor neuron will receive the message to contract. On the other hand, if the synthesis of norepinephrine ceases, the motor neuron receives only inhibitory impulses and does not fire. The effect will be the same if norepinephrine is destroyed as fast as it is formed or if its receptor sites on the motor neuron are blocked. Under these circumstances, the muscle will not contract.

Some people are overactive and continually agitated. Their neurons are firing too often. **Tranquilizers** can be an effective treatment, but different ones act in different ways. One, chlorpromazine, blocks norepinephrine receptors. Another, reserpine, increases the rate at which norepinephrine is destroyed at nerve endings. Lithium compounds, long known for their tranquilizing action, prevent the formation of norepinephrine.

Other people are underactive. They tend to be sleepy and lethargic. These people respond to **stimulants.** One such drug, amphetamine, increases the release of norepinephrine from nerve endings. Iproniazid slows the breakdown of norepinephrine. Another stimulant drug causes norepinephrine to remain on its receptor sites on the motor neuron. This represents a standing order to fire. Still other stimulants interfere with synthesis or release of serotonin.

Although a prescription is not required to obtain alcohol, its effects are similar to those of many tranquilizers. If a large amount of alcohol is consumed, the drinker's judgment may be impaired. Alcohol can suppress self-criticism, and inhibitions learned from earliest childhood may be forgotten. Because alcohol is not changed by digestion, it builds up rather quickly at high levels in the bloodstream. It is broken down, very slowly, primarily in the liver. As alcohol is consumed, the drinker becomes less alert and less aware of the environment. Muscle coordination deteriorates, and the person may become

serotonin [ser uh TOH nun]

norepinephrine [nor ep uh NEF-run]

tranquilizers [TRANG kwuh ly-zurz; Latin: *trans*, across, + *quies*, quiet]

chlorpromazine [klor PROM uh-zeen]

reserpine [rih SUR peen]

amphetamine [am FET uh meen]

iproniazid [eye pruh NY uh zud]

very sleepy. Heavy drinkers may obtain one-half of their caloric needs from alcohol. But this limited diet reduces the intake of proteins, amino acids, vitamins, and other essential nutrients. Excessive consumption of alcohol may eventually impair heart rate or blood pressure. It may even cause permanent damage to the brain or liver.

Some drugs, such as caffeine and alcohol, were in common use long before there were physicians. Other, newer drugs have become what might be called "thrill" drugs. A few of these newer drugs create mental hallucinations. Most of them have little present use for treating disease. Further, their physiological actions are not well known. One that has received much study, lysergic acid (LSD), seems to attach to serotonin receptors. In this way, LSD interferes with all inhibiting effects. Therefore, all neurons affected by it are continuously set to fire. As a result, even very minor stimuli have very large effects. An organism under the effect of LSD seems to act in ways unrelated to its environment.

hallucinations [huh loos un-AYE shunz]: perceptions of objects that are not actually present

lysergic [luh SUR jik]

Prolonged use of drugs can lead to **dependence.** Frequent use of such a drug causes new metabolic pathways to form. Then the constant presence of the drug is needed to keep these pathways functioning. When such a physiological dependence has been established, withdrawal from the drug upsets the new physiological reactions. There usually is a painful process of reestablishing the original metabolic pathways. Unless careful medical supervision is maintained, death may result.

The human brain and its associated nervous system is by far the most complex network in the animal kingdom. Tranquilizers and stimulants can be valuable tools with which physicians can treat nervous disorders. Unfortunately, some people use these drugs without medical advice. To tamper with our complex nervous mechanisms is dangerous. And this is what a person does when he or she uses drugs that alter neural pathways. These pathways are the means by which a person learns to cope with the environment.

Nerve impulses, except for their frequency, are the same in all nerves. Interpretation of nerve impulses occurs in the brain. What might happen if impulses from the ear or tongue were shunted erroneously to the part of the brain normally responsible for sight?

LOOKING AHEAD

Biological and medical scientists have made spectacular advances during the past 25 years. The mechanisms of inheritance are known. The operation of the brain is largely — but still imperfectly — known. The manner in which the immune system works is largely understood — again, however, not completely.

A bioengineer is a scientist who combines the talents of a biologist and an engineer. Tiny control gadgets from space research laboratories and new materials from industry permit bioengineers to make many artificial organs. And no longer are these limited to eyeglasses, false teeth, and artificial limbs.

BIOENGINEERING

No one with poor eyesight complains about wearing eyeglasses (or contact lenses). Similarly, everyone who has had a faulty heart corrected with a pacemaker considers this invention significant. Elderly people unable to walk because of arthritis do not regard plastic hip joints as dangerous inventions. On the contrary, their pain in walking and standing is gone. They can once again lead normal lives.

A chronically ill person is suffering from a disease such as tuberculosis that is not acute, but lasts for a long time. A terminally ill person is suffering from an acute disease that, within the limits of our present medical knowledge, is known to end life rather quickly. Some forms of cancer, such as bone cancer, are examples.

Disputes arise, however, when lifesaving machinery is attached to those who are chronically or terminally ill. These machines were designed to help people survive brief emergencies. From your study of biology you know many things about yourself. The chemical composition of your blood serum is known. So is the function of your kidneys in removing nitrogenous waste, the role of your lungs in oxygenating the blood, and the response of your muscles to electrical stimulation. Bioengineers use this information to design and build mechanical equipment. Hearts can now be made to beat by electrical shocks. Or a mechanical heart can be attached to one of a patient's large arteries. A person's blood can be oxygenated in an artificial chamber. Or a mechanical respirator can be used. An artificial kidney can be attached to a patient's body to remove metabolic wastes from the blood. Glucose and other essential nutrients can be added to the circulating blood by means of tubes.

Questions about these procedures often arise. Should a terminally ill person be prevented from dying? Should anyone be forced to lie motionless, attached to numerous mechanical devices? Should a family's money be spent in keeping someone "alive"? How do physicians define death?

A number of answers have been proposed in response to these questions. None of the answers are completely satisfactory, but all are being debated. We will mention just two. First, terminally ill patients, if they are conscious, may themselves request that all mechanical devices be disconnected. Second, a 24- to 48-hour absence of electrical brain waves, as normally produced by conscious people, may be interpreted as "death." This is true even though individual organs are still biologically active.

GENETIC ENGINEERING

Genetic engineering consists of adding or exchanging "new" genes for "old" ones, functional genes for defective ones. Exchanges of genes have already been made among bacteria. And specific genes can be isolated from yeast and higher organisms (including humans) and transferred to bacteria. The *hope* of molecular geneticists is that specific genes can be obtained— from normal people or by gene-splicing—and transferred to the cells of genetically defective people. The cells with the transferred genes should then produce the chemical that the patient lacks. This type of genetic engineering resembles bioengineering. A defective or handicapped individual, having received suitable treatment, could live a more normal life.

Correcting a person's body cells does not correct that person's reproductive cells. The offspring of a genetically "cured" person would still risk inheriting the abnormality. For this reason, geneticists talk about transferring copies of normal genes into sperm and ova. Once more, some people find the thought of this procedure disturbing. At the moment, the genes carried by children are a random collection of those produced by their parents. With genetic engineering this randomness might be reduced.

EPILOGUE

The problems raised in Chapter 20 (and throughout the rest of the book) must be solved if life on Earth is to continue as we know it. These problems are interrelated. Therefore, their solutions are complex. But the solutions can't come through scientific investigation alone. The right questions must be asked, and facts must be obtained. After a discussion of the facts, *informed* citizens must make decisions. In the text and in your investigations, you have learned many facts and a number of relationships. The problems that await you as you grow up and leave the classroom are challenging. These problems will be constantly changing. The problems and their solutions will have profound effects on the earth. You *do* know that the earth is limited. And so you know that every action influences other actions. Land that is disrupted in order to mine coal, for example, is land on which food crops cannot be raised. Trade-offs are involved.

trade-offs: choices or exchanges; the giving up of some things in return for others. See page 295.

The many interdependent *global* problems include the population explosion, environmental pollution, and the distribution and use of energy and resources. These problems threaten, if not the survival of the human species, at least the quality of our lives.

Examine the conflicts shown in figure 20–32. Think about how you might resolve each one. Your answer, of course,

20—32 The power of humans to shape our environment may lead to continuing usefulness. Or this power may be directed toward waste, depletion, and ruin. Consider the choices shown here and in the world around you.

Choices of a very important resource—people.

Action Photo

Eve Arnold from Magnum

Choices in a grassland ecosystem.

Nebraska Game and Parks Commission

USDA—Soil Conservation Service

will depend on what you believe is important. Identify and examine as many consequences of each action as possible. Consider the trade-offs involved in each situation. (Strip mining, for example, pollutes streams while providing energy for industry. Farmland may be destroyed, but people are given mining jobs.) Finally, realize that conflicts of the sort illustrated are commonplace. Identify some in your own town or city. Discuss your conclusions with others in your class.

Choices in a forest
ecosystem.

Choices in an urban
ecosystem.

You and your classmates should get used to thinking in terms of problem solving — in terms of compromises and trade-offs. Your decisions about population, life styles, and resource conservation should be reasonable and based on sound data. Put your knowledge to good use.

CHECK YOURSELF

X. How is the idea of "waste" related to the idea of "resource"?

Y. Under what conditions may a waste be considered a pollutant?

Z. What environmental problems arise from sewage? From garbage? From junk?

AA. What are some effects that wastes from the burning of fossil fuels have on the environment?

BB. What is the major drawback of nuclear energy as a source of power?

CC. In what forms may metals be toxic?

DD. What is a drug? What is drug dependence?

EE. Distinguish between tranquilizers and stimulants.

FF. What is bioengineering? Genetic engineering?

It is interesting to contemplate a tangled bank, clothed with many plants of many kinds, with birds singing on the bushes, with various insects flitting about, and with worms crawling through the damp earth, and to reflect that these elaborately constructed forms, so different from each other, and dependent upon each other in so complex a manner, have all been produced by laws acting around us. These laws, taken in the largest sense, being Growth with Reproduction; Inheritance which is almost implied by reproduction; Variability from the indirect and direct action of the conditions of life, and from use and disuse; a ratio of increase so high as to lead to a Struggle for Life, and as a consequence to Natural Selection, entailing Divergence of Character and the Extinction of less-improved forms. Thus, from the war of nature, from famine and death, the most exalted object which we are capable of conceiving, namely, the production of the higher animals, directly follows. There is grandeur in this view of life . . . that, whilst this planet has gone cycling on according to the fixed laws of gravity, from so simple a beginning endless forms most beautiful and most wonderful have been, and are being, evolved.

DARWIN, *The Origin of Species*

PROBLEMS

1. Diagram a Stone Age food web centered on humans. Be sure to include protists.

2. Diagram a modern food web centered on yourself.

3. The Agricultural Revolution is not as well known as the Industrial. Find out what archaeologists have learned of this important turning point in our history. You might begin with R. Schery, 1972, *Plants for Man*, 2nd ed., Prentice-Hall, Englewood Cliffs, N. J.

4. An anthropologist studying the Pygmies of the Congo reported this statement by a Pygmy: "When the forest dies, we die." Comment on this human's understanding of ecology.

5. In the 1930's antibiotics were discovered, and many other important drugs to kill pathogens were developed. Which diseases were most affected by these medical advances? Study figure 20–16 to find causes of death that sharply declined after 1940. Find others that continued declining more gradually. And find still others that increased rather than declined. Show examples of each kind on a line graph. Explain the differences.

6. Demographers are concerned with more than changes in the total numbers of persons. They are also interested in the *structure* of populations—the relative numbers of individuals of various kinds. For example, two populations of the same size may have different proportions of males and females. Or two populations of the same size may have different proportions of children and adults. Such data often provide much information about a population.

   a. The total populations of the United States and Sri Lanka are quite different, but more important is the fact that the United States' population has a smaller proportion of children than that of Sri Lanka. What hypotheses can you suggest on the strength of this information?

   b. We may divide the population of the United States into three age groups: (1) persons under 20, most of whom are not self-supporting; (2) persons 20 to 65, most of whom are working; (3) persons over 65, most of whom are retired. In recent years the first and third groups have been increasing more rapidly than the second group. What hypotheses can you suggest to explain this? Can you see a future economic problem in this situation?

   c. In human females reproduction occurs mostly between the ages of 15 and 45. Suppose this age group increases more slowly than the age group over 45 but the number of children per female remains the same. What will happen to the birthrate in the population when expressed as births per 1,000 of population?

   d. The average age at which a female has her first child is higher in Nation A than in Nation B. The average age of death is about the same in both nations. From this information, make a guess about the rate of population growth in the two countries. What additional information would make your guess more reliable?

7. What are the ecological and economic reasons for doubting that the seas can soon become a great food resource? What methods are now being used to increase the yield of human food from seas? What possibilities do marine ecologists see for marine farming? You can make a good start on answering these questions by reading G. B. Pinchot, 1970, Marine Farming, *Scientific American*, December.

8. Poisoning is not the only method used to control organisms that destroy

agricultural crops. Find out what is meant by "biological control." Discuss methods of biological control from the viewpoint of ecological principles. What kinds of information are needed in applying biological controls? How do the effects of biological controls on ecosystems differ from those of chemical controls?

9. This book has included enough history to show something of the international character of biological science. Construct a chart or table to demonstrate this feature of biology, beginning with biologists named in the text. What nationalities can you add through your own efforts?

10. How much land in your state has been set aside by federal, state, and local governments as parks, forests, and recreational areas—open spaces? What percentage of your state's total land area is this? How does this compare with the percentage of such lands in the United States as a whole? Calculate the amount of open space per person in your state. Do you think the amount is adequate?

11. What trade-offs are involved in deciding whether or not to use a poison such as DDT? In deciding whether or not to build a nuclear power plant along a particular river? In deciding whether or not to strip-mine a forested watershed? In deciding whether or not to build a dam across a river?

12. The term "ecology" has become a household word. But it is often used as if it were a synonym for "pollution" or "environment." Sometimes it is merely used as a vague indication of something good. How would you explain the scientific meaning of the word "ecology" to a person who has never studied biology?

SUGGESTED READINGS

Asimov, I. 1975. *Science Past—Science Future.* Doubleday, Garden City, N.Y. Author writes about the significance of science and technology for the future of humans.

BSCS. 1977. *Energy and Society: Investigations in Decision Making.* Hubbard Scientific, Northbrook, Ill. An opportunity to try "managing" energy problems and project the results.

Canby, T. Y. 1975. Can the World Feed Its People? *National Geographic*, July, pp. 2–31.

Cohen, S. N. 1975. Manipulation of Genes. *Scientific American*, July.

Flader, S. L. 1974. *Thinking Like a Mountain: Aldo Leopold and the Evolution of an Ecological Attitude Toward Deer, Wolves and Forests.* University of Missouri Press, Columbia. Describes the person most responsible for modern concepts of wildlife conservation.

Flower, A. R. 1978. World Oil Production. *Scientific American*, March. Before the year 2000, oil supplies will fail to meet demands, even with cutbacks in individual use of gasoline and oil.

Hofmann, F. G. and A. D. Hofmann. 1975. *A Handbook on Drug and Alcohol Abuse: The Biomedical Aspects.* Oxford University Press, New York. Paperback. Concerns and misconceptions are discussed.

Ricciuti, E. R. 1974. *To the Brink of Extinction.* Harper & Row, New York. Comprehensive, well-written account of seven currently endangered species.

Ware, G. W. 1978. *The Pesticide Book.* W. H. Freeman, San Francisco. Paperback. An excellent, short, readable introduction to the history, benefits, and hazards of pesticides.

Wilson, D. G. 1978. Alternative Automobile Engines. *Scientific American*, July. An examination of alternatives in the future design of automobile engines, to increase fuel efficiency rather than power.

Some General Procedures

LABORATORY

Biologists must maintain an unusual amount of orderliness and cleanliness during their scientific work. Their observations and experiments must be verifiable. Therefore, they must know what they did and how they did it. Good order helps ensure this. And many biologists work with disease-producing microscopic organisms. Cleanliness decreases the chance of infection.

In your classroom laboratory there is additional need for orderliness and cleanliness, because you will share space and apparatus with other classes. How you achieve these conditions depends on each classroom situation.

USE OF MATERIALS

Apparatus. Some kinds of biological work still can be done with a few simple tools. But, as biologists probe deeper, they often find it necessary to use complex apparatus for handling and observing their materials.

There are right ways to use each piece of apparatus. "Right" refers to ways that will aid in obtaining accurate scientific information. You must learn how to use apparatus — from beakers and flasks to balances and microscopes.

Living materials. All biologists deal with living things. Though some have no need to handle living things directly in their daily work, no one in a general biology classroom or laboratory can get along without living materials. You, as a biology student, should learn how to care for living organisms.

Animals must be cared for humanely. General rules are as follows:

1. Provide an escape-proof container suitable for the animal.

2. Keep the container clean. This is necessary for the health of the animal. Cages of small birds and mammals should be cleaned daily.

3. Provide water at all times.

4. Feed regularly. The frequency of feeding depends on the animal. Small birds and mammals may be provided with a continuous food supply.

5. Treat laboratory animals with kindness in all situations. Cruelty has no place in biology.

6. When animals must be disposed of or released, your teacher will provide a suitable method.

Plants are just as much living things as are animals; they, too, can be injured or killed. Therefore, handle them carefully and gently.

Most plants must be provided with light, soil, and water. Requirements differ a great deal among plants. Therefore, individual students will care for your classroom plants. They will learn the requirements of the particular kinds of plants in their charge.

Special methods are necessary for handling most microorganisms. Specific instructions are given when needed.

RECORD-KEEPING

Science deals with verifiable observations. No one – not even the original observer – can check an observation that is hazy, indefinite, or half-remembered. All scientists must keep clear and accurate records of what they have observed, made *at the time of observation*.

Data books. The best method of keeping such records is to jot them down in a data book. This should be a stiff-cover book, permanently bound (not loose-leaf), preferably with unlined pages.

Keep records in a diary form, recording the date first. If you make observations on two or more investigations on the same day, use the numbers or abbreviations of the titles as subheadings.

Data may be recorded in words. In the laboratory, time is short, so you should make these notes brief but to the point. Complete sentences are not necessary, but single words are seldom satisfactory. Phrases are usually most useful.

You may choose to sketch your observations. A drawing often records an observation more easily, completely, and accurately than words can. Your sketches need not be works of art. Their success depends on your ability to observe, not on your artistic talent. Keep them simple, usually without shading, and draw them with a hard pencil.

Data may be recorded numerically as counts or measurements. Give the units in which measurements are made. Often numerical data are most easily recorded in the form of a table.

Don't jot down your data on other papers, to be copied into the data book later. This might increase neatness, but it will *decrease* accuracy. Both are virtues in a scientist, but neatness is of value only when it increases accuracy. Your data book is *your* record. Your teacher may want to look at it to help you with your work, but he or she is interested in the accuracy of your data, not in the blots and stains that are a normal hazard of field and laboratory work.

Remember to do the following:
1. Record immediately.
2. Record accurately.
3. Record completely.

More and more, science is becoming a cooperative enterprise – a team activity. You will do much of your own laboratory work as a member of a team. Your data book, therefore, will sometimes contain data contributed by other members of your team. Keep track of what you yourself have observed by encircling (or recording in a different color) observations made by others. You should be able to say: "This I know because I saw it; that I believe because I have confidence in my teammates."

Laboratory reports. Discoveries become a part of science only when they are made known to others. Communication, therefore, is a very important part of science. In writing, scientists must express themselves so clearly that another person can repeat their procedures exactly. The reader must know what material was used (in biology this includes the kind of organism) and must be able to understand every detail of the work. Scientists must be free to communicate, but they can use this freedom only if they know *how* to communicate. For publication, scientific reports are usually written in a rather standard form, somewhat as follows:

1. Title
2. Introduction: section usually stating how the problem arose and often giving a summary of past work
3. Materials and equipment
4. Procedure: complete and exact account of what was done in gathering the data
5. Results: data obtained from the procedure, often in the form of tables and graphs
6. Discussion: part that points up the relationship between the data and the purpose of the work
7. Conclusion: summary of the meaning of the results, often suggesting further work that might be done

8. References: published scientific reports that have been specifically mentioned

If you undertake work on an independent problem, your report should follow this form. But, for the usual work in this course, you do not have to be so elaborate. You are communicating with your fellow students and your teacher, who already know a great deal about the work. Occasionally your teacher may direct you to do a rather complete job of reporting. Usually, however, a much shorter report is all that is required—perhaps merely the answers to the questions in an investigation. In either case, the material in your data book is the basis for your reports.

MEASUREMENT

All major countries of the world use the metric system of measurement except the United States. The metric system is a decimal system—that is, it is based on powers of ten, like our system of currency. Scientists in the United States have long used the metric system.

The official name of the internationally standardized metric system is the International System of Units, abbreviated SI (for Système Internationale). Its units of measure are easily manipulated by doing calculations with ten or powers of ten. Among its basic units of measurement are the **meter** (length), the **kilogram** (mass), the **kelvin** (temperature), and the **second** (time). All lengths are based on that of the meter, and all volumes on a *cubic meter*. All units of mass are based on the kilogram. Units of temperature, which you will become familiar with as *degrees Celsius,* are equal to kelvins.

The major exception you will take to SI measure is in the measure of volume. You will use *liters* and decimals of liters, rather than cubic meters and their decimals. Liter measure is widely used for liquids, and most of your volume measurements in biology will be of liquids. Liter measure is accepted by SI, although not officially as a part of it. Like the cubic meter, the liter is also metric (1 liter = 0.001 cubic meter).

Some of the SI units derived from the basic units for length and mass follow:

1. Length

1 kilometer (km) = 1,000 meters
1 hectometer (hm) = 100 meters
1 dekameter (dkm) = 10 meters
1 meter (m) — the basic unit of length
1 decimeter (dm) = 0.1 meter
1 centimeter (cm) = 0.01 meter
1 millimeter (mm) = 0.001 meter
1 micrometer (μm) = 0.000001 meter
1 nanometer (nm) = 0.000000001 meter

Measurements under microscopes are often made in micrometers. Still smaller measurements, as for wavelengths of light used by plants in photosynthesis, are made in nanometers.

Units of area are derived from units of length by multiplication. One square hectometer is a measure often used for ecological studies; it is commonly called a *hectare* and equals 10,000 square meters.

2. Mass

1 kilogram (kg) = 1,000 grams
1 hectogram (hg) = 100 grams
1 dekagram (dkg) = 10 grams
1 gram (g) — derived from the kilogram, the basic unit
1 decigram (dg) = 0.1 gram
1 centigram (cg) = 0.01 gram
1 milligram (mg) = 0.001 gram
1 microgram (μg) = 0.000001 gram
1 nanogram (ng) = 0.000000001 gram

Measurements of mass in your biology laboratory will usually be made in kilograms, grams, centigrams, and milligrams.

The units you will use for volume and for temperature follow:

3. Volume

1 kiloliter (kl) = 1,000 liters (or 1 cubic meter)
1 hectoliter (hl) = 100 liters
1 dekaliter (dkl) = 10 liters
1 liter (l) — derived from the cubic meter
1 deciliter (dl) = 0.1 liter
1 centiliter (cl) = 0.01 liter
1 milliliter (ml) = 0.001 liter

Your volume measurements in the laboratory will usually be made in glassware marked for milliliters and liters.

4. Temperature

Your laboratory thermometers may read from 0° to 100° Celsius (abbreviated C). Or, since you may be reading temperatures below 0° C, some thermometers may read 30° or 40° below zero.

On the Celsius scale, 0° is the official reading for the triple point of water. At this temperature ice, liquid water, and water vapor pass from any one of these three states to another, staying in equilibrium. Commonly, 0° C is known as the freezing point of water. Atmospheric pressure affects this freezing point.

The boiling point of water is 100° C. Atmospheric pressure also affects this boiling point.

Figure A–1 illustrates the Celsius scale alongside the Fahrenheit scale that is still used in the United States. On the Fahrenheit scale, 32° F is the freezing point of water and 212° F is the boiling point of water. The figure is useful in converting from one scale to the other.

SI measure includes still other basic units (units of electric current, of force, of amount of substance, and so on) that you will not use in your biology studies.

If you wish to learn more about SI measure, write to the U.S. Department of Commerce, National Bureau of Standards, Washington, D.C. 20234.

A–1 Comparison of Fahrenheit and Celsius (centigrade) temperature scales.

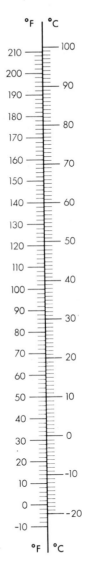

Supplementary Investigations

Investigation A.1   INTRODUCTION TO A MICROSCOPE

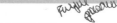

INTRODUCTION

There are many different kinds of microscopes. A magnifying glass is the simplest
kind. But usually the word "microscope"
means an instrument made up of two
groups of glass lenses, one at each end of a
tube — a **compound microscope.**

One type of compound microscope frequently used in biology laboratories is the
monocular microscope. With this kind, you
use only one eye in viewing an object, so
the image you see has length and width but
little depth. Most objects examined under a
monocular microscope must be so small or
thin that light can pass through them. You
can see form and structure in such objects
because some of their parts absorb more
light than others. Things seen in this way
are said to be observed by **transmitted** light.

MATERIALS
(per student or pair of students)

monocular microscope
microscope slide
cover slip
forceps
medicine dropper
finger bowl or beaker
  containing water
lens paper
paper towels
strips of newspaper
scissors
transparent plastic millimeter rule
pieces cut from magazine photograph

PROCEDURE

Setting up a microscope. Remove your microscope from its case or storage cabinet.
Grasp the **arm** of the instrument with one
hand. Place your other hand under the **base.**
Always use two hands to carry a microscope.
Set it down gently on the laboratory table,
with the arm toward you and the **stage** away
from you. The base should be a safe distance
from the edge of the table.

Your teacher will help you identify each
part of the microscope (figure A–2, page 734)
and explain its use. Become familiar with
each part before proceeding.

Preliminary adjustments. Use the coarse-
adjustment knob to raise the **body tube** so
that the **objectives** do not hit the stage when
you rotate the **revolving nosepiece.** Turn the
nosepiece so that the **low-power** (shorter)
objective is in line with the body tube. You
will hear a click when the objective moves
into position. Adjust the substage **diaphragm**
to the largest possible opening. Adjust the
mirror so that it reflects light upward through
the opening in the stage. Never let direct sunlight strike the mirror. Look into the **ocular.**
Make final adjustment of the mirror so that
the circular **field of view** is evenly illuminated.
Adjust the diaphragm to eliminate any glare.

If the lenses of the ocular or the objective
are cloudy or dusty, wipe them gently with a
piece of **lens paper.** Use a circular motion
and light pressure. Never use any other kind
of paper or cloth. When a piece of lens paper

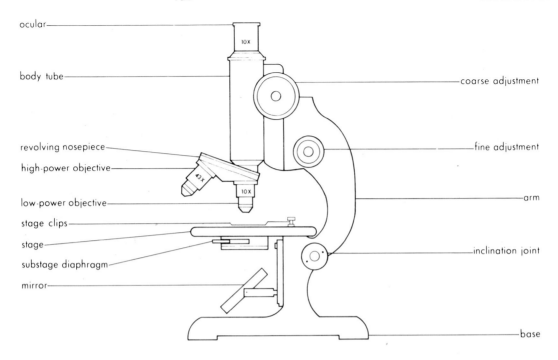

ocular

body tube ———————————————— coarse adjustment

fine adjustment

revolving nosepiece
high-power objective

low-power objective ———————————————— arm

stage clips
stage
substage diaphragm ———————————————— inclination joint

mirror

base

A—2 Two styles of
monocular compound
microscopes.

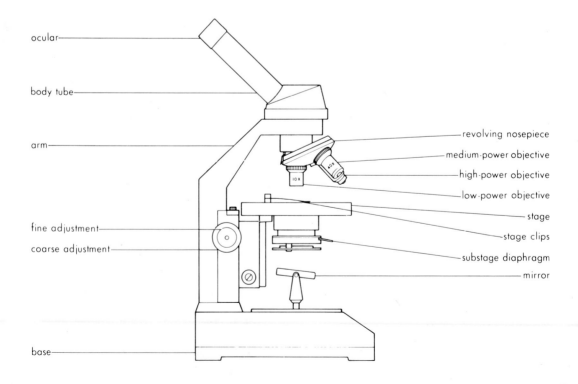

ocular

body tube

arm ———————————————— revolving nosepiece
medium-power objective
high-power objective
low-power objective
stage

fine adjustment
coarse adjustment ———————————————— stage clips
substage diaphragm
mirror

base

has been used once, discard it. If this procedure does not clean the lenses, consult your teacher.

Preparation of materials. Material to be studied under a microscope is usually placed on a piece of glass called a *microscope slide.* In most cases the material is covered with a small, thin piece of glass called a *cover slip.* Both slide and cover slip should be as clean as possible. Always handle them by the edges.

To clean a slide, hold it by the edges, between index finger and thumb, and dip it into water. Then wipe dry, using a piece of soft, clean cloth or paper towel.

Cover slips are much more fragile than slides. To clean a cover slip, hold it by the edges, using the index finger and thumb of one hand, and dip it into water. Fold a piece of thin, soft cloth or lens paper. Hold it between the index finger and thumb of the other hand. Insert the cover slip in the fold and apply pressure to *both* surfaces *at the same time* by bringing thumb and finger together (figure A–3). A gentle, circular motion is most effective.

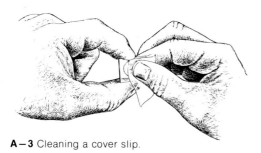

A–3 Cleaning a cover slip.

Now prepare a *wet mount* for microscopic observation. Using scissors, cut out a piece of newspaper that includes at least one letter *e.* The piece should be not more than 3 to 5 mm square. If possible, find a piece that has printing on only one side. Place the piece of newspaper in the center of a slide, printed side up. Put a single drop of water on the newspaper. Some of the water will soak into the paper, but some should remain surround-

ing it. If necessary, add another drop of water. Place a cover slip over the paper. The water will spread out in a thin, even layer between cover slip and slide.

Some skill is required to place the cover slip on the slide so that no air bubbles are included in the mount. The best method is to hold the cover slip at an angle of about 45° to the slide. Bring the cover slip down to the slide until the lower edge touches the drop of water. Continue to lower the slip *slowly* until it is parallel to the surface of the slide (figure A–4). Remaining bubbles may be removed by *gently* tapping the cover slip with the eraser of a pencil.

A–4 Making a wet mount.

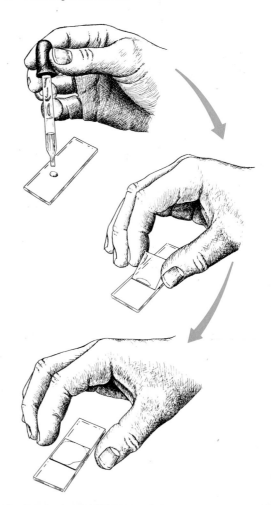

Focusing. Using the coarse adjustment, raise the body tube until there are about 2 cm between the low-power objective and the stage. Place the slide on the stage. Position it so that a letter e is in the center of the stage opening and is right side up. Use the **stage clips** to hold the slide in position. Look at the microscope from the side and use the coarse adjustment to slowly lower the body tube. The lower end of the objective should be about 1 mm above the cover slip. Never allow the objective to touch the cover slip.

Look through the ocular. Slowly raise the body tube until the print on the newspaper becomes visible. If you still see no image after you have raised the objective more than 1 cm, you have missed the position for correct focus. Refocus — look at the microscope from the side, lower the objective to its original position, and try again. *Never* lower the tube with the coarse adjustment while you are looking into the ocular. When you see an image of the printed material, rotate the **fine-adjustment** knob to obtain the best possible focus. Adjusting the diaphragm may improve clearness.

Compare the position of the **image** of the letter e in the ocular with the position of the printed e (the **object**) on the slide. (1) Is the image in the same position as the object seen with the unaided eye? If not, describe its position. (2) While looking into the ocular, slowly move the slide from right to left. Which way does the image move? (3) Move the slide away from you. Which way does the image move?

Rotate the revolving nosepiece so that the **high-power** (longer) objective is in line with the body tube. Make sure that the lower end of the objective does not touch the cover slip. If this happens, you will have to repeat the entire sequence, beginning with focusing the low-power objective. Use *only* the fine adjustment to bring the image into focus. Usually less than one full turn (in either direction) is needed.

(4) Is the field of view now larger or smaller? (5) Does the switch from low power to high power change the position of the image? (6) Is the illumination more or less bright than it is with low power?

Use the coarse adjustment to raise the body tube. Remove the slide and save it for later use.

Magnification. If an object is magnified 50 diameters (50X), the image you see is 50 times longer and wider than if the object were viewed with the unaided eye at a distance of 25.4 cm.

The degree of magnification provided is engraved on each objective and ocular. The magnification of combined ocular and objective equals the product of these numbers. If, for example, the number on the ocular is 5X and that on the low-power objective is 12X, the combined magnification is 5×12, or 60, diameters. Using the same ocular and a high-power objective that magnifies 45X will produce a magnification of 5×45, or 225, diameters. Find the magnification numbers on your microscope. (7) Calculate the magnification with low power. (8) With high power.

Measuring with a microscope. Because objects examined with a microscope are usually quite small, biologists use units of length smaller than centimeters or millimeters for microscopic measurement. One such unit is the **micrometer,** which is 1/1,000th of a mm. The Greek letter μ (called "mu") followed by "m," or μm, is the symbol for micrometer.

You can estimate the size of a microscopic object by comparing it with the size of the circular field of view. To determine the size of the field, place a plastic mm rule on the stage. Use the low-power objective to obtain a clear image of the divisions on the rule. Carefully move the rule until its marked edge passes through the exact center of the field of view. Now, count the number of divisions that you can see in the field of view. The marks on the rule will appear quite wide; 1

mm is the distance from the *center* of one mark to the *center* of the next. (*9*) What is the diameter, in millimeters, of the low-power field of your microscope? (*10*) What is it in micrometers?

To measure the diameter of the high-power field, use the following procedure: First, divide the magnification number of the high-power objective by that of the low-power objective. Then divide the diameter of the low-power field of view by this quotient. The result is the diameter of the high-power field of view. For example, if the magnification of your low-power objective is 12X and that of your high-power objective is 48X, the quotient is 4. If the diameter of the low-power field of view is 1,600μm, the diameter of the high-power field of view is 1,600 ÷ 4, or 400μm. (*11*) Calculate the diameter of your high-power field in micrometers.

Remove the plastic rule and replace it with the wet mount of the letter *e*. (If the mount has dried, add water.) Using low power, compare the height of the letter with the diameter of the field of view. (*12*) Estimate as accurately as possible the actual height of the letter in millimeters. (*13*) In micrometers.

Resolving power. Remove the slide from the stage and carefully lift off the cover slip. Discard the piece of paper. Dry the slide and the cover slip. Prepare another wet mount, using a small piece of a magazine photo-graph. Examine this mount under low power. (*14*) How does the magnified image compare with the photograph as seen with the unaided eye? You have just seen an example of a microscope's **resolving power,** its ability to clearly separate details. With the unaided eye most people cannot see two separate objects that are less than 0.1 mm apart. A microscope permits us to detect space between objects that are much closer together than this.

A microscope actually does two things: it provides magnifying power, and it provides resolving power.

Care of a microscope. Microscopes, like all other laboratory instruments, must be given proper care. At the end of the class, turn the revolving nosepiece until the low-power objective is in place. Adjust the body tube so that the lower end of the objective is about 1 cm above the stage. If you tilted the instrument at the **inclination joint,** return it to its untilted position. Turn the stage clips so that they do not extend beyond the side of the stage. Do not leave a slide on the stage. Return the microscope to its storage space. Clean and dry all slides and cover slips.

FOR FURTHER INVESTIGATION

If you have a stereoscopic microscope in your laboratory, explore its use. This instrument is used most often to view whole objects by **reflected** rather than by transmitted light.

Investigation A.2   USE OF A MICROSCOPE: BIOLOGICAL MATERIAL

MATERIALS
(per student or pair of students)

iodine–potassium-iodide
  (I_2KI) solution in dropper bottle
yeast culture
small piece of white potato
monocular microscope

glass slide
cover slip
medicine dropper
beaker or finger bowl
  containing water
lens paper
paper towel

PROCEDURE

For setting up the microscope, cleaning slides and cover slips, and preparing wet mounts, follow the directions given in Investigation A.1.

Observing starch grains. Place a *small* piece of potato in the center of a clean slide. Place the slide on your laboratory table and carefully press the potato with a finger until some juice is forced out. Distribute the juice evenly over the center of the slide by moving the piece of potato in a circle. Discard the potato. Add a drop of water and a cover slip. Avoid getting air bubbles in the mount.

Examine the mount under low power. Decrease the size of the opening in the substage diaphragm. This increases contrast between the starch grains and the water surrounding them. Move the slide on the stage until you locate a field in which you see well-separated grains. Center a group of these grains in the field and switch to high power. (*1*) Describe the shape of an individual starch grain. (*2*) Can you see any internal structure in these grains? If you can, describe what you observe.

Turn again to low power. Stain the starch grains by placing a small drop of the iodine−potassium-iodide (I_2KI) solution on the slide at one side of the cover slip (figure A−5). Tear off a small piece of paper towel. Place the torn edge in contact with the water at the opposite edge of the cover slip. As water is absorbed by the paper towel at one edge, I_2KI solution will be drawn under the cover slip at the opposite edge. Continue until the I_2KI solution covers half the space under the cover slip. I_2KI solution will continue to spread slowly throughout the mount. Examine various regions of the mount to observe the effects of different concentrations of I_2KI on starch grains. Examine under low power, then under high power. (*3*) What changes occur in the starch grains exposed to relatively high concentrations of I_2KI? (*4*) What differences do you see between these grains

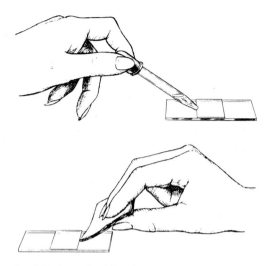

A−5 Putting a liquid under a cover slip.

and others exposed to lower concentrations of I_2KI? (*5*) Can you see internal structure in the stained grains? If so, describe them. (*6*) Using the method given in Investigation A.1, estimate the size (in micrometers) of the larger starch grains.

Remove the slide, lift off the cover slip, and dip both into water. Dry them. Carefully wipe off any liquid from the microscope stage.

Examining yeast cultures. Place one drop of the culture on a clean slide. Add a cover slip. Examine first under low power, then under high power. (*7*) Describe the shape of the yeast organisms.

Study the arrangement of small groups of these organisms. (*8*) From your observations, can you come to any conclusions about how new yeast organisms develop? (*9*) Sketch any internal structures you see.

Using I_2KI solution, stain the yeast as you stained the starch grains. (*10*) Compare the effects of the solution on the yeast organisms with its effects on starch grains. (*11*) Can you see any structures that were not visible in the unstained yeast organisms? If so, describe them. (*12*) Using the method previously described, estimate the size (in micrometers) of an average yeast organism.

A Catalog of Living Things

This Appendix shows one way taxonomists arrange the major groups of living organisms. It does not take into account the many extinct groups known to us only from fossils.

In general the classification is not carried below class level. In some cases, however, examples are given at the family level. In two groups—insects and mammals—a more detailed classification at the order level is given. To show how complicated classification can become at lower levels, the primate order of mammals is carried to the family level.

In examples, common names of groups are used wherever appropriate, as, for example, division Chlorophyta: green algae. The illustrated organisms are identified by common names, if they have them. If not, names of genera rather than of individual species are usually given. References to figures in the text are provided to supplement the Appendix illustrations, thus providing a greater diversity of examples.

A CATALOG OF LIVING PROTISTS

Phylum Schizomycetes

[Greek: *schizein*, to cut, split, + *myketes*, mushrooms]

Bacteria, Actinomycetes, and Rickettsias

Extremely minute (usually 1 to 5 μm). Usually unicellular, without a distinct nucleus. Most lack chlorophyll. They occur singly, as colonies, or as chains of individuals. Unlike "true" bacteria, the actinomycetes produce slender, branched filaments. The relationships of the ultramicroscopic rickettsias are uncertain, but these organisms may be thought of as highly modified Schizomycetes. About 1,600 species. (Figures 6–16, 6–17, and 6–19)

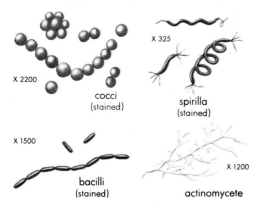

X 2200

cocci
(stained)

X 325

spirilla
(stained)

X 1500

bacilli
(stained)

X 1200

actinomycete

Phylum Cyanophyta

[Greek: *kyaneos*, dark blue, + *phyton*, plant]
Blue-Green Algae

Single cells or colonies in filaments, sheets, or irregular masses. Reproduction by fission. No organized nuclei or plastids. Chlorophyll often masked by other pigments. Mostly aquatic, but some occur on soil or other plants. About 1,500 species. (Figure 6–14)

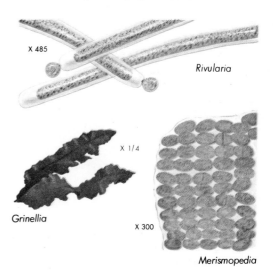

X 485

Rivularia

Grinellia

X 1/4

X 300

Merismopedia

Phylum Mastigophora

[Greek: *mastigo*, whip, + *phoros*, bearing, carrying]
Flagellates

Microscopic or almost so. Locomotion by whiplike flagella. They occur singly or as colonies. Some contain chlorophyll. Colonial forms sometimes considered to be intermediate between protists and multicellular plants or between protists and sponges. About 2,000 species. (Figure 6–13)

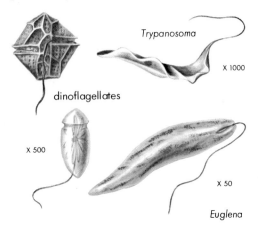

Trypanosoma

X 1000

dinoflagellates

X 500

X 50

Euglena

Phylum Sarcodina

[Greek: *sarx*, flesh, + *eidos*, form]
Sarcodinans

Microscopic or almost so. Locomotion by pseudopods. Many produce intricate shells or skeletal structures. Others are naked. About 8,000 species. (Figures 6–11, ameba; and 6–12)

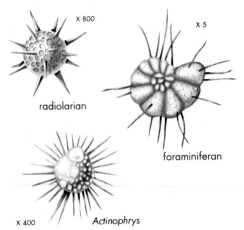

X 800

X 5

radiolarian

foraminiferan

X 400   Actinophrys

Phylum Sporozoa

[Greek: *spora*, seed, + *zoion*, animal]
Sporozoans

Microscopic. Usually no locomotion, but pseudopods or flagella may occur in certain stages of some species. Parasites with complicated life histories. About 2,000 species.

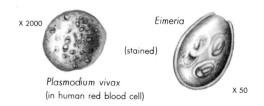

X 2000   Eimeria

(stained)

Plasmodium vivax
(in human red blood cell)   X 50

Phylum Ciliophora

[Latin: *cilium*, eyelash, + Greek: *phoros*]
Ciliates

Microscopic or almost so. Locomotion by cilia. About 5,000 species. (Figures 6–8; 6–9; and 6–11, paramecium)

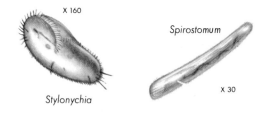

X 160

Spirostomum

X 30

Stylonychia

Phylum Myxomycetes

[Greek: *myxa*, mucus, slime, + *myketes*]
Slime Molds

Macroscopic masses of living substance with hundreds of nuclei inside one membrane. Each mass moves about and engulfs food like a giant ameba. Reproduction by spores, as in fungi. Found on decaying vegetation in damp habitats. About 450 species. (Figure 6–6)

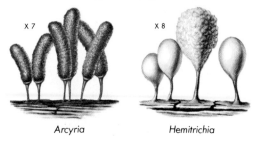

X 7   X 8

Arcyria   Hemitrichia

A CATALOG OF LIVING PLANTS

Division Chlorophyta

[Greek: *chloros*, green, + *phyton*, plant]
Green Algae

Single cells, filaments, ribbons, sheets, tubes, or irregular masses. Chlorophyll seldom masked by other pigments. Food usually stored as starch. About 6,000 species. (Figure 5–33)

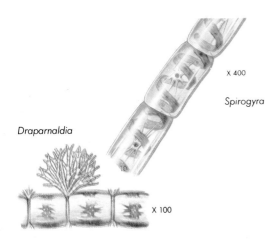

Draparnaldia

X 400

Spirogyra

X 100

Division Chrysophyta

[Greek: *chrysos*, gold, + *phyton*]
Golden Algae

Mostly microscopic. Many with shells of silica. Chlorophyll usually masked by yellow pigments. Food often stored as oil. About 5,700 species.

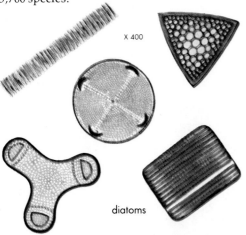

X 400

diatoms

Division Phaeophyta

[Greek: *phaios*, brown, + *phyton*]
Brown Algae

Almost all macroscopic and marine. Chlorophyll usually masked by brownish pigments. Food stored as carbohydrates, but not as starch. About 1,000 species. (Figure 5–31)

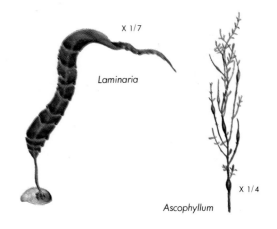

X 1/7

Laminaria

X 1/4

Ascophyllum

Division Rhodophyta

[Greek: *rhodon*, a rose, + *phyton*]
Red Algae

Almost all macroscopic and marine. Chlorophyll usually masked by red pigments. Complex life histories. Reproductive cells not capable of locomotion. Food stored as carbohydrates, but not as starch. About 2,500 species. (Figure 5–30)

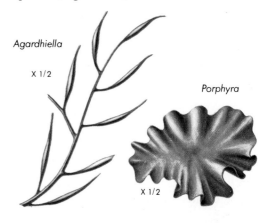

Agardhiella

X 1/2

Porphyra

X 1/2

Division Mycophyta

[Greek: *mykes,* mushroom, + *phyton*]
Fungi

No chlorophyll. No vascular tissues. Structure primarily a system of threadlike cell groups—hyphae. Mostly saprophytic, but many are parasitic on plants or animals. About 75,000 species.

CLASS PHYCOMYCETES

[Greek: *phykos,* seaweed, + *myketes,* mushrooms]
Algalike Fungi

Hyphae usually not divided by cross walls. About 1,500 species. (Figures 5–28, *Rhizopus;* and 5–29)

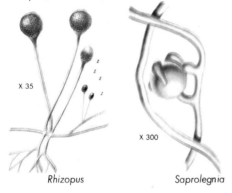

X 35

X 300

Rhizopus   *Saprolegnia*

CLASS ASCOMYCETES

[Greek: *askos,* bag, bladder, + *myketes*]
Sac Fungi

Hyphae divided by cross walls. A few unicellular species. Spores of a definite number (usually 8). Spores produced in a saclike structure, the ascus. Often form lichen partnerships with green or blue-green algae. About 25,000 species. (Figures 5–26; and 5–28, *Penicillium)*

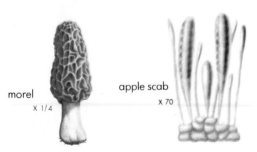

morel
X 1/4

apple scab
X 70

CLASS BASIDIOMYCETES

[Greek: *basis,* base, + *myketes*]
Club Fungi

Hyphae divided by cross walls. Spores produced on the surface of a clublike structure, the basidium. About 23,000 species. (Figures 5–24 and 5–35B)

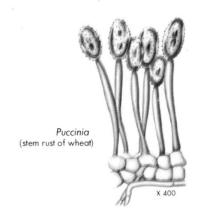

Puccinia
(stem rust of wheat)

X 400

CLASS DEUTEROMYCETES

[Greek: *deuteros,* second, secondary, + *myketes*]
Fungi Imperfecti

Fungi whose life histories are so little known that they cannot be placed in any of the other classes. This is, therefore, a taxonomic grouping of convenience, not of relationship. About 24,000 species.

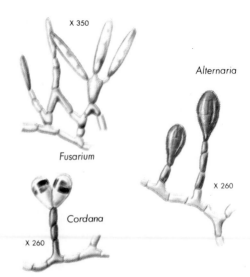

X 350

Alternaria

Fusarium

X 260

Cordana

X 260

Division Bryophyta

[Greek: *bryon,* moss, + *phyton,* a plant]
Bryophytes

Small (less than 40 cm tall). Mostly terrestrial. They often bear structures resembling stems and leaves, but lack vascular (conducting) tissue. Well-developed alternation of generations. Gametophyte generation is the more conspicuous. Sporophyte is more or less dependent on it. About 24,000 species.

CLASS HEPATICAE

[Greek: *hepatikos,* liverlike (from the shape of the leaves)]
Liverworts

Gametophytes flat, often simple, branching masses of green tissue, sometimes with leaflike structures. About 8,500 species.

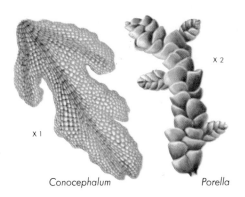

X 1   X 2

Conocephalum   *Porella*

CLASS ANTHOCEROTAE

[Greek: *anthos,* flower, + *keras,* horn]
Hornworts

Gametophytes similar to those of liverworts. Sporophytes live longer and are capable of continuous growth. About 50 species.

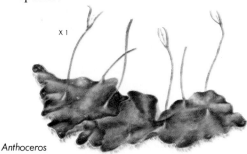

X 1

Anthoceros

CLASS MUSCI

[Latin: *muscus,* moss]
True Mosses

Gametophytes developed from algalike masses of green threads. Plants usually erect (not flat) with leaflike structures arranged in radial symmetry around a stalk. About 15,000 species. (Figures 5–5A and 5–35A)

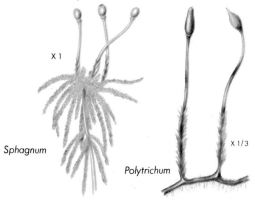

X 1

Sphagnum   X 1/3

Polytrichum

Division Tracheophyta

[Greek: *tracheia,* windpipe, + *phyton*]
Vascular Plants

Vascular (conducting) tissue always present. Alternation of generations. Sporophytes conspicuous. Gametophytes much reduced (often microscopic) and in many cases dependent on the sporophytes. About 211,900 species.

SUBDIVISION PSILOPSIDA

[Greek: *psilos,* bare, + *opsis,* appearance]

No roots. Forking stems, with spore cases at the tips of short branches. 3 species.

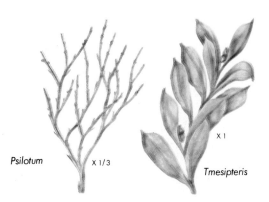

Psilotum   X 1/3

X 1

Tmesipteris

SUBDIVISION SPHENOPSIDA

[Greek: *sphen*, a wedge, + *opsis* (from the shape of the leaves)]
Horsetails

Roots and jointed stems. Small leaves (mere traces in living species) arranged in a circle around each stem joint. Spore cases borne on stem structures resembling cones. 32 species.

Equisetum

X 1/3

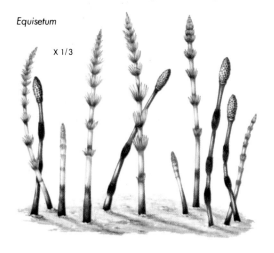

SUBDIVISION LYCOPSIDA

[Greek: *lycos*, wolf, + *opsis* (so named because the roots of a lycopod were thought to resemble a wolf's claw)]
Club Mosses

Roots, stems, and small leaves. Spore cases borne in various ways, usually on modified leaves grouped to form structures something like cones. About 1,100 species. (Figures 5–5B and 5–21)

X 1

Lycopodium

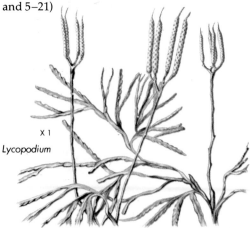

SUBDIVISION PTEROPSIDA

[Greek: *pteron*, feather, + *opsis*]
Ferns and Seed Plants

Most have roots, stems, and leaves. The positions of the leaves are marked in the stem by a gap in the vascular tissue. About 210,700 species.

CLASS FILICINEAE

[Latin: *filix*, ferns]
Ferns

Gametophytes independent of sporophytes. Free-swimming sperm cells. About 10,000 species. (Figures 5–1, 5–19, and 5–20)

X 1/10

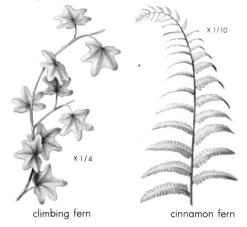

X 1/4

climbing fern   cinnamon fern

CLASS GYMNOSPERMAE

[Greek: *gymnos*, naked, + *sperma*, seed]
Gymnosperms

Gametophytes microscopic, within tissues of sporophytes. Seeds "naked" (not enclosed in a fruit), attached to the surface of a modified leaf. About 700 species. (Figures 5–16, 5–17, 5–18, and 5–35C)

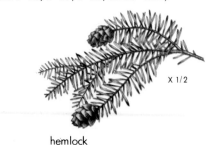

X 1/2

hemlock

CLASS ANGIOSPERMAE

[Greek: *angeion,* a small container, capsule, + *sperma,* seed]

Flowering Plants

Gametophytes microscopic, within tissues of sporophytes. Seeds enclosed in a fruit. Sperm cells in pollen tubes. About 200,000 species. (There are more than 300 families in the class Angiospermae. A few of the common families are given in the following subclasses. Orders are omitted.)

Subclass Dicotyledoneae

[Greek: *dis,* two, double, + *cotyledon*] "Dicots"

Flowering plants. Two cotyledons in the seed. Leaves usually have veins that form a network. Flower parts usually in fours or fives or multiples of these numbers. About 166,000 species. (Figures 5–2, 5–9, 5–12, 5–13, and 5–35 D and E)

Family Fagaceae (Oak Family). Trees and shrubs. Pistils and stamens in separate flowers. Flowers radially symmetrical, with 4 to 7 sepals, no petals, few to many stamens, 1 pistil, and an inferior ovary. (An ovary is the enlarged base of the pistil. It contains the ovules. An inferior ovary is one that is located *below* the attachment of the sepals, petals, and stamens.) (Figure 5–8, oak)

X 1/3

oak

Family Ranunculaceae (Buttercup Family). Herbaceous. Flowers radially symmetrical, with few to many sepals and petals, many stamens and pistils, and a superior ovary. (A superior ovary is one that is located *above* the attach-

ment of sepals, petals, and stamens.) (Figures 5–7, and 5–13, columbine)

X 1/6

larkspur

Family Cruciferae (Mustard Family). Herbaceous. Flowers radially symmetrical, with 4 sepals, 4 petals, 2 sets of stamens (4 long and 2 short), 1 pistil, and a superior ovary. They often have a turniplike or cabbagelike odor.

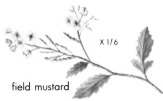

X 1/6

field mustard

Family Rosaceae (Rose Family). Flowers radially symmetrical, with 5 sepals, 5 petals, numerous stamens, 1 to many pistils, and either a superior or more or less inferior ovary.

wild rose

X 1/2

Family Leguminosae (Bean Family). Flowers bilaterally symmetrical, with 5 sepals, 5 petals, 10 stamens, 1 pistil, and a superior ovary.

X 1/2

sweet pea

Family Umbelliferae (Parsley Family). Herbaceous. Flowers radially symmetrical, with 5 small sepals, 5 petals, 5 stamens, 1 pistil, and an inferior ovary.

x 1/2

Queen Anne's lace

Family Polemoniaceae (Phlox Family). Flowers radially symmetrical, with 5 sepals (united), 5 petals (united), 5 stamens, 1 pistil, and a superior ovary.

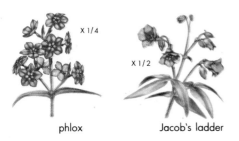

x 1/4

x 1/2

phlox   Jacob's ladder

Family Labiatae (Mint Family). Flowers bilaterally symmetrical, with 5 sepals (united), 5 petals (united), 2 or 4 stamens, 1 pistil, and a superior ovary. Stems usually square in cross section.

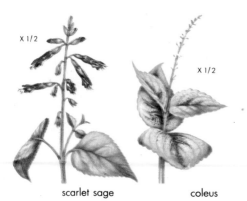

x 1/2

x 1/2

scarlet sage   coleus

Family Scrophulariaceae (Snapdragon Family). Flowers bilaterally symmetrical, with 5 sepals, 5 petals (2 forming an upper lip and 3 forming a lower lip), 4 stamens (in 2 unlike pairs), 1 pistil, and a superior ovary.

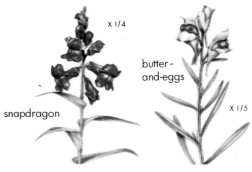

x 1/4

butter-and-eggs

snapdragon

x 1/5

Family Caprifoliaceae (Honeysuckle Family). Flowers radially or bilaterally symmetrical, with 4 or 5 sepals, 4 or 5 petals (united), 4 or 5 stamens, 1 pistil, and an inferior ovary.

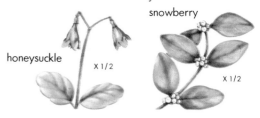

snowberry

honeysuckle

x 1/2

x 1/2

Family Compositae (Composite Family). Small flowers in dense groups. Each group appears to be a single, large flower. Individual flowers radially or bilaterally symmetrical, with sepals reduced to bristles or scales, 5 petals (united), 5 stamens, 1 pistil, and an inferior ovary.

x 1/2

x 1/2

Gaillardia   dandelion

Subclass Monocotyledoneae

[Greek: *monos,* one, single, + *cotyledon*]

"Monocots"

Flowering plants. One cotyledon in the seed. Leaves usually have parallel veins. Flower parts usually in threes or multiples of three. About 34,000 species. (Figures 5–11 and 5–12)

Family Alismataceae (Water Plantain Family). Herbaceous. Aquatic or marsh plants. Flowers radially symmetrical, with 3 sepals, 3 petals, 6 to many stamens, 6 to many pistils, and a superior ovary.

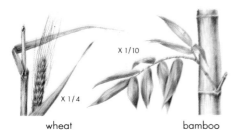

arrowhead

Family Gramineae (Grass Family). Stems usually hollow. Flowers radially symmetrical, with no sepals or petals (but scalelike structures present), 1 to 6 stamens, 1 pistil, and a superior ovary. Leaves sheath the stem.

wheat   bamboo

Family Cyperaceae (Sedge Family). Herbaceous. Stems usually solid. Flowers radially symmetrical, with no sepals or petals (but scalelike structures present), 1 to 3 stamens, 1 pistil, and a superior ovary. Leaves sheath the stem.

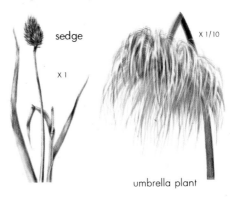

sedge

umbrella plant

Family Commelinaceae (Spiderwort Family). Herbaceous. Flowers radially or somewhat bilaterally symmetrical, with 3 sepals, 3 petals, 3 or 6 stamens, 1 pistil, and a superior ovary.

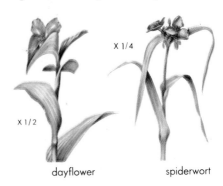

dayflower   spiderwort

Family Liliaceae (Lily Family). Flowers radially symmetrical, with 3 sepals, 3 petals (sepals and petals often colored alike, thus appearing to be 6 petals), 3 or 6 stamens, 1 pistil, and a superior ovary.

tiger lily

tulip

Family Amaryllidaceae (Amaryllis Family). Herbaceous. Flowers radially symmetrical, with 3 sepals, 3 petals, 6 stamens, 1 pistil, and an inferior ovary.

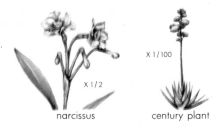

narcissus   century plant

X 1/100

X 1/2

Family Iridaceae (Iris Family). Herbaceous. Flowers radially or somewhat bilaterally symmetrical, with 3 sepals, 3 petals, 3 stamens, 1 pistil, and an inferior ovary.

X 1/8

X 1/5

gladiolus   iris

Family Orchidaceae (Orchid Family). Herbaceous. Flowers bilaterally symmetrical, with 3 sepals, 3 petals (united), 1 or 2 stamens, 1 pistil, and an inferior ovary. (Figure 5–11, orchid)

X 1/2

lady slipper

A CATALOG OF LIVING ANIMALS

Phylum Porifera

[Latin: *porus*, pore, + *ferre*, to bear]
Sponges

Mostly marine. Adults always attached to some solid object. Body wall consists of 2 cell layers. Pores in body wall connected to an internal canal system. About 4,200 species. (Figure 4–31)

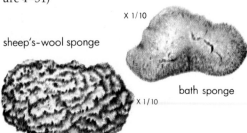

X 1/10

sheep's-wool sponge

bath sponge

X 1/10

Phylum Coelenterata

[Greek: *koilos*, hollow, + *enteron*, intestine]
Coelenterates

Mostly marine. Body wall consists of 2 cell layers and jellylike material between. Saclike digestive cavity with a single opening ("mouth"). Radially symmetrical. Tentacles with stinging cells. About 9,200 species.

CLASS HYDROZOA

[Greek: *hydor*, water, + *zoion*, animal]

Single individuals or colonies. Digestive cavity undivided. Simple sense organs. About 3,000 species.

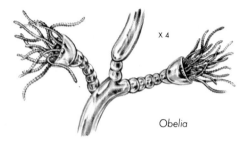

Obelia

CLASS SCYPHOZOA

[Greek: *skyphos*, a cup, can, + *zoion*]

Single individuals that float or swim. A few species have attached stages in the life history. Digestive cavity divided. Rather complex sense organs. About 200 species.

Aurelia

CLASS ANTHOZOA

[Greek: *anthos*, flower, + *zoion*]

Single individuals or massive colonies. Often produce limy skeletons. No floating or swimming stages. Digestive cavity divided. About 6,000 species.

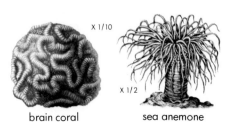

brain coral   sea anemone

Phylum Ctenophora

[Greek: *ktenos*, comb, + *phoros*, carrying or bearing]

Comb Jellies

Marine. Somewhat resembling jellyfish, but without stinging cells. Free-swimming, by means of 8 rows of cilia. About 100 species.

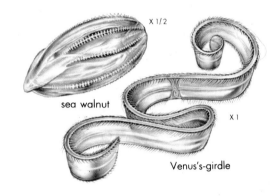

sea walnut

Venus's-girdle

Phylum Platyhelminthes

[Greek: *platys*, flat, + *helmins*, worm]

Flatworms

Free-living or parasitic. Usually flat and bilaterally symmetrical. Branched or unbranched digestive cavity with a single opening, or no digestive cavity. Bodies consist of 3 cell layers. About 6,000 species. (Figure 4–32)

CLASS TURBELLARIA

[Latin: *turba*, disturbance (so named because the cilia cause tiny currents in the water)]

Mostly marine, but some freshwater or terrestrial species. Free-living. Usually have cilia on the outside. About 1,500 species.

planarian

CLASS TREMATODA

[Greek: *trematodes,* having holes]

Parasitic. No external cilia. Usually possess suckers. Digestive system present. About 3,000 species.

X 2

liver fluke
(stained)

CLASS CESTODA

[Greek: *kestos,* girdle]

Parasitic. No external cilia. No digestive system. About 1,500 species.

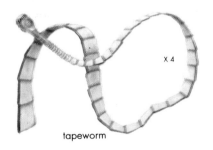

X 4

tapeworm

Phylum Mesozoa

[Greek: *mesos,* middle, + *zoion*]

Parasitic in flatworms, mollusks, and annelids. Minute; worm-shaped. Simple structure; no digestive system. About 45 species.

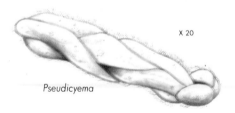

X 20

Pseudicyema

Phylum Nemertinea

[Greek: *Nemertes* (the name of a water nymph in mythology)]

Ribbon Worms

Mostly marine. Flat and unsegmented. Digestive tube with 2 openings (mouth and anus). About 500 species.

X 1/4

Cerebratulus

Phylum Aschelminthes

[Greek: *ascos,* bag, bladder, + *helmins*]

Freshwater, marine, or terrestrial. Free-living or parasitic. Bilaterally symmetrical. Internal organs lie in a body cavity developed between endodermal and mesodermal cell layers. About 12,500 species.

CLASS ROTIFERA

[Latin: *rota,* wheel, + *ferre,* to bear]

Rotifers or Wheel Worms

Microscopic. Freshwater or marine. Bilaterally symmetrical. Numerous cilia around mouth. About 2,000 species.

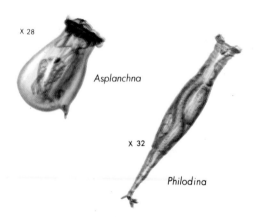

X 28

Asplanchna

X 32

Philodina

CLASS GASTROTRICHA

[Greek: *gaster*, belly, + *thrix*, hair]

Freshwater and marine. Free-living. Microscopic. Cilia on ventral surface. Surface of body covered with cuticular scales. 140 species.

Chaetonotus

X 22

CLASS KINORHYNCHA

[Greek: *kinein*, to set in motion, + *rhynchos*, snout or beak]

Marine. Minute. Protrusible spiny snout. Outer surface of body covered with cuticular plates arranged in rings. 100 species.

Echinoderella

X 19

CLASS PRIAPULIDA

[Greek: *Priapos* (a god of gardens and vineyards)]

Marine. Free-living. Mouth region with spines. Body covered with rings of cuticle. About 5 species.

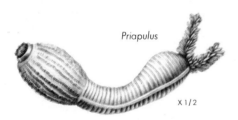

Priapulus

X 1/2

CLASS NEMATOMORPHA

[Greek: *nema*, thread, + *morphe*, form]
Horsehair Worms

Young are parasitic in arthropods. Adults are free-living and have much reduced digestive tubes. About 200 species.

X 1/2

Gordius

CLASS NEMATODA

[Greek: *nema*, thread]
Roundworms

Free-living or parasitic, especially on roots of plants. About 30 species known to live in humans. Cylindrical bodies, bilaterally symmetrical. Digestive tube with mouth and anus. No circulatory system. Many species are decomposers. About 10,000 species.

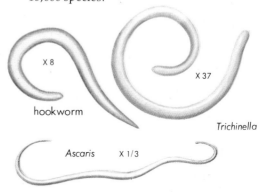

X 8

hookworm

X 37

Trichinella

Ascaris   X 1/3

Phylum Acanthocephala

[Greek: *akantha*, spine, + *kephale*, head]
Spiny-headed Worms

Young parasitic in arthropods. Adults parasitic in intestines of vertebrates. No digestive system. About 100 species.

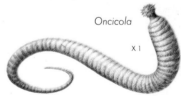

Oncicola

X 1

Phylum Bryozoa

[Greek: *bryon*, moss, + *zoion*, animal]

Mostly marine, living in attached colonies. U-shaped digestive tube. Mouth encircled in a crown of tentacles. About 3,000 species.

Electra

X 10

Phylum Brachiopoda

[Greek: *brachion*, arm, + *pous*, foot]

Marine. Symmetrical, 2-piece shell, enclosing a pair of "arms" bearing tentacles. About 120 species.

Lingula

X 1

Phylum Phoronidea

[Greek: *Phoronis* (the name of a mythological character)]

Marine. Living in tubes in mud. A pair of "arms" bearing tentacles. U-shaped digestive tube. About 15 species.

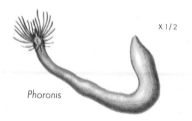

X 1/2

Phoronis

Phylum Chaetognatha

[Greek: *chaite*, hair, + *gnathos*, jaw]

Arrowworms

Marine. Free-swimming or floating. Bilaterally symmetrical. Straight digestive tube. About 30 species.

X 1

Sagitta

Phylum Mollusca

[Latin: *mollis*, soft]

Mollusks

Marine, freshwater, or terrestrial. Bilaterally symmetrical or unsymmetrical. The mantle is a fold of tissue over the body. It usually secretes a hard, limy shell. No segmentation. Well-developed digestive, circulatory, and nervous systems. About 70,000 species.

CLASS AMPHINEURA

[Greek: *amphis*, double, both sides of, + *neuron*, nerve]

Marine. Shell composed of 8 overlapping plates (exposed or hidden). No distinct head. About 630 species.

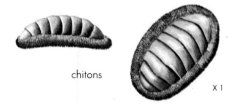

chitons

X 1

CLASS MONOPLACOPHORA

[Greek: *monos*, solitary, + *plax*, tablet, flat plate, + *phoros*, bearing, carrying]

Marine. Single shell with a curved apex. Broad, flattened foot. Found in deep ocean trenches. 3 species.

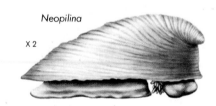

Neopilina

X 2

CLASS GASTROPODA

[Greek: *gastros*, stomach, + *pous*, foot]

Marine, freshwater, or terrestrial. Shell (if present) coiled. Head usually distinct. About 55,000 species. (Figure 4–29, garden snail)

X 1/2

sea slug

X 3/4

banded tulip snail

CLASS SCAPHOPODA

[Greek: *skaphe*, boat, + *pous*]
Tooth Shells

Marine. Shells form a tapering tube. Food-catching tentacles on head. About 200 species.

X 1/2

tooth shell

CLASS PELECYPODA

[Greek: *pelekys*, hatchet, + *pous*]
Bivalves

Marine or freshwater. Some attached; others burrow in mud or sand. Shells in 2 parts, hinged. About 15,000 species. (Figure 4–29, clam)

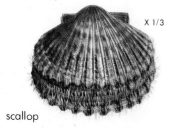

X 1/3

scallop

X 1/3

clam

CLASS CEPHALOPODA

[Greek: *kephale*, head, + *pous*]

Marine. Small, internal shell. In a few cases shell is external, coiled, and internally divided. Several tentacles on head. Locomotion by jet of water. About 400 species. (Figure 4–29, octopus)

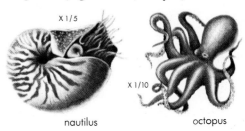

X 1/5

X 1/10

nautilus

octopus

Phylum Annelida

[Latin: *anulus*, a ring]
Segmented Worms

Marine, freshwater, or terrestrial. Bilaterally symmetrical. Body internally and externally segmented. Appendages either not jointed or lacking. Main nerve cord ventral. About 6,500 species. (Figure 4–33)

CLASS POLYCHAETA

[Greek: *polys*, many, + *chaite*, hair]

Mostly marine. Burrowers or tube-builders. Usually with paddlelike appendages on each body segment. About 3,500 species.

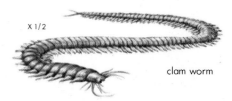

X 1/2

clam worm

CLASS OLIGOCHAETA

[Greek: *oligos*, few, + *chaite*]

Mostly freshwater or terrestrial. Appendages small or lacking. About 2,500 species.

earthworm

X 1

CLASS HIRUDINEA

[Latin: *hirudo*, leech]

Rather flat. Appendages lacking. Suction disks at each end. About 250 species.

leech   X 1/2

Phylum Arthropoda

[Greek: *arthron*, joint, + *pous*]
Arthropods

Marine, freshwater, or terrestrial. Bilaterally symmetrical. Body segmented, but segments often fused. Jointed appendages. Body and appendages covered with a jointed exoskeleton. Main nerve cord ventral. About 750,000 species.

CLASS ONYCHOPHORA

[Greek: *onyx*, nail, claw, + *phoros*, carrying
    or bearing]
Velvet Worms

Terrestrial. Tropical. Wormlike. Paired legs. Poorly developed segmentation. Combine many annelid and arthropod characteristics. About 80 species.

Peripatus

X 1/2

CLASS CRUSTACEA

[Latin: *crusta*, rind]

2 pairs of antennae. Respiration by gills. About 25,000 species. (Figure 4–26)

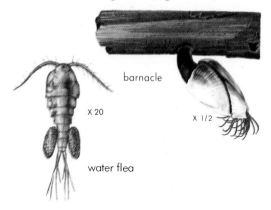

barnacle

X 20

X 1/2

water flea

CLASS ARACHNIDA

[Greek: *arachne*, spider]

No antennae. Segmentation reduced. 4 pairs of legs. No jaws (feeding appendages may resemble claw-bearing legs). About 15,000 species. (Figure 4–25)

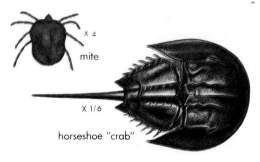

X 4

mite

X 1/6

horseshoe "crab"

CLASS DIPLOPODA

[Greek: *diploos*, two, double, + *pous*]
Millipedes

1 pair of short antennae. Entire body segmented; round in cross section. 2 pairs of legs on each segment. Important forest decomposers. About 6,000 species.

X 1/2

millipede

CLASS CHILOPODA

[Greek: *cheilos*, lip, + *pous*, foot]
Centipedes

1 pair of long antennae. Entire body segmented; flat. 1 pair of legs on each segment. Predators that mostly prey on insects. About 800 species.

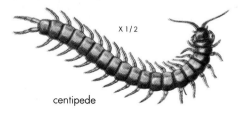

X 1/2

centipede

CLASS INSECTA

[Latin: *in*, into, + *secare*, to cut, divide (from the segmented bodies)]

1 pair of antennae. Body divided into head, thorax, and abdomen. 3 pairs of legs on thorax. About 700,000 species. (The following are the more common orders in the class Insecta.) (Figure 4–24)

Order Thysanura [Greek: *thysanos*, tassel, + *oura*, tail]. Small. Wingless. Soft scales on the body. 3 long bristles at posterior end.

silverfish

X 5

Order Ephemeroptera [Greek: *ephemeros*, temporary (literally, existing but one day), + *pteron*, feather, wing]. 2 pairs of transparent wings; hind wings smaller. 2 or 3 long "tails." Immature forms aquatic.

mayfly

X 1

Order Odonata [Greek: *odous*, tooth]. Two similar pairs of long wings. Antennae short. Abdomen long and slender. Immature forms aquatic. (Figure 4–24, dragonfly)

damselfly

X 1/2

Order Orthoptera [Greek: *orthos*, straight, + *pteron*]. Terrestrial. Front wings leathery. Hind wings folded, fanlike. Chewing mouth parts. (Page 103)

X 1   grasshopper

Order Isoptera [Greek: *isos*, equal, + *pteron*]. 4 wings alike in size, with many fine veins, or wings lacking. Chewing mouth parts. Social.

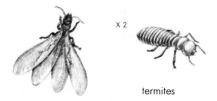

X 2

termites

Order Anoplura [Greek: *anoplos*, unarmed, + *oura*]. Wingless. Flat. Sucking or piercing mouth parts. Parasitic on mammals. (Figure 4–24, louse)

X 20

louse

Order Homoptera [Greek: *homos*, alike, + *pteron*]. 2 pairs of wings, arched above the body, or wings lacking. Jointed sucking beak at base of head.

leafhopper

X 6

Order Hemiptera [Greek: *hemi*, half, + *pteron*]. Front wings thick at the base, thin at the tips. Hind wings thin. Jointed beak on front of head.

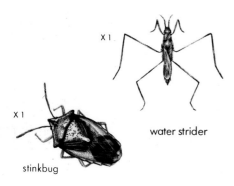

X 1

water strider

X 1

stinkbug

Order Lepidoptera [Greek: *lepidos*, scale, + *pteron*]. 2 pairs of wings covered with soft scales. Coiled, sucking mouth parts in adults. Young are wormlike (caterpillars). (Figure 4–24, moth and butterfly)

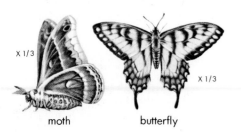

X 1/3

X 1/3

moth   butterfly

Order Diptera [Greek: *dis*, twice, + *pteron*]. 1 pair of wings (hind wings reduced to small rods). Antennae short. Sucking mouth parts. Young are wormlike and either terrestrial (maggots) or aquatic. (Figure 4–24, housefly)

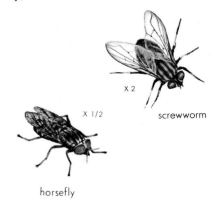

X 2

screwworm

X 1/2

horsefly

Order Coleoptera [Greek: *koleos*, a sheath, + *pteron*]. Front wings form a hard sheath; hind wings folded beneath them. Chewing mouth parts. Young usually wormlike (grubs).

X 2

X 2

hister beetle   cucumber beetle

Order Hymenoptera [Greek: *hymen*, membrane, + *pteron*]. Front wings much larger than hind wings, with the 2 pairs hooked together, or wings lacking. Chewing or sucking mouth parts. Young are wormlike. Many social species.

X 2

wasp

Phylum Echinodermata

[Greek: *echinos*, hedgehog, + *derma*, skin]
Echinoderms

All marine. Adults radially symmetrical. Radiating sections (when present) are called "arms." Larvae bilaterally symmetrical. Internal, limy skeleton, usually with many projecting spines. A system of water-filled tubes, acting on the suction principle, catches food and assists in locomotion. About 5,000 species. (Figure 4–28)

CLASS CRINOIDEA

[Greek: *krinon*, lily, + *eidos*, appearance]

Attached (at least when young). Many highly branched "arms." About 635 species.

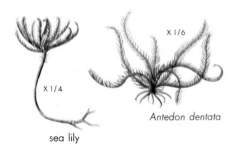

X 1/6

X 1/4

Antedon dentata

sea lily

CLASS ASTEROIDEA

[Greek: *aster*, star, + *eidos*]

Usually 5 "arms," joined to the body at broad bases. About 1,500 species.

X 1/3

starfish

CLASS OPHIUROIDEA

[Greek: *ophis*, serpent, + *oura*, tail, + *eidos*]

Usually 5 long, slim "arms" (sometimes branched), clearly distinguished from the body. About 1,500 species.

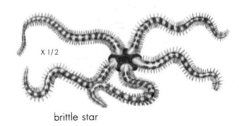

X 1/2

brittle star

CLASS ECHINOIDEA

[Greek: *echinos*, hedgehog, + *eidos*]

Spherical or disk-shaped. No "arms." Long spines or short, hairlike projections from body. Skeleton of interlocking plates. About 770 species.

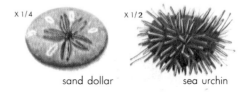

X 1/4   X 1/2

sand dollar   sea urchin

CLASS HOLOTHUROIDEA

[Greek: *holothourion*, a kind of water animal]

Somewhat cylindrical. No "arms." Tentacles around mouth. No spines. Skeleton consists of particles embedded in the leathery skin. About 600 species.

X 1/4

sea cucumber

Phylum Hemichordata

[Greek: *hemi*, half, + *chorde*, string of a musical instrument]

Marine, wormlike. Conspicuous probos-
cis used for burrowing in mud and sand. Dorsal nerve cord and pharyngeal slits. Notochord
doubtfully present. About 100 species.

acorn worm

Phylum Chordata

[Greek: *chorde*, string of a musical instrument]
Chordates

Marine, freshwater, or terrestrial. Bilaterally symmetrical. Hollow dorsal nerve tube and
a stiff notochord beneath it (may be lost or replaced during development). Several pairs of
pharyngeal pouches in the "throat" region.
(These may become perforated during development, forming slits.) Some segmentation,
especially in arrangement of muscles and
nerves. About 46,000 species.

SUBPHYLUM UROCHORDATA

[Greek: *oura*, tail, + *chorde*]
Tunicates

Marine. Larvae free-swimming. Adults
usually attached. Notochord and part of nervous system usually disappear during development. About 700 species.

sea squirt

SUBPHYLUM CEPHALOCHORDATA

[Greek: *kephale*, head, + *chorde*]
Lancelets

Marine. Free-swimming. Translucent. Well-
developed, hollow dorsal nerve cord, notochord, and pharyngeal slits in adults. About
28 species. (Figure 4–14)

lancelet

SUBPHYLUM VERTEBRATA

[Latin: *vertebra*, joint]

Notochord replaced by a "backbone" of
vertebrae during development. Enlarged anterior end of the nerve cord (brain) protected
by cartilage or bone. Most species have appendages in pairs. About 45,000 species.

CLASS AGNATHA

[Greek: *a*, without, + *gnathos*, jaw]

No jaws. No paired fins. Skeleton of
cartilage. Heart with 1 ventricle. 10 species.

hagfish

lamprey

CLASS CHONDRICHTHYES

[Greek: *chondros*, cartilage, + *ichthyes*, fish]
Cartilaginous Fishes

Skeleton of cartilage. 5 or more pharyngeal slits externally visible. Ventral mouth and nostrils. Heart with 1 ventricle. About 600 species. (Figure 4–21)

shark

X 1/24

CLASS OSTEICHTHYES

[Greek: *osteon*, bone, + *ichthyes*]
Bony Fishes

Skeleton of bone (at least in part). Pharyngeal slits covered (not externally visible). Heart with 1 ventricle. About 20,000 species. (Figures 4–13, sunfish; and 4–20)

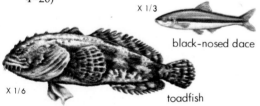

X 1/3

black-nosed dace

X 1/6

toadfish

CLASS AMPHIBIA

[Greek: *amphis*, double, on both sides of, + *bios*, life]

Larvae usually aquatic, with gills. Adults usually terrestrial, with lungs. 2 pairs of appendages (small or lacking in some species). No claws. Heart with 1 ventricle. About 2,800 species. (Figures 4–13, frog; and 4–19)

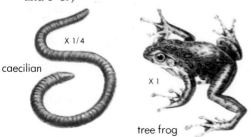

X 1/4

caecilian

X 1

tree frog

CLASS REPTILIA

[Latin: *repere*, to creep]

Both young and adults breathe by lungs. Eggs with leathery shells; membrane in egg encloses water. 2 pairs of appendages (lacking in some species) with claws. Scales on skin. Heart with two ventricles but with an opening in wall separating them (in most species). About 7,000 species. (Figures 4–13, rattlesnake; and 4–18)

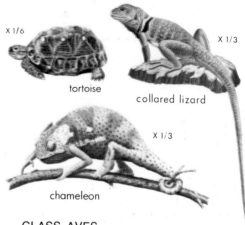

X 1/6

X 1/3

tortoise

collared lizard

X 1/3

chameleon

CLASS AVES

[Latin: *avis*, bird]
Birds

Scales modified as feathers. Eggs as in reptiles, but shell always hard. Front appendages usually modified as wings. Heart with 2 ventricles. About 8,600 species. (Figures 4–7; 4–13, robin; and 4–17)

quetzal

X 1/10

X 1/9

man-of-war

CLASS MAMMALIA

[Latin: *mamma*, breast]

Scales modified as hairs. Mammary glands of females secrete milk. Fewer bones than in reptiles. Teeth usually of 4 well-defined types (incisors, canines, premolars, molars). Heart with 2 ventricles. About 5,000 species. (Figure 4–16)

Order Monotremata [Greek: *monos*, one, + *trema*, hole]. Egg-laying. Mammary glands without nipples. 5 species.

platypus

X 1/8

Order Marsupialia [Greek: *marsypos*, pouch, bag]. Young born in undeveloped state and transferred to a pouch, where they remain tightly attached to the nipples. About 250 species.

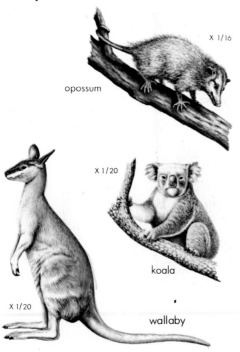

opossum

X 1/16

koala

X 1/20

wallaby

X 1/20

Order Insectivora [Latin: *insectum*, insect, + *vorare*, to eat]. Numerous teeth of all 4 mammalian kinds; none highly specialized. About 400 species.

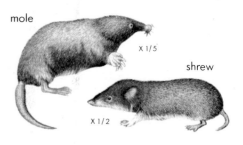

mole

X 1/5

shrew

X 1/2

Order Chiroptera [Greek: *cheir*, hand, + *pteron*, wing]. Bats. Web of skin between fingers and between front limbs and hind limbs, allowing flight. About 900 species. (Figure 4–16, vampire bat)

bat

X 1/4

Order Primates [Latin: *primus*, first]. Eyes usually directed forward. Nails usually present instead of claws. Teeth much like those of insectivores. About 200 species. (Figure 4–16, baboon)

To show how complex classification can become, a complete classification of the order Primates is given on the following page.

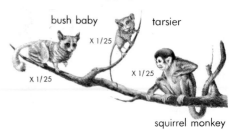

bush baby

tarsier

X 1/25

X 1/25

X 1/25

squirrel monkey

X 1/30

X 1/30

chimpanzee   gorilla

X 1/18

red howler

marmoset

X 1/4

Suborder Prosimii

Infraorder Lemuriformes

Superfamily Tupaioidea

Family Tupaiidae: tree shrews

Superfamily Lemuroidea

Family Lemuridae: lemurs

Family Indriidae: indris

Superfamily Daubentonioidea

Family Daubentoniidae: aye-ayes

Infraorder Lorisiformes

Family Lorisidae: lorises, pottos, galagos

Infraorder Tarsiiformes

Family Tarsiidae: tarsiers

Suborder Anthropoidea

Superfamily Ceboidea

Family Cebidae: New World monkeys   Nu Tails

Family Callithricidae: marmosets

Superfamily Cercopithecoidea

Family Cercopithecidae:
Old World monkeys, baboons   TAILS

Superfamily Hominoidea

Family Pongidae: apes

Family Hominidae: humans

Order Edentata [Latin: *edentare*, to make toothless]. No front teeth; molars in some species. About 30 species.

armadillo

X 1/20

X 1/15

sloth

Order Pholidota [Greek: *pholis*, scale]. Pangolins. No teeth. Body encased in scales formed from modified hairs. 8 species.

pangolin

X 10

Order Tubulidentata [Latin: *tubulus*, small tube, + *dens*, tooth]. Aardvarks. Teeth few in adults but numerous in embryos. Toes ending in "nails" that are intermediate between claws and hoofs. 1 species.

X 1/30

aardvark

Order Rodentia [Latin: *rodere*, to gnaw]. Chisellike incisors, growing continually from the roots; no canines; broad molars. About 1,700 species. (Figure 4–16, porcupine)

squirrel

X 1/12

woodchuck

X 1/17

Order Lagomorpha [Greek: *lagos*, hare, + *morphe*, form]. Harelike mammals. Teeth similar to those of rodents, but with 4 upper incisors instead of 2. Tail very short. About 60 species.

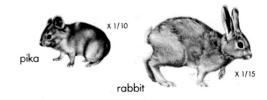

X 1/10

pika

rabbit

X 1/15

Order Cetacea [Greek: *ketos*, whale]. Marine. Front limbs modified as flippers; hind limbs absent. No hair on adults. Eyes small. Head very large. About 80 species.

blue whale

X 1/400

Order Carnivora [Latin: *carnis*, flesh, + *vorare*, to eat]. Incisors small; canines large; premolars adapted for shearing. Claws usually sharp. About 280 species. (Figures 4–3; 4–4; 4–5; and 4–16, cheetah)

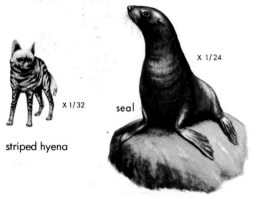

X 1/24

seal

X 1/32

striped hyena

Order Proboscidea [Greek: *pro*, before, in front of, + *boskein*, to feed, graze]. Herbivorous. Upper incisors modified as tusks; molars produced 2 to 4 at a time as older ones wear out. Nose and upper lip modified as a trunk. 2 species.

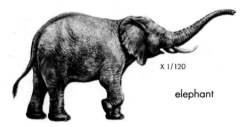

X 1/120

elephant

Order Sirenia [Latin: *siren*, a kind of mermaid]. Aquatic. Herbivorous. No hind limbs. Broad, flat tail, expanded as a fin. Few hairs. 5 species.

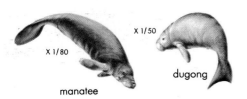

X 1/50

X 1/80

dugong

manatee

Order Perissodactyla [Greek: *perissos*, uneven, + *daktylos*, finger or toe]. Odd-toed, hoofed mammals. 1, 3, or 5 toes, modified as hoofs. Herbivorous. Well-developed molars. About 15 species.

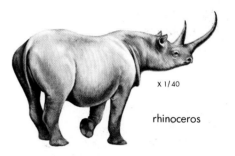

X 1/40

rhinoceros

American tapir

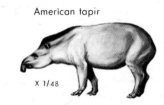

X 1/48

Order Artiodactyla [Greek: *artios*, even, + *daktylos*]. Even-toed, hoofed mammals. 2 or 4 toes, modified as hoofs. Herbivorous. Most have complex stomachs. Often have horns or antlers. About 170 species. (Figure 4–2)

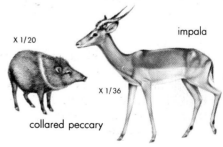

X 1/20

impala

X 1/36

collared peccary

hippopotamus

X 1/60

Dictionary of Biological Terms Used in This Book

All **boldfaced** and other important terms in the book are in this list of terms. Terms not listed include the names of biologists, laboratory apparatus and equipment, and units of measure. The names of phyla, divisions, classes, and orders are listed. The names of families, genera, and species are not listed, except for fossils that have no common name. Chemicals that are important in food, cell metabolism, and genetics are listed. Chemicals from student laboratory investigations are not listed. Some, but not all, of the terms from the index are listed.

abdomen (AB duh mun): the part of an animal's body to the rear of the thorax.

abiogenesis (ay by oh JEN uh sis): the theory of spontaneous generation.

abiotic (AY by OT ik): nonliving.

abortion (uh BOR shun): premature ejection of an embryo from the uterus of a female placental mammal.

absorption (ab SORP shun): taking up materials through the body wall or organ walls, as in absorption of digested foods.

absorption spectrum (ab SORP shun SPEK trum): A visible spectrum produced by light that has passed through a light-absorbing substance. Wavelengths (colors) of light absorbed by the substance are missing from the spectrum.

acid: a substance that in solution is richer in hydrogen (H⁺) ions than in hydroxide (OH⁻) ions.

actinomycetes (ak tuh noh MY seetz): certain bacteria, many of which are decomposers in the soil, and some of which produce antibiotics.

active transport: the movement and concentration of substances against their direction of diffusion, brought about by an expenditure of energy.

adaptation (ad ap TAY shun): a feature of an organism's structure or functioning that fits it to living in a particular environment.

adaptive convergence (uh DAP tiv kun VUR juntz): evolution of descendants of different parent species toward similarities of appearance, structure, and way of life.

adaptive (uh DAP tiv) **radiation:** evolution of a variety of descendant species from one parent species.

adenosine diphosphate (uh DEN uh seen dy FOS fayt): *see* ADP.

adenosine triphosphate (uh DEN uh seen try FOS fayt): *see* ATP.

adhere (ad HIR): to stick to, as one material to another.

ADP: adenosine diphosphate; it results from the use of energy in one phosphate bond of ATP.

adrenal (uh DREEN ul) **glands:** endocrine glands that produce several hormones related to heartbeat and other body functions.

aerobic (a ROH bik): oxygen-requiring; or, open to air with oxygen, as an aerobic environment.

aestivation (es tuh VAY shun): a dormant state of certain animals during the hot, dry season.

African sleeping sickness: a disabling parasitic disease of humans caused by a protist transmitted by the tsetse fly.

afterbirth: the placenta after ejection from the uterus following childbirth.

aggressive (uh GRES iv): bold, forceful, or threatening; or, being first to attack.

Agnatha (AG nuh thuh): a class of fishes without jaws, pairing of fins, or bone in their skeletons; examples are lampreys and hagfish.

algae (AL jee): nonvascular, plantlike organisms usually containing chlorophyll and other pigments. They range in size from a single cell to large kelps. Most are producers, storing foods as starch, other carbohydrates, or oils.

alimentary canal (al uh MENT uh ree kuh NAL): a digestive tract with openings at both ends and specialized organs along its length.

alkaline (AL kuh lin): basic; having in solution more hydroxide (OH⁻) ions than hydrogen (H⁺) ions.

allantois (uh LANT uh wus): one of the four embryonic membranes in vertebrate embryos; in humans, the membrane whose outgrowth develops into the umbilical cord.

allele (uh LEE ul): one of two or more differing forms of a gene for a particular characteristic.

allergic (uh LUR jik): susceptible to some kind of body disorder as a result of a substance introduced into the body that is normally considered harmless.

alpine (AL pyn): mountain elevations above treeline, with some similarities to tundra.

alternation of generations: production of a monoploid generation, then a diploid generation, then monoploid, and so on, as in mosses.

amino (uh MEE noh) **acid:** any of the organic acid molecules of which proteins are made.

ammonia (uh MOH nyuh): a soluble, gaseous nitrogenous waste excreted by aquatic organisms. Also, a stage in nitrogen fixation.

amniocentesis (am nee oh sen TEE sus): withdrawal of a sample of amniotic fluid from a pregnant woman, followed by culture and examination of cast-off embryonic cells in the fluid to determine the genetic health of the embryo.

amnion (AM nee un): one of four embryonic membranes in vertebrate embryos.

Amphibia (am FIB ee uh) or **amphibians** (am FIB ee unz): the class of vertebrates whose members begin life as aquatic organisms but develop into lung-breathing adults that inhabit both land and water. Examples include frogs and salamanders.

anaerobic (AN uh ROH bik): without oxygen, or not requiring oxygen.

anatomy (uh NAT uh mee): the structure of an organism's body.

anemia (uh NEE mee uh): a weakening condition related to oxygen deficiency. It is caused by a disorder or limited supply of hemoglobin or red blood cells.

Angiospermae (AN jee uh SPUR mee) or **angiosperms** (AN jee uh spurmz): the class of flowering plants.

Annelida (uh NEL uh duh) or **annelids** (AN uh lidz): a phylum of segmented worms. Examples include leeches, earthworms, and clam worms.

annual: occurring yearly; also, a plant that dies after one growing season.

antenna (an TEN uh): one of a pair or more of appendages on many invertebrates, most often serving as sensory receptors.

anterior (an TIR ee ur): toward the front end.

antheridium (an thuh RID ee um): a sperm-producing structure in certain plants, as in mosses.

anthocyanin (an thuh SY uh nun): a red pigment of many plants.

anthropology (an thruh POL uh jee): the study of humans and their origin, distribution, characteristics, and culture.

anthropomorphism (an thruh puh MOR fiz um): assigning human motives or interpretations to behavior of other animals.

antibiotic (ant ih by OT ik): a substance produced by microorganisms or synthetically, which inhibits growth of other kinds of organisms.

antibody (ANT ih bod ee): a particle produced by an organism on exposure to a pathogen or its toxin. Effective in disabling or destroying both of the latter.

antigen (ANT ih jun): blood protein of Type A or Type B, on red blood cells in humans.

anus (AY nus): the posterior opening of the digestive tract.

appendage (uh PEN dij): an arm, leg, antenna, or other part attached to the body.

appendicular (ap un DIK yuh lur) **skeleton:** in most vertebrates, the shoulder and hip girdles.

appendix (uh PEN diks): a small appendage to the large intestine near its junction with the small intestine; an appendage of no known function.

aquatic (uh KWAT ik): found in water; water-inhabiting.

Arachnida (uh RAK nuh duh) or **arachnids** (uh RAK nudz): the class of arthropods made up of animals with exo-

skeletons and with four pairs of jointed legs; a spider, scorpion, tick, mite, or horseshoe crab.

arboreal (ar BOR ee ul): tree-dwelling.

Archaeohippus (ar kee oh HIP us): a fossil horse.

Archaeopteryx (ar kee OP tuh riks): a fossil bird, the oldest known until recent fossil discoveries that have not yet been evaluated.

archegonium (ar kih GOH nee um): an ovum-producing structure in certain plants, as in mosses.

arid (AR ud): dry.

artery: a vessel that carries blood away from the heart.

arthritis (ar THRYT us): a painful disorder of bone joints known mainly in mammals, caused by a physiological disorder, aging, or infection.

Arthropoda (ar THRAH puh duh) or **arthropods** (AR thruh-podz): a phylum of invertebrate animals with external skeletons and jointed appendages. The largest animal phylum, including insects, spiders, centipedes, lobsters, crabs, and shrimps.

articulation (ar tik yuh LAY shun): the manner of jointing of bones in a skeleton. Also, the manner of uttering adjoining sounds in speech.

asexual (ay SEK shuh wul) **reproduction:** reproduction that does not involve sex cells or a change in chromosome number (meiosis).

associative neuron: a neuron that transmits impulses between other neurons, usually between sensory and motor neurons.

assumption (uh SUMP shun): something accepted tentatively as true or as a simplified version of what is true.

asthma (AZ muh): a respiratory disorder of humans caused by allergy or physiological disorder.

athlete's foot: a skin disorder of humans caused by a fungus.

atmosphere (AT muh sfir): the gaseous outer layer of Earth.

atom: the smallest particle of an element, consisting of a nucleus surrounded by one or more electrons.

ATP: adenosine triphosphate, the energy-storage compound of cells.

atrium (AY tree um): in vertebrates, a chamber of the heart that receives incoming blood.

Aureomycin (or ee oh MYS un): an antibiotic.

Australopithecus africanus (os tray loh PITH uh kus af rih-KAH nus): an upright-walking primate that coexisted with, and possibly competed with, early humans.

Australopithecus robustus (os tray loh PITH uh kus roh-BUS tus): an upright-walking primate that coexisted with, and possibly competed with, early humans.

autonomic (awt uh NOM ik) **nervous system:** a system of two nerve chains (near the spinal cord) and their associated neurons. Involved in regulating breathing, circulation, and other vital body activities of which a person is unaware.

auxin (OK sun): a plant hormone.

Aves (AY veez): the class of birds.

axial (AK see ul) **skeleton:** in vertebrates, the skull and the vertebrae of the backbone.

bacteria (bak TIR ee uh): certain microscopic, procaryotic, one-celled organisms that are characteristically rod-shaped, spiral-shaped, or spherical. They may be either disease-causing or beneficial to other organisms.

bacteriophage (bak TIR ee uh fayj): a virus that attacks bacteria.

barrier: an obstacle to a species' dispersal, or to interbreeding between two separated populations of the same species.

base: a substance that in solution is richer in hydroxide (OH^-) ions than in hydrogen (H^+) ions.

bathyscaphe (BATH ih skaf): a pressure-resistant vessel for deep-water research.

behavioral isolation: separation or segregation at breeding time because of variations in courtship rituals or the return of individuals to breed in the particular place where they were spawned or born.

bilateral symmetry (by LAT uh rul SIM uh tree): the body plan of animals that have anterior and posterior ends and right and left sides. Each side of the body is symmetrical to the other.

bile: an alkaline secretion of the liver, useful in breaking up fats in the small intestine.

binomial nomenclature (by NOH mee ul NOH mun klay-chur): a two-name system for naming things, and the resulting names. The type of system used to name species of organisms.

biochemist (by oh KEM ust): a scientist who studies the chemical processes of living organisms.

biogenesis (by oh JEN uh sis): the theory that organisms in existence today arise only by reproduction of others of their kind.

biologist (by OL uh just): a scientist in any field of biology; a botanist, ecologist, geneticist, paleontologist, zoologist, and so on.

biology (by OL uh jee): the science of life; the scientific study of living things.

bioluminescent (by oh loo muh NES unt): producing light biochemically, in specialized life processes of certain organisms.

biomass (BY oh mas): the total mass of all individuals of a population or community.

biome (BY ome): all the organisms living in a particular climate.

biosphere (BY uh sfir): the outer region of Earth where life is found.

biota (by OH tuh): all the living things in a place, or on Earth.

biotic (by OT ik): living, or living until recently.

birth: delivery of young from the mother's body.

blade: the flattened portion of a leaf. Also, the flattened or cutting portion of a scalpel.

blastula (BLAS chuh luh): an early stage of an animal embryo as a hollow ball of cells.

blight: any of a group of fungus-caused diseases of crop plants.

blue-green algae (AL jee): a group of photosynthetic, procaryotic protists more like bacteria than algae, and often classified as Cyanobacteria.

bony fish: any fish of the class Osteichthyes, whose skeleton is made mainly of bone rather than cartilage.

botanical (buh TAN ih kul): exclusively devoted to plants.

botanist (BOT un ust): a biologist who specializes in the study of plants.

brachiopod (BRAY kee uh pod): any of a phylum of marine animals with hinged shells, of which only a few species survive today.

breeding: in population studies, a term for sexual reproduction.

bronchus (BRONG kus): either of the two branches of the trachea to the two lungs.

Brontosaurus (bront uh SAWR us): a giant herbivorous dinosaur known from fossils.

brown algae (AL jee): aquatic algae in which the chlorophyll is usually masked, or partly masked, by brownish pigments. Examples range in size from microscopic to large seaweeds.

Bryophyta (bry OFF uh tuh) or **bryophytes** (BRY uh fytz): a plant division of small nonvascular plants without true roots, stems, or leaves but with rhizoids and with leaflike structures. Includes the true mosses and their relatives.

buttress (BUH truhs): a broadening at the base of many trees, radiating from the trunk as natural braces.

caiman (KAY man): a close relative of alligators, but often superficially resembling crocodiles.

calorie (KAL uh ree): the amount of heat necessary to raise the temperature of 1 ml (1 g) of water 1°C; 1,000 calories, the kilocalorie, is the Calorie of food-energy values.

calorimeter (kal uh RIM ut er): an apparatus designed to burn food samples and measure the heat given off.

cambium (KAM bee um): living stem tissue that produces new xylem and phloem cells.

Cambrian (KAM bree un): the first period of the Paleozoic era.

cancer: uncontrolled growth of abnormal cells in an organism.

capillary (CAP uh lair ee): a thin-walled blood vessel connecting an artery and a vein. Exchanges of substances with body cells take place through its walls.

carbohydrate (kar boh HY drayt): any organic compound that contains only carbon, hydrogen, and oxygen with a 2-to-1 ratio of hydrogen to oxygen atoms.

Carboniferous (kar buh NIF uh rus): the fifth period (often divided into two periods) in the Paleozoic era.

Carnivora (kar NIV uh ruh): an order of flesh-eating mammals.

carnivore (KAR nuh vor): any animal that eats other animals; a flesh-eater.

carotene (KER uh teen): an orange pigment of many plants.

carrying capacity: the number of individuals of a given species that an ecosystem with its available resources can support.

cartilage (KART ul ij): a tough, flexible supportive tissue, abundant in vertebrates.

cartilaginous (kart ul AJ uh nus) **fish:** any fish of the class Chondrichthyes, whose skeletons are made entirely of cartilage rather than bone.

catalyst (KAT ul ust): a substance that speeds up a chemical reaction.

cell: the microscopic structural and functional unit of life.

cell membrane: the fragile boundary between a cell and its environment, enclosing the cell's contents.

cell theory: the theory that cells are the units of structure and function in organisms, and that all cells arise from pre-existing cells.

cellular respiration: the energy-releasing breakdown of food molecules in a cell.

cellulose (SEL yuh los): the most common carbohydrate in plants; it serves a support function.

Cenozoic (sen uh ZOH ik): the geologic era that includes the present time.

census: a count of a population.

central nervous system: the brain, spinal cord or nerve cord, and nerves leading directly into or out of them.

centromere (SEN truh mir): a point on a chromosome at which it is attached to the spindle during mitosis or meiosis.

centrosome (SEN truh som): an animal cell structure involved in mitosis. It divides and moves to opposite ends of a cell where the ends of the spindle form.

cerebellum (ser uh BEL um): a part of the vertebrate brain involved with functions such as muscle coordination.

cerebrum (suh REE brum): the part of the vertebrate brain involved with sensory reception, intelligence, memory, and voluntary movement.

cervix (SUR viks): the narrow opening of the uterus in a female mammal.

chaparral (shap uh RAL): a mid-latitude biome in which most of the precipitation comes in the winter. The conspicuous plants are shrubs with small, thick evergreen leaves.

chemical bond: the exchange or sharing of electrons between atoms in forming molecules.

Chilopoda (ky LOP uh duh): the class of arthropods made up of centipedes.

chi-square (KY square): a method for testing the significance of the results of a genetic cross or of certain other experiments.

chitin (KYT un): a substance in the exoskeletons of arthropods.

chlorophyll (KLOR uh fil): a light-absorbing pigment or group of pigments, mostly green, found in algae, certain bacteria, and plants.

chloroplast (KLOR uh plast): a chlorophyll-containing organelle of photosynthesis in cells of producers.

Chondrichthyes (kon DRIK thee eez): the class of cartilaginous fishes.

Chordata (kor DAY tuh): the phylum of animals that includes the vertebrates.

chorion (KOR ee ON): one of the four embryonic membranes in vertebrate embryos. In humans it helps to form the placenta.

chromatid (KROH muh tud): either of two duplicate chromosomes attached to each other at the beginning of mitosis or meiosis.

chromatography (kroh muh TOG ruh fee): a technique for separating chemical compounds from a mixture present in an organic substance, such as chlorophyll.

chromosome (KROH muh som): one of a number of threadlike structures of a cell nucleus, carrying coded hereditary information.

chromosome theory of heredity: the theory that inherited characteristics are determined by genes carried on chromosomes.

chronological (kron ul OJ ih kul): in sequence according to time, with the earliest event first, the next-earliest second, and so on.

chyme (KYM): a food mass when it leaves the stomach and enters the small intestine.

cilia (SIL ee uh): short hairlike projections on cell surfaces in many protists and in certain tissues of many multicellular animals.

ciliate (SIL ee ut): a protist of a species that has cilia covering the body.

circadian (sur KAD ee un) **rhythms:** plant and animal events that occur daily, or in cycles that recur daily.

circannual (sur KAN yuh wul) **rhythms:** plant or animal events that occur at about the same time each year, or in cycles that recur each year.

circulatory system: a fluid-transport system inside the bodies of most multicellular organisms. It supplies cells with their needs and removes their wastes.

class: a group of related orders, in the classification of organisms.

cleavage (KLEE vij): the early cell divisions of a fertilized egg, producing smaller cells.

cleft lip: a genetic disorder of humans in which the upper lip is divided, usually at the middle.

climate (KLY mut): long-term environmental conditions associated with weather, including latitude, temperatures, precipitation, humidity, and hours of sunlight. Variations in most of these conditions occur year-round.

climatogram (kly MA tuh gram): a graph of daily or monthly average temperatures, precipitation, and sometimes other factors of climate for a region.

climax community: the last stage in a succession, relatively permanent until the earth's climates change.

cline (KLYN): continuous increase or decrease in frequency of a trait from one area to another in the geographic range of a species.

clitoris (KLIT uh rus): a small organ anterior to the opening of the vagina in females.

cloning (KLOHN ing): asexual reproduction of offspring genetically identical to the parent.

closed circulatory system: circulation through a continuous set of tubes or vessels. Exchanges with body cells are made through vessel walls.

closed population: a population isolated against immigration and emigration, as an island population.

club fungus (FUNG gus): a mushroom or one of its relatives, named for the club-shaped stalk and cap it produces.

club moss: a vascular plant of the subdivision Lycopsida, named for the club-shaped cones it produces.

codominance: two unlike alleles that express a blended phenotype in an individual. Neither allele is dominant to the other.

codon (KOH don): a triplet of nucleotides. The identities of the three nucleotides and their sequence identify a particular amino acid required to satisfy the code.

Coelenterata (sih LENT uh RAYT uh) or **coelenterates** (sih-

LENT uh rayts): a phylum of marine and freshwater invertebrates that are radially symmetrical and do not have advanced organ systems. Jellyfish, corals, and hydras are examples.

cohesion (ko HEE zhun): attraction of molecules to one another, as in water molecules in the liquid state.

cold-blooded: having an internal body temperature that fluctuates in response to fluctuations in the temperatures of the outer environment.

coleoptile (koh lee OP tul): a closed, tubular structure on a young shoot of many grains and grasses, covering the developing leaves within.

colony: a dense population of microorganisms, or of very small macroscopic organisms.

commensalism (kuh MEN suh liz um): a relationship between two organisms that live together with one benefited, the other unaffected.

communication: visual, sound, or chemical signals that carry meaning between individuals of a species.

community: all populations of organisms that live in the same place at the same time.

companion cell: a cell alongside each sieve cell that regulates the sieve cell in its food transport function.

competition (kom puh TISH un): the relationship existing between two organisms that seek the same food, the same mate, or the same territory. Or, the relationship between two species that share the same environmental niche.

compound (KOM pownd): a substance made of two or more kinds of atoms chemically bonded to one another.

compound leaf: a plant leaf with subdivided leaf blades as leaflets.

conditioning: a learned association of a response with a stimulus.

conifer (KON uh fur): a cone-bearing plant.

coniferous (koh NIF uh rus) **forest:** a biome of northern latitudes, named for the cone-bearing trees that characterize it.

conjugation (kon juh GAY shun): the process during which fusion of gametes occurs in protists, algae, and certain other organisms.

consumer: an organism that obtains its energy and nutrients —its food—by digesting the body materials or waste products of other organisms.

contagious (kun TAY jus): a disease spread directly by its pathogen from one victim to the next.

continental drift: the drifting apart or pushing apart of continents as a result of sea-floor spreading under an ocean between them.

control (kun TROHL): regulation of the effects of all possible variables except for an experimental variable. Accomplished by keeping all the other variables alike for the organisms being compared.

copulate (KOP yuh layt): to mate.

corm: a thickened underground stem base bearing buds and scaly leaves. A vegetative reproduction organ of the plant.

corpus luteum (KOR pus LOOT ee um): a follicle after ovulation. It secretes the hormone progesterone.

cortex: a name for many different outer structures in a vari-

ety of organisms. In a plant root or stem, a region of cells that may later form bark. In a vertebrate brain, the gray matter covering the white tissue underneath.

cotyledon (kot uh LEE dun): the seed-leaf, or one of two seed-leaves, of the embryo plant in a seed.

creodont (KREE uh dont): any of an order of early, carnivorous mammals known only from fossils.

Cretaceous (krih TAY shus): the third period of the Mesozoic era.

Cro-Magnon (kroh MAG nun): a name given to certain modern humans of 25,000 to 50,000 years ago, known from fossils, tools, cave art, and burial customs.

crossing-over: the exchange of segments of DNA between two chromosomes of a pair, resulting in new gene linkages.

Crustacea (kruh STAY shee uh) or **crustaceans** (kruh STAYshunz): the class of arthropods made up of crabs, lobsters, shrimp, crayfish, and related animals. All but a very few, such as sow bugs and pill bugs, are aquatic.

culture: a laboratory population maintained for study or research.

cuticle (KYEWT ih kul): the waxy coating on the epidermis of a plant leaf. Also, a name applied to certain epidermal features of many other organisms.

cycad (SY kud): a gymnosperm of a type closely related to several of the earliest fossil gymnosperms known.

cyclosis (sy KLOH sus): movement or streaming of cell cytoplasm.

cystic fibrosis (SIS tik fy BROH sus): a genetic disorder of humans that affects respiration, pancreatic function, and salt balance.

cytoplasm (SYT uh plaz um): the semiliquid cell medium in which the nucleus and other cell structures are suspended.

data (DAY tuh): information revealed by observation, measurement, or experiment.

debris (duh BREE): rubbish; material left by waves on beaches, or left by glaciers along their sides or at their tip.

deciduous (dih SIJ uh was): shedding leaves in the autumn.

decomposer (dee kum PO zur): an organism that lives on the wastes or decaying remains of other organisms. It digests the materials to simple inorganic molecules.

deficiency disease: a disease resulting from too little of a required nutrient in the diet.

degenerative (dih JEN uh rayt iv) **disease:** a disease caused by aging and often contributed to by diet or by environmental and hereditary factors.

delta (DEL tuh): a mathematical notation of change, symbolized by Δ. The fourth letter of the Greek alphabet.

demographer (dih MOG ruh fur): an ecologist or social scientist who studies the size, density, and distribution of the human population.

denitrifying bacteria (dee NY truh fy ing bak TIR ee uh): soil bacteria that release gaseous nitrogen from nitrates.

density: a ratio of mass to volume. In population studies, the number of individuals per unit of space in an ecosystem.

deoxyribonucleic (DEE ok sih ry boh new KLEE ik) **acid:** *see* DNA.

deoxyribose (dee ok sih RY bose): a five-carbon sugar that differs from ribose in one oxygen atom.

desert: almost any area of less than 40 cm (15 to 16 inches) of annual rainfall. Water and not soil quality is usually the limiting factor.

determiner: a variable that has been confirmed to cause a direct, measurable effect.

deviation (dee vee AY shun): the difference between predicted and observed outcomes of an event.

Devonian (dih VOH nee un): the fourth period of the Paleozoic era.

diaphragm (DY uh fram): the domelike sheet of muscle that separates the thorax from the abdomen in mammals.

diatom (DY uh tom): any of the golden algae that has a shell of silica.

dichotomous (dy KOT uh mus): divided into two groups or two courses of action.

dicotyledon (dy cot uh LEE dun) or **dicot** (DY cot): a plant whose embryo contained two cotyledons.

differentially permeable (PUR mee uh bul): admitting some molecules and ions but not others.

differentiation (dif uh ren chee AY shun): in a developing organism, change of cells from the single type in the egg to the different types in specialized tissues and organs of the body.

diffusion (dif YEW zhun): the random movement of molecules. It results in their dispersion from wherever they are more abundant to where they are less so.

digestion (dy JES chun): the chemical breakdown of food into molecules the body can absorb. Also, the breakdown of foodstuffs in a cell.

digestive system: an internal tract, and the organs along it, present in most multicellular animals and specialized in digesting foods.

digit (DIJ ut): the fingers and toes, or any of the small bones of the toes in vertebrates.

dihybrid (dy HY brud) **cross:** a genetic cross between individuals that differ in two hereditary characteristics being studied.

dilution (dih LOO shun): decreased concentration of a substance by mixture or solution in another substance.

diphtheria (dif THIR ee uh): a disease of humans caused by bacteria, prevented today by artificial immunization. Infection results in formation of false membranes that block the throat and windpipe.

diploid (DIP loid): having the full set of paired chromosomes characteristic of a species.

disaccharide (DY SAK uh ryd): a sugar built of two simple-sugar units. Table sugar (sucrose) is an example.

discontinuous (dis kun TIN yuh wus) **distribution:** separated habitats for a species, often resulting from a wider former distribution which left "pockets."

disease: any disorder serious enough to require medical treatment.

disinfect (dis in FEKT): to kill disease-causing organisms on a surface, on the hands, or on a laboratory instrument.

disinfectant (dis in FEK tunt): a substance or procedure that kills disease-producing organisms where it is applied.

dispersal (dis PUR sul): spreading from the point of origin, as seeds from a parent plant or as animals from where their species originated.

display (dis PLAY): an innate courtship behavior in which the male goes through an elaborate performance that visually stimulates the female. Or, an innate territorial behavior in which the male threatens a male intruder.

dissection (dis EK shun): cutting open of a body part or a dead organism for study.

distribution: the spread of data over a range of values. Or, dispersal or clustering of individuals in a population.

diversity (dih VUR suh tee): different types.

division: a broad classification level for plants, equivalent to a phylum.

DNA: deoxyribonucleic acid, the information-coding compound in chromosomes.

dominant: in social behavior, exerting a controlling influence over other individuals. In genetics, exerting a controlling influence on determination of phenotype.

dormant: inactive but living, as in a seed or a spore that has not germinated or an animal that is hibernating.

dorsal (DOR sul): located in the region of the body commonly called the back. The upper part of the body in animals that maintain a horizontal position.

doubling time: the future time within which a population will double in size.

Down syndrome (SIN drohm): a genetic disorder of humans caused by nondisjunction of chromosome 21 in one of the parents' gametes. Three of that chromosome are present in the offspring, instead of two.

drug: a substance that usually acts on the body by blocking nerve synapses or activating them uncontrollably. Also, any of the many medicinal substances prescribed for illnesses.

drug dependence: addiction or near-addiction.

Dryopithecus (dry oh PITH uh kus): a fossil primate.

duration (dyoo RAY shun): the length of time a condition lasts, as freezing temperatures in a particular environment.

Echinodermata (ih KY nuh DURM uh tuh) or **echinoderms** (ih KY nuh durmz): the phylum of invertebrates including starfish, brittle stars, sea urchins, sand dollars, sea cucumbers, and related animals. All are marine and have radial symmetry as adults.

ecological isolation: populations separated both geographically and because they have adapted to different habitats.

ecology (ih KOL uh jee): study of relationships among organisms, and between organisms and their physical environment.

ecosystem (EE koh sis tum): the community of organisms in a given area, together with their physical environment and its characteristic climate.

ectoderm (EK tuh durm): the outer layer of cells in the body wall of an animal or an animal embryo.

edema (ih DEE muh): a swelling of human body tissues with excess water.

effector: a muscle or gland stimulated by nerve or hormone action.

electron (ih LEK tron): an atomic particle found outside an atom's nucleus and involved in forming chemical bonds.

Also, the basic moving particle of electric current, or electricity.

electron microscope (ih LEK tron MY kruh skohp): a microscope for examining specimens with an electron beam instead of visible light. Images can be seen with an electron microscope that are too small to be seen with a light microscope.

element (EL uh munt): a substance made of a single kind of atom.

elimination (ih lim uh NAY shun): removal of unneeded or undigested substances from the body. In plants, these substances are deposited in dead stem tissue or in leaves that will be shed.

embryo (EM bree oh): an early developmental stage of an offspring of sexual reproduction.

embryology (em bree OL uh jee): the study of formation and development of embryos.

emergent (ih MUR junt) **plant:** a plant rising out of pond, lake, or shallow ocean water. A plant rooted under water but growing above the water surface.

emigration (eh muh GRAY shun): departure of individuals from a population.

endemic (en DEM ik): native to; belonging; usual.

endocrine (EN duh krun) **gland:** a hormone-producing gland that has no delivery duct or tube.

endoderm (EN duh durm): the inner layer of cells in the body wall of an animal or an animal embryo.

endodermis (en duh DUR mus): an inner "skin" or dermal layer of cells around a vascular cylinder in a plant root. Also, any of certain other inner dermal layers in various organisms.

endoplasmic reticulum (en duh PLAZ mik   rih TIK yuhlum): a membranous network throughout the cytoplasm of a cell.

endoskeleton (EN doh SKEL uh tun): an internal skeleton; or, any skeleton covered by at least one layer of tissue on the outside of the body.

endosperm (EN duh spurm): a food-storage tissue in a seed.

energy: the active component of all change. It has no measurable mass but is experienced as heat, light, motion, electricity, chemical energy, nuclear energy, and so on.

environment (en VY run munt): [external] the living and nonliving surroundings of an organism; [internal] the conditions in an organism's body.

environmental disease: a disease caused or aggravated by the body's reaction to certain particles or substances in the environment.

enzyme (EN zym): a protein molecule that functions as a catalyst.

enzyme-substrate complex (EN zym SUB strayt KOM pleks): a temporary chemical bond between an enzyme and its substrate.

Eocene (EE uh seen): the second epoch of the Tertiary period.

epidemic (ep uh DEM ik): a severe outbreak of a disease.

epidermis (ep uh DUR mus): the outer layer of an animal's skin or of a plant leaf, onion bulb, and so on.

epiglottis (ep uh GLOT is): a flap of tissue that closes over the opening to the lungs when food is swallowed.

Epihippus (ep uh HIP us): a fossil horse.

epinephrine (EP uh NEF run): the adrenal hormone also known as adrenalin, important in responding to stress.

epiphytes (EP uh fyts): nonparasitic plants that grow on other, taller plants.

epoch (EP uk): a division of geologic time; part of a period.

equatorial (ee kwuh TOR ee ul) **plate:** a plane through the middle of the cell where chromosomes line up on the spindle at the beginning of mitosis or meiosis. It is an imagined "plate" to indicate the location of the chromosomes, not an actual structure.

era (IR uh): a broad division of geologic time, further divided into periods and epochs.

erosion (ih ROH zhun): wearing away of land surfaces by wind, water, and weathering.

esophagus (ih SOF uh gus): the tube connecting the mouth or pharynx to the stomach in vertebrates and certain invertebrates.

estimate: approximation of a measurement or value in place of determining it precisely.

estrogen (ES truh jun): a primary female hormone with a number of functions; also found in minute amounts in males.

estrous (ES trus) **cycle:** the reproductive cycle of most female mammals.

ethologist (ee THOL uh just): a biologist who specializes in studying animal behavior.

evaporation (ih vap uh RAY shun): change from the liquid to the gaseous state.

evolution (ev uh LOO shun): the theory that, given time and variation among individuals of each species, different species will evolve by natural selection of individuals best-adapted in their variations.

excretion (ik SKREE shun): removal of metabolic wastes from cells and from the blood.

exobiology (EKS oh by OL uh jee): the study of life elsewhere in space than on Earth.

exoskeleton (EKS oh SKEL uh tun): an external skeleton that encloses the body.

experiment (ik SPER uh munt): scientific investigation to test a hypothesis or verify cause and effect with an experimental variable.

experimental variable (VAIR ee uh bul): a condition deliberately varied to observe the experimental effects of its change.

extinct (ik STINKT): no longer existing.

extracellular digestion (EK struh SEL yuh lur dy JES chun): digestion in a body cavity or digestive system that is outside the body cells.

fact: an item of information determined to be true on the basis of repeated observations or experiments by many different scientists.

family: a group of related genera.

famine (FAM un): extreme scarcity of food.

fat: any of a group of compounds made of glycerol and fatty acids.

fatty acid: an organic acid composed of a carbon chain with hydrogen atoms bonded to it, and with only two other atoms (oxygen) at one end in a —COOH group. Acetic acid is the fatty acid with the shortest carbon chain.

feces (FEE seez): undigested food remnants, mucus, and dead cells from the lining of the digestive tract that are eliminated through the rectum and anus.

fermentation (fur mun TAY shun): partial release of energy from foodstuffs in the absence of oxygen.

fern: any of a group of vascular plants in the subdivision Pteropsida that do *not* bear seeds. The leaves are usually subdivided into leaflets on long fronds.

fertile (FUR tul): capable of reproducing sexually. In soils, richness of minerals needed for plant growth.

fertilization: the union of a male and a female gamete, usually a sperm and an egg.

fetus (FEET us): the embryo in its later stages of development.

fiber cells: cells with supportive fibers that strengthen a plant stem.

fibrinogen (fy BRIN uh jun): a blood protein that is converted to fibrin in blood clotting.

fibrous (FY brus) root system: many roots issuing from the base of the stem, each root with branches.

fibrovascular (fy broh VAS kyuh lur) bundle: a bundle of phloem and xylem cells in a cellular sheath.

Filicineae (fil uh SIN ee ee): the class of tracheophytes consisting of ferns.

filtrate (FIL trayt): the liquid portion of a substance, the portion that passes through filter paper.

finite (FY nyt): limited, rather than endless.

first filial (FIL ee ul) generation: the F₁ generation, offspring of a genetic cross.

first-order consumer: a herbivore; an organism that eats plants or other producers.

fission (FISH un): asexual reproduction of a single-celled organism by cell division, in which the parent loses its identity.

flagellum (fluh JEL um): a long, hairlike structure of certain cells, used in locomotion or in creating currents.

flame cell: a type of cell in planarians that functions in removing excess water from the body.

flatworm: a worm flattened in shape from dorsal to ventral sides. A member of the phylum Platyhelminthes.

flocculent (FLOK yuh lunt): soft and flakelike; or fluffy, as in some kinds of chemical precipitates.

fluctuation (fluk chew AY shun): change in numbers or values in both directions—up and down.

follicle (FOL ih kul): a structure of a mammalian ovary in which an egg develops.

follicle-stimulating hormone: *see* FSH.

food: an organic substance that can be digested by an organism's enzymes.

food chain: the food relationship leading from a producer organism to a herbivore that eats the producer, to a carnivore that eats the herbivore, and so on.

food web: all the food chains in an ecosystem, or in the entire biosphere.

foramen magnum (fuh RAY mun MAG num): the large opening in the base of a vertebrate skull where brain and spinal cord meet.

fossil (FOS ul): a trace of an organism of the past, preserved in the earth.

free-living: not parasitic.

fructose (FRUK tose): a simple sugar; fruit sugar.

fruit: the structure formed by the growth and ripening of the pistil around its seeds.

FSH: follicle-stimulating hormone, a pituitary hormone that causes development of an egg in a follicle in the female and production of sperm by the testes in the male.

FSHRH: a releasing hormone (RH) of the hypothalamus that stimulates the pituitary to secrete FSH (follicle-stimulating hormone).

fungus (FUNG gus): a mushroom, mold, or other such organism; usually a decomposer.

fusion (FYEW zhun) nucleus: a diploid nucleus in the ovule of a pistil.

gall bladder: a small sac that stores bile from the liver.

gamete (guh MEET): a sexual reproductive cell, male or female.

gametophyte (guh MEET uh fyt): a monoploid organism that produces gametes, in species with alternation of generations.

ganglion (GANG glee un): a cluster of nerve cell bodies.

gastric (GAS trik) juice: a watery solution of stomach acid and enzymes.

gene: a segment of chromosomal DNA controlling expression of a single hereditary characteristic.

generalization: a summary of a number of separate observations in terms of an apparent pattern among them.

gene-splicing: a chemically controlled procedure for introducing a gene from one organism into the DNA of another organism.

genetic (juh NET ik) drift: changes in gene frequencies due to chance instead of natural selection.

genetics (juh NET iks): the branch of biology that deals with heredity.

genotype (JEE nuh typ): the alleles for a particular characteristic carried by the chromosomes of an individual.

genus (JEE nus): a group of related species; plural, genera (JEN uh ruh).

geographical isolation: separation of populations by mountains, a canyon, a body of water, a desert, and so on.

geographic range: all the known habitats of a particular species, recorded as areas on a map.

geologist (jee OL uh just): a scientist who studies the earth, its minerals, and the causes of its long-term changes.

geotropism (jee AH truh piz um): a response of a plant to gravity.

germinate (JUR muh nayt): to leave the dormant state, as in a spore or seed, and begin growing.

gibberellins (jib ur EL inz): growth substances produced by certain fungi, algae, and plants.

gills: respiratory organs of many aquatic organisms. Also, parts of the reproductive structure of club fungi.

ginkgo (GING koh): a gymosperm tree discovered from fossils and believed extinct until discovered living in China; now widely grown.

gizzard (GIZ urd): a muscular organ in the digestive system of many animals, functioning to grind and break down foods into smaller pieces. In birds, the gizzard is the posterior part of the stomach.

glomerulus (gluh MER yuh lus): a ball of capillaries nested

in the cuplike end of a kidney tubule.

Glossopteris (glos SOP tur us): a type of extinct seed fern.

glucose (GLOO kohs): a simple sugar, the sugar from which many common starches are made.

glycerol (GLIS uh rol): a compound that can be made in cells from glucose and that is used in making fats.

glycogen (GLY kuh jun): the carbohydrate made by the liver in storing excess sugar.

golden algae (AL jee): algae in which the chlorophyll is usually masked by yellow pigments; diatoms are examples.

Golgi (GOL jee) **apparatus:** a cell organelle believed to function in packaging and delivering cell secretions, often through the cell membrane.

gonads (GOH nadz): ovaries and testes; the gamete-producing organs of animals.

gonorrhea (gon uh REE uh): a bacterial disease of humans transmitted by sexual intercourse; a venereal disease.

green algae (AL jee): algae in which the chlorophyll is usually not masked by other pigments, and ranging in size from single cells to large sea lettuce (*Ulva*).

guard cells: a pair of cells that regulates the opening and closing of a stomate.

Gymnospermae (JIM nuh SPURM ee) or **gymnosperms** (JIM nuh spurmz): the class of seed-producing plants in which the seeds are attached to scales, usually in cones. These are mostly woody, coniferous plants.

habitat (HAB uh tat): the place where an organism lives.

half-life: the time required for half an amount of radioactive material to break down into simpler materials and energy.

Hardy-Weinberg principle: a mathematical calculation which demonstrates that random mating in a population tends to leave the population's gene frequencies unchanged from generation to generation, unless natural selection or some other factor is at work.

heartwood: older wood, near the center of a tree trunk or branch, that has lost the conducting function.

hemoglobin (HEE muh gloh bun): the oxygen-transporting pigment in blood. Present in vertebrates and in some invertebrates.

herb: a nonwoody plant.

herbaceous (hur BAY shus): nonwoody and typically small as a result.

herbicide (HUR buh syd): a weed killer.

herbivore (HUR buh vor): an animal that eats plants or other producers.

hereditary (huh RED uh ter ee): determined by genes; transmitted from parent to offspring.

hereditary (huh RED uh ter ee) **disease:** a disease or disorder transmitted by genes.

hermaphrodite (hur MAF ruh dyt): an animal with both ovaries and testes.

herpes (HUR peez): a virus, one strain of which has become the cause of widespread veneral disease.

heterozygous (het uh roh ZY gus): having a genotype of two unlike alleles.

hibernate (HY bur nayt): to fall into a dormant state in which body processes and temperature drop so much below normal that later warming and waking occur only

gradually.

homeostatis (hoh mee oh STAY sis): maintenance of conditions between upper and lower limits tolerable to life.

Homo erectus (HOH moh ih REK tus): an early species of humans known from abundant fossils, stone tools, and charred remains of fires.

homologue (HOH muh log): a biological structure relatively like another and of the same origin. An example is a chromosome and its homologue—the other chromosome of the pair.

Homo sapiens neanderthalensis (HOH moh SAP ee unz nee and ur thawl EN sis): the Neanderthal peoples, known from fossils and many artifacts.

Homo sapiens sapiens (HOH moh SAP ee unz SAP ee unz): the species and subspecies of modern humans.

homozygous (hoh muh ZY gus): having a genotype of two alleles of the same type.

hormone (HOR mohn): any of a group of regulatory substances affecting growth, development, cell metabolism, or a balance of body materials.

horsetail: a plant with hollow, jointed, upright branches, and with needlelike leaves arranged circularly around each joint. A plant of the subdivision Sphenopsida.

horticulturalist (hort uh KULCH uh ruh lust): a person who breeds and grows plants for research or sale.

host: an organism infected by a pathogen or infested with a parasite.

humidity (hew MID uh tee): the water vapor content of air.

humus (HEW mus): decomposed remains of organisms in soil.

hybrid (HY brud): heterozygous; having unlike alleles in a gene pair affecting the characteristic being studied.

hydrolysis (hy DROL uh sus): a type of chemical reaction in which the equivalent of a molecule of water is added for each chemical bond broken, when a large molecule is digested.

hydrosphere (HY droh sfir): all the water on the earth's surface, including in the atmosphere.

hyphae (HY fee): the threadlike filaments of fungi.

hypothalamus (hy poh THAL uh mus): the link between the brain and the endocrine glands in humans and some other vertebrates.

hypothesis (hy POTH uh sis): a trial explanation of available observations, stated to make prediction and experiment possible.

Hyracotherium (hy RAK uh THER ee um): the earliest known fossil horse ancestor.

immigration (im uh GRAY shun): addition of individuals to a population from other populations of the same species.

immunity (im YEW nut ee): effective resistance against a disease.

imprinting (IM print ing): behavior in which the first response to a particular stimulus, early in life, becomes a fixed response to the same stimulus thereafter.

incubation (ing kyuh BAY shun): maintenance at the proper temperature for embryonic development. For microorganisms, maintenance at the proper temperature for reproduction.

indicator: one of two substances that undergoes a visible chemical change in the presence of the other, and is used to test for the latter.

individual: one; single; or, biologically, a single organism.

infectious (in FEK shus) **disease:** any of the diseases caused by microorganisms.

influenza (in floo EN zuh): any of a group of infections with similar symptoms caused by certain viruses or bacteria. Symptoms include fever, congestion, weakness, muscular aches, and digestive upset.

ingestion (in JES chun): feeding; taking in food.

innate (in AYT) **behavior:** behavior determined by heredity; inborn behavior.

inorganic (IN or GAN ik): chemically composed of elements that include no carbon or no more than one carbon atom per molecule.

Insecta (in SEK tuh) or **insects:** the class of invertebrates with segmented exoskeletons and with three pairs of jointed legs appended to the thorax.

insecticide (in SEK tuh syd): a substance poisonous to insects.

insectivorous (in sek TIV uh rus): carnivorous, preying on insects.

instruments: devices to extend the senses in gathering qualitative data, or devices of measurement for quantitative data, or devices that combine both functions.

insulin (IN suh lun): a vertebrate hormone vital to the body's use of sugar.

interbreed: to mate and reproduce.

interrelationship: a connection in ancestry, or way of life in an ecosystem, or some other biological feature, between different organisms or species.

interval: a division of time or space, or of any set of values; or, one of a number of shorter spans or periods so produced.

intestinal juice: an alkaline secretion containing enzymes, produced in the small intestine in vertebrates.

intestine: a digestive organ of many animals, and in some (such as insects) also an organ in which body wastes are concentrated for excretion.

intracellular digestion (IN truh SEL yuh lur dy JES chun): digestion inside the body cells of an organism.

intraspecific (in truh spih SIF ik) **competition:** competition among individuals of the same species, as contrasted to competition between different species that share the same environmental niche.

in vitro (in VEE troh): in the laboratory or in glassware, outside the living body.

in vivo (in VEE voh): in the body; in the living environment.

ion (EYE un): an electrically charged particle resulting from the chemical addition of one or more electrons to, or their removal from, an atom or molecule.

irritability (ir ut uh BIL ut ee): the capability of living things to be affected by stimuli, and to respond.

isopod (EYE suh pod): a member of an order of crustaceans in which an organism's legs are of approximately equal size; example, sow bug.

Jurassic (juh RAS ik): the second period of the Mesozoic era.

kidney: an excretory organ of vertebrates and many in-

vertebrates.

kingdom: the largest grouping in the classification of organisms.

lactose (LAK tohs): milk sugar, a disaccharide.

large intestine: the intestine posterior (in vertebrates) to the small intestine, in which undigested wastes collect for elimination and fluids are reabsorbed by the body.

larva (LAR vuh): an immature stage of development in offspring of many kinds of animals.

larynx (LAR ingks): the voice box, at the anterior end of the trachea or windpipe.

lateral bud: a bud from the side of a plant stem.

latitude (LAT uh tood): distance in degrees north or south of the earth's equator.

leaflet: one of a number of separate portions of a leaf blade into which a leaf is divided, in certain plants.

lenticel (LENT uh sel): one of a system of openings in the bark of a woody plant.

LH: luteinizing hormone, a pituitary hormone that induces ovulation in the female, and production of testosterone by the testes in the male.

LHRH: a releasing hormone (RH) of the hypothalamus that stimulates the pituitary to secrete LH (luteinizing hormone).

lichen (LY kun): a type of organism formed by a mutualistic relationship between an alga and a fungus.

linkage: transmission of certain genes together because they are located on the same chromosome.

lipid (LIP ud): a compound related to fats, but modified chemically.

littoral (LIT uh rul) **zone:** the ocean shore area covered by high tide, but exposed by low tide.

liver: a vertebrate organ of many functions. It excretes wastes to the kidney, secretes bile for use in digestion, stores sugar as glycogen, and removes aged or damaged red blood cells from the bloodstream, among other functions.

locomotion (loh kuh MOH shun): movement from place to place, as by a protist or animal that is motile.

locus (LOH kus): position or location. In genetics, the site of a particular gene on a chromosome.

lungfish: a fish that breathes both with its gills and with a modified air bladder.

luteinizing hormone (LOOT ee un eyz ing HOR mohn): *see* LH.

Lycopsida (ly KOP sih duh): a subdivision of tracheophytes; the club mosses.

lymph (LIMF): blood plasma without its blood proteins; the fluid carrying supplies and wastes that is exchanged between blood and body cells.

lymph (LIMF) **vessels:** a set of vessels into which lymph flows from body cells. The lymph vessels empty into a large vein near the heart.

lysosome (LYE suh som): a cell organelle that contains digestive enzymes and that functions in the digestion of food materials in the cell.

macroscopic (mak ruh SKOP ik): visible without the aid of a microscope.

malaria: a disease of humans caused by a protist of the genus

Plasmodium that attacks red blood cells.

maltose (MAWL tohs): a disaccharide sugar digested from starch.

Mammalia (muh MAY lee uh) or **mammals** (MAM ulz): the class of vertebrates that have hair and that produce milk for their young.

mammary (MAM uh ree) **glands:** milk-producing glands of female mammals.

manometer (muh NOM ut er): an apparatus that measures gas production as a pressure change (*see* Investigation 12.1).

marine (muh REEN): living in the oceans or in seas connected with oceans. Also, for nonliving materials, found in seas or oceans.

marsupial (mar SOO pee ul): a mammal that gives birth to immature young that continue to develop in the mother's abdominal pouch.

mass: the property of substances measured as the amount of matter they contain. Or, in a mass of objects, their accumulation in numbers that appear to form a single larger body.

mass spectrometer (spek TROM ut ur): an instrument that can distinguish heavier from lighter isotopes of the same element.

matter: anything that occupies space and has a measurable mass; a physical characteristic denoting *substance* or *material* as opposed to *energy.*

measles (MEE zulz): a virus-caused disease marked by congestion, fever, and reddened rash on the skin.

medicinal (muh DIS uh nul): used for cleaning or healing of wounds or curing illness.

medium: in a biology laboratory, a nutrient preparation used to feed a population of microorganisms or of small multicellular organisms.

Megahippus (meg uh HIP pus): a fossil horse.

meiosis (my OH sus): reduction of chromosome number in two nuclear divisions preceded by only one duplication of chromosomes. The resulting chromosome number is monoploid—half the parent cell's number of chromosomes.

menstrual (MEN struh wul) **cycle:** the human female reproductive cycle of approximately 28 days.

menstruation (men struh WAY shun): the discharge of blood and material from the uterine lining when pregnancy has not occurred in a reproductive cycle.

meristem (MER uh stem): growth tissue in vascular plants (cambium, stem tips, lateral buds, root tips).

Merychippus (mer ee KIP us): a fossil horse.

mesentery (MES un ter ee): a membrane that in vertebrates holds the intestines in place.

mesoderm (MEZ uh durm): a middle layer of cells in an animal embryo.

Mesohippus (mez uh HIP us): a fossil horse.

mesophyll (MEZ uh fil): loosely arranged cells inside the lower epidermis of a leaf.

Mesozoic (mez uh ZOH ik): the second most recent geologic era, the age of dinosaurs.

messenger RNA: *see* mRNA

metabolism (muh TAB uh liz um): a cell's or an organism's biochemical processes, considered all together.

microbe (MY krob): a microorganism; *microbe* is used chiefly historically, while *microorganism* is used today.

microbiology (MY kroh by OL uh jee): the study of microscopic organisms.

microorganism (my kroh OR guh niz um): an organism invisible to the human eye, but visible under a microscope.

microscope (MY kruh skohp): an instrument for examining small objects in light passed through convex glass lenses to magnify the image.

microscopic (my kruh SKOP ik): invisible to the eye; requiring a microscope to be seen.

mid-latitude (MID LAT uh tood) **desert:** the native biome of some of the southwestern and western states of the United States and of certain other parts of the world.

mid-latitude deciduous (MID LAT uh tood dih SIJ uh was) **forest:** the native biome of much of the United States and of certain other areas of the world. It is named for the types of trees that characterize its forests.

mid-latitude (MID LAT uh tood) **grassland:** the native biome of the prairie states in the United States and of certain other areas of the world.

mid-latitude (MID LAT uh tood) **rain forest:** a biome in a narrow region bordering the Pacific Ocean from northern California to Alaska.

migratory (MY gruh tor ee) **behavior:** an innate behavior of many birds and other animals in having seasonal habitats and traveling between them.

mineral: a general name for inorganic compounds.

Miocene (MY uh seen): the fourth geologic epoch of the Tertiary period.

Miohippus (my uh HIP us): a fossil horse.

mitochondrion (myt uh KON dree un): a cell organelle that carries on cell respiration.

mitosis (my TOH sus): a nuclear division preceded by duplication of the chromosomes, resulting in each new nucleus having the same number and types of chromosomes as the parent nucleus.

mixed culture: a culture of two or more species or varieties of organisms being maintained together.

mixture: two or more substances with their particles intermingled.

model: a physical construction, or a mental picture (sometimes programmed into a computer), used to represent a real situation being investigated.

molecule (MOL ih kewl): the smallest particle of an element or compound usually found naturally occurring.

Mollusca (muh LUS kuh) or **mollusks** (MOL usks): a phylum of unsegmented, soft-bodied invertebrates many of which secrete a shell. Examples are snails, slugs, oysters, clams, squid, octopus, and their relatives.

monocotyledon (mon uh cot uh LEE dun) or **monocot** (MON uh cot): a plant whose embryo contained one cotyledon.

monoploid (MON uh ploid): having only one chromosome of each pair, or half the total set characteristic of a species.

mortality (mor TAL uh tee): the death rate.

motile (MOH tul): capable of moving about in the environment.

motor neuron (NEW ron): a neuron that carries impulses

from the spinal cord or brain to an effector—a muscle or gland.

mRNA: messenger RNA, which carries instructions for making proteins from the DNA of a cell's nucleus to ribosomes in the cell's cytoplasm.

multicellular (mul tih SEL yuh lur): many-celled.

multiple alleles (uh LEE ulz): three or more different alleles for the same genetic characteristic, for which an individual may have any two.

mumps: a virus-caused disease marked by fever and swelling of the salivary glands, producing swollen jaws; ovaries or testes may also be infected.

muscle tone: a state of partial contraction in muscles, but not of their individual fibers (which contract fully or not at all).

mutation (myew TAY shun): a change in a gene resulting in a new allele for a particular trait, thereafter inheritable. Or, a change in a chromosome affecting more than one gene, or the sequence or loci of the genes, and also inheritable.

mutualism (MEW choo uh liz um): a relationship between two organisms that live together, with both benefited.

mycorrhizae (my kuh RY zee): mutualistic relationships between fungi and plant roots, including the tissues formed.

natality (nay TAL uh tee): the rate of reproduction of new individuals.

natural selection: the tendency of individuals best adapted to the environment to survive and reproduce. This accomplishes a selection among the variations in individuals of a species.

nematode (NEM uh tohd): a very small, nonsegmented roundworm found in soil.

nerve cell body: an enlarged region of a neuron, containing the cell nucleus and cytoplasm.

nerve cord: a main trunk of nerve fibers running the length of the body in most animals. It is ventral in invertebrates, dorsal in vertebrates.

nerve fiber: a long extension of a neuron.

nerve impulse: a wave of electrical and chemical changes that moves along a nerve or a nerve fiber.

net productivity (proh duk TIV uh tee): the amount of energy available to consumers from producers, in food.

neuron (NEW ron): a nerve cell.

neutral (pH): a pH value of 7, at which hydrogen (H^+) and hydroxide (OH^-) ions are equal in concentration.

niche (NICH): a way of life described in terms of a suitable environment and how the organism in question will fit into the food web.

nitrifying bacteria (NY truh fy ing bak TIR ee uh): soil bacteria important in nitrogen-fixing reactions in the nitrogen cycle.

nitrogen-fixing: the bonding of nitrogen from the air into nitrogen compounds.

nodule (NOJ ool): a swelling on the root of a plant, housing nitrogen-fixing bacteria.

nomenclature (NOH mun klay chur): a system for naming things, and the resulting names.

nondisjunction (non dis JUNK shun): failure of a pair of chromosomes to separate during meiosis; both go into the same gamete.

nonrenewable resource: a resource that cannot be replaced, such as fuels of biological origin.

notochord (NO tuh kord): a flexible support column in the dorsal region of lower chordates and in embryos of vertebrates.

nuclear membrane: the membrane enclosing a cell nucleus.

nucleic (new KLEE ik) **acid:** DNA or RNA, the kinds of molecules used to code hereditary information in an organism.

nucleolus (new KLEE uh lus): a small, darkly staining body, or one of two or more, in the cell nucleus.

nucleotide (NEW klee uh tyd): a single coding unit in DNA and RNA, consisting of a compound of sugar, phosphate, and a base.

nucleus (NEW klee us): the central portion or controlling part, as in an atom or a cell.

nutrient (NEW tree unt): a needed substance that an organism obtains from its environment in food, or as a mineral. It is used in body regulation or in photosynthesis.

nymph (NIMF): one of the immature young of certain insects.

observation (ob sur VAY shun): information gained by use of the senses, measurement, or experiment.

Olduvai (OLE duh vy): a gorge in East Africa rich in primate fossils.

olfactory (ol FAKT uh ree): associated with smelling.

Oligocene (OL ih goh seen): the third geologic epoch of the Tertiary period.

omnivore (OM nuh vor): an animal that eats both plants and other animals.

open circulatory system: circulation through vessels that open into body spaces, where blood bathes the tissues directly, later reentering vessels.

open population: a population influenced by immigration and emigration.

opposable thumb: articulation of the thumb opposite the four fingers in primates, making grasping and working with objects possible.

optic (OP tik): associated with seeing.

optimum (OP tuh mum): ideal; best.

order: a group of related families in the classification of organisms.

Ordovician (ord uh VISH un): the second period of the Paleozoic era.

organ: a group of tissues organized into a specialized body structure with a specialized function.

organelle (or guh NEL): any structure in the cytoplasm of a cell that is organized for a specific function.

organic (or GAN ik): chemically composed of elements that include carbon atoms linked to one another.

organism (OR guh niz um): a living thing.

organ system: all the organs of an animal that are associated with the same function.

ornithologist (or nuh THOL uh just): a biologist who specializes in studying birds.

Orohippus (or oh HIP us): a fossil horse.

Osteichthyes (os tee IK thee eez): the class of bony fishes.

ovary (OH vuh ree): a female reproductive organ in which eggs mature, and from which they are released.

oviduct (OH vuh dukt): a tube through which an egg passes upon leaving the ovary; in mammals, also called a fallopian tube.

ovulation (ov yuh LAY shun): the bursting of an egg from a follicle in an ovary.

ovule (AHV yewl): a chamber in the pistil of a flower containing several cells, one of which produces an egg nucleus.

ovum (OH vum): an egg cell.

oxyhemoglobin (OKS ih HEE muh gloh bun): hemoglobin combined with oxygen.

ozone (OH zone): a molecular form of oxygen, O_3, that shields the earth from most ultraviolet radiation from the sun.

Paleocene (PAY lee uh seen): the first geologic epoch of the Tertiary period.

paleoecosystem (pay lee oh EE koh sis tum): an ecosystem believed from fossil evidence to have existed in the past.

paleontologist (pay lee un TOL uh just): a scientist who studies the fossil record to reconstruct a picture of life in the past.

Paleozoic (pay lee uh ZOH ik): the geologic era that began with the Cambrian period.

pancreas (PAN kree us): an abdominal gland in vertebrates.

pancreatic (pan kree AT ik) **juice:** a pancreatic secretion containing digestive enzymes.

parasite (PAIR uh syt): an organism that lives on or in another living organism from which it obtains its food as cell or body fluids, or digested foodstuffs.

parathyroid (pair uh THY roid) **glands:** glands that produce hormones which regulate calcium and phosphorous balance between the bones and the blood.

parthenogenesis (par thuh noh JEN uh sus): development of an unfertilized animal egg into a new individual, common among certain insects.

pathogen (PATH uh jun): any organism that infects another.

pathology (puh THOL uh jee): the study of diseases and their causes.

pedigree (PED uh gree): a family chart of the occurrence of a characteristic believed to be hereditary.

pelvis (PEL vus): the fused bones of the hip girdle in many vertebrates.

penicillin (pen uh SIL un): an antibiotic.

penis (PEE nus): the male organ through which urine and semen are discharged; the male organ of sexual intercourse.

perception (pur SEP chun): awareness of environmental objects and events.

perennial (puh REN ee ul): a plant that lives for an indefinite number of years.

pericycle (PAIR uh sy kul): also called pericambium; a tissue in roots that is associated with formation of cambium and of lateral roots.

period: a span of time; in geologic time a division of an era.

permafrost (PUR muh frost): the permanently frozen subsoil of the tundra.

permeable (PUR mee uh bul): admitting molecules and ions, as through a barrier.

Permian (PUR mee un): the last period of the Paleozoic era.

pest: a plant or an animal species that is annoying to humans, or that carries microorganisms of human disease, or that competes with humans for food.

pesticide (PES tuh syd): a substance that is poisonous to certain animals considered by humans as pests. Examples are rat poisons and insecticides.

petal (PET ul): one of a number of leaflike, often brightly colored, parts of a flower that radiate out from the flower's center.

petiole (PET ee ohl): the stemlike portion of a leaf, attaching the leaf to a plant stem.

petrified (PEH truh fyd): changed into rock by mineral replacement of organic parts.

pharyngeal (far un JEE ul): in the throat region; behind the mouth, near the pharynx.

pharynx (FAR ingks): the region posterior to the mouth; the throat in humans.

phenotype (FEE nuh typ): the physical appearance of an individual as determined by its genotype.

pheromone (FER uh mon): any chemical substance used in communication between animals of many species, including as a sex attractant.

phloem (FLOH em): food-conducting cells in a vascular plant.

photosynthesis (FOH tuh SIN thuh sis): conversion of light energy to chemical energy used in the synthesis of organic compounds by producer organisms.

phototropism (foh TAH truh piz um): the response of a plant to light, usually a positive phototropism (growing toward the light).

pH scale: an acid-base scale in chemistry.

phylum (FY lum): a group of related classes, in the classification of organisms. The second-to-largest grouping of organisms, next to kingdom.

physiology (FIZ ee OL uh jee): the functioning of an organism's body. Or, comparing the functions of particular organs or tissues among many organisms.

phytoplankton (fyt oh PLANK tun): microscopic and near-microscopic aquatic producers, mainly algae.

pigment (PIG munt): a richly colored chemical. In organisms, the color of a pigment may be secondary to its function.

pistil (PIS tul): the female reproductive part of a flower.

pith: a central tissue in some plant stems. Also, a procedure for destroying brain and spinal tissue in frogs, permitting painless dissection and study of still-functioning organs.

Pithecanthropus erectus (pith uh KAN thruh pus ih REK tus): fossil primates named before additional discoveries revealed that they were human; now *Homo erectus*.

pituitary (puh TEW uh ter ee) **gland:** the endocrine gland in closest association with the hypothalamus in controlling hormone production and functions.

placenta (pluh SENT uh): an organ formed in early pregnancy from the chorion and an outgrowth of the uterine wall. Through it, exchange of food, oxygen, and wastes occurs between the embryo and mother.

planarian (pluh NAIR ee un): any of a certain group of unsegmented flatworms.

plankton (PLANK tun): microscopic and certain other very small aquatic organisms.

plasma (PLAZ muh): blood without its blood cells.

plasmodium (plaz MOH dee um): the living mass of a slime mold. Also, the name of a genus of protists.

plastid (PLAS tud): a type of cell organelle such as a chloroplast or any of several other structures.

platelet (PLAYT lut): a blood cell in vertebrates that functions in blood clotting.

plate tectonics (tek TON iks): the geologic theory that the earth's crust is made of a number of separate plates that move, accounting for mountain building, earthquakes, and other surface and subsurface activity.

Platyhelminthes (plat ih hel MIN theez): an animal phylum of flatworms.

Pleistocene (PLY stuh seen): the second most recent geologic epoch.

Pliocene (PLY uh seen): the geologic epoch following the Miocene and preceding the Pleistocene.

poliomyelitis (poh lee oh my uh LYT us): a virus-caused disease of humans, often resulting in partial paralysis from nerve damage.

pollen (POL un): monoploid cells produced by the anthers of a flower.

pollen tube: the tube produced by a germinating pollen grain.

pollination (pol uh NAY shun): the transfer of pollen from a stamen to a pistil or ovule.

pollutant (puh LOOT unt): an unneeded substance, or industrial heat waste, present in the environment in an amount or concentration great enough to be irritating or toxic to organisms.

pollution (puh LOO shun): contamination of the environment with materials, heat, or nuclear radiation as byproducts of human activities, volcanic explosions, and other causes.

polygenic (pol ih JEH nik): affected by many genes that are not alleles at one gene locus.

polypeptide (pol ih PEP tyd): a chain of amino acids, used in synthesizing protein.

polyploidy (POL ih ploid ee): the occurrence of individuals with multiple sets of chromosomes because meiosis does not occur or is abnormal.

polysaccharide (pol ih SAK uh ryd): a compound made up of many molecules of simple sugars. Examples are starch and cellulose.

population: all the organisms of a single species that live in the same place at the same time.

population cycle: an up-and-down swing in numbers in a population in which this pattern repeats at measurable intervals.

pore: a functionally adapted hole in living tissue.

Porifera (puh RIF uh ruh): an animal phylum of sponges and their relatives.

posterior (pos TIR ee ur): toward the rear end.

potassium (puh TAS ee um): an element essential to life. A radioactive isotope of it is used in potassium-argon geologic dating.

Pre-Cambrian (pree KAM bree un): the geologic era from the beginning of life to the beginning of the Cambrian period.

precipitation (prih sip uh TAY shun): in weather, falling moisture such as rainfall and snowfall. In a chemical reaction, settling out of a newly formed solid to the bottom of a container.

predator (PRED uh tur): a protist or an animal that preys on other living organisms for food.

prediction (prih DIK shun): anticipation of an undiscovered event in the past, present, or future.

pregnancy (PREG nun see): the embedding of a fertilized egg in the lining of the uterus of a female mammal.

preservative (prih ZUR vuh tiv): a chemical, or high or low temperature, used to prevent or retard spoilage or decay.

prey (PRAY): an organism sought as food by other organisms.

principle of segregation: the principle that genes of a pair are separated in gamete formation.

probability: the field of mathematics dealing with uncertain events.

producer: an organism that uses a nonliving source of energy and inorganic compounds to synthesize organic compounds.

productivity (proh duk TIV uh tee): the amount of available solar energy converted to chemical energy by producers over any given period of time.

progesterone (proh JES tuh rone): a primary female hormone with several functions in the reproductive cycle.

prostaglandin (pros tuh GLAN dun): any of the hormonelike compounds derived from fatty acids and produced by cells and tissues throughout the body.

prostate (PROS tayt) **gland:** a gland in the male that secretes an alkaline fluid which is part of the semen.

protein (PROH teen): a molecule composed of one or more chains, usually two or more, of amino acids.

prothrombin (proh THROM bun): a blood protein that is converted to thrombin in the blood-clotting process.

Protista (proh TIS tuh) or **protists** (PROH tists): a kingdom in the biological classification system. It is used for classifying many microorganisms and certain other organisms that are not plants or animals.

protozoan (proh tuh ZOH un): a protist that is typically nonbacterial, motile, and a consumer rather than a producer; for example, *Paramecium.*

pseudopod (SOO duh pod): a fingerlike extension, or one of two or more such extensions, produced by certain cells and one-celled organisms. It functions in capturing food, engulfing bacteria, and locomotion.

psychologist (sy KOL uh just): a scientist who specializes in studying human and other mammalian behavior.

Pteropsida (tuh ROP sih duh): the subdivision of tracheophytes that includes the ferns, gymnosperms, and flowering plants.

pulsate (PUL sayt): to beat rhythmically.

pupa (PYEW puh): a stage of the development of many insects, in which a larva secretes a covering around itself and then begins to develop into an adult inside its pupal case.

pure culture: a culture free of all organisms except the species or variety desired.

pyloric (py LOR ik) **valve:** a valve between the stomach and intestine of vertebrates, controlling food passage.

qualitative (KWAL uh tay tiv): determined by description and identification, or analysis other than measurement.

quantitative (KWAN tuh tay tiv): determined by measurement.

Quaternary (KWAT ur ner ee): the present period of geologic time.

radial symmetry (RAYD ee ul SIM uh tree): the body plan of animals that have a spherical, wheel-like, or hub-and-spoke appearance, as if all body parts radiated outward from the center.

radiation: energy transmitted in waves of varying wavelengths.

radioactive (rayd ee oh AK tiv): unstable in nuclear organization, breaking down to give off radiation and smaller atomic nuclei.

Ramapithecus (rah muh PITH uh kus): a fossil primate, possibly a descendant of *Dryopithecus*.

random (RAN dum): occurring by chance.

rate: a measure of change with respect to time.

ray cell: any of certain cells through which water, minerals, and food in a woody plant stem move laterally.

reagent (ree AY junt): a chemical taking part in a reaction, and changed by the reaction.

reasoning: intelligent behavior involving thinking about or sizing up a stimulus situation and deciding how to respond. The *first* exposure to the problem is the test, in contrast to trial-and-error learning.

Recent epoch (EP uk): the present geologic time.

receptor: an eye, ear, organ of touch, or any other structure at which stimuli are received from the environment.

recessive: exerting no influence on phenotype unless in a homozygous pair with an identical allele.

recombination: new gene linkages caused by crossing-over of parts of two chromosomes.

red algae (AL jee): algae in which the chlorophyll is masked by red pigments.

red blood cell: a blood cell of vertebrates that contains hemoglobin.

reflex (REE fleks): automatic reception of and response to a stimulus, without intervention by the brain.

reforestation (ree for uh STAY shun): the process of planting new trees on land once forested.

regeneration (rih jen uh RAY shun): the development of a body part to replace a lost or damaged one, as in the new leaves on deciduous trees each spring or a new claw on an injured lobster.

relative humdity (hew MID uh tee): the water vapor content of air expressed as the percentage of the maximum amount of water vapor the air could hold at the existing temperature.

releasing hormone (HOR mohn): any hormone produced by the hypothalamus that helps control secretions of the pituitary gland.

renewable resource: a biological resource that can be recycled or replaced. Examples are carbon dioxide, oxygen, water, soil minerals, and food energy.

replication (rep luh KAY shun): the doubling of chromosome number before mitosis or meiosis. As a result, each chromosome has one strand of DNA from the parent chromosome and one new strand.

reproduction: the asexual and sexual processes by which new organisms are produced.

reproductive isolation: inability of individuals of different species, or varieties within a species, to interbreed because of genetic differences that have changed the breeding season of one or have resulted in some other behavioral or biochemical barrier.

Reptilia (rep TIL ee uh) or **reptiles** (REP tulz): the class of vertebrates that breathe by lungs, have scales on their skin, and lay leathery-shelled eggs on land. Its members include snakes, turtles, lizards, alligators, and crocodiles.

resistance: partial or complete immunity to a disease.

resources: in biology, matter and energy available for use by organisms.

response: anything an organism does in reaction to a stimulus.

rhizoid (RY zoid): a hairlike tissue of ferns, mosses, and liverworts that functions similarly to a root.

rhizome (RY zohm): a horizontal underground stem thickened by food storage. It produces new shoots above and roots below.

ribonucleic (RY boh new KLEE ik) **acid:** *see* RNA.

ribose (RY bose): a five-carbon sugar.

ribosomal (ry buh SOHM ul) **RNA:** the RNA that together with proteins makes up a ribosome.

ribosome (RYE buh som): one of many tiny structures in cell cytoplasm that carry on protein synthesis.

rickettsia (rik ET see uh): one of the smallest kinds of organisms known, smaller than most bacteria; a procaryotic parasite.

ringworm: a skin disorder of many mammals caused by a fungus.

RNA: ribonucleic acid, an information-coding compound of organisms.

root cap: protective cells covering a root tip.

root hair: one of many threadlike extensions of root epidermal cells that absorb water together with dissolved minerals from the soil.

root pressure: a pressure exerted by plant roots that pushes water upward into the stem.

rRNA: ribosomal RNA, which together with proteins makes up a ribosome.

rubidium (roo BID ee um): an element with a radioactive isotope used in a geologic dating method.

rumen (ROO mun): one of four chambers in the stomach of cattle.

sac fungus (FUNG gus): a fungus in which spores are produced in microscopic sacs. *Penicillium* is an example.

salinity (say LIN ut ee): the concentration of salts, or of minerals that are mostly salts, in water.

saliva (suh LY vuh): the secretion of the salivary glands in vertebrates and many invertebrates.

salivary (SAL uh ver ee) **gland:** a gland, or one of two or more, in insects, mammals, and many other animals that produces saliva.

sampling: a method of estimation involving measurement of part of the whole as representative of the whole.

sarcodinan (sar kuh DY nun): any of a group of microorganisms that move by means of pseudopods.

saturated (SACH ur ayt ud): absorbed to capacity; not able to hold more.

savanna (suh VAN uh): an arid tall-grass biome in the tropics or subtropics.

scales: hardened structures on the outer body surface of various animals, mostly vertebrates. Examples are scales of fish, of reptiles, and of the legs of birds.

scapula (SCAP yuh luh): a shoulder blade, in many vertebrates.

scrotum (SKROHT um): the pouch of skin outside the body cavity that holds the testes of a male.

scurvy: a diet-deficiency disease of humans, caused by insufficient vitamin C. Symptoms include bleeding gums, loosening of teeth, and skin disorders.

secondary sexual characteristics: features of appearance and behavior that are linked to the sex and sexual maturity of an individual but are not essential to reproduction. Examples are a rooster's comb (appearance) and the rooster's crowing (behavior).

second filial (FIL ee ul) **generation:** the F_2 generation, offspring of F_1 individuals.

second-order consumer: a flesh-eating animal that feeds on plant-eating animals; a carnivore that eats herbivores.

secretin (sih KREET un): a hormone that stimulates the pancreas to secrete pancreatic juice.

secretion (see KREE shun): the transport from a cell of a useful substance the cell produces.

sediment (SED ih munt): soil, sand, and organic matter that settle to the bottom of a body of water, or that accumulate on land where wind strikes barriers.

sedimentary (sed uh MENT uh ree) **rock:** rock formed from sediments deposited in the past.

seed: a plant embryo surrounded by stored food and a protective seed coat.

seed fern: a fernlike plant, known only from fossils, that produced seeds.

segment (SEG munt): a section or portion. In animals, a section of the body divided from the next by external and muscular structures or by an internal partition (or by both, as in earthworms).

semen (SEE mun): a fluid secreted by glands of the male reproductive system. It provides an alkaline environment for the temporary storage of the sperm produced by the testes.

seminiferous tubule (sem uh NIF uh rus TEW bewl): any of the coiled threadlike tubules in the lining of which sperm are produced in a testis.

sensory neuron (NEW ron): a neuron that carries impulses from a receptor toward the spinal cord and brain.

sepal (SEEP ul): one of several green, leaflike structures that enclose and protect a flower bud, later opening and remaining between the flower's petals and its stem.

sewage: biological wastes of humans.

sex chromosomes (KROH muh somz): the X and Y chromosomes, which determine the sex of an offspring.

sex-linked trait: a trait determined by genes carried on the X chromosome.

shoot: the part of a plant embryo that develops into stem and leaves.

sickle-cell anemia (uh NEE mee uh): a human hereditary disorder causing red blood cells to assume a crescent or sickle shape.

sickle-cell trait: a genotype of one nonsickling and one sickle-cell gene; a heterozygote.

sieve (SIV) **cell:** the food-conducting type of cell in phloem.

significance: the probability that a difference between predicted and observed results of an experiment is due to factors other than chance.

silica (SIL ih kuh): the compound of which sand and glass are made. Also, found in shells of diatoms, in tissues of horsetails, and in skeletons of many invertebrates.

Silurian (sy LUR ee un): the third period of the Paleozoic era.

simple leaf: a plant leaf with one leaf blade.

simple sugar: a sugar that contains no more than six carbon atoms.

simulate (SIM yuh layt): to reproduce conditions that exist elsewhere, or that existed in the past or are predicted in the future.

slime mold: a funguslike organism in which individuals merge into a common amoebalike mass when mating.

small intestine: the intestine posterior to the stomach, in which digestion is completed in vertebrates.

smallpox: a severe, often fatal, disease of humans now prevented by vaccination. Survivors were scarred with pox marks.

smog: the accumulation of industrial and transportation exhaust fumes and particles in the air until they become visible.

smooth muscle: muscle tissue clearly divided into cells that have no cross-striations in the muscle fibers. Characteristic of earthworms and of internal organs of vertebrates except for the heart.

society: an organized population in which individuals have different roles and cooperate in many tasks.

solar (SOH lur): originating in the sun.

somite (SOH myt): a body segment in animals whose bodies are segmented, as in an earthworm. Also, a segment or block of tissue in an animal embryo, as in a chick embryo.

speciation (spee shee AY shun): emergence of new species by natural selection and reproductive isolation from preexisting species.

species (SPEE sheez): all organisms of a similar kind that can interbreed and produce fertile offspring.

specimen (SPES uh mun): a sample or example, as of a kind of organism or some product it makes.

speculation (spek yuh LAY shun): hypothetical thinking in search of further evidence; an early stage of investigation involving assumptions.

sperm: a male reproductive cell.

Sphenopsida (sfee NOP suh duh): a subdivision of tracheophytes; the horsetails.

spina bifida (spy nuh BIF uh duh): a genetic disorder of humans in which the vertebrae are divided, exposing the spinal cord.

spinal cord: the dorsal nerve cord of higher vertebrates.

spindle: fibers along which chromosomes are pulled to opposite ends of a cell in mitosis and meiosis.

spirochete (SPY ruh keet): a spiral-shaped bacterium of the order Spirochaetales.

spleen: an organ of vertebrates that stores blood and removes damaged red cells.

spontaneous abortion (spon TAY nee us   uh BOR shun): premature ejection of an embryo from the uterus of a female placental mammal, because of accident or some disorder.

spontaneous (spon TAY nee us) **generation:** a discredited theory that organisms can arise today not only by reproduction but from nonliving sources and materials. Also called abiogenesis.

spore: a reproductive cell of many plants and certain algae, fungi, and other protists. Depending on the kind of reproductive cycle in the organism, a spore may be sexual or asexual.

sporophyte (SPOH ruh fyt): a diploid organism that produces spores, in species with alternation of generations.

sporozoan (spor uh ZOH un): a type of parasitic microorganism that has no means of locomotion and that reproduces by forming spores.

stamen (STAY mun): a pollen-producing structure in a flower.

sterile (STER ul): incapable of reproducing. Or, in laboratory procedure, treated to destroy all organisms on or in an instrument or a substance in question.

sterilization: destruction of all organisms in or on an object or a substance. Or, as applied to sexually reproducing organisms, destruction of the ability to reproduce.

sternum (STUR num): the breastbone in vertebrates.

stimulant (STIM yuh lunt): a drug that increases nerve activity.

stimulus (STIM yuh lus): anything in an organism's inner or outer environment that causes it to react.

stomach: the digestive organ where protein digestion begins in vertebrates. Also, a digestive organ in many invertebrates, including insects.

stomate (STOH mayt): one of the openings in the lower epidermis of a plant leaf.

stratum (STRAYT um): a layer in sedimentary rock.

strep throat: a throat infection caused by *Streptococcus* bacteria.

striated (STRY ayt ud) **muscle:** muscle tissue that loses individual cell membranes and that has dark and light filaments which give it a cross-striped appearance. It is characteristic of skeletal and heart muscle.

subspecies (SUB SPEE sheez): genetically distinguishable populations of the same species.

substrate (SUB strayt): a substance acted on by an enzyme.

succession (suk SESH un): the replacement of one community of organisms by another as conditions change.

survival (sur VY vul): among organisms, successfully overcoming hazards; continuing to live.

symptom (SIMP tum): the appearance of some sign of a disorder or disease.

syndrome (SIN drohm): a group of symptoms that typically appear together in a particular disease or disorder.

synthesize (SIN thuh syz): to put together a compound, as in a living cell or in the laboratory.

syphilis (SIF uh lus): a bacterial disease of humans, transmitted by sexual intercourse or other sexual contact; a

venereal disease.

tannin (TAN un): a brown pigment of many plants.

taproot system: one major root with smaller roots branching from it.

tassel (TAS ul): flowers arranged along slender or stringlike structures.

taxidermy (TAK suh dur mee): the art of mounting skins and other external organs of animals on bodylike molds for lifelike exhibit.

taxis (TAK sis): a response of a protist or any of certain invertebrates to stimulation by light, chemical change, temperature change, or other environmental cause.

taxonomist (tak SON uh must): a biologist who specializes in classifying organisms.

Tay-Sachs (TAY SAKS): a genetic disorder of humans that is fatal in early childhood.

technology (tek NOL uh jee): the application of scientific discoveries to production of goods and services for human life.

tentacle (TENT ih kul): a slender part of an organism, usually one of a number with which it grasps food or touches its surroundings.

terminal bud: a bud at the tip of a plant stem.

terrestrial (tuh RES tree ul): on land; or, land-inhabiting.

territoriality (ter uh tor ee AL ut ee): a behavior of all animal species whose individual members lay claim to, and defend, a territory.

Tertiary (TUR shee er ee): the first of two periods in the Cenozoic era.

testicle (TES tih kul): a mammalian testis.

testis (TES tus): a male reproductive organ in which sperm are produced. In mammals, also called a testicle.

testosterone (tuh STOS tuh rone): the primary male hormone, also found in minute amounts in females.

tetanus (TET uh nus): an infection of humans caused by bacteria and characterized by muscle spasms, especially in the jaw ("lockjaw").

tetraploid (TET ruh ploid): two diploid sets of chromosomes combined in the same individual.

thalassemia (thal uh SEE mee uh): a genetic disorder of humans that produces severe anemia and skin and other body complications.

theory: the best-tested explanation for relating and organizing knowledge in a scientific field. It fits all or most existing data, explains how events and processes are thought to occur, and leads to prediction of continuing events.

theory of natural selection: the theory that individuals best adapted to the environment are more likely to survive and reproduce, thus accomplishing a selection among the variations in individuals of a species.

theory of organic evolution (ev uh LOO shun): the theory that, given time and variation among individuals of each species, different species will evolve by natural selection of individuals best adapted in their variations.

thorax (THOR aks): the chest area; the part of an animal's body between the head and the abdomen.

thromboplastin (throm boh PLAS tun): the substance released by blood platelets that starts the clotting process.

thyroid (THY roid) **glands:** glands that produce hormones which regulate cellular respiration.

tissue: an organized association of similar cells that carry on the same function, as in muscle tissue or skin tissue.

tolerance (TOL uh runs): the ability of individuals of a species to survive fluctuations in environmental conditions.

toxin (TOK sun): a poisonous substance produced by an organism.

trachea (TRAY kee uh): the windpipe in vertebrates.

tracheid (TRAY kee ud): a kind of xylem.

tracheophyte (TRAY kee uh fyt): a plant with an internal fluid-transport system called a vascular system.

trait: any characteristic of an individual.

tranquilizer (TRANG kwuh ly zur): a drug prescribed to relieve agitation and stress by inhibiting transmission of nerve impulses at synapses.

transfer RNA: *see* tRNA.

transmit: to pass (from one organism) to another.

transpiration (trans spuh RAY shun): loss of water by plant leaves.

trend: a pattern observed in data.

trial-and-error learning: showing different responses to a stimulus until one proves satisfactory or is rewarded.

Triassic (try AS ik): the first period of the Mesozoic era.

trilobite (TRY luh byt): a fossil arthropod.

tripeptide (TRY PEP tyd): a short chain of three amino acids chemically linked together.

triploid (TRIP loid): a monoploid and a diploid set of chromosomes combined, as in the fertilization of a fusion nucleus in an ovule of a flower's pistil.

tRNA: transfer RNA, which carries amino acids to ribosomes for use in protein synthesis.

tropical deciduous (dih SIJ uh was) **forest:** one of several tropical biomes, named for its characteristic type of tree.

tropical rain forest: one of several tropical biomes, in which rain falls almost every day.

tropism (TROH piz um): a plant response, positive if toward a stimulus, negative if away from it.

true-breeding: homozygous as a result of selection or, in plants, as a result of flower construction that prevents cross-pollination.

tsetse (TSET see) **fly:** the vector of African sleeping sickness.

tuber (TOO bur): a thickened underground portion of a stem in which food is stored and buds are found. An example is a potato.

tuberculosis (tew bur kyuh LOH sis): a disease of humans caused by bacteria and chiefly involving destruction of lung tissue, although other tissues are also attacked.

tubule (TEW bewl): a very small tube.

tundra (TUN druh): an arctic biome with permanently frozen subsoil.

turgor (TUR gur): rigidity or support supplied by cell contents exerting pressure on their cell walls.

typhoid (TY foid) **fever:** a disease of humans caused by bacteria. Fever and digestive disorders are the chief symptoms.

umbilical (um BIL ih kul) **cord:** the embryo's link to the placenta, in placental mammals.

unicellular (yew nih SEL yuh lur): one-celled.

uranium (yew RAY nee um): a radioactive element used in the uranium-lead geologic dating method.

urea (yew REE uh): a soluble nitrogenous waste excreted by many vertebrates including humans.

ureter (YEUR uh tur): a tube leading from each kidney to the urinary bladder.

urethra (yew REE thruh): the tube through which urine is eliminated from the body.

uric (YEUR ik) **acid:** a crystalline, insoluble form of nitrogenous waste excreted by insects, many snakes and birds, and some desert mammals.

urinary bladder: a saclike organ in which urine is stored until eliminated from the body.

urine: a watery solution of urea and other wastes from the body of humans and many other terrestrial vertebrates.

uterus (YEWT uh rus): the organ in which the embryo develops in a female mammal.

vaccination (vak suh NAY shun): immunization against smallpox. Today, sometimes used for any injection of dead or weakened viruses or bacteria to induce production of antibodies against a specific disease.

vacuole (VAK yuh wol): a membrane-enclosed, usually fluid-filled cell organelle with any of a number of functions.

vagina (vuh JY nuh): the passage through which the female reproductive tract opens to the outside of the body.

variable (VAIR ee uh bul): any condition subject to change, as temperature. Or, any characteristic not identical for organisms being compared, as size or color.

variation: differences, as among organisms of a species.

vascular (VAS kyuh lur) **system:** the internal fluid-transport system of most plants familiar to people.

vector (VEK tur) **disease:** a disease spread indirectly by its pathogen from a victim to an alternate host—usually a biting insect which transfers the pathogen to another prospective victim by means of a bite.

vegetative (VEJ uh tayt iv) **reproduction:** asexual reproduction in plants.

vein: a vessel that carries blood toward the heart.

venereal (vuh NIR ee ul) **disease:** a disease transmitted by sexual intercourse or other sexual contact.

ventral (VEN trul): located in the areas of the chest or abdomen, in the front of the body. Or, the lower part of the body in animals that maintain a horizontal position.

ventricle (VEN trih kul): in vertebrates, a muscular chamber of the heart that pumps outgoing blood.

verification (ver uh fuh KAY shun): repetition of one scientist's observations or experiments by others, with the same results.

vertebra (VUR tuh bruh): a bone of the backbone.

vertebrate (VURT uh brut): an animal with an internal skeleton of bone or cartilage, including a dorsal backbone or cartilaginous support column.

vessel: any conducting tube; in vascular plants, a kind of xylem.

veterinarian (vet uh run ER ee un): a medical doctor who treats animals, not including humans.

viability (vy uh BIL ut ee): relative ability to survive, as among competing individuals in their environment, or seeds that will be dormant for a year.

villus (VIL us): one of many thousands of tiny, fingerlike extensions of the intestinal wall into the intestinal cavity.

virulence (VIR uh luns): relative danger of a pathogen, or its capability to overcome a host's resistance.

virus (VY rus): an almost lifelike particle composed of DNA and protein, or RNA and protein. It carries on the life process of reproduction inside a living cell.

vitamin (VYT uh mun): a regulatory substance necessary for some of an organism's life processes. It often acts along with an enzyme (as a "co-enzyme") or becomes an actual, nonprotein part of an enzyme molecule.

warm-blooded: having internal body temperature homeostatically regulated against the wide fluctuations in temperature of the outer environment.

wavelength: the distance between the peak of one wave and the peak of the next, in radiant energy and movement of subatomic particles.

white blood cell: any of several types of cells in the blood that engulf and destroy foreign particles and fight infection at wounds.

wild-type trait: the most common form of a characteristic in populations of an organism in the wild.

xanthophyll (ZAN thuh fil): a yellow pigment of many plants.

xylem (ZY lum): water-conducting cells in a vascular plant.

yolk: a food supply in an animal egg.

yolk sac: the membrane that encloses the yolk in an animal egg. One of the four embryonic membranes in vertebrate embryos.

zone of elongation (ee long GAY shun): an area just behind stem-tip and root-tip meristem, where newly formed cells grow longer.

zoological (zoh uh LOJ ih kul): exclusively devoted to animals, as in a zoo.

zoologist (zoh OL uh just): a biologist who specializes in the study of animals.

zooplankton (zoh uh PLANK tun): microscopic and other very small aquatic consumers—protists and little animals.

zygote (ZY gote): a fertilized egg.

Index and Key to Definitions

Boldface numbers indicate pages carrying definitions or explanations of terms.
An asterisk (*) indicates an illustration (chart, diagram, graph, map, or picture).